天津农垦集团总公司

Tianjin Farms Agribusiness Group Corporation

Tianjin Farms Agribusiness Group Corporation is a key group authorized by Tianjin Municipal Committee and Tianjin Municipal Government, and is transformed and built by Tianjin agriculture, industry and commerce head Corporation with the registered assets 235 million RMB. Tianjin Farms Agribusiness Group Corporation has total assets 5,598 million RMB, land with the area of 136,000 mu, 39 companies directly subordinated to it, and 112 business units. In 2006, the total product of industry and agriculture amounted to 2,428 million RMB and the total profit aggregated 129 million RMB. The main businesses of the corporation include: milk business (including cow breeding and HAI HE dairy products producing), wine business (including Dynasty, Welkin and Summer Palace wine), special agriculture (including terrestrial heat cultivating and lawn), real estate (JinKen real estate development) and commercial services (including taxi services, gas station services and office building services). The staff of the group corporation all spare no efforts to develop the spirit of keeping forging ahead and strive to achieve the great development goal in the 21st century. Welcome the friends from diverse fields and both home and abroad to join our Tianjin Farms Agribusiness to achieve a new peak together.

1	2
3	4

1. 天津广大纸业
2. 王朝葡萄酒
3. 场区
4. 海河乳业厂区外景

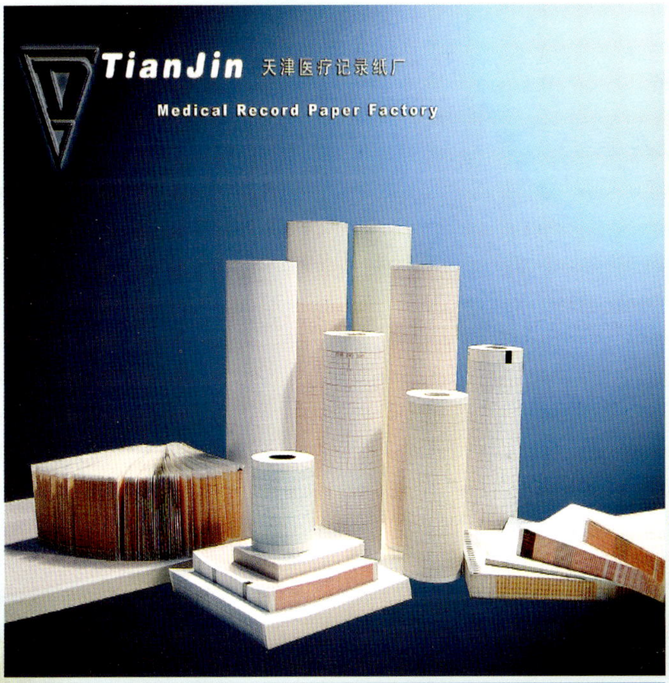

天津统计年鉴

TIANJIN STATISTICAL YEARBOOK

No.23 总第23期

中英文对照
Chinese/English

2007

天津市统计局 编
Compiled by Tianjin Municipal Bureau of Statistics

中国统计出版社
China Statistics Press

天津市生产总值(亿元)
Tianjin's GDP (100 million yuan)

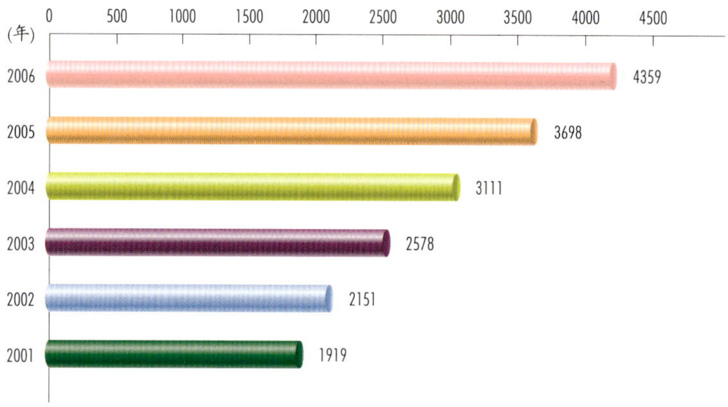

产业结构
Industrial Structure

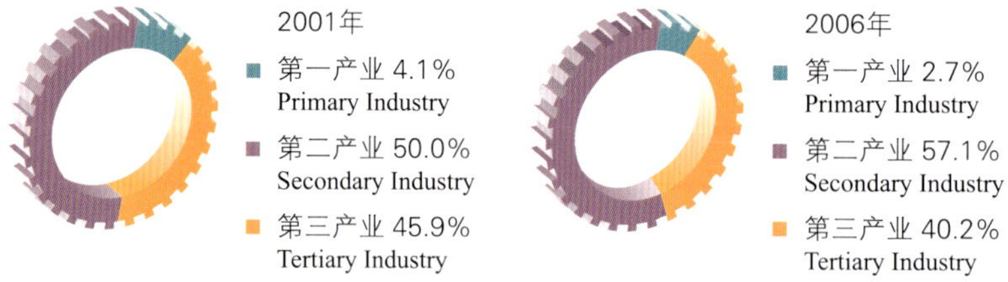

天津全市财政收入(亿元)
Tianjin Municipal Government Revenue (100 million yuan)

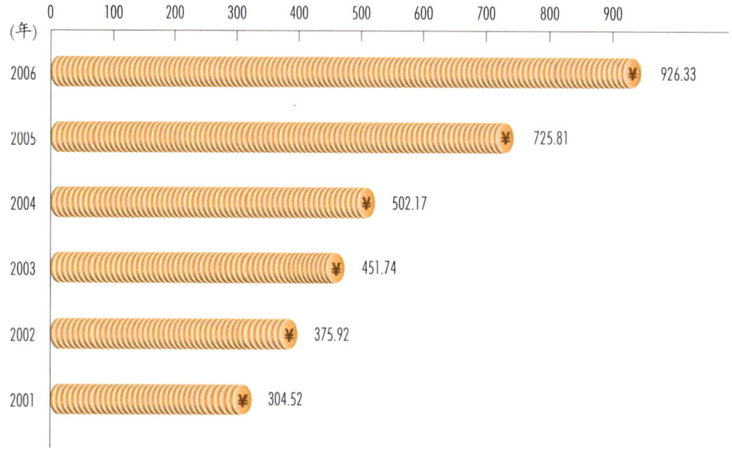

科学发展
Develop Scientifically
和谐发展
Develop Harmoniously
率先发展
Develop Firstly

2006年天津市每天主要社会经济活动情况
Average Daily Social and Economic Activities of Tianjin in 2006

地区生产总值11.94亿元
Gross Domestic Product (1 194 million yuan)

工业增加值6.28亿元
Added Value of Industry (628 million yuan)

第三产业增加值4.80亿元
Added Value of Tertiary Industry (480 million yuan)

全市财政收入25379万元
Total Government Revenue (253.79 million yuan)

原油产量5.32万吨
Output of Crude Oil (53 200 tons)

轿车产量1124辆
Output of Cars (1 124 units)

移动电话机产量27.75万部
Output of Mobile Phones (277 500 pieces)

港口货物吞吐量70.58万吨
Freight Handled at Port (705 800 tons)

社会货物运输量117.43万吨
Freight Transportation (1 174 300 tons)

邮电业务总量6241万元
Business Value of Post and Telecommunications (62.41 million yuan)

社会消费品零售总额3.72亿元
Total Retail Sales of Consumer Goods (372 million yuan)

外贸出口总值9189万美元
Total Value of Exports in Foreign Trade (91.89 million USD)

接待来津国际旅游者2413人次
Reception of International Tourists (2 413 person-times)

全社会竣工房屋建筑面积8.11万平方米
Floor Space of Building Completed (81 100 m²)

天然气和煤气售气量319.43万立方米
Sales of Natural Gas and Fuel Gas (3 194 300 m³)

新增移动电话用户2704户
Increased Mobile Phone Users (2 704 households)

生活用水量74.20万吨
Daily Consumption Water (742 000 tons)

报纸出版259.78万份
Newspaper Issued (2 597 800 copies)

全社会固定资产投资与城市基础设施投资(亿元)
Total Investment in Fixed Assets and Urban Infrastructure Investment (100 million yuan)

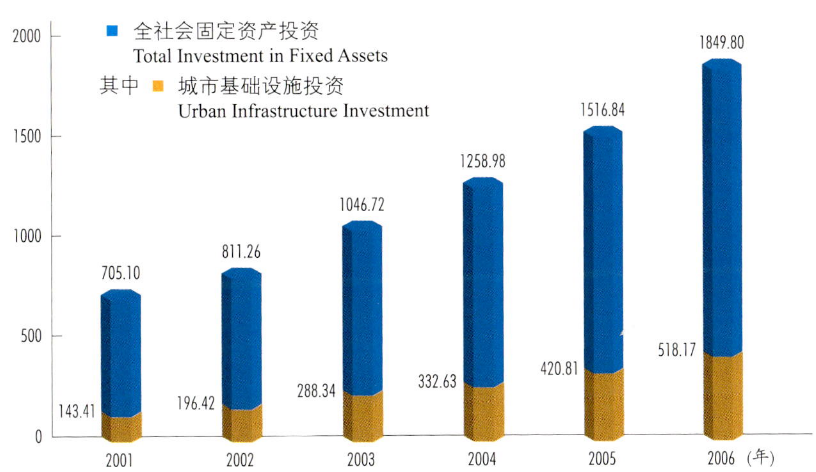

万元地区生产总值、万元工业增加值能耗(吨标准煤)
Energy Consumption of Every 10 000 yuan Gross Domestic Product and Value Added in Industry (tons of SCE)

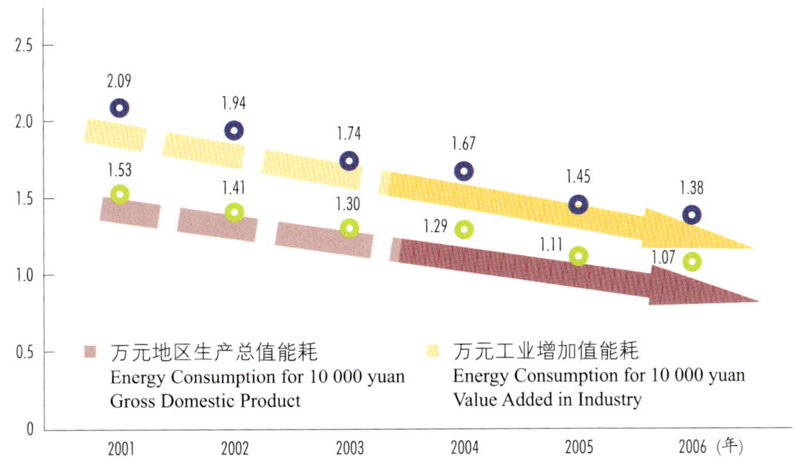

2006年六大优势产业产值构成
Composition of Output Value of Six Advantageous Industries in 2006

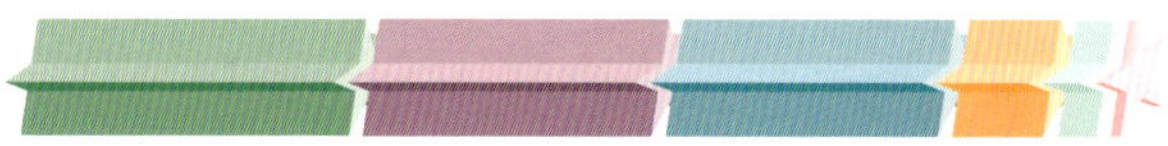

- 电子信息产品制造业 37.5%
  Electronic and Information Products Manufacturing Industry
- 冶金工业 25.9%
  Metallurgical Industry
- 石油及化学工业 24.2%
  Peroleum and Chemical Industry
- 汽车制造业 8.1%
  Automobile Manufacturing Industry
- 生物技术与现代医药制造业 3.4%
  Biotechnology and Modern Pharmaceutical Industry
- 新能源及环保业 0.9%
  New Energy Source and Environment Protection Industry

城市居民家庭生活收支(元)
Domesticity Income and Expenditure of Urban Households (yuan)

- 人均可支配收入
  Per Capita Annual Disposable Income
- 人均消费性支出
  Per Capita Annual Consumptive Expenditure

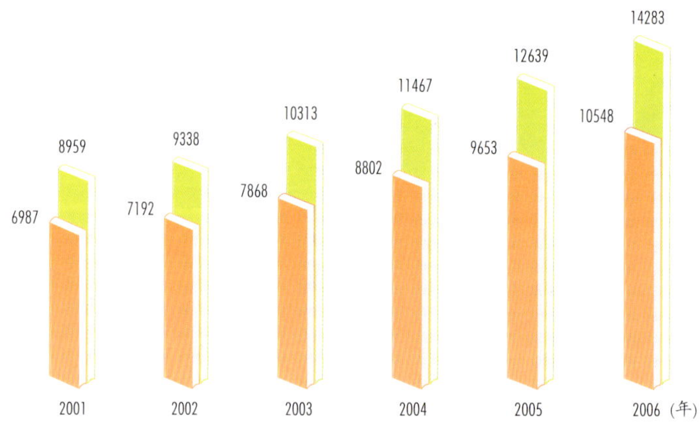

2006年城市居民人均消费性支出构成
Composition of Per Capita Annual Expenditure for Consumption of Urban Households in 2006

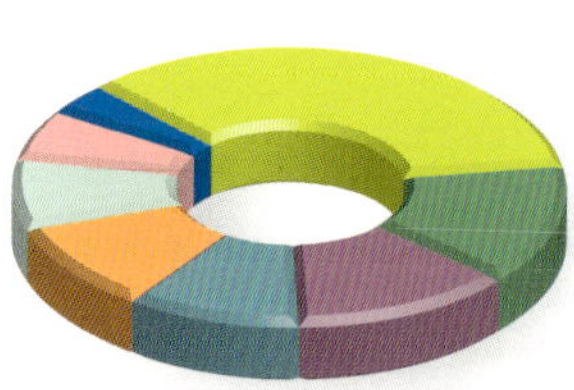

- 食品 34.9% Food
- 娱乐、文教服务 13.8%
  Recreation, Education and Cultural Services
- 居住 13.0% Residence
- 交通和通讯 10.4%
  Transportation and Telecommunication
- 医疗保健 9.9% Medicine and Medical Services
- 衣着 8.2% Clothing
- 家庭设备用品及服务 6.0%
  Household Facilities, Articles and Services
- 杂项商品和服务 3.8%
  Miscellaneous Commodities and Services

科学发展 Develop Scientifically
和谐发展 Develop Harmoniously
率先发展 Develop Firstly

城市居民人均住房建筑面积(平方米)
Per Capita Floor Space of Urban Residential Building (m^2)

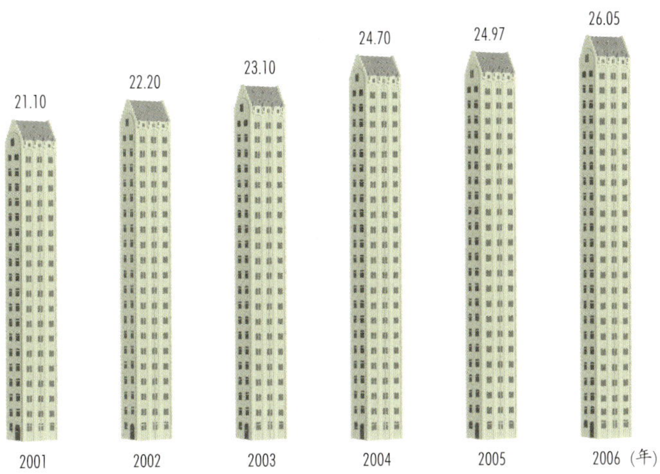

港口货物吞吐量(万吨)
Volume of Freight Handled in Tianjin Port (10 000 tons)

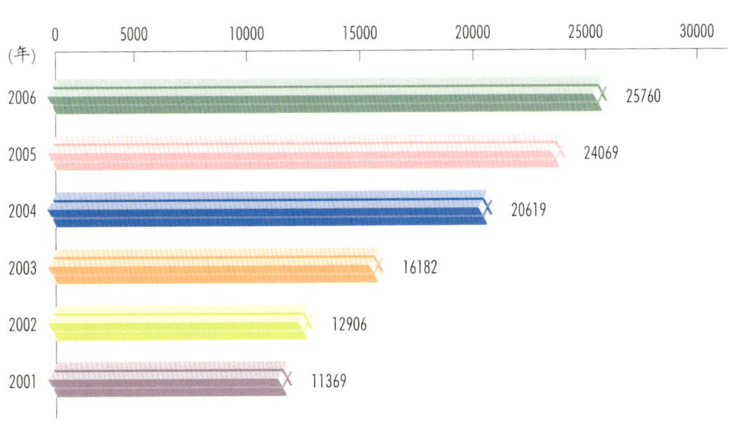

邮电业务总量(亿元)
Bussiness Value of Post and Telecommunications (100 million yuan)

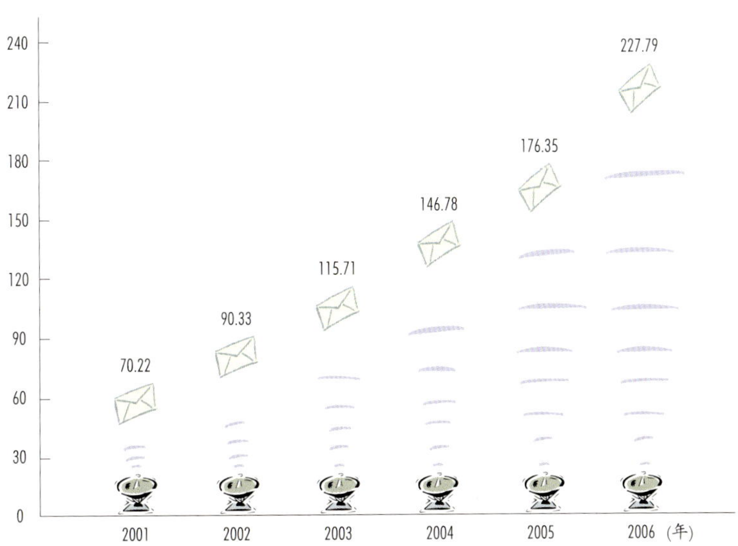

外贸进出口商品总值(亿美元)
Total Value of Import & Export in Foreign Trade (100 million USD)

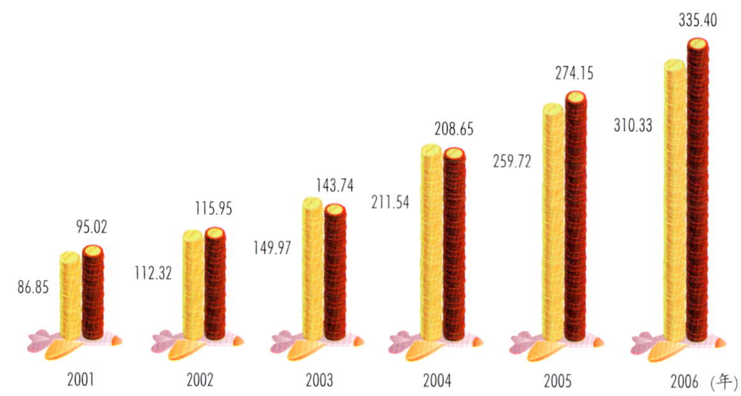

2006年实际直接利用外资额结构
Composition of Actual Used Foreign Direct Investment in 2006

按在天津投资的国家和地区分
By the Countries or Regions Investing in Tianjin

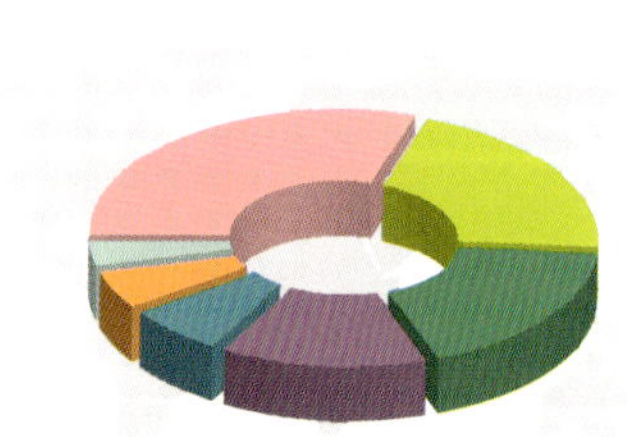

- 中国香港 21.2% Hong Kong, China
- 英属维尔京群岛 18.4% Virgin Islands of the United Kingdom
- 日本 13.9% Japan
- 韩国 6.8% Republic of Korea
- 美国 5.6% United States
- 新加坡 3.9% Singapore
- 其他 30.2% Others

2006年末金融机构(含外资)本外币存贷款余额(亿元)
Balance of Home and Foreign Currency Deposits and Loans in Financial (Including Foreign) Institutions at the End of 2006 (100 million yuan)

科学发展
Develop Scientifically

和谐发展
Develop Harmoniously

率先发展
Develop Firstly

城市绿化覆盖率(%)
Coverage Rate of Afforestation in Urban Areas (%)

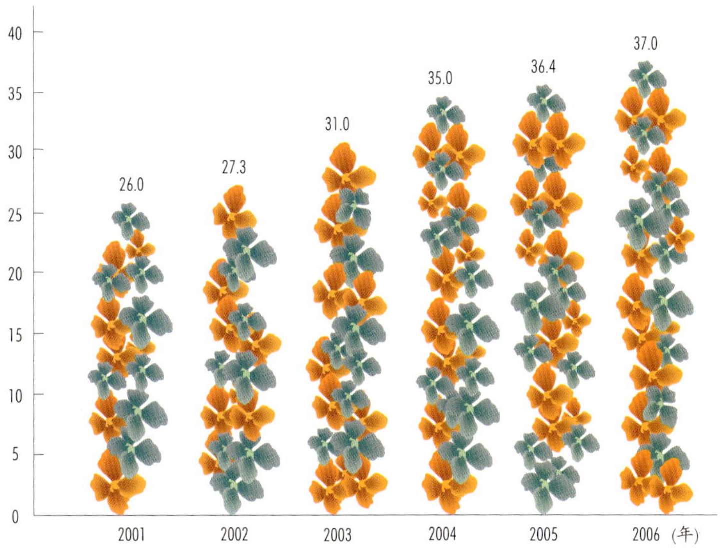

城市物价总指数(上年=100)
The Urban Price Index (preceding year=100)

城市居民消费价格指数
The Urban Residents' Consumption Price Index

城市商品零售价格指数
The Retail Price Index of Commodities in the Urban Area

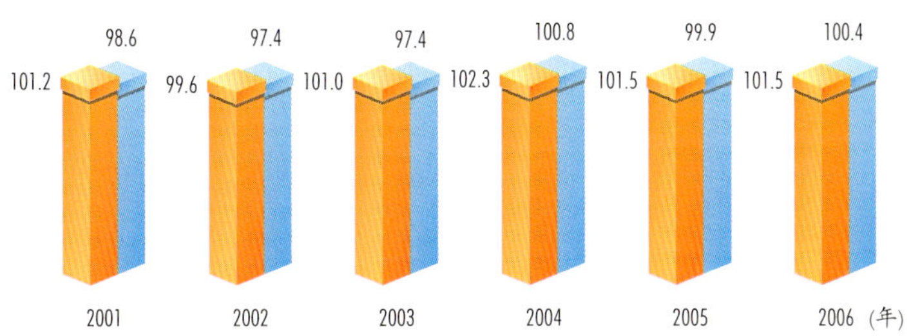

滨海新区地区生产总值(亿元)
Gross Domestic Product of Binhai New Area (100 million yuan)

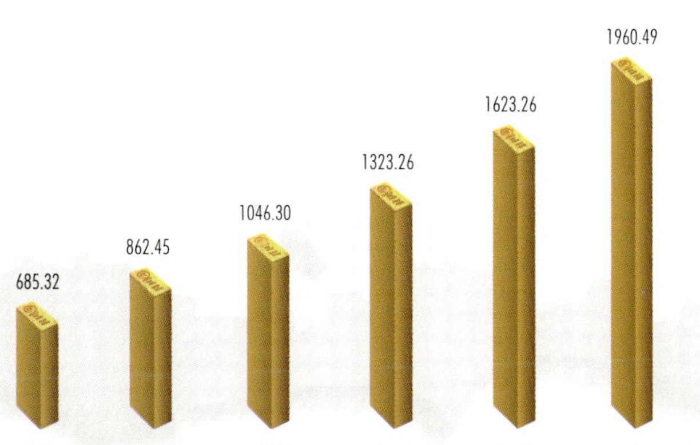

《天津统计年鉴2007》编辑委员会

Tianjin Statistical Yearbook 2007
Editorial Board and Staff

编者说明

一、《天津统计年鉴》是一部全面反映天津市国民经济和社会发展情况的大型资料工具书，创刊于1984年，逐年出版，形成系列。本书以其丰富翔实的统计资料而成为社会各界了解天津、认识天津最具权威性的资料工具书。

二、《天津统计年鉴 2007》全书中英文对照，同步配备电子版光盘。

三、书内文字资料载有《2006 年天津市国民经济和社会发展统计公报》、《2006 年天津市国民经济发展情况综述》、《科学发展，和谐发展》分析文章；书后并附有《2006 年第二次全国残疾人抽样调查天津市主要数据公报》。为方便读者使用，书的篇目索引标明了全书结构。在书中每篇后附有统计指标解释。

四、本年鉴的统计数据主要取自统计年报，一少部分来自抽样调查和专业部门统计资料。

五、本年鉴所使用的度量衡单位均采用国际统一标准计量单位；行业分类标准均采用国家标准 GB/T4754-2002；计算人均指标时，从 2005 年开始采用常住人口计算，2005 年以前采用户籍人口计算。从 2006 年开始，城乡划分标准执行国统字 [2006]60 号文件的新规定。

六、本年鉴中部分数据的合计数和相对数由于四舍五入取舍不同而产生的计算误差，均未做机械调整。

七、本年鉴表中的符号使用说明："空格" 表示该项统计指标无数据、数据不足本表最小单位数或数据不详；"#" 表示其中的主要项。

八、由于国家统计制度变化或主管部门提供的数据有调整等原因，年鉴中部分指标的历史年度数据有变动。读者在使用历史资料时，凡以前年度的年鉴与本年鉴数据有出入的，均以本年鉴为准。

九、《天津统计年鉴》自公开出版以来，得到了国内外广大读者的关心和支持，对本年鉴的内容和编辑工作提出了许多宝贵意见，对此我们深表谢意。限于我们的水平，书中难免有不足之处，敬请广大读者继续给予批评指正，帮助我们进一步改进年鉴编辑工作、提高年鉴编辑水平，更好地为广大读者服务。

Preface

Ⅰ. Tianjin Statistical Yearbook is a large-sized statistics publication to reflect various aspects of Tianjin's economic and social development, which was started in 1984 and published year after year, having become a series of yearbooks. Possessing plentiful and detailed statistical materials, the yearbook has become the most authoritative statistics publication for various circles to understand and know Tianjin.

Ⅱ. Tianjin Statistical Yearbook 2007 is written in Chinese & English, and is equipped with electric CD.

Ⅲ. Written materials in the book include *Statistical Communique on the 2006 National Economic and Social Development of Tianjin*, *Summary of Tianjin National Economy Development*, *Tianjin's Development in a Scientific and Harmonious Way*, together with the appendix *Statistical Communique on the 2006 National Second Handicapped Sample Survey of Tianjin*. In order to help readers using these statistical materials better, Explanatory Notes On Main Statistical Indicators are attached after each chapter.

Ⅳ. The major data sources of this book are obtained from annual statistical report, a few from sample surveys and materials of departments' statistics.

Ⅴ. The units of measurement used in this book are internationally standard measurement units; sector listed in this table is classified by the standard of GB/T4754-2002. When calculating per capital indicators, we use permanent population since 2005 and use registered population before 2005. Since 2006, the division standard of urban and rual areas adopts the new rules of National Bureau of Statistics Regulation 2006[60].

Ⅵ. Statistical discrepancies due to rounding are not adjusted in this book.

Ⅶ. Notations used in this book: "(blank)" indicates the data not available or the figure is not large enough to be measured with the smallest unit in the table. "#" indicates the major items of the total.

Ⅷ. As a result of change of statistics institution, data adjustment of special department and so on, some data in this yearbook are different from former yearbook. When using historical data, users should take the data of this book as standard.

Ⅸ. Since Tianjin Statistical Yearbook had been published openly, we have been concerned and supported by the readers at home and abroad. They advance much valuable suggestion on content and edition of the yearbook, we deeply thanks for this all. Based on our limited level, perhaps there are some mistakes in this book, we welcome all of the readers give us your criticism in order to help us further improving our edition level, and providing services for the readers better.

篇目索引

SUBJECT INDEX

目 录

CONTENTS

第二篇　国民经济核算 / CHAPTER 2　NATIONAL ACCOUNTS

第三篇　人口和劳动就业 / CHAPTER 3　POPULATION, LABOR AND EMPLOYMENT

第四篇　固定资产投资和房地产 / CHAPTER 4 INVESTMENT IN FIXED ASSETS AND REAL ESTATE

第五篇 能源生产和消费 / CHAPTER 5 ENERGY PRODUCTION AND CONSUMPTION

第六篇 财 政 / CHAPTER 6 GOVERNMENT FINANCE

第七篇 价格指数 / CHAPTER 7 PRICE INDICES

第八篇 人民生活 / CHAPTER 8 PEOPLE'S LIFE

第九篇　城市建设和环境保护
CHAPTER 9 URBAN CONSTRUCTION AND ENVIRONMENT PROTECTION

第十篇 农村经济 / CHAPTER 10 RURAL ECONOMY

第十一篇　工　业 / CHAPTER 11 INDUSTRY

第十二篇　建筑业 / CHAPTER 12 CONSTRUCTION

第十三篇　交通运输和邮电
CHAPTER 13 TRANSPORTATION, POST AND TELECOMMUNICATIONS

第十四篇 国内贸易 / CHAPTER 14 DOMESTIC TRADE

第十五篇　对外经济贸易和旅游 / CHAPTER 15 FOREIGN ECONOMY TRADE AND TOURISM

第十六篇　金融业 / CHAPTER 16 FINANCIAL INTERMEDIATION

第十七篇　教育和科技 / CHAPTER 17 EDUCATION AND SCIENCE & TECHNOLOGY

第十八篇　文化和体育 / CHAPTER 18 CULTURE AND SPORTS

第十九篇 卫生、社会保障和社会福利
CHAPTER 19 PUBLIC HEALTH, SOCIAL SECURITY AND SOCIAL WELFARE

第二十篇 公共管理和社会组织
CHAPTER 20 PUBLIC MANAGEMENT AND SOCIAL ORGANIZATIONS

第二十一篇 企业及企业集团 / CHAPTER 21 ENTERPRISES AND ENTERPRISE GROUPS

第二十二篇 滨海新区 / CHAPTER 22 BINHAI NEW AREA

第二十三篇　区县基本情况
CHAPTER 23 BASIC STATISTICS ON DISTRICTS AND COUNTIES

2006年天津市国民经济和社会发展统计公报

天津市统计局
国家统计局天津调查总队
2007年3月21日

2006年是"十一五"发展的第一年。全市人民在市委、市政府的正确领导下，以邓小平理论和"三个代表"重要思想为指导，以科学发展观为统领，认真贯彻落实党中央、国务院关于加快推进滨海新区开发开放的决定和各项部署，扎实推进"三步走"战略和五大战略举措，加快经济增长方式转变，全面推进和谐天津建设，全市经济平稳快速增长，效益质量进一步提高，各项社会事业全面发展，人民生活水平继续提高，实现了"十一五"良好开局。

一、经济发展

经济总量

据初步核算，并经国家统计局联审通过，全市实现地区生产总值(GDP)4337.73亿元，按可比价格计算，比上年增长14.4%，比2000年增长1.2倍，提前四年实现了翻一番，率先完成了"三步走"战略第二步经济总量发展目标(见图1)。按常住人口计算，全市人均地区生产总值达到40961元，比上年增长11.7%，按照当年平均汇率计算，人均地区生产总值为5177美元。

三次产业全面发展。第一产业实现增加值118.97亿元，比上年增长3.5%。第二产业增加值2485.83亿元，增长17.6%。第三产业增加值1732.93亿元，增长11.0%。三次产业结构为2.7∶57.3∶40。

图1　天津市生产总值与增长

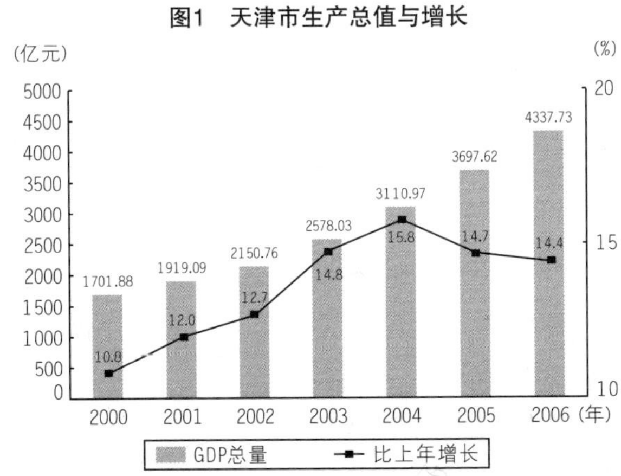

注：本图各年度GDP总量按当年价格计算，增长率按可比价格计算。

财政收入

全市财政收入突破900亿元，达到925.62亿元，比上年增长27.6%，占全市生产总值的比重为21.3%，比上年提高1.7个百分点。其中地方一般预算财政收入416.77亿元，增长25.6%。主要税种收入均增长较快。增值税增长25.6%，消费税增长43.2%，营业税增长20.2%，企业所得税增长29.1%，个人所得税增长12.7%。全市财政支出654.2亿元，比上年增长25.7%。其中，基本建设和城市维护建设支出263.2亿元，增长28.2%；支援农业支出16.1亿元，增长25.1%；社会保障和优抚救济支出62.9亿元，增长36.9%；科技支出18.3亿元，增长33.8%。

劳动与就业

全市新增就业岗位安置就业29万人，比上年增加3.28万人，增长12.5%，其中安置下岗失业人员12.91万人。年末全市社会从业人员总量达到562.92万人，比上年增长3.8%，其中从事第一产业79.93万人，从事第二产业231.36万人，从事第三产业251.63万人。全年人才和劳务市场共接待341.48万人次进场择业洽谈，91.38万人次达成初步意向。城镇登记失业率为3.6%。

价格

城市居民消费价格指数为101.5，即比上年上涨1.5%。八大类价格呈现五升三降格局(见表1)。

表1　居民消费价格指数

指标	指数(上年=100)
城市居民消费价格指数	101.5
食品类	102.7
烟酒及用品类	103.0
衣着类	97.5
家庭设备用品及维修服务类	100.5
医疗保健和个人用品类	101.4
交通和通讯类	98.9
娱乐教育文化用品及服务类	99.0
居住类	104.4

城市商品零售价格指数为100.4。工业品出厂价格指数为100.6。原材料燃料及动力购进价格指数为104.7。房屋销售价格指数为106.7，其中商品住宅价格指数为107.1。

固定资产投资

全社会固定资产投资完成1849.80亿元，比上年增长22.0%(见图2)。其中，城镇固定资产投资1709.66亿元，增长23.4%；农村固定资产投资140.14亿元，增长6.9%。

图2　全社会固定资产投资总额与增长

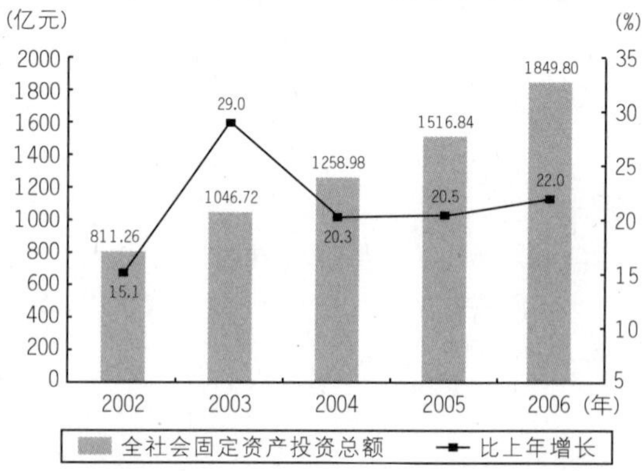

在城镇固定资产投资中，第一产业投资3.38亿元。第二产业投资701.83亿元，增长29.2%。其中工业投资690.34亿元，增长29.6%。第三产业投资1004.45亿元，增长20%。其中交通运输仓储邮政业、房地产业和水利环境公共设施管理业投资分别增长21.5%、22.0%和21.8%。重点项目建设得到加强，10亿元以上的大项目共完成投资746.94亿元，增长51.3%。

农业和农村建设

全市农业总产值完成251.50亿元,比上年增长3.7%。在农业总产值中，种植业产值105.27亿元，增长3.6%；林业产值1.98亿元，增长2.5%；畜牧业产值104.89亿元，增长3.1%；渔业产值39.36亿元，增长6.0%。养殖业（畜牧业和渔业）占农业总产值的比重为57.4%。

农业生产能力继续提高。全年粮食种植面积442.82万亩，比上年增加11.33万亩，粮食总产量143.52万吨，增长4.4%。棉花种植面积106.44万亩，棉花产量9.77万吨，增长17.0%。鱼、肉、蛋、奶等主要农副产品产量比上年增加（见表2）。

表2　主要农副产品产量

产品名称	单位	产量	比上年增长（%）
粮　食	万吨	143.52	4.4
棉　花	万吨	9.77	17.0
肉　类	万吨	59.91	3.7
牛　奶	万吨	65.00	2.5
水产品	万吨	35.80	5.9
禽　蛋	万吨	24.20	3.1
水　果	万吨	30.35	9.2
蔬　菜	万吨	540.13	-0.5

农业产业化经营和机械化水平全面提高。进入农业产业化体系的农户已占总农户的73.6%，比上年提高3.6个百分点。全年组织实施了198项农业科技成果转化与推广项目。农业机械总动力603.39万千瓦，农业机械保有量59.47万台（套），其中，联合收割机0.3万台，农用运输车14.03万辆。机播率和机耕率分别达到58.3%和91.2%。节水灌溉面积达到19.79万公顷。

社会主义新农村建设全面推进，小城镇、文明生态村建设加快。加强了农村公共事业建设，实施了“351”农村劳动力培训工程、农村饮水管网入户工程、农村户厕改造工程等，为广大农村居民带来实惠。

工业

全市完成工业增加值2290.81亿元，比上年增长17.7%，完成工业总产值8907.45亿元，增长25.1%。其中，规模以上工业完成增加值2223.82亿元，增长18.8%，完成工业总产值8527.70亿元，增长25.3%。

优势产业支撑作用继续增强。电子信息、汽车、石油化工、冶金、生物技术与现代医药、新能源及环保等六大优势产业完成工业总产值6391.60亿元，比上年增长27.5%，占全市规模以上工业的比重为74.9%，比上年提高1.2个百分点，对工业增长的贡献率达到80%。高新技术产业产值完成2713.01亿元，增长24.3%，占全市工业的比重为31.8%。全年完成新产品产值2601.30亿元，增长39.9%。

工业品产销形势良好。全市规模以上工业实现销售产值8462.22亿元，比上年增长24.3%，产销率达到99.24%。主要产品产量（见表3）。

表3　主要工业产品产量

产品名称	单位	产量	比上年增长（%）
天然原油	万吨	1943.09	9.0
天然气	亿立方米	10.50	19.5
生　铁	万吨	1131.51	39.3
钢　材	万吨	2117.51	23.2
无缝钢管	万吨	216.58	21.0
水　泥	万吨	607.33	23.9
移动电话	万部	10129.72	48.3
轿　车	万辆	41.03	26.0
自行车	万辆	1707.77	15.7
布	亿米	2.83	24.3
精制食用植物油	万吨	111.27	29.2
家　具	万件	619.47	55.0

工业经济效益连续第四年保持快速增长。全市规模以上独立核算工业企业实现主营业务收入8782.68亿

元，比上年增长24.5%。实现利税总额突破千亿元，达到1004.80亿元，增长31.0%。其中，实现税金313.94亿元，增长30.5%，实现利润690.86亿元，增长31.2%。国有及国有控股工业企业实现利税总额600.52亿元，增长46.0%。其中，实现税金204.29亿元，增长26.8%，实现利润396.24亿元，增长58.4%。分行业看，石油和天然气开采业、通信设备计算机及其他电子设备制造业、黑色金属冶炼及压延加工业、交通运输设备制造业和通用设备制造业等五大行业合计实现利润578.81亿元，占全市利润总额的83.8%。全市工业经济效益综合指数达到240.52，比上年提高32.82点。其中，总资产贡献率为15.48%，比上年提高1.84个百分点；资本保值增值率为115.32%，比上年提高5.76个百分点。

建筑业

全市建筑业完成增加值195.02亿元，比上年增长17.0%；完成总产值924.28亿元，增长27.4 %。全年房屋建筑施工面积4271.14万平方米，增长13.3%；房屋建筑竣工面积1606.92万平方米，增长21.9%。全市有总承包和专业承包资格的建筑企业1152家,实现利润17.45亿元，增长19.3%，实现税金27.70亿元，增长28.3%。

交通运输、仓储和邮政业

全市交通运输、仓储和邮政业完成增加值256.97亿元，比上年增长7.2%。货运量继续增加。全年实现全社会货运量42807.66万吨，比上年增长9.0%，其中，公路运输20290万吨，增长2.2%；水路运输13257.45万吨，增长11.7%；铁路运输8409.43万吨，增长23.5%。公路、水路、铁路三种主要运输方式占货运量比重分别为47.4%、31.0%和19.6%。港口吞吐量完成25759.7万吨，比上年增长7.0%，其中进港10475.1万吨，增长11.8%，出港15284.6万吨，增长4.0%。在港口吞吐量中，集装箱吞吐量完成595万标准箱，比上年净增115万标准箱，增长23.9%。机场货物吞吐量9.68万吨，增长20.7%。

旅客运输增长较快。全年完成客运量5669.62万人，比上年增长21.2%。其中,铁路1632.22万人,增长5.3%；公路3807万人，增长28.6%；滨海国际机场旅客吞吐量276.65万人，增长26.1%。

旅客周转量快速增长，货物周转量略有下降。全年完成旅客周转量163.40亿人公里，比上年增长15.0%。其中，铁路96.51亿人公里，增长6.4%；公路35.64亿人公里，增长34.7%。全年货运周转量12149.29亿吨公里，比上年下降0.4%，其中，公路运输75.80亿吨公里，增长2.4%；水路运输11716.46亿吨公里，下降0.4%；铁路运输352.73亿吨公里，增长0.8%。

年末全市汽车拥有量81.66万辆，比上年增长15.6%，其中轿车43.19万辆，增长26.1%。全市私人汽车达到57.21万辆，占70%，增长19.3%，其中轿车32.57万辆，增长32.0%。

邮政电信规模继续快速扩张。全年邮电业务总量完成225.9亿元，比上年增长26.9%。其中电信业务总量212.32亿元，增长27.3%，邮政业务总量13.58亿元，增长20.1%。年末长途光缆线路总长度达到2884.40公里，局用电话交换机总容量619.19万门，公网固定电话用户达到435.76万户。公网电话本地通话量96.86亿次，长途电话通话量11.99亿次，其中国际及港澳台长途电话0.18亿次。年末移动电话用户600.99万户，比上年增长19.6%，全年短信业务总量104.35亿条，增长36.8%。全年发送邮政函件9279.46万件，增长10.7%，其中特快专递352.32万件，增长6.2%。

国内商业

全市批发和零售贸易业完成增加值487.94亿元，比上年增长11.2%。住宿和餐饮业完成增加值80亿元，比上年增长11.7%。批发零售贸易业购销总规模12947.82亿元，增长27.1%，其中，商品购进总额6280.76亿元，商品销售总额6667.06亿元。

消费品市场趋向活跃。全年社会消费品零售总额完成1356.79亿元，增长14.0%。其中批发和零售贸易业零售额1143.04亿元，增长13.5%，住宿和餐饮业零售额209.97亿元，增长17.4%。交通、通讯和用品类商品保持畅销。限额以上批发零售贸易企业汽车类零售额增长36.0%，石油及制品类增长20.3%，通讯器材类增长19.7%，金银珠宝类增长30.7%，家用电器和音像器材类增长12.1%。

批发交易市场商品物流集散功能增强。年成交额超亿元的批发市场实现成交额995.11亿元，增长20.9%。大型商业设施档次提高。伊势丹、轻纺万象城等大型商业设施竣工开业。社区便民商业设施建设进展迅速，市区累计建成标准化菜市场261个,社区商业网点10368个。农业生产资料连锁经营进乡镇和日用消费品连锁经营进村庄达到2563个，配送中心20个。

金融业

全市金融业完成增加值179.40亿元，比上年增长11.4%。年末全市各类金融机构达2852家，其中，证券营业部74家，保险机构458家。

存贷款规模继续扩大。年末全市金融机构（含外资）本外币各项存款余额6839.20亿元，比年初增加854.52亿元。其中储蓄存款余额2922.70亿元，比年初增加

349.68亿元。年末本外币各项贷款余额5415.72亿元，比年初增加780.14亿元。其中，中长期贷款余额2800.89亿元，比年初增加530.69亿元，占全市贷款增加额的68.0%，对我市基础设施投资和大型重点工程建设发挥了重要作用。年末住房按揭贷款余额419.35亿元，汽车消费贷款余额10.08亿元。金融机构资产质量继续提高，全市不良贷款率降至5.5%。

金融市场交易活跃。年末全市共有境内上市股票25只。全年股票成交额2393.71亿元，债券成交额69.38亿元，基金成交额48.37亿元。期货市场全年成交量598.73万手，增长83.4%，成交金额3000.37亿元，增长1倍。证券帐户开户数96.67万户。全年调剂外汇总额21.11亿美元，比上年下降4.6%，其中调入外汇10.76亿美元，下降17.7%，调出外汇10.35亿美元，增长14.3%。

保险业稳定发展。全年保费收入105.18亿元，增长16.1%，其中财产险保费收入26.62亿元，人身险保费收入78.57亿元。各项赔款和给付21.86亿元，其中财产险12.64亿元，人身险9.22亿元。

房地产业

全市房地产业完成增加值139.27亿元，增长6.6%。完成房地产开发投资402.32亿元，增长22.8%。商品房销售面积1458.60万平方米，增长4.0%；实现销售收入696.27亿元，增长21.2%。完成经济适用房开发投资50.96亿元，增长1.4倍；施工面积380万平方米，其中新开工267万平方米，增长64.8%；竣工141万平方米，增长17.5%。全年存量房交易面积622.9万平方米，实现交易金额214.3亿元。

二、改革开放

所有制结构

在全市生产总值中，公有制经济增加值2082亿元，比上年增长14.2%，占全市的48%；非公有制经济增加值2255.73亿元，增长14.7%，占全市的52%。在非公有制经济中，私营个体经济增加值1063亿元，占全市的24.5%；外资经济增加值1193亿元，占全市的27.5%。

各种所有制工业企业全面发展。全市规模以上工业企业中：国有及国有控股工业企业共完成总产值3341.49亿元，比上年增长28.8%，私营企业完成总产值799.89亿元，增长26.6%；按企业登记注册类型分，外商及港澳台商投资企业完成总产值4308.30亿元，增长29.8%，股份制企业完成总产值3190.25亿元，增长23.0%；股份合作企业完成总产值74.01亿元，增长19.4%。

私营个体经济不断壮大。年末私营个体经济注册资金1924.79亿元，比年初增加304.46亿元。私营和个体经营户达到26.55万户，比年初增加1.12万户；从业人员122.80万人，比年初增加8.62万人；实现销售及营业收入1427.06亿元，比上年增长9.3%；实现税收78.43亿元，增长28.4%。

国有资产管理与国有企业改革

国有资本合理流动的力度加大。全年772宗国有产权进入产权交易市场公开挂牌交易，实现交易额193.38亿元。其中跨区域交易额36.44亿元，市内交易额156.94亿元。

国有企业改革和调整重组步伐加快。年内市属国有企业改制240户，累计达到3183户，改制面达到84.6%，比上年提高8个百分点。股权分置改革和企业上市融资工作取得新成果。相继完成12家国有控股上市公司的股权分置改革工作，通过分拆上市、发行可转换债券和定向募集等方式，累计融资27亿元。

社会保障

社会保障体系建设取得新进展。全市养老保险参保人员328.2万人，增长6.5%，其中，离退休112.7万人；全市失业保险参保职工216.7万人，增长9.7%；医疗保险参保人员329.4万人，增长10.1%；工伤保险参保职工209.7万人；生育保险覆盖180.1万人。出台了农村社会养老保险办法，形成了覆盖城乡的社会养老保险制度体系。启动农民工医疗保险和工伤保险。职工最低工资标准继续提高，月最低工资标准由上年的590元提高到670元。

地区合作

全市引进国内资金到位额431.85亿元，比上年增长27.0%，投资项目1840项。吸引内资来源更加集中，来自环渤海地区、“长三角”地区和“珠三角”地区的资金比重达到89.9%，比上年提高13个百分点。工业和房地产业成为热点行业，吸引内资分别占到全市的27.9%和49.9%。民间资本处于主体地位，到位316.45亿元，占全市利用内资的比重达到73%，比上年提高10个百分点。

继续实施对甘肃省、西藏昌都地区、重庆万州区和新疆喀什的对口支援和帮扶工作，有力地促进了当地经济的发展。全年共援建对口地区项目41个，落实援建资金5000万元。实施合作项目10个，比上年增长25%；实际投资749万元，增长18%。

对外贸易

全市外贸进出口总值突破600亿美元，达到645.73亿美元，增长21.0%。其中，出口335.40亿美元，增长22.3%，进口310.33亿美元，增长19.5%。实现贸易顺差25.07亿美元。在出口产品中：机电产品出口234.7亿美元，增长26.4%，占全市出口的70%；属于高新技术的产品出口154.3亿美元，增长23.7%。电子信息、汽车零部件、新能源、生物医药、海洋石油化工等高附加值商品，成为天津市出口的主导产品。百强企业出口实力雄厚，合计出口242.37亿美元，增长22.3%，占全市出口的比重为72.3%。对美国、欧盟、东盟、日本、韩国和香港等主要贸易伙伴出口278.23亿美元，所占比重达到83.0%。

利用外资

全市新批外商投资企业1050家，其中合同金额1000万美元以上的大项目187家。全市直接利用外资合同金额81.12亿美元，比上年增长10.8%；实际到位41.31亿美元，增长24.1%。服务业合同利用外资42.59亿美元，增长40.7%，占全市合同利用外资额的比重达到52.5%，比上年提高11.2个百分点，实际到位14.43亿美元，增长82.7%。其中交通运输及仓储业增长3倍，房地产业增长1.2倍。新能源领域成为引资新亮点。风力发电、海水淡化、新型电池等一批新能源项目落户津门。截止年末，世界500强跨国公司已经有121家来津投资。

对外经济合作

全市当年对外承包工程及劳务新签合同1098个，合同额12.47亿美元，比上年增长1.9倍，实现营业额6.09亿美元，增长90.2%。年末在境外劳务人员1.2万人。全年新批境外机构72个，其中境外投资生产企业39个。新批境外投资生产企业总投资7545.46万美元，其中中方投资5982.79万美元。引进国外先进技术力度继续加大，全年签定技术引进合同471项，合同金额7.18亿美元。天津被国家批准为服务外包基地城市。成功举办了中日韩十城市市长联席会等大型活动，扩大了天津的影响。

旅 游

全年接待国际旅游者88.06万人次，比上年增长19.0%。其中外国人81.17万人次，增长20.3%。旅游创汇6.26亿美元，增长22.9%。接待外省游客及本市居民市内游人数比上年增长9.3%，旅游收入增长11.2%。全市共有15.3万人次出国出境旅游，增长4.8%，旅游支出20.3亿元，增长5.7%。年末全市拥有星级宾馆、饭店114家；国际、国内旅行社264家，其中国际旅行社29家，国内旅行社235家。

滨海新区

随着滨海新区开发开放被纳入国家总体发展战略，并被批准为全国综合配套改革试验区和设立东疆保税港区，滨海新区掀起新一轮开发开放热潮。基础设施建设全面提速，天津滨海国际机场扩建、天津港25万吨级深水航道、30万吨级原油码头工程和北港池集装箱码头三期工程建设进展顺利，100万吨乙烯、北疆电厂、东疆保税港区等一批重点项目开工建设，空客A320中国总装线项目落户，渤海银行开业，全国第一只产业投资基金——“渤海产业投资基金”正式挂牌成立。

全年滨海新区实现生产总值1960.5亿元，按可比价格计算，比上年增长20.2%，对全市经济增长贡献率为51.4%。电子通信、石油开采、汽车制造、现代冶金为支柱构成的高层次产业结构优势明显，现代医药、航空航天、新材料等高新技术产业群迅速发展。新区全年完成工业总产值5200.52亿元，增长31.3%。完成固定资产投资864.29亿元，增长24.7%。全年直接利用外资合同金额61.80亿美元，占全市的76.2%，增长24.0%，实际到位33.45亿美元，占全市的81.0%，增长31.1%。新区经济外向度不断加大，全年外贸出口达到226.20亿美元，占全市的67.4%，增长22.5%(见表4)。开发区经济总量迅速扩大，增长速度连续6年保持在25%以上，综合实力在全国开发区中继续保持领先；工业总产值完成3004.16亿元，增长25.1%；固定资产投资完成220.09亿元，首次超过200亿元；合同外资额32.54亿美元，实际到位16.08亿美元。

大通关建设成就明显。先后在新疆乌鲁木齐、河北石家庄、河南郑州等地设立了“无水港”。全年天津口岸进出口总值达到1018.85亿美元，增长24.4%，成为全国第四个对外贸易额突破1000亿美元大关的口岸。其中进口447.61亿美元，增长20.2%，出口571.24亿美元，增长27.8%。在天津口岸进出口总值中，北京、河北、山西、

表4 2002-2006年滨海新区主要经济指标

指 标	单位	2002年	2003年	2004年	2005年	2006年
地区生产总值	亿元	862.45	1046.30	1323.26	1623.26	1960.5
比上年增长	%	20.1	20.4	20.1	19.8	20.2
全社会固定资产投资	亿元	280.89	464.08	565.47	693.31	864.29
外贸出口总额	亿美元	72.01	89.38	136.99	184.69	226.20
实际直接利用外资	亿美元	8.23	12.15	17.44	25.31	33.45

内蒙古和甘肃等腹地所占比重达到54.7%。保税区充分发挥国际贸易、保税仓库和物流分拨功能，全年进出区货物总值254.25亿美元，比上年增长35.5%。

三、城市建设和管理

基础设施建设

城市基础设施建设全面推进。全市基础设施建设投资完成518.17亿元，比上年增长23.1%，占全市城镇固定资产投资的比重达到30.3%，有效地提高了城市载体功能。开工建设了京津塘高速公路二线、蓟平高速，实现了京沪高速（天津段）全线通车，高速公路里程达到694公里。中心城区快速路建设进度加快，新增通车里程40公里，累计达到160公里。年末实有城市铺装道路长度5693公里，铺装道路面积7433万平方米。地铁1号线投入试运营，地铁2号线建设全面启动，黄万铁路和神华天津煤炭码头基本建成。

公用事业

公共环境设施建设力度加大。启动了津滨水厂建设，建成咸阳路再生水厂和青光垃圾焚烧厂。实施了南运河、纪庄子河、津港运河改造和铁路专用线综合治理。全年新建绿地面积2172万平方米，建成区绿化覆盖率提高到37%。城市人均公园绿地面积6.59平方米。全市污水处理率达到75%，垃圾处理率达到85%。全市自来水综合生产能力为358万立方米/日，全年自来水售水量6.4亿立方米。顺利完成了35万户居民和1300家企业煤制气转换天然气，年末城市燃气普及率为98.6%。新增供热面积800万平方米，集中供热普及率达到84.6%。我市被建设部授予"优先发展公共交通示范城市"称号，公交运营车辆达到7200标台，年内新辟公交线路31条，年末市内公交线路450条。全年公交客运量9.4亿人次。全市运营出租车31939辆。

海河综合开发

海河综合开发进展迅速。已累计开工商贸、金融、文化等设施282万平方米，新建了大沽桥、保定桥和奉化桥，采用桥梁抬升技术改造了狮子林桥和北安桥。恢复了解放桥和金汤桥的开启功能。拓宽了一批临河道路，累计完成堤岸改造12.5公里。建成音乐公园、解放公园等6处临河绿地。凤凰商贸广场、美博城、港湾中心、少儿艺术中心等一批工程已投入使用。

资源、环境和安全生产

进一步加强土地资源管理。实现了全市经营性土地集中交易和"净地"出让，建立了公开、规范、统一的土地市场，发挥了土地的调控作用。全年土地供应总量4523.1公顷，其中，土地出让3867.06公顷，土地划拨656.04公顷。

我市环保创模通过国家验收，荣获"国家环境保护模范城市"荣誉称号。全市环境质量主要指标保持稳定。全年空气质量二级及以上良好天数为305天，占全年天数的83.6%，比上年提高了2个百分点。城市集中饮用水源地水质达标率100%，城市水环境功能区水质达标率100%。道路交通噪声和区域环境噪声平均声级保持在"好"和"较好"等级，环境噪声控制达标区面积571.5平方公里。当年创建安静居住小区29个，全市安静小区共达到126个。建成烟尘控制区60个，烟尘控制面积589.4平方公里。年末全市有环境监测站21个，生态示范区7个，自然保护区8个，自然保护区面积16.28万公顷。西青区张家窝镇、武清区石各庄镇被命名为"全国环境优美镇"，使我市的全国环境优美乡镇达到6个。

事故发生和人员死亡数量下降。全年发生生产安全事故81起，比上年下降11.9%，死亡92人，下降3.2%；道路交通事故4913起，上升11.5%，死亡878人，下降9.5%；火灾事故4208起，下降18.9%，死亡21人，下降36.4%。全市亿元生产总值生产安全事故死亡率为0.24，下降25%。工矿商贸从业人员生产安全事故10万人死亡率为2.6，下降7.1%。

信息化建设

信息化建设取得新进展。2006年末，全市互联网拨号上网用户308.97万户，宽带用户91.63万户。电子政务专网一期扩容建设已完成并正式运行，启动企业基础信息共享系统建设，依托市电子政务专网，实现工商、地税、国税、质监等15个政府工作部门的企业信息共享，有力地促进了政府职能的转变和行政效率的提高。纺织、机械等20个行业电子商务网站应用效果明显。港口、邮政、公路等行业物流信息系统建设步伐加快，保税区物流公共信息服务平台的建设，加速了口岸贸易的物流速度。

质量监督

2006年新创中国名牌产品3个，累计达到18个；新创天津名牌产品27个，累计达到223个；国家新审定的免检产品18种，累计达到63种。制定、修订企业产品标准3072项，企业标准总计达3.3万项。累计发放体系认证证书3455家。取得"3C"产品认证企业有675家，发证3297张。完成计量仪器检定64.4万台（件），其中强检计量器具占70.45%。2006年，全市共有333家食品生产加工企业取得食品生产许可证。

四、科技和社会事业

科 技

科技创新服务体系和知识创新体系建设取得新成果。一批科技大项目进入国家科技计划，电子信息、生物技术、现代医药、海水淡化等领域的研发取得突破性成果。本市12个科技项目获得2006年度国家科技奖，其中荣获自然科学二等奖1项，科学技术进步二等奖11项。全年市级科技成果登记1559项，其中属于国际领先水平69项，达到国际先进水平397项。在科技成果中，基础理论成果175项，应用技术成果1341项，软科学成果43项。受理专利申请13299件，专利授权4159项。全年签订技术合同10181项，交易额58.86亿元，增长16.1%。新增国家部级重点实验室1个，全市市级以上重点实验室达到50个。

着力增强自主创新能力，切实把科技进步作为转变增长方式的中心环节。召开了全市科技大会，做出了建设创新型城市的决定。大力推进企业技术创新体系建设，建立了一批高新技术联合转化基地，12家企业进入全国大中型工业企业“自主创新能力行业十强”，力神电池、天士力中药、石油钢管位居全行业第一。年末全市共有国家级和市级企业技术中心214家，其中国家级企业技术中心14家。

积极引进海内外优秀人才，全年引进各类人才1.78万余人，新建博士后工作站17家，全市博士后流动站、工作站达到143个，增长13.5%，在站博士后500余人。

新技术产业园区实现快速发展。园区实现技工贸总收入1050亿元，比上年增长26%；技工贸总产值950亿元，增长28%；实现利润总额48亿元，增长26%；实现税金总额55亿元，增长27%；出口销售收入32亿美元，增长19%。华苑产业区继续发挥核心区作用。全年完成工业总产值296亿元，比上年增长40.1%；外贸出口7.7亿美元，增长41.7%。

教 育

高水平大学和重点学科建设加快。天津师范大学等高校新校区一期建成投入使用，商学院、农学院、财经大学改扩建工程全面完成，中医学院、民航学院升级为大学。全市高等教育毛入学率达到53%。当年45所普通高校和高等职业技术学院共招生10.79万人，比上年增加0.43万人，毕业8.20万人，年末共有在校学生35.74万人。当年招收研究生1.09万人，比上年增加0.07万人，毕业0.92万人，年末在学研究生3.06万人。成人高等教育当年招生2.92万人，毕业1.78万人，年末在校学生9.18万人。全市高校19052名贫困学生得到国家助学贷款，发放助学贷款2.43亿元。启动国家职业教育改革试验区建设，建成10个职业教育实验实训基地。

继续推进中等教育资源布局调整。累计建成52所示范中学、16所模范小学和422所村办小学，启动了“历史名校”建设工程，农村80%的中小学教学设备实现了升级换代。建立农村义务教育经费保障机制，率先实施农村中小学生“两免一补”政策，70万学生受益，当年减免学杂费5540万元。全市当年招收普通高中生6.80万人，毕业6.99万人，年末在校学生21.63万人。招收中等职业学校学生4.16万人，年末在校学生13.68万人。招收初中生10.43万人，毕业12.43万人，年末在校学生33.58万人。招收小学生8.21万人，毕业10.61万人，年末在校学生51.68万人。幼儿园在园幼儿19.38万人。高中阶段毛入学率91%，小学生升学率98.41%，学龄儿童入学率99.38%。

文 化

年末全市共有艺术表演团体16个，文化馆18个，博物馆18个，公共图书馆32个，档案馆35个，电影放映单位20个。全市现有广播节目10套，综合人口覆盖率为100%；市级电视节目9套，综合人口覆盖率为99.83%，全市有线电视用户达到200万户。全年共创作9部电影故事片，创作拍摄24部近800集电视连续剧，是我市影视剧创作数量最多的一年。

中华剧院、少儿图书馆等一批文化设施投入使用。结合纪念建党85周年和长征胜利70周年，举办了一系列主题鲜明、内容丰富的文化活动。承办的“永远的辉煌”第八届中国老年合唱节、第八届“和平杯”中国京剧票友邀请赛、第四届农民艺术节等多项全国性文化活动受到广泛好评。

卫 生

年末全市共有各类卫生机构2383个，其中医院、卫生院和社区卫生服务中心472个，卫生防疫、防治机构40个，妇幼保健机构23个。卫生机构拥有床位4.4万张，其中医院、卫生院和社区卫生服务中心4.2万张。全市卫生技术人员6.2万人，其中执业医师及执业助理医师2.54万人，注册护士2万人。卫生资源配置优化。东方器官移植中心、妇女儿童保健中心投入使用，防病中心、传染病医院改扩建工程完工，医大总医院二期和医大二院等建设项目竣工投入使用。出台了《关于进一步发展社区卫生服务的决定》，为群众提供安全、有效、便捷、经济的公共卫生服务和基本医疗服务。农村新型合作医疗扩展到9个区县，人口覆盖率达到48.3%，比上年提高了18.1个百分点。全年无偿献血11.7万人次，增长16.5%。

体育

竞技体育取得新突破。在第15届多哈亚运会上，天津运动员不畏强手，顽强拼搏，共夺得16枚金牌，金牌总数、参赛项目和参赛人数全面超过历届，实现了新的突破。群众健身条件明显改善，建成了社区健身中心、居委会健身路径228个，大型健身广场10个，总面积达到5万余平方米。天津市第二次国民体质监测数据显示，市民体质监测总体达标率为88.6%，高于全国平均水平1.4个百分点。幼儿、成年人和老年人达标率分别高于全国平均水平1.4、0.9和4.5个百分点。

社会福利与救助

政府抚恤、补助各类优抚对象2.41万人，城乡低保对象18.86万人，其中城镇低保对象15.13万人。各种福利院拥有床位18846张，收养13170人。全市有救助站9个，全年救助15829人次。全市社区服务设施2177处。全年销售社会福利彩票5.45亿元，比上年增长35.5%，筹集福利资金1.9亿元，增长35.7%。全年接受社会捐赠3103.5万元，比上年增长1.8倍。

残疾人事业

残疾人康复、就业、社会保障、无障碍建设等项工作稳步推进，为残疾人服务能力增强。完成公共场所无障碍设施改造17182处，为残疾人的出行提供了便利。全年新安置残疾人就业2273人，增长33%；当年全市特殊教育招收新生200余人，在校生达到2500余人，残障儿童入学率保持在95%以上。按照全国统一的调查方案，完成了天津市第二次全国残疾人抽样调查，为我市经济社会和残疾人事业的发展提供了依据。

五、人口与人民生活

人口

年末全市常住人口为1075万人，户籍人口948.88万人。在户籍人口中，农业人口377.85万人，非农业人口571.03万人。人口继续保持低速增长。2006年全市人口出生率为7.67‰，人口死亡率为6.07‰，人口自然增长率为1.60‰。

人民生活

全市城镇单位从业人员人均劳动报酬27252元，比上年增长13.0%。随着提高企业退休人员养老待遇标准和机关事业单位工资改革政策的出台，城市居民人均可支配收入达到14283元，增长13.0%。农村居民人均纯收入7942元，增长10.3%。

居民生活水平继续提高，城市居民人均消费性支出10548元，增长9.3%。居民消费结构向良性变化，恩格尔系数为34.9%，比上年降低1.8个百分点。穿着、家庭设备用品和交通通讯支出分别增长23.8%、21.0%和9.5%。年末城市每百户居民家庭拥有汽车4.6辆、移动电话143.7部、电脑59.2台、微波炉77.9台、热水器87.1台、助力车15.5辆、成套家具95.3套。农村居民人均生活消费支出3829元，增长6.7%。年末农村每百户居民家庭拥有洗衣机96台、电冰箱88台、热水器38台、微波炉20台、移动电话108部、电脑12台。

居民居住条件继续改善，城市居民人均住房建筑面积26.05平方米，农村居民人均住房面积26.43平方米，分别比上年提高1.08和0.37平方米。

经济和社会发展中存在的主要问题是：国民经济结构还需进一步优化，节能降耗、降污减排任务还比较艰巨，就业压力仍然较大等。

注：1. 2006年各项统计数据为快报数。

2. 全市生产总值、各产业增加值绝对数按当年价格计算，增长速度按可比价格计算。

3. 规模以上工业企业包括全部国有和年销售收入在500万元及以上的非国有工业企业。

4. 高等教育毛入学率指在校大学生人数（剔除在津就学的外地籍学生，加入在外地就学的本市籍学生）与学龄组人口的比例，表明一个地区提供高等教育机会的综合水平。

5. 恩格尔系数是指食品消费支出占全部消费性支出的比重。恩格尔系数降低标志着居民生活水平和质量提高。

STATISTICAL COMMUNIQUE ON THE 2006 NATIONAL ECONOMIC AND SOCIAL DEVELOPMENT OF THE CITY OF TIANJIN

Tianjin Municipal Bureau of Statistics
NBS Survey Office in Tianjin
March 21, 2007

In 2006, the beginning of the Eleventh Five-Year Plan, under the correct leadership of Tianjin municipal Party committee of the Communist Party of China and Tianjin Municipal Government, the people of Tianjin followed the guidance of Deng Xiaoping Theory and the principle of "Three Represents", implemented the view of scientific development, carried out the decisions and dispositions of Central Committee of Communist Party of China and State Council about pushing the Binhai district developing and opening. Great efforts were made to boost the implement the "Three-step" development strategy and five strategic measures and construction of harmonious Tianjin. The economic grew steadily and rapidly and social undertakings progressed in a comprehensive way. Peoples' living standard continued to improve. It was a good beginning of the Eleventh-Five-Year Pan.

I. Economic Development

Economic Aggregate

The gross domestic product (GDP) of Tianjin was 433.773 billion yuan, up by 14.4% over the previous year at comparable prices and 1.2 times over 2000. The target of double was achieved 5 years in advance and the economic aggregate of the second-step strategy in the "Three-step" development strategy was fulfilled ahead of schedule. The per capita GDP in Tianjin was 40,961 yuan, up 11.7%, and was 5,177 dollars according to average exchange rate. All of this data were rough calculation and checked by National Bureau of Statistics.

The tertiary industry developed in a comprehensive way. The added value of primary industry was 11.897 billion yuan, up by 3.5% over the previous year. The added value of secondary industry accomplished 248.583 billion yuan, up by 17.6% over the last year. The added value of the tertiary industry achieved 173.293 billion yuan, up 11.0%. The ratio between the three industries is 2.7∶57.3∶40.

Figure 1 GDP and Rate of Tianjin

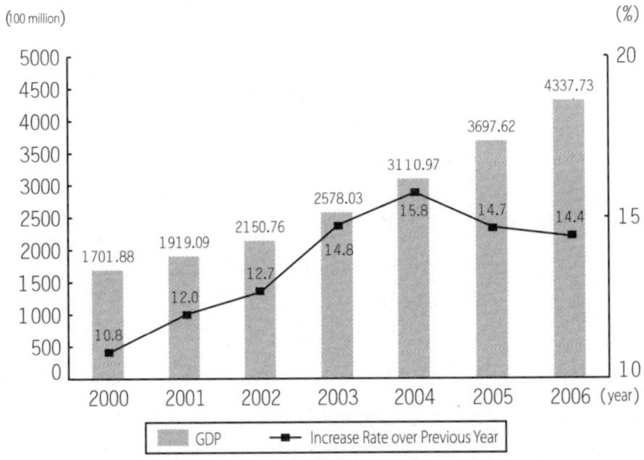

Note: GDP are Calulated at Current Price and Rate are Calulated at Comparable Price.

Government Revenue

Government revenue of Tianjin exceeded 900 billion yuan and achieved 92.562 billion yuan, up by 27.6% over the last year and its ratio to the GDP was 21.3%, 1.7 percentage point higher than the previous year. The budget revenue of Tianjin was 41.677 billion yuan, up 25.6%, of which the main tax items increased rapidly. The value-added tax had increased by 25.6%; consumable tax, 43.2%; business tax, 20.2%; business income tax, 29.1%; individual tax, 12.7%. Government expenditure of Tianjin was 65.42 billion yuan, up 25.7%. Of the total, the expenditure on infrastructure was 26.32 billion yuan, up 28.2%; on agriculture was 1.61 billion yuan, up 25.1%; on social security and subsidies was 6.29 billion yuan, up 36.9%; on technology was 1.83 billion yuan, up 33.8%.

Labor and Employment

The number of people employed in new job posts was 290 thousand, increased of 32.8 thousand and by 12.5%, of which the unemployment was 129.1 thousand. At the end of the year, the total number of employees in Tianjin was 5.6292 million, increased by 3.8%, of which the number of people engaged in the primary industry and the secondary industry were 799.3 thousand and 2313.6 thousand respectively while the number corresponding to the tertiary industry was 2516.3 thousand. In the human resources and labor market, 3414.8 thousand people were interviewed for jobs, and 913.8 thousand people reached preliminary agreement with their potential employers. The registered unemployment rate in the urban area was 3.6%

Price

The urban residents' consumption price index is 101.5, up by

Table 1 Consumer Price Index

Indicator	Index (Previous year = 100)
Urban Residents' Consumption Price Index	101.5
Food	102.7
Tobacco, Liquor and Related Articles	103.0
Clothing	97.5
Household Appliances, Articles and Repair	100.5
Medical, Health Care and Individual Goods	101.4
Transportation and Telecommunication	98.9
Recreational, Educational & Cultural Articles and Services	99.0
Residence	104.4

1.5% over the last year. Five kinds of merchandises' price rose while three fallen.

The retail price index of commodities in the urban was 100.4. The ex-factory price index of industrial products was 100.6. The purchasing price index of raw material, fuels and motive power was 104.7. The sales price index of housing was 106.7 of which price index of the commodity housing was 107.1.

Investment in Fixed Assets

The total investment in fixed assets in Tianjin was 184.980 billion yuan, up by 22.0% over the last year. Of the total, the fixed assets investment in the urban was 170.966 billion yuan, up 23.4% and the fixed assets investment in the country was 14.014 billion yuan, increased by 6.9%.

Figure 2 Total Investment in Fixed Assets and Increase Rate

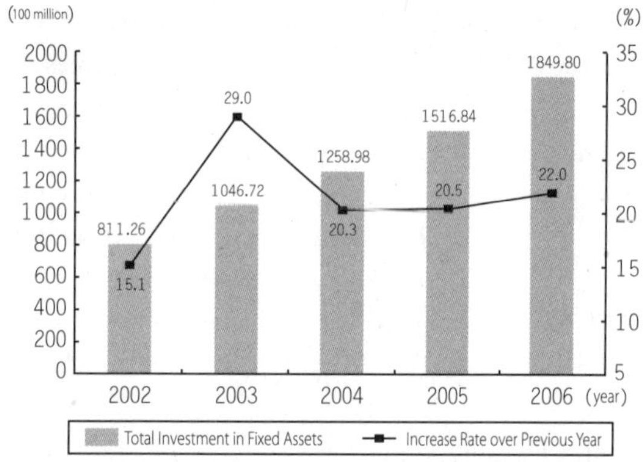

Of the fixed assets investment in the urban, the primary industry was 0.338 billion yuan. The secondary industry accounted for 70.138 billion yuan, up 29.2%, of which investment on industry was 69.034 billion yuan, grown by 29.6% and 100.445 billion yuan went to the tertiary industry, up 20%. The investment on transportation and post and storage, real estate industry and environment were increased by 21.5%, 22.0% and 21.8% respectively. The construction of major projects were strengthened so that the large projects on which the investment were exceeded 1 billion yuan had finished investment of 74.694 billion yuan, up 51.3%.

Agriculture

The total agricultural output value had reached 25.150 billion yuan, up by 3.7% over the previous year. Of the total, planting industry was 10.527 billion yuan, up 3.6%; forest industry 0.198 billion yuan, up 2.5%; stockbreeding 10.489 billion yuan, up 3.1%; fishery industry 3.936 billion yuan, up 6.0%. Stockbreeding and fishery industry accounted for 57.4% of the total agriculture output value.

The agriculture productivity was growing steadily. The crop planting area in the year was 4.4282 million acres, increased of 0.1133 million acres over the last year. The total output of grains was 1.4352 million tons, up 4.4%. The planting area of crop was 1.0644 million tons and the output of crop was 97.7 thousand tons, grew by 17.0%. The radios of fish, meat, eggs, milk, etc., agriculture products were higher than the last year.

Table 2 Yield of Major Agricultural Products

Name of Products	Unit	Output	Increase Rate over Previous Year (%)
Grain	10 000 tons	143.52	4.4
Cotton	10 000 tons	9.77	17.0
Meat	10 000 tons	59.91	3.7
Milk	10 000 tons	65.00	2.5
Aquatic Products	10 000 tons	35.80	5.9
Poultry Eggs	10 000 tons	24.20	3.1
Fruits	10 000 tons	30.35	9.2
Vegetables	10 000 tons	540.13	-0.5

Agricultural industrialization and mechanization were advanced all around. Farmers joined the agriculture industrialization accounted for 73.6% of the total farmers, 3.6 percentage point higher than the last year. 198 projects on transformation and application of achievements in agricultural science and technology had been implemented in the year. The total powers of agricultural machine was 603.39 ten thousand kilowatt and the number of agriculture machine was 594.7 thousand, of which the numbers of the seeds combine harvester and the agricultural vehicles were 3 and 140.3 thousand respectively. The radio of seeding by machines was 58.3% and the number was 91.2% for the radio of culturing by machines. The area of water-saving irrigation was 19.79 ten thousand ha..

The construction of the new country of socialist had advanced in a comprehensive way. The construction of country public works were strengthened, because many projects had been implemented, such as "351" country labor training project, country watering pipe project and country toilet reconstruction project. Thus, farms' living conditions were improved greatly.

Industry

The added value of industry in Tianjin was 229.081 billion yuan, a rise of 17.7% over the last year and realized the total industrial output of 890.745 billion yuan, up 25.1%. The added value of the industry enterprises above the designated size reached 222.382 billion yuan, increased by 18.8% and accomplished the total industrial output of 852.770 billion yuan, grown by 25.3%.

The advantageous industries play more important roles as under props. Six advantageous industries in Tianjin (electronic information, automobile, petrochemical industry, metallurgy, biotechnology and modern medicine, new energy resources and environment) achieved a total industrial output of 639.160 billion yuan, up 27.5%, accounting for 74.9%, higher 1.2% than the previous year and their contribution rate to industrial growth in Tianjin was 80%. The output value of the new and high-tech industries accomplished 271.301 billion yuan, increased by 24.3%, proportion of which was 31.8% to the total industrial output. The new products value was 260.130 billion yuan, grew by 39.9%.

The production and marketing situations were adapted to each other better. The sales output value of industries above designated size was 846.222 billion yuan, increased by 24.3% over the last year and the sales rate was 99.24% to the output.

Table 3 Yield of Major Industrial Products

Name of Products	Unit	Output	Increase Rate over Previous Year (%)
Crude Oil	10 000 tons	1943.09	9.0
Natural Gas	100 million cu. m	10.50	19.5
Pig Iron	10 000 tons	1131.51	39.3
Steel Products	10 000 tons	2117.51	23.2
Seamless Steel Pipe	10 000 tons	216.58	21.0
Cement	10 000 tons	607.33	23.9
Mobile Phone	10 000 units	10129.72	48.3
Car	10 000 units	41.03	26.0
Bicycle	10 000 units	1707.77	15.7
Cloth	100 million m	2.83	24.3
Refined Edible Vegetable Oilc	10 000 tons	111.27	29.2
Furniture	10 000 pieces	619.47	55.0

The industrial economic benefit increased rapidly in consecutive four years. The independent industrial enterprises above the designated size in Tianjin earned an revenue of 878.268 billion yuan, grew by 24.5%. Their profit payments and tax turnover exceeded thousand billion yuan and reached 100.480 billion yuan, up 31.0%. Of the total, tax turnover was 31.394 billion yuan, grew by 30.5% and profit payment was 69.086 billion yuan, increased by 31.2%. The total profit payments and tax turnover of state-owned and state-controlled industrial enterprises was 60.052 billion yuan, up 46.0%. Of the total, tax turnover was 20.429 billion yuan, grew by 26.8% and profit payment was 39.624 billion yuan, increased by 58.4%. The profit payments of five industries (petroleum and natural gas extraction industries, telecommunications equipment and computer & other electronic equipments manufacturing, smelting and pressing of ferrous metal, transport equipment manufacturing and all-purpose equipment manufacturing) were 57.881 billion yuan, of which the proportion was 83.8% to the total profit payment in Tianjin. The comprehensive index on economic profit of industrial enterprises was 240.52, 32.82–percentage point higher than the previous year. The radio of total assets to industrial output value was 15.48%, 1.84–percentage point higher. The rate of value-sustained and value-added assets was 115.32%, up 5.76%.

Construction

The added value of construction was 19.502 billion yuan, up 17.0%. The total output value of Tianjin was 92.428 billion yuan, up 27.4%. Construction area of houses was 4,271.14 ten thousand square meters, increased by 13.3%. Area of houses completed was 1,606.92 ten thousand square meters, grew by 21.9%. There are 1,152 general contractors and specialized contractors in Tianjin, whose total profit payment was 1.745 billion yuan, up 19.3%, and tax turnover was 2.770 billion yuan, up 28.3%.

Transportation, Posts & Telecommunications and Storage

The transportation, posts & telecommunications and storage accomplished an added value of 25.697 billion yuan, up 7.2%. Cargo transport continues to grow. In 2006, the total cargo transport was 42,807.66 ten thousand tons, up 9.0%. Of the total, the cargo transport by highways was 20,290 ten thousand tons, increased by 2.2%; by water transport, 13,257.45 ten thousand tons, up 11.7%; by railways, 8,409.43 ten thousand tons, up 23.5%. Share of transportation volume by three means of highway, waterway and railway was 47.4%, 31.0%, and 19.6% respectively. The cargo loaded and unloaded at Tianjin Port weighted 25,759.7 ten thousand tons, up 7.0%. Of which the import transportation volume was 10,475.1 ten thousand tons, up 11.8% and the export transportation volume was 15,284.6 ten thousand tons, by 4.0%. The transportation volume of containers was 595 ten thousand standard containers, increased 115 ten thousand and up 23.9%. The freight turnover was 96.8 thousand tons, up 20.7%.

Passenger transportation grew rapidly. In 2006, the volume of passenger traffic was 56.6962 million, up 21.2%. Of the total, passengers carried by railway were 16.3222 million, up 5.3%; by highway, 38.07 million, up 28.6%. The turnover volume of passenger of Binhai International Airport was 2.7665, up 26.1%.

The turnover volume of passenger increased greatly but turnover volume of freight traffic decreased a little. The turnover volume of passenger was 16.340 billion passengers per km, up 15.0%. Of the total, railway turnover was 9.651 billion passengers per km, up 6.4% and highway turnover was 3.564 billion passenger-km, up 34.7%. The turnover volume of freight traffic was 1214.929 billion tons per km, down 0.4%. The transportation by highway was 7.580 billion tons per km, up 2.4%; water transportation, 1171.646 billion tons per km, down 0.4%; railway transportation, 35.273 billion tons per km, up 0.8%.

At the end of the year, there were 816.6 thousand automobiles, up 15.6%, of which 431.9 thousand were cars, up 26.1%. The number of private automobile was 572.1 thousand, accounting for 70% to the total number, up 19.3%, of which 325.7 thousand were the cars, up 32.0%.

The business in post and telecommunication industry had developed rapidly. The total business of post and telecommunication industry was 22.59 billion yuan, up 26.9%. The telecommunication business was 21.232 billion yuan, up 27.3% and the post business was 1.358 billion yuan, up 20.1%. At the end of the year, the long-distance optic cable reached a length of 2884.40km. The total exchange capacity was 6191.9 thousand telephones and the number of fixed telephone users reached 4357.6 thousand. Local calls numbered 9.686 billion times and long-distance calls were 1.199 billion times, of which the international and Hong Kong, Macao and Taiwan calls numbered 0.018 billion times. The number of mobile phone users was 6009.9 thousand, up 19.6%. A total of 10.435 billion messages were sent through mobile phones, increased by 36.8%. Throughout the year, 92794.6 thousand mailing matters were posted, up

10.7%, including 3523.2 thousand EMS matters, up 6.2%.

Domestic Commerce

In 2006, the wholesale and retail trades achieved an added value of 48.794 billion yuan, up by 11.2% over the previous year. The total added value of accommodation service and catering service was 8 billion yuan, increased by 11.7%. The total purchases and sales of wholesales and retail trade was 1294.782 billion yuan, up 27.1%, of which the total purchase was 628.076 billion yuan and the total sales was 666.706 billion yuan.

The consumable market tended to be active. The total retail volume of consumer goods was 135.679 billion yuan, up 14.0%. The total value of the wholesale and retail trades was 114.304 billion yuan, up 13.5% and the total value of the accommodation service and catering service was 20.997 billion yuan, increased by 17.4%. The supplies of transportation, communication and commodity products were enough. The total retail of automobile above the designated size raised by 36.0% and petroleum was increased by 20.3%. Telecommunication equipments, jewelry and household appliance grew by 19.7%, 30.7% and 12.1% respectively.

The function of wholesale trading markets as places to assemble and disperse commodities has been strengthened. The wholesale markets whose bargain value over 100 million yuan annually have total bargain value of 99.511 billion yuan, up 20.9%. The rank of large-scaled commercial establishment has been heightened. Some large-sized commercial established have been put into use, such as Isetan and Wanxiang textile house. The constructions of community convenience commercial establishments are developing rapidly, including constructing 261 standard food markets, 10368 community commercial nets. There are 2,563 production materials multiple shops and 20 distribution centers in towns and countries.

Financial Industry

In 2006, the added value of finance industry was 17.940 billion yuan, up 11.4% over the last year. There were 2852 financial institutions of different kinds, including 74 securities sales department and 458 insurance institutes.

The deposit and loan continued to increase. At the end of the year, the total amount of home and foreign currency deposited in Tianjin financial institutes was worth 683.920 billion yuan, an increase of 85.452 billion yuan compared to the beginning of the year. Of the total, savings reached 292.270 billion yuan, increased 34.968 billion yuan to the beginning of the year. At the end of the year, the total amount of loan was 541.572 billion yuan, grew 78.014 billion yuan to the beginning of the year. Of the total, medium-term and long-term loans reached 280.089 billion yuan and up 53.069 billion yuan compared to the beginning of the year, a percent of 68.0% to the added value of loan in Tianjin. These loans made a great contribution to the investment on infrastructure and the construction of large projects. Housing loans were 41.935 billion yuan and automobiles consume loans were 1.008 billion yuan. The quality of financial institutes' assets had been improved steadily and the rate of non-performing reduced to 5.5%.

The financial market traded actively. At the end of 2006, there were 25 kinds of listed stocks in domestic stock market in Tianjin. The transaction volume of stocks was 239.371 billion yuan and that of treasure bonds, 6.938 billion yuan and that of funds was 4.837 billion yuan. In the futures market, 598.73 ten thousand transactions were made, up 83.4%, with a business volume of 300.037 billion yuan, increased double. Account-openings by investors in stock market reached 96.67 ten thousand households. Over the year, the total volume of foreign exchange swap was 2.111 billion yuan; decreased by 4.6% and foreign exchange swap from Tianjin was 1.035 billion dollars, up 14.3%.

The insurance market has developed steadily in general. In 2006, the insurance premium brought an income of 10.518 billion yuan, increased by 16.1%. Of the total, the premium income from property insurance was 2.662 billionyuan and the personal insurance income was 7.857 billion yuan. The total expenditure on insurance was 2.186 billion yuan, of which the property insurance expenditure was 1.264 billion yuan and the personal insurance expenditure was 0.922 billion yuan.

Real Estate

The added value in the real estate industry was 13.927 billion yuan, up 6.6%. The investment in this industry was 40.232 billion yuan, increased by 22.8%. The commercial housing that has been sold covers 145.860 ten thousand squares, up by 4.0% and the sales revenue was 69.627 billion yuan, grew by 21.2%. The economically affordable housing has been invested 5.096 billion yuan, up 1.4 times than the last year's. The area under development was 380 ten thousand squares, 267 ten thousand squares of which was new developed, up 64.8% and 141 ten thousand squares was 141 ten thousand squares, increased by 17.5%. In the year, the amount of stock housing transaction was 622.9 ten thousand squares and the total money was 21.43 billion yuan.

Ⅱ Reform and Opening up to the Outside World

Ownership Structure

Of the total GDP in Tianjin, public-owned economy completed added value 208.2 billion yuan, up 14.2%, accounting for 48%; the non-public-owned economy completed 225.573 billion yuan, up 14.7%, accounting for 52%. Of the non-public-owned economy, added value of private enterprise was 106.3 billion yuan, accounting for 24.5% of the total in Tianjin; foreign capital 119.3 billion yuan, accounting for 27.5% of the total in Tianjin.

The ownership structures of the industries are quite diversified. Of the industrial enterprises above the designated size in Tianjin, the state-owned and state-owned holding industrial enterprises completed an output value of 334.149 billion yuan, up 28.8%; the private industry accomplished 79.989 billion yuan, up 26.6%. According to the status of registration, the enterprise with investment from abroad or Hong Kong, Macao or Taiwan accomplished an output value of 430.830 billion yuan, up 29.8%; the stock ownership enterprise completed that of 319.025 billion yuan, up 23.0%; the cooperative enterprise reached that of 7.401 billion yuan, up 19.4%.

The private individual economic is growing rapidly. At the

end of the year, registered capital of the private individual economic was 192.479 billion yuan, increased 30.446 billion yuan than the beginning of the year. The number of private or individual businesses was 265.5 thousand, increased 11.2 thousand than the last year, and the number of employment personnel was 1228.0 thousand, increased 86.2 thousand than the beginning of the year such that the business income reached 142.706 billion yuan, up 9.3% and revenue accomplished 7.843 billion yuan, up 28.4%.

Management of State-owned Assets and Reform of State-owned Enterprise

The state-owned capital is flowing reasonably. 772 state-owned assets were registered at the Tianjin Property Right Exchange and the transaction volume was 19.338 billion yuan, of which the transaction volume among districts was 3.644 billion yuan and that of the transaction volume between Tianjin was 15.694 billion yuan.

The reform and adjustment of state-owned enterprises have been performing rapidly. 240 municipal state-owned enterprises were reformed such that the total number has reached 3183 covering 84.6% of all the stated-owned enterprises in Tianjin, up 8% than the last year. New progresses were made in the reform of non-tradable shares and the work on listing and financing of enterprises. 12 state-owned listing companies have been completed the reform of non-tradable shares and have financed 2.7 billion yuan by means of equity cover-out, issuing convertible bonds and fixed directed collection.

Social Security

New progress has been made to the construction of the social security system. In 2006, 3282 thousand workers were involved in endowment insurance, up 6.5%, of which 1127 thousand were retired. 2167 thousand workers were involved in unemployment insurance, up 9.7%. 3294 thousand workers were involved in medical insurance, up 10.1%. 2097 thousand workers were involved in employment injury insurance and 1801 thousand people in maternity insurance. The regulation for country pension insurance has been issued and the social pension insurance system has covered towns and countries. Besides, medical insurance and employment injury insurance have offered to off-farm workers. The minimum standard of wages of staff and workers was improved steadily and the minimum salary of enterprise workers in Tianjin was set at 670 Yuan from 590 yuan.

Domestic Cooperation

The actual investment in Tianjin was 43.185 billion yuan on 1,840 projects, up 27.0%. As for the sources of capital, the proportion of actual investment in Tianjin from Loop-Bohai Region, "Yangtze Delta", "Peal River Delta" reached 89.9%, up 13-percentage point. Industry and real estate industry became hot, attracted 27.9% and 49.9% of the domestic capital respectively. Civilian capital played a main role, 31.645 billion yuan of which was fully funded, 73% of the total domestic capital, up 10%.

Assistance and support of Tianjin to GanShu Province, Changdu of Tibet, Wanzhou District of ChongQing and KaShi of XinJiang was further enhanced and promoted the development of local economy. During the year, 41 projects has been planned to support these areas, 10 of which has been implemented, up 25% and 50 million finance has been authorized, of which the actual investment was 7.49 million yuan, up 18%.

Foreign Trade

In 2006, the total import and export through foreign trade broke 60 billion dollars, reached 64.573 billion dollars, up 21.0%. Of the total, the export was 33.540 billion dollars, up 22.3%; the import was 31.033 billion dollars, up 19.5%. A favorable trade balance of US $ 2.507 billion has been achieved. The export of electromechanical equipments reached US $ 23.47 billion, up 26.4%, accounting for 70%of the total export in Tianjin. The export of high-tech products reached US $ 15.43 billion, up 23.7%. The high added value products of electronic information, automotives spare parts, biological and medical, ocean petrochemical has become the main export products in Tianjin. The first hundred enterprises export goods worth US $ 24.237 billion, a growth of 22.3% over the previous year, accounting for 72.3% of the total export. The exports to US, EU, ASEAN, Japan, Korea and Hong Kong reach US $ 27.823 billion, accounting for 83.0%.

Foreign Investment

In 2006, 1050 enterprises with foreign investment were approved in Tianjin, among of which, big projects with contracted value over US $ 10 million reached 187. The contracted value of foreign capital to be directly used was US $ 8.112 billion, up 10.8%; the foreign capital actually used was US $ 4.131 billion, up 24.1%. The contracted value of foreign capital to be directly used in service industry was US $ 4.259 billion, up 40.7%, accounting for 52.5% of the total contracted value foreign capital to be directly used, a growth of 11.2 percentage point over the previous year; the foreign capital was actually used was US $ 1.443 billion, up 82.7%, among of which, transport, storage and post services increase 3 times, real estate increase 1.2 times. New energy resources became the new point in attracting foreign investment. New energy projects like wind electric power generation, seawater desalination and new cell came to Tianjin. Until the end of 2006, 121 enterprises in world 5000 multinational companies have invested to Tianjin.

Foreign Economic Cooperation

In 2006, Tianjin signed 1098 contracts with foreign enterprises on projects undertaking and cooperation of labor service, with the contract value of US $ 1.247 billion, a rise of 1.9 times over the previous year, yielding a business turnover of US $609 million, up 90.2%. Year-end workers abroad reached 12 thousand. 72 overseas institutions and 39 overseas manufacturing enterprises were approved in 2006, with a total investment of US $ 75454.6 thousand, including Chinese investment US $ 59827.9 thousand. Greater efforts were made in introducing advanced technology from abroad. In 2006, 471 contracts were signed on technology introduction, with a contract value of US $ 718 million. Tianjin was approved by nation to be out-service base city and enlarged affection with successful activities hosted, such as Mayors' Meeting of China-Japan-Korea 10 cities.

Tourism

In 2006, 880.6 thousand tourists from all over the world visited Tianjin, up 19.0%, including 8117 thousand foreign tourists, 20.3% more than in the previous year. Tourist industry earned foreign exchange US $ 626 million, a growth of 22.9%. The number of domestic tourists increased by 9.3% and the income from domestic tourists increased by 11.2%. In the year, 153 thousand Tianjin citizens traveled abroad, up 4.8%, causing an expenditure of 2.03 billion yuan, up 5.7%. By the end of 2006, there were 114 hotels above star level in Tianjin, together with 264 traveling agencies, including 29 international agencies and 235 domestic agencies.

Binhai New Area

Along with the adoption of Binhai New Area development and opening-up into national overall development strategy, the warrant to be national comprehensive supporting reform trial place and the foundation of Dongjiang bonded port, a new development and opening-up rush is booming in Binhai New Area. The pace of infrastructure construction was quickened. Many key projects went well, including expansion of Tainjin Binhai Airport, Tianjin deep channel of 250 thousand tons, crude oil dock of 300 thousand tons level and phrase Ⅲ project of Beigang container dock. And many key projects started to construct, including ethane project with annual productive power over 1 million tons, Beijiang power plant and Dongjiang bonded port area. The project of airbus A320 China assembly line was approved, Bohai Bank set up, and the first industry investment fund in China–"Bohai Industry investment fund" was listed formally.

The total output value in Binhai New Area was 196.05 billion yuan, a growth of 20.2% according to comparable price, and the share to Tianjin economy increase is 51.4%. The high level industries of electronic information, oil extraction, automotive manufacturing and modern metallurgy showed their obvious advantages, and the high-tech industries, like medical and pharmaceutical industry, aeronautics and astronautics and new materials developed quickly. The total industry output value was 520.052 billion yuan, an increase of 31.3%.The total investment on fixed assets was 86.429 billion yuan, increased 24.7%. The contracted value of foreign capital was US $ 6.18 billion, up 24.0%, accounting for 76.2% of the total; and the foreign capital actually used was US $ 3.345 billion, up 31.1%, accounting for 81.0%. The opening-up of the area continually increased. The export through foreign trade was US $ 22.62 billion, up 22.5%, accounting for 67.4%. As for TEDA, the gross economy was developed quickly, the development speed kept over 25% in continual 6 years and the comprehensive strength retained the leading position in the development areas of China. The total industry output value was 300.416 billion yuan, a growth of 25.1%; the investment of fixed assets was 22.009 billion yuan, the first time exceeding 20 billion yuan; the contracted foreign investment was US $ 3.254 billion and the foreign investment actually used was US $ 1.608 billion.

The construction of Datongguan gained outstanding achievement. "Dry Ports" were set up in Wulumuqi, Shijianzhuang, Zhengzhou, and etc.. orderly. In 2006, the total volume of import and export through Tianjin port reached US $ 101.885 billion, increased 24.4%, which made it to be the 4th port in China with the foreign trade volume exceeding US $ 10 million. The import was US $ 44.761 billion, up 20.2% and the export was US $ 57.124 billion, up 27.8%, thereinto, the goods transported from Beijing, Hebei, Shanxi, Inner Mongolia, Gansu accounting for 54.7%. The function of international trade, free trade and logistic park of TFTZ operated well. The total goods getting in and out of TFTZ worth US $ 25.425 billion, up 35.5% than in the previous year.

Table 4 Main Indicators of Binhai New Area, 2002-2006

Indicator	Unit	2002	2003	2004	2005	2006
GDP	100 million yuan	862.45	1046.30	1323.26	1623.26	1960.50
Increase Rate over Previous Year	%	20.1	20.4	20.1	19.8	20.2
Total Investment in Fixed Assets	100 million yuan	280.89	464.08	565.47	693.31	864.29
Total Value of Exports	USD 100 million	72.01	89.38	136.99	184.69	226.20
Foreign Direct Capital Actually Used	USD 101 million	8.23	12.15	17.44	25.31	33.45

Ⅲ Urban Construction and Management

Construction of Infrastructure

The construction of infrastructure in Tianjin progressed quickly. The investment to infrastructure construction reached 51.817 billion yuan, a growth of 23.1% over previous year, accounting for 30.3% of the total rural investment to fixed asset, which strengthen the city function effectively. The second line of Jing-jin-tang expressway and Jiping expressway came into construction. Jinhu expressway (Tianjin part) was put to use successfully. The total length of expressway reached 694 km. The construction of fast road in central city was quickened. With 40 km fast road newly used, the total used length reached 160 km. By the end of 2006, the length of paved roads was 5963 km; the area of paved roads was 74.33 million sq.m. Line No.1 of underground subway was put to test, line No.2 began to construct and the construction of Huangwan railway and Shenhua Tianjin Coal Port Base almost finished.

Public Utilities

Public utilities construction became more active. Construction of Jinbin Water Plant has started. Constructions of Xianyang Road Water Recycling Plant and Qingguang Sewage Processing Factory have finished. Comprehensive treatment of South Canal,

Jizhuangzi River, Tianjin Port Canal reconstruction and special railway line were also implemented. In 2006, new increased green land was 21.72 million sq. m. The green coverage rate in the built-up area reached 37%. The urban average area of parks was 6.59 sq. m. The sewage-processing rate and rubbish-processing rate reached 75% and 85% respectively. The production capacity of tap water was 3.58 million m^3 and total annual volume of water sold reached 0.64 billion m^3. After the successful transform from coal gas to natural gas for 350 thousand households and 1300 enterprises, the year-end percentage of population access to gas reached 98.6%. With new increased heating capacity of 8 million sq. m, percentage of population access to central heating supply reached 84.6%. Tianjin was awarded "Advanced Development in Public Transportation Demonstration City" by National Construction Ministry. The public transportation operation vehicles reached 7200 units. With 31 new routes newly opened, the year-end public transportation routes reached 450. The passengers carried by public transportation vehicles reached 0.94 billion. The operating taxis were 31939 units.

Comprehensive Development along Haihe River

The steps were quickened to comprehensively develop the belt along Haihe River. Until the end of 2006, the construction of commerce, trade, finance and culture have covered 2.82 million sq.m. Dagu Bridge, Baoding Bridge and Fenghua Bridge were newly built; Shizilin Bridge and Bei'an Bridge were reconstruction by bridge rising technology; Jiefang Bridge and Jintang Bridge's open function were recovered. The roads along Haihe River were widened and the reconstruction of bank reached 12.5 km accumulatively. 6 green fields along river were built, including Music Park and Jiefang Park. A set of projects, such as Fenghuang Commerce Hall, Meibo Center, Gangwan Center, Children's Art Center, has already put to use.

Resource, Environment and Safe Production

Tianjin implemented more rigid measures for land administration, realized central exchang of operating land and remising of "empty land", and established an open, normative, uniform land market. Land supply was controlled rigidly. In 2006, 4523.1 hectares of land were supplies, there into, 3867.06 hectares were sold and 656.04 hectares were planned.

In 2006, Tianjin passed the evaluation of the National Environment Protection Administration and gained the title "National Environment Protection Demonstration City". The main indicators of environment quality keep well. There were 305 days with high-quality air, accounting for 83.6% in the total year, 2-percentage point up over the previous year. The up-to-standard rate of drinking water and that of the water quality in the urban water function area are both 100%. The level of road transportation noise and urban environment noise were kept at "good" and "preferable". The area with up-to-standard urban environment noise level is 571.5 square kilometers. With 29 new communities, 126 quiet residential communities have been established. 60 smoke control areas have been established, and the smoke control area is 589.4 sq. km. At the end of 2006, there were 21 environment-monitoring stations, 7 ecological areas, and 8 nature reserves with an area of 162.8 thousand hectare in Tianjin. Zhangjiawo Town in Xiqing District and Shigezhuang Town in Wuqing District were named "National Town with Beautiful Environment", which made the number of national town with beautiful environment in Tianjin reached 6.

The number of accident and persons died decreased. In 2006, 81 production accidents happened, down 11.9%, 92 persons died, down 3.2%; 4913 traffic accidents happened, up 11.5%, 878 persons died, down 9.5%; 4208 fire accidents happened, down 18.9%, 21 persons died, down 36.4%. The rate of production accident per 100 million yuan GDP was 0.24, down 25%. And the dead rate of employees of industry, mining, business and commerce in production accidents was 2.6, 7.1% lower than in 2005.

Information Construction

In 2006, information construction made new achievement. By the end of the year, the number of subscriber of Internet dialing number was 3089.7 thousand, and the number of subscriber of wild-belt Internet was 916.3 thousand. The first phrase expansion of the municipal e-government network has finished and started to operate formally. With the municipal e-government network and the construction of enterprises basic information share system, 15 government departments, including industry and commerce, local tax, national tax, quality supervision and inspection, etc., have realized the share of enterprise information, which effectively improved the transfer of government function and the efficiency of government operation. The construction of logistic distribution information system, like ports, post and roads, had a quicker pace and the construction of public logistic distribution information service system in TFTZ also quickened the speed of logistic distribution in port trade.

Quality Supervision and Inspection

In 2006, 3 products became name-brand products in China, making the total to be 18; 27 products became name-brand products in Tianjin, making the total to be 223. 18 products were approved to be exempted from inspection, making the total to be 63. 3072 enterprise and product standards were established or amended, making the total number of enterprise standards to be 33 thousand. A total of 3455 system authentification certificates had been issued. 675 enterprises had won China Compulsory Certification (3C) for their products, and a total of 3297 certificates had been issued. 644 thousand sets (pieces) of measurement instrument were verified in 2006. The up-to-standard rate of the production batches was 70.45%. In 2006, a total of 333 enterprises had food production licenses.

Ⅳ Science, Technology and Social Undertakings

Science and Technology

In 2006, the construction of science and technology innovation service system has made new achievements. A series of big technology projects were adopted by national technology program. The R&D of electronic information, biotechnology, medical and pharmaceutical, seawater desalination has made outstanding achievements. In 2006, Tianjin won 12 national awards, among of which, 1 award was second class of natural science, and 11 awards were second class of national scientific and technological progress. In 2006, Tianjin won 1559 municipal awards for its scientific achievements, 69 of which reached the leading level in the world and 397 of which came up to the advanced world standard. There were 175 basic research achievements, 1341 applied achievements, and 43 soft science achievements. The number of patent application in Tianjin was 13299, and the number of patents granted was 4159. The number of technology contracts was 10181, and the transaction value was 5.886 billion Yuan in 2006, up 16.1%. There was one newly increased national lab of ministry level and the key labs of municipal level reached 50.

The ability of independent innovation has increased materially. The development of technology has been the key link of the transformation of the ways to achieve economic growth. In the municipal technology convention, the decision of innovation city construction was made. In order to improve the construction of enterprise technology innovation system, a series of high-tech transformation bases were established and 12 enterprises have entered the "10 big enterprises of independent innovation ability in industry". Lishen batteries, Tasley Chinese medicine and steel tubes for oil took the first position in the industry. At the end of year, there were 214 enterprise technology centers above the municipal level in Tianjin, including 14 enterprise technology centers at the state level.

Proactive efforts have been made to attract excellent talents from homeland and abroad. In 2006, a total of over 17.8 thousand talents were introduced to Tianjin. 17 post-doctoral workstations were established. Thus, there were in total 143 post-doctoral mobile stations and workstations in Tianjin, up 13.5%, with over 500 post-doctors working there.

The New Technology Industrial Park has been developing at a high speed. In 2006, the park had a total income of 105.0 billion yuan through technology, industry and trade, a rise of 26% over the previous year. The total output value of technology, industry and technology was 95.0 billion yuan, up 28%; the total profit was 4.8 billion yuan, up 26%; the total tax payment was 5.5 billion yuan, up 27%; the total revenue from export and sales was US $3.2 billion, up 19%. HuaYuan Industrial Park has played a leading role as a kernel park: it achieved a total industrial output value of 29.6 billion yuan, 40.1% more than in the previous year; its export volume through foreign trade was US $0.77 billion, up 41.7%.

Education

Both the universities of high level and the key subjects have been developed with a higher speed. The phrase I new school district of Tianjin Normal University, etc.. The reconstruction and expansion of Tianjin University of Commerce, Tianjin University of Agriculture and Tianjin University of Finance & Economics finished completely. Tianjin College of Traditional Chinese Medicine and Tianjin Civil Aviation College have upgraded to be universities. The gross rate of admission to higher education institutions was 53%. In 2006, 45 institutions of higher education and senior vocational schools enrolled 107.9 thousand students, 4.3 thousand more than in the previous year. 82.0 thousand students graduated, and at the end of the year, there were 357.4 thousand students studying in these schools. The year 2006 also saw the recruitment of 10.9 thousand graduate students, 0.7 thousand more than in the previous year. 9.2 thousand graduate students graduated in 2006, and at the end of the year, there were 3.06 thousand graduate students. In 2006, the adult education institutions of higher learning in Tianjin enrolled 29.2 thousand students, thus the total number of these students was 91.8 thousand, and 17.8 thousand students graduated from these schools. In 2006, a total of 19052 students from poverty-stricken families got student loans totaling 243 million yuan. The construction of vocational education reform trial place started and 10 vocational education reform bases were finished.

The adjustment of high school resource continued. 52 demonstrated high schools, 16 demonstrated primary schools and 422 village schools were built accumulatively. "Historical famous schools" constructions have started. 80% of teaching appliances in rural high schools and primary schools were upgraded. The safeguard mechanism of rural compulsory education outlays was established. With the implementing of " two free & one subsidy" for rural primary and high school students, 700 thousand students got benefits of 55.4 million yuan tuition and fees reduction. In 2006, 68.0 thousand students were admitted to senior high schools and 69.9 thousand students graduated. At the end of the year, there were 216.3 thousand students studying in these schools. There were 136.8 thousand enrolled students in secondary vocational schools, with 41.6 thousand new entrants. In 2006, 104.3 thousand students were admitted to junior high schools, and 124.3 thousand students graduated. At the end of the year, there were 516.8 thousand students in senior high schools. In primary schools, 82.1 thousand children were enrolled, and 106.1 thousand students graduated. The number of students studying the primary schools was 516.8 thousand. In kindergartens, there were 193.8 thousand children. 91% of senior high school students were enrolled to colleges, 98.41% of the primary school graduates were admitted to junior high schools and 99.38% of school-age children were enrolled to schools to receive education.

Culture

At the end of the year, there were 16 arts performing troupes, 18 cultural centers, 18 museums, 32 public libraries, 35 archives and 20 film-projecting units. In 2006, there are 10 radio channels (accessible to 100% of Tianjin citizens), and 9 TV channels (accessible to 99.83% of Tianjin citizens). In the whole city, 2 million families have access to cable TV programs. 9 films and nearly 800 sets of 24 series TV plays were produced, which made year 2006 to be the year with the most films and TV plays produced in Tianjin.

A series of cultural instruments were put in use, including China Theatre and Children's Library. Combined with Party's 85th birthday and the 70th anniversary of Long March victory, a set of culture activities were held. Also, a lot of national culture activities were held and welcomed widely, including "Forever Glory" the 8th China Agedness Chorus Festival, the 8th " Peace Cup" China Beijing Opera Invitational Tournament and the 4th farmers' Arts Fair.

Public Health

At the end of 2006, there were in Tianjin 2383 public health organizations, including 472 hospitals, clinics, and community health centers, 40 disease control organizations, and 23 health centers for women and children. There were 44000 beds in the public health organizations, including 42000 beds in hospitals and clinics. In Tianjin, there were 62000 health personnel, including 25400 practicing physicians and practicing assistant physicians, and 20000 registered nurses. New progress has been made in the improvement of public health. Dongfang Organ Transplantation Center, Women & Children Health Center have already put to use. The expansion and reconstruction of Disease Prevention and Control Center and Infection Hospital have finished. After the <Decision on the development of community health service>, much more safe, effective, convenient and economical public health service and basic medical service were provided to the citizens. New-style cooperative medical services in the rural areas are available to 9 districts and counties with the coverage rate reached 48.3%, 18.1 percentage point more than in the previous year. In the year, 117 thousand people donated their blood for free, up 16.5%.

Sports

At the 15th Doha Asian Games, Tianjin athletes won 16 gold medals. The number of gold medals, race events and athletes all achieved the best record in the history of Tianjin sports. The conditions of citizens body-shaping improved a lot. There were 228 community body-shaping centers and residents' committee fitness paths, 10 large fitness grounds. The total area reached 50 thousand sq.m and more. According to the data of the second National Physique Monitoring, 88.6% of the citizens reached the standards, 1.4 percentage point higher than the average national level. The attainment rates of children, adults and agedness were 1.4,0.9 and 4.5 percentage point higher than average national level respectively.

Social Welfare and Relief

In 2006, 24100 people were subject to special care given to servicemen and the family members of revolutionary martyrs and servicemen. 188600 people from the urban or rural areas received subsistence allowances, among of which 151300 people were urban citizens. The welfare institutions have 18846 beds and 13170 people are living there. There are 9 rescue stations in Tianjin, which offered help to 15829 people in 2006. There are 2177 community service facilities. With the sale of 545 million yuan social welfare lotteries, which was 35.5% higher than in the previous year, a total of 190 million yuan has been raised as welfare fund, up 35.7%. Throughout the year, 31.035 million yuan was donated from all walks of life, increased 1.8 times.

Disable Undertaking

The healing, employment, social insurance and non-hinder facilities construction of disabled developed steadily. In 2006, 17182 non-hinder facilities reconstruction finished, providing more conveniences to the disabled. 2273 disable people were newly employed, a growth of 33% than in the previous year. With over 200 new entrants, there were 2500 more students receiving special education. Enrollment rate of handicapped children compulsory education kept over 95%. According to the uniform investigation plans, Tianjin finished the Second Sample Survey of National Disabled, proving figures for the development of municipal economy, society and disabled programs.

V Population and People's Life

Population

At the end of 2006, the total number of permanent residents in Tianjin was 10.75 million. The registered population was 9.4888 million, among of which, the agricultural population was 3.7785 million, and the non-agricultural population was 5.7103 million. With a birth rate of 7.67‰, and a death rate of 6.07‰, the natural population change rate in Tianjin was 1.60‰ in 2006. The population of Tianjin increased with a low growth rate.

People's Life

In 2006, per capita remuneration payment for urban workers in Tianjin was 27252 yuan, up 13.0% over 2005. With the increase of elder pension for enterprise retired staff and the issue of payment reform policy for government agencies and institutions, per capita disposable income in urban families reached 14283 yuan in 2006, up 13.0%. The per capita net income of peasants was 7,942 yuan, up 10.3% over the previous year.

The citizens' living conditions continued to improve. In 2006, the nonproductive expenditure in Tianjin urban families was 10548 yuan, up 9.3% over the previous year. The consume structure continued to upgrade. The Engel's Coefficient was 34.9%, 1.8 percentage point lower than in 2005. The expenditures on clothing, household facilities & articles, and transportation & telecommunications increased by 23.8%, 21.0% and 9.5% respectively. By the end of 2006, for every 100 urban households in Tianjin, there were 4.6 cars, 143.7 mobile phones, 59.2 computers, 77.9 microwave ovens, 87.1 hot-water shower baths, 15.5 helping hand cars and 95.3 sets of composite furniture. In the countryside, the per capita personal consumption is 3829 yuan, up 6.7%. For every 100 rural households, there were 96 washing machines, 88 refrigerators, 38 water heaters, 20 microwave ovens, 108 mobile phones, and 12 computers.

The housing conditions and living environment have been improved both in the urban and rural areas. In 2006, per capita floor space of urban residents was 26.05 square meters, and per capita floor space floor space of rural residents was 26.43 square meters, an increase of 1.08 and 0.37 square meters more than 2005.

The main problems in national economy and social development were as follows: the structure of national economy still need to be adjusted; the task of energy saving and pollution reduction is yet arduous; heavier pressure of employment needs to be solved, etc..

Note: 1. All figures in the communique are preliminary statistics.

2. Figures in value term on added value and output value of GDP and all industries are at current prices, where as growth rates are calculated at comparable prices.

3. Industrial enterprises above designated size refer to all state-owned enterprises and other enterprises with annual sales of over 5 million yuan.

4. The gross rate of admission to higher education institutions refer to the proportion of students of higher education institutions and population at school age, it indicates the general level of providing chances of higher education.

5. The Engel Coefficient is the ratio of the expenditure on foodstuffs share in the average consuming expenditure, the decrease of the Engel Coefficient identify the improvement of living standards of the people.

2006 年天津市国民经济发展情况综述

2006 年是我市“十一五”发展的第一年，也是滨海新区纳入国家发展战略的第一年。全市各地区、各部门在市委市政府的领导下，以科学发展观为统领，认真贯彻党中央、国务院的重大战略部署，全面落实市委八届九次、十次全会精神，坚持更高标准，追求更高水平，进一步加强和改善宏观调控，扎实推进“三步走”战略和五大战略举措的实施，积极推动滨海新区的开发开放，全年国民经济在新的上升期呈现高增长、高效益的运行态势，实现了全市“十一五”开局又好又快的发展。

一、经济总量比 2000 年翻一番，发展水平迈上新台阶

2006 年全市经济继续在高位平稳运行，经初步核算，全市地区生产总值完成 4337.73 亿元，按可比价格计算，比上年增长 14.4%，比 2000 年增长 1.2 倍，提前四年实现了GDP 翻一番，率先完成了“三步走”战略第二步总量发展目标。按常住人口计算，全市人均地区生产总值达到 40961 元，增长 11.7%，约合 5177 美元，比 2003 年的 3126 美元增加了 2051 美元，三年时间跨越两个 1000 美元台阶。按照世界银行 2002 年标准，我市经济发展已达到上中等收入国家平均水平，在全国 31 个省（自治区、直辖市）中，成为继上海、北京之后第三个人均 GDP 达到 5000 美元以上的地区。

经济发展水平又迈上了一个新台阶。2006 年，全市工业增加值超过 2000 亿元，工业利税总额超过 1000 亿元，口岸进出口超过 1000 亿美元，全市外贸进出口超过 600 亿美元，商品购销总额超过 1 万亿元，港口吞吐量超过 2.5 亿吨，直接利用外资到位额超过 40 亿美元，城市居民人均消费超过万元，全市财政收入三年翻了一番。

二、全市经济在高增长、高效益平台上稳定运行

经济发展持续在高增长平台上稳定运行。自 2003 年下半年以来，我市经济进入新一轮增长周期的高峰期，至 2006 年，全市地区生产总值已连续四年增长 14% 以上，经济增长的稳定性进一步增强。2006 年三次产业保持稳定快速增长。第一产业完成增加值 118.97 亿元，增长 3.5%；第二产业完成增加值 2485.83 亿元，增长 17.6%。其中工业增加值完成 2290.81 亿元，增长 17.7%，拉动全市经济增长 9.0 个百分点；建筑业增加值完成 195.02 亿元，增长 17.0%。第三产业增加值完成 1732.93 亿元，增长 11.0%。

财政收入连续第二年跨越两个百亿元台阶。全年全市财政收入突破 900 亿元，达到 925.62 亿元，比上年增加 200 亿元，增长 27.6%，占全市生产总值的比重达到 21.3%，比上年提高 1.7 个百分点。收入增幅连续三年保持在 26% 以上，收入总量三年翻了一番，为经济社会发展提供了坚实的财力保障。地方一般预算收入为 416.77 亿元，增长 25.6%。主要税种收入都保持较快增长。其中增值税收入增长 25.6%，消费税增长 43.2%，营业税增长 20.2%，企业所得税增长 29.1%，个人所得税增长 12.7%。

工业经济效益连续第四年保持快速增长。全市规模以上独立核算工业企业完成主营业务收入 8782.68 亿元，比上年增长 24.5%。实现利税总额突破千亿元，达到 1004.80 亿元，比上年增长 31.0%。其中，实现税金 313.94 亿元，增长 30.5%。实现利润 690.86 亿元，增长 31.2%，连续四年保持快速增长，与 2002 年相比，净增利润 504.67 亿元，增长 2.7 倍。石油和天然气开采业、通信设备计算机及其他电子设备制造业、黑色金属冶炼及压延加工业、交通运输设备制造业和通用设备制造业等五大行业成为工业利润的主力军，合计实现利润 578.81 亿元，占全市利润总额的 83.8%。全市工业经济效益综合指数达到 240.52，比上年提高 32.82 个点。总资产贡献率为 15.48%，比上年提高 1.84 个百分点。资本保值增值率为 115.32%，比上年提高 5.76 个百分点。

三、农业生产势头良好

2006 年我市认真落实工业反哺农业、城市支持农村和“多予、少取、放活”的方针，加大支农惠农政策落实力度，农业生产保持了稳定增长。全年农业总产值完成 251.50 亿元，增长 3.7%。种植业比重扩大，全年粮食播种面积达到 442.82 万亩，连续三年保持增长，优质粮种植比重超过总面积的 60%。棉花种植面积超过 100 万亩，达到 106.44 万亩，增长 15.9%。全年粮食生产再获丰收，总产量达到 143.52 万吨，比上年增长 4.4%，创五年来最好水平。棉花产量达到 9.77 万吨，比上年增长 17.0%。养殖业发展稳定，全年总产值完成 144.25 亿元，占到农业总产值的 57.4%。主要农副产品产量全面增长，肉类总产量 59.91 万吨，增长 3.7%；禽蛋产量 24.20 万吨，增长 3.1%；水产品产量 35.80 万吨，增长 5.9%；牛奶产量 65 万吨，增长 2.5%。

四、工业结构进一步优化，优势产业和高新技术产业引领工业快速增长

全市规模以上工业完成工业增加值2223.82亿元，增长18.8%，完成工业总产值8527.70亿元，增长25.3%。工业结构继续调整，以高新技术产业为引领、优势产业为支撑的格局逐渐形成。全年全市高新技术产业产值完成2713.01亿元，增长24.3%，占全市工业的比重达到31.8%。电子信息、汽车、石油化工、冶金、生物技术与现代医药、新能源及环保等六大优势产业完成产值6391.60亿元，增长27.5%，占规模以上工业的比重达到74.9%，比上年提高1.2个百分点，对工业增长的贡献率为80%。其中，汽车制造业增长49.3%，电子信息产品制造业增长26.0%，石油及化学工业增长26.3%，冶金工业增长24.7%。外商及港澳台商投资工业企业继续担当领头羊，完成工业增加值914.81亿元，增长30.1%，增幅快于全市平均水平11.3个百分点。大中型工业企业主体地位更加突出，完成工业增加值1695.32亿元，占到全市工业的76.2%。从行业看，通信设备计算机及其他电子设备制造业、黑色金属冶炼及压延加工业和交通运输设备制造业等三大行业对全市工业的拉动作用较强，合计完成工业增加值占全市的35.7%，共同拉动全市工业增长11.6个百分点。重点工业产品保持较快增长。全年天然原油开采1943.09万吨，增长9.0%。水泥生产超过600万吨，达到607.33万吨，增长23.9%。成品钢材产量2117.51万吨，增长23.2%。无缝钢管产量突破200万吨,达到216.58万吨，增长21.0%。全年轿车产量突破40万辆，达到41.03万辆，增长26.0%。移动电话机产量突破1亿部，达到1.01亿部，增长48.3%。

五、服务业竞相发展，行业规模继续扩大

交通运输仓储和邮政业、房地产业稳定发展，批发零售业、住宿餐饮业和金融业增幅较高。全年交通运输、仓储和邮政业完成增加值256.97亿元，比上年增长7.2%。全年实现全社会货运量4.28亿吨，增长9.0%；客运量5669.62万人，增长21.2%。滨海国际机场货邮和旅客吞吐量快速增长，分别达到9.68万吨和276.65万人次，比上年增长20.7%和26.1%。全年港口吞吐量达到2.58亿吨，比上年增长7.0%；集装箱吞吐量完成595万标准箱，比上年净增115万标准箱，增长23.9%。邮电业务总量225.89亿元，增长26.9%。批发和零售业增加值完成487.94亿元，增长11.2%。批发零售贸易业购销总额达到1.3万亿元，全年销售额超亿元的大型商业企业已达501家。住宿餐饮业增加值完成80亿元，增长11.7%。旅游休闲餐饮市场火爆，成为服务业发展中的新亮点。金融业增加值完成179.40亿元，增长11.4%，信贷规模进一步扩大。房地产业增加值完成139.27亿元，增长6.6%。商品房销售面积达到1458.60万平方米，实现销售收入696.27亿元，分别增长4.0%和21.2%。

六、投资结构不断优化，城市载体功能进一步增强

固定资产投资快速增长。全年全社会固定资产投资完成1849.80亿元，比上年增长22.0%，净增加投资332.96亿元，是历年增加最多的一年。其中城镇固定资产投资完成1709.66亿元，增长23.4%。在固定资产投资总体保持较快增长的同时，投资结构进一步优化。主要表现在：一是工业优势产业投资力度继续加大，全市工业投资完成690.34亿元，增长29.6%，拉动全市城镇固定资产投资增长11.4个百分点，其中六大优势产业共完成投资451.90亿元，增长29.2%，占工业投资比重为65.5%。二是能源工业投资得到加强，全市共完成280.39亿元，增长48.0%，占城镇固定资产投资的16.4%，比上年提高2.7个百分点。其中，石油天然气开采业投资增长47.6%，电力燃气及水的生产供应业投资增长45.2%，石油加工炼焦业及核燃料加工业投资增长72.8%。三是服务业投资保持较快增长，全年完成1004.45亿元，增长20.0%，占全市城镇投资的比重为58.8%，其中交通运输仓储邮政业投资增长21.5%，房地产业增长22.0%，水利环境公共设施管理业增长21.8%。四是重点大项目建设得到加强。全年投资在10亿元以上的大项目共完成投资746.94亿元，增长51.3%，增幅比全市整体水平高出27.9个百分点，有力地拉动了我市城镇整体投资的增长。五是建设资金更加充足。全市城镇固定资产投资资金到位2330.79亿元,增长24.6%,总量高于实际完成621.13亿元。其中国内贷款到位534.11亿元，增长26.4%；自筹资金到位1042.71亿元,增长25.4%;利用外资到位150.46亿元，增长32.2%，为我市投资增长提供了有利支撑。

城市基础设施建设力度加大。全年全市基础设施建设投资完成518.17亿元，增长23.1%，占全市城镇固定资产投资的比重达到30.3%，有效的带动了经济增长和城市载体功能的提升。京津城际快速铁路、京津塘高速公路二线、天津滨海国际机场扩建等工程进展顺利，京沪高速公路天津段竣工通车，地铁1号线投入试运营，地铁2号线开工建设，市区快速路新增40公里，累计达到160公里，海河综合开发和旧路改造等城市基础设施建设取得新进展。

七、市场活跃，居民消费跃上新台阶

2006年全市社会消费品零售总额完成1356.79亿元，比上年增长14.0%。其中批发和零售业零售额完成1143.04亿元，增长13.5%。住宿和餐饮业零售额突破200亿元，完成209.97亿元，增长17.4%。消费层次提升，购买力显著增强。全年汽车类零售额增长36.0%，石油及制品类增长20.3%，通讯器材类增长19.7%，金银珠宝类增长30.7%，家用电器和音像器材类增长12.1%。

城市居民人均消费突破万元，消费结构发生明显变化。2006年，我市城市居民家庭人均消费性支出达到10548元，增长9.3%，恩格尔系数为34.9%，比上年下降1.8个百分点，城市居民用于服务性消费支出3111元，增长11.2%，占居民消费性支出的29.5%，比上年提高0.5个百分点，充分说明居民生活质量在不断提高。居民消费能力进一步增强，促进了消费结构的变化。人均在外用餐支出980元，增长15.6%。人均衣着类支出865元，增长23.8%。其中服装支出增长24.1%，服装消费呈现量平价增档次提高的趋势。人均家庭设备用品类支出634元，增长21.0%，每百户家庭拥有家用汽车达到4.6辆，比2004年增长了1倍，每百户家庭拥有手机143.7部，超过每家一部的水平，固定电话出现下降趋势，手机已开始替代固定电话成为居民的主要通信工具。

八、利用外资向优势产业和新领域集中，吸引内资大幅增长

2006年全市新批外商投资企业1050家，其中合同金额1000万美元以上的大项目187家；全市直接利用外资合同金额81.12亿美元，增长10.8%；实际到位41.31亿美元，增长24.1%。外商及港澳台商独资企业合同利用外资仍为主体，全年达到60.25亿美元，增长11.6%，占全市合同外资额的74.3%。服务业合同外资比重过半。全年服务业合同利用外资42.59亿美元，增长40.7%，占全市合同利用外资额的比重达到52.5%，比上年提高11.2个百分点；实际到位达到14.43亿美元，增长82.7%，增幅快于制造业73.5个百分点，其中交通运输及仓储业增长3倍，房地产业增长1.2倍。新能源领域成为引资新亮点。风力发电、海水淡化、工业气体、新型电池等一批新能源项目落户津门。世界500强跨国公司来津投资继续增加，截止到目前，已达121家。三区成为利用外资的主要地区，全年开发区、保税区和高科技产业园区实际直接利用外资26.23亿美元，占全市的比重为63.5%。

吸引国内资金继续保持旺盛势头。投资环境的改善和良好的发展前景进一步吸引国内资金的流入。全年全市吸引国内投资项目1840项，实际利用内资431.85亿元，增长27.0%。吸引内资来源更加集中。来自环渤海地区、“长三角”地区和“珠三角”地区的资金合计达到388.24亿元，占全市实际到位内资的89.9%，比上年提高13个百分点。工业和房地产业成为热点行业，吸引内资分别为120.55亿元和215.31亿元，占到全市的27.9%和49.9%。民间资本成为内资的主体，全年实际到位316.45亿元，占全市利用内资的73%，比上年提高10个百分点。

九、对外贸易规模迅速扩大，进出口总额三年翻番

2006年全市外贸进出口总值突破600亿美元，达到645.73亿美元，增长21.0%，连续五年保持在20%以上快速增长，比2003年增长1.2倍，翻了一番多。出口和进口均跃上300亿美元台阶，分别达到335.40亿美元和310.33亿美元，比上年增长22.3%和19.5%。实现贸易顺差25.07亿美元，是历史上最多的一年。工业结构调整效果显著，机电产品和高新技术产品出口增长快速。全市机电产品出口234.7亿美元，增长26.4%，占全市出口的70%。高新技术产品出口154.3亿美元，增长23.7%，其中电子技术与光电技术产品出口分别增长61.6%和1.1倍。百强企业出口实力雄厚，合计出口242.37亿美元，增长22.3%，占全市出口的比重为72.3%。外贸出口的大幅增加，保持了对全市经济的拉动力。美国、欧盟、东盟、日本、韩国和香港等国家和地区仍是我市的主要贸易伙伴，全年我市对上述国家和地区出口达到278.23亿美元，占全市比重为83.0%。

十、滨海新区总体实力进一步增强，开发开放热潮正在形成

随着滨海新区纳入国家总体发展战略，以及一系列政策措施的出台，滨海新区新的一轮开发开放建设热潮正加速形成，成为我市进入新的上升期的强大引擎。全年滨海新区生产总值完成1960.5亿元，按可比价格计算，比上年增长20.2%，对全市经济增长贡献率为51.4%。全年滨海新区完成工业总产值5200.52亿元，增长31.3%，比全市平均水平高6个百分点。完成固定资产投资864.29亿元，增长24.7%。100万吨乙烯、北疆电厂等一批重点工业项目开始建设。新区基础设施建设全面提速，完成投资218亿元，增长24.6%。天津港25万吨级深水航道、30万吨级原油码头工程和北港池集装箱码头三期工程建设进展顺利，东疆港区各项工程建设也正在抓紧进行之中。新区对外资的强大吸引力进一步显现，成为我市利用外资的主要集中地，全年直接利用外资合同金额61.80亿美元，占全市的比重为76.2%，增长24.0%，

比全市平均水平高13.2个百分点；实际到位33.45亿美元，占全市的比重为81.0%，增长31.1%，比全市平均水平高7个百分点。新区经济外向度不断加深，全年外贸出口达到226.20亿美元，占全市的67.4%，增长22.5%。

口岸进出口迈上千亿美元台阶，滨海新区对外开放门户功能进一步增强。全年天津口岸进出口总值达到1018.85亿美元，增长24.4%，成为全国第四个贸易值突破1000亿美元大关的口岸。其中进口447.61亿美元，增长20.2%，出口571.24亿美元，增长27.8%。北方国际航运中心和国际物流中心建设步伐不断加快，对腹地的辐射带动作用不断增强。

十一、金融形势稳定，物价总体保持平稳

新增贷款创新高，有力的支持了全市经济增长。截止2006年末，全市金融机构（含外资）本外币各项贷款余额5415.72亿元，增长14.2%，比年初增加780.14亿元，比上年多增131.20亿元。其中，新增中长期贷款占全市贷款增加额的68.0%，对我市基础设施投资和大型重点工程建设发挥了重要作用。年末全市金融机构（含外资）本外币各项存款余额6839.20亿元，增长12.2%，比年初增加854.52亿元，其中储蓄存款2922.70亿元，当年增加349.68亿元，比上年多增27亿元。

物价总体保持平稳。全年城市居民消费价格指数为101.5，涨幅与上年持平。从主要商品和服务类别看，食品类和居住类价格涨幅相对较高，但比上年涨幅有所回落，全年分别上涨2.7%和4.4%，涨幅比上年分别回落0.7个和2.3个百分点。家庭设备用品及维修服务类、医疗保健和个人用品类上涨平稳，分别上涨0.5%和1.4%。衣着类、交通通讯类、娱乐教育文化用品及服务类呈现不同程度的下跌。城市商品零售价格指数为100.4，保持稳定。

工业品出厂价格涨幅波动不大。全年工业品出厂价格指数为100.6，涨幅比上年略升0.5个点，其中生产资料价格上涨1.2%，生活资料价格下降1.4%。原材料燃料及动力购进价格指数为104.7，比上年回落0.2个点。出厂价格与购进价格离差为4.1个点，比上年缩小0.7个点。房屋销售价格继续上涨，涨幅为6.7%，其中商品住宅价格上涨7.1%。

十二、就业和劳动报酬继续增加，居民收入增幅提高

2006年我市继续采取多种措施积极引导、支持、组织就业，成效显著。全年全市新增就业岗位安置就业29万人。年末全市城镇单位从业人员人数达到了194.9万人，比上年增长0.4%，连续四年保持增长势头。其中三资企业从业人员快速增长，人数达到54.2万人，比上年末增加3.1万人，增长6.1%。全市城镇单位从业人员劳动报酬总额达到521.64亿元，增长13.8%。人均劳动报酬27252元，增长13.0%。其中企业单位和中央单位从业人员人均劳动报酬增长较快。全年企业单位从业人员人均劳动报酬增长13.4%，快于事业机关单位1.7个百分点，中央单位增长18.2%，快于地方单位6.9个百分点。

城乡居民收入保持较快增长。随着经济的快速发展，企业退休人员养老待遇标准的提高和机关事业单位工资改革政策的出台，拉动了城市居民人均可支配收入增长提速，全年达到14283元，增长13.0%，增幅比上年提高2.8个百分点。其中工薪收入的较快增长起到了主要拉动作用，全年增长13.3%，拉动可支配收入增长了8.6个百分点。农村居民人均纯收入为7942元，增长10.3%，其中来自家庭成员的工资性收入比重超过一半，达到53.3%，来自家庭经营二、三产业收入增幅较高，比上年增长17.2%。

总体来看，2006年我市经济发展呈现快速、高效、稳步运行态势，这主要是得益于我市“三五八十”四大奋斗目标和“三步走”战略第一步目标完成所积聚能量的进一步释放，特别是滨海新区新一轮开发开放的推进，更为我市经济发展进入新的上升期注入了新的强大动力。

自2002年我市第八次党代会召开以来，全市人民在市委、市政府的正确领导下，以邓小平理论和“三个代表”重要思想为指导，深入贯彻党的十六大精神，认真落实党中央、国务院各项重大战略部署，以科学发展观统领经济社会发展全局，全面加快社会主义和谐社会建设，天津经济和社会发展取得了举世瞩目的成就。“三五八十”四大奋斗目标提前一年全面实现，“三步走”战略第一步目标和第二步总量发展目标圆满完成，以滨海新区纳入国家总体发展战略为标志，天津正以科学发展、和谐发展的崭新面貌迈入新的上升期。

科学发展　和谐发展

天津市第八次党代会以来我市经济社会发展综述

一、经济发展位于全国前列，综合实力显著增强

五年来，我市以“三五八十”四大奋斗目标的实现为起点，以全面推进“三步走”战略和五大战略举措为动力，坚持科学发展、和谐发展，不断加快发展步伐，努力提高发展水平，综合经济实力显著增强，经济发展始终位于全国前列，进入了经济增长最快、持续时间最长、运行质量最好的新阶段。

1. 经济发展迈上新台阶

全市生产总值由2001年的1919.09亿元增加到2006年的4337.73亿元，按可比价格计算，五年年均增长14.5%，高于全国同期年均增长水平4.5个百分点，始终位于全国经济发展前列。

五年累计，实现财政收入2981.26亿元，实现工业总产值30351.59亿元，实现工业利税总额3155.76亿元，完成全社会固定资产投资6483.6亿元，完成外贸进出口总值2121.77亿美元，分别相当于前10年的1.9倍、1.4倍、2倍、1.4倍和2.3倍。五年来，我市经济发展不断取得新成就。集聚能量奠定基础，2002年提前一年全面实现了“三五八十”四大奋斗目标。进入新起点实现高起步，2003年人均GDP突破3000美元，圆满完成“三步走”战略第一步目标。乘势而上迈上新台阶，2006年全市生产总值提前四年比2000年翻一番，完成了“三步走”战略第二步总量发展目标，按常住人口计算，人均GDP突破5000美元，达到5177美元，为全面实现市八次党代会确定的2010年率先基本实现现代化目标打下坚实的基础。

2. 经济运行质量显著提高

财政收入五年跨越6个百亿台阶。全市财政收入由2001年的304.52亿元增加到2006年的925.62亿元，年均增长24.9%。

五年来，全市财政收入净增加621.10亿元，跨越了6个百亿元台阶，其中2005年和2006年两年年均净增200亿元。全市财政收入占GDP的比重，由2001年的15.9%提高到2006年的21.3%，提高了5.4个百分点。

工业经济效益大幅提高。规模以上工业实现利税突破千亿元，由2001年的326.55亿元增加到2006年的1004.8亿元，五年增长2.1倍，年均增长25.2%。其中实现利润由2001年的185亿元增加到2006年的690.86亿元，五年增长2.7倍，年均增长30.1%，五年累计实现利润2074.73亿元，相当于前10年的2.7倍。

3. 经济在高增长平台上实现又好又快运行

五年中，我市经济发展进入新一轮经济增长周期，随着总体实力的增强，我市经济适应市场、调控市场、抵御风险的能力显著提高，在经济持续、快速发展的同时，保持了物价总体平稳。五年来，城市居民消费价格指数年均上涨1.2%，工业品出厂价格年均上涨0.6%，原材料燃料及动力购进价格年均上涨5.7%，分别比上一轮经济增长周期（1993−1997年）低12.4、9.9和7.3个百分点。在新一轮经济增长周期中，我市经济已连续四年保持在14%以上的高增长平台上持续快速稳定运行，经济增长的稳定性、协调性和持续性明显增强，成为改革开放以来经济增长最快、持续时间最长、运行质量最好、物价水平最稳定的时期。

二、滨海新区纳入国家发展战略，带动作用显著提升

举全市之力，经过九年发展，我市滨海新区基本建成。近五年来，滨海新区开发开放取得重大进展，综合实力显著增强，服务辐射功能进一步完善，以纳入国家总体发展战略为标志，滨海新区开发开放进入新的发展阶段。

1. 滨海新区成为全市最大的增长点

五年来，滨海新区生产总值由2001年的685.32亿元增加到2006年的1960.49亿元，五年年均增长20.1%，对全市经济的贡献率达到52.7%。

工业总产值由2001年的1463.38亿元增加到2006年的5200.52亿元，年均增长20.1%，占全市工业总产值的比重达到58.4%，比2001年提高14.9个百分点。五年累计，滨海新区固定资产投资完成2868.04亿元，年均增长30.1%；外贸出口709.27亿美元，年均增长33.0%，占全市同期的65.8%。五年来，新区基础设施日臻完善，现代化工业基地实力不断壮大，研发转化能力日益提高，成为全国发展最具活力的地区之一，为我市经济发展注入了强大动力。随着滨海新区纳入国家总体发展战略和一系列配套政策措施的陆续出台，滨海新区新一轮开发开放的热潮正在形成。

2. 对外开放门户作用显著提升

五年来，滨海新区实际直接利用外资累计达到96.58

亿美元，占全市同期的73.9%。坚持高水平集约化发展，引进和启动了一批项目规模大、产业关联度强、技术水平高、集聚效果好、带动作用突出的重大项目，成为世界跨国公司在中国投资最密集的地区。五年来，丰田整车、三星手机、飞思卡尔芯片、LG化工、100万吨乙烯炼化一体化、空客A320系列飞机总装线及配套项目相继落户滨海新区。电子信息、汽车制造、石油开采、冶金等支柱产业快速增长。绿色能源、环保、生物医药、民航科技等新兴科技产业加快聚集。2006年，《国务院关于推进天津滨海新区开发开放有关问题的意见》，批准天津滨海新区为全国综合配套改革试验区，天津滨海新区成为我国北方最大的对外开放门户。

3. 辐射服务功能明显增强

北方国际航运中心和物流中心建设步伐加快，国家级保税物流园区、空港保税物流园区、天津港集装箱和散货物流中心等建设提速。扩大港口辐射范围，在北京、河北、山西、新疆等地区设立"无水港"，辐射服务功能向腹地进一步延伸。天津口岸进出口总值突破1000亿美元，五年累计达到3342.82亿美元，年均增长25.8%，其中外地经由天津口岸进出口货值占到54%。2006年，国务院批准天津港东疆港区设立全国最大的保税港区，滨海新区整体的辐射服务功能进一步提升。

三、经济增长方式明显转变，经济发展充满生机活力

五年来，我市积极推进国民经济全面、协调、可持续发展，不断深化结构调整，着力增强自主创新能力，全面提高对外开放水平，努力构建集约型、节约型、生态型发展模式，经济发展迈出坚实步伐。

1. 结构调整成效显著，增长方式转变加快

农业生产结构得到有效调整，新农村建设进展顺利。连续三年认真贯彻落实中央一号文件精神，极大地改善了农业生产条件，有力地促进了农业生产的稳定增长。全市农业总产值由2001年的169.51亿元增加到2006年的251.50亿元，五年年均增长5.3%。粮食生产连续三年获得丰收，2006年粮食总产量达到143.52万吨，为五年来最好水平。

养殖业产值比重达到57.4%，五年提高了9.4个百分点。农业产业化经营水平进一步提高，进入产业化体系的农户比重达到73.6%。无公害蔬菜基地面积比重达到80%以上。主要农副产品产量保持稳定增长。小城镇、文明生态村建设加快，农村城市化率达到49.2%，五年累计支农支出达到55亿元，实施了农村劳动力培训、农村饮水管网入户、农村户厕改造等一系列农村公共事业工程。农村新型合作医疗覆盖面扩大到9个区县，覆盖率达到48.3%。

优势产业进一步集聚，工业经济增长方式出现积极变化。新一轮"嫁改调"开发度更深、技术水平更高、聚集效应更强、资源配置更合理，以天钢东移、纺织工业园、丰田汽车、大无缝（二、三套）、三星手机扩能等一大批重点项目建成投产为标志，先进的现代化制造业基地初步建成，带动工业快速增长，成为全市经济快速发展的火车头。全市工业完成增加值由2001年的869.15亿元增加到2006年的2290.81亿元，五年增长1.3倍，年均增长18.0%，对全市经济增长的贡献率达到61.9%。全部工业总产值由2001年的3366.53亿元增加到2006年的8907.45亿元，五年增长1.9倍，年均增长23.8%。

五年来，我市电子信息、汽车、石油化工、冶金、生物技术与现代医药、新能源及环保等六大优势产业迅速集聚壮大，2006年合计完成工业总产值6391.60亿元，占全市规模以上工业的比重达到74.9%。手机产量突破1亿部，占全国产量的四分之一。无缝钢管产量达到216.58万吨，居全国之首。轿车产量达到41.03万辆，占全国产量的十分之一，其中经济型轿车市场占有率居全国第一。百万吨级PVC基地提前建成，成为全国最大的聚氯乙烯生产基地。

现代服务业功能更加完善，对优化经济增长结构发挥了重要作用。全市服务业完成增加值由2001年的881.30亿元增加到2006年的1732.93亿元，年均增长11.6%。

交通运输、仓储和邮政业增加值由2001年的172.63亿元增加到2006年的256.97亿元，五年增长45.8%。港口货物吞吐量五年累计完成9.95亿吨，年均增长17.8%；集装箱吞吐量累计完成2000万标箱，年均增长24.2%。2006年天津机场旅客吞吐量达到276.65万人次，货邮吞吐量达到9.68万吨，分别比2001年增长1.9倍和1.1倍。邮电业务总量五年累计750.94亿元，年均增长26.4%。

批发和零售贸易业增加值由2001年的204.23亿元增加到2006年的487.94亿元，五年增长98.9%，年均增长14.7%。旅游休闲餐饮市场活跃，成为服务业发展中的新亮点。

金融业增加值由2001年的66.52亿元增加到2006年的179.40亿元，五年增长1.1倍，年均增长16.0%，占服务业的比重达到10.4%，五年提高了2.9个百分点，五年累计新增贷款3045.71亿元，年均增长18%，高于全国

同期平均增长水平3.3个百分点，是我市历史上信贷增长最快、金融对经济增长支持最强的时期。

房地产业增加值由2001年的65.07亿元增加到2006年的139.27亿元，五年增长69.6%。五年累计销售商品房4602.56万平方米，对相关产业发挥了重要的拉动作用。

所有制结构调整成效明显，经济发展活力进一步增强。2006年，我市公有制经济完成增加值2082亿元，占全市生产总值的比重为48%，非公有制经济完成增加值2255.73亿元，占全市生产总值的52%，五年提高13.2个百分点。其中，外资经济增加值由2001年的366.05亿元增加到2006年的1193亿元，五年年均递增20.8%；私营个体经济增加值由2001年的373.68亿元增加到2006年的1063亿元，五年年均递增22.1%。非公有制经济快速发展壮大，对提高全市经济整体效率、增添发展活力发挥了重要作用。

经济结构的调整优化，促进了经济增长方式的加快转变，全市能源消耗水平稳步降低。2002-2005年我市万元生产总值能耗下降17.6%，平均每年下降4.7%，2006年继续保持下降趋势。

2. 自主创新能力明显增强，技术进步成为经济快速增长的重要因素

五年来，我市始终把加快技术创新作为经济工作的三件大事之一，摆在重要位置，坚持高水平是财富，低水平是包袱的发展理念，技术创新能力显著增强。五年中全市共完成市级科技成果6698项，其中属于国际领先水平310项，国际先进水平1508项，共获得国家科技奖62项。

五年累计授权专利1.41万项。研发经费（R&D）占全市生产总值的比例逐年提高，2005年达到1.97%，比2001年提高了0.46个百分点，电子信息、生物技术、现代医药、海水淡化等一大批科技研发项目取得突破性成果，推动了产业结构的优化升级。全市高新技术产业产值年均增长25.8%，占全市工业的比重达到31.8%。大中型工业企业技术创新能力明显增强，建立了一批高新技术转化基地，12家企业进入全国自主创新能力行业十强，力神电池、天士力中药、石油钢管等位居全行业第一。国家级和市级企业技术中心达到214家，其中国家级企业技术中心14家。

3. 固定资产投资年均超过千亿，城市建设呈现勃勃生机

五年累计，全社会固定资产投资完成6483.60亿元，年均增长21.1%，年均投资规模达到1296.72亿元。随着投资总量的迅速扩大，有力地促进了产业结构优化升级，加快了城市布局调整，带动了区域经济融合发展。

投资对经济增长和结构调整的作用进一步加大。工业投资五年累计完成2195.57亿元，年均增长19.4%。加快了工业战略东移步伐，一汽丰田汽车、大沽化聚氯乙烯、天钢东移改造、力神锂离子电池等一大批重点项目先后竣工投产，为工业发展增添了后劲。能源工业投资得到加强，五年累计完成869.02亿元，年均增长21.0%。服务业投资大幅增长，促进了社会公共资源的优化调整，支持了科教文卫各项社会事业的全面发展。服务业五年累计完成投资3608.35亿元，年均递增24.0%，占全市城镇固定资产投资的比重达到58.8%。

基础设施建设成绩斐然，城市载体功能显著增强，海河综合开发为城市发展增添了新的生机。五年累计，全市基础设施建设投资完成1756.37亿元，年均增长31.5%。其中，港口建设累计完成投资190.4亿元，路桥建设累计投资674亿元，城乡电网改造累计投资96.6亿元。五年净增道路长度1800公里，净增道路面积3160万平方米，新建和改造桥梁500多座，高速公路里程达到694公里，市区快速路通车里程达到160公里。现代化大交通体系不断完善，唐津、津蓟等6条高速和京沪高速公路天津段竣工通车，京津城际快速铁路、天津滨海国际机场扩建等工程进展顺利。城市轨道交通体系格局初现，津滨轻轨、地铁1号线投入运营，地铁2号线建设全面启动。港口辐射功能显著提升，黄万铁路和神华天津煤炭码头基本建成。海河两岸综合开发进展加快，一批旧桥整修一新，数座新桥建成通车，累计改造建成堤岸景观12.5公里，一批风貌建筑完成整修，一批新的金融商贸设施建成交付使用，海河两岸服务型经济带、文化带和景观带的综合效益开始显现。

4. 对内对外开放全面扩大，城市发展充满活力

五年来，我市紧紧抓住我国加入WTO和经济全球化带来的战略机遇，进一步加大对外开放力度，努力提高对外开放水平，外向型经济发展强劲，成为拉动全市经济快速增长的重要引擎。五年来，全市外贸进出口总值累计达到2121.77亿美元，五年年均增长28.8%。其中出口累计1077.89亿美元，年均增长28.7%。出口结构明显改善，机电产品第一大类出口产品地位更加稳固，机电产品出口占全市出口的比重由2001年的52.4%提高到2006年的70%。高附加值的电子信息、汽车零部件、新能源、生物医药、海洋石油化工产品成为我市出口的主导产品。

招商引资成效显著。五年来,我市不断改善投资环境,加大招商引资力度,利用外资快速增长。全市实际直接利用外资五年累计达到130.65亿美元,年均增长24.2%。来津投资的世界500强跨国公司已达121家。利用外资结构发生明显变化。服务业合同外资迅速扩大,2001年服务业合同外资比重尚不足18%,到2006年时已经超过一半。其中交通运输及仓储业和房地产业发展势头强劲。新能源领域成为引资新亮点,风力发电、海水淡化、工业气体、新型电池等一批新能源项目落户津门。吸引国内资金大幅增长。五年来,全市实际利用内资累计达到1183.83亿元,年均增长53.2%,成为吸引国内资金的热点地区。

5. 流通集散功能显著增强,商贸中心城市魅力聚增

2006年全市批发和零售贸易业商品购销总额超过1万亿元,达到1.29万亿元,其中销售总额达到6667.06亿元,比2001年增长3.3倍。五年来,全市社会消费品零售总额累计完成5455.26亿元,年均增长13.8%。其中餐饮业年均增长15.7%。多层次商贸流通格局进一步优化。

截止2006年底,全市年销售额过亿元的大型商业企业达到501家,伊势丹、轻纺万象城等一批新的上万平米大型商业设施竣工开业,年成交额超亿元的大型批发市场达到48家,其中超10亿元的达到19家;社区商业网点达到10368个,农村连锁超市和便利店达到2600个。基本形成了以大型批发市场为龙头,以大型商业企业为骨干,以农村和城市社区网点为基础的多层次、多门类的商贸流通体系,有力地促进了天津作为经济中心城市商贸集散功能和作用的提升。

四、人民群众得到更多实惠,社会发展更加和谐

五年来,我市积极促进经济社会协调发展,坚持经济发展不欠社会进步的账,在推动经济发展的同时,更加注重发展社会事业和完善公共服务体系,人与环境更加和谐,城乡居民生活水平稳步提高,社会发展综合水平始终位于全国前列。

1. 民生之本更加稳固,就业规模不断扩大

积极实施再就业工程,多渠道创造公益性岗位,努力拓宽就业渠道,就业总量迅速扩大,就业结构明显改善。全市社会从业人员由2001年的488.34万人增加到2006年的562.92万人,五年增加74.58万人。其中第三产业增加58.64万人,对全市就业增长的贡献率达到78.6%,第三产业成为扩大就业的主要渠道。五年累计新增就业岗位108.38万个,实现新增就业岗位数量多于新增下岗失业人员数量,累计分流安置下岗失业人员61.91万人。城镇登记失业率由2002年的3.91%下降到2006年的3.6%。劳动力素质稳步提高,新增劳动力平均受教育年限达到14年。

2. 城乡居民收入协调增长,居民生活水平稳步提高

城镇单位从业人员人均劳动报酬由2001年的14242元增加到2006年的27252元,五年增加13010元,年均递增13.9%。城市居民人均可支配收入由2001年的8959元增加到2006年的14283元,五年增加5324元,年均递增11.3%。农村居民人均纯收入由2001年的4825元增加到2006年的7942元,五年增加3117元,年均递增10.5%。城乡居民收入比由2001年的1.86∶1变为2006年的1.80∶1。城乡居民储蓄存款由2001年的1284.95亿元增加到2006年的2811.02亿元,五年增加1526.07亿元。

城市居民人均消费性支出突破万元,由2001年的6987元增加到2006年的10548元,五年增长51%。城市居民恩格尔系数为34.9%,五年下降2.1个百分点。城市居民消费结构明显升级,住房、汽车成为新的消费热点,旅游休闲消费成为时尚,通讯设备、家庭设备用品不断更新换代。城市居民人均住房建筑面积由2001年21.1平方米增加到2006年的26.05平方米,五年增加4.95平方米。城市居民家庭每百户拥有手机143.7部,五年增加122.5部;拥有空调器115.7台,增加41.9台;拥有电脑59台,增加37.8台;拥有家用汽车达到4.6辆。农村居民人均生活消费支出由2001年的2618元增加到3829元,五年增长46.3%。农村居民恩格尔系数为38.0%,五年下降2.5个百分点。农村居民人均住房面积达到26.43平方米,五年增加2.53平方米。农村居民家庭每百户家庭拥有手机108部,五年增加89部;拥有空调器50台,增加30台;拥有冰箱88台,增加22台。

3. 社会保障体系进一步完善,保障能力显著提高

基本建立了城镇职工养老、医疗、失业、工伤、生育保险体系和城乡最低生活保障制度。2006年末,全市养老保险覆盖328.2万职工,失业保险覆盖216.7万职工,医疗保险覆盖329.4万人,工伤保险覆盖209.7万职工,生育保险覆盖180.1万人。符合低保条件的困难群众实现了应保尽保。积极发展社会福利、社会救济、优抚安置等社会保障事业,建立并完善了社会救助体系、社会互助体系和灾害救助体系,加大了抚恤和救济投入,提高了优抚和救济对象保障标准,为困难群众和弱势群体撑起"保护伞"。2006年末全市共有收养性福利单位249所,拥有床位总数1.61万张,在院收养人员1.16万人。

4. 环境保护取得积极进展，人与环境更加和谐

五年来，我市环境保护累计投入400多亿元，实施了蓝天、碧水、安静、生态、工业污染防治等环保工程。环保创模通过国家验收，荣获“国家环境保护模范城市”荣誉称号。主要环境质量指标保持稳定，2006年空气质量二级以上良好天数达到305天，比2001年增加131天，占全年天数的83.6%，五年提高35.9个百分点。城市集中饮用水源地水质达标率和城市水环境功能区水质达标率均达到100%。道路交通噪声和区域环境噪声平均声级保持在好和较好等级，环境噪声控制达标区面积达到571.5平方公里，五年增加196.5平方公里，全市安静小区达到126个。建成烟尘控制区60个，烟尘控制面积589.4平方公里，五年增加125.4平方公里。2006年末全市共有环境监测站21个、生态示范区7个、自然保护区8个、自然保护区面积16.28万公顷。

5. 社会事业全面进步，公共服务体系日益完善

大力调整教育资源布局，教育整体水平位居全国前列。基础教育不断加强，累计建成52所示范中学，启动了“历史名校”建设工程。全市普通高中五年累计招收学生34.35万人，高中阶段毛入学率达到91%，比2001年提高10.9个百分点。高等教育进入普及化阶段，五年累计招收学生46.33万人，高等教育毛入学率达到53%，累计培养毕业生27.04万人。职业教育继续保持优势，全市中等职业学校五年累计招收学生21.58万人。

文化设施建设成就显著，文艺创作精品迭出。五年来先后建成天津博物馆、泰达会展中心、华夏未来少儿艺术中心、中华剧院、少儿图书馆等一批文化设施，京剧《华子良》、话剧《为你喝彩》、芭蕾舞剧《精卫》等一批独具天津特色的优秀文艺作品在全国屡屡获奖。

公共卫生体系建设不断完善，医疗卫生设施条件和医疗整体水平有了显著提高。2006年末全市共有各类卫生机构2383个，拥有床位数4.4万张，卫生技术人员6.2万人。人民医院、眼科医院、东方器官移植中心、妇女儿童保健中心、医大总医院二期投入使用，防病中心、传染病医院改扩建完工。

竞技体育成绩辉煌。五年累计，天津市运动员在国际和全国重大比赛中共获得金牌106块，银牌77块，铜牌60.5块。在雅典奥运会和多哈亚运会上，我市体育健儿取得较好成绩。2003-2005年天津女排全国女排联赛中取得“三连冠”。群众体育工作始终保持全国领先，天津市第二次国民体质监测数据显示，2006年我市国民体质监测总体达标率为88.6%，高于全国平均水平1.4个百分点。

回首过去五年，这是一个快速发展的五年，我市国民经济发展始终走在全国前列；这是一个科学发展的五年，经济增长方式在不断加快结构调整和技术创新中得到明显转变；这是一个和谐发展的五年，城乡发展更加协调，人民得到更多实惠，整体环境明显改善；这是一个收获的五年，滨海新区纳入国家总体发展战略，城市面貌变化巨大，天津的整体竞争力和影响力明显提高；这是一个积极进取、不断创新的五年，“三五八十”四大奋斗目标提前实现，“三步走”战略扎实推进。五年发展取得的成就，必将为天津发展进入新的上升期，实现又好又快发展奠定坚实的基础。

（杜威、黄瑛、王雪飞）

自然资源（2006年）

Natural Resources, 2006

天津自然资源丰富。一是充足的油气资源。天津有渤海和大港两大油田，是国家重点开发的油气田，已探明的石油地质储量40亿吨，油田面积100多平方公里，2006年年产原油1943万吨。已探明的天然气地质储量1500多亿立方米，2006年年天然气10.5亿立方米。二是取之不尽的海盐资源。天津有153多公里的海岸线，中国最著名的海盐产区长芦盐场就位于这里，2006年年产原盐236万吨，占全国海盐总产量的1/10。三是丰富的金属和非金属矿产资源。金属矿产主要有锰硼石、锰、金、钨、钼、铜、锌、铁等20多种。非金属矿产主要有水泥石灰岩、重晶石、迭层石、大理石、天然石、紫砂陶土、麦饭石等，都具有较高的开采价值。四是蕴藏较为丰富的地下热水资源。具有埋藏浅、水质好的特点，已发现的10个具有勘探和开发利用价值的地热异常区，面积2434平方公里，水温在30—90摄氏度之间。五是土地资源丰富。天津市土地总面积119.19万公顷。其中耕地面积44.52万公顷，占全市土地总面积的37.3%；居民点及工矿用地26.40万公顷；未利用土地3.99万公顷。全市的土地，除北部蓟县山区、丘陵外，其余地区都是在深厚积沉物上发育的土壤。在海河下游的滨海地区有待开发的近200平方公里的荒地、滩涂。这些地区交通条件好，开发费用低，是国内其他大城市所不具备的。

Tianjin enjoys a rich supply of natural resources. First of all, Tianjin has abundant oil and gas resources. Its Bohai and Dagang Oil Fields are key state oil and gas projects with 4 billion tons known oil deposits and more than 150 billion m^3 known natural gas. The area of oil field reached more than 100 km^2. In 2006, 19.43 million tons of crude oil and 1.05 billion m^3 of natural gas were turned out. Secondly, with its coastline stretching 153 km, Tianjin has inexhaustible sea salt resources. In 2006, with an annual output of 2.36 million tons of salt (10% of the total sea salt output in China), Changlu Salt Field is the most famous sea salt production base in China. Thirdly, Tianjin possesses rich mineral resources, including metal and nonmetal. The major metal minerals include jimboite, manganese, gold, wolfram, molybdenum, copper, zinc, iron, etc.. The nonmetal minerals here–cement rock, barytes, stromatolith, marble, natural rock, purple sand porcelain clay, maifan stone, etc.–are of considerable mining values. Fourthly, plentiful underground warm water is available in Tianjin. In addition to its excellent quality, the warm water is deposited at a shallow position. There are ten areas with geothermal resources worth further prospecting and tapping. The total area is 2434 km^2 and the warm water temperature ranges from 30℃ to 90℃. Fifthly, Tianjin has abundant land resources. The total area of land in Tianjin is 1,191,900 ha., including arable land 445,200 ha. (37.3% of the total land area of Tianjin), residential, industrial and mining land 264,000 ha., and unused land area 39,900 ha.. Except for the mountainous and hilly areas in the north, the land in Tianjin abounds in fertile soil formed on a deep layer of sediments. In the coastal area at the lower reaches of Haihe River, about 200 km^2 salt and alkaline wasteland and shallows have great potentials for development. Because of the convenient transportation in these areas, it is possible to develop the land at low cost. Such favorable conditions are not available in other large cities in China.

自然状况（2006年）

Natural Conditions, 2006

地理位置 天津市位于北纬38度34分至40度15分，东经116度43分至118度4分之间，处于国际时区的东八区。地处华北平原的东北部，海河流域下游，东临渤海，北依燕山，西靠首都北京，距北京120公里。

地　势 天津市是"退海之地"，绝大部分是由古黄河三次北徙冲积而成的平原，地势由西北山区向东南逐渐降低，呈簸箕形向渤海倾，有山地、丘陵和平原三种地形。平原面积占总面积的94%，一般海拔2—5米。最北部燕山南麓的低山丘陵区一般海拔在100—500米之间，最高处九山顶海拔1078米。

行政区域面积 天津市区域总面积11760平方公里。南北长189公里，东西宽117公里。其中市辖区面积7399平方公里，市辖县面积4361平方公里。疆域周长约1290.814公里，其中海岸线长153.334公里，陆界长约1137.48公里。

河　流 天津市地处海河流域下游，是海河五大支流南运河、子牙河、大清河、永定河、北运河的汇合处和入海口，素有"九河下梢"、"河海要冲"之称。

气　候 天津地处北温带半干旱半湿润季风气候区，四季分明。冬季受蒙古冷高压控制，盛行西北风，天气寒冷干燥；夏季受西北太平洋副热带高压西侧影响，多偏南风，且高温高湿，雨热同季；春季干旱多风，冷暖多变；秋季天高云淡，风和日丽。天津主要为大陆性气候特征，但受渤海影响，有时也显现出海洋性气候特征，海陆风现象比较明显。

天津市全年平均气温在11.4—12.9℃之间，一月最冷，月平均气温在-3.0—-5.4℃之间；七月最热，月平均气温在25.9—26.7℃之间。年平均降水量为566毫米，全年85%左右的降水集中在夏秋季。年平均日照时数在2471—2769小时之间。年平均风速为2.3米/秒。

Geographic Location Located at latitude 38°34'N-40°15'N and longitude 116°43'E-118°04'E, Tianjin belongs to the 8th eastern international time zone. Tianjin lies on the northeast of North China Plain and the lower reaches of Haihe River Basin. On its east is Bohai Sea; north, Yanshan Mountain; and west, Beijing. Tianjin is only 120 kilometers away from Beijing,

Topography Most parts of Tianjin area are alluvial plain, created by ancient Yellow River's moving to north part three times. The topography is higher in the Northwest, lower in the Southeast; the whole topography inclines to Bohai Sea. There are three topographlies, including mountain, hill and plain. Plain occupies 94% of the total area. The general sea level elevation is 2~5 meters, that of North part hills is 100~500 meters, the highest site, Jiushanding, is 1,078 meters.

Area of the Administrative Region The administrative region of Tianjin covers an area of 11,760 km^2, Tianjin is 189 km long from south to north and 117 km wide from east to west. Its urban districts cover an area of 7,399 km^2 and its rural counties cover 4,361 km^2. The circumference of the whole city is about 1290.814 km, including a coastline of 153.334 km and a land line of over 1137.48 km.

River Tianjin locates at the lower reaches of Haihe River Basin, five major branches of Haihe River–South Canal, Ziya River, Daqing River, Yongding River, and North Canal – converge and flow into the sea. The city of Tianjin is well-known for its abundance in rivers and closeness to the sea.

Climate Located in the north warm temperate zone, Tianjin has sub-dry and sub-humid monsoon climate with four seasons clearly cut. It is influenced by Mongolia cold anticyclone in winter, which results in a cold, dry climate with northwest wind. In summer, influenced by northwest pacific subtropical anticyclone, it always has a high temperature and humidity with south wind and plentiful rain. In spring, the climate is dry and windy, with a great different temperature. In autumn, it has a kind climate and beautiful sceneries. Tianjin has continental climate mainly, however, influenced by Bohai Ocean, it has maritime climate with sea-land breeze sometimes.

The average temperature in a year is 11.4-12.9℃. January is the coldest month and the average temperature is -3.0-5.4℃; July is the hottest month and the average temperature is 25.9-26.7℃. The annual average precipitation is 566 mm, 85% of which concentrated in summer and autumn. The annual average sunshine is between 2471 and 2769 hours and the annual average wind speed is 2.3m per second.

第1篇
CHAPTER 1
综　合
General Survey

1-1 行政建制(2006年底)
ADMINISTRATIVE DIVISIONS (END OF 2006)

单位：个 (unit)

项　目	Item	行政区域面积(平方公里) (sq. km)	街道办事处 Subdistrict Offices	居民委员会 Residents' Committees	镇政府 Town Governments	乡政府 Township Governments	村民委员会 Village Committees
全市总计	**Total**	**11760.3**	**104**	**1636**	**118**	**20**	**3830**
市辖区	**Districts Under City Administration**	**7398.9**	**103**	**1538**	**71**	**9**	**2214**
和平区	Heping District	10.0	6	62			
河东区	Hedong District	39.6	12	137			
河西区	Hexi District	38.0	12	251			
南开区	Nankai District	38.6	12	254			
河北区	Hebei District	29.6	10	196			
红桥区	Hongqiao District	21.3	10	171			
塘沽区	Tanggu District	782.4	11	83	1		32
汉沽区	Han'gu District	409.2	4	44	4		58
大港区	Dagang District	1041.0	5	81	3		74
东丽区	Dongli District	478.5	6	45	2	1	114
西青区	Xiqing District	566.3	2	45	7		149
津南区	Jinnan District	387.8		26	8		165
北辰区	Beichen District	473.0	4	91	9		126
武清区	Wuqing District	1574.8	6	26	19	5	731
宝坻区	Baodi District	1508.8	3	26	18	3	765
市辖县	**Counties Under City Administration**	**4361.4**	**1**	**98**	**47**	**11**	**1616**
宁河县	Ninghe County	1296.0		26	11	3	283
静海县	Jinghai County	1475.7		52	16	2	384
蓟　县	Jixian County	1589.7	1	20	20	6	949

资料来源：天津市民政局。
Sources: Tianjin Civil Affairs Bureau.

1-2 土地面积(2006年)
AREA OF LAND, 2006

项　目	Item	面　积 Area (平方公里) (sq. km)	占全市土地总面积比重(%) Percentage to Total Area (%)
全市土地总面积	**Total Land Area**	**11919.70**	**100.0**
农用地	**Land for Agricultural Production**	**7067.18**	**59.3**
耕　地	Cultivated Land	4452.55	37.3
园　地	Garden Plot	371.23	3.1
林　地	Afforested Land	367.17	3.1
牧草地	Grassland	6.04	0.1
其他农用地	Others	1870.19	15.7
建设用地	**Land for Construction**	**3487.00**	**29.3**
居民点及工矿用地	Land for Residents and Industry	2640.29	22.2
交通用地	Land for Transportation	191.85	1.6
水利设施用地	Land for Water Conservancy	654.86	5.5
未利用地面积	**Unused Area**	**1365.52**	**11.4**
未利用土地	Unused Soil	399.22	3.3
其他土地	Other Land	966.30	8.1

资料来源：天津市国土资源和房屋管理局。
Sources: Bureau of Land Resources and Housing Management of Tianjin.

1-3 各月份气象资料(2006年)
METEOROLOGICAL DATA OF EACH MONTH, 2006

月 份 Month	平均气温 Average Temperature (℃)	最高气温 The Highest Temperature (℃)	最低气温 The Lowest Temperature (℃)	相对湿度 Average Relative Humidity (%)	日照时数 (小时) Hours of Sunshine (hour)	降水量 (毫米) Precip-itation (mm)	一日最大降水量 (毫米) Largest Precipitation in a Day (mm)	平均风速 (米/秒) Average Wind Speed (m/sec)
一 月 January	-2.8	2.1	-6.3	68	99.1	0.6	0.4	2.2
二 月 February	-1.4	3.8	-5.4	56	144.3	4.4	4.1	2.6
三 月 March	7.5	13.9	2.1	38	247.7	0	0	3.3
四 月 April	13.2	19.3	8	48	193.2	3.7	2.4	3.4
五 月 May	20.3	26.2	15.3	55	201	62.8	28	3
六 月 June	26.4	32.5	21.1	54	213.3	33.5	12.1	2.5
七 月 July	25.9	30.1	22.5	78	173.3	131.4	53.6	2.4
八 月 August	26.4	30.7	22.8	77	169.7	161.5	71.5	1.8
九 月 September	21.3	27.4	16.5	68	223.3	0.9	0.4	2
十 月 October	16.3	22.1	11.7	67	177.3	7.8	3.6	2
十一月 November	6.5	11.9	2.2	60	151.5	7.3	4.3	2.4
十二月 December	-1.7	3.3	-5.3	62	136.3	1.3	0.9	2.1

1-4 各区县气象资料(2006年)
METEOROLOGICAL DATA OF DISTRICTS AND COUNTIES, 2006

地 区 Region	全年平均气温 Annual Average Temperature (℃)	平均相对湿度 Average Relative Humidity (%)	日照时数(小时) Hours of Sunshine (hour)	降水量(毫米) Precipitation (mm)	无霜期(天) Non-Frosting Period (day)	雾天数(天) Foggy Days (day)
市 区 Urban District	14.1	58	1857.3	323.6	248	22
塘沽区 Tanggu District	13.5	64	2048	411.5	236	27
汉沽区 Han'gu District	12.5	68	2394.1	436.4	213	54
大港区 Dagang District	13.5	64	2039.3	423.9	248	15
东丽区 Dongli District	13.6	63	2252.1	367.6	247	34
西青区 Xiqing District	13.2	61	2130	415.2	248	23
津南区 Jinnan District	13.5	62	2187.8	380.9	248	17
北辰区 Beichen District	12.9	60	2006.9	422	217	28
武清区 Wuqing District	12.6	65	2088.5	373.9	217	38
宝坻区 Baodi District	12.1	63	1991	563.9	206	35
宁河县 Ninghe County	12.5	65	2383.2	479.4	236	33
静海县 Jinghai County	13.4	62	2070.4	328.9	229	31
蓟 县 Jixian County	13.1	55	2133.5	510.8	222	17

资料来源：天津市气象信息中心。
Sources: Tianjin Meteorological Information Center.

1-5 法人和产业活动单位数（2006年底）(按登记注册类型分)

NUMBER OF INSTITUTIONAL UNITS AND UNIT WITH INDUSTRIAL UNDERTAKINGS, THE END OF 2006 (Grouped by Registered Type)

项目	Item	合计(个) Total (unit)	法人单位 Institutional Units	# 企业法人 Enterprise Institution
总计	**Total**	**118932**	**102132**	**87199**
内资企业	**Domestic-funded**	**111107**	**95617**	**80703**
国有	State-owned	17575	12029	4932
集体	Collective-owned	12276	10048	9587
股份合作	Cooperative	1508	1145	1124
联营企业	Joint Ownership Enterprises	469	384	371
国有联营	State Joint Ownership	115	90	88
集体联营	Collective Joint Ownership	150	116	112
国有与集体联营	State-owned and Collective Joint Ownership	95	87	85
其他联营	Others	109	91	86
有限责任公司	Limited Liability Corporations	15364	13365	13322
国有独资公司	Sole State-owned Corporations	335	242	239
其他有限责任公司	Other Limited Liability Corporations	15029	13123	13083
股份有限公司	Share Holding Corporations Ltd.	3128	1591	1499
私营企业	Private Enterprises	49423	46981	46767
私营独资	Sole Private Enterprises	9510	9131	9027
私营合伙	Private Partnership	2906	2811	2759
私营有限责任公司	Private Limited Liability Corporations	35214	33354	33306
私营股份有限公司	Private Share Holding Corporations Ltd.	1793	1685	1675
其他	Others	11362	10072	3099
港、澳、台商投资企业	**Enterprises with Investment from Hong Kong, Macao and Taiwan**	**2006**	**1691**	**1686**
与港澳台商合资经营	Hong Kong, Macao and Taiwan Joint Venture	833	686	684
与港澳台商合作经营	Hong Kong, Macao and Taiwan Cooperative Operation	68	53	52
港澳台商独资	Hong Kong, Macao and Taiwan Funded Solely	1078	925	923
港澳台商投资股份有限公司	Hong Kong, Macao and Taiwan Share Holding Corporations Ltd.	27	27	27
外商投资企业	**Foreign Funded Enterprises**	**5819**	**4824**	**4810**
中外合资经营	Chinese-foreign Joint Venture	1810	1542	1539
中外合作经营	Chinese-foreign Cooperative Operation	182	154	148
外资企业	Foreign Investment Enterprise	3728	3074	3070
外商投资股份有限公司	Foreign-funded Share Holding Corporations Ltd.	99	54	53

1-5 续表 Continued

项　目	Item	产业活动单位 Unit with Industrial Undertakings	# 企 业 Enterprise
总　计	**Total**	**16800**	**12912**
内资企业	**Domestic-funded**	**15490**	**11660**
国　有	State-owned	5546	2666
集　体	Collective-owned	2228	1890
股份合作	Cooperative	363	357
联营企业	Joint Ownership Enterprises	85	77
国有联营	State Joint Ownership	25	21
集体联营	Collective Joint Ownership	34	34
国有与集体联营	State-owned and Collective Joint Ownership	8	5
其他联营	Others	18	17
有限责任公司	Limited Liability Corporations	1999	1965
国有独资公司	Sole State-owned Corporations	93	84
其他有限责任公司	Other Limited Liability Corporations	1906	1881
股份有限公司	Share Holding Corporations Ltd.	1537	1522
私营企业	Private Enterprises	2442	2385
私营独资	Sole Private Enterprises	379	363
私营合伙	Private Partnership	95	92
私营有限责任公司	Private Limited Liability Corporations	1860	1827
私营股份有限公司	Private Share Holding Corporations Ltd.	108	103
其　他	Others	1290	798
港、澳、台商投资企业	**Enterprises with Investment from Hong Kong, Macao and Taiwan**	**315**	**294**
与港澳台商合资经营	Hong Kong, Macao and Taiwan Joint Venture	147	145
与港澳台商合作经营	Hong Kong, Macao and Taiwan Cooperative Operation	15	15
港澳台商独资	Hong Kong, Macao and Taiwan Funded Solely	153	134
港澳台商投资股份有限公司	Hong Kong, Macao and Taiwan Share Holding Corporations Ltd.		
外商投资企业	**Foreign Funded Enterprises**	**995**	**958**
中外合资经营	Chinese-foreign Joint Venture	268	257
中外合作经营	Chinese-foreign Cooperative Operation	28	27
外资企业	Foreign Investment Enterprise	654	630
外商投资股份有限公司	Foreign-funded Share Holding Corporations Ltd.	45	44

1-6 法人活动单位数（2006年底）（按行业类别分）
NUMBER OF INSTITUTIONAL UNITS, THE END OF 2006 (Grouped by Sector)

项 目	Item	合 计（个）Total (unit)	法人单位 Institutional Units	#企业法人 Enterprise Institution	产业活动单位 Unit with Industrial Undertakings
总 计	Total	118932	102132	87199	16800
农、林、牧、渔业	Farming, Forestry, Animal Husbandry and Fishery	789	697	527	92
农 业	Farming	128	123	100	5
林 业	Forestry	53	53	33	
畜牧业	Animal Husbandry	247	244	206	3
渔 业	Fishery	123	122	82	1
农、林、牧、渔服务业	FFAF Services	238	155	106	83
采矿业	Minerals Mining	141	122	122	19
煤炭开采和洗选业	Mining and Washing of Coal	10	9	9	1
石油和天然气开采业	Extraction of Petroleum and Natural Gas	55	39	39	16
黑色金属矿采选业	Mining and Processing of Ferrous Metal Ores	5	5	5	
有色金属矿采选业	Mining and Processing of Non-Ferrous Metal Ores	7	6	6	1
非金属矿采选业	Mining and Processing of Nonmetal Ores	62	62	62	
其他采矿业	Mining of Other Ores	2	1	1	1
制造业	Manufacturing	32805	32140	32140	665
农副食品加工业	Processing of Food from Agricultural Products	856	837	837	19
食品制造业	Manufacture of Foods	890	854	854	36
饮料制造业	Manufacture of Beverages	282	270	270	12
烟草制品业	Manufacture of Tobacco	2	2	2	
纺织业	Manufacture of Textile	1301	1284	1284	17
纺织服装、鞋、帽	Manufacture of Textile Wearing Apparel, Footware and Caps	1462	1433	1433	29
皮革、毛皮、羽毛（绒）及其制品业	Manufacture of Leather, Fur, Feather and Related Products	306	300	300	6
木材加工及木、竹、藤、棕、草制品业	Processing of Timber, Manufacture of Wood, Bamboo, Rattan, Palm, and Straw Products	454	444	444	10
家具制造业	Manufacture of Furniture	489	479	479	10
造纸及纸制品业	Manufacture of Paper and Paper Products	1063	1054	1054	9
印刷业和记录媒介的复制	Printing, Reproduction of Recording Media	844	829	829	15
文教体育用品制造业	Manufacture of Articles For Culture, Education and Sport Activity	395	385	385	10
石油加工、炼焦及核燃料加工业	Processing of Petroleum, Coking, Processing of Nuclear Fuel	168	163	163	5

1-6 续表 1 Continued

项　目	Item	合　计 (个) Total (unit)	法　人 单　位 Institutional Units	#企　业 法　人 Enterprise Institution	产业活动 单　位 Unit with Industrial Under -takings
化学原料及化学制品制造业	Manufacture of Raw Chemical Materials and Chemical Products	2591	2535	2535	56
医药制造业	Manufacture of Medicines	356	339	339	17
化学纤维制造业	Manufacture of Chemical Fibers	60	60	60	0
塑料制品业	Manufacture of Rubber	582	573	573	9
橡胶制品业	Manufacture of Plastics	1665	1632	1632	33
非金属矿物制品业	Manufacture of Non-metallic Mineral Products	1465	1429	1429	36
黑色金属冶炼及压延加工业	Smelting and Pressing of Ferrous Metals	950	937	937	13
有色金属冶炼及压延加工业	Smelting and Pressing of Non-ferrous Metals	448	443	443	5
金属制品业	Manufacture of Metal Products	3786	3731	3731	55
通用设备制造业	Manufacture of General Purpose Machinery	3485	3435	3435	50
专用设备制造业	Manufacture of Special Purpose Machinery	1826	1782	1782	44
交通运输设备制造业	Manufacture of Transport Equipment	2446	2401	2401	45
电气机械及器材制造业	Manufacture of Electrical Machinery and Equipment	1733	1688	1688	45
通信设备、计算机及其他电子设备制造业	Manufacture of Communication Equipment, Computers and Other Electronic Equipment	1083	1051	1051	32
仪器仪表及文化、办公用机械制造业	Manufacture of Measuring Instruments and Machinery for Cultural Activity and Office Work	781	766	766	15
工艺品及其他制造业	Manufacture of Artwork and Other Manufacturing	934	904	904	30
废弃资源和废旧材料回收加工业	Recycling and Disposal of Waste	102	100	100	2
电力、燃气及水的生产和供应业	**Production and Supply of Electric Power and Heat Power**	**398**	**221**	**221**	**177**
电力、热力的生产和供应业	Production and Supply of Electric & Heat Energy	259	120	120	139
燃气生产和供应业	Production and Supply of Gas	57	38	38	19
水的生产和供应业	Production and Supply of Water	82	63	63	19
建筑业	**Construction**	**4750**	**3895**	**3895**	**855**
房屋和土木工程建筑业	Building and Civil Engineering	1578	1077	1077	501
建筑安装业	Building Installation	1340	1205	1205	135
建筑装饰业	Building Decoration	1275	1137	1137	138
其他建筑业	Others	557	476	476	81

1-6 续表 2 Continued

项　目	Item	合计(个) Total (unit)	法人单位 Institutional Units	#企业法人 Enterprise Institution	产业活动单位 Unit with Industrial Under-takings
交通运输、仓储和邮政业	**Transportation, Storage and Post Services**	**4951**	**4116**	**4091**	**835**
铁路运输业	Railway Transport	101	48	48	53
道路运输业	Highway Transport	974	858	838	116
城市公共交通业	City Public Traffic	142	114	112	28
水上运输业	Waterway Transport	222	191	191	31
航空运输业	Air Transport	32	14	14	18
管道运输业	Pipeline Transport	9	5	5	4
装卸搬运和其他运输服务业	Load & Unload and Others	2379	2145	2142	234
仓储业	Storage Services	809	705	705	104
邮政业	Post Services	283	36	36	247
信息传输、计算机服务和软件业	**Information Transmitting, Computer Services and Software**	**1617**	**1388**	**1320**	**229**
电信和其他信息传输服务业	Telecommunication and Other Information Transmitting Service	345	170	146	175
计算机服务业	Computer Services	760	725	684	35
软件业	Software	512	493	490	19
批发和零售业	**Wholesale and Retail Trade**	**30775**	**25891**	**25891**	**4884**
批发业	Wholesale	18940	17284	17284	1656
零售业	Retail	11835	8607	8607	3228
住宿和餐饮业	**Accommodation and Catering Services**	**2494**	**1788**	**1778**	**706**
住宿业	Accommodation	637	527	517	110
餐饮业	Catering Service	1857	1261	1261	596
金融业	**Finance Intermediation**	**2824**	**541**	**537**	**2283**
银行业	Banking	2333	276	274	2057
证券业	Securities	121	78	77	43
保险业	Insurance	282	106	106	176
其他金融活动	Others	88	81	80	7
房地产业	**Real Estate**	**3631**	**2758**	**2758**	**873**
租赁和商务服务业	**Leasing and Business Services**	**7416**	**6524**	**5848**	**892**
租赁业	Leasing Serving	321	269	264	52
商务服务业	Business Serving	7095	6255	5584	840

1-6 续表 3 Continued

项 目	Item	合计(个) Total (unit)	法人单位 Institutional Units	#企业法人 Enterprise Institution	产业活动单位 Unit with Industrial Undertakings
科学研究、技术服务和地质勘查业	**Scientific Research,Technical Services and Geological Prospecting**	**4520**	**4244**	**3533**	**276**
研究与试验发展	R&D	299	279	179	20
专业技术服务业	Special Technical Services	2185	2014	1604	171
科技交流和推广服务业	Science Exchanges and Technology Expansion	2000	1917	1727	83
地质勘查业	Geological Prospecting	36	34	23	2
水利、环境和公共设施管理业	**Management for Water Conservancy Environment and Public Facilities**	**967**	**832**	**265**	**135**
水利管理业	Management for Water Conservancy	285	276	29	9
环境管理业	Management for Environment	287	214	70	73
公共设施管理业	Management for Public Facilities	395	342	166	53
居民服务和其他服务业	**Resident Services and Other Social Services**	**4911**	**4219**	**3607**	**692**
居民服务业	Resident Services	2024	1664	1214	360
其他服务业	Others	2887	2555	2393	332
教 育	**Education**	**3604**	**2528**	**122**	**1076**
卫生、社会保障和社会福利业	**Health Care, Social Security and Social Welfare**	**1889**	**995**	**98**	**894**
卫 生	Health Care	1597	738	87	859
社会保障业	Social Security	130	117	7	13
社会福利业	Social Welfare	162	140	4	22
文化、体育和娱乐业	**Culture, Sports and Recreational Services**	**1015**	**919**	**446**	**96**
新闻出版业	News Publication	123	107	50	16
广播、电视、电影和音像业	Broadcast, TV, Movies Record and Video Industry	171	159	44	12
文化艺术业	Culture and Art	280	262	85	18
体 育	Sports	153	141	46	12
娱乐业	Recreational Services	288	250	221	38
公共管理和社会组织	**Public Management and Social Organizations**	**9435**	**8314**		**1121**
中国共产党机关	Chinese Communist Party Agencies	157	157		
国家机构	Government Agencies	2780	1741		1039
人民政协和民主党派	The People's Political Consultative Conference Committees and Democracy Party Groupings	62	62		
群众团体、社会团体和宗教组织	Mass Organizations, Social Organizations and Religious Groups	1131	1061		70
基层群众自治组织	Grass-roots Mass Autonomy Organizations	5305	5293		12

1-7 主要年份国民经济主要指标和增长速度
MAIN INDICATORS AND INCREASE RATE OF NATIONAL ECONOMY IN MAIN YEARS

单位：亿元 (100 million yuan)

年 份 Year	户籍人口 (万人) Registered Population (10 000 persons)	社会从业人员 (万人) Number of Employment Personnel (10 000 persons)	#城镇单位从业人员 Persons Employed in Urban Units	地区生产总值 (亿元) Gross Domestic Product (100 million yuan)	人均地区生产总值 (元) Per Capital GDP (yuan)	社会劳动生产率 (元/人) Society Labour Productivity (yuan/person)
1952	439.22	159.50	45.18	12.80	298	825
1957	529.65	186.50	86.24	24.11	465	1311
1962	595.63	203.80	106.48	24.25	406	1166
1965	637.80	227.50	120.30	35.96	560	1602
1970	652.70	270.20	135.81	50.99	781	1960
1975	702.86	328.60	181.46	69.73	991	2232
1978	724.27	366.70	217.40	82.65	1133	2300
1980	748.91	394.79	242.69	103.53	1357	2671
1985	804.80	455.98	276.48	175.78	2169	3892
1990	866.25	470.07	284.31	310.95	3487	6617
1995	894.67	515.30	289.59	931.97	9769	18126
1996	898.45	512.00	283.98	1121.93	11734	21842
1997	899.80	513.33	281.34	1264.63	13142	24668
1998	905.09	508.10	218.56	1374.60	14243	26915
1999	910.17	508.14	211.76	1500.95	15405	29539
2000	912.00	486.89	201.75	1701.88	17353	34208
2001	913.98	488.34	192.30	1919.09	19141	39357
2002	919.05	492.61	185.50	2150.76	21387	43851
2003	926.00	510.90	191.01	2578.03	25544	51380
2004	932.55	527.78	193.91	3110.97	30575	59902
2005	939.31	542.52	194.12	3697.62	35783	69095
2006	948.89	562.92	195.00	4359.15	41163	78867
平均每年递增(%) Average Annual Increase Rate (%)						
1953-1957	3.8	3.2	13.8	13.5	9.3	9.7
1958-1962	2.4	1.8	4.3	-1.7	-4.4	-4.1
1963-1965	2.3	3.7	4.2	15.5	12.7	12.6
1966-1970	0.5	3.5	2.5	8.3	7.9	5.1
1971-1975	1.5	4.0	6.0	7.2	5.6	3.4
1976-1980	1.3	3.7	6.0	7.4	5.7	2.9
1981-1985	1.4	2.9	2.6	9.3	8.0	6.0
1986-1990	1.5	0.6	0.6	5.2	3.2	4.4
1991-1995	0.6	1.9	0.4	11.7	10.2	9.7
1996-2000	0.4	-1.1	-7.0	11.3	10.7	12.0
2001-2005	0.6	2.2	-0.8	14.0	12.8	12.3
1981-1990	1.5	1.8	1.6	7.3	5.6	5.2
1991-2000	0.5	0.4	-3.4	11.5	10.4	10.9
1953-2006	1.4	2.4	2.7	9.0	7.2	6.5
1979-2006	1.0	1.5	-0.4	10.4	8.9	8.7
2006比2005	1.0	3.8	0.5	14.5	11.9	10.9

注：1. 本表地区生产总值、人均地区生产总值按现价计算，速度按可比价计算。2. 社会劳动生产率按现价地区生产总值计算，速度按可比价计算。
Note: a) Gross domestic product and per capita GDP are calculated at current prices; increase rate are based on comparable prices. b) Society labour productivity are calculated at current prices of GDP, increase rate are based on comparable prices.

1-7 续表 1 Continued

单位：亿元 (100 million yuan)

年 份 Year	农业总产值 Gross Output Value of Agriculture	工业总产值 Gross Output Value of Industry	轻工业 Light Industry	重工业 Heavy Industry	中资金融机构人民币存款余额 RMB Deposits of Chinese Financial Institutions	# 储蓄存款余额 Savings Deposit Balance
1952	2.73	19.71	16.36	3.35	2.66	0.50
1957	3.23	40.44	29.01	11.43	3.08	1.05
1962	2.78	45.39	29.12	16.27	10.33	0.93
1965	4.82	66.35	39.08	27.27	12.19	1.57
1970	5.20	102.77	54.83	47.94	14.54	1.59
1975	5.39	145.57	74.47	71.10	25.69	2.88
1978	6.72	157.90	81.47	76.43	33.24	4.02
1980	9.25	195.94	106.00	89.94	44.92	7.96
1985	20.44	319.47	164.22	155.25	114.25	29.38
1990	51.72	679.94	354.50	325.44	263.21	126.92
1995	125.44	1879.65	752.03	1127.62	1079.97	549.97
1996	133.53	2177.42	1014.46	1162.96	1399.06	724.91
1997	140.47	2450.21	1130.04	1320.17	1634.95	863.36
1998	156.16	2562.62	1157.09	1405.53	1860.84	1020.14
1999	150.11	2751.37	1128.47	1622.90	2060.02	1130.19
2000	156.30	3080.74	1263.10	1817.64	2281.55	1172.40
2001	169.51	3366.53	1153.73	2212.80	2562.55	1284.95
2002	181.07	3717.72	1207.88	2509.84	3018.26	1486.38
2003	193.44	4370.76	1254.68	3116.08	4033.51	1825.32
2004	221.35	6186.04	1398.65	4787.39	4729.61	2116.73
2005	238.34	7169.62	1569.06	5600.56	5684.40	2462.41
2006	250.28	8907.45	1664.03	7243.42	6531.94	2811.02
平均每年递增(%) Average Annual Increase Rate (%)						
1953-1957	3.8	16.6	13.5	29.5	3.0	16.0
1958-1962	-2.6	0.4	-1.3	4.5	27.4	-2.3
1963-1965	18.8	15.5	12.8	20.6	5.7	19.0
1966-1970	1.1	10.3	7.5	14.5	3.6	0.3
1971-1975	1.1	8.5	6.7	10.6	12.1	12.6
1976-1980	3.5	6.0	7.7	4.1	11.8	22.5
1981-1985	9.7	9.7	10.1	9.1	20.5	29.8
1986-1990	8.6	10.6	10.2	11.2	18.2	34.0
1991-1995	7.0	20.7	16.3	24.9	32.6	34.1
1996-2000	6.2	15.2	15.8	14.8	16.1	16.3
2001-2005	6.1	21.5	10.4	27.4	20.0	16.0
1981-1990	9.2	10.2	10.1	10.1	19.6	31.9
1991-2000	6.6	17.9	16.0	19.7	24.1	24.9
1953-2006	5.2	12.2	9.7	15.3	15.6	17.3
1979-2006	7.7	15.4	12.4	16.8	20.8	26.4
2006比2005	3.6	25.1	6.1	29.3	14.9	14.2

注：1. 农业总产值按现价计算，速度按可比价计算。2. 工业总产值1995年以后为现价新规定，以前为原规定，速度按可比价计算，以下各表同。3. 金融机构人民币存、贷款余额为当年年末数。

Note: a) Gross output value of agriculture are calculated at current prices; increase rate are based on comparable prices. b) Gross output value of industry are calculated at current prices of new stipulation after 1995, others are former stipulation.Increase rate are based on comparable prices, same as following next. c) RMB deposits and loans of financial institutions are year-end figures.

1-7 续表 2 Continued

单位：亿元 (100 million yuan)

年 份 Year	中资金融机构人民币贷款余额 RMB Loans of Chinese Financial Institutions	全市财政收 入 Total Government Revenue	全市财政支 出 Total Government Expenditures	全社会固定资产投资额 Total Investment in Fixed Assets	#地 方 Local	全社会新增固定资产 Total Newly Increased in Fixed Assets
1952	0.46	3.88	1.08	1.03	0.32	
1957	10.91	7.99	1.63	2.40	1.13	
1962	24.96	9.77	2.49	1.86	1.33	
1965	25.25	13.33	3.50	2.91	1.84	
1970	39.04	28.02	6.40	6.17	4.34	
1975	68.59	39.17	10.61	16.25	8.88	
1978	80.14	39.25	14.51	20.30	10.03	
1980	102.66	40.94	14.67	23.92	14.53	17.84
1985	191.04	48.21	26.97	65.90	50.80	42.62
1990	415.91	44.88	40.20	87.69	57.47	65.16
1995	1113.95	117.34	90.37	393.18	309.75	300.86
1996	1357.38	137.45	110.19	435.81	325.71	313.12
1997	1502.91	169.12	140.08	498.66	376.69	320.46
1998	1629.12	186.55	155.15	575.86	452.11	439.58
1999	1825.26	206.89	177.62	567.36	405.31	459.54
2000	1863.60	244.81	209.57	608.80	463.83	434.28
2001	2159.86	304.52	259.78	705.10	567.40	476.92
2002	2519.04	375.92	300.07	811.26	677.60	537.98
2003	3426.02	451.74	350.63	1046.72	893.73	656.99
2004	3821.38	502.17	431.49	1258.98	1067.97	696.56
2005	4417.45	725.81	520.28	1516.84	1288.85	847.79
2006	5106.94	926.33	654.15	1849.80	1523.01	1423.73
平均每年递增(%) Average Annual Increase Rate (%)						
1953-1957	88.3	15.5	8.6	20.8	36.6	
1958-1962	18.0	4.1	8.8	24.4	45.7	
1963-1965	0.4	10.9	12.0	26.4	20.7	
1966-1970	9.1	16.0	12.8	6.7	4.1	
1971-1975	11.9	6.9	10.6	22.0	14.0	
1976-1980	8.4	0.9	6.7	6.5	7.7	
1981-1985	13.2	3.3	12.9	20.8	29.6	23.6
1986-1990	16.8	-1.4	8.3	6.7	2.3	13.4
1991-1995	21.8	21.2	17.6	36.8	43.3	35.1
1996-2000	10.8	15.9	18.3	10.6	9.1	9.1
2001-2005	18.8	24.3	19.9	19.4	22.9	13.4
1981-1990	15.1	0.9	10.6	16.8	19.6	17.9
1991-2000	16.2	18.5	18.0	26.3	28.9	25.9
1953-2006	18.8	10.7	12.6	14.5	16.8	
1979-2006	16.0	12.0	14.6	17.3	19.8	
2006比2005	15.6	27.7	25.7	22.0	18.2	67.9

注：1994年以前全市财政收支为原地方预算内财政收支口径；1994年以后为分税制后的全市财政收支数。

Note: Before 1994, total government revenue and expenditure intra-budgetary refer to original local government budgetary revenue and expenditure; but it has been total government revenue and expenditure of the city since the reform of tax system was implemented in 1994.

1-7 续表 3 Continued

年 份 Year	全社会房屋建筑竣工面积 (万平方米) Total Floor Space of Buildings Completed (10 000 sq. m)	#住 宅 Residential Buildings	社 会 货运量 (万吨) Freight Traffic (10 000 tons)	港口货物吞吐量 (万吨) Freight Handled at Ports (10 000 tons)	邮电业务总量 (万元) Total Business Value of Post and Telecommunications (10 000 yuan)	社会消费品零售总额 (亿元) Total Retail Sales of Consumer Goods (100 million yuan)
1952			1748	74	894	7.19
1957			2984	284	935	10.55
1962			3498	391	1436	12.31
1965			3450	549	1621	12.32
1970			4837	817	1660	14.57
1975			6766	826	2385	21.18
1978			9241	1131	2710	25.20
1980			13949	1192	3163	34.64
1985	1220.89	853.91	18249	1856	5290	64.12
1990	686.39	468.84	15929	2063	32735	139.88
1995	1263.82	690.68	24040	5787	187195	375.64
1996	1470.04	965.55	24133	6188	256978	470.04
1997	1210.02	678.43	25090	6789	342848	535.02
1998	1142.49	689.63	24505	6818	474067	587.12
1999	1330.66	852.35	27052	7298	567242	657.28
2000	1459.36	910.30	26400	9582	753669	736.63
2001	1614.93	958.73	28608	11369	702206	832.70
2002	1835.39	1043.38	31016	12906	903296	941.36
2003	2072.31	1121.97	35252	16182	1157060	922.27
2004	2353.92	1428.39	37934	20619	1467836	1044.78
2005	2863.36	1662.53	40263	24069	1763477	1190.06
2006	2960.32	1726.71	42863	25760	2277902	1356.79
平均每年递增(%) Average Annual Increase Rate (%)						
1953-1957			11.3	30.9	0.9	5.5
1958-1962			3.2	6.6	9.0	0.8
1963-1965			-0.5	12.0	4.1	4.0
1966-1970			7.0	8.3	0.5	3.7
1971-1975			6.9	0.2	7.5	7.8
1976-1980			15.6	7.6	5.8	8.8
1981-1985			5.5	9.3	10.8	9.3
1986-1990	-10.9	-11.3	-2.7	2.1	24.9	6.5
1991-1995	13.0	8.1	8.6	22.9	41.7	9.2
1996-2000	2.9	5.7	2.0	10.6	32.1	14.8
2001-2005	14.4	12.8	8.8	20.2	26.0	15.0
1981-1990			1.3	5.6	17.7	7.8
1991-2000	7.8	6.9	5.2	16.6	36.8	12.0
1953-2006			6.1	11.4	14.8	7.6
1979-2006			5.6	11.8	25.4	10.6
2006比2005	3.4	3.9	6.5	7.0	29.2	13.6

注：2003年起社会消费品零售总额为新口径。增长速度均为可比口径，并已扣除物价因素。

Note: Since 2003, retail sales of consumer goods has been calculated on new statistical coverage. The increase rate of retail on sales of consumer goods are calculated at comparable price and have deducted price sectors.

1-7 续表 4 Continued

年　份 Year	实际利用外资额 (万美元) Foreign Capital Actually Used (USD 10 000)	#客商直投 Foreign Direct Investment	天津口岸进出口总值 (亿美元) Total Value of Imports & Exports In Tianjin Port (USD 100 million)	#出　口 Exports	外贸进出口总值 (亿美元) Total Value of Imports & Exports in Foreign Trade (USD 100 million)	#出　口 Exports
1952						1.90
1957					2.50	2.48
1962					2.40	2.34
1965					3.54	3.41
1970					3.58	3.19
1975					8.86	7.72
1978					9.88	8.65
1980	271	271			18.27	15.42
1985	7558	4409	96.18	20.07	14.86	11.53
1990	33467	8315	85.95	42.53	22.10	17.86
1995	211010	152064	217.46	127.81	65.46	29.98
1996	298358	200587	216.85	122.89	82.97	40.49
1997	342301	251135	215.62	131.24	100.23	50.18
1998	305787	251803	223.19	134.84	106.16	54.99
1999	274535	253203	248.29	139.18	126.05	63.32
2000	282467	256000	298.03	165.29	171.57	86.29
2001	329688	322000	323.71	178.13	181.86	95.02
2002	386901	380591	365.35	190.55	228.27	115.95
2003	170550	163325	461.67	259.57	293.71	143.74
2004	270236	247243	677.66	384.80	420.19	208.65
2005	364573	332885	819.29	446.83	533.87	274.15
2006	436896	413077	1018.85	571.24	645.73	335.40
平均每年递增(%) Average Annual Increase Rate (%)						
1953-1957						5.5
1958-1962					-0.8	-1.2
1963-1965					13.8	13.5
1966-1970					0.2	-1.4
1971-1975					19.9	19.4
1976-1980					15.6	14.8
1981-1985	94.6	74.7			-4.1	-5.7
1986-1990	34.7	13.5	-2.2	16.2	8.3	9.1
1991-1995	44.5	78.8	20.4	24.6	24.3	10.9
1996-2000	6.0	11.0	6.5	5.3	21.3	23.5
2001-2005	27.2	32.0	22.4	22.0	25.5	26.0
1981-1990	61.9	40.8			1.9	1.5
1991-2000	23.8	40.9	13.2	14.5	22.7	17.1
1953-2006						10.1
1979-2006					16.1	14.0
2006比2005	19.8	24.1	24.4	27.8	21.0	22.3

注：2003年实际利用外资额采用商务部口径，速度按可比口径计算；以下相关表同。

Note: Since 2003, foreign direct investment refer to new coverage of Ministry of Commerce,its increase rate is calculated on the basis of comparable coverage, same as following next.

1-7 续表 5 Continued

年 份 Year	城镇单位从业人员劳动报酬总额(亿元) Total Remuneration of Persons Employed in Urban Units (100 million yuan)	# 国有单位 State-owned Units	城镇单位从业人员人均劳动报酬(元) Per Capita Annual Remuneration of Persons Employed in Urban Units (yuan)	# 国有单位 State-owned Units	城市居民人均可支配收入(元) Disposable Income of Urban Households (yuan)	城市居民人均消费性支出(元) Expenditure for Consumption of Urban Households (yuan)
1952	2.56	2.56		573	200	176
1957	5.05	5.05		749	240	216
1962	7.11	7.11		685	252	238
1965	8.48	7.29	714	745	261	234
1970	8.58	7.17	652	673	281	255
1975	10.66	8.61	618	663	324	295
1978	14.00	11.51	640	690	388	345
1980	19.32	15.77	820	865	527	475
1985	34.14	24.69	1250	1223	876	771
1990	69.38	55.50	2438	2611	1639	1440
1995	184.80	135.22	6501	6963	4930	4064
1996	212.05	154.34	7643	8072	5968	4680
1997	223.25	160.47	8238	8689	6609	5204
1998	225.39	151.80	9895	10169	7111	5471
1999	234.42	151.93	11046	11169	7650	5852
2000	253.53	161.86	12414	12690	8141	6121
2001	277.56	176.26	14242	14823	8959	6987
2002	304.23	182.27	16223	16632	9338	7192
2003	350.60	194.80	18511	18929	10313	7868
2004	407.99	222.60	21146	22031	11467	8802
2005	458.26	247.30	24122	24832	12639	9653
2006	530.29	283.14	27628	29135	14283	10548
平均每年递增(%) Average Annual Increase Rate (%)						
1953-1957	12.1	12.1		3.3	1.5	2.0
1958-1962	4.7	4.7		-3.9	-1.3	-0.3
1963-1965	10.0	4.6		6.7	5.0	3.2
1966-1970	0.6	0.1	-1.4	-1.5	1.9	2.1
1971-1975	4.4	3.7	-1.1	-0.3	2.9	3.0
1976-1980	11.2	11.5	4.5	4.1	8.8	8.6
1981-1985	8.4	5.8	5.3	3.7	7.2	6.6
1986-1990	5.2	7.4	4.4	6.3	3.5	3.5
1991-1995	5.2	3.4	5.3	5.3	7.8	6.4
1996-2000	4.4	1.6	11.6	10.5	8.4	6.4
2001-2005	11.3	7.6	12.9	13.1	8.0	8.3
1981-1990	6.8	6.6	4.8	4.4	5.1	5.0
1991-2000	4.9	2.5	8.4	7.9	8.1	6.5
1953-2006	7.0	5.8		4.3	5.1	4.6
1979-2006	7.7	6.0	8.2	8.1	7.8	6.9
2006比2005	14.0	12.8	12.8	15.6	11.3	7.7

注: 1. 1998年以前有关劳动报酬指标的绝对数为职工工资，计算增长速度时已扣除物价因素。2. 计算城市居民人均收支增长速度按可比口径，并已扣除物价因素。

Note: a) Before 1998, total remuneration and per capita remuneration refer to wage of staff and workers, average annua lincrease rate of these indicators have deducted price sectors. b) The increase rate of income and expenditure are calculated at comparable coverage and have deducted price sectors.

1-7 续表 6 Continued

年　份 Year	农村居民人均纯收入(元) Per Capita Annual Net Income of Rural Households (yuan)	农村居民人均生活消费支出(元) Per Capita Annual Expenditure for Consumption of Rural Households (yuan)	各类学校在校学生数(万人) Students Enrollment by Level of School (10 000 persons)	国有单位自然科学技术人员数(人) Natural Scientific & Technical Personnel of State-owned Units (person)	医　院卫生院床位数(张) Hospital Beds (unit)	卫生技术人员数(人) Medical Technical Personnel (person)	#执业及助理医师 Certified & Assistant Doctors
1952	70		57.14		3457	8481	3326
1957	92		83.92		6156	15124	5522
1962	65		106.37		10521	23858	8627
1965	92		148.10		11266	26393	10585
1970	145		148.17		11361	23591	9046
1975	147		169.71		15961	33734	12326
1978	153	132	162.30	102022	17288	40653	15776
1980	278	208	139.06	127803	18753	50662	20474
1985	564	426	121.09	194837	25191	60412	25555
1990	1069	733	134.97	271761	33382	67485	32034
1995	2531	1717	155.28	248739	37280	71806	33693
1996	3142	2101	161.40	265924	38284	71014	32975
1997	3548	2110	164.41	260927	39467	70431	32475
1998	3890	2260	164.11	259374	39134	68070	31482
1999	4055	2334	162.53	257169	38579	65901	30273
2000	4370	2393	162.22	249934	38842	65145	30031
2001	4825	2618	160.54	240361	40394	63475	29215
2002	5315	2778	161.69	226639	38837	56705	23888
2003	5861	3015	163.23	232324	38074	55629	22780
2004	6525	3297	161.67	212049	38876	60722	25299
2005	7202	3590	162.05	206222	39491	61284	25088
2006	7942	3829	158.84	207958	38893	62258	25358
平均每年递增(%) Average Annual Increase Rate (%)							
1953-1957	5.6		8.0		12.2	12.3	10.7
1958-1962	-6.7		4.9		11.3	9.5	9.3
1963-1965	12.3		11.7		2.3	3.4	7.1
1966-1970	9.5				0.2	-2.2	-3.1
1971-1975	0.3		2.8		7.0	7.4	6.4
1976-1980	13.6		-3.9		3.3	8.5	10.7
1981-1985	15.2	15.4	-2.7	8.8	6.1	3.6	4.5
1986-1990	13.6	11.5	2.2	6.9	5.8	2.2	4.6
1991-1995	18.8	18.6	2.8	-1.8	2.2	1.2	1.2
1996-2000	11.5	6.7	0.9	0.1	0.8	-1.9	-2.3
2001-2005	10.5	8.5		-3.8	0.3	-1.2	-3.5
1981-1990	14.4	13.4	-0.3	7.8	5.9	2.9	4.6
1991-2000	15.1	12.6	1.9	-0.8	1.5	-0.4	-0.6
1953-2006	9.2		1.9		4.6	3.8	3.8
1979-2006	15.1	12.8	-0.1	2.6	2.9	1.5	1.7
2006比2005	10.3	6.7	-2.0	0.8	-1.5	1.6	1.1

1-8 国民经济和社会发展结构指标(2003-2006年)
STRUCTURAL INDICATORS ON NATIONAL ECONOMY AND SOCIAL DEVELOPMENT, 2003-2006

单位: % (%)

指 标	Item	2003	2004	2005	2006
人 口	**Population**				
农非结构	Grouped by Non-agricultural and Agricultural				
非农业	Non-agricultural	59.4	59.6	59.9	60.2
农 业	Agricultural	40.6	40.4	40.1	39.8
性别结构	Grouped by Sex				
男	Male	50.5	50.5	50.4	50.4
女	Female	49.5	49.5	49.6	49.6
就 业	**Employment**				
社会从业人员产业结构	Grouped by Industry				
第一产业	Primary Industry	16.3	15.7	15.1	14.4
第二产业	Secondary Industry	42.9	42.4	41.9	41.7
第三产业	Tertiary Industry	40.8	41.9	43.0	43.9
国民经济核算	**National Accounting**				
地区生产总值产业结构	Grouped by Industry				
第一产业	Primary Industry	3.5	3.4	3.0	2.7
第二产业	Secondary Industry	51.9	54.2	55.5	57.1
第三产业	Tertiary Industry	44.6	42.4	41.5	40.2
投 资	**Investment**				
全社会固定资产投资结构	Structure of Total Investment in Fixed Assets				
建设工程	Construction	56.8	54.8	56.2	54.4
安装工程	Installation	5.8	4.9	5.0	6.1
设备、工具、器械购置	Purchase of Equipment and Instruments	18.9	22.5	20.8	21.3
其他费用	Others	18.5	17.8	18.0	18.2
资金来源结构	Structure of Sources of Funds				
国家预算内投资	State Budgetary Appropriation	1.4	1.5	1.8	1.1
国内贷款	Domestic Loans	30.2	28.1	24.7	25.0
利用外资	Foreign Investment	5.9	7.3	6.7	7.0
自筹和其他投资	Fundraising and Others Investment	62.5	63.1	66.8	66.9
财 政	**Government Finance**				
地方财政收入结构	Structure of Local Government Revenue				
#增值税	Value-added Tax	18.4	11.6	15.6	15.3

1-8 续表 1 Continued

单位: % (%)

指　标	Item	2003	2004	2005	2006
营业税	Business Tax	26.2	25.9	23.4	21.9
企业所得税	Income Tax of Enterprises	9.7	10.6	10.0	10.1
个人所得税	Individual Income Tax	5.1	5.3	4.6	4.0
利用外资	**Utilization of Foreign Capital**				
实际利用外资结构	Structure of Foreign Capital Actually Utilized				
对外借款	Foreign Loans	4.2	8.5	8.7	5.5
客外商直接投资	Foreign Direct Investment	95.8	91.5	91.3	94.5
能　源	**Energy**				
能源使用结构	Structure of Energy Consumption				
#第一产业	Primary Industry	1.9	1.8	1.9	1.8
第二产业	Secondary Industry	64.0	65.2	65.7	67.5
第三产业	Tertiary Industry	21.1	20.9	20.3	19.3
农　业	**Agriculture**				
农林牧渔业产值结构	Structure of Gross Output Value of FFAF				
农　业	Farming	45.6	43.1	40.9	42.1
林　业	Forestry	0.8	0.7	0.8	0.8
牧　业	Animal Husbandry	39.9	41.8	43.1	41.6
渔　业	Fishery	13.7	14.4	15.2	15.5
工　业	**Industry**				
全部工业总产值结构	Structure of Gross Output Value of Industry				
轻工业	Light Industry	28.7	22.6	21.9	18.7
重工业	Heavy Industry	71.3	77.4	78.1	81.3
建筑业	**Construction**				
建筑业总产值结构	Structure of Gross Output Value of Construction				
房屋和土木工程建筑业	Building and Civil Engineering	81.9	81.0	80.9	82.4
建筑安装业	Equipment Installation	13.8	12.2	13.9	12.4
建筑装饰业	Building Decoration	3.1	4.1	3.0	2.5
其他建筑业	Others	1.2	2.7	2.2	2.7
交通运输业	**Transportation**				
货运量结构	Structure of Freight Traffic				
铁　路(天津地区)	Railway (Tianjin Area)	16.1	16.1	18.0	19.6

1-8 续表 2 Continued

单位: % (%)

指　标	Item	2003	2004	2005	2006
公　路	Highway	56.9	51.6	49.3	47.3
水运、民航	Waterway and Civil Aviation	25.4	30.6	30.7	31.1
管道运输	Pipelines	1.6	1.7	2.0	2.0
国内商业	**Domestic Trade**				
社会消费品零售总额构成	Composition of Retail Sales of Consumer Goods				
市	City	93.2	93.4	93.5	94.0
县	County	3.8	3.7	3.6	3.3
县以下	Under County Level	3.0	2.9	2.9	2.7
对外经济贸易	**Foreign Trade**				
进出口贸易总值结构	Structure of Imports and Exports				
出口总值	Exports	48.9	49.7	51.4	51.9
进口总值	Imports	51.1	50.3	48.6	48.1
国际旅游	**International Tourism**				
来津旅游人员结构	Structure of Tourists				
外国人、华侨	Foreigners and Overseas Chinese	83.7	85.6	86.1	88.2
港澳台同胞	Compatriots form Hong Kong, Macao and Taiwan	16.3	14.4	13.9	11.8
金融业	**Financial Intermediation**				
金融机构存款结构	Structure of Deposits in Financial Institution				
# 企事业存款	Deposits of Enterprises and Institutions	38.5	40.1	40.2	41.4
储蓄存款	Savings Deposits	45.7	44.0	42.4	42.7
金融机构贷款结构	Structure of Loans in Financial Institution				
# 短期贷款	Short-term Loans	47.8	46.4	44.0	41.3
中长期贷款	Medium-term & Long-term Loans	41.5	44.6	47.8	51.7
教　育	**Education**				
在校学生结构	Strurcture of Student Enronllment				
大学生	University and College Students	15.0	17.7	20.5	22.2
中学生	Secondary Students	49.1	48.0	46.6	45.7
小学生	Primary Students	35.9	34.3	32.9	32.1

1-8 续表 3 Continued

单位：% (%)

指标	Item	2003	2004	2005	2006
专任教师结构	Full-time Teachers by Type				
大学	University and College	13.8	16.7	18.9	21.0
中学	Secondary Schools	47.5	46.1	45.2	44.6
小学	Primary Schools	38.7	37.2	35.9	34.4
科技	**Science and Technolgy**				
科技经费筹集额结构	Structure of Funding for Scientific and Technological				
# 政府资金	Government Fund	18.7	17.8	18.4	14.2
企业资金	Enterprises Fund	67.9	71.4	73.6	76.3
金融机构贷款	Loans from Banks	7.6	6.1	5.0	4.3
卫生	**Health Care**				
卫生机构结构	Structure of Health Care Institution				
# 医院、卫生院	Hospitals and Health Care Centers	18.2	18.4	18.5	16.8
卫生技术人员结构	Structure of Medical Professionals				
# 执业及助理医师	Certified and Assistant Doctors	40.9	41.7	40.9	40.7
注册护士	Registered Nurses	34.5	32.3	32.0	32.2
生活	**People's Livelihood**				
城市居民消费结构	Consumption Structure of Urban Residents				
食品类	Food	37.7	37.2	36.7	34.9
衣着类	Clothing	7.4	7.1	7.2	8.2
用品及其他	Articles for Daily Use and Others	41.0	41.7	42.7	43.9
居住	Residence	13.9	14.0	13.4	13.0
农村居民消费结构	Consumption Structure of Rural Residents				
食品类	Food	38.3	38.5	38.3	38.0
衣着类	Clothing	8.8	8.9	10.1	9.7
用品及其他	Articles for Daily Use and Others	29.9	29.6	28.1	27.6
居住	Residence	23.0	23.0	23.5	24.7
环境	**Environment**				
空气质量结构	Strcuture of Air Quality				
二级和好于二级的天数	Days of Grade II and Better than Grade II	72.3	81.7	81.6	83.6

1-9 国民经济和社会发展比例和效益指标(2003-2006年)
MAIN INDICATORS ON PROPORTION AND EFFICIENCY IN NATIONAL ECONOMY AND SOCIAL DEVELOPMENT, 2003-2006

单位: % (%)

指 标	Item	2003	2004	2005	2006
人 口	**Population**				
出生率(‰)	Birth Rate (‰)	7.1	7.3	7.4	7.7
死亡率(‰)	Death Rate (‰)	6.0	6.0	6.0	6.1
自然增长率(‰)	Natural Growth Rate (‰)	1.1	1.3	1.4	1.6
就 业	**Employment**				
城镇登记失业率	Unemployment Rate in Urban Areas	3.8	3.8	3.7	3.6
国民经济核算	**National Accounting**				
经济增长贡献率	Contribution to Gross Domestic Product				
第一产业	Primary Industry	1.6	1.2	0.9	0.7
第二产业	Secondary Industry	63.0	66.6	66.1	67.5
#工 业	Industy	59.2	66.1	62.4	62.1
第三产业	Tertiary Industry	35.4	32.2	33.0	31.8
固定资产投资	**Investment in Fixed Assets**				
全社会固定资产投资相当于地区生产总值比例	Proportion of Total Investment in Fixed Assets to GDP	40.6	40.5	41.0	42.4
新增固定资产交付使用率	Rate of Fixed Assets Transferred and in Use	62.8	55.3	55.9	77.0
财 政	**Government Finance**				
全市财政收入相当于地区生产总值比例	Proportion of Total Government Revenue to GDP	17.5	16.1	19.6	21.3
全市财政支出相当于地区生产总值比例	Proportion of Total Government Expenditures to GDP	13.6	13.9	14.1	15.0
预算外资金收入相当于全市财政收入比例	Proportion of Extra-budgetaty Receipt to Total Government Revenue	13.2	9.5	8.3	6.1
利用外资	**Utillization of Foreign Capital**				
客商直接投资相当于签约额比例	Proportion of Foreign Direct Investment to Foreign Investment Contracted	46.5	44.2	45.5	50.9
能 源	**Energy**				
能源消费弹性系数	Elasticity Ratio of Energy Consumption	0.43	0.95	0.77	0.69
万元地区生产总值耗能(吨标准煤)	Energy Consumption per 10 000 yuan GDP (ton of SCE)	1.3	1.29	1.11	1.07

1-9 续表 1 Continued

单位：% (%)

指　　标	Item	2003	2004	2005	2006
农　业	Agriculture				
每公顷耕地农业机械总动力(千瓦)	Total Power of Agricultural Machinery per Hectare of Cultivated Land (kW)	14.38	14.64	14.76	
每公顷播种面积农产品产量(吨)	Output of Crops per Hectare of Sown Area (ton)				
粮　食	Grain	4.62	4.75	4.78	4.86
棉　花	Cotton	1.34	1.38	1.37	1.38
油　料	Oil-bearing Crops	1.95	2.54	2.53	2.61
工　业	Industry				
总资产贡献率	Ratio of Total Assets to Industrial Output Value	9.9	12.8	14.5	15.9
成本费用利润率	Ratio of Profits to Industrial Cost	6.0	7.5	8.5	8.7
工业增加值率	Ratio of Value Added to Gross Industrial Output Value	26.5	26.1	27.1	28.7
建筑业	Construction				
技术装备率(万元/人)	Value of Machinery per Labor (10000 yuan/person)	2.42	2.74	2.61	2.54
产值利税率	Ratio of Per-tax Profits to Gross Output Value	4.8	4.9	5.3	5.8
全员劳动生产率(万元/人)	Overall Labor Productivity (10 000 yuan/person)	14.65	17.12	19.29	25.51
邮电通信业	Post and Telecommunications				
电话普及率(含移动电话)(部/百人)	Access to Telephones (include mobile phone (set/100 person)	82.3	89.5	90.1	106.7
移动电话普及率(部/百人)	Access to Mobile Phones (set/100 person)	41.4	45.4	48.2	56.0
每一邮电局所服务面积(平方公里)	Average Service Area per Post and Telecommunications Office (sq. km)	19.26	17.03	14.41	14.57
对外经济贸易	Foreign Economy Trade				
进出口总值相当于地区生产总值比例	Proportion of Total Value of Imports & Exports in Foreign Trade to GDP	94.3	111.8	118.3	118.09
出口总值相当于地区生产总值比例	Proportion of Total Value of Exports to GDP	46.1	55.5	60.7	61.3
国际旅游	International Tourism				
每一来津游客花费(美元)	Expenditure Per International Tourist in Tianjin (USD)	674	670	688	711

1-9 续表 2 Continued

单位: % (%)

指　标	Item	2003	2004	2005	2006
金融业	**Financial Intermediation**				
中资金融机构人民币存款相当于地区生产总值比例	Chinese Bank Deposits of RMB as Percentage of GDP	156.5	152.0	153.7	149.8
中资金融机构贷款相当于地区生产总值比例	Chinese Bank Loans of RMB as Percentage of GDP	132.1	122.8	119.5	117.2
教　育	**Education**				
学龄儿童入学率	Percentage of School-aged Children Enrolled	100	100	100	101.1
初中毕业升学率	Percentage of Entering Junior Secondary Schools	93.1	94.0	94.5	99.8
每一教师负担学生数(人)	Student-teacher Ratio (person)	14	14	14	14
科　技	**Science**				
研究与实验发展经费支出相当于地区生产总值比例	R&D Expenditures as Percentage of GDP	1.65	1.81	1.97	2.18
文　化	**Culture**				
每百万人有艺术表演团体(个)	Number of Troupes per Million Persons (unit)	1.5	1.6	1.5	1.5
每百万人有公共图书馆(个)	Number of Public Libraries per Persons (unit)	3.1	3.1	3.1	3.0
每百万人有博物馆(个)	Number of Museums per Million Persons (uint)	1.7	1.7	1.7	1.8
婚　姻	**Marriages and Divorces**				
离婚率(‰)	Divorces Rate (‰)	2.4	3.2	3.3	3.7
生　活	**People's Livelihood**				
城市与农村居民收入增长率比例(以农村居民收入指数为100)	Proportion of Growth Rate of Annual Income of Urban Residents to the Growth Rate of Annual Net Income of Rural Residents (rural=100)	100.1	99.9	99.8	102.4
福　利	**Welfare**				
离退休退职费相当于劳动报酬比例	Pensions for Retired Veterans, Retired and Resigned Persons as Percentage of Total Wages	30.0	30.3	32.7	32.5
离退休退职人员相当于在职人员比例	Proportion of Retired or Resigned Workers to Employed Ones	63.6	68.7	77.2	79.1
环境保护	**Environmental Protection**				
污水处理率	Percentage of Sewage Disposed	43.9	53.7	58.0	58.9
工业固体废物综合利用率	Rate of Comprehensive Using Industrial Waste Residue	96.1	97.3	98.3	98.4

1-10 平均每天社会经济活动(2003-2006年)
AVERAGE DAILY SOCIAL AND ECONOMIC ACTIVITIES, 2003-2006

指　标	Item	单　位	Unit	2003	2004	2005	2006
全市每天创造的财富	Daily Production						
地区生产总值	Gross Domestic Product	万　元	10 000 yuan	70631	85232	101305	119428
第一产业	Primary Industry	万　元	10 000 yuan	2463	2884	3079	3239
第二产业	Secondary Industry	万　元	10 000 yuan	36639	46191	56197	68172
工　业	Industry	万　元	10 000 yuan	33367	42458	51645	62815
建筑业	Construction	万　元	10 000 yuan	3272	3733	4552	5358
第三产业	Tertiary Industry	万　元	10 000 yuan	31529	36158	42029	48017
全市财政收入	Total Government Revenue	万　元	10 000 yuan	12376	13758	19885	25379
主要工业产品产量	Output of Major Industrial Products						
钢	Steel	吨	ton	15505	21602	26172	35215
钢　材	Steel Products	吨	ton	28259	47127	45590	58014
水　泥	Cement	吨	ton	12310	14261	14223	16639
原　油	Crude Oil	吨	ton	36063	39622	48846	53235
原　盐	Salt	吨	ton	6041	6608	6304	6469
发电量	Electricity	万千瓦时	10 000 kWh	8766	9308	10019	9842
汽　车	Motor Vehicle	辆	unit	473	628	898	1135
彩色电视机	Color Television	台	set	3080	2998	1778	2688
摩托车	Motorcycle	辆	unit	3145	3421	3053	532
自行车	Bicycle	辆	unit	22847	52823	35800	46788
微波炉	Microwave Oven	台	set	26572	37720	39210	39309
移动电话	Mobile Phone	部	unit	86020	134989	173146	277527
布	Cloth	万　米	10 000 m	69	84	71	78
纱	Yarn	吨	ton	205	206	201	209
农用化肥	Chemical Fertilizer	吨	ton	449	437	464	447
化学农药	Chemical Pesticide	吨	ton	58	12	35	34
硫　酸	Sulfuric Acid	吨	ton	300	274	327	377
烧　碱	Caustic Soda	吨	ton	2189	2223	2204	2435
合成洗涤剂	Synthetic Detergents	吨	ton	139	138	38	20
饮料酒	Alcoholic Beverages	吨	ton	677	648	570	816
主要农产品产量	Output of Major Farm Products						
粮　食	Grain	吨	ton	3268	3432	3767	3932
棉　花	Cotton	吨	ton	259	330	229	298
油　料	Oil bearing Crops	吨	ton	84	42	35	33
肉　类	Meat	吨	ton	1436	1472	1583	1631
蛋　类	Eggs	吨	ton	664	668	643	632
牛　奶	Milk	吨	ton	1184	1486	1737	1871
蔬　菜	Vegetables	吨	ton	16515	16039	14870	12916
水产品	Aquatic Products	吨	ton	817	849	926	972

1-10 续表 Continued

指　标	Item	单　位	Unit	2003	2004	2005	2006
全市每天消费量	**Daily Consumption**						
最终消费	Final Consumption Expenditure	万　元	10 000 yuan	32686	36812	41285	48305
居民消费	Resident Consumption	万　元	10 000 yuan	21403	24032	26850	30651
城镇居民	Urban	万　元	10 000 yuan	18479	20896	23499	27112
农村居民	Rural	万　元	10 000 yuan	2925	3133	3351	3539
政府消费	Government Consumption Expenditure	万　元	10 000 yuan	11283	12781	14435	17654
社会消费品零售总额	Total Retail Sales of Consumer Goods	万　元	10 000 yuan	25268	28624	32604	37172
生活用煤、气、水、电	Coal, Gas, Water & Electricity For Living						
煤	Coal	万　吨	10 000 tons	0.25	0.23	0.24	0.21
液化石油气	Liquid Petroleum Gas	吨	ton	293	245	195	193
天然气和煤气	Natural Gas And Coal Gas	万立方米	10 000 cu. m	82.5	78.9	105	99
水	Water	万　吨	10 000 tons	81.7	78.9	79.1	74.2
电	Electricity	万千瓦时	10 000 kWh	869	916	1040	1179
每天其他经济活动	**Other Daily Economic Activities**						
社会货物运输量	Freight Traffic	万　吨	10 000 tons	96.6	103.9	110.3	117.4
客运量	Passenger Traffic	万人次	10 000 person-times	9.6	11.2	12.8	15.5
港口货物吞吐量	Freight Handled at Ports	万　吨	10 000 tons	44.3	56.5	65.9	70.6
邮电业务总量	Total Business of Post and Telecommunications Service	万　元	10 000 yuan	3170	4021	4831	6241
出版图书	Books Published	万　册	10 000 copies	18.6	22.7	16.2	14.0
出版报纸	Newspapers Issued	万　份	10 000 copies	225.7	237.5	239.9	259.8
出版杂志	Magazines Issued	万　册	10 000 copies	12.6	12.3	11.5	11.1
邮寄函件	Letters Delivered	万　件	10 000 copies	60.4	29	23	24.4
外贸出口总值	Total Value of Exports in Foreign Trade	万美元	USD 10 000	3938	5716	7511	9189
实际利用外资额	Foreign Capital Actually Used	万美元	USD 10 000	467	740	999	1197
全社会竣工房屋建筑面积	Total Floor Space of Buildings Completed	万平方米	10 000 sq. m	5.68	6.45	7.84	8.11
接待来津国际旅游人数	Accommodated International Tourists (Stay for Night)	人　次	person-times	472	755	849	1157
每天人口和婚姻动态	**Daily Population Changes And Marriages**						
出生人口	Births	人	person	197	204	211	223
死亡人口	Deaths	人	person	167	166	170	176
结婚对数	Marriages	对	couple	173	211	174	229
离婚对数	Divorces	对	couple	33	44	47	54

1-11 国民经济主要指标人均水平(2003-2006年)
PER CAPITA ANNUAL LEVEL OF MAIN INDICATORS ON NATIONAL ECONOMY, 2003-2006

指　标	Item	单　位	Unit	2003	2004	2005	2006
1. 地区生产总值	Gross Domestic Product	元	yuan	21387	25544	35783	41163
2. 全市财政收入	Total Government Revenue	元	yuan	4897	5404	7024	8747
3. 全市财政支出	Total Government Expenditures	元	yuan	3801	4643	5035	6177
4. 全社会固定资产投资	Total Investment in Fixed Assets	元	yuan	11346	13548	14679	17467
5. 工业总产值	Gross Output Value of Industry	元	yuan	47378	62026	69383	84112
6. 主要工业产品产量	Output of Major Industrial Products						
原　油	Crude Oil	吨	ton	1.43	1.55	1.73	1.83
天然气	Natural Gas	立方米	cu. m	92	93	85	99
发电量	Electricity	千瓦时	kWh	3468	3630	3539	3392
钢	Steel	吨	ton	0.61	0.84	0.92	1.21
钢　材	Steel Products	吨	ton	1.12	1.84	1.61	2
水　泥	Cement	吨	ton	0.49	0.56	0.5	0.57
布	Cloth	米	m	27	33	25	27
纱	Yarn	公　斤	kg	8.1	8	7.1	7.2
7. 农业总产值	Gross Output Value of Agriculture	元	yuan	2097	2382	2307	2363
8. 主要农产品产量	Output of Major Farm Products						
粮　食	Grain	公　斤	kg	129	135	133	136
棉　花	Cotton	公　斤	kg	10.3	12.9	8.1	10.3
油　料	Oil-bearing Crops	公　斤	kg	3.3	1.7	1.2	1.1
蔬　菜	Vegetables	公　斤	kg	653	630	525	445
肉　类	Meat	公　斤	kg	57	58	56	56
蛋　类	Eggs	公　斤	kg	26	26	23	22
奶　类	Milk	公　斤	kg	47	58	61	64
水产品	Aquatic Products	公　斤	kg	32.3	33.3	32.7	33.5
鲜　果	Fresh Fruits	公　斤	kg	34.3	31.8	26.9	28.3
9. 社会消费品零售额	Total Retail Sales of Consumer Goods	元	yuan	9997	11243	11517	12812
10. 城市居民主要商品购买量	Perchase Volume of Major Products of Urban Households						
粮　食	Grain	公　斤	kg	80.8	80.8	81.4	75.8
食用植物油	Edible Vegetable-oil	公　斤	kg	9.3	9.7	8.7	9.7
猪牛羊肉	Pork, Beef and Mutton	公　斤	kg	24.2	24	24	24.2
鸡　蛋	Eggs	公　斤	kg	18.8	16.8	18.5	17.8
鲜　菜	Fresh Vegetables	公　斤	kg	138.9	138.9	132.4	126.9
鱼	Fish	公　斤	kg	9.5	9.3	9.6	9.1
鲜　奶	Milk	公　斤	kg	23.1	23.1	23.6	23.2
鲜瓜果	Fresh Fruits	公　斤	kg	80.4	71.1	73.4	73.0
服　装	Garments	件	piece	6.3	6.1	6.1	6.4
鞋　类	Shoes	双	pair	2.4	2.4	2.3	2.3
11.外贸出口总值	Total Value of Exports in Foreign Trade	美　元	USD	1558	2245	2653	3167
12.社会货物运输量	Freight Traffic	吨	ton	38.2	40.8	39	40.5

112 天津在全国的地位
POSITION OF TIANJIN IN THE WHOLE NATION

指 标	Item	2001		2006	
		天 津 Tianjin	占全国比重(%) As Percentage To Nation (%)	天 津 Tianjin	占全国比重(%) As Percentage To Nation (%)
年末常住人口(万人)	**Permanent Population (year-end) (10 000 persons)**	**1004.06**	**0.8**	**1075.00**	**0.8**
社会从业人员(万人)	**Total Employment Personnel (10 000 persons)**	**488.34**	**0.7**	**562.92**	**0.7**
地区生产总值(亿元)	**Gross Domestic Product (100 million yuan)**	**1919.09**	**1.8**	**4359.15**	**2.1**
第一产业	Primary Industry	78.73	0.5	118.23	0.5
第二产业	Secondary Industry	959.06	1.9	2488.29	2.4
第三产业	Tertiary Industry	881.30	2.0	1752.63	2.1
财政、金融(亿元)	**Government Finance and Banking (100 million)**				
地方一般预算财政收	Local General Budgetary Government Revenue	163.64	2.1	417.05	2.3
一般预算财政支出	General Budgetary Government Expenditure	234.67	1.8	543.12	1.8
金融机构本外币存款余额	Balance of Home and Foreign Currency Deposits	2562.55	1.8	6839.20	2.0
金融机构本外币贷款余额	Balance of Home and Foreign Currency Loans	2159.86	1.9	5415.72	2.3
保费收入	Premium	41.70	2.0	105.18	1.9
规模以上工业增加值(亿元)	**Gross Output Value of Industry (Above Designated Size) (100 million yuan)**	728.10	2.6	2443.84	3.1
轻工业	Light Industry	207.95	2.0	392.85	1.6
重工业	Heavy Industry	520.14	2.9	2050.99	3.7
主要工业产品产量	**Output of Major Industrial Products**				
钢(万吨)	Steel (10 000 tons)	395.30	2.6	1285.34	3.0
生 铁(万吨)	Pig Iron (10 000 tons)	228.74	1.5	1131.51	2.8
水 泥(万吨)	Cement (10 000 tons)	338.99	0.5	607.33	0.5
发电量(亿千瓦时)	Electricity (100 million kWh)	217.43	1.5	359.24	1.3
原 油(万吨)	Crude Oil (10 000 tons)	970.29	5.9	1943.09	10.6
原 盐(万吨)	Salt (10 000 tons)	238.49	7.0	236.10	4.4
天然气(亿立方米)	Natural Gas (100 million cu. m)	8.95	3.0	10.50	1.8
轿 车(万辆)	Motor Vehicles (10 000 units)	5.10	7.3	41.03	10.6
自行车(万辆)	Bicycles (10 000 units)	322.26	11.1	1707.77	25.4
移动电话机(万部)	Mobile Phone (10 000 units)	1497.52	18.6	10129.72	21.1
化学纤维(万吨)	Chemical Fibers (10 000 tons)	22.96	2.7	18.68	0.9
纱(万吨)	Yarn (10 000 tons)	8.13	1.1	7.62	0.4
布(亿米)	Cloth (100 million m)	2.59	0.9	2.83	0.5
彩色电视机(万台)	Color Television Sets (10 000 sets)	51.42	1.3	98.11	1.2

1-12 续表 Continued

指　标	Item	2001 天津 Tianjin	2001 占全国比重(%) As Percentage To Nation (%)	2006 天津 Tianjin	2006 占全国比重(%) As Percentage To Nation (%)
空调器(万台)	Air Conditioners (10 000 sets)	89.50	3.8	482.13	7.0
主要农产品产量(万吨)	**Output of Major Farm Products (10 000 tons)**				
粮　食	Grain	143.33	0.3	143.52	0.3
肉　类	Meat	36.40	0.6	59.53	0.7
蛋　类	Eggs	26.00	1.1	23.08	0.8
水产品	Aquatic Products	26.46	0.6	35.49	0.7
全社会固定资产投资额(亿元)	**Total Investment in Fixed Assets (100 million yuan)**	705.10	1.9	1849.80	1.7
# 房地产开发投资额	Real Estate Development	161.27	2.5	402.32	2.1
运输、邮政、电信	**Transportation, Post & Telecommunications Service**				
港口货物吞吐量(万吨)	Freight Handled at Ports (10 000 tons)	11369	8.0	25760	7.5
社会货物运输量(万吨)	Freight Traffic (10 000 tons)	28608	2.0	42863	2.1
邮电业务总量(亿元)	VAlue of Post & Telecommunications (100 million yuan)	70.22	1.5	227.79	1.5
商业、外贸、外经	**Commerce, Foreign Trade & Foreign Capital**				
社会消费品零售总额(亿元)	Total Retail Sales of Consumer Goods (100 million yuan)	832.70	1.9	1356.79	1.8
外贸出口总额(亿美元)	Total Value of Exports in Foreign Trade (USD 100 million)	95.02	3.6	335.40	3.5
实际利用外资额(亿美元)	Foreign Capital Actually Used (USD 100 million)	32.97	6.6	43.69	5.9
教育、科技、卫生、文化	**Education,Science & Technology, Health Care, Culture**				
高等学校在校学生数(万人)	Number of Students at Colleges and Universities (10 000 persons)	15.40	2.1	35.74	2.1
技术市场成交额(亿元)	Transaction Volume in the Technology Market (100 million yuan)	30.60	3.9	58.86	3.2
专利申请授权量(项)	Patent Applications Granted (item)	1829	1.8	4159	1.9
医院、卫生院(个)	Number of Hospitals (unit)	495	0.8	401	0.7
医院、卫生院床位(万张)	Number of Hospital Beds (10 000 units)	4.04	1.4	3.89	1.2
图书出版数(万册)	Number of Books Published (10 000 copies)	6236	1.0	5106	0.8
杂志出版数(万册)	Number of Magazines Issued (10 000 copies)	4898	1.7	4060	1.4
报纸出版数(亿份)	Number of Newspapers Issued (100 million copies)	7.21	2.1	9.48	2.3

主要统计指标解释

行业划分标准　本年鉴中各专业指标的行业分类标准均采用《国民经济行业分类》标准（GB/T 4754-2002）。

国民经济行业分类标准（GB/T 4754-2002）

门　类	大类	中类	小类
A 农、林、牧、渔业	5	18	38
B 采矿业	6	15	33
C 制造业	30	169	482
D 电力、燃气及水的生产和供应业	3	7	10
E 建筑业	4	7	11
F 交通运输、仓储和邮政业	9	24	37
G 信息传输、计算机服务和软件业	3	10	14
H 批发和零售业	2	18	93
I 住宿和餐饮业	2	7	7
J 金融业	4	16	16
K 房地产业	1	4	4
L 租赁和商务服务业	2	11	27
M 科学研究、技术服务和地质勘查业	4	19	23
N 水利、环境和公共设施管理业	3	8	18
O 居民服务和其他服务业	2	12	16
P 教育	1	5	13
Q 卫生、社会保障和社会福利业	3	11	17
R 文化、体育和娱乐业	5	22	29
S 公共管理和社会组织	5	12	24
T 国际组织	1	1	1
（合计）　20	95	396	913

三次产业　根据《国民经济行业分类》标准（GB/T 4754-2002）规定，三次产业划分范围如下：

第一产业：包括农、林、牧、渔业。

第二产业：包括采矿业，制造业，电力、燃气及水的生产和供应业，建筑业。

第三产业：包括除第一、二产业以外的其他行业，具体包括 交通运输、仓储和邮政业，信息传输、计算机服务和软件业，批发和零售业，住宿和餐饮业，金融业，房地产业，租赁和商务服务业，科学研究、技术服务和地质勘查业，水利、环境和公共设施管理业，居民服务和其他服务业，教育，卫生、社会保障和社会福利业，文化、体育和娱乐业，公共管理和社会组织等。

现行价格（或称当年价格）　指报告期的实际价格，如工业品的出厂价格，农副产品的收购价格，商业的零售价格等。它反映当年的实际情况，使国民经济各项指标互相衔接，便于对生产、流通、分配、消费之间进行综合平衡。

可比价格　指计算各种总量指标所采用的扣除了价格变动因素的价格，可进行不同时期总量指标的对比。按可比价格计算总量指标有两种方法：一种是直接用产品产量乘某一年的不变价格计算；另一种是用价格指数进行缩减。

平均增长速度　我国计算平均增长速度有两种方法：一种是习惯上经常使用的“水平法”，又称几何平均法，是以间隔期最后一年的水平同基期水平对比来计算平均每年增长（或下降）速度；另一种是“累计法”，又称代数平均法或方程法，是以间隔期内各年水平的总和同基期水平对比来计算平均每年增长（或下降）速度。在一般正常情况下，两种方法计算的平均每年增长速度比较接近；但在经济发展不平衡、出现大起大落时，两种方法计算的结果差别较大。

本年鉴内所列的平均增长速度，除固定资产投资类指标用“累计法”计算外，其余均用“水平法”计算。从某年到某年平均增长速度的年份，均不包括基期年在内。

企业注册类型　以工商行政管理部门对企业登记注册的类型为依据，将企业登记注册类型划分为三大类：第一类是内资企业，包括国有企业、集体企业、股份合作企业、私营企业、股份有限公司、有限责任公司、联营企业和其他内资企业。第二类是港、澳、台商投资企业，包括合资经营企业、合作经营企业、港澳台商独资经营企业、港澳台商投资股份有限公司。第三类是外商投资企业，包括中外合资、中外合作、外资企业和外商投资股份有限公司。由于个体经营不属于企业，因此在《关于划分企业登记注册类型的规定》中，未将个体经营列入。但国家明确规定其仍属于国家统计范围，并在分类中单列。企业登记注册类型不同于经济类型，特别是其中的国有企业和集体企业不同于经济类型中的国有经济和集体经济。

主要统计指标解释

内资企业 包括国有企业、集体企业、股份合作企业、私营企业、股份有限公司、有限责任公司、联营企业和其他内资企业。

国有企业 指企业全部资产归国家所有，并按《中华人民共和国企业法人登记管理条例》规定登记注册的非公司制的经济组织。不包括有限责任公司中的国有独资公司和联营企业中的国有与国有联营企业。

集体企业 指企业资产归集体所有，并按《中华人民共和国企业法人登记管理条例》规定登记注册的经济组织。不包括股份合作企业和联营企业中的集体与集体联营企业。

股份合作企业 指以合作制为基础，由企业职工共同出资入股，吸收一定比例的社会资产投资组建，实行自主经营，自负盈亏，共同劳动，民主管理，按劳分配与按股分红相结合的一种集体经济组织。

私营企业 指由自然人投资设立或由自然人控股，以雇佣劳动为基础的营利性经济组织。包括按照《公司法》、《合伙企业法》、《私营企业暂行条例》规定登记注册的私营有限责任公司、私营股份有限公司、私营合伙企业和私营独资企业。

股份有限公司 指根据《中华人民共和国公司登记管理条例》规定登记注册，其全部注册资本由等额股份构成并通过发行股票筹集资本，股东以其认购的股份对公司承担有限责任，公司以其全部资产对其债务承担责任的经济组织。

有限责任公司 指根据《中华人民共和国公司登记管理条例》规定登记注册，由两个以上，五十个以下的股东共同出资，每个股东以其所认缴的出资额对公司承担有限责任，公司以其全部资产对其债务承担责任的经济组织。有限责任公司包括国有独资公司以及其他有限责任公司。

国有独资公司 指国家授权的投资机构或者国家授权的部门单独投资设立的有限责任公司。

其他有限责任公司 指国有独资公司以外的其他有限责任公司。

联营企业 指两个及两个以上相同或不同所有制性质的企业法人或事业单位法人，按自愿、平等、互利的原则共同投资组成的经济组织。

其他内资企业 指上述内资企业之外的其他内资经济组织。

港澳台商投资企业 包括合资经营企业（港或澳、台资）、合作经营企业（港或澳、台资）、港澳台商独资经营企业和港澳台商投资股份有限公司。

港、澳、台商独资经营企业 指依照《中华人民共和国外资企业法》及有关法律的规定，在内地由港澳台地区投资者全额投资设立的企业。

港、澳、台商投资股份有限公司 指根据国家有关规定，经商务部（原外经贸部）依法批准设立，其中港、澳、台商的股本占公司注册资本的比例达25%以上的股份有限公司。凡其中港、澳、台商的股本占公司注册资本的比例小于25%的，属于内资企业中的股份有限公司。

外商投资企业 包括中外合资经营企业、中外合作经营企业、外资（独资）企业和外商投资股份有限公司。

个体经营 指除农户外，生产资料归劳动者个人所有，以个体劳动为基础，劳动成果归劳动者个人占有和支配的一种经营单位。包括按照《民法通则》和《城乡个体经营户管理暂行条例》规定登记注册的个体工商户和个人合伙，以及没有领取营业执照，但从事个体经营活动的城镇、农村个体经营单位。

行政机关、事业单位和社会团体 填写登记注册类型参照企业登记注册类型，主要按其经费来源和管理方式划分。具体规定如下：

(1) 行政机关：包括国家机关和政党机关，原则上均列为“国有”。但有特殊规定的，如供销社等，则列为“集体”。

主要统计指标解释

(2) 事业单位：包括经国家机构编制部门和有关业务主管部门批准成立的各类事业单位，不包括实行企业化管理的事业单位。事业单位的划分办法如下：

① 由国家财政预算拨款或列入财政预算外资金管理以及经费主要来源于国有主管部门或国有上级单位的事业单位，列为"国有"。

② 经费主要来源于集体单位的事业单位，列为"集体"。

③ 公民个人（或个人合伙）开办的事业单位，列为"私营"。

④ 上述以外的其他事业单位，如果其经费来源不明确，按管理方式进行归类。

(3) 社会团体：包括经民政部门批准成立以及未纳入社会团体管理条例范围的工会、妇联等各类社会团体。社会团体的划分办法如下：

① 未纳入民政部社会团体管理条例范围的工会、妇联、共青团、青联、工商联、科协、侨联等社会团体，国家拨款设立的基金会或基金管理组织以及经费主要来源于国有业务主管部门或国有上级单位的社会团体，列为"国有"。

② 经费主要来源于集体单位的社会团体，列为"集体"。

③ 公民个人（或个人合伙）开办的社会团体，划为"私营"。

④ 上述以外的其他社会团体，如果其经费来源不明确，改按管理方式进行归类。

经济类型　本年鉴中的经济类型分组，从1998年开始是在企业登记注册类型分组基础上的再加工，其中国有经济包括国有企业、国有独资和国有与国有联营企业；集体经济包括集体企业、股份合作企业和集体与集体联营企业。私有经济包括私营企业和个体经营。

Explanastory Notes on Main Statistical Indicators

Standard of Industry Categorized In this statistical yearbook, the industry category adopts the standard (GB/T 4754-2002).

National Economy Industry Category(GB/T 4754-2002)

Industry	Large	Middle	Small
A Farming, Forestry, Animal Husbandry and Fishery	5	18	38
B Minerals Mining	6	15	33
C Manufacturing	30	169	482
D Production & Supply of Power, Gas and Water	3	7	10
E Construction	4	7	11
F Transport, Storage, Post Services	9	24	37
G Information Transmitting,Computer Services and Software	3	10	14
H Wholesale and Retail Trade	2	18	93
I Accommodation and Catering Services	2	7	7
J Finance	4	16	16
K Real Estate	1	4	4
L Leasing and Business Services	2	11	27
M Scientific Research, Technical Services and Geological Prospecting	4	19	23
N Management for Water Conservancy, Environment and Public Facilities	3	8	18
O Resident Services and Other Social Services	2	12	16
P Education	1	5	13
Q Health Care, Social Security and Social Welfare	3	11	17
R Culture, Sports and Recreational Services	5	22	29
S Public Management and Social Organizations	5	12	24
T International Organizations	1	1	1
(Total) 20	95	396	913

Three Industries According to the standard of national economy industry category (GB/T 4754-2002), three industries are categorized as following.

Primary Industry includes agriculture, forestry, animal husbandry and fishery.

Secondary Industry includes minerals mining, manufacturing, production and supply of electricity, gas and water, construction.

Tertiary Industry includes all other industries not included in primary or secondary industry, including transport, storage, post services; information transmitting, computer services and software; wholesale and retail trade; accommodation and catering services; finance; real estate; leasing and business services; scientific research, technical services and geological prospecting; management for water conservancy, environment and public facilities; resident services and other social services; education; health care, social security and social welfare; culture, sports and recreational services; public management and social organizations and so on.

Actual Price (current year price) includes all other industries not included in primary or secondary industry, including transport, storage, post services; information transmitting, computer services and software; wholesale and retail trade; accommodation and catering services; finance; real estate; leasing and business services; scientific research, technical services and geological prospecting; management for water conservancy, environment and public facilities; resident services and other social services; education; health care, social security and social welfare; culture, sports and recreational services; public management and social organizations and so on.

Comparable Prices refer to prices that are used to remove the factors of price change in calculating economic aggregates, so as to facilitate comparison of aggregates over time. Two methods are used for calculating economic aggregates at comparable prices, a) Multiplying the output of products by their constant prices of certain year; b) Deflation of data at current prices by relevant price index.

Average Annual Growth Rate Two methods for calculating average annual growth rate are applied in China, one is often called "level approach", or the method of calculating geometric average, which is derived by comparing the level of the last year of the interval with that of the beginning year; the other is called "accumulative approach" or algebraic average or equation method, which is derived by the summation of the actual figure of each year in the interval divided by the figure in the base year. Usually the results calculated by the two methods are fairly close, but they differed sharply when uneven economic development occurred with striking fluctuations in growth.

The average annual growth rate listed in this statistical yearbook are calculated by "level approach" except for the growth rate of investment in fixed assets. The base years are not listed when the years are listed for average annual growth rates.

Registration Status of Enterprises Enterprises are classified into 3 categories, in the light of the registration status of an enterprise in industrial and commercial administration agencies. Domestic-funded enterprises include state-owned enterprises, collective-owned enterprises, cooperative enterprises, private enterprises, share-holding

Explanastory Notes on Main Statistical Indicators

corporations Ltd., limited liability corporations, joint ownership enterprises and other domestic-funded enterprises. Hong Kong, Macao and Taiwan funded enterprises include joint venture enterprises, cooperative enterprises, sole investment enterprises and share-holding corporations Ltd. Foreign funded enterprises include Chinese-foreign joint venture enterprises, Chinese-foreign cooperative enterprises, sole foreign funded enterprises and share-holding corporations Ltd. with foreign investment. Due to individuals don't belong to enterprises, individuals don't be listed according to the "Regulation of Registered Status of Enterprises". But individuals belong to statistical category. Registered status of enterprises is different to ownership, especially, state-owned and collective-owned enterprises are different to state-owned and collective-owned economy.

Domestic-funded Enterprises include state-owned enterprises, collective-owned enterprises, cooperative enterprises, private enterprises, share-holding corporations Ltd., limited liability corporations, joint ownership enterprises and others.

State-owned Enterprises refer to non-corporation economic units where the entire assets are owned by the state and which have registered in accordance with the Regulation of the People's Republic of China on the Management of Registration of Corporate Enterprises. Excluded from this category are sole state-funded corporations in the limited liability corporations. Excluded from this category are enterprises with exclusive investment from state-owned, state-owned cooperative enterprises in the join ownership enterprises.

Collective-owned Enterprises refer to economic units where the assets are owned collectively and which have registered in accordance with the Regulation of the People's Republic of China on the Management of Registration of Corporate Enterprises. Excluded from this category are collective-owned and collective-owned cooperative enterprises in joint ownership enterprises, excluded cooperative enterprises.

Cooperative Enterprises refer to a form of collective economic units (enterprises) where capitals come mainly from employees as their shares, with certain proportion of capital from the outside, where production is organized on the basis of independent operation, independent accounting for profits and losses, joint work, democratic management, and a distribution system that integrates remuneration according to work with divided according to capital share.

Private Enterprises refer to profit-making economic units invested and established by natural persons, or controlled by natural persons using employed labor. Included in this category are private limited liability corporations, private share-holding corporations Ltd., private partnership enterprises and private-funded enterprises registered in accordance with the Corporation Law, Partnership Enterprises Law and Interim Regulations on Private Enterprises.

Share-holding Corporations Ltd. refer to economic units registered in accordance with the Regulation of the People's Republic of China on the Management of Registration of Corporations, with total registered capitals divided into equal shares and raised through issuing stocks. Each investor bears limited liability to the corporation depending on the holding of shares, and the corporation bears liability to its debt to the maximum of its total assets.

Limited Liability Corporations refer to economic units established with investment from 2-50 investors and registered in accordance with the Regulation of the People's Republic of China on the Management of Registration of Corporations, each investor bearing limited liability to the corporation depending on its share of investment, and the corporation bearing liability to its debt to the maximum of its total assets. Limited liability corporations include exclusive state-funded limited liability corporations and other limited liability corporations.

Sole State-funded Corporations refer to limited liability corporations established with exclusive investment from investment institutions or departments authorized by the state.

Other Limited Liability Corporations refer to the limited liability corporations other than sole state-funded corporations.

Joint Ownership Enterprises refer to economic units established by two or more corporate enterprises or corporate institutions of the same or different ownership, through joint investment on the basis of equality, voluntary participation and mutual benefits. They include state joint ownership enterprises, collective joint ownership enterprises, joint state-collective enterprises, and other joint ownership enterprises.

Other Domestic-funded Enterprises refer to domestic-funded economic units other than those mentioned above.

Enterprises with Investment from Hong Kong, Macao and Taiwan include joint venture enterprises with funds from Hong Kong, Macao and Taiwan, cooperative enter-

Explanastory Notes on Main Statistical Indicators

prises with funds from Hong Kong, Macao and Taiwan, enterprises with exclusive investment from Hong Kong, Macao and Taiwan, share-holding corporations Ltd. with investment from Hong Kong, Macao and Taiwan.

Enterprises with Exclusive Investment from Hong Kong, Macao and Taiwan refer to enterprises established in the mainland of China with exclusive investment from investors from Hong Kong, Macao and Taiwan in accordance with the Law of the People's Republic of China on Foreign-Funded Enterprises and other relevant laws.

Share-holding Corporations Ltd. with Investment from Hong Kong, Macao and Taiwan refer to share-holding corporations Ltd. established with the approval from the Ministry of Commerce Relations (the Ministry of Foreign Trade and Economic) in line with relevant state regulations, where the share of investment from Hong Kong, Macao or Taiwan business men exceeds 25% of the total registered capital of the corporation. In case, the share of investment from Hong Kong, Macao or Taiwan is less than 25% of the total registered capital, the enterprise is to be classified as domestic-funded share-holding corporation Ltd.

Foreign Funded Enterprises include joint venture enterprises with foreign investment, cooperation enterprises with foreign investment, enterprises with exclusive foreign investment, share-holding corporations Ltd. with foreign investment.

Individual refer to economic units which the production materials are owned by individual, where production is organized on the basis of individual operation, labors results are owned and used by laborer, including economic units where have registered in accordance with Civil Law General Rule and individual industrialists and businessmen or a group of citizens which have registered in urban and rural industrial and commercial administration agencies, urban and rural individual where have no business licenses but undertake individual operation.

Government Agencies, Institutions and Social Organizations are classified into following categories by source of funds and way of management taking reference of the registration status of enterprises.

a. Government agencies include state and party agencies, classified in principle as "state-owned". There are exceptions, such as supply and marketing cooperatives which are classified as "collective-owned".

b. Institutions include institutions of various types established with the approval by organization and staffing department of the government, but exclude institutions where enterprise management system is introduced. Institutions are further classified as follows:

(a) Institutions whose main budget is listed in the government budget appropriations or extra-budget funds, or allocated from the budget of their competent government agencies. Such institutions are classified as "state-owned".

(b) Institutions whose budget mainly comes from collective units. Such institutions are classified as "collective-owned".

(c) Institutions established by individual (individual partnership), which are classified as "private".

(d) Institutions other than those mentioned above whose source of budget are not clear. Such institutions are classified by way of management.

c. Social organizations include social organizations established with the approval from the Ministry of Civil Affairs, and organizations that are not covered by social organizations management regulations such as trade unions, women's federations etc.. Social organizations are further classified as follows:

(a) Social organizations that are not covered by social organizations management regulations of the Ministry of Civil Affairs, such as trade unions, women's federations, communist youth leagues, youth associations, industrial and commerce associations, scientists associations, overseas Chinese associations, etc., foundations and fund management organization established with funds from state, and social organizations whose funds mainly come from the budget of their competent government agencies. Such institutions are classified as "state-owned".

(b) Social organizations whose budget mainly comes from collective units. Such institutions are classified as "collective-owned".

(c) Social organizations established by individual (individual partnership), which are classified as "private".

(d) Social organizations other than those mentioned above whose source of budget is not clear. Such institutions are classified by way of management.

Type of Ownership refers to enterprises classified as various type of ownership in accordance with registered categories of enterprises after 1998.In which, state-owned economy refer to state-owned enterprises, sole state-funded enterprises, state joint ownership enterprises, collective-owned economy refer to collective-owned enterprises, co-operative enterprises, collective joint ownership enterprises; private economy refer to private enterprises and individual.

第2篇
CHAPTER 2

国民经济核算
National Accounts

2-1 历年地区生产总值(1949-2006年) GROSS DOMESTIC PRODUCT BY YEAR, 1949-2006

单位：亿元 (100 million yuan)

年份 Year	地区生产总值 Gross Domestic Product	第一产业 Primary Industry	第二产业 Secondary Industry	工业 Industry	建筑业 Construction	第三产业 Tertiary Industry	人均地区生产总值(元) GDP Per Capita (yuan)	社会劳动生产率(元/人) Society Labour Productivity (yuan/person)
1949	4.07	0.94	1.48			1.65		
1950	7.55	1.22	3.59			2.74		556
1951	11.45	1.62	6.13			3.70		795
1952	12.80	1.85	6.31	6.12	0.19	4.64	298	825
1953	17.58	1.76	8.49	8.18	0.31	7.33	393	1103
1954	16.98	1.79	8.93	8.51	0.42	6.26	362	1047
1955	17.12	2.35	9.16	8.89	0.27	5.61	356	1024
1956	20.70	2.26	10.83	10.54	0.29	7.61	417	1182
1957	24.11	2.49	13.28	12.86	0.42	8.34	465	1311
1958	32.49	2.28	22.21	21.34	0.87	8.00	600	1643
1959	41.25	2.80	29.10	28.08	1.02	9.35	735	1973
1960	42.66	2.65	29.65	28.46	1.19	10.36	736	1976
1961	28.41	2.52	16.56	15.98	0.58	9.33	482	1307
1962	24.25	2.12	14.08	13.69	0.39	8.05	406	1166
1963	26.65	2.27	16.20	15.63	0.57	8.18	433	1305
1964	30.59	2.30	20.08	19.28	0.80	8.21	483	1436
1965	35.96	3.91	22.96	22.34	0.62	9.09	560	1602
1966	39.31	2.69	26.87	26.17	0.70	9.75	605	1729
1967	33.62	3.50	20.93	20.30	0.63	9.19	514	1449
1968	34.77	3.60	21.26	20.64	0.62	9.91	523	1456
1969	42.87	3.46	29.03	28.39	0.64	10.38	649	1747
1970	50.99	3.80	35.80	35.08	0.72	11.39	781	1960
1971	55.12	3.89	39.52	38.33	1.19	11.71	832	2016
1972	56.37	3.46	40.53	38.95	1.58	12.38	832	1999
1973	60.33	3.92	42.51	40.68	1.83	13.90	875	2076
1974	66.69	4.79	46.81	44.52	2.29	15.09	960	2261
1975	69.73	4.37	50.29	47.73	2.56	15.07	991	2232
1976	65.25	4.01	45.57	43.84	1.73	65.25	908	1941
1977	67.73	3.56	46.97	44.81	2.16	67.73	938	1946

注：1. 本表数据已依据2004年第一次经济普查结果进行了修订，以下各表同。2. 本表按当年价格计算。
Note: a) The historical data in this table were adjusted correspondingly in accordance with the result of the first economic census in 2004, same as following tables. b) Data in this table are calculated at current prices.

2-1 续表 Contiuned

单位：亿元 (100 million yuan)

年 份 Year	地区生产总值 Gross Domestic Product	第一产业 Primary Industry	第二产业 Secondary Industry	工 业 Industry	建筑业 Construction	第三产业 Tertiary Industry	人均地区生产总值(元) GDP Per Capita (yuan)	社会劳动生产率(元/人) Society Labour Productivity (yuan/person)
1978	82.65	5.03	57.53	54.39	3.14	20.09	1133	2300
1979	93.01	6.54	64.82	61.01	3.81	21.65	1241	2489
1980	103.53	6.53	72.56	67.48	5.08	24.44	1357	2671
1981	107.96	5.18	76.97	71.06	5.91	25.81	1458	2672
1982	114.11	7.00	79.86	72.30	7.56	27.24	1469	2737
1983	123.42	7.60	84.47	76.69	7.78	31.35	1555	2883
1984	147.53	11.13	96.47	87.97	8.50	39.93	1853	3342
1985	175.78	12.95	114.92	104.80	10.12	47.91	2169	3892
1986	194.74	16.51	123.33	111.90	11.43	54.90	2352	4220
1987	220.12	19.63	138.02	125.05	12.97	62.47	2621	4694
1988	259.71	26.21	160.96	146.73	14.23	72.54	3035	5549
1989	283.49	26.85	177.54	160.73	16.81	79.10	3261	6064
1990	310.95	27.32	181.38	165.59	15.79	102.25	3487	6617
1991	342.65	29.26	196.60	179.75	16.85	116.79	3777	7216
1992	411.04	30.26	233.41	212.80	20.61	147.37	4481	8516
1993	538.94	35.40	308.40	280.73	27.67	195.14	5800	10901
1994	732.89	46.55	414.95	371.43	43.52	271.39	7751	14426
1995	931.97	60.80	518.55	467.93	50.62	352.62	9769	18126
1996	1121.93	67.67	609.10	549.81	59.29	445.16	11734	21842
1997	1264.63	69.52	676.01	609.65	66.36	519.10	13142	24668
1998	1374.60	74.14	697.99	622.15	75.84	602.47	14243	26915
1999	1500.95	71.14	758.51	682.52	75.99	671.30	15405	29539
2000	1701.88	73.69	863.83	785.96	77.87	764.36	17353	34208
2001	1919.09	78.73	959.06	869.15	89.91	881.30	19141	39357
2002	2150.76	84.21	1069.08	968.44	100.64	997.47	21387	43851
2003	2578.03	89.91	1337.31	1217.88	119.43	1150.82	25544	51380
2004	3110.97	105.28	1685.93	1549.70	136.26	1319.76	30575	59902
2005	3697.62	112.38	2051.17	1885.04	166.13	1534.07	35783	69095
2006	4359.15	118.23	2488.29	2292.73	195.56	1752.63	41163	78867

2-2 历年地区生产总值构成(1949-2006年)
COMPOSITION OF GROSS DOMESTIC PRODUCT BY YEAR, 1949-2006

单位：% (%)

年份 Year	地区生产总值 Gross Domestic Product	第一产业 Primary Industry	第二产业 Secondary Industry	工业 Industry	建筑业 Construction	第三产业 Tertiary Industry
1949	100	23.1	36.4			40.5
1950	100	16.2	47.5			36.3
1951	100	14.2	53.5			32.3
1952	100	14.5	49.3	47.8	1.5	36.2
1953	100	10.0	48.3	46.5	1.8	41.7
1954	100	10.5	52.6	50.1	2.5	36.9
1955	100	13.7	53.5	51.9	1.6	32.8
1956	100	10.9	52.3	50.9	1.4	36.8
1957	100	10.3	55.1	53.3	1.8	34.6
1958	100	7.0	68.4	65.7	2.7	24.6
1959	100	6.8	70.5	68.0	2.5	22.7
1960	100	6.2	69.5	66.7	2.8	24.3
1961	100	8.9	58.3	56.3	2.0	32.8
1962	100	8.7	58.1	56.5	1.6	33.2
1963	100	8.5	60.8	58.7	2.1	30.7
1964	100	7.5	65.6	63.0	2.6	26.9
1965	100	10.9	63.8	62.1	1.7	25.3
1966	100	6.8	68.4	66.6	1.8	24.8
1967	100	10.4	62.3	60.4	1.9	27.3
1968	100	10.4	61.1	59.3	1.8	28.5
1969	100	8.1	67.7	66.2	1.5	24.2
1970	100	7.5	70.2	68.8	1.4	22.3
1971	100	7.1	71.7	69.5	2.2	21.2
1972	100	6.1	71.9	69.1	2.8	22.0
1973	100	6.5	70.5	67.4	3.1	23.0
1974	100	7.2	70.2	66.8	3.4	22.6
1975	100	6.3	72.1	68.4	3.7	21.6
1976	100	6.2	69.8	67.2	2.6	24.0
1977	100	5.3	69.3	66.2	3.1	25.4

注：本表按当年价格计算。
Note: Data in this table are calculated at current prices.

2-2 续表 Contiuned

单位：% (%)

年 份 Year	地区生产总值 Gross Domestic Product	第一产业 Primary Industry	第二产业 Secondary Industry	工 业 Industry	建筑业 Construction	第三产业 Tertiary Industry
1978	100	6.1	69.6	65.8	3.8	24.3
1979	100	7.0	69.7	65.6	4.1	23.3
1980	100	6.3	70.1	65.2	4.9	23.6
1981	100	4.8	71.3	65.8	5.5	23.9
1982	100	6.1	70.0	63.4	6.6	23.9
1983	100	6.2	68.4	62.1	6.3	25.4
1984	100	7.5	65.4	59.6	5.8	27.1
1985	100	7.4	65.4	59.6	5.8	27.2
1986	100	8.5	63.3	57.4	5.9	28.2
1987	100	8.9	62.7	56.8	5.9	28.4
1988	100	10.1	62.0	56.5	5.5	27.9
1989	100	9.5	62.6	56.7	5.9	27.9
1990	100	8.8	58.3	53.2	5.1	32.9
1991	100	8.5	57.4	52.5	4.9	34.1
1992	100	7.4	56.8	51.8	5.0	35.8
1993	100	6.6	57.2	52.1	5.1	36.2
1994	100	6.4	56.6	50.7	5.9	37.0
1995	100	6.5	55.7	50.2	5.5	37.8
1996	100	6.0	54.3	49.0	5.3	39.7
1997	100	5.5	53.5	48.2	5.3	41.0
1998	100	5.4	50.8	45.3	5.5	43.8
1999	100	4.7	50.6	45.5	5.1	44.7
2000	100	4.3	50.8	46.2	4.6	44.9
2001	100	4.1	50.0	45.3	4.7	45.9
2002	100	3.9	49.7	45.0	4.7	46.4
2003	100	3.5	51.9	47.3	4.6	44.6
2004	100	3.3	54.2	49.8	4.4	42.5
2005	100	3.0	55.5	51.0	4.5	41.5
2006	100	2.7	57.1	52.6	4.5	40.2

2-3 历年地区生产总值指数(1949-2006)
INDICES OF GROSS DOMESTIC PRODUCT BY YEAR, 1949-2006

上年=100 (preceding year=100)

年 份 Year	地区生产总值 Gross Domestic Product	第一产业 Primary Industry	第二产业 Secondary Industry	工 业 Industry	建筑业 Construction	第三产业 Tertiary Industry	人均地区生产总值 GDP Per Capita	社 会 劳动生产率 Society Labour Productivity
1950	180.5	132.0	243.4			169.5		
1951	143.2	133.1	164.4			128.5		
1952	112.2	112.4	104.4			121.1		
1953	133.4	96.6	135.6	134.2	172.1	147.8	127.9	130.7
1954	95.3	101.9	105.8	104.4	136.3	83.6	91.9	94.7
1955	102.5	131.6	104.7	107.1	65.6	89.4	100.1	99.5
1956	123.6	97.8	124.2	125.2	95.4	136.4	119.7	118.6
1957	113.5	108.3	119.2	117.7	170.3	108.3	108.5	108.8
1958	129.8	93.5	163.6	161.9	204.9	87.2	124.3	123.9
1959	124.4	122.4	128.1	129.1	110.3	116.5	120.2	118.1
1960	103.3	94.5	102.2	101.7	113.3	109.4	99.9	100.0
1961	64.1	93.9	51.8	51.9	48.8	83.5	63.0	62.0
1962	85.5	85.0	87.0	87.8	70.2	83.5	84.4	89.6
1963	109.0	102.8	115.6	114.5	144.6	101.1	105.8	111.6
1964	115.9	102.3	126.8	126.0	143.0	102.0	112.6	112.2
1965	121.5	169.4	115.9	117.7	80.9	115.4	119.8	114.1
1966	106.2	68.7	115.1	115.2	111.8	108.0	105.0	106.8
1967	87.9	127.7	78.7	78.2	93.8	84.9	87.3	84.4
1968	107.9	103	109.1	109.7	94.5	108.1	106.2	105.2
1969	122.6	95.7	138.5	139.7	104.9	104.1	123.3	121.5
1970	117.5	109.3	121.2	121.5	110.5	111.5	118.9	111.4
1971	109.0	100.7	112.5	111.1	166.1	102.7	107.5	104.0
1972	104.3	87.3	106.1	105.2	130.9	105.7	102.0	101.4
1973	107.8	117.3	105.5	105.1	113.5	111.7	105.9	104.2
1974	110.5	119.7	110.0	109.3	124.1	109.0	109.8	108.7
1975	104.3	91.9	107.4	107.4	108.0	99.9	103.0	98.9
1976	94.1	91.7	91.2	92.6	66.3	104.0	92.1	87.4
1977	103.6	88.2	103.2	102.4	124.0	109.5	103.1	100.2

注：本表按可比价格计算。
Note: Data in this table are calculated at comparable prices.

2-3 续表 Continued

上年=100 (preceding year=100)

年 份 Year	地区生产总值 Gross Domestic Product	第一产业 Primary Industry	第二产业 Secondary Industry	工 业 Industry	建筑业 Construction	第三产业 Tertiary Industry	人均地区生产总值 GDP Per Capita	社 会 劳动生产率 Society Labour Productivity
1978	120.9	115.6	123.3	121.1	167.9	116.0	119.6	117.1
1979	110.0	117.4	110.4	110.4	110.7	107.0	107.1	105.9
1980	110.0	99.8	111.4	110.6	122.0	108.7	108.0	106.0
1981	104.8	79.1	107.0	106.6	112.2	104.8	108.0	100.5
1982	104.3	112.9	103.5	102.4	117.5	105.3	99.4	101.1
1983	108.3	109.2	106.0	106.0	106.3	114.8	106.0	105.5
1984	119.3	122.8	116.6	117.5	106.2	125.9	118.9	115.6
1985	110.6	121.1	110.5	110.0	116.5	108.8	108.7	108.1
1986	105.8	108.0	105.5	105.0	111.8	106.0	103.6	103.6
1987	107.6	106.0	108.3	108.2	108.9	106.3	106.1	105.9
1988	105.8	107.7	107.7	108.3	101.2	100.4	103.8	106.0
1989	101.6	111.4	98.1	97.8	101.2	109.3	100.0	101.8
1990	105.4	104.6	101.1	102.0	91.6	116.4	102.7	104.8
1991	106.0	103.4	105.5	105.8	102.1	107.5	104.2	104.9
1992	111.7	100.7	111.5	112.4	101.2	114.6	110.4	109.8
1993	112.1	107.4	112.9	113.6	103.6	111.7	110.6	109.4
1994	114.3	105.3	114.7	114.1	122.7	115.6	112.3	111.2
1995	114.9	106.3	114.1	114.5	109.9	117.9	113.9	113.5
1996	114.3	108.2	114.3	114.6	110.1	115.4	114.0	114.4
1997	112.1	107.7	111.7	111.8	110.1	113.4	111.4	112.3
1998	109.3	106.7	107.4	107.0	112.7	113.0	109.0	109.9
1999	110.0	100.1	111.7	112.6	99.2	108.9	109.0	110.5
2000	110.8	103.7	111.5	112.2	100.9	110.5	110.0	113.1
2001	112.0	106.3	112.8	112.7	114.3	111.7	109.6	114.3
2002	112.7	106.1	114.3	114.6	112.2	111.4	112.3	111.9
2003	114.8	106.1	118.0	118.6	112.4	111.9	114.4	112.2
2004	115.8	105.1	119.8	121.5	101.7	111.9	114.9	111.8
2005	114.7	104.3	117.6	117.9	113.5	111.7	112.9	111.3
2006	114.5	103.3	117.7	117.8	117.0	111.1	111.9	110.9

2-4 地区生产总值指数(1979-2006年)
INDICES OF GROSS DOMESTIC PRODUCT, 1979-2006

1978年=100 (year of 1978=100)

年份 Year	地区生产总值 Gross Domestic Product	第一产业 Primary Industry	第二产业 Secondary Industry	工业 Industry	建筑业 Construction	第三产业 Tertiary Industry
1978	100.0	100.0	100.0	100.0	100.0	100.0
1979	110.0	117.4	110.4	110.4	110.7	107.0
1980	121.0	117.1	123.0	122.2	135.1	116.3
1981	126.7	92.6	131.6	130.2	151.6	121.9
1982	132.2	104.6	136.1	133.3	178.1	128.3
1983	143.2	114.3	144.4	141.3	189.3	147.3
1984	170.8	140.3	168.3	166.1	201.0	185.5
1985	188.9	169.9	186.0	182.7	234.2	201.7
1986	199.8	183.4	196.3	191.8	261.8	213.8
1987	215.0	194.4	212.5	207.6	285.1	227.3
1988	227.4	209.3	228.8	224.8	288.5	228.1
1989	231.1	233.2	224.4	219.8	292.0	249.4
1990	243.6	244.0	226.9	224.2	267.5	290.3
1991	258.2	252.3	239.3	237.1	273.1	312.2
1992	288.2	254.2	266.9	266.6	276.3	357.9
1993	323.0	272.9	301.2	302.8	286.2	399.9
1994	369.2	287.4	345.3	345.4	351.1	462.3
1995	424.2	305.4	394.1	395.4	385.8	545.0
1996	484.9	330.6	450.4	453.0	424.7	629.0
1997	543.4	356.0	503.1	506.6	467.4	713.4
1998	594.2	379.9	540.1	542.0	526.5	805.9
1999	653.8	380.2	603.3	610.4	522.5	877.4
2000	724.5	394.3	672.7	684.9	527.2	969.6
2001	811.6	419.1	759.1	771.9	602.5	1082.6
2002	914.4	444.6	867.9	884.2	675.9	1205.6
2003	1050.0	471.7	1024.4	1048.5	759.7	1348.5
2004	1216.3	496.0	1227.0	1273.6	772.6	1508.3
2005	1395.1	517.1	1443.2	1502.0	876.9	1684.1
2006	1597.4	534.2	1698.6	1769.4	1025.9	1871.0

注:本表按可比价格计算。
Note: Data in this table are calculated at comparable prices.

2-5 地区生产总值
GROSS DOMESTIC PRODUCT

单位：亿元 (100 million yuan)

项　目 Item	2004	2005	2006	2006比2005年增长(%) Increase Rate in 2006 over 2005 (%)
地区生产总值 Gross Domestic Product	**3110.97**	**3697.62**	**4359.15**	**14.5**
第一产业 Primary Industry	**105.28**	**112.38**	**118.23**	**3.3**
第二产业 Secondary Industry	**1685.93**	**2051.17**	**2488.29**	**17.7**
工　业 Industry	1549.67	1885.04	2292.73	17.8
建筑业 Construction	136.26	166.13	195.56	17.0
第三产业 Tertiary Industry	**1319.76**	**1534.07**	**1752.63**	**11.1**
交通运输、仓储和邮政业 Transportation, Storage and Post Services	222.83	227.16	252.86	6.8
信息传输、计算机服务和软件业 Information Transmitting, Computer Services and Software	65.14	77.13	84.35	9.0
批发和零售业 Wholesale and Retail Trade	372.32	436.14	468.12	11.2
住宿和餐饮业 Accommodation and Catering Services	56.45	70.15	79.41	10.5
金融业 Finance Intermediation	136.97	159.24	186.87	11.9
房地产业 Real Estate	106.14	128.77	160.72	7.3
租赁和商务服务业 Leasing and Business Services	26.92	45.6	61.40	23.8
科学研究、技术服务和地质勘查业 Scientific Research, Technical Service and Geological Prospecting	63.12	78.98	99.23	19.8
水利、环境和公共设施管理业 Management for Water Conservancy, Environment and Public Facilities	18.65	21.89	30.85	18.4
居民服务和其他服务业 Resident Services and Other Social Services	60.96	66.9	74.65	9.9
教　育 Education	77.01	93.25	102.39	10.3
卫生、社会保障和社会福利业 Health Care, Social Security and Social Welfare	39.05	40.35	44.59	10.1
文化、体育和娱乐业 Culture, Sports and Recreational Services	13.12	13.24	20.08	15.0
公共管理和社会组织 Public Management and Social Organizations	61.08	75.27	87.11	14.0

注:本表按当年价格计算，增长速度按可比价计算。
Note: Data in this table are calculated at current prices,increase rate are based on comparable prices.

2-6 三次产业贡献率(1990-2006年)
SHARE OF THE THREE INDUSTRIES TO THE INCREASE OF GDP, 1990-2006

单位：% (%)

年 份 Year	地区生产总值 Gross Domestic Product	第一产业 Primary Industry	第二产业 Secondary Industry	#工 业 Industry	第三产业 Tertiary Industry
1990	100	5.7	13.8	22.4	80.5
1991	100	5.0	53.4	51.6	41.6
1992	100	0.5	57.4	56.9	42.1
1993	100	4.7	61.8	60.5	33.5
1994	100	2.7	60.0	53.4	37.3
1995	100	2.9	55.5	52.6	41.6
1996	100	3.6	58.1	55.1	38.3
1997	100	3.8	56.4	53.0	39.8
1998	100	4.1	45.7	40.3	50.2
1999	100	0.1	66.5	66.9	33.4
2000	100	1.8	61.9	61.6	36.3
2001	100	2.3	54.2	48.8	43.5
2002	100	2.0	57.8	53.4	40.2
2003	100	1.5	63.1	59.2	35.4
2004	100	1.2	66.6	66.1	32.2
2005	100	0.9	66.1	62.4	33.0
2006	100	0.7	67.5	62.1	31.8

注：1. 产业贡献率指各产业增加值增量与GDP增量之比。2. 本表按可比价格计算。
Note: a) Share of the three industries refers to the proportion of the increment of every industrial value added to the increment of GDP. b) Data in this table are calculated at comparable prices.

2-7 三次产业对地区生产总值增长的拉动(1990-2006年)
CONTRIBUTION OF THE THREE INDUSTRIES TO GDP GROWTH, 1990-2006

单位：百分点 (percentage points)

年 份 Year	地区生产总值 Gross Domestic Product	第一产业 Primary Industry	第二产业 Secondary Industry	#工 业 Industry	第三产业 Tertiary Industry
1990	5.4	0.3	0.8	1.2	4.3
1991	6.0	0.3	3.2	3.1	2.5
1992	11.7	0.1	6.7	6.7	4.9
1993	12.1	0.6	7.5	7.3	4.0
1994	14.3	0.4	8.6	7.6	5.3
1995	14.9	0.4	8.3	7.8	6.2
1996	14.3	0.5	8.3	7.9	5.5
1997	12.1	0.5	6.8	6.4	4.8
1998	9.3	0.4	4.2	3.7	4.7
1999	10.0	0.0	6.7	6.7	3.3
2000	10.8	0.2	6.7	6.7	3.9
2001	12.0	0.3	6.5	5.9	5.2
2002	12.7	0.2	7.4	6.8	5.1
2003	14.8	0.2	9.3	8.8	5.3
2004	15.8	0.2	10.5	10.4	5.1
2005	14.7	0.1	9.7	9.2	4.9
2006	14.5	0.1	9.8	9.0	4.6

注：1. 产业拉动指GDP增长速度与各产业贡献率之乘积。2. 本表按可比价格计算。
Note: a) Contribution of the three industies to GDP growth refers to the growth rate of GDP multiplying the industrial shares. b) Data in this table are calculated at comparable prices.

2-8 地区生产总值项目结构（1978-2006年）
COMPONENTS OF GROSS DOMESTIC PRODUCT, 1978-2006

单位：亿元 (100 million yuan)

年 份 Region	地区生产总值 Gross Domestic Product	劳动者报酬 Compensation of Employees	固定资产折旧 Depreciation of Fixed Assets	生产税净额 Net Taxes on Production	营业盈余 Operating Surplus
1978	82.65	26.80	6.10	15.68	34.07
1979	93.01	31.64	6.80	16.28	38.29
1980	103.53	31.35	8.75	19.99	43.44
1981	107.96	31.40	10.40	17.92	48.24
1982	114.11	34.42	11.97	17.68	50.04
1983	123.42	36.21	13.83	20.95	52.43
1984	147.53	51.85	14.58	23.44	57.66
1985	175.78	51.45	17.97	30.39	75.97
1986	194.74	63.11	23.09	32.29	76.25
1987	220.12	76.71	23.41	34.24	85.76
1988	259.71	90.11	27.10	41.82	100.68
1989	283.49	103.47	44.91	43.63	91.48
1990	310.95	135.54	48.41	43.64	83.36
1991	342.65	144.25	55.15	51.14	92.11
1992	411.04	166.13	68.74	61.39	114.78
1993	538.94	223.72	72.44	83.56	159.22
1994	732.89	319.98	99.10	117.22	196.59
1995	931.97	417.02	139.84	150.51	224.60
1996	1121.93	534.48	178.28	160.57	248.60
1997	1264.63	634.76	189.31	186.38	254.18
1998	1374.60	699.85	210.58	223.85	240.32
1999	1500.95	748.05	217.46	274.62	260.82
2000	1701.88	715.11	264.63	328.92	393.22
2001	1919.09	774.46	308.13	387.17	449.33
2002	2150.76	835.23	358.80	416.97	539.76
2003	2578.03	892.22	446.50	534.87	704.44
2004	3110.97	1050.14	483.73	571.81	1005.29
2005	3697.62	1164.82	515.77	727.37	1289.66
2006	4359.15	1383.36	775.09	595.09	1605.61

注：本表按当年价格计算。
Note: Data in this table are calculated at current prices.

2-9 支出法地区生产总值（1978-2006年）
GROSS DOMESTIC PRODUCT BY EXPENDITURE APPORACH, 1978-2006

年份 Year	地区生产总值（亿元） Gross Domestic Product (100 million yuan)	最终消费支出 Final Consumption Expenditures	资本形成总额 Gross Capital Formation	货物和服务净出口 Net Exports of Goods and Services	最终消费率（消费率）(%) Final Consumption Rate (%)	资本形成率（投资率）(%) Capital Formation Rate (%)
1978	82.65	30.79	26.19	25.67	37.3	31.7
1979	93.01	34.68	33.00	25.33	37.3	35.5
1980	103.53	40.43	35.36	27.74	39.1	34.2
1981	107.96	44.48	25.06	38.42	41.2	23.2
1982	114.11	47.61	34.73	31.77	41.7	30.4
1983	123.42	53.50	41.82	28.10	43.3	33.9
1984	147.53	60.58	48.31	38.64	41.1	32.7
1985	175.78	72.45	87.92	15.41	41.2	50.0
1986	194.74	83.37	100.20	11.17	42.8	51.5
1987	220.12	98.70	92.29	29.13	44.8	41.9
1988	259.71	128.62	140.56	-9.47	49.5	54.1
1989	283.49	145.79	135.58	2.12	51.4	47.8
1990	310.95	147.62	132.93	30.40	47.5	42.7
1991	342.65	170.29	162.86	9.50	49.7	47.5
1992	411.04	196.37	225.42	-10.75	47.8	54.8
1993	538.94	253.74	312.64	-27.44	47.1	58.0
1994	732.89	338.13	427.16	-32.40	46.1	58.3
1995	931.97	423.04	509.92	-0.99	45.4	54.7
1996	1121.93	537.07	594.24	-9.38	47.9	53.0
1997	1264.63	604.46	662.27	-2.10	47.8	52.4
1998	1374.60	652.88	725.40	-3.68	47.5	52.8
1999	1500.95	750.83	718.26	31.86	50.0	47.9
2000	1701.88	843.89	811.06	46.93	49.6	47.7
2001	1919.09	948.42	927.90	42.77	49.4	48.4
2002	2150.76	1040.49	1048.50	61.77	48.4	48.8
2003	2578.03	1193.05	1313.06	71.92	46.3	50.9
2004	3110.97	1343.65	1661.24	106.08	43.2	53.4
2005	3697.62	1506.91	1968.45	222.26	40.8	53.2
2006	4359.15	1763.14	2364.41	231.60	40.4	54.2

注：本表按当年价格计算。
Note: Data in this table are calculated at current prices.

2-10 最终消费及构成（1978-2006）
FINAL CONSUMPTION EXPENDITURE AND COMPOSITION, 1978-2006

年 份 Year	最终消费（亿元） Final Consumption Expenditures (100 million yuan)	居民消费 Household Consumption Expenditures			政府消费 Government Consumption Expenditures	构 成(%)(最终消费=100) Composition(%) (Final Consumption Expenditures=100)	
			农村居民 Rural Households	城镇居民 Urban Households		居民消费 Household Consumption Expenditures	政府消费 Government Consumption Expenditures
1978	30.79	27.13	5.55	21.58	3.66	88.1	11.9
1979	34.68	30.57	6.4	24.17	4.11	88.1	11.9
1980	40.43	36.29	7.6	28.69	4.14	89.8	10.2
1981	44.48	38.07	8.22	29.85	6.41	85.6	14.4
1982	47.61	41.11	10.03	31.08	6.50	86.3	13.7
1983	53.50	45.78	10.8	34.98	7.72	85.6	14.4
1984	60.58	50.84	13.02	37.82	9.74	83.9	16.1
1985	72.45	61.19	14.86	46.33	11.26	84.5	15.5
1986	83.37	69.92	15.59	54.33	13.45	83.9	16.1
1987	98.70	77.78	17.2	60.58	20.92	78.8	21.2
1988	128.62	99.36	21.32	78.04	29.26	77.3	22.7
1989	145.79	111.74	23.55	88.19	34.05	76.6	23.4
1990	147.62	119.32	23.03	96.29	28.30	80.8	19.2
1991	170.29	135.19	25.08	110.11	35.10	79.4	20.6
1992	196.37	154.19	27.69	126.5	42.18	78.5	21.5
1993	253.74	195.20	33.53	161.67	58.54	76.9	23.1
1994	338.13	255.93	39.38	216.55	82.20	75.7	24.3
1995	423.04	337.71	50.49	287.22	85.33	79.8	20.2
1996	537.07	413.10	63.76	349.34	123.97	76.9	23.1
1997	604.46	472.58	71.04	401.54	131.88	78.2	21.8
1998	652.88	500.24	76.19	424.05	152.64	76.6	23.4
1999	750.83	537.85	80.02	457.83	212.98	71.6	28.4
2000	843.89	596.52	87.26	509.26	247.37	70.7	29.3
2001	948.42	667.57	94.35	573.22	280.85	70.4	29.6
2002	1040.49	706.66	99.33	607.33	333.83	67.9	32.1
2003	1193.05	781.22	106.75	674.47	411.83	65.5	34.5
2004	1343.65	877.16	114.36	762.8	466.49	65.3	34.7
2005	1506.91	980.05	122.32	857.73	526.86	65.0	35.0
2006	1763.14	1118.76	129.18	989.58	644.38	63.5	36.5

注：本表按当年价格计算。
Note: Data in this table are calculated at current prices.

2-11 最终消费总指数（1978-2006年）
FINAL CONSUMPTION INDICES, 1978-2006

年 份 Year	最终消费 （以1978年为100） Final Consumption Expenditures (year of 1978=100)	居民消费 Household Consumption Expenditures	农村居民 Rural Households	城镇居民 Urban Households	政府消费 Government Consumption Expenditures
1978	100.0	100.0	100.0	100.0	100.0
1979	112.6	111.7	115.5	110.4	111.0
1980	124.4	122.4	130.5	119.7	106.0
1981	135.2	128.3	141.1	124.0	161.7
1982	145.4	138.4	164.9	129.3	163.1
1983	162.3	152.6	182.1	142.4	192.8
1984	182.5	169.3	220.0	151.9	239.1
1985	197.7	184.6	240.0	165.4	242.7
1986	210.5	194.7	248.4	176.4	270.3
1987	235.2	204.9	254.6	188.2	393.0
1988	260.8	222.9	279.0	204.2	467.3
1989	257.9	219.1	275.1	200.5	472.5
1990	257.9	224.4	262.7	211.7	471.5
1991	272.1	231.8	270.4	218.9	540.8
1992	283.6	237.8	276.3	224.8	594.4
1993	307.9	254.4	283.8	244.2	677.0
1994	337.8	272.0	297.1	262.5	810.4
1995	358.4	292.7	322.1	281.9	821.7
1996	409.7	330.1	368.8	316.6	978.7
1997	452.3	369.4	404.2	356.5	1033.5
1998	495.7	397.8	440.5	382.8	1201.9
1999	567.6	423.3	469.2	407.3	1695.9
2000	628.3	458.9	511.4	440.7	1977.4
2001	689.9	499.2	545.6	482.6	2218.7
2002	760.2	524.7	580.0	505.8	2686.8
2003	861.3	570.3	617.7	553.3	3280.6
2004	967.3	650.8	644.9	640.2	3575.9
2005	1075.6	723.6	683.6	716.4	3976.4
2006	1240.2	813.4	711.6	813.8	4791.5

注：本表数据按可比价格计算。
Note: Data in this table are calculated at comparable prices.

2-12 最终消费
FINAL CONSUMPTION EXPENDITURE

单位：亿元 (100 million yuan)

项　目 Item	2004	2005	2006
最终消费 Final Consumption Expenditure	**1343.65**	**1506.91**	**1763.14**
居民消费 Household Consumption	**877.16**	**980.05**	**1118.76**
农村居民 Rural Households	**114.36**	**122.32**	**129.18**
食品类支出 Food	35.60	38.61	39.42
衣着类支出 Clothing	8.24	10.16	10.04
居住类支出 Residence	11.99	12.60	17.60
家庭设备、用品及服务类支出 Household Facilities, Articles and Services	3.28	3.03	3.17
医疗保健类支出 Medicine and Medical Services	7.29	7.52	7.28
公共医疗消费支出 Commonality Medicine and Medical Services		0.01	
交通和通信类支出 Transportation and Communication Services	6.76	7.58	8.07
文教娱乐用品及服务类支出 Recreation, Education and Cultural Services	6.95	7.07	6.77
金融中介服务虚拟支出 Invented Expenditure for Finance Agent Service	15.31	17.69	18.83
自有住房服务虚拟支出 Invented Expenditure for Owned Housing Service	15.86	14.96	14.72
其他商品和服务类支出 Other Goods and Services	3.08	3.09	3.28
城镇居民 Urban Households	**762.80**	**857.73**	**989.58**
食品类支出 Food	241.65	266.70	290.09
衣着类支出 Clothing	46.04	52.61	68.17
居住类支出 Residence	90.68	97.23	107.85
家庭设备、用品及服务类支出 Household Facilities, Articles and Services	36.67	39.46	50.01
医疗保健类支出 Medicine and Medical Services	60.74	75.00	82.71
公共医疗消费支出 Commonality Medicine and Medical Services	34.50	42.23	50.52
交通和通信类支出 Transportation and Communication Services	58.07	75.12	86.15
文教娱乐用品及服务类支出 Recreation, Education and Cultural Services	90.85	96.63	114.47
金融中介服务虚拟支出 Invented Expenditure for Finance Agent Service	43.92	47.47	57.83
自有住房服务虚拟支出 Invented Expenditure for Owned Housing Service	23.97	30.28	36.63
实物消费支出 Practicality	11.54	11.09	13.15
其他商品和服务类支出 Other Goods and Services	24.17	23.91	32.00
政府消费 Government Consumption	**466.49**	**526.86**	**644.38**

2-13 资本形成总额和指数（1978-2006年）
GROSS CAPTIAL FORMATION AND INDICES, 1978-2006

年 份 Year	资本形成总额(亿元) Gross Capital Formation (100 million)	固定资本形成总额 Gross Fixed Capital Formation	存货增加 Change in Inventory	总指数(以1990年为100) Indices of Gross Captial Formation (year of 1990=100)	固定资本形成总额 Gross Fixed Capital Formation	存货增加 Change in Inventory
1978	26.19	18.55	7.64			
1979	33.00	23.91	9.09			
1980	35.36	25.56	9.8			
1981	25.06	25.00	0.06			
1982	34.73	32.36	2.37			
1983	41.82	38.27	3.55			
1984	48.31	48.67	-0.36			
1985	87.92	67.60	20.32			
1986	100.20	75.89	24.31			
1987	92.29	81.63	10.66			
1988	140.56	96.85	43.71			
1989	135.58	95.43	40.15			
1990	132.93	98.03	34.90	100.0	100.0	100.0
1991	162.86	144.19	18.67	115.6	137.2	57.1
1992	225.42	185.12	40.3	140.8	155.0	102.4
1993	312.64	246.16	66.48	156.3	167.7	125.5
1994	427.16	345.46	81.70	186.9	202.0	145.8
1995	509.92	417.95	91.97	215.5	236.3	157.0
1996	594.24	491.90	102.34	243.5	269.2	170.7
1997	662.27	556.43	105.84	274.5	308.4	176.7
1998	725.40	640.15	85.25	305.2	358.7	148.4
1999	718.26	631.92	86.34	305.8	356.9	156.1
2000	811.06	695.10	115.96	342.5	389.8	204.2
2001	927.90	805.34	122.56	392.5	451.0	221.0
2002	1048.50	926.65	121.85	447.5	521.3	229.6
2003	1313.06	1180.54	132.52	545.9	647.5	246.1
2004	1661.24	1446.49	214.75	615.8	683.1	422.6
2005	1968.45	1753.92	214.53	731.6	840.9	410.3
2006	2364.41	2122.35	242.06	862.5	1004.0	434.5

注：本表总量按当年价格计算，指数按可比价格计算
Note: Data in this table are calculated at current prices,increase rate are based on comparable prices.

2-14 最终消费和资本形成总额对地区生产总值增长的贡献率和拉动（1978-2006年）
SHARE AND CONTRIBUTION OF FINAL CONSUMPTION EXPENDITURE AND GROSS CAPITAL FORMATION TO GDP GROWTH, 1978-2006

年 份 Year	最终消费支出 Final Consumption Expenditure		资本形成总额 Gross Capital Formation	
	贡献率(%) Share (%)	拉 动(百分点) Contribution (percentage points)	贡献率(%) Share (%)	拉 动(百分点) Contribution (percentage points)
1978	15.1	3.2		
1979	40.2	4.0		
1980	27.3	2.7		
1981	78.8	3.8		
1982	57.7	2.5		
1983	56.5	4.7		
1984	26.8	5.2		
1985	29.3	3.1		
1986	44.7	2.6		
1987	61.3	4.7		
1988	76.8	4.5		
1989	-28.3	-0.5		
1990	18.1	1.0		
1991	43.7	2.6	116.0	7.0
1992	16.8	2.0	87.1	10.2
1993	32.6	3.9	46.3	5.6
1994	29.7	4.2	69.0	9.9
1995	16.7	2.5	53.6	8.0
1996	37.9	5.4	47.8	6.8
1997	32.9	4.0	54.4	6.6
1998	39.0	3.6	60.7	5.6
1999	57.3	5.7	1.2	0.1
2000	40.1	4.3	54.8	5.9
2001	41.3	5.0	58.0	7.0
2002	37.8	4.8	54.0	6.9
2003	42.6	6.3	73.6	10.9
2004	36.3	5.7	41.8	6.6
2005	34.5	5.1	65.4	9.6
2006	42.8	6.2	65.5	9.5

注：1. 贡献率指最终消费和资本形成总额的增量与支出法地区生产总值增量之比。2. 拉动指地区生产总值增长速度与最终消费和资本形成总额贡献率的乘积。3. 本表按可比价格计算。

Note: a) Share of final consumption expenditure and gross capital formation refer to the proportion of the increment of the three components of GDP to the increment of GDP. b)Contribution of final consumption expenditure and gross capital formation refer to the growth rate of GDP multiplies the share of the three components. c) Data in this table are calculated at comparable prices.

2-15 居民消费水平(1978-2006年)
HOUSEHOLD CONSUMPTION, 1978-2006

年 份 Year	全 市 居 民 (元) All Households (yuan)	农 村 居 民 Rural Households	城 镇 居 民 Urban Households	城乡消费水平对比(农村居民=1) Urban/Rural Consumption Ratio (Rural Households=1)	全市居民消费指数(以1978年为100) All Households Index (year of 1978=100)	农 村 居 民 Rural Households	城 镇 居 民 Urban Households
1978	372	178	533	2.99	100.0	100.0	100.0
1979	408	206	562	2.73	108.7	115.0	104.6
1980	475	248	639	2.58	117.1	131.0	109.2
1981	514	271	682	2.52	121.2	142.0	110.2
1982	529	328	653	1.99	128.6	163.4	112.4
1983	577	352	714	2.03	139.0	179.0	120.8
1984	639	425	751	1.77	152.5	215.5	126.3
1985	755	493	898	1.82	164.2	237.9	132.8
1986	845	518	1011	1.95	171.3	245.5	138.9
1987	926	564	1114	1.98	177.6	246.5	146.8
1988	1161	696	1398	2.01	190.4	267.4	156.1
1989	1285	774	1531	1.98	184.9	263.9	149.5
1990	1338	749	1635	2.18	186.1	248.1	155.2
1991	1490	813	1832	2.25	189.7	253.1	158.2
1992	1681	903	2067	2.29	193.3	258.4	160.4
1993	2101	1094	2603	2.38	205.3	264.3	172.6
1994	2707	1287	3435	2.67	218.0	275.9	183.8
1995	3540	1658	4495	2.71	233.5	298.9	195.9
1996	4321	2109	5389	2.56	256.6	335.9	212.8
1997	4911	2369	6117	2.58	286.9	368.8	239.0
1998	5181	2561	6374	2.49	307.8	403.1	254.5
1999	5520	2715	6758	2.49	325.7	430.9	267.2
2000	6083	2994	7398	2.47	351.7	472.3	286.2
2001	6763	3267	8231	2.52	382.0	505.8	311.4
2002	7120	3466	8604	2.48	399.9	538.7	323.8
2003	7789	3758	9377	2.50	431.9	575.4	349.4
2004	8621	4079	10348	2.54	484.2	620.2	394.5
2005	9484	4360	11394	2.61	529.7	656.8	432.3
2006	10564	4771	12554	2.63	581.1	708.7	469.1

注：1. 本表绝对数按当年价格计算，指数按可比价格计算。2. 城乡消费水平对比未剔除城乡价格不可比因素。
Note: a) Absolute figures in this table are calculated at current prices, while indices are calculated at comparable prices. b) The effect of price differentials between urban and rural areas has not been removed in the calculation of the urban/rural consumption ratio.

主要统计指标解释

生产总值（原国内生产总值）　指按市场价格计算的一个国家（或地区）所有常住单位在一定时期内生产活动的最终成果。

从价值形态看，它是所有常驻单位在一定时期内所生产的全部货物和服务价值超过同期投入的全部非固定资产货物和服务价值的差额，即所有常驻单位的增加值之和；从收入形态看，它是所有常驻单位在一定时期内所创造并分配给常驻单位和非常驻单位的初次分配收入之和；从产品形态看，它是最终使用的货物和服务减去进口货物和服务。在实际核算中，其三种表现形态体现为三种计算方法，即生产法、收入法和支出法。三种方法分别从不同的方面反映生产总值及其构成。根据国务院和国家统计局有关我国 GDP 核算和数据发布制度的规定，天津市国内生产总值自 2004 年起更名为"天津市生产总值" 简称"天津市 GDP"。

绿色 GDP　人类的经济活动包括两方面的活动。一方面为社会创造着财富，即所谓"正面效应"，但另一方面又在以种种形式和手段对社会生产力的发展起着阻碍作用，即所谓"负面效应"。改革现行的国民经济核算体系，对环境资源进行核算，从现行 GDP 中扣除环境资源成本和对环境资源的保护服务费用，其计算结果可称之为"绿色 GDP"。绿色 GDP 指标，实质上代表了国民经济增长的净正效应。绿色 GDP 占 GDP 的比重越高，表明国民经济增长的正面效应越高，负面效应越低，反之亦然。

劳动者报酬　指劳动者因从事生产活动所获得的全部报酬。包括劳动者获得的各种形式的工资、奖金和津贴，既包括货币形式的，也包括实物形式的，还包括劳动者所享受的公费医疗和医药卫生费、上下班交通补贴和单位支付的社会保险费、住房公积金等。对于个体经济来说，其所有者所获得的劳动报酬和经营利润不易区分，这两部分统一作为劳动者报酬处理。

生产税净额　指生产税减生产补贴后的余额。生产税指政府对生产单位生产、销售和从事经营活动以及因从事生产活动使用某些生产要素（如固定资产、土地、劳动力）所征收的各种税、附加费和规费。生产补贴与生产税相反，指政府对生产单位的单方面转移支付，因此视为负生产税，包括政策亏损补贴、价格补贴等。

固定资产折旧　指一定时期内为弥补固定资产损耗按照核定的固定资产折旧率提取的固定资产折旧，或按国民经济核算统一规定的折旧率虚拟计算的固定资产折旧。它反映了固定资产在当期生产中的转移价值。各类企业和企业化管理的事业单位的固定资产折旧是指实际计提的折旧费；不计提折旧的政府机关、非企业化管理的事业单位和居民住房的固定资产折旧是按照统一规定的折旧率和固定资产原值计算的虚拟折旧。原则上，固定资产折旧应按固定资产的重置价值计算，但是目前我国尚不具备对全社会固定资产进行重估价的基础，所以暂时只能采用这种办法。

营业盈余　指常住单位创造的增加值扣除劳动者报酬、生产税净额和固定资产折旧后的余额。它相当于企业的营业利润加上生产补贴，但要扣除从利润中开支的工资和福利等。

最终消费　指常住单位在一定时期内对于货物和服务的全部最终消费支出，也就是常住单位为满足物质、文化和精神生活的需要，从本国经济领土和国外购买的货物和服务的支出。不包括非常住单位在本国经济领土内的消费支出。最终消费分为居民消费和政府消费。

居民消费　指常住住户对货物和服务的全部最终消费支出。它除了常住住户直接以货币形式购买货物和服务的消费之外，还包括以其他方式获得的货物和服务的消费，即单位以实物报酬及实物转移的形式提供给劳动者的货物和服务；住户生产并由住户自己消费的货物和服务，其中的服务仅指住户的自有住房服务和支付报酬的家庭服务；金融机构提供的金融媒介服务；保险公司提供的保险服务。

政府消费　指政府部门为全社会提供公共服务的消费支出和免费或以较低价格向住户提供的货物和服务

主要统计指标解释

的净支出。前者等于政府服务的产出价值减去政府单位所获得的经营收入后的价值，政府服务的产出价值等于它的经常性业务支出加上固定资产折旧；后者等于政府部门免费或以较低价格向住户提供的货物和服务的市场价值减去向住户收取的价值。

资本形成总额 指常住单位在一定时期内获得的减去处置的固定资产加存货的净变动额，包括固定资本形成总额和存货增加。

固定资本形成总额 指生产者在一定时期内获得的固定资产减处置的固定资产的价值总额，固定资产是通过生产活动生产出来的，其使用年限在一年以上，单位价值在规定标准以上的资产，不包括自然资产。固定资本形成总额可分为有形固定资本形成总额和无形固定资本形成总额。有形固定资本形成总额包括一定时期内完成的建筑工程、安装工程、设备工器具购置（减处置）价值以及土地改良、新增役、种、奶、毛、娱乐用牲畜和新增经济林木价值。无形固定资本形成总额包括矿藏的勘探、计算机软件等获得减处置。

存货增加 指常住单位在一定时期内存货实物量变动的市场价值，即期末价值减期初价值的差额，再扣除当期由于价格变动而产生的持有收益。存货增加可以是正值，也可以是负值；正值表示存货增加，负值表示存货减少。它包括生产单位购进的原材料、燃料和储备物资等存货，以及生产单位生产的产成品、在制品存货等。

货物和服务净出口 指货物和服务出口减货物和服务进口的差额。出口包括常住单位向非常住单位出售和无偿转让的各种货物和服务的价值；进口包括常住单位从非常住单位购买或无偿得到的各种货物和服务的价值。由于服务活动的提供与使用同时发生，因此服务的进出口业务并不发生出入境现象，一般把常住单位从国外得到的服务作为进口，常住单位向国外提供的服务作为出口。货物的出口和进口都按离岸价格计算。在计算地区货物和服务净出口时，还包括地区间货物和服务的流入流出。用公式表示：

货物和服务净出口（净流出）=货物和服务出口（流出）－进口（流入）

Explanastory Notes on Main Statistical Indicators

Gross Domestic Product refers to the final products at market prices produced by all resident units in a country (or a region) during a certain period of time.

From the aspect of value added form, GDP refers to the total value of all products and services produced by all resident units during a certain period of time minus total value of inputs of non-fixed-assets products and services or the summation of the value added of all resident units; the form of products refers to all final goods and services minus imports of goods and services. In the practice of national accounting, it is calculated by three approaches, i.e. product approach, income approach and expenditure approach, respectively, to reflect Gross Product and its composition of different aspects. According to the regulations of GDP national accounting as Tianjin Gross Product Value, for short Tianjin GDP.

Green Economic GDP The human economic activities include two components. On one hand, creating wealth for social, namely so-called "positive effect" but on the other hand, obstructing the development of the social productivity with all kinds of measures, namely so-called "negative effect" Green Economic GDP, i.e. the current GDP minus the environment resources cost and the protection service charge of the environment resources through reforming the current national economy accounts system and accounting the environment resources. Green Economic GDP represents the net positive effect of national economy growth. The higher the weight of the Green Economic GDP accounted for the GDP, the higher the positive effect of national economy is, the lower the negative effect is, contrarily, the lower the positive effect of national economy is, the higher the negative effect is.

Labor Remuneration refers to the whole payment of various forms earned by the laborers from the productive activities they are engaged in. It includes wages, bonuses and allowances the laborers earned in monetary form and in kind. It also includes the free medical services provided to the laborers and the medicine expenses, traffic subsidies, social insurance fee and housing provident fund paid by the laborer's working units for them. As the individual economy is concerned, since the laborer's remuneration is not easily distinguished from the operating profit, both are treated as laborer's remuneration.

Net Taxes on Production refers to the residual of the taxes on production minus the subsidies on production. The taxes on production refers to the various taxes, extra charges and fees levied on the production units on their production, sale and business activities as well as on some sectors of production, such as fixed assets, land and labor force, used in the production activities they are engaged in. In contrast to the taxes on production, the subsidies on production refer to the unilateral transfer of part of the government's revenue to the production units and are therefore regarded as negative taxes on production. They include subsidies on the loss due to implementation of government policies, price subsidies, etc.

Depreciation of Fixed Assets refers to the depreciation of fixed assets of a given period, drawn in accordance with the stipulated depreciation rate for the purpose of compensating the wear loss of the fixed assets or the depreciation of fixed assets calculated in a fictitious way in accordance with the stipulated unified depreciation rate in the national economic accounting system. It reflects the value of transfer of the fixed assets in the production of the current period. The depreciation of fixed assets in various enterprises and institutions managed as enterprises refers to the depreciation expenses actually drawn. In government agencies and institutions not managed as enterprises which do not draw the depreciation expenses, as well as for the houses of residents, the depreciation of fixed assets is the imputed depreciation, which is calculated in accordance with the stipulated unified depreciation rate. In principle, the depreciation of fixed assets should be calculated on the basis of the re-purchased value of the fixed assets. However, there is no actual condition to re-evaluate all the fixed assets in China. Therefore, this method is temporarily adopted at present.

Operating Surplus refers to the balance of the value added created by the resident units deducting the laborer's remuneration, net taxes on production and the depreciation of fixed assets. It is equivalent to the business profit of the enterprises plus subsidies on production, but the wages and welfare expenses paid from the profits should be deducted.

Final Consumption refers to the total expenditure of resident units on final consumption of goods and services in a certain period, namely the expenditure of the resident units for purchases of goods and services from domestic economic territory and abroad to meet the requirements of material, cultural and spiritual life. It excludes the consumption expenditure of non-resident units on consumption in the economic territory of the country. The final consumption is classified into households' consumption and government consumption.

Households Consumption refers to the total expenditure of resident households on the final consumption of goods and services. In addition to the consumption of goods and services bought by the households directly with money, the households consumption also includes expenditure on

Explanastory Notes on Main Statistical Indicators

goods and services obtained by the households on other ways, i.e. the goods and services provided to the households by the units in the form of payment in kind and transfer in kind; the goods and services produced and consumed by the households themselves, in which the services refer only to the owner-occupied housing and domestic services provided by the paid household workers; financial intermediate services provided by financial institutions; insurance services provided by insurance companies.

Government Consumption refers to the expenditure on the consumption of the public services provided by the government to the whole society and the net expenditure on the goods and services provided by the government to the households at free charge or lower prices. The former equals to the output value of the government services minus the value of operating income obtained by the government departments, the output value of the government services equals to its current operating expenditure plus depreciation of fixed assets. The latter equals to the market value of the goods and services provided by the government free of charge or at low prices to the households minus the value received by the government from the households.

Total Capital Formation refers to the fixed assets acquired minus those disposed and the net value of inventory, including the total fixed assets formation and the increase in inventory.

Total Fixed Capital Formation refers to the value of fixed assets acquired minus those disposed of during a given period. Fixed assets are the assets produced through production activities with specified unit value which could be used for over one year, excluding natural assets. Total fixed capital formation can be categorized into total tangible assets formation and total intangible assets formation. The total tangible assets formation include the value of the construction projects, installation projects completed and the equipment, apparatus and instruments purchased as well as the value of land improved, the value of draught animals, breeding stock, animal for milk, wool and for recreational animals purpose and the newly increased forest with economic value during a given period. The total intangible assets formation includes the prospecting of minerals, the acquisition of computer software minus the disposal of them.

Increase in Inventory refers to the market value of the change in inventory of resident units during a given period, i.e. the difference of value between the beginning and the end of the period minus the current gains due to the change in prices. The increase in inventory can be positive or negative. A positive value indicates the increase in inventory while a negative value indicates the decrease in stock. The inventory includes the raw materials, fuel and reserve materials purchased by the production units as well as the inventory of finished products, semi-finished products, etc.

Net Export of Goods and Services refers to the difference of the exports of goods and services minus the imports of goods and services. The imports include the value of various goods and services sold or gratuitously transferred by the resident units to the non-resident units. The imports include the value of various goods and services purchased or gratuitously acquired by the resident units from the non-resident units. Because the provision of services and the use of them happen simultaneously, the import and export of services do not appear to have the phenomena of crossing the border of the country. The acquisition of services by the resident units from abroad is usually treated as import while the acquisition of services by non-resident units in this country is usually treated as export. The export and import of goods are calculated at FOB. The formula for calculating is as follows:

Net export of goods and services =value of export of goods and services - value of import of goods and services

第3篇
CHAPTER 3

人口和劳动就业
Population, Labor and Employment

3-1 人口主要指标(1990-2006年)
MAJOR POPULATION STATISTICS, 1990-2006

年 份 Year	常住人口 (万人) Permanent Population (10 000 persons)	户籍人口 (万人) Registered Population (10 000 persons)	户籍户数 (万户) Registered Households (10 000 households)	人口密度 (人/平方公里) Population Density (person/sq. km)	人口出生率 Birth Rate (‰)	人口死亡率 Death Rate (‰)	人口自然增长率 Natural Growth Rate (‰)
1990	884.03	866.25	258.31	764	15.62	5.79	9.83
1991	908.89	872.63	262.75	770	11.94	5.78	6.16
1992	920.41	878.97	266.77	776	12.50	6.00	6.50
1993	928.02	885.89	270.77	782	10.71	6.20	4.51
1994	935.28	890.55	273.87	745	10.98	6.19	4.79
1995	941.83	894.67	276.89	749	10.23	6.23	4.00
1996	948.19	898.45	279.62	752	10.09	6.53	3.56
1997	952.59	899.80	284.08	753	9.98	6.95	3.03
1998	956.64	905.09	288.20	757	9.89	6.49	3.40
1999	959.48	910.17	291.32	762	9.68	6.73	2.95
2000	1001.14	912.00	293.04	763	7.72	6.17	1.55
2001	1004.06	913.98	295.63	765	7.58	5.94	1.64
2002	1007.18	919.05	299.67	769	7.49	6.04	1.45
2003	1011.30	926.00	303.27	775	7.14	6.04	1.10
2004	1023.67	932.55	316.62	780	7.31	5.97	1.34
2005	1043.00	939.31	322.95	797	7.44	6.01	1.43
2006	1075.00	948.89	328.66	805	7.67	6.07	1.60

注：1. 人口密度2005年以后按市民政局行政区划面积计算，2005年以前按市规划局土地面积计算。2. 人口自然变动"三率"为历年人口调查数据。"三率"为历年人口调查数据。

Note: a) After 2005, the population density is calculated with administrative areas measured by Tianjin Civil Administration Bureau, and those before 2005 are calculated with areas measured by Tianjin Bureau of Planning. b) The three ratio of population changing are obtained from population surveys.

3-2 户籍人口主要构成(1990-2006年)
COMPOSITION OF REGISTERED POPULATION, 1990-2006

单位：% (%)

年 份 Year	按户口性质分 By Registered Character		按性别分 By Sex		
	非农业 Non-agricultural	农 业 Agricultural	男 性 Male	女 性 Female	性别比(女=100) Sex Ratio (Female=100)
1990	56.04	43.96	50.79	49.21	103.20
1991	56.19	43.81	50.76	49.24	103.07
1992	56.29	43.71	50.73	49.27	102.96
1993	56.44	43.56	50.71	49.29	102.87
1994	56.60	43.40	50.70	49.30	102.85
1995	56.77	43.23	50.66	49.34	102.67
1996	57.12	42.88	50.62	49.38	102.50
1997	57.27	42.73	50.58	49.42	102.33
1998	57.60	42.40	50.53	49.47	102.14
1999	58.09	41.91	50.51	49.49	102.06
2000	58.39	41.61	50.51	49.49	102.05
2001	58.56	41.44	50.48	49.52	101.92
2002	58.88	41.12	50.45	49.55	101.84
2003	59.37	40.63	50.47	49.53	101.89
2004	59.64	40.36	50.46	49.54	101.86
2005	59.87	40.13	50.44	49.56	101.77
2006	60.18	39.82	50.41	49.59	101.65

3-3 按地区分的户数、人口数及人口密度
HOUSEHOLDS,POPULATION AND POPULATION DENSITY BY REGION

地　区	Region	年末户数 (万户) Year-end Households (10 000 households)		年末人口数 (万人) Year-end Population (10 000 persons)		年平均人口 (万人) Average Annual Population (10 000 persons)	人口密度 (人/平方公里) Population Density (person/sq. km)
		2005	2006	2005	2006	2006	2006
全市常住人口	**Total Permanent Population**	**346.18**	**359.83**	**1043.00**	**1075.00**	**1059.00**	**914**
全市户籍人口	**Total Registered Population**	**322.95**	**328.66**	**939.31**	**948.89**	**944.10**	**805**
市辖区	**Districts Under City Administration**	**270.08**	**274.78**	**769.60**	**777.91**	**773.76**	**1048**
# 市内六区	Six Urban Districts	135.24	136.61	384.57	384.18	384.38	21696
滨海区	Coastal District	37.21	37.95	101.22	104.19	102.71	467
和平区	Heping District	13.01	12.99	43.84	38.51	41.18	38507
河东区	Hedong District	25.35	25.65	69.23	69.94	69.59	17648
河西区	Hexi District	26.01	26.34	73.96	75.45	74.71	19849
南开区	Nankai District	27.79	28.05	79.73	81.08	80.41	21033
河北区	Hebei District	22.85	23.16	62.65	63.44	63.05	21419
红桥区	Hongqiao District	20.23	20.42	55.16	55.76	55.46	26227
塘沽区	Tanggu District	17.62	17.97	48.85	50.13	49.49	641
# 经济技术开发区	TEDA	0.82	0.89	2.65	3.21	2.93	
汉沽区	Han'gu District	6.39	6.54	16.91	17.09	17.00	418
大港区	Dagang District	13.20	13.44	35.46	36.97	36.22	355
东丽区	Dongli District	12.45	12.83	31.82	32.35	32.09	676
西青区	Xiqing District	11.96	12.32	31.48	33.24	32.36	587
津南区	Jinnan District	13.78	14.33	38.07	39.06	38.57	1007
北辰区	Beichen District	12.51	12.88	33.02	34.22	33.62	724
武清区	Wuqing District	25.60	26.16	81.72	82.49	82.11	524
宝坻区	Baodi District	20.37	20.73	65.28	65.71	65.50	435
天津铁厂	Tianjin Iron Works	0.96	0.97	2.42	2.47	2.45	
市辖县	**Counties Under City Administration**	**52.87**	**53.88**	**169.71**	**170.98**	**170.35**	**392**
宁河县	Ninghe County	11.28	11.43	36.74	36.89	36.82	285
静海县	Jinghai County	17.30	17.64	52.27	52.88	52.58	358
蓟　县	Jixian County	24.29	24.81	80.70	81.21	80.96	511

3-4 按户口性质分的户籍户数
HOUSEHOLDS BY REGISTERED CHARACTER

单位：万户 (10 000 households)

地 区	Region	非农业 Non-agricultural Households		农 业 Agricultural Households	
		2005	2006	2005	2006
全市总计	**Total**	**206.68**	**210.28**	**116.27**	**118.38**
市辖区	**Districts Under City Administration**	**193.56**	**196.57**	**76.52**	**78.21**
# 市内六区	Six Urban Districts	134.41	135.79	0.83	0.82
滨海区	Coastal District	29.70	30.24	7.51	7.71
和平区	Heping District	13.01	12.99		
河东区	Hedong District	25.31	25.61	0.04	0.04
河西区	Hexi District	25.86	26.20	0.15	0.14
南开区	Nankai District	27.29	27.55	0.50	0.50
河北区	Hebei District	22.83	23.15	0.02	0.01
红桥区	Hongqiao District	20.11	20.29	0.12	0.13
塘沽区	Tanggu District	15.25	15.55	2.37	2.42
# 经济技术开发区	TEDA	0.82	0.89		
汉沽区	Han'gu District	4.83	4.91	1.56	1.63
大港区	Dagang District	9.62	9.78	3.58	3.66
东丽区	Dongli District	4.97	5.13	7.48	7.70
西青区	Xiqing District	3.50	3.60	8.46	8.72
津南区	Jinnan District	4.20	4.31	9.58	10.02
北辰区	Beichen District	5.39	5.65	7.12	7.23
武清区	Wuqing District	5.51	5.75	20.09	20.41
宝坻区	Baodi District	4.92	5.13	15.45	15.60
天津铁厂	Tianjin Iron Works	0.96	0.97		
市辖县	**Counties Under City Administration**	**13.12**	**13.71**	**39.75**	**40.17**
宁河县	Ninghe County	3.59	3.65	7.69	7.78
静海县	Jinghai County	4.07	4.23	13.23	13.41
蓟 县	Jixian County	5.46	5.83	18.83	18.98

3-5 按户口性质分的户籍人口数
REGISTERED POPULATION BY REGISTERED CHARACTER

单位：万人 (10 000 persons)

地　区	Region	非农业 Non-agricultural Households		农　业 Agricultural Households	
		2005	2006	2005	2006
全市总计	**Total**	**562.40**	**571.04**	**376.91**	**377.85**
市辖区	**Districts Under City Administration**	**532.42**	**540.02**	**237.18**	**237.89**
#市内六区	Six Urban Districts	382.86	382.47	1.71	1.71
滨海区	Coastal District	80.23	83.09	20.99	21.10
和平区	Heping District	43.84	38.51		
河东区	Hedong District	69.17	69.87	0.06	0.07
河西区	Hexi District	73.66	75.17	0.30	0.28
南开区	Nankai District	78.65	79.99	1.08	1.09
河北区	Hebei District	62.63	63.42	0.02	0.02
红桥区	Hongqiao District	54.91	55.51	0.25	0.25
塘沽区	Tanggu District	42.81	44.08	6.04	6.05
#经济技术开发区	TEDA	2.65	3.21		
汉沽区	Han'gu District	12.36	12.48	4.55	4.61
大港区	Dagang District	25.06	26.53	10.40	10.44
东丽区	Dongli District	12.06	12.50	19.76	19.85
西青区	Xiqing District	8.34	9.93	23.14	23.31
津南区	Jinnan District	10.38	11.08	27.69	27.98
北辰区	Beichen District	13.21	14.58	19.81	19.64
武清区	Wuqing District	12.48	13.05	69.24	69.44
宝坻区	Baodi District	10.44	10.85	54.84	54.86
天津铁厂	Tianjin Iron Works	2.42	2.47		
市辖县	**Counties Under City Administration**	**29.98**	**31.02**	**139.73**	**139.96**
宁河县	Ninghe County	8.77	8.95	27.97	27.94
静海县	Jinghai County	9.20	9.53	43.07	43.35
蓟　县	Jixian County	12.01	12.54	68.69	68.67

3-6 按性别分的户籍人口数
REGISTERED POPULATION BY SEX

单位：万人 (10 000 persons)

地　区	Region	男性 Male		女性 Female		性别比(女=100) Sex Ratio (Female=100)	
		2005	2006	2005	2006	2005	2006
全市总计	**Total**	**473.77**	**478.34**	**465.54**	**470.55**	**101.77**	**101.65**
市辖区	**Districts Under City Administration**	**387.38**	**391.28**	**382.22**	**386.63**	**101.35**	**101.20**
#市内六区	Six Urban Districts	192.79	192.39	191.78	191.79	100.53	100.31
滨海区	Coastal District	52.25	53.71	48.97	50.48	106.67	106.40
和平区	Heping District	21.43	18.59	22.41	19.92	95.65	93.33
河东区	Hedong District	34.89	35.22	34.34	34.72	101.58	101.45
河西区	Hexi District	36.62	37.22	37.34	38.23	98.10	97.34
南开区	Nankai District	40.36	41.09	39.37	39.99	102.50	102.74
河北区	Hebei District	31.61	32.00	31.04	31.44	101.82	101.76
红桥区	Hongqiao District	27.88	28.27	27.28	27.49	102.23	102.87
塘沽区	Tanggu District	25.19	25.83	23.66	24.30	106.44	106.26
#经济技术开发区	TEDA	1.35	1.64	1.30	1.57	103.45	104.58
汉沽区	Han'gu District	8.57	8.64	8.34	8.45	102.69	102.37
大港区	Dagang District	18.49	19.24	16.97	17.73	108.94	108.51
东丽区	Dongli District	16.00	16.22	15.82	16.13	101.09	100.60
西青区	Xiqing District	15.61	16.54	15.87	16.70	98.36	98.97
津南区	Jinnan District	19.04	19.55	19.03	19.51	100.09	100.23
北辰区	Beichen District	16.53	17.12	16.49	17.10	100.30	100.16
武清区	Wuqing District	40.96	41.31	40.76	41.18	100.49	100.31
宝坻区	Baodi District	32.96	33.17	32.32	32.54	101.95	101.94
天津铁厂	Tianjin Iron Works	1.24	1.27	1.18	1.20	105.61	105.69
市辖县	**Counties Under City Administration**	**86.39**	**87.06**	**83.32**	**83.92**	**103.70**	**103.74**
宁河县	Ninghe County	18.65	18.73	18.09	18.16	103.16	103.15
静海县	Jinghai County	26.63	26.95	25.64	25.93	103.88	103.93
蓟　县	Jixian County	41.11	41.38	39.59	39.83	103.83	103.88

3-7 计划生育情况（2003-2006年）
FAMILY PLANNING, 2003-2006

指　标 Item	2003	2004	2005	2006
政策生育率(%)				
Family Planning Rate (%)	98.73	98.99	99.02	98.95
一孩率(%)				
One-child Rate (%)	76.36	78.25	73.62	72.88
二孩率(%)				
Two-child Rate (%)	22.59	20.55	24.91	25.30
多孩率(%)				
Multi-child Rate (%)	1.05	1.20	1.47	1.82
总和生育率				
General Fertility Rate	1.03	1.00	1.00	1.11

资料来源：政策生育率为计生委年报数；其余指标为历年人口抽样调查数据.
Sources: Family planning rate is obtained from annual reports of Tianjin Birth Control Committee; other data of this table are obtained from annual sample survey

3-8 人口婚姻登记情况（2003-2006年）
MARRIAGE REGISTRATION, 2003-2006

指　标 Item	2003	2004	2005	2006
结婚对数合计(对)				
Total Marriages (couple)	**62973**	**76950**	**63600**	**83580**
# 恢复结婚对数				
Remarriage with Former Spouse	515	1446	1303	1361
涉外婚姻				
Chinese-Foreigner Marriage	343	361	399	452
# 女　性(人)				
Female (person)	278	298	345	384
初婚人数(万人)				
First Marriages (10 000 persons)	10.9	13.2	10.3	14.34
再婚人数(万人)				
Remarriages (10 000 persons)	1.6	2.2	2.4	2.4
离婚对数(对)				
Divorces (couple)	**12041**	**16146**	**17073**	**19769**
法院判决离婚				
Mediated by The Court	3647	3590	3554	4031
民政协议离婚				
Approved by Civil Administration Agencies	8394	12556	13519	15738

3-9 各种特征年龄组的户籍人口（2006年）
REGISTERED POPULATION BY AGE GROUPS, 2006

单位：万人 (10 000 persons)

年龄组	Age Groups	合计 Total	# 市内六区 Six Urban Districts	男性 Male	# 市内六区 Six Urban Districts	女性 Female	# 市内六区 Six Urban Districts
按学龄人口分组	**Grouped by School Age**						
0-2 岁	Age 0-2	20.21	4.84	10.73	2.49	9.48	2.35
3-5 岁	Age 3-5	18.62	4.13	9.88	2.13	8.74	2.00
6-14岁	Age 6-14	72.80	18.28	38.28	9.34	34.52	8.94
15-17岁	Age 15-17	39.46	11.95	20.38	6.03	19.08	5.92
18-21岁	Age 18-21	66.73	27.41	34.06	13.99	32.67	13.42
按婚育人口分组	**Grouped by Marriage Age and Child-bearing Age**						
进入法定婚龄人口	Reaching Legal Marriage Age	16.94	7.97	8.21	4.30	8.73	3.67
育龄妇女人口 (15-49岁)	Women at Child-bearing Age (Between 15-49)	265.13	105.45			265.13	105.45
按劳龄人口分组	**Grouped by Labor Age**						
进入劳龄人口	Reaching Labor Age						
(国内标准)	(Domestic Standard)	13.79	4.02	7.10	2.02	6.69	2.00
(国际标准)	(International Standard)	10.02	2.68	5.22	1.35	4.80	1.33
劳动年龄内人口	Within Labor Age						
(国内标准)	(Domestic Standard)	647.90	268.67	342.48	142.88	305.42	125.79
(国际标准)	(International Standard)	730.01	302.01	368.21	153.02	361.80	148.99
退出劳龄人口	Over Labor Age						
(国内标准)	(Domestic Standard)	12.22	5.26	4.97	2.08	7.25	3.18
(国际标准)	(International Standard)	7.41	3.36	3.63	1.64	3.78	1.72
按老年人口分组	**Grouped by Aged Population**						
60岁及以上人口	Age 60 and over	148.81	72.59	71.76	34.19	77.05	38.40
占总人口比重(%)	Proportion in Total (%)	15.68	18.89	15.00	17.77	16.38	20.02
65岁及以上人口	Age 65 and over	107.25	54.92	51.24	25.40	56.01	29.52
占总人口比重(%)	Proportion in Total (%)	11.30	14.29	10.71	13.20	11.90	15.39
80岁及以上人口	Age 80 and over	19.65	11.01	8.89	5.05	10.76	5.96
占总人口比重(%)	Proportion in Total (%)	2.07	2.87	1.86	2.62	2.29	3.11

3-10 常住人口主要数据
MAIN STATISTICS OF PERMANENT POPULATION

指　标	Item	2005	2006	2006比2005年增长(%) Increase Rate in 2006 over 2005 (%)
常住人口(万人)	**Permanent Population (10 000 persons)**	**1043.00**	**1075.00**	**3.1**
按性别分	By Sex			
男性人口	Male	523.71	546.41	4.3
女性人口	Female	519.29	528.59	1.8
性别比(女=100)	Sex Ratio (Female=100)	100.85	103.37	2.5
按户别分组	By Household Type			
家庭户	Family	989.52	1010.13	2.1
集体户	Collective	53.48	64.87	21.3
按城乡分组	By Residence			
城　镇	Urban Population	783.40	814.10	3.9
占总人口比重(%)	Proportion in Total (%)	75.11	75.73	
乡　村	Rural Population	259.60	260.90	0.5
按年龄分组	By Age			
0-14岁	Age 0-14	131.42	135.55	3.1
15-64岁	Age 15-64	810.65	835.81	3.1
65岁及以上	Age 65 and above	100.93	103.64	2.7
人口负担系数(%)	Population Dependency Ratio (%)			
人口总负担系数	Total Dependency Ratio	28.66	28.62	
负担少儿系数	Children Dependency Ratio	16.21	16.22	
负担老年系数	The Aged Dependency Ratio	12.45	12.40	
老少比	Ratio of Aged to Children	76.80	76.46	
常住人口户数(万户)	**Number of Households (10 000 households)**	**346.34**	**359.83**	**3.9**
家庭户	Family Households	335.25	341.13	1.8
集体户	Collective Households	11.09	18.70	68.6
家庭平均户规模(人/户)	**Average Family Size (person/household)**	**2.95**	**2.96**	**0.3**
人口变动情况(万人)	**Change of Population (10 000 persons)**			
出生人口	Birth	7.75	8.12	4.8
死亡人口	Death	5.72	6.43	12.4
净迁入人口	Net Immigration	114.35	139.00	21.6

注：此表为人口抽样调查推算数据。
Note: Data in this table are calculated according to population sample survey.

3-11 按年龄分的6岁及以上各种受教育程度人口（2006年）
EDUCATION STATUS OF POPULATION AGED 6 AND ABOVE BY AGE, 2006

单位：人 (person)

年 龄 Age	6岁及以上人口合计 Aged 6 and abover	#小 学 Primary School	#初 中 Junior Middle School	#高 中 Senior Middle School	#大学专科 Junior College	#大学本科 Undergraduate	#研究生 Graduate
全市总计							
Total	**75579**	**16529**	**28494**	**16527**	**6003**	**4306**	**347**
6-9	2512	2272	5				
10-14	3936	2088	1787	41			
15-19	6194	355	2420	2657	442	292	2
20-24	6071	239	1893	1431	1300	1114	63
25-29	5272	342	2003	1345	777	708	69
30-34	5406	526	2505	1205	600	472	55
35-39	6632	908	3297	1358	535	416	57
40-44	8097	953	3768	2375	530	323	65
45-49	6986	995	2772	2531	399	178	12
50-54	7757	1802	3629	1391	548	158	11
55-59	5037	1722	1856	794	332	108	2
60-64	3425	1174	1097	567	210	156	2
65岁及以上							
(≥65)	8254	3153	1462	832	330	381	9
#女 性							
Female	**37975**	**8793**	**13302**	**8155**	**2943**	**2061**	**148**
6-9	1189	1087	2				
10-14	1826	945	859	18			
15-19	3054	169	1066	1363	272	173	
20-24	3094	117	906	675	735	615	31
25-29	2626	182	982	644	388	377	37
30-34	2733	295	1239	611	319	214	29
35-39	3310	509	1618	669	261	188	22
40-44	4087	590	1795	1256	241	131	21
45-49	3494	633	1258	1293	170	68	5
50-54	3956	1089	1716	664	237	63	2
55-59	2546	986	817	395	130	38	
60-64	1760	682	487	272	78	63	
65岁及以上							
(≥65)	4300	1509	557	295	112	131	1

注：此表为2006年人口抽样调查数据，3-12至3-14表相同。
Note: Data in this table are obtained from population sample survey in 2006. Same as 3-12 to 3-14.

3-12 按年龄分的15岁及以上各种婚姻状况人口（2006年）
MARRIAGE STATUS OF POPULATION AGED 15 AND ABOVE BY AGE, 2006

单位：人 (person)

年 龄 Age	15岁及以上 人口合计 Aged 15 and above	未 婚 Unmarried	初婚有配偶 First Marriages	再婚有配偶 Remarriages	离 婚 Divorces	丧 偶 Widowed
全市总计						
Total	**69131**	**13262**	**50131**	**1082**	**913**	**3743**
15-19	6194	6194				
20-24	6071	4607	1434	13	16	1
25-29	5272	1500	3674	36	57	5
30-34	5406	369	4871	74	79	13
35-39	6632	176	6104	187	143	22
40-44	8097	122	7517	182	203	73
45-49	6986	72	6506	132	172	104
50-54	7757	83	7207	148	117	202
55-59	5037	40	4566	105	54	272
60-64	3425	34	2981	61	24	325
65岁及以上						
(≥65)	8254	65	5271	144	48	2726
#女 性						
Female	**34960**	**6208**	**25104**	**585**	**453**	**2610**
15-19	3054	3054				
20-24	3094	2231	845	9	8	1
25-29	2626	630	1950	18	24	4
30-34	2733	131	2507	42	45	8
35-39	3310	61	3055	111	64	19
40-44	4087	24	3810	105	96	52
45-49	3494	21	3246	61	93	73
50-54	3956	27	3642	85	61	141
55-59	2546	14	2257	60	24	191
60-64	1760	9	1466	29	12	244
65岁及以上						
(≥65)	4300	6	2326	65	26	1877

3-13 按地区分的家庭户规模（2006年）
FAMILY HOUSEHOLDS BY SIZE AND REGION, 2006

单位：户 (household)

地区	Region	合计 Total	一人户 One-Person	二人户 Two-Person	三人户 Three-Person	四人户 Four-Person	五人户 Five-Person	六人及以上户 Six-Person and Over
全市总计	**Total**	**26107**	**2124**	**6258**	**11043**	**4100**	**2015**	**567**
市辖区	**Districts under City Administration**	**21735**	**1919**	**5349**	**9697**	**2996**	**1469**	**305**
和平区	Heping District	1139	163	348	437	125	47	19
河东区	Hedong District	1932	175	470	968	213	84	22
河西区	Hexi District	2188	262	603	1041	187	84	11
南开区	Nankai District	2247	246	615	1080	225	71	10
河北区	Hebei District	1746	179	447	862	182	71	5
红桥区	Hongqiao District	1751	210	497	830	136	70	8
塘沽区	Tanggu District	1398	153	351	670	149	63	12
汉沽区	Han'gu District	551	65	183	220	57	23	3
大港区	Dagang District	1085	72	287	545	136	37	8
东丽区	Dongli District	762	43	157	364	126	67	5
西青区	Xiqing District	1068	52	254	429	200	114	19
津南区	Jinnan District	1022	37	222	476	171	98	18
北辰区	Beichen District	927	71	184	430	153	76	13
武清区	Wuqing District	2156	119	367	795	490	313	72
宝坻区	Baodi District	1763	72	364	550	446	251	80
市辖县	**Counties under City Administration**	**4372**	**205**	**909**	**1346**	**1104**	**546**	**262**
宁河县	Ninghe County	993	35	199	303	266	144	46
静海县	Jinghai County	1389	57	313	530	331	125	33
蓟　县	Jixian County	1990	113	397	513	507	277	183

3-14 按地区分有65岁及以上老年人口的家庭户(2006年)
HOUSEHOLDS WITH POPULATION AGED 65 AND OVER BY REGION, 2006

单位：户 (household)

地 区	Region	合 计 Total	#单身老人户 Single	#一对老夫妇户 One Couple	#一个老人与亲属户 One Aged Population and Relatives	#二个老人与亲属户 Two Aged Population and Relatives
全市总计	**Total**	**4404**	**977**	**1232**	**1464**	**717**
市辖区	**Districts under City Administration**	**3898**	**877**	**1076**	**1302**	**631**
和平区	Heping District	377	73	84	143	77
河东区	Hedong District	364	82	66	147	69
河西区	Hexi District	469	118	118	156	76
南开区	Nankai District	492	118	161	132	77
河北区	Hebei District	449	84	110	174	79
红桥区	Hongqiao District	414	115	121	118	59
塘沽区	Tanggu District	204	44	62	66	32
汉沽区	Han'gu District	116	35	40	30	10
大港区	Dagang District	125	25	46	37	17
东丽区	Dongli District	79	13	21	32	13
西青区	Xiqing District	160	29	35	69	27
津南区	Jinnan District	114	13	43	39	19
北辰区	Beichen District	130	36	36	36	22
武清区	Wuqing District	229	52	62	78	37
宝坻区	Baodi District	176	40	71	45	17
市辖县	**Counties under City Administration**	**506**	**100**	**156**	**162**	**86**
宁河县	Ninghe County	91	14	29	33	15
静海县	Jinghai County	147	28	40	58	21
蓟 县	Jixian County	268	58	87	71	50

3-15 社会从业人员(1990-2006年) TOTAL PERSONS EMPLOYED, 1990-2006

单位：万人 (10 000 persons)

年份 Year	劳动力资源总数 Number of Labour Force	社会从业人员合计 Number of Persons Employed	按城乡分组 Grouped by Urban and Rural Areas					
			城镇 Urban Areas	国有单位 State-owned Units	集体单位 Collective-owned Units	其他 Others	个体、私营单位 Private and Individual Units	乡村 Rural Areas
1990	558.93	470.07	290.01	217.26	62.55	4.50	5.70	180.06
1991	564.15	479.67	300.58	219.34	66.17	6.05	9.02	179.09
1992	569.70	485.70	303.70	212.73	72.39	8.85	9.73	182.00
1993	566.10	503.10	312.70	210.90	75.50	16.30	10.00	190.40
1994	694.30	513.00	318.60	206.50	71.40	24.40	16.30	194.40
1995	701.60	515.30	319.80	202.10	68.40	29.20	20.10	195.50
1996	708.80	512.00	317.10	199.10	62.80	31.00	24.20	194.90
1997	716.26	513.33	318.60	196.16	58.19	35.80	28.45	194.73
1998	728.68	508.10	312.65	183.49	53.00	41.58	34.58	195.45
1999	740.76	508.14	313.89	176.54	47.54	49.80	40.01	194.25
2000	753.27	486.89	296.61	163.84	40.58	55.37	36.82	190.28
2001	761.11	488.34	295.37	153.25	32.13	60.94	49.05	192.97
2002	771.69	492.61	295.71	137.81	26.60	82.54	48.76	196.90
2003	793.86	510.90	299.95	128.52	22.80	93.72	54.91	210.95
2004	798.43	527.78	302.47	126.36	20.21	103.59	52.31	225.31
2005	858.88	542.52	312.76	99.18	11.31	148.01	54.26	229.76
2006	888.51	562.92	402.12	97.34	30.00	158.21	116.57	160.80

年份 Year	按三次产业分 Grouped by Three Industries					
	绝对数 Number			构成(%) Composition in Percentage (%)		
	第一产业 Primary Industry	第二产业 Secondary Industry	第三产业 Tertiary Industry	第一产业 Primary Industry	第二产业 Secondary Industry	第三产业 Tertiary Industry
1990	93.63	232.17	144.27	19.9	49.4	30.7
1991	94.27	237.24	148.16	19.7	49.5	30.8
1992	92.50	238.40	154.80	19.0	49.1	31.9
1993	89.00	245.20	168.90	17.7	48.7	33.6
1994	85.60	246.50	180.90	16.7	48.0	35.3
1995	82.90	247.10	185.30	16.1	47.9	36.0
1996	82.10	241.40	188.50	16.0	47.2	36.8
1997	81.26	235.69	196.38	15.8	45.9	38.3
1998	80.88	233.21	194.01	15.9	45.9	38.2
1999	79.57	230.33	198.24	15.7	45.3	39.0
2000	81.29	222.15	183.45	16.7	45.6	37.7
2001	82.70	212.65	192.99	16.9	43.6	39.5
2002	82.25	205.38	204.98	16.7	41.7	41.6
2003	83.19	219.44	208.27	16.3	42.9	40.8
2004	82.83	223.89	221.06	15.7	42.4	41.9
2005	81.79	227.38	233.35	15.1	41.9	43.0
2006	81.11	234.85	246.96	14.4	41.7	43.9

注：1. 1998-2004年城镇从业人员中包括由于各种原因已经离开本人的生产或工作岗位，但仍与本单位保留劳动关系的职工。2. 2006年社会从业人员城乡划分标准是按照国家统计局新确定的标准统计的。

Note: a) From 1998 to 2004, the number of urban employment personnel include those staff and workers who still keep their relation with their units, but have left their working post at there. b) In 2006, the division of urban and rural persons employed adopt the new standard of National Bureau of Statistics of People's Republic of China.

3-16 城镇单位从业人员(1990-2006年)
PERSONS EMPLOYED IN URBAN UNITS, 1990-2006

单位：万人 (10 000 persons)

年份 Year	合计 Total	按三次产业分 Grouped by Three Industries			按登记注册类型分 Grouped by Registration Status		
		第一产业 Primary Industry	第二产业 Secondary Industry	第三产业 Tertiary Industry	国有单位 State-owned Units	集体单位 Collective-owned Units	其他单位 Others
总计 Total							
1990	284.31	4.10	167.68	112.53	217.26	62.55	4.50
1991	291.56	4.34	171.57	115.65	219.34	66.17	6.05
1992	293.97	4.10	171.41	118.46	212.73	72.39	8.85
1993	293.45	2.55	171.18	119.72	206.52	70.89	16.04
1994	291.94	2.30	168.72	120.92	201.75	66.21	23.98
1995	289.59	1.90	167.33	120.36	197.01	64.19	28.39
1996	283.98	1.73	163.07	119.18	194.32	59.62	30.04
1997	281.34	1.71	158.68	120.95	191.64	55.28	34.42
1998	218.56	1.43	113.47	103.66	144.18	36.26	38.12
1999	211.76	1.10	110.27	100.39	135.08	30.46	46.22
2000	201.75	1.11	105.63	95.01	125.00	25.82	50.93
2001	192.30	1.09	99.82	91.39	116.24	20.05	56.00
2002	185.50	1.09	92.68	91.73	107.79	16.47	61.24
2003	191.01	0.97	97.60	92.44	101.57	13.95	75.49
2004	193.91	0.87	96.82	96.22	102.09	12.46	79.36
2005	194.12	0.81	97.52	95.79	99.18	11.33	83.61
2006	195.00	0.73	98.37	95.90	97.34	9.61	88.05
#女性 Female							
1990	120.90	1.25	71.76	47.89	84.44	34.39	2.07
1991	124.24	1.44	73.87	48.93	85.78	35.61	2.85
1992	124.05	1.23	73.38	49.44	83.89	35.89	4.27
1993	123.14	0.86	72.00	50.28	81.46	34.00	7.68
1994	123.73	0.81	72.00	50.92	80.64	31.79	11.30
1995	123.60	0.68	72.03	50.89	79.27	30.81	13.52
1996	120.23	0.57	69.84	49.82	77.39	28.59	14.25
1997	118.75	0.55	67.48	50.72	76.61	26.15	15.99
1998	89.89	0.46	46.11	43.32	56.17	15.93	17.79
1999	82.95	0.31	41.33	41.31	51.80	13.22	17.93
2000	77.28	0.33	38.85	38.10	47.26	10.76	19.26
2001	77.40	0.36	40.09	36.95	43.26	8.11	26.03
2002	73.59	0.33	36.00	37.26	39.60	6.52	27.47
2003	76.27	0.28	38.49	37.50	37.73	5.33	33.21
2004	73.66	0.26	35.30	38.10	37.56	4.39	31.71
2005	68.66	0.23	33.01	35.42	33.94	4.09	30.63
2006	70.28	0.22	33.95	36.11	33.13	3.41	33.74

注：1998年以前为职工人数。
Note: The data before 1998 of this table refer to staff and workers.

3-17 按国民经济行业分各类从业人员(2006年)
PERSONS EMPLOYED GROUPED BY SECTOR, 2006

单位：万人 (10 000 persons)

项　目 Item	社会从业人员 Persons Employed	城镇单位从业人员 Persons Employed In Urban Units	在岗职工人数 On-post Staff and Workers	其他从业人员 Other Persons Employed
总　计 Total	**562.92**	**195.00**	**172.03**	**22.97**
按三次产业分 Grouped by Three Industries				
第一产业 Primary Industry	81.11	0.73	0.72	0.01
第二产业 Secondary Industry	234.85	98.37	90.62	7.75
第三产业 Tertiary Industry	246.96	95.90	80.69	15.21
按国民经济行业分 Grouped by Sector				
农、林、牧、渔业 Farming, Forestry, Animal Husbandry and Fishery	81.11	0.73	0.72	0.01
采矿业 Minerals Mining	11.68	7.49	6.36	1.13
制造业 Manufacturing	186.29	78.48	72.90	5.58
电力、燃气及水的生产和供应业 Production & Supply of Power, Gas and Water	5.53	3.47	3.18	0.29
建筑业 Construction	31.35	8.93	8.18	0.75
交通运输、仓储及邮政业 Transportation, Storage and Post Services	39.90	11.58	9.96	1.62
信息传输、计算机服务和软件业 Information Transmitting, Computer Services and Software	4.52	2.30	2.10	0.20
批发和零售业 Wholesale and Retail Trade	67.21	11.04	8.75	2.29
住宿和餐饮业 Accommodation and Catering Services	14.29	3.43	2.30	1.13
金融业 Finance Intermediation	8.07	5.15	3.58	1.57
房地产业 Real Estate	4.98	2.23	1.67	0.56
租赁和商务服务业 Leasing and Business Services	11.88	6.53	5.01	1.52
科学研究、技术服务和地质勘察业 Scientific Research, Technical Services and Geological Prospecting	8.12	5.35	4.69	0.66
水利、环境和公共设施管理业 Management for Water Conservancy, Environment and Public Facilities	5.62	3.57	3.13	0.44
居民服务和其他服务业 Resident Services and Other Social Services	20.32	5.00	2.96	2.04
教　育 Education	25.34	16.75	15.98	0.77
卫生、社会保障和社会福利业 Health Care, Social Security and Social Welfare	12.51	7.76	6.85	0.91
文化、体育和娱乐业 Culture, Sports and Recreational Services	3.74	1.84	1.62	0.22
公共管理和社会组织 Public Management and Social Organizations	20.46	13.37	12.09	1.28

3-18 社会从业人员及构成
NUMBER AND COMPOSITION OF PERSONS EMPLOYED

项　目	Item	绝对数(万人) Number (10 000 persons) 2005	2006	构 成(%) Composition in Percentage (%) 2005	2006
总　计	**Total**	**542.52**	**562.92**	**100.0**	**100.0**
按登记注册类型分	**Grouped by Registration Status**				
内资单位	Domestic Investment Units				
国有单位	State-owned Units	99.18	100.81	18.3	17.9
集体单位	Collective-owned Units	181.18	113.93	33.4	20.2
联营单位	Joint-owned Units	1.35	5.71	0.2	1.0
股份有限公司	Share Holding Corporations Ltd.	10.20	34.47	1.9	6.1
有限责任公司	Limited-Liability Corporations	14.78	56.32	2.7	10.0
股份合作单位	Cooperative Units	1.08	4.81	0.2	0.9
私营单位	Private	88.71	93.48	16.4	16.6
个　体	Individual	25.46	75.83	4.7	13.5
其他单位	Others	69.44	20.49	12.8	3.6
港澳台商投资单位	Units with Funds from Hong Kong, Macao and Taiwan	9.94	11.60	1.8	2.1
外商投资单位	Foreign Funded Units	41.20	45.47	7.6	8.1
按国民经济行业分	**Grouped by Sector**				
农、林、牧、渔业	Farming, Forestry, Animal Husbandry and Fishery	81.79	81.11	15.1	14.4
采矿业	Minerals Mining	7.41	11.68	1.4	2.1
制造业	Manufacturing	186.14	186.29	34.3	33.1
电力、燃气及水的生产和供应业	Production & Supply of Power, Gas and Water	4.40	5.53	0.8	1.0
建筑业	Construction	29.43	31.35	5.4	5.6
交通运输、仓储及邮政业	Transportation, Storage and Post Services	33.86	39.90	6.2	7.1
信息传输、计算机服务和软件业	Information Transmitting, Computer Services and Software	3.73	4.52	0.7	0.8
批发和零售业	Wholesale and Retail Trade	67.09	67.21	12.4	11.9
住宿和餐饮业	Accommodation and Catering Services	11.27	14.29	2.1	2.6
金融业	Finance Intermediation	5.81	8.07	1.1	1.4
房地产业	Real Estate	5.83	4.98	1.1	0.9
租赁和商务服务业	Leasing and Business Services	12.45	11.88	2.3	2.1
科学研究、技术服务和地质勘察业	Scientific Research, Technical Services and Geological Prospecting	6.10	8.12	1.1	1.4
水利、环境和公共设施管理业	Management for Water Conservancy, Environment and Public Facilities	5.08	5.62	0.9	1.0
居民服务和其他服务业	Resident Services and Other Social Services	37.58	20.32	6.9	3.6
教　育	Education	16.97	25.34	3.1	4.5
卫生、社会保障和社会福利业	Health Care, Social Security and Social Welfare	8.95	12.51	1.7	2.2
文化、体育和娱乐业	Culture, Sports and Recreational Services	3.58	3.74	0.6	0.7
公共管理和社会组织	Public Management and Social Organizations	15.05	20.46	2.8	3.6

3-19 城镇单位从业人员及构成
NUMBER AND COMPOSITION OF PERSONS EMPLOYED IN URBAN UNITS

项 目	Item	绝对数(万人) Number (10 000 persons) 2005	2006	构 成(%) Composition in Percentage (%) 2005	2006
总 计	**Total**	**194.12**	**195.00**	**100.0**	**100.0**
按登记注册类型分	**Grouped by Registration Status**				
国有单位	State-owned Units	99.18	97.34	51.1	49.9
集体单位	Collective-owned Units	11.33	9.61	5.8	4.9
其他单位	Others	83.61	88.05	43.1	45.2
#外商及港澳台商投资单位	Units with Funds from Foreign Countries, Hong Kong, Macao & Taiwan	51.15	54.98	26.3	28.2
股份有限公司	Share Holding Corporations Ltd.	10.20	9.87	5.3	5.1
按国民经济行业分	**Grouped by Sector**				
农、林、牧、渔业	Farming, Forestry, Animal Husbandry and Fishery	0.81	0.73	0.4	0.4
采矿业	Minerals Mining	7.31	7.49	3.8	3.9
制造业	Manufacturing	77.72	78.48	40.1	40.2
电力、燃气及水的生产和供应业	Production & Supply of Power, Gas and Water	3.36	3.47	1.7	1.8
建筑业	Construction	9.12	8.93	4.7	4.6
交通运输、仓储及邮政业	Transportation, Storage and Post Services	11.77	11.58	6.1	5.9
信息传输、计算机服务和软件业	Information Transmitting, Computer Services and Software	2.43	2.30	1.2	1.2
批发和零售业	Wholesale and Retail Trade	11.74	11.04	6.0	5.7
住宿和餐饮业	Accommodation and Catering Services	3.00	3.43	1.6	1.8
金融业	Finance Intermediation	5.12	5.15	2.6	2.6
房地产业	Real Estate	2.32	2.23	1.2	1.1
租赁和商务服务业	Leasing and Business Services	6.59	6.53	3.4	3.3
科学研究、技术服务和地质勘察业	Scientific Research, Technical Services and Geological Prospecting	5.31	5.35	2.7	2.7
水利、环境和公共设施管理业	Management for Water Conservancy, Environment and Public Facilities	3.60	3.57	1.9	1.8
居民服务和其他服务业	Resident Services and Other Social Services	4.20	5.00	2.2	2.6
教 育	Education	16.97	16.75	8.7	8.6
卫生、社会保障和社会福利业	Health Care, Social Security and Social Welfare	7.71	7.76	4.0	4.0
文化、体育和娱乐业	Culture, Sports and Recreational Services	1.75	1.84	0.9	0.9
公共管理和社会组织	Public Management and Social Organizations	13.29	13.37	6.8	6.9
按企业、事业、机关分	**Grouped By Enterprise, Institution and Agency**				
企 业	Enterprises	147.93	148.77	76.2	76.3
中 央	Central	26.27	27.02	13.5	13.9
地 方	Local	121.66	121.75	62.7	62.4
#国 有	State-owned	35.08	33.12	18.1	17.0
事 业	Institutions	33.63	33.61	17.3	17.2
中 央	Central	2.36	2.31	1.2	1.2
地 方	Local	31.27	31.30	16.1	16.0
机 关	Government Agencies	12.56	12.62	6.5	6.5
中 央	Central	1.14	1.15	0.6	0.6
地 方	Local	11.42	11.47	5.9	5.9

3-20 城镇单位在岗职工及构成
NUMBER AND COMPOSITION OF ON-POST STAFF AND WORKERS IN URBAN UNITS

项 目	Item	绝对数(万人) Number (10 000 persons)		构 成(%) Composition in Percentage (%)	
		2005	2006	2005	2006
总 计	**Total**	**169.90**	**172.03**	**100.0**	**100.0**
按登记注册类型分	**Grouped by Registration Status**				
国有单位	State-owned Units	87.53	86.21	51.5	50.1
集体单位	Collective-owned Units	9.12	7.80	5.4	4.5
其他单位	Others	73.25	78.02	43.1	45.4
#外商及港澳台商投资单位	Units with Funds from Foreign Countries, Hong Kong, Macao & Taiwan	46.08	50.30	27.1	29.2
股份有限公司	Share Holding Corporations Ltd.	8.55	8.35	5.0	4.9
按国民经济行业分	**Grouped by Sector**				
农、林、牧、渔业	Farming, Forestry, Animal Husbandry and Fishery	0.80	0.72	0.5	0.4
采矿业	Minerals Mining	6.42	6.36	3.8	3.7
制造业	Manufacturing	71.45	72.90	42.1	42.4
电力、燃气及水的生产和供应业	Production & Supply of Power, Gas and Water	3.09	3.18	1.8	1.8
建筑业	Construction	8.32	8.18	4.9	4.8
交通运输、仓储及邮政业	Transportion, Storage, Post Services	10.45	9.96	6.1	5.8
信息传输、计算机服务和软件业	Information Transmitting, Computer Services and Software	2.18	2.10	1.3	1.2
批发和零售业	Wholesale and Retail Trade	8.81	8.75	5.2	5.1
住宿和餐饮业	Accommodation and Catering Services	2.19	2.30	1.3	1.4
金融业	Finance Intermediation	3.55	3.58	2.1	2.1
房地产业	Real Estate	1.70	1.67	1.0	1.0
租赁和商务服务业	Leasing and Business Services	4.49	5.01	2.6	2.9
科学研究、技术服务和地质勘察业	Scientific Research, Technical Services and Geological Prospecting	4.74	4.69	2.8	2.7
水利、环境和公共设施管理业	Management for Water Conservancy, Environment and Public Facilities	3.13	3.13	1.8	1.8
居民服务和其他服务业	Resident Services and Other Social Services	2.14	2.96	1.3	1.7
教 育	Education	16.20	15.98	9.5	9.3
卫生、社会保障和社会福利业	Health Care, Social Security and Social Welfare	6.77	6.85	4.0	4.0
文化、体育和娱乐业	Culture, Sports and Recreational Services	1.52	1.62	0.9	0.9
公共管理和社会组织	Public Management and Social Organizations	11.95	12.09	7.0	7.0

3-21 城镇单位其他从业人员及构成
NUMBER AND COMPOSITION OF OTHER PERSONS EMPLOYED IN URBAN UNITS

项　目	Item	绝对数(万人) Number (10 000 persons)		构 成(%) Composition in Percentage (%)	
		2005	2006	2005	2006
总　计	**Total**	**24.22**	**22.97**	**100.0**	**100.0**
按登记注册类型分	**Grouped by Registration Status**				
国有单位	State-owned Units	11.65	11.13	48.1	48.5
集体单位	Collective-owned Units	2.21	1.81	9.1	7.8
其他单位	Others	10.36	10.03	42.8	43.7
#外商及港澳台商投资单位	Units with Funds from Foreign Countries, Hong Kong, Macao & Taiwan	5.07	4.68	20.9	20.4
股份有限公司	Share Holding Corporations Ltd.	1.65	1.52	6.8	6.7
按国民经济行业分	**Grouped by Sector**				
农、林、牧、渔业	Farming, Forestry, Animal Husbandry and Fishery	0.01	0.01	0.1	
采矿业	Minerals Mining	0.89	1.13	3.7	4.9
制造业	Manufacturing	6.27	5.58	25.9	24.3
电力、燃气及水的生产和供应业	Production & Supply of Power, Gas and Water	0.27	0.29	1.1	1.3
建筑业	Construction	0.80	0.75	3.3	3.3
交通运输、仓储及邮政业	Transportation, Storage and Post Services	1.32	1.62	5.5	7.0
信息传输、计算机服务和软件业	Information Transmitting, Computer Services and Software	0.25	0.20	1.0	0.9
批发和零售业	Wholesale and Retail Trade	2.93	2.29	12.1	10.0
住宿和餐饮业	Accommodation and Catering Services	0.81	1.13	3.3	4.9
金融业	Finance Intermediation	1.57	1.57	6.5	6.8
房地产业	Real Estate	0.62	0.56	2.5	2.4
租赁和商务服务业	Leasing and Business Services	2.10	1.52	8.7	6.6
科学研究、技术服务和地质勘察业	Scientific Research, Technical Services and Geological Prospecting	0.57	0.66	2.3	2.9
水利、环境和公共设施管理业	Management for Water Conservancy, Environment and Public Facilities	0.47	0.44	1.9	1.9
居民服务和其他服务业	Resident Services and Other Social Services	2.06	2.04	8.5	8.9
教　育	Education	0.77	0.77	3.2	3.4
卫生、社会保障和社会福利业	Health Care, Social Security and Social Welfare	0.94	0.91	3.9	4.0
文化、体育和娱乐业	Culture, Sports and Recreational Services	0.23	0.22	0.9	0.9
公共管理和社会组织	Public Management and Social Organizations	1.34	1.28	5.6	5.6

3-22 城镇单位从业人员变动情况(2006年)
CHANGES OF PERSONS EMPLOYED IN URBAN UNITS, 2006

单位：人 (person)

项 目 Item	合 计 Total	按登记注册类型分 Grouped by Registration Status			按企事业机关分 Grouped by Enterprise, Institution and Agency		
		国有单位 State-owned Units	集体单位 Collective-owned Units	其他单位 Others	企 业 Enterprise	事 业 Institution	机 关 Government Agency
从业人员增加合计 Number of Persons Employed Increased	**286767**	**92851**	**12497**	**181419**	**258371**	**22279**	**6117**
1. 从农村招收人员 Recruited from Rural Area	68061	9852	1934	56275	67525	297	239
2. 从城镇招收失业人员 Recruited from Urban Area	32698	7857	1808	23033	31035	1325	338
3. 录用的退伍军人 Employment of Demobilized Soldiers	2069	1478	93	498	1353	216	500
4. 录用及使用的大中专技校毕业生 Employment of Graduate	53577	19079	1301	33197	43133	8116	2328
5. 调入人数 Job Changes	59751	27945	3383	28423	50230	7490	2031
# 市外调入 From Outside Tianjin	4396	3103	10	1283	3981	400	15
6. 其 他 Others	70611	26640	3978	39993	65095	4835	681
从业人员减少合计 Number of Persons Employed Decreased	**291076**	**103089**	**23792**	**164195**	**264065**	**22142**	**4869**
1. 离退休退职人员 Retire and Quit	35645	20299	2595	12751	25624	8260	1761
2. 开除、除名、辞退 Discharge	14076	2746	1513	9817	13508	449	119
3. 终止、解除合同 Contract Expiration	97579	20468	5295	71816	94972	2218	389
4. 在岗人员转不在岗 Not On-post from On-post	20159	11707	2394	6058	19119	993	47
5. 死 亡 Death	1668	1169	91	408	1133	390	145
6. 调出人数 Job Changes	54578	24695	5154	24729	46589	6318	1671
# 调至市外 To Outside Tianjin	1816	515	5	1296	1606	195	15
7. 其 他 Others	67371	22005	6750	38616	63120	3514	737

3-23 市属部分局(总公司)国有经济单位从业人员年末人数
YEAR-END NUMBER OF PERSONS EMPLOYED BY STATE-OWNED UNITS IN PART OF BUREAUS (CORPORATIONS)

单位:人 (person)

局(总公司)	Bureau (Corporation)	2005	2006
经委系统	**Tianjin Economical Committee System**		
机电工业控股集团公司	Tianjin Machinery & Electric Industry Holding Group Company	10129	6090
中环电子信息集团有限公司	Tianjin Zhonghuan Electronics & Information Group	12991	12608
冶金集团(控股)有限公司	Tianjin Metallurgical Group (Holding) Corporation	9107	9619
渤海化工集团公司	Tianjin Bohai Chemical Industry Group Corporation	29597	29903
纺织集团(控股)有限公司	Tianjin Textile Industrial General Corporation	24343	21099
一轻集团(控股)有限公司	Tianjin First Light Industry Group (Holding) Co., Ltd.	4340	3348
二轻集团(控股)有限公司	Tianjin Second Light Industry Group (Holding) Co., Ltd.	2318	1989
医药集团有限公司	Tianjin Pharmaceutical Holdings	2340	2389
汽车工业(集团)有限公司	Tianjin Automobile Industry Group Co., Ltd.	556	907
飞鸽集团有限公司	Tianjin Flying Pigeon Group Co., Ltd.	1195	1039
塑料集团	Tianjin Plastics Group	763	508
天铁冶金集团有限公司	Tianjin Tian Tie Metallurgical Group Co., Ltd.	19267	19346
建筑材料集团(控股)有限公司	Tianjin Building Materials Group (Holding) Co., Ltd.	3187	2764
农委系统	**Tianjin Agricultural Committee System**		
农业局	Tianjin Agriculture Bureau	435	439
畜牧局	Tianjin Animal Husbandry Bureau	323	342
农垦集团总公司	Tianjin State Farms Agribusiness Group Company	3465	3206
水产局	Tianjin Aquatic Products Bureau	847	736
建委系统	**Tianjin Construction Committee System**		
建工集团总公司	Tianjin Construction Engineering Group Corporation	3707	2138
市政工程局	Tianjin Municipal Engineering Bureau	13985	13740
房地产管理局	Tianjin Real Estate Administrative Bureau	9164	9300
住宅建设发展集团	Tianjin House Construction Development Group	1285	1138
公共交通集团公司	Tianjin Public Traffic Group Corporation	10507	10680
自来水集团	Tianjin Tap Water Group	3737	3535
燃气集团	Tianjin Gas Group	6630	6589
交委系统	**Tianjin Transportation Committee System**		
天津港(集团)有限公司	Tianjin Port Group Corporation Ltd.	11143	11998
天津交通运输总公司	Tianjin Communication Corporation	6181	5776
商委系统	**Tianjin Commercial Committee System**		
粮食粮油集团有限公司	Tianjin Grain & Oil Group Co., Ltd.	2978	2549
一商集团有限公司	Tianjin First Commercial Group Co., Ltd.	1933	1665
二商集团有限公司	Tianjin Second Commercial Group Co., Ltd.	3332	2932

3-24 市属部分局(总公司)国有经济单位从业人员年平均人数

AVERAGE NUMBER OF PERSONS EMPLOYED BY STATE-OWNED UNITS IN PART OF BUREAUS (CORPORATIONS)

单位:人 (person)

局(总公司)	Bureau (Corporation)	2005	2006
经委系统	**Tianjin Economical Committee System**		
机电工业控股集团公司	Tianjin Machinery & Electric Industry Holding Group Company	10531	6787
中环电子信息集团有限公司	Tianjin Zhonghuan Electronics & Information Group	13136	12709
冶金集团(控股)有限公司	Tianjin Metallurgical Group (Holding) Corporation	9380	9712
渤海化工集团公司	Tianjin Bohai Chemical Industry Group Corporation	30791	30038
纺织集团(控股)有限公司	Tianjin Textile Industrial General Corporation	24637	21941
一轻集团(控股)有限公司	Tianjin First Light Industry Group (Holding) Co., Ltd.	4584	3765
二轻集团(控股)有限公司	Tianjin Second Light Industry Group (Holding) Co., Ltd.	2551	2091
医药集团有限公司	Tianjin Pharmaceutical Holdings	2496	2454
汽车工业(集团)有限公司	Tianjin Automobile Industry Group Co., Ltd.	861	796
飞鸽集团有限公司	Tianjin Flying Pigeon Group Co., Ltd.	1288	1125
塑料集团	Tianjin Plastics Group	741	480
天铁冶金集团有限公司	Tianjin Tian Tie Metallurgical Group Co., Ltd.	18927	19259
建筑材料集团(控股)有限公司	Tianjin Building Materials Group (Holding) Co., Ltd.	3574	2915
农委系统	**Tianjin Agricultural Committee System**		
农业局	Tianjin Agriculture Bureau	430	443
畜牧局	Tianjin Animal Husbandry Bureau	317	336
农垦集团总公司	Tianjin State Farms Agribusiness Group Company	3707	3299
水产局	Tianjin Aquatic Products Bureau	971	804
建委系统	**Tianjin Construction Committee System**		
建工集团总公司	Tianjin Construction Engineering Group Corporation	4082	2118
市政工程局	Tianjin Municipal Engineering Bureau	14027	13819
房地产管理局	Tianjin Real Estate Administrative Bureau	9096	9326
住宅建设发展集团	Tianjin House Construction Development Group	1461	1153
公共交通集团公司	Tianjin Public Traffic Group Corporation	10316	10586
自来水集团	Tianjin Tap Water Group	3710	3647
燃气集团	Tianjin Gas Group	6540	6748
交委系统	**Tianjin Transportation Committee System**		
天津港(集团)有限公司	Tianjin Port Group Corporation Ltd.	11446	12144
天津交通运输总公司	Tianjin Communication Corporation	6316	5940
商委系统	**Tianjin Commercial Committee System**		
粮食粮油集团有限公司	Tianjin Grain & Oil Group Co., Ltd.	3080	2820
一商集团有限公司	Tianjin First Commercial Group Co., Ltd.	2706	1780
二商集团有限公司	Tianjin Second Commercial Group Co., Ltd.	3991	2971

3-25 离退休退职人员情况（2003-2006年）
BASIC STATISTICS ON RETIRED AND QUITED PERSONNEL, 2003-2006

指 标 Item	2003	2004	2005	2006
离退休、退职人数(万人) **Number of Retired and Quited Personnel (10 000 persons)**	**111.2**	**118.6**	**131.2**	**136.1**
劳动部门 Labour Department	110.6	118.0	130.6	135.6
国有单位 State-owned Units	76.6	83.0	94.6	98.2
集体单位 Collective-owned Units	18.6	19.1	20.9	21.7
其他单位 Others	15.4	15.9	15.1	15.7
民政部门 Civil Administration Department	0.6	0.6	0.6	0.5
离退休退职人员与在职职工之比(以在职职工为100) **Ratio of Retired and Quited Personnel to On-post Staff and Workers (take on-post staff and workers as 100)**	**63.6**	**68.7**	**77.2**	**79.2**

资料来源:天津市劳动和社会保障局、民政局。
Sources: Tianjin Municipal Labour & Social Insurance Bureau and Tianjin Civil Administration Bureau.

3-26 城镇登记失业人员情况（2003-2006年）
BASIC STATISTICS ON REGISTERED PERSONS UNEMPLOYED IN URBAN AREA, 2003-2006

单位：万人 (10 000 persons)

指 标 Item	2003	2004	2005	2006
新登记失业人数 **Number of Newly Registered Unemployed Personnel**	**7.61**	**6.61**	**6.03**	**8.51**
#女 性 Female	3.96	3.33	3.14	4.42
由就业转失业人数 Unemployment Turned from Employment	5.60	4.01	4.11	6.90
本期失业人员就业人数 **Newly Employed Personnel Turning from Unemployment**	**8.48**	**6.87**	**6.09**	**8.55**
期末实有登记失业人数 **Registered Unemployed Personnel Year-end**	**12.03**	**11.77**	**11.72**	**11.67**
#女 性 Female	6.25	5.92	6.09	6.07
长期失业者 Permanent Unemployed Personnel	4.81	5.20		4.67
登记失业率(%) **Registered Unemployed Rate (%)**	**3.80**	**3.76**	**3.70**	**3.60**

资料来源：天津市劳动和社会保障局。
Sources: Tianjin Municipal Labour & Social Insurance Bureau.

3-27 职业技能培训与就业服务情况（2003-2006年）
STATISTICS ON VOCATIONAL SKILL TRAINING AND EMPLOYMENT SERVICE, 2003-2006

项 目 Item	2003	2004	2005	2006
参加职业技能鉴定人次 (person-times) Persons Attending Vocational Technical Appraisal	**155120**	**206427**	**227984**	**236060**
初级工 Junior Worker	106367	138398	144874	133502
中级工 Middle Worker	39554	49393	59594	73171
高级工 Senior Worker	8350	14634	17058	22243
技 师 Technician	809	3596	6082	6678
高级技师 Senior Technician	40	406	376	466
取得职业资格证书人数 (person) Persons Gaining Vocational Certificate	**145246**	**193218**	**215217**	**223313**
初级工 Junior Worker	99820	131097	137961	128219
中级工 Middle Worker	36847	44877	55256	68195
高级工 Senior Worker	7761	13565	16102	20307
技 师 Technician	784	3292	5549	6151
高级技师 Senior Technician	34	387	349	441
人才和劳务市场情况(万人次) Statistics on Talent and Labor Force Market (10 000 person-times)				
进场择业洽谈人次 Number of Person Times Entering for Interview	292.26	329.57	331.83	341.48
# 劳动力市 场 Labour Force Market	249.00	271.00	275.80	276.90
达成初步意向人次 Number of Person Times Reached Preliminary Initial Intent	61.22	90.43	90.19	91.39
# 劳动力市场 Labour Force Market	45.50	69.00	70.10	70.60

3-28 全市就业和再就业情况（2003-2006年）
STATISTICS ON EMPLOYMENT AND RE-EMPLOYMENT, 2003-2006

单位：万人 (10 000 persons)

项 目 Item	2003	2004	2005	2006
新增就业岗位人数 Persons Employed on New Job Posts	**18.12**	**21.45**	**26.21**	**29.49**
下岗失业人员 Laid-off and Unemployed	12.08	13.70	14.22	12.91
下岗人员 Laid-off	6.10	6.83	7.16	4.31
失业人员 Unemployed	5.98	6.87	7.06	8.60
其他人员 Others	6.04	7.75	11.99	16.58
领取再就业优惠证人数 Persons Gaining Re-employment Favourable Prove	**12.09**	**11.10**	**6.14**	**3.30**
# “4050”人员 Female of 40s and Male of 50s	7.08	3.01	2.05	1.29

主要统计指标解释

常住人口　指实际经常居住在某地区一定时间（指半年以上）的人口。按人口普查和抽样调查规定，主要包括：1. 除离开本地半年以上（不包括在国外工作或学习的人）的全部常住本地的户籍人口；2. 户口在外地，但在本地居住半年以上者，或离开户口地半年以上而调查时在本地居住的人口；3. 调查时居住在本地，但在任何地方都没有登记常住户口，如手持户口迁移证、出生证、退伍证、劳改劳教释放证等尚未办理常住户口的人，即所谓"口袋户口"的人。

户籍人口　指公民依照《中华人民共和国户口登记条例》，已在其经常居住地的公安户籍管理机关登记了常住户口的人。这类人口不管其是否外出，也不管外出时间长短，只要在某地注册有常住户口，则为该地区的户籍人口。

人口密度　指单位土地面积上的人口数。通常使用常住人口计算人口密度，用于说明人口的拥挤程度。通常以每平方公里的居民人数来表示。计算公式：

人口密度 =（常住人口 / 总土地面积）

人口出生率　指一定时期内出生的人口数与该时期内平均人口数之比，通常以年为单位计算，用千分比来表示，表明某年1000人中活产的人数。计算公式：

人口出生率 =（年内出生人数 / 年平均人口数）×1000‰

人口死亡率　指一定时期内死亡的人口数与该时期内平均人口数之比，通常以年为单位计算，用千分比来表示，表明某年1000人中死亡的人数。计算公式：

人口死亡率 =（年内死亡人数 / 年平均人口数）×1000‰

人口自然增长率　指一定时期内人口自然增长数（出生人数减死亡人数）与该时期内平均人口数之比，通常以年为单位计算，用千分比来表示，计算公式：

人口自然增长率 =〔（年内出生人数－年内死亡人数）/ 年平均人口数〕×1000‰

人口自然增长率 = 人口出生率－人口死亡率

总和生育率　总和生育率是将特定时点上全体妇女生育率综合起来，以一个数字来表示。实际上，它就是假设一个妇女在整个育龄期都按照某一年的年龄别生育率生育，她所生育孩子的总数，即平均每个妇女在育龄期生育的孩子数。

总负担系数　指14岁及以下少年儿童人口数和65岁及以上老年人口数与15-64岁劳动力年龄人口数的比例。表明的是每百名劳动年龄人口负担多少非劳动年龄人口。计算公式：

总负担系数 =〔（14岁及以下人数 +65岁及以上人数）/15-64岁人数〕×100%

劳动力资源　指在劳动年龄内，具有劳动能力，在正常情况下，可能或实际参加社会劳动的总人口数。具体的范围是：劳动年龄内（16周岁及以上），有劳动能力、实际参加社会劳动和未参加社会劳动的人员。

社会从业人员　是指在劳动年龄内，有劳动能力，参加社会劳动取得劳动报酬或经营收入的人员。具体指城镇单位从业人员，乡镇企业从业人员，乡村农林牧渔劳动者，私营、个体雇员，私营、个体雇主以及其他从业人员。从空间范围上讲社会从业人员既包括城镇中的从业人员，又包括乡村中的从业人员。

城镇单位从业人员　是指在各级国家机关、政党机关、社会团体、事业单位以及城镇范围内的各类企业中工作，并取得劳动报酬的全部人员。包括在岗职工和其他从业人员，但不包括不在岗职工。

城镇私营和个体从业人员　城镇私营从业人员指在工商管理部门注册登记，其经营地址设在县城关镇（含城关镇）以上的私营企业从业人员；包括私营企业投资者和雇工。城镇个体从业人员指在工商管理部门注册登记，并持有城镇户口或在城镇长期居住，经批准从事个体工商经营的从业人员；包括个体经营者和在个体工商户劳动的家庭帮工和雇工。

在岗职工　是指调查时期（时点）在单位工作并领取工资的职工。具体是指那些与本单位签有劳动合同或在本单位在册，并在本单位从事有报酬的劳动人员，在岗职工还包括单位派出学习、工作及病伤产假（六个月内）且仍在单位支付劳动报酬的人员。

主要统计指标解释

单位其他从业人员 劳动统计规定不作在岗职工统计，但实际参加各单位生产或工作并取得劳动报酬的人员。包括再就业的离退休人员、民办教师、在各单位工作的港、澳、台、外籍人员、聘用的外单位不在岗人员、聘用的失业人员、聘用和使用的外来人员、聘用的其他人员以及在本单位从事第二职业的外单位人员，但不包括在单位中工作并领取报酬的在校学生。

城镇登记失业人员 指有非农业户口，在一定的劳动年龄（16 岁至退休年龄）内，有劳动能力，无业且要求就业，并在当地劳动保障机构进行求职登记的人员。

城镇登记失业率 报告期末城镇登记失业人数占期末从业人员总数与期末实有城镇登记失业人数之和的比重。计算公式：

城镇登记失业率＝〔期末实有城镇登记失业人数 /（期末从业人员总数＋期末实有城镇登记失业人数）〕×100%

法定婚龄、劳龄人口 我国进入婚龄法定人口标准为男 22 岁、女 20 岁；进入劳龄人口、劳动年龄内人口、退出劳龄人口的国内标准分别是男 16 岁、16-59 岁、60 岁和女 16 岁、16-54 岁、55 岁；国际标准男女均为 15 岁、15-64 岁、65 岁。

城乡划分标准 根据国家统计局 2006[60] 号文件中《关于统计上划分城乡的暂行规定》，新的城乡划分标准为：城镇是指在我国市镇建制和行政区划的基础上，经该规定划定的区域，包括城区和镇区。城区是指在市辖区和不设区的市中，经该规定划定的区域。镇区是指在城区以外的镇和其他区域中，经该规定划定的区域。乡村是指该规定划定的城镇以外的其他区域。

2006 年人口抽样调查资料说明 2006 年人口抽样调查登记的标准时点为 2006 年 11 月 1 日零时；调查样本采取分层、多阶段、整群、概率比例的抽样方法，在全市 18 个区县中，抽取了 199 个街（乡、镇）级行政单位的 391 个居（村）委会和 780 个调查小区，其样本量为 8 万人，占全市总人口的 0.74%，实际调查登记了 2.39 万户、7.88 万人。表 3-11 至 3-14 为这次调查加权汇总数据。

劳务人才市场交易情况 劳务人才市场是指劳动力供求双方实现劳务交换和劳动力流动的场所。主要反映进场单位数、进场人次、达成意向人次等情况。

Explanastory Notes on Main Statistical Indicators

Permanent Resident Population refers to the total number of people alive at a given area within a period (over half a year). According to the regulation of population census and sample survey, permanent resident population include (a) registered population in this area except those who have left this area over half a year (exclude those going abroad to work or study). (b) population with residence registered in other area, but having actually resided in this area over half a year or having left place of residence registration over half a year and resided in this area during the period of population survey.(c) population with residence registration in this enumeration area not yet settled, i.e. residence card on hand, migration certificate, birth certificate, demobilized soldier card, release certificate, etc.

Registered Population refers to the population with registered in accordance with the regulation of the People's Republic of China on the Management of Registration Residence in public security organs in this area. No matter he is out or not, how long the time is, which is often expressed in.

Population Density refers to the total number of people within unit land area. Usually, population density is calculated using permanent resident population and indicates crowd degree of population. It is often expressed in the number of people per square kilometer. The following formula is used :

Population Density=(permanent resident population)/(Total Area of Land)

Birth Rate refers to the ratio of the number of births to the average population during a certain period of time, usually using a year as unit for calculation, which is often expressed in ‰ and indicates the alive births per 1000 persons. The following formula is used

Birth Rate=(Number of Births)/(Annual Average Number of Population)×1000‰

Death Rate refers to the ratio of the number of deaths to the average population during a certain period of time, usually using a year as unit for calculation, which is often expressed in ‰ and indicates the deaths per 1000 persons. The following formula is used

Death Rate=(Number of Deaths)/(Annual Average Number of Population)×1000‰

Natural Growth Rate of Population refers to the ratio of natural increase in population (number of births minus number of deaths) in a certain period of time to the average population of the same period, usually using a year as unit for calculation, which is often expressed in ‰. The following formula is used :

Natural Growth Rate of Population=(Number of Births-Number of Deaths)/(Annual Average Number of Population)×1000‰

Natural Growth Rate of Population=Birth Rate-Death Rate

Total of Birth Rate refers to the total of birth rate of women aged 15-49 during a certain period of time, which is expressed in a data. It actually refers to the number of children of average woman aged 15-49.

Gross Dependency Coefficient refers to the ratio of children aged 0-14 and elderly population aged 65 and over to the working-age population aged 15-64.It describes in general the number of non-working-age population that every 100 people at working ages will take care of. The following formula is used:

Gross Dependency Coefficient=[(population aged 0-14)+(population aged 65 and over)]/(population aged 15-64)×100%

Labour Force Resources refer to the number of population at working ages (aged 16 and over) who have capacity for physical labor, have engaged in social labor or not.

Social Employment Personnel refer to the persons aged 16 and over who are engaged in social labor and receive remuneration payment or earn business income, including employment personnel worked in units in urban areas, employment personnel worked in township enterprises, rural labor engaged in farming, forestry, animal husbandry and fishery, employees in private enterprises and individual economy, employers of private enterprises and individual economy and other employment personnel. Social employment personnel not only include those in urban areas, also include those in rural areas.

Persons Employed in Urban Units refer to all the persons working in government agencies of various levels, political and party organizations, social organizations, enterprises and institutions, and receiving remuneration payment. They include on-post staff and workers and other employment personnel in various units, but exclude staff and workers who have left their working units.

Persons Employed in Private Enterprises and Individual Economy in Urban Areas Persons employed in private enterprises refer to the persons employed in the private enterprises which have been registered at the departments of industrial and commercial administration and are situated at a town (i.e. at own where the county government is located) for business operation or at urban areas with the level higher than a county town. The individual economy in

Explanastory Notes on Main Statistical Indicators

urban areas refer to persons who hold the certificates of residence in urban areas or have resided in the urban areas for a long time and have been registered at the departments of industrial and commercial administration and approved to be engaged in individual industrial or commercial business, including self-employed persons as well as helpers and hired laborers who work in the individual households engaged in industrial or commercial business.

On-post Staff and Workers refer to staff and workers who work in and receive wages from their working units during a survey period. They include the persons who have signed working contracts with units or registered in units, also include those receive wages from units but are temporarily absent from work for reasons of study, work or on sick, injury or maternal leave no more than six months.

Other Persons Employed in Various Units refer to the numbers receiving wages or other forms of payment, include re-employed retirees, teachers in schools run by the local people, foreigners and Chinese compatriots from Hong Kong, Macao, and Taiwan working in various units, employees of other units working temporarily at current posts, unemployment personnel, non-locals, and employees holding the second job of other units, exclude students enrolled in universities and colleges who work at the units and receive wages.

Registered Urban Unemployed Persons refer to the persons who are registered as permanent residents in the urban areas engaged in non-agricultural activities, aged within the range of working age (16-retired age), capable to labor, unemployed but desirous to be employed and have been registered at the local employment service agencies to apply for a job.

Registered Urban Unemployment Rate refers to the ratio of the number of the registered unemployed persons to the sum of the number of employed persons and the registered unemployed persons. The formula is as follows
Registered urban unemployment rate=number of urban registered unemployed persons/ (urban employed persons + number of registered urban unemployed persons)×100%

Legal Marriage Age, Labor Age Population The standard of legal marriage age is 22 for male and 20 for female the domestic standard of "reaching labor age", "within labor age" and "over labor age" are 16,16 to 59,60 for male respectively and 16,16 to 54,55 for female respectively the international standard of these items are 15,15-64 and 65 respectively for both male and female.

The Division Standard of Urban and Rural Areas According to <The Temporary Regulation on The Division of Urban and Rural Areas in Statistics > of National Bureau of Statistics 2006 [60], The new division standard of Urban and Rural Areas is as follow: Urban Area refers to the areas defined by the temporary regulation on the base of administrative divisions, including city and township. City refers to the areas in the districts of city and the city without districts, which defined by the temporary regulation. Township refers to the towns outside city zones and other areas, which defined by the temporary regulation. Rural areas refer to the other areas besides urban areas defined by the temporary regulation.

Brief introduction for Sample Survey on Population in 2006 The reference time of 2006 sample survey was zero o'clock of November 1,2006. The sample survey was conducted with a multi-stage systematic cluster-sampling scheme. A total of 80 thousand people, which take 0.74% of total population in Tianjin, were selected as the sample from 780 areas in 391 resident's committees & village committees in 199 streets (towns) of 18 districts (counties). The exact sample of registration is 78.8 thousand people from 23.9 thousand households. From Table 3-11 to Table 3-14,data were calculated by the weighted sum method.

Employees Supply and Demand Dealings Market It is often known as an office to which employees made an application for having been either supplied or demanded daily. The principal datum there of are including numbers of the market entrance-making sectors or enterprises, of employees suppliers and demanders registered together with their agreements to have been reached between them.

第4篇
CHAPTER 4

固定资产投资和房地产
Investment in Fixed Assets and Real Estate

4-1 全社会固定资产投资(1990-2006年)
TOTAL INVESTMENT IN FIXED ASSETS, 1990-2006

单位：亿元 (100 million yuan)

年 份 Year	全社会固定资产投资 Total Investment in Fixed Assets	国有经济 State-owned	集体经济 Collective -owned	# 农村非农户 Rural Non-agricultural	个体经济 Individuals	# 农村农户 Rural Agricultural
总 计 Total						
1990	87.69	72.18	10.56	9.48	4.95	4.36
1991	128.95	109.69	12.18	10.84	7.08	6.68
1992	169.88	137.81	25.21	23.59	6.86	6.08
1993	226.56	187.83	30.51	27.34	8.22	6.36
1994	315.97	265.32	40.14	36.98	10.51	8.51
1995	393.18	324.20	58.65	46.52	10.33	9.36
1996	435.81	351.59	66.67	57.35	17.55	15.28
1997	498.66	422.84	61.77	52.39	14.05	10.63
1998	575.86	491.87	68.39	56.70	15.60	12.45
1999	567.36	488.45	61.59	49.00	17.32	11.50
2000	608.80	526.20	61.80	56.47	20.80	13.10
2001	705.10	612.50	66.10	61.50	26.50	16.40
2002	811.26	695.75	85.90	74.00	29.61	20.01
2003	1046.72	919.59	98.04	89.73	29.09	22.86
2004	1258.98	1114.98	109.72	99.06	34.28	27.20
2005	1516.84	1364.07	123.34	101.85	29.43	29.29
2006	1849.80	1678.70	141.10	110.14	30.00	30.00
# 地 方 Local Investment						
1990	57.47	41.96	10.56	9.48	4.95	4.36
1991	93.13	73.87	12.18	10.84	7.08	6.68
1992	123.85	91.78	25.21	23.59	6.86	6.08
1993	176.14	137.41	30.51	27.34	8.22	6.36
1994	256.88	206.23	40.14	36.98	10.51	8.51
1995	309.75	240.77	58.65	46.52	10.33	9.36
1996	325.71	241.49	66.67	57.35	17.55	15.28
1997	376.69	300.87	61.77	52.39	14.05	10.63
1998	452.11	368.12	68.39	56.70	15.60	12.45
1999	405.31	326.40	61.59	49.00	17.32	11.50
2000	463.83	381.23	61.80	56.47	20.80	13.10
2001	567.40	474.80	66.10	61.50	26.50	16.40
2002	677.60	562.09	85.90	74.00	29.61	20.01
2003	893.73	766.60	98.04	89.73	29.09	22.86
2004	1067.91	923.91	109.72	99.06	34.28	27.20
2005	1288.85	1136.08	123.34	101.85	29.43	29.29
2006	1523.01	1360.45	132.56	110.14	30.00	30.00

注：本表国有经济中包括"三资"、股份制、联营、私营经济。以下各表同。

Note: State-owned units of this table include foreign funded economic units, share holding economic units, joint ownership economic units and private economic units. Same as following tables.

4-2 全社会新增固定资产(1990-2006年) TOTAL NEWLY INCREASED FIXED ASSETS, 1990-2006

单位：亿元 (100 million yuan)

年份 Year	全社会新增固定资产 Total Newly Increased Fixed Assets	国有经济 State-owned	集体经济 Collective-owned	#农村非农户 Rural Non-agricultural	个体经济 Individuals	#农村农户 Rural Agricultural
总计 Total						
1990	65.16	49.66	10.55	9.55	4.95	4.36
1991	74.11	54.99	12.03	10.85	7.09	6.68
1992	102.27	73.24	22.17	21.26	6.86	6.08
1993	140.00	105.82	25.96	24.11	8.22	6.36
1994	261.12	216.98	33.63	32.36	10.51	8.51
1995	300.86	247.08	43.45	40.19	10.33	9.36
1996	313.12	246.63	48.94	41.61	17.55	15.28
1997	320.46	259.08	47.33	41.76	14.05	10.63
1998	439.58	379.21	44.77	42.54	15.60	12.45
1999	459.54	383.73	58.49	47.78	17.32	11.50
2000	434.28	372.48	50.48	46.15	11.32	7.140
2001	476.92	385.67	64.75	61.00	26.50	16.40
2002	537.98	427.98	80.39	71.14	29.61	20.01
2003	656.99	534.66	96.66	87.03	25.67	22.86
2004	696.56	567.65	98.46	92.64	30.45	27.20
2005	847.79	711.58	109.26	95.97	26.95	26.81
2006	1423.73	1255.52	138.21	110.14	30.00	30.00
#地方 Local Investment						
1990	49.46	33.96	10.55	9.55	4.95	4.36
1991	47.38	28.26	12.03	10.85	7.09	6.68
1992	69.15	40.12	22.17	21.26	6.86	6.08
1993	93.59	59.41	25.96	24.11	8.22	6.36
1994	244.01	199.87	33.63	32.36	10.51	8.51
1995	218.06	164.28	43.45	40.19	10.33	9.36
1996	241.66	175.17	48.94	41.61	17.55	15.28
1997	243.63	182.25	47.33	41.76	14.05	10.63
1998	351.27	290.90	44.77	42.54	15.60	12.45
1999	353.35	277.54	58.49	47.78	17.32	11.50
2000	350.97	289.17	50.48	46.15	11.32	7.140
2001	356.46	263.86	66.10	61.50	26.50	16.40
2002	434.61	324.61	80.39	71.14	29.61	20.01
2003	543.59	421.26	96.66	87.03	25.67	22.86
2004	522.43	393.52	98.46	92.64	30.45	27.20
2005	727.65	591.44	109.26	95.97	26.95	26.81
2006	1223.30	1063.64	129.66	110.14	30.00	30.00

4-3 全社会固定资产投资和房屋建筑面积
TOTAL INVESTMENT IN FIXED ASSETS AND FLOOR SPACE OF BUILDINGS

指　标	Item	2004	2005	2006	2006比2005年增长(%) Increase Rate in 2006 over 2005 (%)
投资总额(亿元)	**Total Investment (100 million yuan)**	**1258.98**	**1516.84**	**1849.80**	**22.0**
按经济类型分	**Grouped by Ownership**				
国有经济	State-owned	1114.98	1364.07	1678.70	23.1
集体经济	Collective-owned	109.72	123.34	141.10	14.4
# 农村非农户	Rural Non-agricultural	99.06	101.85	110.14	8.1
个体经济	Individuals	34.28	29.43	30.00	1.9
# 农村农户	Rural Agricultural	27.2	29.29	30.00	2.4
按隶属关系分	**Grouped by Administrative Relationship**				
中　央	Central Government	191.07	227.99	326.79	43.3
地　方	Local Government	1067.91	1288.85	1523.01	18.2
按城乡分	**By Urban and Rural**				
城镇投资	Urban Investment	1132.33	1385.56	1709.66	23.4
# 房地产开发	Real Estate Development	263.92	327.54	402.32	22.8
农村投资	Rural Investment	126.26	131.14	140.14	6.9
按构成分	**Grouped by Use of Funds**				
建筑工程	Construction	690.33	852.6	1006.09	18.0
安装工程	Installation	61.76	75.59	113.26	49.8
设备工器具购置	Purchases of Equipment and Instruments	282.48	316.1	394.28	24.7
其他费用	Others	224.41	272.55	336.17	23.3
按三次产业分	**Grouped by Industry**				
第一产业	Primary Industry	11.55	13.71	16.04	17.0
第二产业	Secondary Industry	501.7	614.63	765.49	24.5
第三产业	Tertiary Industry	745.73	888.5	1068.27	20.2
房屋建筑面积(万平方米)	**Floor Space of Buildings (10 000 sq. m)**				
施工面积	Floor Space Under Construction	5242.05	6295.19	7248.78	15.1
# 住　宅	Residential Buildings	3439.04	3450.97	4048.30	17.3
竣工面积	Floor Space Completed	2353.92	2863.36	2960.32	3.4
# 住　宅	Residential Buildings	1428.39	1662.53	1726.71	3.9

4-4 按行业分全社会固定资产投资
TOTAL INVESTMENT IN FIXED ASSETS GROUPED BY SECTOR

单位：万元 (10 000 yuan)

行 业 Sector	2005	2006	2006比2005年增长(%) Increase Rate in 2006 over 2005 (%)
总 计 Total	**15168404**	**18497987**	**22.0**
农、林、牧、渔业 Farming, Forestry, Animal Husbandry and Fishery	137077	160392	17.0
采矿业 Minerals Mining	1243053	1828278	47.1
制造业 Manufacturing	4178023	4817537	15.3
电力、燃气及水的生产和供应业 Production & Supply of Power, Gas and Water	577491	838526	45.2
建筑业 Construction	147804	170512	15.4
交通运输、仓储和邮政业 Transportation, Storage and Post Services	1722811	2117386	22.9
信息传输、计算机服务和软件业 Information Transmitting, Computer Services and Software	265065	271309	2.4
批发和零售业 Wholesale and Retail Trade	274144	268414	-2.1
住宿和餐饮业 Accommodation and Catering Services	57925	81874	41.3
金融业 Finance Intermediation	5841	1173	-79.9
房地产业 Real Estate	3718385	4573036	23.0
租赁和商务服务业 Leasing and Business Services	59873	121342	102.7
科学研究、技术服务和地质勘查业 Scientific Research, Technical Services and Geological Prospecting	46199	22456	-51.4
水利、环境和公共设施管理业 Management for Water Conservancy, Environment and Public Facilities	1798851	2188194	21.6
居民服务和其他服务业 Resident Services and Other Social Services	60222	76256	26.6
教 育 Education	404478	413713	2.3
卫生、社会保障和社会福利业 Health Care, Social Security and Social Welfare	95672	139106	45.4
文化、体育和娱乐业 Culture, Sports and Recreational Services	147388	167148	13.4
公共管理和社会组织 Public Management and Social Organizations	228102	241335	5.8

4-5 全市固定资产投资及新增固定资产
MUNICIPAL INVESTMENT IN FIXED ASSETS AND NEWLY INCREASED FIXED ASSETS

单位：万元 (10 000 yuan)

项　目	Item	2005	2006	2006比2005年增长(%) Increase Rate in 2006 over 2005 (%)
固定资产投资	**Total Investment in Fixed Assets**	**13855642**	**17096567**	**23.4**
按三次产业分	**Grouped by Industry**			
第一产业	Primary Industry	50472	33840	-33.0
第二产业	Secondary Industry	5429365	7018329	29.3
#工　业	Industry	5323543	6903357	29.7
第三产业	Tertiary Industry	8375805	10044398	19.9
按隶属关系分	**Grouped by Administrative Relationship**			
中　央	Central Government	2279888	3267865	43.3
地　方	Local Government	11575754	13828702	19.5
按建设性质分	**Grouped by Type of Construction**			
#新　建	New Construction	5906967	8107851	37.3
改、扩建及其他	Expansion, Reconstruction and Others	4673272	4965532	6.3
按构成分	**Grouped by Use of Funds**			
建筑工程	Construction	7876445	9355628	18.8
安装工程	Installation	710873	1083887	52.5
设备工器具购置	Purchases of Equipment and Instruments	2660897	3405465	28.0
其他费用	Others	2607427	3251587	24.7
按登记注册类型分	**Grouped by Registered Status**			
内资企业	Domestic-funded Enterprises	11723920	14210480	21.2
国有企业	State-owned Enterprises	4229851	5762904	36.2
集体企业	Collective-owned Enterprises	190026	265754	39.9
股份合作企业	Cooperative Enterprises	130828	106856	-18.3
私　营	Private Enterprises	1383094	1388885	0.4
股份有限公司	Share Holding Corporations Ltd.	1666833	3335708	100.1
有限责任公司	Limited Liability Corporations	3802831	3080017	-19.0
#国有独资	Sole State-funded Corporations	1940401	1178453	-39.3
联营企业	Joint Ownership Enterprises	122206	73763	-39.6
#国有与国有联营企业	State Joint Ownership Enterprises	99593	64918	-34.8
集体与集体联营企业	Collective Joint Ownership Enterprises	4313	6285	45.7
其他内资企业	Other Domestic-funded Enterprises	198251	196593	-0.8
港澳台商投资企业	Enterprises with Investment from Hong Kong, Macao and Taiwan	496515	540484	8.9
外商投资企业	Foreign Funded Enterprises	1616264	2344893	45.1
个体经济	Individuals	18943	710	-96.3
新增固定资产	**Newly Increased Fixed Assets**	**7233152**	**12680334**	**75.3**
第一产业	Primary Industry	41660	22390	-46.3
第二产业	Secondary Industry	2920481	5801706	98.7
#工　业	Industry	2867340	5728786	99.8
第三产业	Tertiary Industry	4271011	6856238	60.5
固定资产交付使用率(%)	**Rate of Fixed Assets Put into Use (%)**	**52.2**	**74.2**	

注：1. 全市固定资产投资为城镇口径，不含农村非农户和农户的投资，4-13、4-14表同。2. 表中按建设性质分组数据不含房地产开发投资。
Note: a) Municipal investment in fixed assets refers to urban data, excluding rural non-agricultural and agricultural households. Same as following tables 4-13 and 4-14. b) Investment grouped by type of construction of this table excludes real estate development.

4-6 按行业分全市固定资产投资
MUNICIPAL INVESTMENT IN FIXED ASSETS BY SECTOR

单位：万元 (10 000 yuan)

行业 Sector	2005	2006	2006 比2005年增长(%) Increase Rate in 2006 over 2005 (%)
总计 Total	**13855642**	**17096567**	**23.4**
农、林、牧、渔业 Farming, Forestry, Animal Husbandry and Fishery	50472	33840	-33.0
采矿业 Minerals Mining	1243053	1828278	47.1
制造业 Manufacturing	3502999	4236553	20.9
电力、燃气及水的生产和供应业 Production & Supply of Power, Gas and Water	577491	838526	45.2
建筑业 Construction	105822	114972	8.6
交通运输、仓储和邮政业 Transportation, Storage and Post Services	1678371	2039652	21.5
信息传输、计算机服务和软件业 Information Transmitting, Computer Services and Software	264845	271124	2.4
批发和零售业 Wholesale and Retail Trade	233653	231822	-0.8
住宿和餐饮业 Accommodation and Catering Services	48426	72829	50.4
金融业 Finance Intermediation	5841	1173	-79.9
房地产业 Real Estate	3394727	4142624	22.0
租赁和商务服务业 Leasing and Business Services	48753	112003	129.7
科学研究、技术服务和地质勘查业 Scientific Research, Technical Services and Geological Prospecting	46199	22456	-51.4
水利、环境和公共设施管理业 Management for Water Conservancy, Environment and Public Facilities	1786977	2177124	21.8
居民服务和其他服务业 Resident Services and Other Social Services	18385	39139	112.9
教育 Education	394620	405433	2.7
卫生、社会保障和社会福利业 Health Care, Social Security and Social Welfare	92424	136379	47.6
文化、体育和娱乐业 Culture, Sports and Recreational Services	141542	157234	11.1
公共管理和社会组织 Public Management and Social Organizations	221042	235406	6.5

4-7 按制造业主要行业分全市固定资产投资
MUNICIPAL INVESTMENT IN FIXED ASSETS OF MAIN MANUFACTURING

单位：万元 (10 000 yuan)

行业	Sector	2005	2006	2006比2005年增长(%) Increase Rate in 2006 over 2005 (%)
总计	**Total**	**3502999**	**4236553**	**20.9**
#农副食品加工业	Processing of Food from Agricultural Products	90764	36586	-59.7
食品制造业	Manufacture of Foods	64945	81805	26.0
饮料制造业	Manufacture of Beverages	46857	63883	36.3
纺织业	Manufacture of Textile	163631	96722	-40.9
纺织服装、鞋、帽制造业	Manufacture of Textile Wearing Apparel, Footware and Caps	41363	13114	-68.3
皮革、皮毛、羽毛及其制品业	Manufacture of Leather, Fur, Feather and Related Products	7729	14050	81.8
木材加工及木、竹、藤、棕、草制品业	Processing of Timber, Manufacture of Wood, Bamboo, Rattan, Palm and Straw Products	4028	1578	-60.8
家具制造业	Manufacture of Furniture	25843	28141	8.9
造纸及纸制品业	Manufacture of Paper and Paper Products	14741	28234	91.5
印刷和记录媒介的复制	Printing, Reproduction of Recording Media	19448	27115	39.4
文教体育用品制造业	Manufacture of Articles for Culture, Education and Sport Activity	12762	15341	20.2
石油加工、炼焦及核燃料加工	Processing of Petroleum, Coking, Processing of Nuclear Fuel	83060	143491	72.8
化学原料及化学制品制造业	Manufacture of Raw Chemical Materials and Chemical Products	256040	406263	58.7
医药制造业	Manufacture of Medicines	118674	94313	-20.5
化学纤维制造业	Manufacture of Chemical Fibers	7240	1	-100.0
橡胶制品业	Manufacture of Rubber	68075	124902	83.5
塑料制品业	Manufacture of Plastics	113249	110099	-2.8
非金属矿物制品业	Manufacture of Non-metallic Mineral Products	116501	120489	3.4
黑色金属冶炼及压延加工业	Smelting and Pressing of Ferrous Metals	826155	938461	13.6
有色金属冶炼及压延加工业	Smelting and Pressing of Non-Ferrous Metals	21628	40959	89.4
金属制品业	Manufacture of Metal Products	132857	136264	2.6
通用设备制造业	Manufacture of General Purpose Machinery	155789	196470	26.1
专用设备制造业	Manufacture of Special Purpose Machinery	125804	155943	24.0
交通运输设备制造业	Manufacture of Transport Equipment	397093	645824	62.6
电气机械及器材制造业	Manufacture of Electrical Machinery and Equipment	102206	189234	85.1
通信设备、计算机及其他电子设备制造业	Manufacture of Communication Equipment,Computers and Other Electronic Equipment	450622	469240	4.1
仪器仪表及文化、办公用机械制造业	Manufacture of Measuring Instruments and Machinery for Cultural Activity and Office Work	26872	31994	19.1

4-8 按行业分全市新增固定资产
MUNICIPAL NEWLY INCREASED FIXED ASSETS BY SECTOR

单位：万元 (10 000 yuan)

行　业　Sector	2005	2006	2006 比2005年 增长(%) Increase Rate in 2006 over 2005 (%)
总　计 Total	**7233152**	**12680334**	**75.3**
农、林、牧、渔业 Farming, Forestry, Animal Husbandry and Fishery	41660	22390	-46.3
采矿业 Minerals Mining	716585	1535368	114.3
制造业 Manufacturing	1865570	3758398	101.5
电力、燃气及水的生产和供应业 Production & Supply of Power, Gas and Water	285185	435020	52.5
建筑业 Construction	53141	72920	37.2
交通运输、仓储和邮政业 Transportation, Storage and Post Services	660215	1182775	79.1
信息传输、计算机服务和软件业 Information Transmitting, Computer Services and Software	127659	91801	-28.1
批发和零售业 Wholesale and Retail Trade	132891	239126	79.9
住宿和餐饮业 Accommodation and Catering Services	13092	65416	399.7
金融业 Finance Intermediation	5841	1013	-82.7
房地产业 Real Estate	2704969	4008336	48.2
租赁和商务服务业 Leasing and Business Services	6634	42820	545.5
科学研究、技术服务和地质勘查业 Scientific Research, Technical Services and Geological Prospecting	14929	8083	-45.9
水利、环境和公共设施管理业 Management for Water Conservancy, Environment and Public Facilities	284966	545526	91.4
居民服务和其他服务业 Resident Services and Other Social Services	4800	22470	368.1
教　育 Education	152792	256837	68.1
卫生、社会保障和社会福利业 Health Care, Social Security and Social Welfare	102374	104195	1.8
文化、体育和娱乐业 Culture, Sports and Recreational Services	3755	134268	3475.7
公共管理和社会组织 Public Management and Social Organizations	56094	153572	173.8

4-9 按制造业主要行业分全市新增固定资产 MUNICIPAL NEWLY INCREASED FIXED ASSETS OF MAIN MANUFACTURING

单位：万元 (10 000 yuan)

行业	Sector	2005	2006	2006比2005年增长(%) Increase Rate in 2006 over 2005 (%)
总计	**Total**	**1865570**	**3758398**	**101.5**
#农副食品加工业	Processing of Food from Agricultural Products	37097	31920	-14.0
食品制造业	Manufacture of Foods	30634	76636	150.2
饮料制造业	Manufacture of Beverages	11120	94501	749.8
纺织业	Manufacture of Textile	35470	168735	375.7
纺织服装、鞋、帽制造业	Manufacture of Textile Wearing Apparel, Footware and Caps	36003	10485	-70.9
皮革、皮毛、羽毛及其制品业	Manufacture of Leather, Fur, Feather and Related Products	829	2500	201.6
木材加工及木、竹、藤、棕、草制品业	Processing of Timber, Manufacture of Wood, Bamboo, Rattan, Palm and Straw Products	9639	472	-95.1
家具制造业	Manufacture of Furniture	8777	14970	70.6
造纸及纸制品业	Manufacture of Paper and Paper Products	7280	26756	267.5
印刷和记录媒介的复制	Printing, Reproduction of Recording Media	11518	15438	34.0
文教体育用品制造业	Manufacture of Articles for Culture, Education and Sport Activity	4500	6715	49.2
石油加工、炼焦及核燃料加工	Processing of Petroleum, Coking, Processing of Nuclear Fuel	48662	74880	53.9
化学原料及化学制品制造业	Manufacture of Raw Chemical Materials and Chemical Products	97191	182042	87.3
医药制造业	Manufacture of Medicines	72887	79473	9.0
化学纤维制造业	Manufacture of Chemical Fibers	4280		
橡胶制品业	Manufacture of Rubber	13675	119576	774.4
塑料制品业	Manufacture of Plastics	76807	117231	52.6
非金属矿物制品业	Manufacture of Non-metallic Mineral Products	71742	140543	95.9
黑色金属冶炼及压延加工业	Smelting and Pressing of Ferrous Metals	619942	1465894	136.5
有色金属冶炼及压延加工业	Smelting and Pressing of Non-Ferrous Metals	10535	31259	196.7
金属制品业	Manufacture of Metal Products	62437	126244	102.2
通用设备制造业	Manufacture of General Purpose Machinery	81257	146873	80.8
专用设备制造业	Manufacture of Special Purpose Machinery	54430	122925	125.8
交通运输设备制造业	Manufacture of Transport Equipment	182401	147457	-19.2
电气机械及器材制造业	Manufacture of Electrical Machinery and Equipment	56903	89283	56.9
通信设备、计算机及其他电子设备制造业	Manufacture of Communication Equipment,Computers and Other Electronic Equipment	202825	412639	103.4
仪器仪表及文化、办公用机械制造业	Manufacture of Measuring Instruments and Machinery for Cultural Activity and Office Work	11171	30264	170.9

4-10 全市固定资产投资资金来源
SOURCE OF FUNDS FOR MUNICIPAL INVESTMENT IN FIXED ASSETS

单位：万元 (10 000 yuan)

项　目	Item	2005	2006	2006 比2005年增长(%) Increase Rate in 2006 over 2005 (%)
资金来源合计	**Total Funds**	**18706157**	**23303457**	**24.6**
上年末结余资金	Balance of Funds Brought Forward from The Previous Year	1595826	1897210	18.9
本年资金来源小计	Subtotal of The Sources of Funds in Current Year	17110331	21406247	25.1
国家预算内资金	State Budgetary Appropriation	311579	234157	-24.8
国内贷款	Domestic Loans	4227194	5341054	26.3
债　券	Bonds		78469	
利用外资	Foreign Investment	1137705	1504615	32.3
# 外商直接投资	Foreign Direct Investment	1046214	823153	-21.3
自筹资金	Fundraising	8322423	10427108	25.3
# 企、事业单位自有资金	Owned by Enterprises and Institutions	6333895	7927731	25.2
其他资金	Others	3111430	3820844	22.8

4-11 全市施工和竣工房屋建筑面积
MUNICIPAL FLOOR SPACE OF BUILDINGS UNDER CONSTRUCTION AND COMPLETED

单位:：平方米 (10 000 sq. m)

项　目	Item	2005	2006	2006 比2005年增长(%) Increase Rate in 2006 over 2005 (%)
全市房屋建筑施工面积	**Floor Space of Buildings under Construction**	**5210.19**	**6134.1**	**17.7**
# 房地产开发企业	Real Estate Development	3470.57	4142.6	19.4
# 住宅施工面积	Residential Buildings	2896.83	3459.18	19.4
# 房地产开发企业	Real Estate Development	2827.87	3396.45	20.1
全市房屋建筑竣工面积	**Floor Space of Buildings Completed**	**2023.09**	**2098.05**	**3.7**
# 房地产开发企业	Real Estate Development	1479.22	1520.24	2.8
# 住宅竣工面积	Residential Buildings	1305.08	1333.01	2.1
# 房地产开发企业	Real Estate Development	1270.96	1308.95	3.0

注：房屋竣工面积不含农村非农户和农户建房数。
Note: Floor space of buildings completed exclude rural non-agricultural and agricultural houses.

4-12 按行业分全市固定资产投资资金来源（2006年）
SOURCE OF FUNDS FOR MUNICIPAL INVESTMENT IN FIXED ASSETS BY SECTOR, 2006

行业 Sector	资金来源合计 Total Funds	上年末结余资金 Balance of Funds Brought Forward From The Previous Year	本年资金来源小计 Subtotal of the Sources of Funds in Current Year
总计 Total	**23303457**	**1897210**	**21406247**
农、林、牧、渔业 Farming, Forestry, Animal Husbandry and Fishery	36646	3359	33287
采矿业 Minerals Mining	1924309		1924309
制造业 Manufacturing	4505208	123228	4381980
电力、燃气及水的生产和供应业 Production & Supply of Power, Gas and Water	906553	8858	897695
建筑业 Construction	116972	794	116178
交通运输、仓储和邮政业 Transportation, Storage and Post Services	2252793	4931	2247862
信息传输、计算机服务和软件业 Information Transmitting, Computer Services and Software	278455	5986	272469
批发和零售业 Wholesale and Retail Trade	240514	14243	226271
住宿和餐饮业 Accommodation and Catering Services	72640	2211	70429
金融业 Finance Intermediation	1199		1199
房地产业 Real Estate	9240358	1460750	7779608
租赁和商务服务业 Leasing and Business Services	101479	2500	98979
科学研究、技术服务和地质勘查业 Scientific Research, Technical Services and Geological Prospecting	25126	471	24655
水利、环境和公共设施管理业 Management for Water Conservancy, Environment and Public Facilities	2485349	116352	2368997
居民服务和其他服务业 Resident Services and Other Social Services	42225	1848	40377
教育 Education	369535	42017	327518
卫生、社会保障和社会福利业 Health Care, Social Security and Social Welfare	204350	67428	136922
文化、体育和娱乐业 Culture, Sports and Recreational Services	179632	13256	166376
公共管理和社会组织 Public Management and Social Organizations	320114	28978	291136

单位: 万元 (10 000 yuan)

国家预算内资金 State Budgetary Appropriation	国内贷款 Domestic Loans	债　券 Bonds	利用外资 Foreign Investment	#外　商直接投资 Foreign Direct Investment	自筹资金 Fundraising	#企事业单位自有资金 Owned by Enterprises and Institutions	其他资金 Others
234157	**5341054**	**78469**	**1504615**	**823153**	**10427108**	**7927731**	**3820844**
3375	95				22927	18429	6890
	90		454410	454410	1467119	1273197	2690
1430	542933		922494	303282	2905050	2611759	10073
3202	230138		19632	15872	293818	135232	350905
20580	4000				89958	89958	1640
90514	906100	75769	27212	6000	1139342	1125691	8925
480	6732				265257	265004	
1840	28481		129	129	189503	170221	6318
	5100		1660	1660	63669	63619	
					1199	699	
	1834819		60939	30949	2596175	1482704	3287675
	96		123	123	94730	81279	4030
1500	4362				12488	12488	6305
59296	1565787	2700	11288	4000	696368	221613	33558
	300		2106	2106	37971	18920	
5212	76094		286	286	222899	162655	23027
18781	48339				62196	48591	7606
16630	23055		4336	4336	66046	27831	56309
11317	64533				200393	117841	14893

4-13 按行业分全市固定资产投资施工项目个数
NUMBER OF MUNICIPAL INVESTMENT PROJECTS UNDER CONSTRUCTION IN FIXED ASSETS BY SECTOR

单位：个 (unit)

项　目 Item	2005	2006	2006 比2005年增长(%) Increase Rate in 2006 over 2005 (%)
总　计 Total	**1770**	**1923**	**8.6**
农、林、牧、渔业 Farming, Forestry, Animal Husbandry and Fishery	58	43	-25.9
采矿业 Minerals Mining	24	32	33.3
制造业 Manufacturing	753	730	-3.1
电力、燃气及水的生产和供应业 Production & Supply of Power, Gas and Water	105	184	75.2
建筑业 Construction	23	27	17.4
交通运输、仓储和邮政业 Transportation, Storage and Post Services	78	72	-7.7
信息传输、计算机服务和软件业 Information Transmitting, Computer Services and Software	44	25	-43.2
批发和零售业 Wholesale and Retail Trade	87	95	9.2
住宿和餐饮业 Accommodation and Catering Services	24	32	33.3
金融业 Finance Intermediation		2	
房地产业 Real Estate	24	11	-54.2
租赁和商务服务业 Leasing and Business Services	17	25	47.1
科学研究、技术服务和地质勘查业 Scientific Research, Technical Services and Geological Prospecting	16	12	-25.0
水利、环境和公共设施管理业 Management for Water Conservancy, Environment and Public Facilities	254	311	22.4
居民服务和其他服务业 Resident Services and Other Social Services	8	20	150.0
教　育 Education	124	132	6.5
卫生、社会保障和社会福利业 Health Care, Social Security and Social Welfare	31	58	87.1
文化、体育和娱乐业 Culture, Sports and Recreational Services	26	34	30.8
公共管理和社会组织 Public Management and Social Organizations	74	78	5.4

4-14 按行业分全市固定资产投资建成投产项目个数
NUMBER OF MUNICIPAL INVESTMENT PROJECTS IN FIXED ASSETS COMPLETED AND PUT INTO USE BY SECTOR

单位：个 (unit)

项 目 Item	2005	2006	2006 比2005年增长(%) Increase Rate in 2006 over 2005 (%)
总 计 Total	**826**	**1085**	**31.4**
农、林、牧、渔业 Farming, Forestry, Animal Husbandry and Fishery	36	19	-47.2
采矿业 Minerals Mining	16	5	-68.8
制造业 Manufacturing	335	369	10.1
电力、燃气及水的生产和供应业 Production & Supply of Power, Gas and Water	48	85	77.1
建筑业 Construction	14	18	28.6
交通运输、仓储和邮政业 Transportation, Storage and Post Services	41	47	14.6
信息传输、计算机服务和软件业 Information Transmitting, Computer Services and Software	7	6	-14.3
批发和零售业 Wholesale and Retail Trade	55	76	38.2
住宿和餐饮业 Accommodation and Catering Services	6	24	300.0
金融业 Finance Intermediation		1	
房地产业 Real Estate	8	5	-37.5
租赁和商务服务业 Leasing and Business Services	3	10	233.3
科学研究、技术服务和地质勘查业 Scientific Research, Technical Services and Geological Prospecting	6	4	-33.3
水利、环境和公共设施管理业 Management for Water Conservancy, Environment and Public Facilities	147	236	60.5
居民服务和其他服务业 Resident Services and Other Social Services	1	17	1600.0
教 育 Education	57	80	40.4
卫生、社会保障和社会福利业 Health Care, Social Security and Social Welfare	16	31	93.8
文化、体育和娱乐业 Culture, Sports and Recreational Services	3	19	533.3
公共管理和社会组织 Public Management and Social Organizations	27	33	22.2

4-15 全市能源工业固定资产投资
MUNICIPAL INVESTMENT IN FIXED ASSETS OF ENERGY INDUSTRY

单位：万元 (10 000 yuan)

项　目	Item	2005	2006	2006 比2005年增长(%) Increase Rate in 2006 over 2005 (%)
总　计	**Total**	**1894661**	**2803922**	**48.0**
石油和天然气开采业	Petroleum and Natural Gas Extraction	1234110	1821905	47.6
电力、热力的生产和供应业	Production and Supply of Electric Power and Heating Energy	412464	702096	70.2
水的生产和供应业	Production and Supply of Water	102969	109445	6.3
燃气生产和供应业	Production and Supply of Gas	62058	26985	-56.5
石油加工、炼焦业及核燃料加工	Petroleum Processing, Coking and Nuclear Fuel Processing	83060	143491	72.8
能源投资占全市固定资产投资比重(%)	**As Percentage of Total Investment in Fixed Assets (%)**	**13.7**	**16.4**	

4-16 全市城市基础设施固定资产投资
MUNICIPAL URBAN INFRASTRUCTURE INVESTMENT IN FIXED ASSETS

单位：万元 (10 000 yuan)

项　目	Item	2005	2006	2006 比2005年增长(%) Increase Rate in 2006 over 2005 (%)
总　计	**Total**	**4208066**	**5181674**	**23.1**
交通运输、仓储和邮政业	Transportation, Storage and Post Services	1678371	2039652	21.5
电信和其他信息传输服务业	Telecommunication and Other Information Transmitting Services	263845	260795	-1.2
电力、热力的生产和供应业	Production and Supply of Electric Power and Heating Energy	412464	702096	70.2
燃气生产和供应业	Production and Supply of Gas	62058	26985	-56.5
水的生产和供应业	Production and Supply of Water	102969	109445	6.3
公共设施管理	Management for Public Facilities	1688359	2042701	21.0
城市基础设施占全市固定资产投资比重(%)	**As Percentage of Total Investment in Fixed Assets (%)**	**30.4**	**30.3**	

4-17 全市地方固定资产投资
MUNICIPAL LOCAL INVESTMENT IN FIXED ASSETS

单位：万元 (10 000 yuan)

项　目	Item	2005	2006	2006比2005年增长(%) Increase Rate in 2006 over 2005 (%)
总　计	Total	11575754	13828702	19.5
按构成分	Grouped by Use of Funds			
建筑工程	Construction	6393726	6996370	9.4
安装工程	Installation	531180	728271	37.1
设备工器具	Equipment and Instruments	2336711	3042768	30.2
其他费用	Others	2314137	3061293	32.3
按建设性质分	Grouped by Type of Construction			
新　建	New Construction	5122917	6933183	35.3
扩　建	Expansion	1398027	1158647	-17.1
改　建	Reconstruction	981039	800432	-18.4
其　他	Others	798368	913256	14.4
按行业分	Grouped by Sector			
农、林、牧、渔业	Farming, Forestry, Animal Husbandry & Fishery	50472	33840	-33.0
采矿业	Minerals Mining	8943	7703	-13.9
制造业	Manufacturing	3391942	4096505	20.8
电力、煤气及水的生产和供应业	Production & Supply of Power, Gas and Water	368289	330569	-10.2
建筑业	Construction	102040	114972	12.7
交通运输、仓储和邮政	Transportation, Storage and Post Services	1309803	1539134	17.5
信息传输、计算机服务和软件业	Information Transmitting, Computer Services and Software	10387	13799	32.8
批发和零售业	Wholesale and Retail Trade	217709	231822	6.5
住宿和餐饮业	Accommodation and Catering Services	48426	72829	50.4
金融业	Finance Intermediation		1173	
房地产业	Real Estate	3394727	4142624	22.0
租赁和商务服务业	Leasing and Business Services	48753	112003	129.7
科学研究、技术服务和地质勘查业	Scientific Research, Technical Services and Geological Prospecting	41023	20361	-50.4
水利、环境和公共设施管理业	Management for Water Conservancy, Environment and Public Facilities	1786917	2177124	21.8
居民服务和其他服务业	Resident Services and Other Social Services	18385	39139	112.9
教　育	Education	326756	371308	13.6
卫生、社会保障和社会福利业	Health Care, Social Security and Social Welfare	92424	132879	43.8
文化、体育和娱乐业	Culture, Sports and Recreational Services	141542	157054	11.0
公共管理和社会组织	Public Management and Social Organizations	217216	233864	7.7

注：表中按建设性质分组数据不包括房地产开发投资。
Note: Investment grouped by type of construction excludes real estate development.

4-18 全市房地产开发投资、建设情况（1990-2006年）
INVESTMENT AND CONSTRUCTION OF MUNICIPAL REAL ESTATE DEVELOPMENT, 1990-2006

单位：万元 (10 000 yuan)

年 份 Year	本年完成投资额 Investment Completed in Current Year	住 宅 Residential Buildings	办公楼 Office Buildings	商业营业用 Buildings for Business Use	其 他 Others
1990	24934	19589			
1991	32403	27237			
1992	45842	33994			
1993	180957	136882			
1994	256571	136627			
1995	694364	444015	86703	78455	85191
1996	715103	428672	66798	124930	94703
1997	808041	396370	86881	140582	184208
1998	1067035	630053	65161	111459	260362
1999	1169569	868972	36045	46569	217983
2000	1339294	900198	31251	71834	336011
2001	1612662	963985	45157	156497	447023
2002	1758446	1031788	75122	147244	504292
2003	2113876	1509252	77808	242564	284252
2004	2639165	1752377	157504	282388	446896
2005	3275403	2349240	119477	417449	389237
2006	4023184	3113391	237419	356585	315789

单位：万平方米 (10 000 sq. m)

年 份 Year	施工面积 Floor Space of Building under Construction	#住 宅 Residential Buildings	竣工面积 Floor Space of Building Completed	#住 宅 Residential Buildings
1990	129.71	117.3	60.79	53.03
1991	117.7	104.5	50.9	46.37
1992	185.29	157.66	64.81	55.71
1993	377.66	296.42	89.03	80.13
1994	418.46	313.11	128.08	111.43
1995	1016.95	788.22	394.75	344.58
1996	988.66	712.76	366.51	318.5
1997	1116.23	773.92	299.63	254.39
1998	1379.77	1093.69	428.74	357.17
1999	1596.67	1274.32	454.81	431.12
2000	1783	1582.15	583.51	532.63
2001	1863.48	1590.62	690.48	626.63
2002	2135.56	1746.13	746.44	673
2003	2314.43	1953.5	911.27	750.67
2004	2865.55	2352.98	1108.13	1014.46
2005	3470.57	2827.87	1479.22	1270.96
2006	4142.6	3396.45	1520.24	1308.95

4-19 全市房地产开发投资情况
MUNICIPAL INVESTMENT IN REAL ESTATE DEVELOPMENT

单位：万元 (10 000 yuan)

项　目	Item	2005	2006	2006 比2005年增长(%) Increase Rate in 2006 over 2005 (%)
本年完成投资额	**Investment Completed in Current Year**	**3275403**	**4023184**	**22.8**
按隶属关系分	**Grouped by Administrative Relationship**			
中　央	Central Government			
地　方	Local Government	3275403	4023184	22.8
按登记注册类型分	**Grouped by Registered Status**			
1. 内资企业	Domestic-funded Enterprises	3031982	3519255	16.1
国有企业	State-owned Enterprises	527458	569503	8.0
集体企业	Collective-owned Enterprises	54111	25949	-52.0
股份合作企业	Cooperative Enterprises	24911	43340	74.0
私　营	Private Enterprises	1027038	1160336	13.0
股份有限公司	Share Holding Corporations Ltd.	239426	251575	5.1
有限责任公司	Limited Liability Corporations	1091243	1398156	28.1
# 国有独资	Sole State-funded Corporations	111421	117036	5.0
联营企业	Joint Ownership Enterprises	30590	21372	-30.1
# 国有联营	State Joint Ownership Enterprises	28877	21372	-26.0
集体联营	Collective Joint Ownership Enterprises	713		-100.0
其他内资企业	Other Domestic-funded Enterprises	37205	49024	31.8
2. 港澳台商投资企	Enterprises with Investment from Hong Kong, Macao and Taiwan	124790	180522	44.7
3. 外商投资企业	Foreign Funded Enterprises	118631	323407	172.6
按构成分	**Grouped by Use of Funds**			
建筑工程	Construction	1773711	2406112	35.7
安装工程	Installation	203581	254804	25.2
设备工器具	Equipment and Instruments	51975	54786	5.4
其他费用	Others	1246136	1307482	4.9
按工程用途分	**Grouped by Use of Projects**			
住　宅	Residential Buildings	2349240	3113391	32.5
# 别墅、高档公寓	Top Grade Apartment	311449	346048	11.1
办公楼	Office Buildings	119477	237419	98.7
商业营业用房	Commerce Buildings	417449	356585	-14.6
其　他	Others	389237	315789	-18.9
本年新增固定资产	**Newly Increased Fixed Assets in Current Year**	**2659678**	**3960974**	**48.9**

4-20 全市房地产开发建设情况
CONSTRUCTION OF MUNICIPAL REAL ESTATE DEVELOPMENT

项　目	Item	2005	2006	2006 比 2005 年增长 (%) Increase Rate in 2006 over 2005 (%)
施工房屋面积(万平方米)	**Floor Space of Buildings Under Construction (10 000 sq. m)**	**3470.57**	**4142.6**	**19.4**
住　宅	Residential Buildings	2827.87	3396.45	20.1
办公楼	Office Buildings	159.19	193.21	21.4
商业营业用房	Houses for Business Use	368.41	401.17	8.9
其　他	Others	115.1	151.77	31.9
竣工房屋面积(万平方米)	**Floor Space of Buildings Completed (10 000 sq. m)**	**1479.22**	**1520.24**	**2.8**
住　宅	Residential Buildings	1270.96	1308.95	3.0
办公楼	Office Buildings	39.3	43.68	11.1
商业营业用房	Houses for Business Use	121.07	139.29	15.0
其　他	Others	47.89	28.32	-40.9
竣工房屋价值(万元)	**Value of Buildings Completed (10 000 yuan)**	**2787124**	**3537483**	**26.9**
住　宅	Residential Buildings	2174910	2934495	34.9
办公楼	Office Buildings	137296	162982	18.7
商业营业用房	Houses for Business Use	340606	375546	10.3
其　他	Others	134312	64460	-52.0
资金来源合计(万元)	**Total Funds (10 000 yuan)**	**7277942**	**9119485**	**25.3**
上年末结余资金	Balance of Funds Brought Forward from The Previous Year	1001288	1460385	45.9
本年资金来源合计	Subtotal of The Sources of Funds in Current Year	6216654	7659100	23.2
国家预算内资金	State Budgetary Appropriation			
国内贷款	Domestic Loans	1383517	1810468	30.9
债　券	Bonds			
利用外资	Foreign Investment	34895	60939	74.6
#外商直接投资	Foreign Direct Investment	27229	30949	13.7
自筹资金	Fundraising	2017535	2507418	24.3
#企、事业单位自有资金	Owned by Enterprises and Institutions	1202589	1434019	19.2
其他资金	Others	2780707	3280275	18.0

4-21 房地产销售、中介服务和物业管理情况
BASIC STATISTICS ON REAL ESTATE SALES,AGENCY SERVICES AND PROPERTY MANAGEMENT

指　标	Item	2005	2006
商品房销售情况	**Statistics on Commercial Houses Sales**		
商品房销售面积(万平方米)	Floor Space of Commercial Houses Sold (10 000 sq. m)	1408.37	1458.60
住　宅	Residential Buildings	1264.38	1332.49
办公楼	Office Buildings	43.47	37.08
商业营业用房	Houses for Business Use	79.12	61.72
其　他	Others	21.40	27.31
商品房销售额(万元)	Total Sales of Commercial Houses (10 000 yuan)	5710574	6962674
住　宅	Residential Buildings	5041379	6195083
办公楼	Office Buildings	218322	228792
商业营业用房	Houses for Business Use	373821	386330
其　他	Others	77052	152469
房地产中介服务情况	**Statistics on Real Estate Agency Services**		
房屋代理总面积(万平方米)	Total Floor Space (10 000 sq. m)	232.32	312.63
房屋代理成交面积(万平方米)	Transaction Floor Space by Agency (10 000 sq. m)	222.32	312.63
房屋代理成交合同金额(万元)	Transaction Value by Agency (10 000 yuan)	1054655	1502800
房地产物业管理情况	**Statistics on Real Estate Property Management**		
企业总数(个)	Number of Enterprises (unit)	764	842
物业管理项目个数(个)	Number of Projects Managed (unit)	1976	2356
房屋建筑面积(万平方米)	Floor Space of Buildings (10 000 sq. m)	11505.96	14071.46
住　宅	Residential Buildings	9938.63	12326.58
办公用房	Office Buildings	787.55	705.75
商业营业用房	Houses for Business Use	279.3	388.37
工业仓储用房	Houses for Industry and Storage	285.55	375.08
其　他	Others	214.93	275.68
从业人员(人)	Personnel (person)	100786	102407
# 管理人员	Administrative Personnel	16898	17983
年经营收入(万元)	Annual Income (10 000 yuan)	104350	130915.9
从业人员报酬(万元)	Remuneration of Employment Personnel (10 000 yuan)	36695	43220.06

4-22 农村非农户固定资产投资
TOTAL INVESTMENT IN FIXED ASSETS OF RURAL NON-AGRICULTURAL HOUSEHOLDS

项　目	Item	2005	2006
投资额(万元)	**Total Investment (10 000 yuan)**	**1018499**	**1101420**
按主要行业分	Grouped by Sector		
#农、林、牧、渔业	Farming, Forestry, Animal Husbanday, Fishery	38528	41665
工　业	Industry	663884	717934
建筑业	Construction	16031	17336
交通运输业	Transportation	6006	6495
批发和零售业	Wholesale and Retail Trade	38511	41646
房地产业	Real Estate	163804	177140
水利、环境和公共设施管理业	Management for Water Conservancy, Environment and Public Facilities	10823	11704
新增固定资产(万元)	**Newly Increased Fixed Assets (10 000 yuan)**	**959718**	**1101420**
房屋面积(万平方米)	**Floor Space of Buildings (10 000 sq. m)**		
施工面积	Under Construction	766.89	765.73
#住　宅	Residential Buildings	291.1	302.27
竣工面积	Completed	610.29	615.3
#住　宅	Residential Buildings	161.12	163.53
竣工住宅价值(万元)	**Value of Residential Buildings Completed (10 000 yuan)**	**142302**	**295171**
竣工住宅造价(元/平方米)	**Cost of Residential Buildings Completed (yuan/sq. m)**	**883**	**1805**

4-23 农村农户固定资产投资
TOTAL INVESTMENT IN FIXED ASSETS OF RURAL AGRICULTURAL HOUSEHOLDS

项　目	Item	2005	2006
投资额(万元)	**Total Investment (10 000 yuan)**	**292900**	**300000**
按主要行业分	Grouped by Sector		
#农、林、牧、渔业	Farming,Forestry, Animal Husbanday, Fishery	48076	53814
工　业	Industry	11140	14044
建筑业	Construction	25951	20280
交通运输业	Transportation	38434	40410
批发和零售业	Wholesale and Retail Trade	1980	2584
房地产业	Real Estate	158491	159719
水利、环境和公共设施管理业	Management for Water Conservancy, Environment and Public Facilities	1051	1098
房屋面积(万平方米)	**Floor Space of Buildings (10 000 sq. m)**		
施工面积	Under Construction	317.89	348.95
#住　宅	Residential Buildings	262.88	286.85
竣工面积	Completed	229.75	246.97
#住　宅	Residential Buildings	196.17	230.18
竣工住宅价值(万元)	**Value of Residential Buildings Completed (10 000 yuan)**	**142302**	**168768**
竣工住宅造价(元/平方米)	**Cost of Residential Buildings Completed (yuan/sq. m)**	**725**	**733**

4-24 重点建设项目一览表(2006年)
BASIC STATISTICS ON KEY PROJECTS, 2006

项 目 名 称 Name of Project	开工时间 Starting Time	计划总投资(万元) Total Planned Investment (10 000 yuan)	累计完成投资(万元) Investment Accumulated (10 000 yuan)	本年完成投资(万元) Investment in 2006 (10 000 yuan)
总　计(61项)		**27479955**	**8737614**	**5667495**
一、工业项目(18项)		**7709750**	**1836733**	**1401215**
1. 100万吨/年乙烯及配套项目	2006.06	2197053	112519	104856
2. 蓝星集团化工新材料基地一期工程		663000	7046	7046
3. LG渤化35万吨/年氯乙烯项目	2005.05	248255	212793	162073
4. 锦湖轮胎525万条子午线轮胎项目	2005.06	152529	155560	113483
5. 天碱搬迁		935499	3000	3000
6. 天津一汽丰田汽车有限公司新花冠项目	2005.07	410368	287054	194958
7. 一汽发动机(改良型)国产化项目	2005.05	224673	157000	139073
8. 天铁板材基地项目	2005.05	864453	363521	365492
9. 天津钢管公司三期扩建项目	2004.05	390835	57550	82478
10. 中芯国际芯片扩能		640000	62278	62278
11. 三星移动通信及终端设备制造项目	2006.01	55485	26550	26550
12. 力神公司锂离子电池及相关产品项目	2006.04	20000	4900	4790
13. 天士力中药数字化提取与粉针剂项目	2001.06	48100	59087	17512
14. 金耀生物工程产业化基地	2005.06	210000	17600	6023
15. 高新纺织工业基地	2004.02	465900	252415	78534
16. 金威啤酒公司40万千升/年啤酒项目	2005.04	82600	40100	15309
17. 歌美飒风电有限公司厂房建设	2006.01	29000	9760	9760
18. 新泉海水淡化项目		72000	8000	8000
二、能源交通项目(13项)		**7050248**	**3054028**	**1822653**
19. 杨柳青热电厂四期扩建工程	2005.05	242046	117624	99860
20. 东北郊热电厂		312898		
21. 陈塘庄热电厂三期扩建工程	2006.06	278817	20147	19077
22. 京津塘高速公路二线	2004.01	986000	300129	206000
23. 京沪高速公路天津段(一、二期工程)	2003.12	826490	558481	240190
24. 津蓟高速公路延长线	2006.01	113000	36000	36000
25. 津汕高速公路天津段		400000	6000	6000
26. 黄骅南至万家码头铁路工程	2004.11	139900	138199	44431
27. 京津城际铁路客运专线项目	2005.07	1234000	427759	319808
28. 天津滨海机场扩建工程	2005.08	259600	165000	100000
29. 机场配套工程	2006.08	80000	200	200
30. 天津港扩建工程	2006.01	1977497	1219056	696544
31. 天津国际贸易与航运服务区工程	2005.02	200000	65433	54543

4-24 续表 Continued

项目名称 Name of Project	开工时间 Starting Time	计划总投资 (万元) Total Planned Investment (10 000 yuan)	累计完成投资 (万元) Investment Accumulated (10 000 yuan)	本年完成投资 (万元) Investment in 2006 (10 000 yuan)
三、基础设施和环保项目(19项)		**10868867**	**2787880**	**1907441**
32. 海河开发基础设施建设	2003.02	1960000	987567	456847
33. 城市快速路	2006.04	1730000	314500	262313
34. 津滨大道		430000		
35. 地铁2、3号线	2006.12	2100000	42000	42000
36. 津滨轻轨西段工程	2005.01	316500	49073	20501
37. 天津站交通枢纽工程	2006.1	800000	40100	40100
38. 大孟庄等电网工程建设	2004.06	140000	50012	13600
39. 城市电网建设与改造工程	2006.03	707162	405417	403307
40. 城市供热管网改造工程	2006.06	112490	25763	25763
41. 津滨自来水厂	2006.06	157000	14527	7527
42. 城市污水处理及再生水工程		137515		13028
43. 贯庄垃圾焚烧厂		54000		3500
44. 公交场站	2004.01	100000	42093	12398
45. 公共停车场(楼)		73200	7331	7331
46. 市内道路改造工程	2004.01	50000	292916	228590
47. 河道改造工程	2004.04	300000	105917	11079
48. 快速路及铁路专用线两侧环境改造工程	2006.04	420000	314500	314500
49. 公园绿化工程	2005.08	81000	46377	14900
50. 天津临港工业区滩涂开发工程	2005.06	1200000	49787	30157
四、农林水利和小城镇建设项目(4项)		**617038**	**229209**	**195971**
51. 永定新河治理一期工程		96000	5000	5000
52. 华明示范镇建设	2006.01	305038	201209	170971
53. 大良示范镇建设(一期工程)	2006.1	50000	5000	5000
54. 小站示范镇建设	2006.08	166000	18000	15000
五、社会事业及其它项目(7项)		**1234052**	**829764**	**340215**
55. 高等教育布局调整项目	2003.01	615206	523136	213452
56. 基础教育布局调整项目	2004.01	70578	35457	17113
57. 卫生资源调整项目	2002.12	152996	143309	45923
58. 天津奥林匹克中心体育场	2003.08	141920	87612	20080
59. 今晚传媒大厦	2006.09	13352	1603	5000
60. 凤凰商贸广场		60000	15100	15100
61. 现代城大型商业设施		180000	23547	23547

4-25 建设项目主要新增生产能力(2006年)
MAIN NEWLY INCREASED PRODUCTION CAPACITY OF CONSTRUCTION PROJECTS, 2006

生产能力名称	Item	建设规模 Construction Size	累计新增生产能力 Accumulated Newly Increased
天然原油(万吨/年)	Natural Petroleum (10 000 tons/year)	96	23
生　铁(万吨/年)	Pig Iron (10 000 tons/year)	530	530
粗　钢(万吨/年)	Steel-Making (10 000 tons/year)	570	480
钢　材(万吨/年)	Steel Products (10 000 tons/year)	1006	410
热轧钢材(万吨/年)	Steel-Rolling (10 000 tons/year)	830	400
输电线路长度(公里)	Length of Transmit Electricity Line (km)	629.77	415.12
平板玻璃(万重量箱/年)	Plate Glass (10 000 weight cases)	360	360
乙　烯 (吨/年)	Ethene (ton/year)	1000000	
汽车制造 (辆/年)	Car (unit/year)	200000	
塑料树脂及共聚合物(吨/年)	Plastic Resin and Plastic Resin Polymer (ton/year)	610000	
烧　碱(吨/年)	Caustic Soda (ton/year)	160000	
程控交换机(万线/年)	Telephone Exchanges (10 000 lines/year)	4	4
新建公路(公里)	Length of New Roads (km)	173	56
#高速公路(公里)	Highway (km)	173	56
高等院校：学生席位(个)	Universities and Colleges:Students Capacity (unit)	26102	18872
建筑面积(平方米)	Floor Space of Construction (sq. m)	349652	271830
啤　酒(万吨/年)	Beer (10 000 tons/year)	20	20
医院病床(张)	Number of Hospital Beds (bed)	5545	1615
城市道路扩建长度(公里)	Length of Urban Roads Expanded (km)	236.1	6.8
城市道路扩建面积(万平方米)	Areas of Urban Roads Expanded (10 000 sq. m)	1070.35	18.7
城市排水管道铺设长度(公里)	Length of Urban Drain Pipes Paved (km)	672.06	37.31
城市永久性桥梁(座)	Urban Permanent Bridges (unit)	68	
新(扩)建港口码头(年吞吐量)	Newly Built and Expanded Ports (annual handling capacity, 10 000 tons/year)	6320	6320
新(扩)建港口码头(泊位:个)	Newly Built and Expanded Ports (number of berths : unit)	9	9

4-26 房地产开发企业投资额、销售额五十强（2006年）
TOP 50 REAL ESTATE ENTERPRISES ORDERED BY INVESTMENT AND SALES, 2006

投资额名次 Position of Investment	企业名称 Name of Enterprises	销售额名次 Position of Sales	企业名称 Name of Enterprises
1	天津市东丽区滨丽小城镇建设开发投资有限公司	1	天津泰瑞房地产开发有限公司
2	天津市房地产发展(集团)股份有限公司	2	天津融创奥城投资有限公司
3	天津市河东区东美安居建设有限公司	3	天津泰达建设集团有限公司
4	天津富力城房地产开发有限公司	4	天津富力城房地产开发有限公司
5	天津融创奥城投资有限公司	5	天津市塘沽经济开发区鸿发房地产有限公司
6	天津优联投资发展集团有限公司	6	天津市房地产发展(集团)股份有限公司
7	天津泰达建设集团有限公司	7	天津阳光壹佰房地产开发有限公司
8	天津中新置地有限公司	8	天津万科房地产有限公司
9	天津泰瑞房地产开发有限公司	9	天津市红磡房地产开发有限公司
10	河西区建设开发总公司	10	天津浩天房地产开发有限公司
11	天津融创置地有限公司	11	天津经济技术开发区房地产开发公司
12	天津市塘沽区正通房地产开发公司	12	天津优联投资发展集团有限公司
13	天津市先行房地产开发有限公司	13	天津合生珠江房地产开发有限公司
14	天津富铭置业有限公司	14	天津乐康置业有限公司
15	金地(集团)天津房地产开发有限公司	15	天津滨海发展投资控股有限公司
16	天津市远驰房地产开发有限公司	16	天津星运(集团)有限公司
17	天津市凯兴安居建设有限公司	17	天津国信置业有限公司
18	天津市美震房地产开发有限公司	18	天津朗钜地产有限公司
19	天津万科新锐房地产有限公司	19	天津万通时尚置业有限责任公司
20	天津合生珠江房地产开发有限公司	20	天津融创置地有限公司
21	天津阳光鑫地投资有限公司	21	天津市美震房地产开发有限公司
22	天津耀华投资发展有限公司	22	天津市宁发发展有限公司
23	天津中新嘉业房地产开发有限公司	23	天津市安居建设发展总公司
24	天津星运(集团)有限公司	24	天津塘沽贻成实业有限公司
25	天津万通时尚置业有限责任公司	25	天津市宁发集团有限公司
26	天津塘沽贻成实业有限公司	26	天津开发区福林发展有限公司
27	天津顺潮房地产开发有限公司	27	天津滨海快速交通发展有限公司
28	天津松江集团有限公司	28	天津津滨创辉发展有限公司
29	天津市红鼎房地产开发有限公司	29	天津瀚华置业发展有限公司
30	天津奥林匹克花园置业投资有限公司	30	天津市塘沽区正通房地产开发公司
31	天津万事兴房地产开发集团有限公司	31	天津中新嘉业房地产开发有限公司
32	天津市津房置业发展有限责任公司	32	天津梅江建设发展有限公司
33	天津市西青区环城安居建设有限公司	33	天津市金厦中天房地产开发有限公司
34	天津津滨雅都置业发展有限公司	34	河西区建设开发总公司
35	天津津滨创辉发展有限公司	35	天津大众集团有限公司
36	天津天保控股有限公司	36	天津鸿正集团有限公司
37	天津市宁发发展有限公司	37	天津市万顺置业有限公司
38	港通(天津)置业有限公司	38	天津天保控股有限公司
39	天津万科房地产有限公司	39	天津金色领地房地产开发有限公司
40	天津市现代投资有限公司	40	天津市远驰房地产开发有限公司
41	天津澳中发展有限公司	41	天津市荣丰兆业房地产开发有限公司
42	天津滨海快速交通发展有限公司	42	天津市恒星置业发展有限公司
43	天津市河北区环金安居建设有限公司	43	金地(集团)天津房地产开发有限公司
44	天津鸿正集团有限公司	44	天津兴海房地产开发有限公司
45	天津泰达广洋置业有限公司	45	天津广顺房地产开发有限责任公司
46	天津市新创置业有限公司	46	天津耀华投资发展有限公司
47	天津鑫茂科技园有限公司	47	天津市世纪华明房地产开发有限公司
48	天津市宏佳安居建设有限公司	48	天津开发区福祺置业发展有限公司
49	天津国信置业有限公司	49	天津顺驰北岸置地有限公司
50	天津市金厦中天房地产开发有限公司	50	天津兴利房地产开发公司

主要统计指标解释

固定资产投资额 是以货币表现的在一定时期内建造和购置固定资产的工作量以及与此有关的费用的总称。全社会固定资产投资的统计范围包括城镇固定资产投资、农村非农户投资和农村农户投资。全市固定资产投资的统计范围是全社会固定资产投资中扣除农村非农户投资和农村农户投资。(从2006年开始，按国家制度规定，个体投资中取消“城镇和工矿区私人建房投资”)。

房地产开发投资 指房地产开发公司、商品房建设公司及其他房地产开发单位进行土地开发工程、商品房屋建设工程所完成的投资额。是以货币表现的房地产开发工作量。

固定资产投资按构成分组

建筑工程 指各种房屋建筑物的建造工程，又称建筑工程量。这部分投资额必须兴工动料，通过施工才能实现。建筑工程包括各种房屋的建造，设备基础及各种窑炉的砌筑和金属结构工程，为施工而进行的建筑场地布置、地质勘探、平整场地、施工用水、电、气、路和清理绿化等。矿井的开凿、铁路、公路、桥梁、水利及防空、地下建筑等特殊工程。

安装工程 指各种设备、装置的安装工程，又称安装工作量。在安装工程投资额中，不包括被安装设备本身的价值。安装工程包括生产、动力、起重、运输、传动和医疗试验等各种需安装设备的装配与设备相连的工作台、梯子栏杆以及管线敷设、保温、油漆、防腐和单机试运系统联动无负簧试运(不包括投料试运)。

设备、工具、器具购置 指购置和自制达到固定资产标准的设备、工具、器具的价值。但新建单位、扩建单位的新建车间，按照设计和计划要求购置或自制的全部设备、工具、器具，不论是否达到固定资产标准均计入“设备、工具、器具购置”中。

其他费用 指除建筑安装、设备工具器具购置和商品房屋购置以外的构成固定资产投资完成额的各种费用。主要包括牲畜购置费、林木营建费、办公和生活家具、器具购置费、土地青苗补偿费和安置补助费、建设单位管理费、研究试验费、勘察设计费、联合试运转费、引进技术和进口设备项目的其他费用、生产职工培训费、施工机构迁移费、报废工程损失费和供电站费、矿山巷道维修费等。

固定资产投资按建设性质分组 是反映固定资产投资使用方向，研究各类性质的比重和对比分析投资效果。具体包括：

新建 一般指从无到有“平地起家”新开始建设的企事业和行政单位及新建输电线路、输油管道、铁路、公路等独立工程。有的项目原有基础很小，经扩大建设后，其新增加的固定资产价值(原值)超过原有固定资产价值三倍以上的也应算为新建。

扩建 指为扩大原有产品生产能力或新的产品能力，在厂内或其他地点增建主要生产车间(或主要工程)，独立的生产线等。事业单位和行政单位在原单位增建业务用房，也作为扩建。

改建 现有企事业单位为了技术进步对现有设施、工艺条件进行技术改造或更新(包括相应配套的辅助性生产、生活设施建设)。有的还充分发挥现有的生产能力，进行填平补齐而增建不直接增加本单位主要产品生产能力的车间等，也属于改建。

新增固定资产 指报告期内交付使用的固定资产价值，包括建成投入生产或交付使用的工程投资和达到固定资产标准的设备、工具器具的投资以及有关的摊入费用和属于增加固定资产价值的其他建设费用。

固定资产交付使用率 指报告期内新增固定资产与同期完成投资额的比率。它反映各个时期固定资产动用速度，衡量建设过程中投资效果的一个综合性指标。

施工房屋建筑面积 指报告期内施工的全部房屋建筑面积。包括本期新开工的面积和上期开工跨入本期继续施工的房屋面积，以及上期已停建在本期复工的房屋面积。

主要统计指标解释

竣工房屋建筑面积 指在报告期内房屋建筑按设计要求已全部完工，达到住人和使用条件，经验收鉴定合格（或达到竣工验收标准），可正式移交使用的各栋房屋建筑面积的总和。

商品房销售面积 指报告期内出售商品房屋的合同总面积（即双方签署的正式买卖合同中所确定的建筑面积）。由现房销售建筑面积和期房销售建筑面积两部分组成。

商品房销售额 指报告期内出售商品房屋的合同总价款（即双方签署的正式买卖合同中所确定的合同总价）。该指标与商品房销售面积同口径，由现房销售额和期房销售额两部分组成。

别墅、高档公寓 指建筑造价和销售价格明显高于一般商品住宅的商品住宅。别墅一般指地处郊区，独立成栋的商品住宅；高档公寓一般指地处市内高尚社区，高层或多层的商品住宅。别墅、高档公寓的确定标准：一是经有房地产投资计划审批权的主管部门审批建设的别墅、高档公寓开发项目；二是销售价格高于当地同等地段商品住宅平均销售价格一倍以上的别墅、公寓开发项目。该指标可以分析房地产投资结构，反映高收入家庭商品住宅的供求平衡情况。

Explanastory Notes on Main Statistical Indicators

Total Investment in Fixed Assets refers to the volume of activities in construction and purchases of fixed assets and related fees, expressed in monetary terms. Total investment in fixed assets in the whole country includes urban investment, rural non-agricultural investment and rural agricultural investment. Investment in fixed assets in Tianjin refers to total investment in fixed assets in the whole country deducting rural non-agricultural investment and rural agricultural investment. (Since 2006, "Private Investment in House Construction in Urban Areas, Industrial and Mining Areas" in individual investment was canceled according to national system.)

Investment in Real Estate Development refers to the investment by the real estate development companies, commercial buildings construction companies and other real estate development units of various types of ownership in the construction of house buildings. It is finished work in monetary terms.

Investment in Fixed Assets by Structure

Construction Project refers to the construction of various houses and buildings, it also is called the work volume of construction, including construction of various houses, equipment foundations and industrial kilns and stoves, preparation works for project construction, and clearing up works post project construction, geological examination, land-leveling, water, electricity, gas road-cleaning, planting trees, drilling of mines, pavement of railways and roads, highway, bridge, construction of projects of water conservancy, construction of underground air-raid shelters and construction of other special projects.

Installation Project refers to the installation of various kinds of equipment and instruments (work volume of installation). The value of equipment installed is excluded in the value of installation projects. Including various kinds of equipment, i.e. production, power-driven, lifting, transport, transmission, medical experiment etc. and working table, stepladder railing, putting up of pipes, keep warm, paint, rot-proofing, try operation (excluding put in material try operation).

Purchase of Equipment and Instruments refers to the total value of equipment, tools, and vessels purchased or self-produced which come up to standards for fixed assets. Equipment, tools and vessels purchased or self- produced for new workshops by newly established or expanded units are categorized as "purchase of equipment and instruments" no matter whether they come up to the standards for fixed assets or not.

Other Expenses refers to investment excluded in above items, which consist of construction and installation, purchase of equipment and instruments, purchase of commercial buildings, including purchase of animals by agricultural and forestry units, planting and operating of various economic forest, purchase of office and home furniture, purchase of instruments and vessels, compensation for the loss of land and young crops, subsidies for moving, administration expenses of construction units, and expenses on research and testing, geological prospecting and designing, joint trial running, and the other purchase introduction of technology and imports of equipment, expenses on training of staff and workers, transportation of construction machines, loss of discarded projects, powers supply station, mine harbor maintenance.

Investment in Fixed Assets by Type of Construction

refers to reflect use direction of investment in fixed assets, researching various proportions and analyzing result of investment. It includes:

New Construction refers to newly constructed units. In the case, in which the value of the original fixed assets is quite small, and the value of newly added fixed assets exceeds the original ones by three times, the expansion construction is considered as new construction.

Expansion Construction refers to construction of new major production workshop or independent production line within a factory or in other locations, or construction of a branch factory so as to increase the production capacity of the original products. Newly constructed business houses in institutions and administrative organizations are also classified as expansion.

Reconstruction refers to technical innovation and transformation of the existing equipment and technical conditions undertaken by enterprises and institutions for the purposes of technological advancement, (including accessory facilities for production or for living and welfare purposes). The construction of new workshops for improving existing production capacity rather than increasing production capacity is also considered as reconstruction.

Newly Increased Fixed Assets refers to the newly increased value of fixed assets through investment, including the value of projects completed and put into production, the value of equipment, tools, and vessels considered as fixed assets, as well as the relevant expenses as investment in fixed assets and other construction expansion of increased the volume in fixed assets.

Explanastory Notes on Main Statistical Indicators

Rate of Projects of Fixed Assets Completed and Put into Operation refers to the ratio of the newly increased fixed assets to the total investment made in the same period. This is a comprehensive indicator, reflecting the speed of the employment of fixed assets and the investment efficiency.

Floor Space of Buildings under Construction refers to total floor space of all buildings under construction during the reference period, including floor space of newly started buildings during the reference period, floor space of construction extended from the previous year to the current period, and floor space of construction suspended during the previous period and resumed in the current period.

Floor Space of Buildings Completed refer to the floor space of all buildings completed in the reference period, which have been appraised and accepted(or come up to the designed standards) and have been transferred to the owners for use.

Area of Commercial Housing Sold refers to total contracted area of commercial housing (i.e. area of floor space as designated in the formal contracts signed by both sides) during the reference time. It constitutes floor space of completed housing and floor space of future housing.

Value of Commercial Housing Sold refer to total value of contracts (i.e. value of sales/purchase for selling/purchase of commercial housing as designated in the contracts signed by both sides) during the reference time. It has the same coverage as the area of commercial housing sold, constituting completed housing and floor space of future housing

Villas, High-Grade Apartments refers to commercial houses whose construction costs and marketing prices are significantly higher than ordinary housing. Villas are independent structures generally located in the suburbs; high-grade apartments are multi-story buildings located in elegant urban neighborhoods. Criteria for villas and high-grade apartments include: 1) projects for the construction of villas or high-grade apartments have to be approved by competent departments in charge of real estate development and investment plans, and 2) prices for projects on villas or high-grade apartments are higher by over 100% compared with the average prices of ordinary commercial housing projects in similar location. This indicator helps to analyze the investment structure of the real estate industry and the demand and supply of housing for high-income households.

第5篇
CHAPTER 5

能源生产和消费
Energy Production and Consumption

5-1 能源生产总量及构成（1990-2006年）
TOTAL PRODUCTION OF ENERGY AND ITS COMPOSITION, 1990-2006

年 份 Year	能源生产总量 (万吨标准煤) Total Energy Production (10 000 tons of SCE)	占能源生产总量的比重(%) As Percentage of Total Energy Production (%)	
		原 油 Crude Oil	天然气 Natrual Gas
1990	719.41	93.23	6.77
1991	726.45	93.39	6.61
1992	757.45	92.75	7.25
1993	790.99	93.38	6.62
1994	936.65	89.84	10.16
1995	978.82	90.61	9.39
1996	1036.17	89.15	10.85
1997	1014.77	90.93	9.07
1998	1079.73	91.46	8.54
1999	1084.63	90.45	9.55
2000	1201.94	90.81	9.19
2001	1494.84	92.73	7.27
2002	1844.92	94.16	5.84
2003	1983.56	94.80	5.20
2004	2171.95	95.12	4.88
2005	2663.93	95.61	4.39
2006	2915.55	95.21	4.79

5-2 能源终端消费量（1990-2006年）
FINAL CONSUMPTION OF ENERGY, 1990-2006

单位：万吨标准煤 (10 000 tons of SCE)

年 份 Year	能源终端消费量 Final Consumption of Energy	第一产业 Primary Industry	第二产业 Secondary Industry	第三产业 Tertiary Industry	生活消费 Living Consumption
1990	1961.58	64.12	1320.02	365.11	212.33
1991	1920.61	56.99	1260.45	381.56	221.61
1992	2062.35	65.24	1383.16	394.86	219.09
1993	2233.06	65.80	1540.61	412.10	214.55
1994	2250.85	55.70	1583.40	424.92	186.83
1995	2539.46	69.30	1773.03	478.40	218.73
1996	2374.07	70.72	1735.50	311.33	256.52
1997	2312.79	44.76	1605.60	420.96	241.47
1998	2353.71	44.00	1588.62	437.27	283.82
1999	2352.21	53.61	1435.11	535.14	328.35
2000	2553.60	58.17	1570.08	635.23	290.12
2001	2724.32	68.83	1694.78	608.05	352.66
2002	2966.56	76.64	1935.92	575.96	378.04
2003	3084.49	58.86	1975.56	650.27	399.80
2004	3522.15	62.00	2296.39	737.35	426.41
2005	3901.28	73.28	2562.80	791.21	473.99
2006	4294.93	76.41	2897.63	827.14	493.76

5-3 综合能源平衡表(标准量)
OVERALL ENERGY BALANCE SHEET(STANDARD EQUIVALENT)

单位：万吨标准煤 (10 000 tons of SCE)

项目	Item	2005	2006
可供本地区消费的能源量	**Volume of Energy Available for Consumption**	**4115.52**	**4524.02**
年初库存量	Stock at the Beginning of the Year	323.55	416.78
一次能源生产量	Primary Energy Output	2663.93	2915.55
回收能	Recovery of Energy	27.71	21.91
外省(区、市)调入量	Inflow from Other Provinces (Regions, Cities)	6790.41	7336.03
进口量	Import	632.50	748.90
我轮、机在外国加油量	Our Steamship and Plane Oiled Abroad	93.86	81.27
本市调出量(–)	Outflow to Other Provinces (Regions, Cities) (–)	-5681.20	-6185.92
出口量(–)	Export (–)	-302.68	-333.46
外轮、机在本市加油量(–)	Foreign Steamship and Plane Oiled in Tianjin (–)	-53.54	-58.24
年末库存量(–)	Stock at Year-end	-379.02	-417.81
加工转换投入(–)产出(+)量	**Input (–) or Output (+) of Processing and Transformation**	**-108.19**	**-121.61**
火力发电	Fuel Power Generation		
供　热	Heating		
洗选煤	Clean Coal		
炼　焦	Coke Making	-9.00	-33.36
炼　油	Oil Refining	-99.18	-88.25
制　气	Gas Making		
# 焦炭再投入量(–)	Input of Coke (–)		
煤制品加工	Processing of Coal Products		
损失量	**Loss Volume**	**105.72**	**108.60**
终端消费量	**Final Consumption**	**3901.28**	**4294.93**
第一产业	Primary Industry	73.28	76.41
第二产业	Secondary Industry	2562.80	2897.63
工　业	Industry	2512.38	2837.56
建筑业	Construction	50.42	60.07
第三产业	Tertiary Industry	791.21	827.14
交通运输、仓储及邮政业	Transportation, Storage and Post Services	336.94	348.93
批发和零售业、住宿和餐饮业	Wholesale and Retail Trade, Accommodation and Catering Services	296.59	308.49
其　他	Others	157.68	169.72
生活消费	Living Consumption	473.99	493.76
平衡差额	**Balance**	**0.33**	**-0.97**
消费量合计	**Total of Consumption**	**4115.19**	**4525.14**

5-4 能源消耗基本情况（1990-2006年）
BASIC INDICATORS OF ENERGY CONSUMPTION, 1990-2006

年 份 Year	能源消耗 (万吨标准煤) Energy Consumption (10 000 tons of SCE)	#工 业 Industry	电力消耗(亿千瓦小时) Electricity Power Consumption (100 million kWh)	#工 业 Industry
1990	2037.93	1355.97	124.15	97.78
1991	1989.63	1294.48	130.11	102.72
1992	2140.73	1433.05	134.29	103.08
1993	2292.67	1565.67	151.55	117.36
1994	2345.10	1653.91	167.42	128.55
1995	2568.79	1714.57	178.99	122.14
1996	2500.22	1816.55	187.51	111.35
1997	2452.34	1698.19	194.09	142.45
1998	2502.24	1698.82	200.38	147.43
1999	2553.07	1608.66	211.19	151.09
2000	2793.71	1776.94	236.55	171.83
2001	2918.04	1855.60	250.47	181.89
2002	3022.15	1969.20	281.00	205.33
2003	3214.97	2087.57	313.00	230.16
2004	3696.68	2434.14	350.97	259.61
2005	4115.19	2726.29	396.33	292.49
2006	4525.14	3067.77	445.73	330.51

年 份 Year	生产总值能耗 (吨标准煤/万元) Energy Consumption of GDP (tons of SCE/10 000 yuan)	生产总值电耗 (千瓦小时/万元) Electricity Power Consumption of GDP (kWh/10 000 yuan)	工业增加值能耗 (吨标准煤/万元) Energy Consumption of Value Added in Industry (tons of SCE/10 000 yuan)	工业增加值电耗 (千瓦小时/万元) Electricity Power Consumption of Value Added in Industry (kWh/10 000 yuan)
1990	3.56	2169.35	5.27	3800.23
1991	3.28	2145.44	4.76	3774.25
1992	3.16	1983.31	4.68	3368.99
1993	3.02	1997.23	4.50	3376.83
1994	2.70	1930.33	4.17	3242.53
1995	2.58	1796.02	3.78	2691.53
1996	2.19	1646.08	3.49	2141.55
1997	1.92	1520.31	2.92	2450.07
1998	1.79	1434.95	2.73	2369.84
1999	1.66	1374.94	2.30	2156.90
2000	1.64	1389.94	2.26	2186.25
2001	1.53	1313.51	2.09	2053.52
2002	1.41	1308.20	1.94	2023.65
2003	1.30	1268.95	1.74	1912.95
2004	1.29	1228.33	1.67	1776.40
2005	1.11	1040.80	1.45	1551.64
2006	1.07	1024.05	1.38	1488.98

注：1. 能源消耗指标采用等价值计量。2. 生产总值、工业增加值的能耗和电耗2005年及以后年份为2005年可比价，2005年以前年份为2000年可比价。
Note: a) Indicators of energy consumption are converted into equal value. b) Since 2005, energy or electricity power consumption of GDP and energy or electricity power consumption of value added in industry are calculated at 2005 comparable prices; data before 2005 are calculated at 2000 comparable prices.

5-5 电力平衡表（2001-2006年）
ELECTRICITY BALANCE SHEET, 2001-2006

单位：亿千瓦小时 (100 million kWh)

项 目 Item	2001	2002	2003	2004	2005	2006
可供量 Total Energy Available for Consumption	**250.48**	**281.00**	**313.00**	**350.97**	**396.33**	**445.73**
生产量 Output	224.53	276.10	325.60	343.22	376.36	366.74
火 电 Thermal Power	224.53	276.10	325.60	343.22	376.36	366.74
外省(区、市)调入量 Inflow from Other Provinces (Regions, Cities)	26.19	5.18	4.10	8.08	20.38	79.58
本市调出量 Outflow to Other Provinces	0.24	0.28	16.70	0.33	0.41	0.59
消费量 Total Energy Consumption	**250.47**	**281.00**	**313.00**	**350.97**	**396.33**	**445.73**
在消费量中: Consumption by Sector						
农、林、牧、渔、水利业 Farming, Forestry, Animal Husbandry, Fishery and Water Conservancy	8.12	10.54	9.49	8.93	9.73	10.88
工 业 Industry	181.89	205.33	230.16	259.61	292.49	330.51
建筑业 Construction	1.48	1.53	1.74	1.99	3.77	4.80
交通运输、仓储和邮政业 Transportation, Storage and Post Services	4.55	4.88	5.68	6.72	6.52	6.90
批发和零售业、住宿和餐饮业 Wholesale & Retail Trade, Accommodation & Catering Services	11.03	12.82	15.28	17.59	19.31	21.14
其 他 Others	17.26	16.56	18.92	22.68	26.55	28.46
生活消费 Living Consumption	26.14	29.34	31.73	33.45	37.96	43.04
在消费量中: Consumption by Usage						
终端消费 Final Consumption	236.55	265.39	293.85	329.38	373.37	420.40
#工 业 Industry	167.97	189.72	211.01	238.02	269.53	305.18
输配电损失量 Losses in Transmission	13.92	15.61	19.15	21.59	22.96	25.33
平衡差额 Balance	**0.01**					

5-6 能源消费弹性系数（1991-2006年）
ELASTICITY OF ENERGY CONSUMPION, 1991-2006

年 份 Year	能源消费比上年增长(%) Growth Rate of Energy Consumption over Preceding Year (%)	电力消费比上年增长(%) Growth Rate of Electricity Power Consumption over Preceding Year (%)	生产总值比上年增长(%) Growth Rate of GDP over Preceding Year (%)	能源消费弹性系数 Elasticity Ratio of Energy Consumption	电力消费弹性系数 Elasticity Ratio of Electric Power Consumption
1991	-2.4	4.8	6.0		0.80
1992	7.6	3.2	11.7	0.65	0.28
1993	7.1	12.9	12.1	0.59	1.07
1994	2.3	10.5	14.3	0.16	0.73
1995	9.5	6.9	14.9	0.64	0.46
1996	-2.7	4.8	14.3		0.33
1997	-1.9	3.5	12.1		0.29
1998	2.0	3.2	9.3	0.22	0.34
1999	2.0	5.4	10.0	0.20	0.54
2000	9.4	12.0	10.8	0.87	1.11
2001	4.5	5.9	12.0	0.37	0.49
2002	3.6	12.2	12.7	0.28	0.96
2003	6.4	11.4	14.8	0.43	0.77
2004	15.0	12.1	15.8	0.95	0.77
2005	11.3	12.9	14.7	0.77	0.88
2006	10.0	12.5	14.5	0.69	0.87

5-7 平均每天能源消费量（2001-2006年）
AVERAGE DAILY ENERGY CONSUMPTION, 2001-2006

能源品种	Item	单 位	Unit	2001	2002	2003	2004	2005	2006
合 计	**Total**	**万吨标准煤**	**10 000 tons of SCE**	**7.99**	**8.28**	**8.81**	**10.13**	**11.27**	**12.40**
煤 炭	Coal	万 吨	10 000 tons	7.22	8.02	8.78	9.61	10.41	10.44
焦 炭	Coke	万 吨	10 000 tons	0.35	0.41	0.39	0.90	0.90	1.48
原 油	Crude Oil	万 吨	10 000 tons	2.05	1.85	2.06	2.15	2.36	2.47
燃料油	Fuel Oil	万 吨	10 000 tons	0.24	0.24	0.31	0.31	0.31	0.29
汽 油	Gasoline	万 吨	10 000 tons	0.32	0.26	0.29	0.33	0.33	0.35
煤 油	Kerosene	万 吨	10 000 tons	0.03	0.04	0.05	0.04	0.04	0.04
柴 油	Diesel Oil	万 吨	10 000 tons	0.50	0.50	0.53	0.62	0.67	0.68
天然气	Natural Gas	亿立方米	100 million cu. m	0.02	0.02	0.02	0.02	0.02	0.03
电 力	Electricity	亿千瓦小时	100 million kWh	0.69	0.77	0.86	0.96	1.09	1.22

5-8 生活能源消费量（2001-2006年）
ENERGY CONSUMPTION FOR NON-PRODUCTION PURPOSE, 2001-2006

能源品种 Item	单 位 Unit	2001	2002	2003	2004	2005	2006
合 计	**万吨标准煤**						
Total	**10 000 tons of SCE**	**352.66**	**378.04**	**399.80**	**426.41**	**473.99**	**493.76**
煤 炭	万 吨						
Coal	10 000 tons	88.20	79.87	91.44	84.27	88.98	75.86
液化石油气	万 吨						
LPG	10 000 tons	10.77	9.59	10.70	8.93	7.13	7.04
天然气和煤气	亿立方米						
Natural Gas and Coal Gas	100 million cu. m	3.94	3.83	3.01	2.88	3.85	3.60
热 力	万百万千焦						
Heat	10 billion kilo-joule	3302.62	3803.57	3983.72	4340.00	4482.00	4701.0
电 力	亿千瓦小时						
Electricity	100 million kWh	26.14	29.34	31.73	33.45	37.96	43.04

5-9 人均生活能源消费量（1990-2006年）
ANNUAL PER CAPITA ENERGY CONSUMPTION FOR NON-PRODUCTION PURPOSE, 1990-2006

年 份 Year	平均每人生活消费能源 (千克标准煤) Annual Per Capita Consumption for Non-production Purpose (kg of SCE)	煤 炭 (千克) Coal (kg)	电 力 (千瓦小时) Electricity (kWh)	液化石油气 (千克) LGP (kg)	天然气和煤气 (立方米) Natural Gas and Coal Gas (cu. m)
1990	247	247	93	3	21
1991	255	254	102	3	27
1992	250	224	116	3	25
1993	243	212	127	3	24
1994	210	168	151	4	31
1995	245	165	161	5	31
1996	286	214	189	6	21
1997	269	188	211	5	22
1998	315	141	227	5	22
1999	362	131	265	19	22
2000	318	109	271	13	47
2001	386	97	286	12	43
2002	413	87	320	11	42
2003	433	99	344	12	33
2004	459	91	360	10	31
2005	459	86	367	7	37
2006	466	51	406	7	35

5-10 工业行业主要能源终端消费量(2006年)
THE FINAL CONSUMPTION OF MAIN ENERGY BY INDUSTRIAL SECTOR, 2006

行业	Sector	煤炭(万吨) Coal (10 000 tons)	焦炭(万吨) Coke (10 000 tons)	原油(万吨) Crude Oil (10 000 tons)	汽油(万吨) Gasoline (10 000 tons)
总计	**Total**	**824.13**	**541.1**	**15.4**	**9.87**
煤炭开采和洗选业	Mining and Washing of Coal				0.02
石油和天然气开采业	Extraction of Petroleum and Natural Gas	16		15.34	1.15
有色金属矿采选业	Mining and Processing of Non-Ferrous Metal Ores	1.76			0.01
非金属矿采选业	Mining and Processing of Nonmetal Ores	3.6			0.06
农副食品加工业	Processing of Food from Agricultural Products	9.3			0.13
食品制造业	Manufacture of Foods	11.81			0.15
饮料制造业	Manufacture of Beverages	39.61			0.06
烟草制品业	Manufacture of Tobacco	2.45			0.19
纺织业	Manufacture of Textile	28.73			0.31
纺织服装鞋帽制造业	Manufacture of Textile Wearing Apparel, Footware and Caps	8.32			0.08
皮革毛皮羽毛(绒)及其制品业	Manufacture of Leather, Fur, Feather and Related Products	1.59			0.1
木材加工及木、竹、藤、棕、草制品业	Processing of Timber, Manufacture of Wood, Bamboo, Rattan, Palm, and Straw Products	6.33	0.01		0.14
家具制造业	Manufacture of Furniture	4.67			0.2
造纸及纸制品业	Manufacture of Paper and Paper Products	13.81	0.11	0.02	0.16
印刷业和记录媒介的复制	Printing, Reproduction of Recording Media	2.04			0.08
文教体育用品制造业	Manufacture of Articles For Culture, Education and Sport Activity	3.26	0.02	0.04	0.13
石油加工炼焦及核燃料加工业	Processing of Petroleum, Coking, Processing of Nuclear Fuel	10.72			0.73
化学原料及化学制品制造业	Manufacture of Raw Chemical Materials and Chemical Products	122.85	1.65		0.14
医药制造业	Manufacture of Medicines	17.77			0.02
化学纤维制造业	Manufacture of Chemical Fibers	3.77			0.44
橡胶制品业	Manufacture of Rubber	19.47		0.02	0.29
塑料制品业	Manufacture of Plastics	7.5	0.01		0.4
非金属矿物制品业	Manufacture of Non-Metallic Mineral Products	105.69	0.07	0.13	0.34
黑色金属冶炼及压延加工业	Smelting and Pressing of Ferrous Metals	289.66	532.64		0.08
有色金属冶炼及压延加工业	Smelting and Pressing of Non-Ferrous Metals	4.78	0.14		1.06
金属制品业	Manufacture of Metal Products	19.67	0.93		0.71
通用设备制造业	Manufacture of General Purpose Machinery	11.2	4.76		0.39
专用设备制造业	Manufacture of Special Purpose Machinery	3.2	0.22		0.98
交通运输设备制造业	Manufacture of Transport Equipment	21.62	0.4	0.04	0.4
电气机械及器材制造业	Manufacture of Electrical Machinery and Equipment	9.59	0.1	0.01	0.29
通信设备计算机及其他电子设备制造业	Manufacture of Communication Equipment, Computers and Other Electronic Equipment	4.38			0.13
仪器仪表及文化办公用机械制造业	Manufacture of Measuring Instruments and Machinery for Cultural Activity and Office Work	0.74			0.09
工艺品及其他制造业	Manufacture of Artwork and Other Manufacturing	5.29			0.01
废弃资源和废旧材料回收加工业	Recycling and Disposal of Waste	0.01			0.01
电力热力的生产和供应业	Production and Supply of Electric Power and Heat Power	13.95			0.24
燃气生产和供应业	Production and Supply of Gas	1.57	0.04		0.12
水的生产和供应业	Production and Supply of Water	0.51			0.03

5-10 续表 1 Continued

行　业	Sector	柴　油 (万吨) Diesel Oil (10 000 tons)	燃料油 (万吨) Fuel Oil (10 000 tons)	天然气 (亿立方米) Natural Gas (100 million cu.m)
总　计	**Total**	**26.74**	**48.16**	**4.92**
煤炭开采和洗选业	Mining and Washing of Coal	0.01		
石油和天然气开采业	Extraction of Petroleum and Natural Gas	12.55		1.16
有色金属矿采选业	Mining and Processing of Non-Ferrous Metal Ores	0.07		
非金属矿采选业	Mining and Processing of Nonmetal Ores	0.15		
农副食品加工业	Processing of Food from Agricultural Products	0.65	0.01	0.03
食品制造业	Manufacture of Foods	0.1	0.66	0.04
饮料制造业	Manufacture of Beverages	0.31		
烟草制品业	Manufacture of Tobacco			
纺织业	Manufacture of Textile	0.17	0.01	0.04
纺织服装鞋帽制造业	Manufacture of Textile Wearing Apparel, Footware and Caps	0.14		0.02
皮革毛皮羽毛(绒)及其制品业	Manufacture of Leather, Fur, Feather and Related Products	0.02		
木材加工及木、竹、藤、棕、草制品业	Processing of Timber, Manufacture of Wood, Bamboo, Rattan, Palm, and Straw Products	0.06		0.03
家具制造业	Manufacture of Furniture	0.09		0.02
造纸及纸制品业	Manufacture of Paper and Paper Products	0.28	0.11	
印刷业和记录媒介的复制	Printing, Reproduction of Recording Media	0.05		
文教体育用品制造业	Manufacture of Articles For Culture, Education and Sport Activity	0.1	0.01	
石油加工炼焦及核燃料加工业	Processing of Petroleum, Coking, Processing of Nuclear Fuel	0.43	12.67	0.04
化学原料及化学制品制造业	Manufacture of Raw Chemical Materials and Chemical Products	1.51	23.43	0.49
医药制造业	Manufacture of Medicines	0.21		0.04
化学纤维制造业	Manufacture of Chemical Fibers	0.07	0.01	
橡胶制品业	Manufacture of Rubber	0.2	0.75	0.09
塑料制品业	Manufacture of Plastics	0.42	0.01	0.05
非金属矿物制品业	Manufacture of Non-Metallic Mineral Products	2.68	4.41	0.22
黑色金属冶炼及压延加工业	Smelting and Pressing of Ferrous Metals	1.45	3.6	1.86
有色金属冶炼及压延加工业	Smelting and Pressing of Non-Ferrous Metals	0.17	0.41	0.06
金属制品业	Manufacture of Metal Products	0.87	1.58	0.08
通用设备制造业	Manufacture of General Purpose Machinery	0.33	0.04	0.05
专用设备制造业	Manufacture of Special Purpose Machinery	0.35	0.02	0.02
交通运输设备制造业	Manufacture of Transport Equipment	0.85	0.01	0.1
电气机械及器材制造业	Manufacture of Electrical Machinery and Equipment	0.46	0.01	0.05
通信设备计算机及其他电子设备制造业	Manufacture of Communication Equipment, Computers and Other Electronic Equipment	0.33	0.35	0.33
仪器仪表及文化办公用机械制造业	Manufacture of Measuring Instruments and Machinery for Cultural Activity and Office Work	0.04	0.01	0.03
工艺品及其他制造业	Manufacture of Artwork and Other Manufacturing	0.04	0.04	
废弃资源和废旧材料回收加工业	Recycling and Disposal of Waste			
电力热力的生产和供应业	Production and Supply of Electric Power and Heat Power	1.54	0.01	0.02
燃气生产和供应业	Production and Supply of Gas	0.04		0.05
水的生产和供应业	Production and Supply of Water			

5-10 续表 2 Continued

行　业	Sector	热　力(万百万千焦) Heat(10 000 million kilo-joule)	电　力(亿千瓦时) Electricity (100million kWh)	其他石油制品(万吨) Other Petroleum Product (10 000 tons)
总　计	**Total**	**5719.63**	**305.18**	**124.2**
煤炭开采和洗选业	Mining and Washing of Coal		0.01	
石油和天然气开采业	Extraction of Petroleum and Natural Gas	1.97	10.73	
有色金属矿采选业	Mining and Processing of Non-Ferrous Metal Ores		0.73	
非金属矿采选业	Mining and Processing of Nonmetal Ores	293.57	1.26	
农副食品加工业	Processing of Food from Agricultural Products	174.79	2.9	
食品制造业	Manufacture of Foods	99.38	2.62	
饮料制造业	Manufacture of Beverages	60.68	3.16	
烟草制品业	Manufacture of Tobacco		0.17	
纺织业	Manufacture of Textile	115.24	7.88	
纺织服装鞋帽制造业	Manufacture of Textile Wearing Apparel, Footware and Caps	8.1	1	
皮革毛皮羽毛(绒)及其制品业	Manufacture of Leather, Fur, Feather and Related Products	0.27	0.7	
木材加工及木、竹、藤、棕、草制品业	Processing of Timber, Manufacture of Wood, Bamboo, Rattan, Palm, and Straw Products	0.02	0.82	
家具制造业	Manufacture of Furniture	1.73	1.74	
造纸及纸制品业	Manufacture of Paper and Paper Products	66.24	3.44	
印刷业和记录媒介的复制	Printing, Reproduction of Recording Media	16.72	0.78	
文教体育用品制造业	Manufacture of Articles For Culture, Education and Sport Activity	4.49	0.74	
石油加工炼焦及核燃料加工业	Processing of Petroleum, Coking, Processing of Nuclear Fuel	1026.65	16.42	122.64
化学原料及化学制品制造业	Manufacture of Raw Chemical Materials and Chemical Products	3106.62	51.32	
医药制造业	Manufacture of Medicines	121.69	5.4	0.01
化学纤维制造业	Manufacture of Chemical Fibers		0.15	
橡胶制品业	Manufacture of Rubber	75.74	5.48	0.01
塑料制品业	Manufacture of Plastics	11.45	8.15	
非金属矿物制品业	Manufacture of Non-Metallic Mineral Products	1.37	9.12	0.81
黑色金属冶炼及压延加工业	Smelting and Pressing of Ferrous Metals	55.5	75.48	0.03
有色金属冶炼及压延加工业	Smelting and Pressing of Non-Ferrous Metals	1.15	1.69	
金属制品业	Manufacture of Metal Products	9.95	9.2	0.01
通用设备制造业	Manufacture of General Purpose Machinery	28.02	8.79	0.09
专用设备制造业	Manufacture of Special Purpose Machinery	35.82	2.73	0.03
交通运输设备制造业	Manufacture of Transport Equipment	110	11.84	0.47
电气机械及器材制造业	Manufacture of Electrical Machinery and Equipment	14.62	7.94	0.06
通信设备计算机及其他电子设备制造业	Manufacture of Communication Equipment, Computers and Other Electronic Equipment	79.11	20.33	
仪器仪表及文化办公用机械制造业	Manufacture of Measuring Instruments and Machinery for Cultural Activity and Office Work	15.87	1.04	0.02
工艺品及其他制造业	Manufacture of Artwork and Other Manufacturing	0.41	0.85	
废弃资源和废旧材料回收加工业	Recycling and Disposal of Waste		0.1	
电力热力的生产和供应业	Production and Supply of Electric Power and Heat Power	182.46	27.85	0.02
燃气生产和供应业	Production and Supply of Gas		0.55	
水的生产和供应业	Production and Supply of Water		2.07	

主要统计指标解释

能源生产总量 指一定时期内全市一次能源生产量的总和。该指标是观察全市能源生产水平、规模、构成和发展速度的总量指标。一次能源生产量包括原煤、原油、天然气、水电、核能及其他动力能（如风能、地热能等）发电量，不包括低热值燃料生产量、生物质能、太阳能等的利用和由一次能源加工转换而成的二次能源产量。

能源消费总量 指一定时期内全市物质生产部门、非物质生产部门和生活消费的各种能源的总和。该指标是观察能源消费水平、构成和增长速度的总量指标。能源消费总量包括原煤和原油及其制品、天然气、电力，不包括低热值燃料、生物质能和太阳能等的利用。能源消费总量分为终端能源消费量、能源加工转换损失量和能源损失量三部分。

终端能源消费量 指一定时期内全市生产和生活消费的各种能源在扣除了用于加工转换二次能源消费量和损失量以后的数量。

能源加工转换损失量 指一定时期内全市投入加工转换的各种能源数量之和与产出各种能源产品之和的差额。该指标是观察能源在加工转换过程中损失量变化的指标。

能源损失量 指一定时期内能源在输送、分配、储存过程中发生的损失和由客观原因造成的各种损失量，不包括各种气体能源放空、放散量。

能源消费弹性系数 反映能源消费增长速度与国民经济增长速度之间比例关系的指标。计算公式为：

能源消费弹性系数＝能源消费量年平均增长速度／国民经济年平均增长速度

电力消费弹性系数 反映电力消费增长速度与国民经济增长速度之间比例关系的指标。计算公式为：

电力消费弹性系数＝电力消费量年平均增长速度／国民经济年平均增长速度

Explanastory Notes on Main Statistical Indicators

Total Energy Production refers to the total production of primary energy by all energy producing enterprises in the city in a given period of time. It is a comprehensive indicator to show the capacity, scale, composition and development of energy production of the country. The production of primary energy includes that of coal, crude oil, natural gas, hydropower and electricity generated by nuclear energy and other means such as wind power and geothermal power. However, it excludes the production of fuels of low calorific value, bio-energy, solar energy and the secondary energy converted from the primary energy.

Total Energy Consumption refers to the total consumption of energy of various kinds by material production sectors, non material production sectors and households in the city in a given period of time. It is a comprehensive indicator to show the scale, composition and development of energy consumption. The total energy consumption includes that of coal, crude oil and their products, natural gas and electricity; however, it excludes the consumption of fuel of low calorific value, bio-energy and solar energy. Total domestic energy consumption can be divided into three parts: final energy consumption, loss during the process of energy conversion, and energy loss.

Final Energy Consumption refers to the total energy consumption by material production sectors, non material production sectors and households in the city in a given period of time, but excludes the consumption in conversion of the primary energy into the secondary energy and the loss in the process of energy conversion.

Loss during the Process of Energy Conversion refers to the total input of various kinds of energy for conversion, minus the total output of various kinds of energy in the city in a given period of time. It is an indicator to show the loss that occurs during the process of energy conversion.

Energy Loss refers to the total of the loss of energy during the course of energy transport, distribution and storage and the loss caused by any objective reason in a given period of time. The loss of various kinds of gas due to gas discharges and stocktaking is excluded.

Elasticity Ratio of Energy Consumption is an indicator to show the relationship between the growth rate of energy consumption and the growth rate of the national economy. The formula is:
Elasticity Ratio of Energy Consumption = (Average Annual Growth Rate of Energy Consumption)/(Average Annual Growth Rate of National Economy)

Elasticity Ratio of Electricity Consumption is an indicator to show the relationship between the growth rate of electricity consumption and the growth rate of the national economy. The formula is:
Elasticity Ratio of Electricity Consumption = (Average Annual Growth Rate of Electricity)/(Average Annual Growth Rate of National Economy)

第6篇
CHAPTER 6

财　政
Government Finance

6-1 全市财政收支（1994-2006年）
TOTAL GOVERNMENT REVENUE AND EXPENDITURE, 1994-2006

年份 Year	全市财政收入合计 Total Government Revenue	一般预算收入 General Budgetary Government Revenue	基金预算收入 Fund Revenue	全市财政支出合计 Total Government Expenditure	一般预算支出 General Budgetary Government Expenditure	基金预算支出 Fund Expenditure
绝对数(亿元) Value (100 million yuan)						
1994	95.99	95.99		69.00	69.00	
1995	117.34	117.34		90.37	90.37	
1996	137.45	137.45		110.19	110.19	
1997	169.12	151.42	17.70	140.08	122.78	17.30
1998	186.55	170.07	16.47	155.15	137.93	17.22
1999	206.89	187.14	19.75	177.62	157.41	20.21
2000	244.81	222.70	22.11	209.57	187.05	22.52
2001	304.52	279.41	25.12	259.78	234.67	25.11
2002	375.92	339.81	36.11	300.07	265.21	34.86
2003	451.74	410.95	40.79	350.63	312.08	38.56
2004	502.17	445.15	57.03	431.49	375.02	56.47
2005	725.81	645.09	80.71	520.28	442.12	78.16
2006	926.33	814.53	111.79	654.15	543.12	111.03
比上年增长(%) Increase Rate over Preceding Year (%)						
1995	22.2	22.2		31.0	31.0	
1996	15.8	15.8		21.9	21.9	
1997	13.5	10.2		13.8	11.4	
1998	10.3	12.3	-6.9	8.0	6.9	16.8
1999	10.9	10.0	19.9	14.5	14.1	17.3
2000	18.3	19.0	11.9	16.4	17.1	11.2
2001	24.4	25.5	13.6	25.7	27.3	11.8
2002	18.4	14.7	43.8	15.5	13.0	39.6
2003	20.2	21.0	12.9	16.8	17.8	10.0
2004	26.7	25.4	39.8	23.3	20.2	48.8
2005	26.8	26.3	41.5	20.6	17.9	38.4
2006	27.7	26.3	38.5	25.7	22.8	42.1

资料来源：天津市财政局。
Sources: Tianjin Municipal Finance Bureau.
注：1. 本表收支均未含以港养港收支。2. 增长速度均按可比口径计算。3. 6-2至6-7表同。
Note: a) Revenue and expenditure in this table exclude expenses charged and used for operation of Tianjin Port. b) Increase rate is calculated on the basis of comparable coverage. c) Same as following table 6-2 to 6-7.

6-2 地方一般预算财政收入(1994-2006年)
LOCAL GENERAL BUDGETARY GOVERNMENT REVENUE, 1994-2006

年 份 Year	地方一般预算收入 Local General Budgetary Government Revenue	# 增值税(25%) Value-added Tax (25%)	# 营业税 Business Tax	# 企业所得税 Income Tax of Enterprises	# 个人所得税 Individual Income Tax
绝对数(亿元) Value (100 million yuan)					
1994	46.83	14.26	15.17	11.21	2.41
1995	58.94	16.66	19.86	12.67	3.77
1996	76.02	17.25	24.67	19.06	5.30
1997	89.91	17.30	27.60	21.48	6.49
1998	101.40	18.99	30.71	20.34	7.91
1999	112.81	20.83	33.88	24.02	8.86
2000	133.61	26.12	38.16	29.25	11.34
2001	163.64	34.87	42.99	39.38	16.58
2002	171.83	38.73	51.65	26.24	13.20
2003	204.53	45.19	64.32	23.80	12.53
2004	246.18	35.17	78.39	32.12	15.98
2005	331.85	64.24	96.45	41.11	18.82
2006	417.05	80.67	115.92	53.20	21.21
比上年增长(%) Increase Rate over Preceding Year (%)					
1995	16.0	28.8	42.6	13.0	56.5
1996	29.0	3.6	24.2	50.4	40.4
1997	18.3	0.3	11.9	12.7	22.5
1998	12.8	9.8	11.3	-5.3	21.9
1999	11.3	9.7	10.3	18.1	12.1
2000	18.4	25.4	12.6	21.8	27.9
2001	22.5	33.5	12.7	34.6	46.2
2002	16.9	11.1	20.1	9.6	23.1
2003	24.8	16.7	24.5	13.6	18.7
2004	28.9	16.7	21.9	34.8	27.5
2005	28.2	21.8	23.0	27.8	17.5
2006	25.7	25.6	20.2	29.8	12.7

注：2002年开始中央与地方实施所得税收入分享改革，所得税中央与地方分享比例2002年为5∶5，2003年以来为6∶4。下同。
Note: Since 2002, the distribution of income tax has reformed. Central government and local government shared income tax at equal share of 50% each in 2002; central government shares 60% and local government shares 40% since 2003. Same as following tables.

6-3 一般预算财政支出(1994-2006年)
GENERAL BUDGETARY GOVERNMENT EXPENDITURE, 1994-2006

年 份 Year	一般预算支出 General Budgetary Government Expenditure	# 基本建设 Capital Construction	# 支援农业 Supporting Agriculture	# 教育支出 Operating Expense on Education	# 城市维护费 City Maintenance	# 科技三项费用 Science and Technology Promotion
绝对数(亿元) Value (100 million yuan)						
1994	69.00	9.69	2.29	11.41	6.88	0.94
1995	90.37	17.95	2.81	13.41	7.82	0.99
1996	110.19	23.20	3.11	16.62	10.33	1.16
1997	122.78	22.69	3.72	19.07	12.30	1.43
1998	137.93	24.16	4.00	21.74	15.13	1.58
1999	157.41	22.87	4.38	25.33	14.89	2.32
2000	187.05	29.71	4.65	30.87	15.90	3.69
2001	234.67	37.43	5.74	36.26	16.09	6.06
2002	265.21	39.36	7.05	41.57	20.44	6.68
2003	312.08	52.43	8.04	47.58	27.61	7.80
2004	375.02	69.39	10.93	55.40	40.81	9.20
2005	442.12	73.23	12.85	67.20	52.02	10.86
2006	543.12	83.29	16.08	81.58	66.90	14.97
比上年增长(%) Increase Rate over Preceding Year (%)						
1995	31.0	85.3	22.7	17.5	13.7	10.3
1996	21.9	29.3	10.6	23.9	32.1	17.4
1997	11.4	-2.2	19.6	14.7	19.1	22.8
1998	6.9	6.5	7.6	14.0	23.0	10.4
1999	14.1	-5.4	9.5	16.5	-1.6	47.0
2000	17.1	29.9	6.2	21.9	6.7	59.2
2001	27.3	26.0	23.4	17.4	1.2	64.0
2002	13.0	5.2	22.9	14.7	27.0	10.2
2003	17.8	33.2	14.3	14.4	35.1	16.8
2004	20.2	30.9	35.6	16.4	48.3	17.9
2005	17.9	5.5	17.6	21.3	27.5	18.0
2006	22.8	13.7	25.1	21.4	28.6	37.9

6-4 全市财政收入
TOTAL GOVERNMENT REVENUE

单位：万元 (10 000 yuan)

项　　目	Item	2005	2006	2006比2005年增长(%) Increase Rate in 2006 over 2005 (%)
合　　计	**Total**	**7258066**	**9263251**	**27.7**
#一般预算收入	General Budgetary Government Revenue	6450919	8145316	26.3
一、地方财政收入	**Local Governmentl Revenue**	**4125654**	**5288414**	**28.2**
1. 一般预算收入	**General Budgetary Government Revenue**	**3318507**	**4170479**	**25.7**
#税收收入	Revenue from Taxs	2705011	3426480	26.7
#增值税(25%)	Value-added Tax (25%)	642377	806681	25.6
营业税	Business Tax	964545	1159176	20.2
个人所得税	Individual Income Tax	188224	212141	12.7
企业所得税	Income Tax of Enterprises	411131	531963	29.8
国有企业计划亏损补贴	Planning Subsidies to Loss-suffering State-owned Enterprises	-25000	-25000	
罚没收入	Penalty and Confiscatory Income	67835	89009	31.2
行政性收费收入	Income from Administrative Fees	458474	535075	16.7
专项收入	Special Project Income	89995	109381	21.5
基金预算收入	**Budgetary Fund Revenue**	**807147**	**1117935**	**38.5**
2. 市级财政收入	**Government Revenue at City Level**	**2071234**	**2667933**	**27.5**
一般预算收入	General Budgetary Government Revenue	1483171	1861827	23.8
基金预算收入	Budgetary Fund Revenue	588063	806106	37.1
区县级财政收入	**Government Revenue at District & County Level**	**2054420**	**2620481**	**27.6**
一般预算收入	General Budgetary Government Revenue	1835336	2308652	25.8
基金预算收入	Budgetary Fund Revenue	219084	311829	42.5
二、上划中央收入小计	**Revenue Transferred to Central Government**	**3132412**	**3974840**	**27.0**

6-5 全市财政支出
TOTAL GOVERNMENT EXPENDITURE

单位：万元 (10 000 yuan)

项 目	Item	2005	2006	2006 比2005年增长(%) Increase Rate in 2006 over 2005 (%)
合 计	Total	5202795	6541504	25.7
1. 一般预算支出	General Budgetary Government Expenditure	4421207	5431219	22.8
# 基本建设支出	Capital Construction	732323	832874	13.7
企业挖潜改造资金	Innovation Funds of Enterprises	291198	346945	19.1
科技三项费用	Science and Technology Promotion	108550	149692	37.9
支援农村生产支出	Supporting Agricultural Production	128503	160785	25.1
工交流通等部门事业费	Operating Expenses of Industrial, Transportation and Commercial Departments	19374	25658	32.4
城市维护费	Expenditure for City Maintenance	520168	668999	28.6
文体广播事业费	Operating Expenses on Culture, Sports and Broadcasting	107471	135239	25.8
教育支出	Operating Expense on Education	672034	815828	21.4
科学支出	Operating Expense for Science	27989	33063	18.1
医疗卫生支出	Expenditure for Health Care	189803	237784	25.2
社会保障和优抚救济支出	Social Security and Pensions, Relief	459111	625467	36.2
政策性补贴支出	Expenditure for Price Subsidies	30072	46433	54.4
基金预算支出	Budgetary Fund Expenditure	781588	1110285	42.1
2. 市级财政支出	Government Expenditure at City Level	2560824	3390950	32.4
一般预算支出	General Budgetary Government Expenditure	2000867	2558032	27.8
基金预算支出	Budgetary Fund Expenditure	559957	832918	48.7
区县级财政支出	Government Expenditure at City Level	2641971	3150554	19.3
一般预算支出	General Budgetary Government Expenditure	2420340	2873187	18.7
基金预算支出	Budgetary Fund Expenditures	221631	277367	25.3

6-6 区县级一般预算财政收入(2006年)
GENERAL BUDGETARY GOVERNMENT REVENUE AT DISTRICT & COUNTY LEVEL, 2006

单位：万元 (10 000 yuan)

地　区	Region	一般预算财政收入 General Budgetary Government Revenue	个人所得税 Individual Income Tax	营业税 Business Tax	增值税 Value-added Tax
总　计	**Total**	**2308652**	**83820**	**528267**	**506220**
区级合计	**Total at District Level**	**2179066**	**81238**	**509864**	**479286**
和平区	Heping District	120385	4712	35498	8665
河东区	Hedong District	93880	3119	27889	10300
河西区	Hexi District	136078	4787	39894	13090
南开区	Nankai District	139702	3617	34691	13763
河北区	Hebei District	57421	1649	17004	6809
红桥区	Hongqiao District	37302	835	8866	3875
塘沽区	Tanggu District	159900	2889	39656	16044
汉沽区	Han'gu District	22964	437	4011	6369
大港区	Dagang District	61386	1935	12082	10800
东丽区	Dongli District	131002	3741	20587	32645
西青区	Xiqing District	148452	3714	29500	32648
津南区	Jinnan District	82566	2289	14866	21315
北辰区	Beichen District	117394	3167	18405	39413
武清区	Wuqing District	110021	5159	31090	21248
宝坻区	Baodi District	49392	1563	15022	6834
天津经济技术开发区	TEDA	528871	26635	104262	197087
天津保税区	TFTZ	101578	5512	35215	17038
天津新技术产业园区	THIP	80772	5478	21326	21343
县级合计	**Total at County Level**	**129586**	**2582**	**18403**	**26934**
宁河县	Ninghe County	29958	727	4963	3871
静海县	Jinghai County	43906	867	7374	11116
蓟　县	Jixian County	55722	988	6066	11947

6-6 续表 Continued

单位：万元 (10 000 yuan)

地　区	Region	城市维护建设税 Tax on Urban Maintenance and Construction	企业所得税 Income Tax of Enterprises	其他各项收入 Others
总　计	**Total**	**142566**	**350974**	**696805**
区级合计	**Total at District Level**	**132561**	**332870**	**643247**
和平区	Heping District	7196	22384	41930
河东区	Hedong District	7485	7377	37710
河西区	Hexi District	8475	9615	60217
南开区	Nankai District	8131	11843	67657
河北区	Hebei District	4237	6345	21377
红桥区	Hongqiao District	2652	2698	18376
塘沽区	Tanggu District	10970	13703	76638
汉沽区	Han'gu District	2549	1360	8238
大港区	Dagang District	5021	6843	24705
东丽区	Dongli District	18251	16502	39276
西青区	Xiqing District	11975	20934	49681
津南区	Jinnan District	7212	15360	21524
北辰区	Beichen District	11425	12498	32486
武清区	Wuqing District	7555	15295	29674
宝坻区	Baodi District	3451	2271	20251
天津经济技术开发区	TEDA	7620	129995	63272
天津保税区	TFTZ	3156	23256	17401
天津新技术产业园区	THIP	5200	14591	12834
县级合计	**Total at County Level**	**10005**	**18104**	**53558**
宁河县	Ninghe County	1632	1415	17350
静海县	Jinghai County	3041	4370	17138
蓟　县	Jixian County	5332	12319	19070

6-7 区县级一般预算财政支出（2006年）
GENERAL BUDGETARY GOVERNMENT EXPENDITURE AT DISTRICT & COUNTY LEVEL, 2006

单位：万元 (10 000 yuan)

地 区	Region	一般预算财政支出 General Budgetary Government Expenditure	#基本建设支出 Capital Construction	#支援农村生产支出 Supporting Agricultural Production	#教育支出 Operating Expense on Education
总 计	**Total**	**2873187**	**636562**	**71493**	**537122**
区级合计	**Total at District Level**	**2630972**	**636042**	**52905**	**464708**
和平区	Heping District	130816	16689		33240
河东区	Hedong District	107843			33059
河西区	Hexi District	130336	4776		36075
南开区	Nankai District	137300	3089		32931
河北区	Hebei District	83270			32705
红桥区	Hongqiao District	76855			26581
塘沽区	Tanggu District	202654	11510	3667	44634
汉沽区	Han'gu District	46174		2176	12161
大港区	Dagang District	102620	9686	3256	40067
东丽区	Dongli District	132466	6577	3711	22356
西青区	Xiqing District	171528	78821	4259	21073
津南区	Jinnan District	121314	28881	8459	19540
北辰区	Beichen District	93683	20422	3429	24078
武清区	Wuqing District	192608		16039	43018
宝坻区	Baodi District	99940	1000	7909	30700
天津经济技术开发区	TEDA	598372	335570		9290
天津保税区	TFTZ	133418	80106		
天津新技术产业园区	THIP	69775	38915		3200
县级合计	**Total at County Level**	**242215**	**520**	**18588**	**72414**
宁河县	Ninghe County	58405	20	3781	16750
静海县	Jinghai County	83878	500	8834	25231
蓟 县	Jixian County	99932		5973	30433

6-7 续表 Continued

单位：万元 (10 000 yuan)

地　区	Region	# 医疗卫生支　出 Expenditure for Health Care	# 社会保障补助支出 Subsidies for Social Security	# 公检法司支出 Public Security Agency, Procuratorial Agency & Court of Justice
总　计	**Total**	**124288**	**31598**	**165531**
区级合计	**Total at District Level**	**103848**	**30219**	**145380**
和平区	Heping District	7821	1401	11233
河东区	Hedong District	6742	2679	11440
河西区	Hexi District	8018	1940	13600
南开区	Nankai District	8557	3118	14190
河北区	Hebei District	6746	1554	8014
红桥区	Hongqiao District	7660	1760	7126
塘沽区	Tanggu District	6430	6700	19983
汉沽区	Han'gu District	4925	977	4061
大港区	Dagang District	4410	1339	6983
东丽区	Dongli District	6612	2854	8443
西青区	Xiqing District	5789	392	7241
津南区	Jinnan District	5734	908	5968
北辰区	Beichen District	5996	910	5868
武清区	Wuqing District	8763	549	8488
宝坻区	Baodi District	3490	1550	5550
天津经济技术开发区	TEDA	6112	690	5593
天津保税区	TFTZ		800	1413
天津新技术产业园区	THIP	43	98	186
县级合计	**Total at County Level**	**20440**	**1379**	**20151**
宁河县	Ninghe County	2128	316	4109
静海县	Jinghai County	5825	477	6668
蓟　县	Jixian County	12487	586	9374

6-8 天津市国家税务局各项税收情况（2003-2006年）
TAX REVENUE OF TIANJIN NATIONAL TAX BUREAU, 2003-2006

单位：万元 (10 000 yuan)

项 目	Item	2003	2004	2005	2006
总 计	**Total**	**4064420**	**5087574**	**7189915**	**9294321**
税收合计	**Total Tax**	**4693511**	**6306091**	**8377271**	**10540397**
# 增值税	Value-added Tax	3595089	4631805	5836010	7115949
消费税	Consumption Tax	289421	352408	447750	785393
营业税	Business Tax	28396	30143	32106	40761
企业所得税	Income Tax of Enterprises	134168	203579	365496	513778
# 国有企业	State-owned Enterprises	22144	27551	37525	66681
集体企业	Collective-owned Enterprises	4933	10022	8410	11796
股份合作企业	Cooperative Enterprises	711	706	1462	523
联营企业	Joint Ownership Enterprises	322	1028	2704	5570
股份有限公司	Share-holding Corporations Ltd.	82605	92248	291765	380637
私营企业	Private Enterprises	1396	7676	23583	48229
外商投资企业和外国企业所得税	Income Tax of Foreign and Foreign-founded Enterprises	553412	982337	1470901	1937033
个人所得税	Individual Income Tax	86507	96567	107602	130658
城市维护建设税	Tax on Urban Maintenance and Construction	3223	5042	7036	9632
房产和城市房地产税	Tax on Real Estates and Land	574	626	681	880
印花税	Stamp Tax	2562	3440	4970	6157
城镇土地使用税	Tax on the Use of Urban Land	129	124	136	138
车船使用和牌照税	Vehicle and Vessel License Tax	30	20	24	18
出口退税合计	**Total Tax Returned from Export Enterprises**	**-679190**	**-1266686**	**-1232311**	**-1313082**
其他收入合计	**Total Others**	**50099**	**48169**	**44955**	**67006**
# 教育费附加收入	Revenue from Extra-Charges for Education	1381	2156	3014	4128

主要统计指标解释

财政收入 指国家可直接支配的财力，主要包括税收收入和其他收入两大类。1994 年我国统一实行分税制财政体制，按税种分为上划中央收入和地方财政收入。上划中央收入包括：增值税的 75% 和消费税的 100% 等；地方财政收入包括：增值税的 25%、营业税（不含银行总行、铁道、保险总公司的营业税）、地方企业交纳的企业所得税、外商投资企业和外国企业所得税、个人所得税、土地使用税、固定资产投资方向调节税、城市维护建设税（不含银行总行、铁道、保险总公司集中交纳的部分）、资源税（不包括海洋石油资源税）、房产税、车船使用税、印花税、屠宰税、农牧业税、耕地占用税、契税、遗产和赠与税、土地增值税、国有土地有偿使用收入以及基金收入等。地方财政收入加上划中央收入为全市财政收入。需要指出的是 1994 年以后地方财政收入与以前实行的总额分成财政体制下的地方财政收入在内容和范围上有一定差别，历年数据不完全可比。

一般预算财政收入 是通过一定的形式和程序，由各级财政部门组织并纳入预算管理的各项收入，也就是会计制度改革以前所称的“预算收入”。

基金预算收入 是按规定收取，转入或通过当年财政安排，由财政管理并具有指定用途的政府性基金预算收入等。

一般预算财政支出 是各级财政部门对集中的一般预算收入有计划地分配和使用而安排的支出。

基金预算支出 是各级财政部门用基金预算收入安排的支出。

基本建设支出 指按国家有关规定，属于基本建设范围内的基本建设有偿使用、拨款、资本金支出以及经国家批准对专项和政策性基建投资贷款，在部门的基建投资额中统筹支付的贴息支出。

企业挖潜改造资金 指国家预算内拨给的用于企业挖潜、革新和改造方面的资金。包括各部门企业挖潜改造资金和企业挖潜改造贷款资金，为农业服务的县办“五小”企业技术改造补助，挖潜改造贷款贴息资金。

科技三项费用 指国家预算用于科技支出的费用，包括新产品试制费、中间试验费、重要科学研究补助费。

支援农村生产支出 指国家财政支援农村集体（户）各项生产的支出。包括对农村举办的小型农田水利和打井、喷灌等的补助费，对农村水土保持措施的补助费，对农村举办的小水电站的补助费，特大抗旱的补助费，农村开荒补助费，扶持乡镇企业资金，支援农村合作生产组织资金、农村农技推广和植保补助费，农村草场和畜禽保护补助费，农村造林和林木保护补助费，农村水产补助费，发展粮食生产专项资金。

工业交通商业等部门的事业费 指国家预算支付给工交商各部门用于事业发展的人员和公用经费支出，包括勘探设计费、中等专业学校经费、技术学校经费、干部训练费。

政策性补贴支出 指经国家批准，由国家财政拨给用于粮棉油等产品的价格补贴支出。主要包括粮、棉、油差价补贴，平抑物价和储备糖补贴，农业生产资料价差补贴，粮食风险基金，副食品风险基金，地方煤炭风险基金等。

Explanastory Notes on Main Statistical Indicators

Government Revenue refers to the revenue of the government directly disposable finance, including various tax revenue and other revenue. In accordance with the classification of the structure of the government finance in 1994 on the basis of the classification of channels for collection of tax revenue, the revenue of the central government and the revenue of the local governments have different coverage. Revenue of the central government includes 75% of the value added tax and 100% of the value consumption tax, etc, The revenue of the local governments includes 25% of the value added tax, business tax, (excluding business taxes of head offices of bank, profits of railways, head office of insurance company) , income tax of the local enterprises subordinated to the local government, income tax of foreign, Hong Kong, Macao and Taiwan funded enterprises, personal income tax, tax on the use of urban land, tax on the adjustment of the investment in fixed assets, tax on town maintenance and construction, tax on resources (excluding tax on ocean petroleum resources), tax on real estates, tax on the use of vehicles and ships, stamp tax, slaughter tax, tax on agriculture and animal husbandry, tax on the occupancy of cultivated land, contract tax, inheritance tax, gift tax, land value added tax, income of non -gratuitous use on the state-owned land and income of funds. Total of government revenue included the revenue of the central government and the revenue of the local governments. Now the content and coverage of the local financial revenue is difference from that before 1994, the figures in 2002 are not comparable with the previous years, please pay attention to distinguish when you use.

General Budgetary Government Revenue refers to financial revenue with budgetary management through certain form and procedure by financial departments at each level, also called "budgetary revenue" before reformation of accounting system.

Fund Budgetary Revenue refers to government fund budgetary revenue with financial management and assigned uses gathered by rules or through financial arrangement.

General Budgetary Government Expenditure refers to expenditure distributed and used from general budgetary financial revenue by financial departments at each level.

Fund Budgetary Expenditure refers to expenditure arranged from fund budgetary revenue by financial departments at each level.

Expenditure for Capital Construction refers to the non-gratuitous use and appropriation of funds for capital construction in the range of capital construction, outlay of capital as well as the loans on capital construction approved by the government for special purpose or policy purpose and the expenditure with discount paid in an overall way within the amount of the funds appropriated to the departments for capital construction.

Innovation Funds of the Enterprises refer to the funds appropriated from the government budget for the enterprises to tap the latent power, upgrade the technology and carry out innovation, including the innovation fund of the departments, loan of the enterprises for innovation, subsidies on the innovation of the small fertilizer plant, small cement plant, small coal mines, small machinery plant and small steel plant, the expenditure of interest for the loan for innovation.

Expenditures for Science and Technology Promotion refer to the expenses appropriated from the government budget for the scientific and technological expenditure, including new products development expenditure, expenditure for intermediate trial and subsidies on important scientific researches.

Expenditure for Supporting Rural Production refers to the expenditures appropriated from the government budget for supporting the various expenditures of the rural collective units or households for production, including the subsidies to the small water conservancy projects and well drilling, sprinkling irrigation projects run by the villages; subsidies on the rural water and soil conserving measures; subsidies to the small power stations run by the villages; subsidies to the expenditure for fighting against particularly severe draughts; subsidies on the rural waste land exclamation; fund for supporting the township enterprises; fund for supporting rural cooperative production organizations, subsidies to the expenditure for popularization of the agricultural technologies and plant protection in the rural areas; subsidies to the expenditure for the protection of grasslands and cattle and fowls; subsidies on afforestation and forest protection in rural areas; subsidies on the rural aquatic products industry; special fund for developing grain production.

Operating Expenses of the Departments of Industry, Transport and Commerce refer to the expenses appropriated from the government budget to cover the expenditure on salaries and operational expenditure of the departments of industry, transport and commerce for the expenditure of business development, including expenses for prospecting and designing, expenditures of specialized secondary schools, expenditures of the technical training schools and expenditures for cadres training, etc..

Explanastory Notes on Main Statistical Indicators

Expenditure on Policy-related Subsidies refers to the expenditure appropriated, with the approval of the government, from the state budget for price subsidies on such products as grain, cotton and edible oil. More specifically, it includes subsidies to the difference between the selling prices and purchasing prices of grains, cotton and edible oil, subsidies for curtaining prices and for sugar reserve, subsidies to the difference between the selling prices and purchasing prices of means pf agricultural production, risk fund for grains, risk fund for non-staple food, risk fund for local production of coal, etc..

第7篇
CHAPTER 7

价格指数
Price Indices

7-1 城市物价总指数（1978-2006年）
URBAN GENERAL PRICE INDICES, 1978-2006

年份 Year	上年=100 Preceding Year=100		1978年=100 Year of 1978=100		1990年=100 Year of 1990=100	
	商品零售价格指数 Retail Price Index	居民消费价格指数 Consumer Price Index	商品零售价格指数 Retail Price Index	居民消费价格指数 Consumer Price Index	商品零售价格指数 Retail Price Index	居民消费价格指数 Consumer Price Index
1978	100.0	100.0	100.0	100.0		
1979	101.1	101.0	101.1	101.0		
1980	105.5	105.1	106.7	106.2		
1981	101.5	101.3	108.3	107.5		
1982	100.5	100.5	108.8	108.1		
1983	100.5	100.5	109.3	108.6		
1984	101.8	101.8	111.3	110.6		
1985	113.9	113.1	126.8	125.0		
1986	107.2	106.8	135.9	133.6		
1987	106.9	106.8	145.3	142.6		
1988	117.7	116.9	171.0	166.7		
1989	115.1	114.7	196.8	191.2		
1990	102.7	103.0	202.1	197.0	100.0	100.0
1991	108.0	110.2	218.3	217.1	108.0	110.2
1992	109.4	111.4	238.8	241.8	118.2	122.8
1993	114.3	117.6	273.0	284.4	135.0	144.4
1994	115.6	124.0	315.6	352.6	156.1	179.0
1995	110.6	115.3	349.0	406.6	172.7	206.4
1996	105.1	109.0	366.8	443.2	181.5	225.0
1997	100.7	103.1	369.4	456.9	182.7	232.0
1998	96.6	99.5	356.8	454.6	176.5	230.8
1999	97.5	98.9	347.9	449.6	172.1	228.3
2000	98.6	99.6	343.1	447.8	169.7	227.3
2001	98.6	101.2	338.2	453.2	167.3	230.1
2002	97.4	99.6	329.5	451.4	163.0	229.2
2003	97.4	101.0	320.9	455.9	158.7	231.4
2004	100.8	102.3	323.5	466.4	160.0	236.8
2005	99.9	101.5	323.1	473.4	159.8	240.3
2006	100.4	101.5	324.4	480.5	160.5	243.9

7-2 城市居民消费价格分类指数
URBAN CONSUMER PRICE INDICES BY CATEGORY

上年=100 (Preceding Year=100)

项　目　Item	2004	2005	2006
居民消费价格总指数 General Consumer Price Index	**102.3**	**101.5**	**101.5**
#服务项目价格指数 Services	100.3	101.6	101.5
1.食　品 Food	**109.9**	**103.4**	**102.7**
粮　食 Grain	123.7	103.8	103.7
淀　粉 Starches	102.3	109.3	107.4
干豆类及豆制品 Beans and Related Products	119.9	100.8	98.6
油脂类 Oil or Fat	120.1	94.7	97.6
肉禽及其制品 Meat, Poultry and Related Products	113.9	104.5	96.6
蛋　类 Eggs	123.8	103.5	95.5
水产品 Aquatic Products	131.6	95.7	103.7
菜　类 Vegetables	94.5	112.1	110.9
调味品 Flavoring	104.3	101.7	101.0
糖 Sugar	99.8	103.0	105.6
茶及饮料 Tea and Drink	99.7	101.0	99.8
干鲜瓜果 Dried and Fresh Melons and Fruits	109.2	109.6	111.9
糕点饼干面包 Pasty, Biscuit and Bread	105.9	105.3	102.9
液体乳及乳制品 Liquid Dairy and Related Products	100.0	100.3	100.9
在外用膳食品 Catering Trade	103.9	104.1	102.7
其他食品 Other Food	101.9	101.4	101.4
2.烟酒及用品 Tobacco, Liquor and Related Goods	**101.0**	**99.7**	**103.0**
烟　草 Tobacco	101.5	101.2	101.5
酒 Liquor	106.0	103.2	102.7
吸烟饮酒用品 Related Goods	91.4	88.6	107.1
3.衣　着 Clothing	**92.1**	**96.3**	**97.5**
服　装 Garments	92.5	99.9	98.3

注：根据国家统计制度的新规定，2006年以前淀粉为淀粉及薯类；液体乳及乳制品为奶及奶制品；其他食品为其他食品及食品加工服务。7-3表同。

Note: According to the new regulations of national statistics system, before 2006, Starche sand Tubers were used instead of Starches;Milk and Related Products were used instead of Liquid Dairy and Related Products; Other Food and Cooking Services were used instead of Other Food. Same as 7-3.

7-2 续表 Continued

项　目　Item	2004	2005	2006
衣着材料 Clothing Materials	100.6	100.0	100.7
鞋袜帽 Shoes, Socks and Hats	88.7	85.2	94.8
衣着加工服务 Processing Services	100.0	99.7	98.3
4. 家庭设备用品及维修服务 Household Appliances, Articles and Repair Services	**98.3**	**99.1**	**100.5**
耐用消费品 Durable Consumer Goods	97.5	97.6	98.9
室内装饰品 Indoors Decorations	100.0	95.9	89.6
床上用品 Bed Articles	89.0	103.2	94.6
家庭日用杂品 Daily Use Household Articles	101.2	100.4	103.3
家庭服务及加工维修服务 Household Services and Repair Services	98.4	107.2	116.3
5. 医疗保健和个人用品 Medical, Health Care and Individual Goods	**93.4**	**97.6**	**101.4**
医疗保健 Medicine and Medical Services	91.6	97.6	101.5
个人用品及服务 Individual Goods and Services	98.7	97.4	101.0
6. 交通和通信 Transportation and Communications	**96.8**	**98.6**	**98.9**
交　通 Transportations	98.7	104.1	103.4
通　信 Communications	95.5	94.8	94.7
7. 娱乐教育文化用品及服务 Recreational, Educational & Cultural Articles and Services	**99.2**	**100.0**	**99.0**
文娱用耐用消费品及服务 Durable Consumer Goods & Services for Recreational Use	91.9	95.1	91.9
教　育 Education	101.5	100.5	100.0
文化娱乐 Recreation and Culture	94.9	103.5	97.1
旅　游 Tourism	106.5	100.8	111.2
8. 居　住 Residence	**103.6**	**106.7**	**104.4**
建房及装修材料 Building and Decoration Materials	100.7	102.1	107.8
租　房 Rent	100.3	102.1	100.7
自有住房 Individual Housing	100.4	103.6	101.7
水、电、燃料 Water, Electricity and Fuel	108.4	112.5	104.9

注：根据国家统计制度的新规定，2006年以前交通和通信为交通和通讯；文化娱乐为文化娱乐用品；旅游为旅游及外出。7-3表同。

Note: According to the new regulations of national statistics system, before 2006, Transportation and Telecommunications were used instead of Transportation and Communications; Recreation and Culture Articles were used instead of Recreation and Culture; Tourism and Going-out were used instead of Tourism. Same as 7-3.

7-3 城市商品零售价格分类指数
URBAN RETAIL PRICE INDICES BY CATEGORY

上年=100 (Preceding Year=100)

项 目 Item	2004	2005	2006
商品零售价格总指数 General Retail Price Index	**100.8**	**99.9**	**100.4**
1.食 品 Food	**110.2**	**103.5**	**102.8**
粮 食 Grain	123.7	103.8	103.7
淀 粉 Starches	102.3	109.3	107.4
干豆类及豆制品 Beans and Related Products	119.9	100.8	98.6
油脂类 Oil or Fat	120.1	94.7	97.6
肉禽及其制品 Meat, Poultry and Related Products	113.9	104.5	96.6
蛋 类 Eggs	123.8	103.5	95.5
水产品 Aquatic Products	131.6	95.7	103.7
菜 类 Vegetables	94.5	112.1	110.9
调味品 Flavoring	104.3	101.7	101.0
糖 Sugar	99.8	103.0	105.6
茶及饮料 Tea and Drink	109.2	109.6	111.9
干鲜瓜果 Dried and Fresh Melons and Fruits	105.9	105.3	102.9
糕点饼干面包 Pasty, Biscuit and Bread	100.0	100.3	100.9
液体乳及乳制品 Liquid Dairy and Related Products	103.9	104.1	102.7
在外用膳食品 Catering Trade	101.9	101.3	101.4
其他食品 Other Food	102.3	101.8	101.4
2.烟酒及用品 Tobacco, Liquor and Related Goods	**99.7**	**101.0**	**99.8**
烟 草 Tobacco	101.5	101.2	101.5
酒 Liquor	106.0	103.2	102.7
吸烟饮酒用品 Related Goods	91.7	96.1	97.4
3.衣 着 Clothing	**92.6**	**99.9**	**98.3**
服 装 Garments	88.9	85.2	94.8
其 他 Others	95.7	98.3	98.0

7-3 续表 1 Continued

项　目　Item	2004	2005	2006
4. 纺织品 Textiles	**94.5**	**102.2**	**97.7**
衣着材料 Clothing Materials	100.6	100.0	100.7
床上用品 Bed Articles	88.4	103.2	96.3
5. 家用电器及音像器材 Household Appliances and Stereo Sets & Camera Facilities	**93.5**	**96.3**	**95.0**
家庭设备 Hosehold Facilities	96.1	98.3	98.2
文娱用耐用消费品 Durable Consumer Goods for Recreational Use	87.3	92.7	90.4
音像器材类 Stereo Sets & Camera Facilities	98.4	96.5	97.6
6. 文化办公用品 Culture and Office Articles	**96.2**	**98.8**	**95.2**
7. 日用品 Articles for Daily Use	**100.3**	**100.4**	**101.2**
日用百货 General Merchandise for Daily Use	101.6	99.6	100.5
日用杂品 Sundry Articles	98.1	100.4	106.6
洗涤用品 Washing Articles	100.1	100.6	103.0
其他日用品 Other Articles for Daily Use	99.5	101.4	98.8
8. 体育娱乐用品 Sport and Recreation Articles	**95.3**	**97.6**	**97.7**
体育用品 Sport Articles	98.7	100.6	100.0
娱乐用品 Recreation Articles	93.1	95.8	97.0
9. 交通、通信用品 Transportation and Communications Articles	**87.8**	**88.6**	**90.0**
交通运输机械 Transportation Machinery	93.0	99.1	98.2
通信器材 Communications Facilities	72.2	70.5	68.0
10. 家　具 Furniture	**99.9**	**97.2**	**99.7**
11. 化妆品 Cosmetics	**100.9**	**98.2**	**101.7**
12. 金银珠宝 Gold, Silver and Jewelry	**119.1**	**102.9**	**123.5**
13. 中西药品及医疗保健用品 Traditional Chinese & Western Medicine and Medical, Health Care Goods	**86.9**	**96.5**	**102.3**
医疗器具及用品 Medical Facilities and Goods	100.0	98.4	99.5
中药材及中成药 Traditional Chinese Raw Medicine and Medicine	94.0	95.3	105.0

7-3 续表 2 Continued

项　目 Item	2004	2005	2006
西　药 Western Medicine	81.1	96.2	100.3
保健器具及用品 Health Care Facilities and Goods	93.4	98.6	103.2
14. 书报杂志及电子出版物 Books, Newspapers and Magazines, Electronics Publications	**99.5**	**100.6**	**99.0**
教材及参考书 Teaching Materials and Reference Books	97.0	100.9	98.0
书报杂志 Books, Newspapers and Magazines	100.5	100.0	100.0
电子音像制品 Electronics Stereo Goods	104.3	101.8	99.3
15. 燃　料 Fuels	**110.5**	**112.9**	**106.8**
煤炭及制品类 Coal and Related Products	124.3	121.9	102.2
石油及制品类 Petroleum and Related Products	109.7	112.4	107.0
16. 建筑材料及五金电料 Construction Materials and Hardware Materials	**100.6**	**101.6**	**107.7**
建筑装璜材料 Construction and Decoration Materials	100.7	102.1	109.4
五金电料类 Hardware Materials	100.0	100.0	100.5

7-4 居民货币购买力指数（1991-2006年）
INDICES OF MONETARY PURCHASING POWER OF RESIDENTS, 1991-2006

年　份 Year	上年=100 Preceding Year=100	年　份 Year	1990年=100 Year of 1990=100
1991	90.7	1991	90.7
1992	89.8	1992	81.4
1993	85.0	1993	69.3
1994	80.6	1994	55.9
1995	86.7	1995	48.4
1996	91.7	1996	44.4
1997	97.0	1997	43.1
1998	100.5	1998	43.3
1999	101.1	1999	43.8
2000	100.4	2000	44.0
2001	98.8	2001	43.5
2002	100.4	2002	43.6
2003	99.0	2003	43.2
2004	97.8	2004	42.2
2005	98.5	2005	41.6
2006	98.5	2006	41.0

7-5 固定资产投资价格指数（2003-2006年）
PRICE INDICES OF INVESTMENT IN FIXED ASSETS, 2003-2006

上年=100 (Preceding Year=100)

项 目 Item	2003	2004	2005	2006
固定资产投资价格总指数 General Price Index of Investment In Fixed Assets	**102.6**	**107.3**	**101.2**	**100.7**
建筑安装、装饰工程 Building Installation	104.9	111.3	101.4	100.3
# 材料费用 Expense of Materials	106.0	114.8	101.1	99.2
设备工器具购置 Purchase of Equipment, Tools and Instruments	97.8	100.5	99.1	99.9
其他费用 Others	100.4	101.0	102.6	102.9

7-6 工业品出厂价格指数（2003-2006年）
EX-FACTORY PRICE INDICES OF INDUSTRIAL PRODUCTS, 2003-2006

上年=100 (Preceding Year=100)

项 目 Item	2003	2004	2005	2006
工业品出厂价格总指数 General Industrial Products Price Index	**102.5**	**104.1**	**100.1**	**100.6**
轻工业 Light Industry	99.6	101.2	98.2	98.7
以农产品为原料 Using Farm Products as Raw Materials	103.6	104.0	98.9	99.5
以非农产品为原料 Using Non-farm Products as Raw Materials	98.1	100.3	98.0	98.5
重工业 Heavy Industry	105.1	106.3	101.5	101.7
采掘业 Mining and Quarrying Industry	124.7	121.0	131.0	124.5
原料工业 Raw Materials Industry	113.5	118.4	108.1	106
加工工业 Processing Industry	97.5	97.2	92.9	95.1
生产资料 Production Goods	103.3	105.6	101.0	101.2
采掘业 Mining and Quarrying Industry	124.7	121.1	130.4	122.8
原料工业 Raw Materials Industry	113.0	117.7	107.4	107
加工工业 Processing Industry	98.2	99.7	95.4	96.2
生活资料 Consumer Goods	100.0	99.2	97.3	98.6
食 品 Food	103.1	103.5	98.3	99.9
衣 着 Clothing	101.2	100.9	98.0	99.4
一般日用品 Daily Use Articles	99.9	99.8	101.0	98.5
耐用消费品 Durable Consumer Goods	96.4	95.6	95.1	97.8

7-7 按行业分工业品出厂价格指数（2006年）
EX-FACTORY PRICE INDICES OF INDUSTRIAL PRODUCTS BY SECTOR, 2006

上年=100 (Preceding Year=100)

行业 Sector	指数 Index	行业 Sector	指数 Index
煤炭开采和洗选业 Mining and Washing of Coal	95.1	医药制造业 Manufacture of Medicines	96.2
石油和天然气开采业 Extraction of Petroleum and Natural Gas	124.4	化学纤维制造业 Manufacture of Chemical Fibers	100.3
有色金属矿采选业 Mining and Processing of Non-Ferrous Metal Ores	133.1	橡胶制品业 Manufacture of Rubber	105.6
非金属矿采选业 Mining and Processing of Nonmetal Ores	88.3	塑料制品业 Manufacture of Plastics	100.0
农副食品加工业 Processing of Food from Agricultural Products	98.1	非金属矿物制品业 Manufacture of Non-Metallic Mineral Products	102.8
食品制造业 Manufacture of Foods	101.6	黑色金属冶炼及压延加工业 Smelting and Pressing of Ferrous Metals	94.4
饮料制造业 Manufacture of Beverages	101.4	有色金属冶炼及压延加工业 Smelting and Pressing of Nonferrous Metals	139.7
烟草制品业 Manufacture of Tobacco	101.2	金属制品业 Manufacture of Metal Products	95.0
纺织业 Manufacture of Textile	101.9	通用设备制造业 Manufacture of General Purpose Machinery	99.5
纺织服装、鞋、帽制造业 Manufacture of Textile Wearing Apparel, Footware, and Caps	97.7	专用设备制造业 Manufacture of Special Purpose Machinery	100.1
皮革、毛皮、羽毛(绒)及其制品业 Manufacture of Leather, Fur, Feather and Related Products	100.0	交通运输设备制造业 Manufacture of Transport Equipment	98.9
木材加工及木、竹、藤、棕、草制品业 Processing of Timber, Manufacture of Wood, Bamboo, Rattan, Palm and Straw Products	101.6	电气机械及器材制造业 Manufacture of Electrical Machinery and Equipment	108.0
家具制造业 Manufacture of Furniture	100.3	通信设备、计算机及其他电子设备制造业 Manufacture of Communication Equipment, Computers and Other Electronic Equipment	91.2
造纸及纸制品业 Manufacture of Paper and Paper Products	98.6	仪器仪表及文化、办公用机械制造业 Manufacture of Measuring Instruments and Machinery for Cultural Activity and Office Work	91.4
印刷业和记录媒介的复制 Printing and Record Medium Reproduction	99.7	工艺品及其他制造业 Manufacture of Artwork and Other Manufacturing	99.6
文教体育用品制造业 Cultural, Educational and Sports Goods	99.6	废弃资源和废旧材料回收加工业 Recycling and Disposal of Waste	122.5
石油加工、炼焦及核燃料加工业 Processing of Petroleum, Coking, Processing of Nuclear Fuel	119.5	电力、热力的生产和供应业 Production and Supply of Electric Power and Heat Power	104.9
化学原料及化学制品制造业 Manufacture of Raw Chemical Materials and Chemical Products	100.1	煤气生产和供应业 Production and Supply of Gas	104.3
		水的生产和供应业 Production and Supply of Water	120.0

7-8 工业主要原材料、燃料及动力购进价格指数(2003-2006年)
MAIN RAW MATERIALS, FUELS AND MOTIVE POWER PURCHASING PRICE INDICES OF INDUSTRY, 2003-2006

上年=100 (Preceding Year=100)

项　目 Item	2003	2004	2005	2006
原材料燃料动力购进价格总指数 Raw Materials Fuel and Motive Power Purchasing Price Index	**108.7**	**115.4**	**104.9**	**104.7**
燃料、动力类 Fuels and Energy	113.1	118.3	122.9	111.9
黑色金属材料类 Ferrous Metals	119.6	134.3	103.3	93.9
有色金属材料及电线类 Non ferrous Metals	107.8	130.5	117.3	153.6
化工原料类 Chemical Raw Materials	111.3	114.4	111.7	102.0
木材及纸浆类 Wood and Paper Pulps	100.9	99.0	104.6	103.4
建筑材料及非金属矿类 Construction Materials	106.9	106.3	114.5	96.6
其他工业原材料及半成品类 Other Industrial Raw Materials and Semi-products	95.9	105.5	98.3	101.9
农副产品类 Farm and Sideline Products	122.5	115.6	91.9	108.5
纺织原料类 Textile Raw Materials	106.2	118.6	97.9	100.0

7-9 房地产价格指数(2003-2006年)
PRICE INDICES OF REAL ESTATE, 2003-2006

上年=100 (Preceding Year=100)

项　目 Item	2003	2004	2005	2006
房屋销售价格指数 Price Index of Real Estate Sales	**104.1**	**113.5**	**106.0**	**106.7**
商品房 Commercial House	104.0	111.7	106.3	106.9
经济适用房 Low-cost and Policy Related House	106.6	111.2	104.7	104.7
普通住宅 Common Residence	103.2	111.7	107.1	108.2
高档住宅 High-grade Residence	100.6	110.3	107.2	105.5
二手房 Second-hand House	105.0	119.5	105.0	106.2
房屋租赁价格指数 Price Index of Real Estate Rent	**100.7**	**101.2**	**101.3**	**100.2**
住　宅 Residence	107.9	100.4	101.6	100.0
办公楼 Office	96.1	101.7	102.7	100.6
商业娱乐用房 Business and Entertainment Housing	99.9	103.1	100.4	100.5
工业仓储用房 Industry storehouses	90.3	101.4	100.4	100.1
土地交易价格指数 Price Index of Land Transaction	**103.0**	**116.3**	**103.9**	**103.4**

主要统计指标解释

商品零售价格指数 是工业、商业、餐饮业和其他零售企业向城乡居民、机关团体出售生活消费品和办公用品的价格水平变动趋势和变动程度的相对数。其目的在于掌握零售商品价格的变动趋势，为国家宏观调控和国民经济核算提供参考依据。

商品零售价格的调查范围涉及到各种类型的工业、商业、餐饮业和其他行业的零售商品以及农民对非农业居民出售商品的价格。包括食品、饮料烟酒、服装鞋帽、纺织品、家用电器及音像器材、文化办公用品、日用品、体育娱乐用品、交通通信用品、家具、化妆品、金银珠宝、中西药品及医疗保健用品、书报杂志及电子出版物、燃料、建筑材料及五金电料等16个大类。

居民消费价格指数 是反映居民家庭购买的消费品及服务价格水平的变动趋势和变动程度的相对数。它是宏观经济分析和决策、价格总水平监测和调控以及国民经济核算的重要指标。其按年度计算的变动率通常被用来作为反映通货膨胀（或紧缩）程度的指标。

居民消费价格的调查范围包括居民家庭购买并用于日常生活消费的商品和服务项目价格。按用途划分为8个大类，包括食品、烟酒及用品、衣着、家庭设备用品及维修服务费、医疗保健及个人用品、交通和通信、娱乐教育文化用品及服务、居住等。

固定资产投资价格指数 是反映一定时期内固定资产投资额价格变动趋势和程度的相对数。固定资产投资额是由建筑安装工程投资完成额、设备、工器具购置投资完成额和其他费用投资完成额三部分组成的。编制固定资产投资价格指数首先分别编制上述三部分投资的价格指数，然后采用加权算术平均法求出固定资产投资价格总指数。该指数可以准确地反映固定资产投资中涉及的各类商品和取费项目价格变动趋势和变动幅度，消除按现价计算的固定资产投资指标中的价格变动因素，真实地反映固定资产投资的规模、速度、结构和效益，为国家科学地制定、检查固定资产投资计划并提高宏观调控水平，为完善国民经济核算体系提供科学的、可靠的依据。

工业品出厂价格指数 是反映一定时期内全部工业产品出厂价格总水平的变动趋势和程度的相对数，包括工业企业售给本企业以外所有单位的各种产品和直接售给居民用于生活消费的产品。通过工业品出厂价格指数能观察出厂价格变动对工业总产值的影响。

工业原材料、燃料及动力购进价格指数 是反映一定时期内全部工业企业作为生产投入，从物资交易市场和能源、原材料生产企业购买原材料、燃料和动力产品时，所支付的价格水平变动趋势和程度的相对数，是扣除工业企业物质消耗成本中的价格变动影响的重要依据。

房地产价格指数 是反映全部房地产价格总水平的变动趋势和程度的相对数。包括土地交易价格指数、房地产销售价格指数、房地产租赁价格指数。

土地交易价格指数 是反映一定时期内房地产开发商或其他建设单位在进行商品房、生产和商业用房及其他生产经营用地开发前为取得土地使用权而实际支付的价格的变动趋势和程度的相对数。

房屋销售价格指数 是反映一定时期内房屋销售价格总水平变动趋势和程度的相对数。

房屋租赁价格指数 是反映一定时期内房屋租赁价格总水平变动趋势和程度的相对数。

Explanastory Notes on Main Statistical Indicators

Retail Price Index reflects the trend and degree of changes in retail prices of living consumer goods and office equipment which are sold to residents and organizations by retail enterprises. It can be used to know about the change tendency of the price of retailed goods, provides reliable data for government decision making and further improving the current national accounting system.

Its survey field covers the retail price of industry, commerce, catering trade and other sectors and prices of goods sold to non-agricultural population by farmers. Now it is classified into 16 categories by food, beverages, tobacco and liquor, garments, shoes and hats, textiles, household appliances, stereo sets & camera facilities, cultural and office goods, articles for daily use, sports and recreational goods, transport and communications goods, furniture, cosmetics, jewelry, traditional Chinese and western medicines, newspapers, magazines and electronics publications, fuels, building decoration materials, hardware materials.

Consumer Price Index reflects the trend and degree of changes in prices of consumer goods and services purchased by citizens. It is an indicator used for government decision making, price monitoring & controlling and improving the current national accounting system. The annual price index is used to reflect the degree of inflation and deflation.

Its survey field covers the prices of goods and services purchased by citizens and used for living. It is classified into 8 categories by food, tobacco and use articles, clothing, household facilities and articles, repair services, medicine and medical articles, means of transportation and communication, recreation, education and culture articles, residence, services.

Price Index of Investment in Fixed Assets reflects the trend and degree of changes in prices of investment in fixed assets during a given period. The investment in fixed assets consists of three components, namely the investment in construction and installation, the investment in purchases of equipment and instrument, and the investment in other items. Price index of investment in fixed assets is calculated as the weighted arithmetic mean of the price indices of the three components of investment in fixed assets. Removing the factor of price change in the aggregates of investment at current prices, this indicator shows the changes in the prices of commodities and fees involved in the investment of fixed assets, and can be used to observe the actual size, growth, structure, and efficiency of investment in fixed assets and provides reliable and scientific data for government planning, management, decision making, and further improving the current national accounting system.

Ex-factory Price Index of Industrial Products reflects the trend and degree of changes in general ex-factory prices of all industrial products during a given period, including sales of industrial products by an industrial enterprise to all units outside the enterprise, as well as sales of consumer goods to residents. It can be used to analyze the impact of ex-factory prices on gross industrial output value.

Purchasing Price Index of Raw Material, Fuel and Power reflects the trend and degree of changes in purchasing price of raw material, fuel and power paid by industrial enterprises when they purchase production as input from the market or other energy and raw material producers during a given period, and provide basis for measuring the material consumption of industrial enterprises after removing influence of price from cost.

Price Index of Real Estate reflects the trend and degree changes in real estate price, including price index of land transaction, price index of real estate sales, price index of real estate leasing.

Price Index of Land Transaction reflects the trend and degree changes in land transaction price which paid actually by developing enterprises or construction units to get land use rights before development of commodity buildings during a given period.

Price Index of Housing Sales reflects the trend and degree changes in housing sales during a given period.

Price Index of Housing Leasing reflects the trend and degree changes in housing leasing during a given period.

第8篇
CHAPTER 8
人民生活
People's Life

8-1 城乡居民物质文化生活水平提高情况(2002-2006年)
IMPROVEMENT IN URBAN AND RURAL RESIDENTS' MATERIAL AND CULTURAL LIFE, 2002-2006

指　　标	Item	2002	2003	2004	2005	2006
居民收入支出(元)	**Income and Expenditure of Urban and Rural Residents (yuan)**					
城镇单位从业人员人均劳动报酬	Per Capita Annual Remuneration of Persons Employed in Urban Units	16223	18511	21146	24122	27628
城市居民人均可支配收入	Per Capita Annual Disposable Income of Urban Residents	9338	10313	11467	12639	14283
城市居民人均消费性支出	Per Capita Annual Expenditures for Consumption of Urban Residents	7192	7868	8802	9653	10548
农村居民人均纯收入	Per Capita Annual Net Income of Rural Residents	5315	5861	6525	7202	7942
农村居民人均生活消费支出	Per Capita Annual Living Expenditures of Rural Residents	2778	3015	3297	3590	3829
储　蓄(万元)	**Savings (10 000 yuan)**					
人均年末储蓄存款余额	Per Capita Saving Deposit Balance	1.62	1.97	2.27	2.36	2.61
住　房(平方米)	**Floor Space of Residential Buildings (sq. m)**					
城市人均住宅建筑面积	Per Capita Floor Space of Urban Residential Buildings	22.2	23.1	24.7	25.0	26.1
农村人均住房面积	Per Capita Living Floor Space of Rural Residents	24.3	24.4	25.2	26.1	26.4
交通和通信	**Transportation and Communications**					
城市每万人拥有公共交通车辆(标台)	Number of Public Transportations Vehicles per 10 000 Persons in City (standard vehicles)	9.3	9.4	10.7	11.2	14.2
城市每万人拥有铺装道路长度(公里)	Length of Paved Roads per 10 000 Persons in City (km)	6.57	6.55	6.71	8.52	10.6
每人每年函件交寄(件)	Per Capita Annual Letters Delivered (piece)	22	23.9	11.4	8.1	8.4
全市每百人拥有电话机(含移动)(部)	Telephones Owned per 100 Persons (Include Mobile) (set)	65.4	82.3	89.5	90.1	106.7
电、水、燃气、供热	**Electricity, Water, Gas and Heating**					
全市人均生活用电量(千瓦小时)	Per Capita Electric Consumption for Living of All Residents (kWh)	320	344	360	367	406
城市人均生活用水量(吨)	Per Capita Water Consumption for Living of Urban Households (ton)	48.5	47.8	45.6	45.1	47.6
城市用气普及率(%)	Popularization Rate of Urban Households in Gas Use (%)	95.1	97.1	98.5	98.5	99.2
城市住宅集中供热面积(万平方米)	Heating Area of Urban Residential Buildings (10 000 sq. m)	7381	8118	8970	10967	12041

8-1 续表 Continued

指　标	Item	2002	2003	2004	2005	2006
文　化	**Culture**					
每百户城市居民	Per 100 Urban Households					
家庭拥有(台)	Possession (set)					
彩色电视机	Color TV Sets	135	135	137	136	136
家用电脑	Personal-Computers	26	34	41	51	59
每百户农村居民	Per 100 Urban Households					
家庭拥有(台)	Possession (set)					
彩色电视机	Color TV Sets	105	110	115	116	120
家用电脑	Personal-Computers	5	7	8	10	12
平均每人每年有图书(册)	Annual Per Capita Number of Books (copy)	6.9	6.7	8.2	5.7	4.8
平均每百人每天	Number of Newspapers per 100					
有报纸(份)	Persons Per Day (copy)	22	22.4	23.3	23.2	24.5
教　育	**Education**					
每万人口中有各级	Number of Students Enrollment					
学校在校学生(人)	Per 10 000 Population (person)	1608	1617	1589	1615	1519
# 大学生	University Students	196	243	281	330	337
卫　生	**Public Health**					
每万人拥有医院、	Number of Hospital Beds Per 10 000					
卫生院床位(张)	Persons (bed)	35.7	35.6	36.0	37.1	34.6
每万人拥有医生(人)	Number of Doctors Per 10 000 Persons (person)	26.9	25.7	24.9	25.0	24.0
赡养人口(人)	**Persons Supported by Others (person)**					
城镇每一就业者	Number of Persons Supported by					
赡养人口	Each Urban Employee	1.46	1.46	1.41	1.38	1.69
农村每一劳动力	Number of Persons Supported by					
负担人口	Each Rural Labour	1.48	1.48	1.48	1.42	1.40
城市绿化	**City Afforestation**					
建成区绿化覆盖率(%)	Coverage Rate of Afforestation					
	in Developed Area (%)	27.3	31.0	35.0	36.4	37
环境卫生与保护	**Environment Sanitation and Protection**					
年末拥有公共厕所(座)	Public Lavatories (unit)	2723	2430	2731	2778	2458
城市环境噪声达标	Standardization Areas of City					
面积(平方公里)	Environment Noise (sq. km)	477	539	560	570	572

8-2 城镇单位从业人员劳动报酬总额(1990-2006年)
TOTAL REMUNERATION OF PERSONS EMPLOYED IN URBAN UNITS, 1990-2006

单位：万元 (10 000 yuan)

年 份 Year	合 计 Total	按三次产业分 Grouped by Three Industries			按登记注册类型分 Grouped by Registration Status		
		第一产业 Primary Industry	第二产业 Secondary Industry	第三产业 Tertiary Industry	国有单位 State-owned Units	集体单位 Collective-owned Units	其他单位 Others
1990	693799.9	7922.4	384745.7	301131.8	555045.8	126263.4	12490.7
1991	797340.6	9044.1	448747.2	339549.3	623445.1	154187.4	19708.1
1992	915613.9	10256.6	540256.4	365100.9	719664.3	165127.4	30822.2
1993	1167779.8	7155.8	691240.2	469383.8	903227.9	192110.6	72441.3
1994	1540420.1	7987.2	869252.5	663180.4	1160716.0	216900.1	162804.0
1995	1848027.9	8603.4	1055034.7	784389.8	1352214.5	259963.3	235850.1
1996	2120491.6	9611.0	1163182.5	947698.1	1543422.3	271357.8	305711.5
1997	2232525.8	10438.1	1187059.3	1035028.4	1604714.3	264608.8	363202.7
1998	2253865.6	10749.2	1185574.2	1057542.2	1517991.3	239448.3	496426.0
1999	2344186.1	9713.4	1215273.1	1119199.6	1519302.4	212537.6	612346.1
2000	2535342.8	10707.3	1311485.3	1213150.2	1618601.9	198578.4	718162.5
2001	2775592.7	11572.1	1374770.9	1389249.7	1762580.1	168567.3	844445.3
2002	3042326.7	13831.2	1457423.5	1571072.0	1822701.1	154713.5	1064912.1
2003	3506036.0	13186.3	1727566.1	1765283.6	1947978.7	154880.0	1403177.3
2004	4079878.3	13776.8	1991231.4	2074870.1	2225960.7	162127.1	1691790.5
2005	4582620.0	13168.1	2197189.1	2372262.8	2472988.3	166904.2	1942727.5
2006	5302914.1	13536.7	2566324.2	2723053.2	2831413.4	179922.6	2291578.1

注：1. 1998年以前为职工工资总额。2. 1993年以前各项指标中均不包括交通费、洗理费。下同。
Note: a) Data before 1998 of this table refer to total wages of staff and workers. b) Each item before 1993 excludes expenses of transport and washing.Same as following next.

8-3 城镇单位从业人员人均劳动报酬(1990-2006年)
PER CAPITA REMUNERATION OF PERSONS EMPLOYED IN URBAN UNITS, 1990-2006

单位：元 (yuan)

年 份 Year	合 计 Total	按三次产业分 Grouped by Three Industries			按登记注册类型分 Grouped by Registration Status		
		第一产业 Primary Industry	第二产业 Secondary Industry	第三产业 Tertiary Industry	国有单位 State-owned Units	集体单位 Collective-owned Units	其他单位 Others
1990	2438	1932	2270	2715	2611	1866	2946
1991	2724	3102	2572	2980	2912	2114	3455
1992	3118	2430	3088	3188	3383	2285	3553
1993	4080	2972	4167	3980	4410	2780	5869
1994	5364	2610	5116	5297	5806	3370	7100
1995	6501	4844	6237	6357	6963	4138	8640
1996	7643	5710	7131	7787	8072	4745	10522
1997	8238	6476	7691	8372	8689	5083	10599
1998	9895	7541	9778	10062	10169	6020	12818
1999	11046	8476	11000	11127	11169	6821	13601
2000	12414	9414	12259	12622	12690	7485	14317
2001	14242	10333	13503	15107	14823	8159	15263
2002	16223	12492	15432	17081	16632	9152	17449
2003	18511	13257	17772	19357	18929	10865	19424
2004	21146	15450	20398	21972	22031	12545	21421
2005	24122	15954	23370	24936	24832	14693	24583
2006	27628	17975	26711	28631	29135	17752	27081

8-4 城镇单位从业人员劳动报酬总额
TOTAL REMUNERATION OF PERSONS EMPLOYED IN URBAN UNITS

单位：万元 (10 000 yuan)

项　目	Item	2005	2006	2006比2005年增长(%) Increase Rate in 2006 over 2005 (%)
总　计	**Total**	**4582620.0**	**5302914.1**	**15.7**
按登记注册类型分	**Grouped by Registration Status**			
国有单位	State-owned Units	2472988.3	2831413.4	14.5
集体单位	Collective-owned Units	166904.2	179922.6	7.8
其他单位	Others	1942727.5	2291578.1	18.0
#外商及港澳台商投资单位	Foreign Countries, Hong Kong, Macao & Taiwan Funded Units	1192183.1	1428767.1	19.8
股份有限公司	Share Holding Corporations Ltd.	328255.0	358118.5	9.1
按国民经济行业分	**Grouped by Sector**			
农、林、牧、渔业	Farming, Forestry, Animal Husbandry and Fishery	13168.1	13536.7	2.8
采矿业	Minerals Mining	201973.4	250784.0	24.2
制造业	Manufacturing	1606401.2	1858456.3	15.7
电力、燃气及水的生产和供应业	Production & Supply of Power, Gas and Water	155120.0	179151.7	15.5
建筑业	Construction	233694.5	277932.2	18.9
交通运输、仓储及邮政业	Transportation, Storage and Post Services	352055.3	392461.0	11.5
信息传输、计算机服务和软件业	Information Transmitting, Computer Services and Software	84530.3	92559.7	9.5
批发和零售业	Wholesale and Retail Trade	227133.8	253400.3	11.6
住宿和餐饮业	Accommodation and Catering Services	44198.9	52315.5	18.4
金融业	Finance Intermediation	203182.3	255140.3	25.6
房地产业	Real Estate	50001.0	52240.5	4.5
租赁和商务服务业	Leasing and Business Services	92766.9	102464.4	10.5
科学研究、技术服务和地质勘察业	Scientific Research, Technical Services and Geological Prospecting	188409.0	219036.1	16.3
水利、环境和公共设施管理业	Management for Water Conservancy, Environment and Public Facilities	74351.8	77682.3	4.5
居民服务和其他服务业	Resident Services and Other Social Services	54087.5	71097.0	31.4
教　育	Education	417452.3	480787.0	15.2
卫生、社会保障和社会福利业	Health Care, Social Security and Social Welfare	192381.9	221974.8	15.4
文化、体育和娱乐业	Culture, Sports and Recreational Services	44785.9	51637.2	15.3
公共管理和社会组织	Public Management and Social Organizations	346925.9	400257.1	15.4
按企业、事业、机关分	**Grouped By Enterprise, Institution and Agency**			
企　业	Enterprises	3430435.7	3981068.6	16.1
中　央	Central	907068.2	1110372.9	22.4
地　方	Local	2523367.5	2870695.7	13.8
#国　有	State-owned	686183.5	751919.5	9.6
事　业	Institutions	823225.8	943091.2	14.6
中　央	Central	69603.2	87484.8	25.7
地　方	Local	753622.6	855606.4	13.5
机　关	Government Agencies	328958.5	378754.3	15.1
中　央	Central	35703.6	43001.5	20.4
地　方	Local	293254.9	335752.8	14.5

8-5 城镇单位从业人员人均劳动报酬
PER CAPITA REMUNERATION OF PERSONS EMPLOYED IN URBAN UNITS

单位：元 (yuan)

项　目	Item	2005	2006	2006 比2005年 增长(%) Increase Rate in 2006 over 2005 (%)
总　计	**Total**	**24122**	**27628**	**14.5**
按登记注册类型分	**Grouped by Registration Status**			
国有单位	State-owned Units	24832	29135	17.3
集体单位	Collective-owned Units	14693	17752	20.8
其他单位	Others	24583	27081	10.2
#外商及港澳台商投资单位	Foreign Countries, Hong Kong, Macao & Taiwan Funded Units	25705	27763	8.0
股份有限公司	Share Holding Corporations Ltd.	31846	36161	13.5
按国民经济行业分	**Grouped by Sector**			
农、林、牧、渔业	Farming, Forestry, Animal Husbandry and Fishery	15954	17975	12.7
采矿业	Minerals Mining	28248	34097	20.7
制造业	Manufacturing	21595	24354	12.8
电力、燃气及水的生产和供应业	Production & Supply of Power, Gas and Water	46625	53764	15.3
建筑业	Construction	25540	30613	19.9
交通运输、仓储及邮政业	Transportation, Storage and Post Services	30117	34260	13.8
信息传输、计算机服务和软件业	Information Transmitting, Computer Services and Software	37375	40591	8.6
批发和零售业	Wholesale and Retail Trade	19116	22677	18.6
住宿和餐饮业	Accommodation and Catering Services	14458	15424	6.7
金融业	Finance Intermediation	39528	49810	26.0
房地产业	Real Estate	22462	24184	7.7
租赁和商务服务业	Leasing and Business Services	15081	15810	4.8
科学研究、技术服务和地质勘察业	Scientific Research, Technical Services and Geological Prospecting	36398	41473	13.9
水利、环境和公共设施管理业	Management for Water Conservancy, Environment and Public Facilities	19247	22215	15.4
居民服务和其他服务业	Resident Services and Other Social Services	13119	14863	13.3
教　育	Education	24608	28752	16.8
卫生、社会保障和社会福利业	Health Care, Social Security and Social Welfare	25109	28959	15.3
文化、体育和娱乐业	Culture, Sports and Recreational Services	25481	28349	11.3
公共管理和社会组织	Public Management and Social Organizations	26322	30156	14.6
按企业、事业、机关分	**Grouped By Enterprise, Institution and Agency**			
企　业	Enterprises	23820	27265	14.5
中　央	Central	34899	41217	18.1
地　方	Local	21380	24108	12.8
#国　有	State-owned	19165	22578	17.8
事　业	Institutions	24579	28260	15.0
中　央	Central	29866	38250	28.1
地　方	Local	24183	27524	13.8
机　关	Government Agencies	26391	30176	14.3
中　央	Central	30966	37850	22.2
地　方	Local	25925	29413	13.5

8-6 在岗职工工资总额
TOTAL WAGES OF ON-POST STAFF AND WORKERS

单位：万元 (10 000 yuan)

项　目	Item	2005	2006	2006比2005年增长(%) Increase Rate in 2006 over 2005 (%)
总　计	**Total**	**4198023.7**	**4874598.0**	**16.1**
按登记注册类型分	**Grouped by Registration Status**			
国有单位	State-owned Units	2354416.8	2700999.0	14.7
集体单位	Collective-owned Units	143864.6	157287.4	9.3
其他单位	Others	1699742.3	2016311.6	18.6
# 外商及港澳台商投资单位	Foreign Countries, Hong Kong, Macao & Taiwan Funded Units	1031654.6	1245797.5	20.8
股份有限公司	Share Holding Corporations Ltd.	292090.9	320993.8	9.9
按国民经济行业分	**Grouped by Sector**			
农、林、牧、渔业	Farming, Forestry, Animal Husbandry and Fishery	13035.4	13411.4	2.9
采矿业	Minerals Mining	188186.0	228469.2	21.4
制造业	Manufacturing	1448728.4	1680374.0	16.0
电力、燃气及水的生产和供应业	Production & Supply of Power, Gas and Water	149981.4	175431.7	17.0
建筑业	Construction	224434.9	267557.7	19.2
交通运输、仓储及邮政业	Transportation, Storage and Post Services	330296.5	364309.3	10.3
信息传输、计算机服务和软件业	Information Transmitting, Computer Services and Software	81893.5	90345.1	10.3
批发和零售业	Wholesale and Retail Trade	184406.1	208946.5	13.3
住宿和餐饮业	Accommodation and Catering Services	34346.2	42229.2	23.0
金融业	Finance Intermediation	166445.0	215706.6	29.6
房地产业	Real Estate	42506.8	44464.2	4.6
租赁和商务服务业	Leasing and Business Services	72594.6	85078.9	17.2
科学研究、技术服务和地质勘察业	Scientific Research, Technical Services and Geological Prospecting	180484.0	207540.7	15.0
水利、环境和公共设施管理业	Management for Water Conservancy, Environment and Public Facilities	70267.1	73255.6	4.3
居民服务和其他服务业	Resident Services and Other Social Services	39019.0	55941.7	43.4
教　育	Education	409435.9	470694.2	15.0
卫生、社会保障和社会福利业	Health Care, Social Security and Social Welfare	184482.6	212575.1	15.2
文化、体育和娱乐业	Culture, Sports and Recreational Services	39655.8	48332.9	21.9
公共管理和社会组织	Public Management and Social Organizations	337824.5	389934.0	15.4

8-7 在岗职工平均工资
PER CAPITA WAGES OF ON-POST STAFF AND WORKERS

单位：元 (yuan)

项　目	Item	2005	2006	2006比2005年增长(%) Increase Rate in 2006 over 2005 (%)
总　计	**Total**	**25271**	**28682**	**13.5**
按登记注册类型分	**Grouped by Registration Status**			
国有单位	State-owned Units	26759	31287	16.9
集体单位	Collective-owned Units	15713	19125	21.7
其他单位	Others	24642	26743	8.5
#外商及港澳台商投资单位	From Foreign Countries, Hong Kong, Macao & Taiwan Funded Units	24683	26213	6.2
股份有限公司	Share Holding Corporations Ltd.	33770	38064	12.7
按国民经济行业分	**Grouped by Sector**			
农、林、牧、渔业	Farming, Forestry, Animal Husbandry and Fishery	16034	18092	12.8
采矿业	Minerals Mining	29571	35847	21.2
制造业	Manufacturing	21183	23545	11.2
电力、燃气及水的生产和供应业	Production & Supply of Power, Gas and Water	48417	56971	17.7
建筑业	Construction	26777	32107	19.9
交通运输、仓储及邮政业	Transportation, Storage and Post Services	31836	36666	15.2
信息传输、计算机服务和软件业	Information transmitting, Computer Services and Software	40569	43366	6.9
批发和零售业	Wholesale and Retail Trade	20603	23750	15.3
住宿和餐饮业	Accommodation and Catering Services	15861	18286	15.3
金融业	Finance Intermediation	46874	59796	27.6
房地产业	Real Estate	26727	27939	4.5
租赁和商务服务业	Leasing and Business Services	17898	17528	-2.1
科学研究、技术服务和地质勘察业	Scientific Research, Technical Services and Geological Prospecting	38973	44993	15.4
水利、环境和公共设施管理业	Management for Water Conservancy, Environment and Public Facilities	21113	24401	15.6
居民服务和其他服务业	Resident Services and Other Social Services	18895	19099	1.1
教　育	Education	25268	29512	16.8
卫生、社会保障和社会福利业	Health Care, Social Security and Social Welfare	27435	31299	14.1
文化、体育和娱乐业	Culture, Sports and Recreational Services	25892	30148	16.4
公共管理和社会组织	Public Management and Social Organizations	28432	32524	14.4

8-8 其他从业人员劳动报酬总额
TOTAL REMUNERATION OF OTHER PERSONS EMPLOYED

单位：万元 (10 000 yuan)

项　目	Item	2005	2006	2006比2005年增长(%) Increase Rate in 2006 over 2005 (%)
总　计	**Total**	**384596.3**	**428316.1**	**11.4**
按登记注册类型分	**Grouped by Registration Status**			
国有单位	State-owned Units	118571.5	130414.4	10.0
集体单位	Collective-owned Units	23039.6	22635.2	-1.8
其他单位	Others	242985.2	275266.5	13.3
#外商及港澳台商投资单位	Foreign Countries, Hong Kong, Macao & Taiwan Funded Units	160528.5	182969.6	14.0
股份有限公司	Share Holding Corporations Ltd.	36164.1	37124.7	2.7
按国民经济行业分	**Grouped by Sector**			
农、林、牧、渔业	Farming, Forestry, Animal Husbandry and Fishery	132.7	125.3	-5.6
采矿业	Minerals Mining	13787.4	22314.8	61.8
制造业	Manufacturing	157672.8	178082.3	12.9
电力、燃气及水的生产和供应业	Production & Supply of Power, Gas and Water	5138.6	3720.0	-27.6
建筑业	Construction	9259.6	10374.5	12.0
交通运输、仓储及邮政业	Transportation, Storage and Post Services	21758.8	28151.7	29.4
信息传输、计算机服务和软件业	Information Transmitting, Computer Services and Software	2636.8	2214.6	-16.0
批发和零售业	Wholesale and Retail Trade	42727.7	44453.8	4.0
住宿和餐饮业	Accommodation and Catering Services	9852.7	10086.3	2.4
金融业	Finance Intermediation	36737.3	39433.7	7.3
房地产业	Real Estate	7494.2	7776.3	3.8
租赁和商务服务业	Leasing and Business Services	20172.3	17385.5	-13.8
科学研究、技术服务和地质勘察业	Scientific Research, Technical Services and Geological Prospecting	7925.0	11495.4	45.1
水利、环境和公共设施管理业	Management for Water Conservancy, Environment and Public Facilities	4084.7	4426.7	8.4
居民服务和其他服务业	Resident Services and Other Social Services	15068.5	15155.3	0.6
教　育	Education	8016.4	10092.8	25.9
卫生、社会保障和社会福利业	Health Care, Social Security and Social Welfare	7899.3	9399.7	19.0
文化、体育和娱乐业	Culture, Sports and Recreational Services	5130.1	3304.3	-35.6
公共管理和社会组织	Public Management and Social Organizations	9101.4	10323.1	13.4

8-9 其他从业人员人均劳动报酬
PER CAPITA REMUNERATION OF OTHER PERSONS EMPLOYED

单位：元 (yuan)

项 目	Item	2005	2006	2006比2005年增长(%) Increase Rate in 2006 over 2005 (%)
总 计	**Total**	**16124**	**19481**	**20.8**
按登记注册类型分	**Grouped by Registration Status**			
国有单位	State-owned Units	10221	12017	17.6
集体单位	Collective-owned Units	10453	11845	13.3
其他单位	Others	24182	29846	23.4
# 外商及港澳台商投资单位	Foreign Countries, Hong Kong, Macao & Taiwan Funded Units	35032	46473	32.7
股份有限公司	Share Holding Corporations Ltd.	21808	25248	15.8
按国民经济行业分	**Grouped by Sector**			
农、林、牧、渔业	Farming, Forestry, Animal Husbandry and Fishery	10702	10619	-0.8
采矿业	Minerals Mining	17535	22733	29.6
制造业	Manufacturing	26295	36034	37.0
电力、燃气及水的生产和供应业	Production & Supply of Power, Gas and Water	22410	14709	-34.4
建筑业	Construction	12050	13911	15.4
交通运输、仓储及邮政业	Transportation, Storage and Post Services	16552	18526	11.9
信息传输、计算机服务和软件业	Information Transmitting, Computer Services and Software	10847	11242	3.6
批发和零售业	Wholesale and Retail Trade	14575	18705	28.3
住宿和餐饮业	Accommodation and Catering Services	11051	9318	-15.7
金融业	Finance Intermediation	23115	26031	12.6
房地产业	Real Estate	11791	13676	16.0
租赁和商务服务业	Leasing and Business Services	9628	10685	11.0
科学研究、技术服务和地质勘察业	Scientific Research, Technical Services and Geological Prospecting	14531	17191	18.3
水利、环境和公共设施管理业	Management for Water Conservancy, Environment and Public Facilities	7636	8946	17.2
居民服务和其他服务业	Resident Services and Other Social Services	7323	8172	11.6
教 育	Education	10547	13065	23.9
卫生、社会保障和社会福利业	Health Care, Social Security and Social Welfare	8427	10762	27.7
文化、体育和娱乐业	Culture, Sports and Recreational Services	22700	15137	-33.3
公共管理和社会组织	Public Management and Social Organizations	7012	8042	14.7

8-10 市属部分局（总公司）国有经济单位从业人员劳动报酬总额
TOTAL REMUNERATION OF PERSONS EMPLOYED BY STATE-OWNED UNITS IN PART OF BUREAUS (CORPORATIONS)

单位：万元 (10 000 yuan)

局(总公司)	Bureau (Corporation)	2005	2006
经委系统	**Tianjin Economical Committee System**		
机电工业控股集团公司	Tianjin Machinery & Electric Industry Holding Group Company	17124.2	12743.0
中环电子信息集团有限公司	Tianjin Zhonghuan Electronics & Information Group	24271.5	26600.9
冶金集团(控股)有限公司	Tianjin Metallurgical Group (Holding) Corporation	14445.7	21203.4
渤海化工集团公司	Tianjin Bohai Chemical Industry Group Corporation	71409.2	79279.2
纺织集团(控股)有限公司	Tianjin Textile Industrial General Corporation	32746.7	31775.0
一轻集团(控股)有限公司	Tianjin First Light Industry Group (Holding) Co., Ltd.	8248.8	9117.3
二轻集团(控股)有限公司	Tianjin Second Light Industry Group (Holding) Co., Ltd.	3900.7	3900.9
医药集团有限公司	Tianjin Pharmaceutical Holdings	5302.2	6033.6
汽车工业(集团)有限公司	Tianjin Automobile Industry Group Co., Ltd.	2980.7	2043.9
飞鸽集团有限公司	Tianjin Flying Pigeon Group Co., Ltd.	1340.3	1469.1
塑料集团	Tianjin Plastics Group	934.2	805.1
天铁冶金集团有限公司	Tianjin Tiantie Metallurgical Group Co., Ltd.	41434.5	47573.8
建筑材料集团(控股)有限公司	Tianjin Building Materials Group (Holding) Co., Ltd.	5648.8	5548.4
农委系统	**Tianjin Agricultural Committee System**		
农业局	Tianjin Agriculture Bureau	971.7	1090.4
畜牧局	Tianjin Animal Husbandry Bureau	686.2	848.3
农垦集团总公司	Tianjin State Farms Agribusiness Group Company	7321.2	8305.0
水产局	Tianjin Aquatic Products Bureau	2386.7	1396.7
建委系统	**Tianjin Construction Committee System**		
建工集团总公司	Tianjin Construction Engineering Group Corporation	7425.6	4759.1
市政工程局	Tianjin Municipal Engineering Bureau	32913.3	35552.0
房地产管理局	Tianjin Real Estate Administrative Bureau	22903.5	27865.1
住宅建设发展集团	Tianjin House Construction Development Group	3017.6	3346.4
公共交通集团公司	Tianjin Public Traffic Group Corporation	14708.8	17656.4
自来水集团	Tianjin Tap Water Group	10348.8	11037.7
燃气集团	Tianjin Gas Group	17992.7	20159.7
交委系统	**Tianjin Transportation Committee System**		
天津港(集团)有限公司	Tianjin Port Group Corporation Ltd.	68353.4	81954.7
天津交通运输总公司	Tianjin Communication Corporation	9013.8	10001.6
商委系统	**Tianjin Commercial Committee System**		
粮食粮油集团有限公司	Tianjin Grain & Oil Group Co., Ltd.	5385.7	5545.8
一商集团有限公司	Tianjin First Commercial Group Co., Ltd.	4494.1	3751.9
二商集团有限公司	Tianjin Second Commercial Group Co., Ltd.	6167.5	6340.4

8-11 市属部分局（总公司）国有经济单位从业人员人均劳动报酬
PER CAPITA REMUNERATION OF PERSONS EMPLOYED BY STATE-OWNED UNITS IN PART OF BUREAUS (CORPORATIONS)

单位：元 (yuan)

局(总公司)	Bureau (Corporation)	2005	2006
经委系统	**Tianjin Economical Committee System**		
机电工业控股集团公司	Tianjin Machinery & Electric Industry Holding Group Company	16261	18776
中环电子信息集团有限公司	Tianjin Zhonghuan Electronics & Information Group	18477	20931
冶金集团(控股)有限公司	Tianjin Metallurgical Group (Holding) Corporation	15401	21832
渤海化工集团公司	Tianjin Bohai Chemical Industry Group Corporation	23192	26393
纺织集团(控股)有限公司	Tianjin Textile Industrial General Corporation	13292	14482
一轻集团(控股)有限公司	Tianjin First Light Industry Group (Holding) Co., Ltd.	17995	24216
二轻集团(控股)有限公司	Tianjin Second Light Industry Group (Holding) Co., Ltd.	15291	18656
医药集团有限公司	Tianjin Pharmaceutical Holdings	21243	24587
汽车工业(集团)有限公司	Tianjin Automobile Industry Group Co., Ltd.	34619	25677
飞鸽集团有限公司	Tianjin Flying Pigeon Group Co., Ltd.	10406	13059
塑料集团	Tianjin Plastics Group	12607	16773
天铁冶金集团有限公司	Tianjin Tiantie Metallurgical Group Co., Ltd.	21892	24702
建筑材料集团(控股)有限公司	Tianjin Building Materials Group (Holding) Co., Ltd.	15805	19034
农委系统	**Tianjin Agricultural Committee System**		
农业局	Tianjin Agriculture Bureau	22598	24614
畜牧局	Tianjin Animal Husbandry Bureau	21647	25247
农垦集团总公司	Tianjin State Farms Agribusiness Group Company	19750	25174
水产局	Tianjin Aquatic Products Bureau	24580	17372
建委系统	**Tianjin Construction Committee System**		
建工集团总公司	Tianjin Construction Engineering Group Corporation	18191	22470
市政工程局	Tianjin Municipal Engineering Bureau	23464	25727
房地产管理局	Tianjin Real Estate Administrative Bureau	25180	29879
住宅建设发展集团	Tianjin House Construction Development Group	20654	29023
公共交通集团公司	Tianjin Public Traffic Group Corporation	14258	16679
自来水集团	Tianjin Tap Water Group	27894	30265
燃气集团	Tianjin Gas Group	27512	29875
交委系统	**Tianjin Transportation Committee System**		
天津港(集团)有限公司	Tianjin Port Group Corporation Ltd.	59718	67486
天津交通运输总公司	Tianjin Communication Corporation	14271	16838
商委系统	**Tianjin Commercial Committee System**		
粮食粮油集团有限公司	Tianjin Grain & Oil Group Co., Ltd.	17486	19666
一商集团有限公司	Tianjin First Commercial Group Co., Ltd.	16608	21078
二商集团有限公司	Tianjin Second Commercial Group Co., Ltd.	15454	21341

8-12 职工劳保福利费发放情况(2003-2006年)
TOTAL INSURANCE WELFARE OF STAFF AND WORKERS, 2003-2006

指 标 Item	2003	2004	2005	2006
在职职工保险福利费用总额(万元) Total Insurance Welfare of On-post Staff & Workers (10 000 yuan)	**265528.4**	**323589.0**	**227405.7**	**251658.9**
国有单位 State-owned Units	176980.3	219670.2	150358.8	158377.0
集体单位 Collective-owned Units	7738.1	26307.8	5761.8	4266.5
其他单位 Others	80810.0	77611.0	71285.1	89015.4
非在职职工保险福利费用总额(万元) Total Insurance Welfare of Staff & Workers not On-post (10 000 yuan)	**1136250.0**	**1358726.3**	**1672527.2**	**1771984.8**
# 国有单位 State-owned Units	864488.0	1075570.6	1303996.9	1389785.6
在职职工人均保险福利费(元) Per Capita Insurance Welfare of On-post Staff & Workers (yuan)	**1246**	**1539**	**1369**	**1472**
国有单位 State-owned Units	1432	1864	1699	1846
集体单位 Collective-owned Units	373	1460	663	581
其他单位 Others	1175	1044	1034	1143
非在职职工人均保险福利费(元) Per Capita Insurance Welfare of Staff & Workers not On-post (yuan)	**10270**	**11513**	**12809**	**13072**
# 国有单位 State-owned Units	11281	12954	13791	14158

注：1. 资料来源:天津市劳动和社会保障局、民政局。2. 非在职职工保险福利费不含民政部门支付。
Note: a) Data are obtained from Tianjin Municipal Labour & Social Insurance Bureau and Tianjin Civil Administration Bureau. b) Insurance welfare of staff and workers not on-post exclude those paid by civil administration department.

8-13 职工保险福利费构成(2003-2006年)
COMPOSITION OF INSURANCE WELFARE OF STAFF AND WORKERS, 2003-2006

单位：万元 (10 000 yuan)

指 标 Item	2003	2004	2005	2006
在职职工 On-post Staff & Workers	**265528.4**	**323589.0**	**227405.7**	**251658.9**
集体福利设施、事业补贴费 Collective Welfare Facilities,Insurance Subsidies	46666.4	43561.9	37976.7	42299.4
文体宣传费 Culture and Sport Expenses	9300.5	8833.1	9287.7	8080.4
医疗卫生费 Medical,Health Care Expenses	102014.0	96968.3	82265.7	80228.5
其 他 Others	107547.5	174225.7	97875.6	121050.6
非在职职工 Staff and Workers not On-post	**1136250.0**	**1358726.3**	**1672527.2**	**1771984.8**
离休费 Retirement Pensions	51122.5	69304.2	60036.0	66784.3
退休费 Pension Pensions	978888.5	1158782.4	1440551.5	1654875.5
退职生活费 Resignation Living Expenses	7165.5	7019.0		
医疗卫生费 Medical, Health Care Expenses	64498.4	70006.1	90251.9	
其 他 Others	34575.1	53614.6	81687.8	50325.0

8-14 城市居民家庭人均收支及增幅（1990-2006年）
PER CAPITA INCOME & EXPENDITURES AND INCREASE RATE OF URBAN HOUSEHOLDS, 1990-2006

年 份 Year	人均可支配收入(元) Per Capita Annual Disposable Income (yuan)	人均消费性支出(元) Per Capita Annual Expenditures for Consumption (yuan)	人均可支配收入增幅(%) Increase Rate of Per Capita Annual Disposable Income (%)		人均消费支出增幅(%) Increase Rate of Per Capita Annual Expenditures for Consumption (%)	
			扣除物价 Deducting Price Factor	未扣除物价 Including Price Factor	扣除物价 Deducting Price Factor	未扣除物价 Including Price Factor
1990	1638.92	1440.47	7.7	10.9	8.3	11.6
1991	1844.98	1585.71	2.2	12.6	-0.1	10.1
1992	2238.38	1907.17	8.9	21.3	8.0	20.3
1993	2769.26	2322.19	5.2	23.7	3.6	21.8
1994	3982.13	3301.37	16.0	43.8	14.7	42.2
1995	4929.53	4064.1	7.4	23.8	6.8	23.1
1996	5967.71	4679.61	11.1	21.1	5.6	15.1
1997	6608.56	5204.29	7.4	10.7	7.9	11.2
1998	7110.54	5471.01	8.1	7.6	5.6	5.1
1999	7649.83	5851.53	8.8	7.6	8.1	7.0
2000	8140.55	6121.07	6.8	6.4	5.0	4.6
2001	8958.7	6987.22	8.7	10.1	12.8	14.2
2002	9337.54	7191.97	12.1	11.6	5.8	5.4
2003	10312.91	7867.53	9.4	10.4	8.3	9.4
2004	11467.16	8802.44	8.7	11.2	9.4	11.9
2005	12638.55	9653.26	8.6	10.2	8.0	9.7
2006	14283.09	10548.05	11.3	13.0	7.7	9.3

8-15 城市居民家庭基本情况（2003-2006年）
BASIC STATISTICS OF URBAN HOUSEHOLDS, 2003-2006

指 标	Item	2003	2004	2005	2006
调查户数(户)	Number of Households Surveyed (household)	1500	1500	1500	1500
平均每户人口(人)	Average Persons Per Household (person)	2.99	2.96	2.92	2.88
平均每户就业人口(人)	Average Employees Per Household (person)	1.41	1.47	1.45	1.42
平均每户就业面(%)	Percentage of Employment Per Household (%)	47.2	49.7	49.7	49.3
平均每一就业者负担人口(人)	Persons Supported By Each Employee (person)	2.12	2.01	2.01	2.03
居民家庭人均收入(元)	**Per Capita Annual Income (yuan)**				
人均总收入	Gross Income per Capita	10971.57	12279.73	13563.32	15476.04
#可支配收入	Average per Capita Disposable Income	10312.91	11467.16	12638.55	14283.09
工薪收入	Salaries	6663.54	7508.72	8174.64	9259.72
经营净收入	Net Income from Household Business	468.96	600.40	665.53	742.97
财产性收入	Property Income	96.41	123.55	148.15	165.05
转移性收入	Transferred Income	3742.66	4047.06	4574.99	5308.30
#养老金或离退休金	Pensions and Retirement Pay	2851.34	3126.76	3376.79	4214.27
居民家庭人均支出(元)	**Per Capita Annual Expenditures (yuan)**				
人均总支出	Gross Expenditures Per Capita	11087.99	13322.83	14450.32	15900.27
#消费性支出	Consumption Expenditures	7867.53	8802.44	9653.26	10548.05
#服务性消费支出	Service Consumption Expenditure	2125.33	2502.25	2798.38	3110.93

8-16 城市不同收入水平居民家庭基本情况(2006年)(按平均每人每年可支配收入分组)
BASIC STATISTICS OF URBAN HOUSEHOLDS WITH DIFFERENT INCOME LEVEL, 2006
(Grouped by Annual Per Capita Disposable Income)

项 目	Item	调查户数(户) Number of Households Surveyed (household)	平均每户人口(人) Average Persons per Household (person)	平均每户就业人口(人) Average Employees per Household (person)	平均每一就业者负担人口(人) Persons Supported by Each Employee (person)
全 市	**Total**	**1500**	**2.88**	**1.42**	**2.03**
1. 最低收入户	Lowest Income Households				
(6453.33元以下)	(Below 6453.33 yuan)	150	3.13	1.31	2.39
# 更低收入户	Even More Lowest Income				
(5327.14元以下)	Households (Below 5327.14 yuan)	75	3.11	1.06	2.93
2. 低收入户	Low Income Households				
(6458.00-8110.80元)	(6458.00-8110.80 yuan)	150	3.17	1.45	2.19
3. 中等偏下收入户	Lower Middle Income Households				
(8111.67-11115.00元)	(8111.67-11115.00 yuan)	300	3.07	1.49	2.06
4. 中等收入户	Middle Income Households				
(11118.06-14530.28元)	(11118.06-14530.28 yuan)	300	2.77	1.27	2.18
5. 中等偏上收入户	Upper Middle Income Households				
(14530.32-20048.00元)	(14530.32-20048.00 yuan)	300	2.80	1.45	1.93
6. 高收入户	High Income Households				
(20061.67-24974.41元)	(20061.67-24974.41 yuan)	150	2.69	1.54	1.75
7. 最高收入户	Highest Income Households				
(24979.02元以上)	(Over 24979.02 yuan)	150	2.55	1.46	1.75

单位：元 (yuan)

项 目	Item	人均总收入 Per Capita Annual Actual Income	# 可支配收入 Disposable Income	人均消费性支出 Per Capita Annual Expenditures for Consumption	# 人均服务性消费支出 Expenditures for Services
全 市	**Total**	**15476.04**	**14283.09**	**10548.05**	**3110.93**
1. 最低收入户	Lowest Income Households				
(6453.33元以下)	(Below 6453.33 yuan)	5653.09	5185.24	5740.06	1757.44
# 更低收入户	Even More Lowest Income				
(5327.14元以下)	Households (Below 5327.14 yuan)	4640.48	4376.29	5118.35	1512.24
2. 低收入户	Low Income Households				
(6458.00-8110.80元)	(6458.00-8110.80 yuan)	7959.58	7270.81	6862.06	2047.13
3. 中等偏下收入户	Lower Middle Income Households				
(8111.67-11115.00元)	(8111.67-11115.00 yuan)	10377.34	9579.83	8272.45	2386.15
4. 中等收入户	Middle Income Households				
(11118.06-14530.28元)	(11118.06-14530.28 yuan)	13719.53	12670.24	9602.55	2506.66
5. 中等偏上收入户	Upper Middle Income Households				
(14530.32-20048.00元)	(14530.32-20048.00 yuan)	18348.96	16887.96	11641.18	3617.24
6. 高收入户	High Income Households				
(20061.67-24974.41元)	(20061.67-24974.41 yuan)	24386.30	22255.50	14972.09	4360.73
7. 最高收入户	Highest Income Households				
(24979.02元以上)	(Over 24979.02 yuan)	37287.22	34889.90	21506.44	6722.42

8-17 城市居民家庭人均消费性支出分类（2006年）
THE CLASSIFICATION OF PER CAPITA ANNUAL EXPENDITURES FOR CONSUMPTION OF URBAN HOUSEHOLDS, 2006

单位：元 (yuan)

项　目	Item	总平均 Average	最低收入 10% Lowest Income 10 percent	低收入 10% Low Income 10 percent	中等偏下收入 20% Lower Middle Income 20 percent
人均消费性支出	Per Capita Total Expenditures for Consumption	10548.05	5740.06	6862.06	8272.45
一、食　品	Food	3680.22	2412.27	2747.07	3202.29
（一）粮油类	Grain and Oil	406.54	386.75	389.71	402.73
1. 粮　食	Grain	247.29	242.01	242.63	245.68
2. 淀粉及薯类	Starches and Tubers	29.50	28.68	29.55	29.79
3. 干豆类及豆制品	Beans and Bean Products	31.40	27.13	29.94	29.06
4. 油脂类	Oil and Fats	98.36	88.94	87.58	98.21
（二）肉禽蛋水产品类	Meat, Poultry, Egg and Related Products	902.85	664.26	771.24	853.87
1. 肉　类	Meat	438.35	343.11	393.56	429.11
2. 禽　类	Poultry	75.85	51.16	65.70	75.81
3. 蛋　类	Eggs	96.02	81.48	84.83	91.83
4.水产品类	Aquatic Products	292.63	188.51	227.15	257.11
（三）蔬菜类	Vegetables	308.16	238.60	267.10	290.24
（四）调味品	Flavouring	61.28	47.27	53.77	58.65
（五）糖烟酒饮料类	Sugar, Tobacco, Liquor and Beverages	378.34	200.05	245.59	308.60
1. 糖　类	Sugar	32.50	17.82	21.39	26.52
2. 烟草类	Tobacco	157.25	94.87	102.20	122.42
3. 酒　类	Liquor	103.68	48.69	70.91	88.72
4. 饮　料	Beverages	84.91	38.67	51.10	70.94
（六）干鲜瓜果类	Dry and Fresh Melons and Fruits	303.39	187.27	228.45	261.35
（七）糕点、奶及奶制品	Cake, Milk and Related Produts	256.29	174.27	196.97	225.38
（八）其他食品	Other Food	83.38	43.91	53.78	67.47
（九）饮食服务	Dining	979.98	469.88	540.46	733.99
#在外饮食	Dining Out	979.60	469.77	540.22	733.63
二、衣　着	Clothing	864.89	332.90	494.14	624.39
#服　装	Garments	606.70	219.38	326.63	430.31
衣着材料	Clothing Materials	13.86	5.65	7.69	10.17
鞋　类	Shoes	199.71	88.12	130.23	149.22
衣着加工服务费	Tailoring and Laundering Service Fees	9.41	4.03	6.96	8.16
三、家庭设备、用品及服务	Household Facilities, Articles and Services	634.39	204.98	286.26	407.12
#耐用消费品	Durable Consumer Goods	329.82	80.99	118.35	204.87
室内装饰品	Room Decorations	40.23	4.83	16.19	13.93
家庭服务	Household Services	48.12	10.74	24.61	15.54
四、医疗保健	Medicine and Medical Services	1049.33	359.52	583.76	942.59
五、交通与通讯	Transportation and Communication Services	1092.87	430.47	580.62	736.70
六、娱乐、教育、文化服务	Recreation, Education and Cultural Services	1452.17	1083.51	1125.00	1117.61
#文化娱乐用品	Cultural and Recreational Articles	432.74	205.83	194.38	295.02
七、居　住	Residence	1368.20	754.00	896.82	961.99
#燃　料	Fuels	107.75	93.23	100.44	98.73
八、杂项商品与服务	Miscellaneous Commodities and Services	405.99	162.40	148.37	279.77

8-17 续表 Continued

单位：元 (yuan)

项　目	Item	中等收入 20% Middle Income 20 percent	中等偏上收入 20% Upper Middle Income 20 percent	高收入 10% High Income 10 percent	最高收入 10% Highest Income 10 percent
人均消费性支出	**Per Capita Total Expenditures for Consumption**	**9602.55**	**11641.18**	**14972.09**	**21506.44**
一、食　品	Food	3640.72	3909.92	4818.54	5932.18
（一）粮油类	Grain and Oil	424.00	392.06	417.27	443.68
1. 粮　食	Grain	255.76	232.79	253.24	270.56
2. 淀粉及薯类	Starches and Tubers	30.57	27.25	29.71	32.09
3. 干豆类及豆制品	Beans and Bean Products	32.23	32.49	36.79	34.24
4. 油脂类	Oil and Fats	105.44	99.52	97.53	106.79
（二）肉禽蛋水产品类	Meat, Poultry, Egg and Related Products	966.40	927.19	1041.85	1140.46
1. 肉　类	Meat	471.09	449.24	468.40	507.03
2. 禽　类	Poultry	81.84	80.62	76.99	94.33
3. 蛋　类	Eggs	105.57	97.74	98.53	110.86
4. 水产品类	Aquatic Products	307.89	299.59	397.93	428.24
（三）蔬菜类	Vegetables	316.51	313.77	360.86	401.94
（四）调味品	Flavouring	60.83	65.57	72.71	73.63
（五）糖烟酒饮料类	Sugar, Tobacco, Liquor and Beverages	387.07	396.97	500.64	742.01
1. 糖　类	Sugar	32.14	32.28	53.50	57.90
2. 烟草类	Tobacco	174.07	156.01	202.21	305.27
3. 酒　类	Liquor	101.18	108.78	133.04	211.34
4. 饮　料	Beverages	79.68	99.89	111.89	167.49
（六）干鲜瓜果类	Dry and Fresh Melons nad Fruits	295.14	340.24	407.48	467.96
（七）糕点、奶及奶制品	Cake, Milk and Related Produts	259.62	288.27	305.10	376.67
（八）其他食品	Other Food	74.78	105.92	117.42	140.42
（九）饮食服务	Dining	856.38	1079.95	1595.21	2145.40
#在外饮食	Dining Out	856.07	1079.24	1594.92	2144.95
二、衣　着	Clothing	799.62	927.92	1432.65	1962.82
#服　装	Garments	545.04	655.29	1035.09	1430.61
衣着材料	Clothing Materials	15.52	16.68	13.72	30.96
鞋　类	Shoes	193.52	210.41	315.26	412.80
衣着加工服务费	Tailoring and Laundering Service Fees	7.33	10.81	11.64	21.10
三、家庭设备、用品及服务	Household Facilities, Articles and Services	552.14	682.59	977.60	1852.78
#耐用消费品	Durable Consumer Goods	308.50	338.83	468.83	1079.60
室内装饰品	Room Decorations	33.34	42.95	73.49	150.78
家庭服务	Household Services	29.77	63.08	89.68	164.75
四、医疗保健	Medicine and Medical Services	1054.07	1321.40	1439.08	1717.29
五、交通与通讯	Transportation and Communication Services	921.01	1139.10	1968.03	2748.18
六、娱乐、教育、文化服务	Recreation, Education and Cultural Services	1171.16	1609.30	1796.60	3017.88
#文化娱乐用品	Cultural and Recreational Articles	390.75	486.43	577.37	1160.97
七、居　住	Residence	1204.55	1597.76	1951.18	2923.82
#燃　料	Fuels	119.15	114.30	112.72	112.23
八、杂项商品与服务	Miscellaneous Commodities and Services	259.29	453.19	588.40	1351.49

8-18 城市居民家庭平均每人主要消费品全年购买量（2006年）
PER CAPITA ANNUAL PURCHASES OF MAJOR CONSUMER GOODS OF URBAN HOUSEHOLDS, 2006

商品名称	Item	单位 Unit	总平均 Average	最低收入10% Lowest Income 10 percent	低收入10% Low Income 10 percent	中等偏下收入20% Lower Middle Income 20 percent
粮　食	Grain	公　斤 kg	75.84	78.89	77.09	75.82
淀粉及薯类	Starches and Tubers	公　斤 kg	12.91	13.81	13.62	13.23
油脂类	Oil and Fats	公　斤 kg	9.72	9.58	9.29	10.09
#食用植物油	Edible Vegetable Oil	公　斤 kg	9.71	9.58	9.28	10.08
肉　类	Meat	公　斤 kg	28.01	22.50	25.71	27.51
#猪　肉	Pork	公　斤 kg	17.55	14.59	16.13	17.30
牛　肉	Beef	公　斤 kg	3.89	3.39	3.29	3.73
羊　肉	Mutton	公　斤 kg	2.75	2.07	2.66	2.88
禽　类	Poultry	公　斤 kg	4.94	3.63	4.60	5.03
#鸡	Chicken	公　斤 kg	2.96	2.28	2.96	3.11
蛋　类	Eggs	公　斤 kg	17.84	15.46	16.17	17.02
#鲜　蛋	Fresh Eggs	公　斤 kg	16.87	14.67	15.39	16.05
鱼	Fish	公　斤 kg	9.11	8.18	8.12	8.34
虾	Shrimp	公　斤 kg	4.06	2.87	3.28	3.83
鲜　菜	Fresh Vegetables	公　斤 kg	126.85	113.34	114.53	120.92
干　菜	Dry Vegetables	公　斤 kg	0.32	0.28	0.23	0.28
酒　类	Liquor	公　斤 kg	8.85	5.82	7.24	8.57
#白　酒	Wine	公　斤 kg	1.90	1.39	1.88	2.08
啤　酒	Beer	公　斤 kg	6.75	4.35	5.23	6.34
碳酸饮料	Beverages	公　斤 kg	3.44	1.74	2.49	3.19
茶　叶	Tea	公　斤 kg	0.28	0.20	0.22	0.30
鲜　果	Fresh Fruits	公　斤 kg	44.89	31.04	34.96	39.69
鲜　瓜	Fresh Melons	公　斤 kg	28.10	21.68	24.03	23.76
糕　点	Cake	公　斤 kg	6.45	4.45	5.81	6.19
鲜　奶	Milk	公　斤 kg	23.20	16.44	15.74	18.65
服　装	Garments	件 piece	6.42	3.84	4.48	5.59
#男士服装	Men's Clothing	件 piece	2.56	1.58	1.93	2.13
女士服装	Women's Clothing	件 piece	3.39	2.03	2.30	3.06
童　装	Children's Clothing	件 piece	0.48	0.22	0.24	0.40
鞋　类	Shoes	双 pair	2.29	1.61	2.02	2.07

8-18 续表 Continued

商品名称	Item	单位 Unit	中等收入 20% Middle Income 20 percent	中等偏上收入 20% Upper Middle Income 20 percent	高收入 10% High Income 10 percent	最高收入 10% Highest Income 10 percent
粮 食	Grain	公 斤 kg	79.26	69.68	76.20	76.32
淀粉及薯类	Starches and Tubers	公 斤 kg	13.59	11.51	12.29	12.45
油脂类	Oil and Fats	公 斤 kg	10.41	9.56	8.70	9.48
#食用植物油	Edible Vegetable Oil	公 斤 kg	10.40	9.55	8.69	9.47
肉 类	Meat	公 斤 kg	30.10	28.47	29.61	31.65
#猪 肉	Pork	公 斤 kg	18.40	17.12	19.33	20.83
牛 肉	Beef	公 斤 kg	4.41	4.38	3.35	3.97
羊 肉	Mutton	公 斤 kg	3.38	2.56	2.63	2.54
禽 类	Poultry	公 斤 kg	5.28	5.03	4.85	5.86
#鸡	Chicken	公 斤 kg	3.10	2.90	2.71	3.50
蛋 类	Eggs	公 斤 kg	19.52	17.88	18.15	20.74
#鲜 蛋	Fresh Eggs	公 斤 kg	18.48	16.98	16.98	19.58
鱼	Fish	公 斤 kg	9.60	8.90	10.15	11.60
虾	Shrimp	公 斤 kg	4.22	4.09	5.26	5.35
鲜 菜	Fresh Vegetables	公 斤 kg	134.70	124.20	139.76	148.24
干 菜	Dry Vegetables	公 斤 kg	0.35	0.34	0.39	0.40
酒 类	Liquor	公 斤 kg	9.56	8.83	9.27	13.31
#白 酒	Wine	公 斤 kg	2.17	1.80	1.68	1.94
啤 酒	Beer	公 斤 kg	7.22	6.84	7.38	10.68
碳酸饮料	Beverages	公 斤 kg	3.11	3.89	3.99	6.45
茶 叶	Tea	公 斤 kg	0.32	0.29	0.31	0.30
鲜 果	Fresh Fruits	公 斤 kg	43.90	50.29	55.74	65.70
鲜 瓜	Fresh Melons	公 斤 kg	28.35	30.79	35.62	37.10
糕 点	Cake	公 斤 kg	6.43	7.03	7.88	7.65
鲜 奶	Milk	公 斤 kg	25.24	27.93	25.58	34.46
服 装	Garments	件 piece	6.49	7.10.	8.67	9.99
#男士服装	Men's Clothing	件 piece	2.56	2.85	3.56	3.84
女士服装	Women's Clothing	件 piece	3.36	3.66	4.55	5.40
童 装	Children's Clothing	件 piece	0.58	0.59	0.55	0.74
鞋 类	Shoes	双 pair	2.37	2.43	2.61	3.11

8-19 城市居民家庭平均每百户主要消费品购买量（2002-2006年）
PER 100 URBAN HOUSEHOLDS ANNUAL PURCHASES OF MAJOR CONSUMER GOODS, 2002-2006

商品名称	Item	2002	2003	2004	2005	2006
摩托车(辆)	Motorcycle (unit)	0.3	0.2	0.2	0.1	0.1
自行车(辆)	Bicycle (unit)	18.9	19.7	18.8	21.1	19.7
助力车(辆)	Helping Hand Car (unit)	0.9	2.9	4.1	4.7	4.6
家用汽车(辆)	Automobile (unit)	0.3	0.5	0.5	1.0	0.7
电风扇(台)	Electric Fan (unit)	5.3	6.4	3.7	6.6	7.0
洗衣机(台)	Washing Machine (unit)	4.8	6.8	6.1	5.8	6.2
电冰箱(台)	Refrigerator (unit)	5.7	4.9	5.2	5.2	4.2
冰　柜(台)	Freezer (unit)	0.9	0.5	0.2	0.5	0.6
彩色电视机(台)	Color TV Set (unit)	9.9	6.8	8.6	7.0	7.6
影碟机(台)	Video Disc Player (unit)	4.7	4.4	5.3	4.7	4.7
录放像机(台)	Videorecorder (unit)	0.1	0.2	0.2	0.2	0.1
摄像机(台)	Vidicon (unit)	0.1	0.1	0.5	0.6	0.5
组合音响(台)	Hi-Fi Stereo Component System (unit)	1.5	1.1	0.7	0.8	0.8
收录机(台)	Recorder (unit)	6.9	6.4	5.4	3.4	2.3
家用电脑(台)	Personal-computer (unit)	5.7	5.6	5.3	5.9	5.9
照像机(架)	Camera (set)	1.1	1.1	2.3	1.7	3.2
微波炉(台)	Microwave Oven (unit)	6.3	7.0	4.6	3.7	2.6
空调器(台)	Air-conditioner (unit)	6.7	6.7	5.9	7.1	7.2
电炊具(台)	Electric Cooking Appliance (unit)	8.7	9.5	7.4	7.2	9.2
淋浴热水器(台)	Shower (unit)	6.9	6.2	6.8	6.6	7.9
排油烟机(台)	Smoke Absorber (unit)	5.1	6.2	5.0	4.9	5.0
吸尘器(台)	Dust Catcher (unit)	1.5	1.9	1.0	0.7	0.7
移动电话(部)	Mobile Telephone (unit)	11.9	22.0	22.3	18.8	24.2

8-20 城市居民家庭平均每百户耐用消费品年末拥有量（2002-2006年）
PER 100 URBAN HOUSEHOLDS YEAR-END POSSESSIONS OF MAJOR DURABLE CONSUMER GOODS, 2002-2006

商品名称	Item	2002	2003	2004	2005	2006
成套家具(套)	Composite Furniture (set)	85.0	91.9	98.5	95.7	95.3
摩托车(辆)	Motorcycle (unit)	8.5	8.9	8.5	8.1	6.3
自行车(辆)	Bicycle (unit)	226.1	228.5	222.4	202.4	189.0
助力车(辆)	Helping Hand Car (unit)	2.1	4.4	7.4	11.1	15.5
家用汽车(辆)	Automobile (unit)	1.2	2.2	2.3	3.0	4.6
电风扇(台)	Electric Fan (unit)	118.7	119.9	114.6	95.8	107.5
洗衣机(台)	Washing Machine (unit)	96.0	96.3	95.9	109.1	96.8
电冰箱(台)	Refrigerator (unit)	102.1	98.5	98.9	97.8	98.3
冰　柜(台)	Freezer (unit)	18.0	16.7	16.8	14.5	13.9
彩色电视机(台)	Color TV Set (unit)	135.0	134.5	136.5	136.3	135.9
影碟机(台)	Video Disc Player (unit)	45.1	49.6	55.3	56.1	56.9
录放像机(台)	Video-recorder (unit)	30.4	30.3	28.0	24.2	23.3
摄像机(台)	Vidicon (unit)	2.7	3.4	3.9	5.7	7.9
组合音响(台)	Hi-Fi Stereo Component System (unit)	25.1	26.8	28.9	28.8	27.7
收录机(台)	Recorder (unit)	55.7	56.8	54.7	46.2	38.1
家用电脑(台)	Personal-computer (unit)	26.3	34.1	41.2	51.1	59.2
照像机(架)	Camera (unit)	60.0	56.3	54.3	52.5	59.5
钢　琴(架)	Piano (unit)	1.5	1.4	1.1	1.3	1.3
微波炉(台)	Microwave Oven (unit)	51.1	61.4	68.9	74.3	77.9
空调器(台)	Air-conditioner (unit)	80.9	90.9	95.3	102.1	115.7
电炊具(台)	Electric Cooking Appliance (unit)	91.9	101.1	103.0	97.3	100.0
淋浴热水器(台)	Shower (unit)	79.0	82.7	85.8	86.5	87.1
排油烟机(台)	Smoke Absorber (unit)	75.9	82.4	87.1	85.1	86.1
吸尘器(台)	Dust Catcher (unit)	21.1	24.3	26.7	24.7	23.7
移动电话(部)	Mobile Telephone (unit)	45.2	77.8	107.1	122.1	143.7

8-21 农村居民家庭基本情况（2003-2006年）
BASIC STATISTICS OF RURAL HOUSEHOLDS, 2003-2006

项　目	Item	单 位	Unit	2003	2004	2005	2006
户均常住人口	Average Permanent Residents Per Household	人	person	3.60	3.56	3.55	3.47
#劳动力	Labors Per Household	人	person	2.44	2.41	2.49	2.48
平均每个劳动力负担人口	Dependents per Labor	人	person	1.48	1.48	1.42	1.40
年末户均生产性固定资产原值	Year-end Productive Original Value of Fixed Assets per Household	元	yuan	7051	8311	10150	10837
#役畜、产品畜	Draught Animals and Commodity Animals	元	yuan	729	469	515	522
大中型铁木农具	Large and Medium Wood and Iron Farm Tools	元	yuan	263	363	162	172
农林牧渔业机械	Machinery for Farming, Forestry, Animal Husbandry and Fishery	元	yuan	1300	1480	1910	1809
户均经营耕地面积	Cultivated Land Areas per Household	公　顷	hectare	0.31	0.32	0.32	0.29
年内人均新建住房面积	New Living Space per Capita in Current Year	平方米	sq. m	0.29	0.31	0.73	0.21
年末人均住房面积	Year-end Living Space per Capita	平方米	sq. m	24.44	25.22	26.06	26.43
全年人均纯收入	Annual Net Income per Capita	元	yuan	5861	6525	7202	7942
全年人均生活消费支出	Annual per Capita Living Expenditures	元	yuan	3015	3297	3590	3829
年末百户生产性固定资产拥有量	Year-end Productive Original Value of Fixed Assets per 100 Households						
汽　车	Motor Vehicles	辆	set	5.83	5.50	6.67	6.50
大中型拖拉机	Large and Medium Tractors	台	set	1.67	2.50	1.67	1.67
小型和手扶拖拉机	Mini-tractors	台	set	22.33	21.67	18.00	17.83
水　泵	Pumps	台	set	18.67	19.25	19.00	19.00

8-22 农村居民家庭劳动力文化程度（2003-2006年）
EDUCATION LEVEL OF LABORS IN RURAL HOUSEHOLDS, 2003-2006

单位：人 (person)

项　目	Item	2003	2004	2005	2006
每百个劳动力中：	In per 100 Labors:				
不识字或识字很少	Illiterate or Semi-illiterate	1.65	1.64	1.64	1.60
小　学	Primary School	25.37	24.65	18.08	18.28
初　中	Junior Middle School	55.84	53.13	59.68	59.63
高　中	Senior Middle School	11.13	14.78	13.90	13.37
中　专	Specialized Secondary School	4.64	4.35	4.89	5.17
大专及以上	Junior College and Above	1.37	1.45	1.81	1.95

8-23 农村居民人均纯收入
PER CAPITA NET INCOME OF RURAL RESIDENTS

单位：元 (yuan)

项　目	Item	2004	2005	2006
人均纯收入	**Per Capita Annual Net Income**	**6525**	**7202**	**7942**
1. 工资性收入	Rewards of Labours	3579	3840	4234
# 在非企业组织中劳动得到	From Collective Organization	710	684	689
在本地企业中劳动得到	From Labour in Local Enterprises	2366	2512	2595
# 从乡镇集体企业中劳动得到	From Collective Enterprises	882	654	618
2. 家庭经营纯收入	Income from Family Business	2604	2959	3210
# 农　业	Farming	1316	1399	1454
畜牧业	Animal Husbandry	192	191	174
采矿业和制造业	Minerals Mining and Manufacturing	29	38	50
建筑业	Construction	147	182	194
交通运输、仓储和邮政业	Transportation, Storage and Post Service	277	371	460
批发和零售业	Wholesale and Retail Trade	121	165	226
住宿和餐饮业	Accommodation and Catering Service	62	82	82
3. 转移性、财产性纯收入	Transfer and Property Income	342	403	498

8-24 农村居民人均纯收入构成
COMPOSITION OF PER CAPITA NET INCOME OF RURAL RESIDENTS

单位：% (%)

项　目	Item	2004	2005	2006
人均纯收入	**Per Capita Annual Net Income**	**100.0**	**100.0**	**100.0**
1. 工资性收入	Rewards of Labours	54.9	53.3	53.3
# 在非企业组织中劳动得到	From Collective Organization	10.9	9.5	8.7
在本地企业中劳动得到	From Labour in Local Enterprises	36.3	34.9	32.7
# 从乡镇集体企业中劳动得到	From Collective Enterprises	13.5	9.1	7.8
2. 家庭经营纯收入	Income from Family Business	39.9	41.1	40.4
# 农　业	Farming	20.2	19.4	18.3
畜牧业	Animal Husbandry	2.9	2.7	2.2
采矿业和制造业	Minerals Mining and Manufacturing	0.4	0.5	0.6
建筑业	Construction	2.3	2.5	2.4
交通运输、仓储和邮政业	Transportation, Storage and Post Service	4.2	5.2	5.8
批发和零售业	Wholesale and Retail Trade	1.9	2.3	2.9
住宿和餐饮业	Accommodation and Catering Service	1.0	1.1	1.0
3. 转移性、财产性纯收入	Transfer and Property Income	5.2	5.6	6.3

8-25 农村居民人均生活消费支出
PER CAPITA ANNUAL LIVING EXPENDITURES OF RURAL RESIDENTS

单位：元 (yuan)

项　目	Item	2004	2005	2006
人均生活消费支出	**Per Capita Annual Living Expenditures**	**3297**	**3590**	**3829**
食　品	Food	1270	1376	1456
衣　着	Clothing	294	362	371
居　住	Residence	757	844	947
家庭设备、用品及服务	Household Facilities, Articles and Services	117	108	117
医疗保健	Medicine and Medical Services	260	268	269
交通通讯	Transportation and Communications	241	270	298
文教娱乐用品及服务	Culture, Education and Recreation Articles and Services	248	252	250
其他商品和服务	Other Commodities and Services	110	110	121

8-26 农村居民人均生活消费支出构成
COMPOSITION OF PER CAPITA LIVING EXPENDITURES OF RURAL RESIDENTS

单位：% (%)

项　目	Item	2004	2005	2006
人均生活消费支出	**Per Capita Annual Living Expenditure**	**100.0**	**100.0**	**100.0**
食　品	Food	38.5	38.3	38.0
衣　着	Clothing	8.9	10.1	9.7
居　住	Residence	23	23.5	24.7
家庭设备、用品及服务	Household Facilities, Articles & Services	3.6	3.0	3.1
医疗保健	Medicine and Medical Services	7.9	7.5	7.0
交通通讯	Transportation and Communications	7.3	7.5	7.8
文教娱乐用品及服务	Culture, Education and Recreation Articles and Services	7.5	7.0	6.5
其他商品和服务	Other Commodities and Services	3.3	3.1	3.2

8-27 农村居民家庭每百户耐用消费品年末拥有量（2002-2006年）
PER 100 RURAL HOUSEHOLDS YEAR-END POSSESSIONS OF DURABLE CONSUMER GOODS, 2002-2006

商品名称	Item	2002	2003	2004	2005	2006
自行车(辆)	Bicycle (unit)	204	198	191	183	181
电动自行车(辆)	Electric Bicycle (unit)	2	3	4	8	16
摩托车(辆)	Motorcycle (unit)	41	45	49	50	48
生活用汽车(辆)	Car (unit)	3	3	4	6	7
电风扇(台)	Electric Fan (set)	180	171	158	137	140
空调器(台)	Air-Conditioner (set)	26	32	36	42	50
洗衣机(台)	Washing Machine (set)	86	90	92	95	96
电冰箱(台)	Refrigerator (set)	72	75	78	84	88
微波炉(台)	Microwave Oven (set)	7	10	12	16	20
吸尘器(台)	Dust Catcher (unit)	5	6	6	6	7
热水器(台)	Shower (set)		15	21	32	38
抽油烟机(台)	Smoke Absorber (set)		12	14	18	22
普通电话(部)	Telephone (unit)	80	84	87	88	86
移动电话(部)	Mobile Telephone (unit)	36	54	65	89	108
家用电脑(台)	Personal-computer (unit)	5	7	8	10	12
彩色电视机(台)	Color TV Set (set)	105	110	115	116	120
照相机(架)	Camera (set)	20	20	20	20	20
影碟机(台)	Video Disc Player (set)	27	31	33	40	38
收录机(台)	Tape Recorder (set)	19	19	18	19	18
摄像机(台)	Vidicon (set)		1	1	1	1

8-28 农村居民人均食品消费量（2002-2006年）
PER CAPITA ANNUAL CONSUMPTION ON FOOD OF RURAL HOUSEHOLDS, 2002-2006

单位：千克 (kg)

商品名称	Item	2002	2003	2004	2005	2006
粮　食	Grain	199.0	195.0	182.3	173.5	165.5
蔬菜及其制品	Vegetables and Related Products	132.4	134.3	136.4	124.7	132.2
食用植物油	Vegetable Oil	10.8	9.3	9.4	9.4	9.3
食用动物油	Animal Oil	0.9	0.7	0.5	0.3	0.4
猪　肉	Pork	8.9	9.4	9.3	9.8	11.2
牛　肉	Beef	0.6	0.7	0.9	1.0	0.8
羊　肉	Mutton	1.1	1.0	1.1	1.2	1.4
家　禽	Poultry	1.1	1.1	0.9	0.7	0.6
肉禽制品	Meat, Poultry and Related Products	0.9	1.2	1.1	1.1	1.3
蛋类及其制品	Eggs and Related Products	14.4	16.6	18.0	17.4	17.6
奶及其制品	Milk and Related Products	1.3	1.9	2.4	3.4	5.7
水产品	Aquatic Products	8.7	9.4	10.2	12.8	14.8
水果及其制品	Fruits and Related Products	30.2	30.1	31.4	28.8	32.0
食　糖	Sugar	2.0	1.1	0.7	0.6	0.7
白　酒	Wine	3.3	3.2	3.1	3.5	3.5
啤　酒	Beer	7.3	7.0	7.3	7.3	6.9

主要统计指标解释

城镇单位从业人员劳动报酬 是指各单位在一定时期内直接支付给本单位全部从业人员的劳动报酬总额。包括在岗职工工资总额和本单位其他从业人员劳动报酬两部分。

在岗职工工资总额 指各单位在一定时期内直接支付给本单位在岗职工的全部劳动报酬总额。在岗职工工资总额构成包括：计时工资（含计时标准工资）、计件工资、奖金、计件超额工资、津贴和补贴、加班加点工资、特殊情况下支付的工资等。

其他从业人员劳动报酬 指各单位在一定时期内直接支付给本单位其他从业人员的全部劳动报酬。包括支付给再就业的离退休人员的劳动报酬和民办教师、港澳台和外籍人员的劳动报酬总额。还包括支付给聘用的外单位不在岗人员、聘用的失业人员、聘用和使用的外来人员、聘用的在本单位从事第二职业人员的劳动报酬。

职工保险福利费总额 指各单位在工资以外实际支付给职工个人和用于集体的劳动保险福利费用总额。

城市居民家庭就业人口 指从事社会劳动并取得报酬或经营收入的人口，不论在全民、集体和其他所有制单位工作或从事个体劳动，不论有固定性职业或临时性职业都是就业人口。

城市居民家庭总收入 指城市居民家庭中生活在一起的所有家庭成员在调查期得到的工薪收入、经营净收入、财产性收入、转移性收入的总和，不包括出售财物收入和借贷收入。收入的统计标准以实际发生的数额为准，无论收入是补发还是预发，只要是调查期得到的都应如实计算，不作分摊。

城市居民家庭可支配收入 指城市居民家庭可用于最终消费支出和其他非义务性支出以及储蓄的总和，即居民家庭可以用来自由支配的收入。它是家庭总收入扣除交纳的所得税、个人交纳的社会保障费以及调查户的记帐收入补贴后的收入。计算公式为：

可支配收入＝家庭总收入－交纳所得税－个人交纳的社会保障支出－记帐补贴

城市居民家庭消费支出 指城市居民家庭用于本家庭日常生活消费需要的全部支出，包括食品、衣着、家庭设备用品及服务、医疗保健、交通和通讯、娱乐教育文化服务、居住、杂项商品和服务等八大类。

城市居民家庭服务性消费支出 指城市居民家庭用于本家庭支付社会提供的各种文化和生活方面的非商品性服务费用。不包括为别人付款的服务费用。

农村居民常住人口 指全年经常在家或在家居住六个月以上，而且经济和生活与本户连成一体的人口。外出从业人员在外居住时间虽然在六个月以上，但收入主要带回家中，经济与本户连成一体，仍视为家庭常住人口；在家居住、生活和本户连成一体的国家职工、退休人员也视为家庭常住人口。但是现役军人、中专及以上（走读生除外）的在校学生、以及常年在外（不包括探亲、看病等）且已有稳定的职业与居住场所的外出从业人员，不应当作为家庭常住人口。

农村居民纯收入 指农村住户当年从各个来源得到的总收入相应地扣除所发生的费用后的收入总和。纯收入主要用于再生产投入和当年生活消费支出，也可用于储蓄和各种非义务性支出。计算公式为：

农村居民纯收入＝总收入－家庭经营费用支出－税费支出—生产性固定资产折旧－农村亲友赠送

农村居民工资性收入 指农村住户成员受雇于单位或个人，靠出卖劳动而获得的收入。包括：

（1）在非企业组织中劳动得到的收入：指农村住户成员在不具备企业性质的行政事业单位和各种组织中劳动得到的收入。包括村干部和民办教师的工资（奖金、补贴），乡及以上行政、事业单位工作人员的工资（奖金、补贴）等。

（2）在本地劳动得到的收入：指农村住户成员在所属乡（镇）地域范围内受雇于单位或个人，靠出卖劳动而获得的收入。

主要统计指标解释

（3）常住人口外出从业得到的收入：指农村住户成员到住户所属乡镇地域范围以外从业得到的收入。

农村居民家庭经营收入　指农村住户以家庭为生产经营单位进行生产筹划和管理而获得的收入。家庭经营活动按行业划分为农业、林业、畜牧业、渔业、工业、建筑业、交通运输和邮电业、批发和零售贸易餐饮业、社会服务业、文教卫生业和其他家庭经营。

农村居民财产性收入　指金融资产或有形非生产性资产的所有者向其他机构单位提供资金或将有形非生产性资产供其支配，作为回报而从中获得的收入。包括利息收入、股息收入、租金收入、土地征用补偿收入等。

农村居民转移性收入　指农村住户和住户成员无须付出任何对应物而获得的货物、服务、资金或资产所有权等，不包括无偿提供的用于固定资本形成的资金。一般情况下，指农村住户在二次分配中的所有收入。包括家庭非常住人口寄回或带回、城市亲友赠送、农村亲友赠送等。

农村居民生活消费支出　指农村住户用于物质生活和精神生活方面的支出。包括食品，衣着，居住，家庭设备、用品及服务，医疗保健，交通和通讯，文化教育娱乐用品及服务，其他商品和服务等消费支出。

Explanastory Notes on Main Statistical Indicators

Remuneration of Employment Personnel Worked in Urban Units refer to total reward payment of employment personnel worked in units during a certain period. It includes total wages of working staff and workers and reward of other employment personnel.

Total Wages of On-post Staff and Workers refer to the total reward payment to working staff and workers in their units during a certain period of time. It includes time wage, piece wage, cash awards, exceed wage, subsidy, working overtime wage and other special wage.

Total Remuneration to Other Employment Personnel refers to the total reward payment to other persons employed in their units during a certain period of time. It includes reward payment to re-employed retirees, teachers in schools run by the local people, foreigners and Chinese compatriots from Hong Kong, Macao, and Taiwan working in various units, employees of other units working temporarily at current posts, unemployment personnel, non-locals, and employees holding the second job of other unit.

Total Insurance Welfare Funds of Staff and Workers refer to the total labor insurance welfare funds payment to every staff and worker in various units and collective of the units.

Employment Personnel of Urban Households refer to the persons who are engaged in social labor and receive payment or earn business income, including the staff and workers in the state-owned, the staff and workers in collective-owned, other employed, employed persons individual business, etc. No matter he is permanent or temporary.

Total Income of Urban Households refers to the total income of the sample households, including wage, income from business, income from property, transfer income, excluding proceeds from sales of belongings and credit income. It is calculated on real income, no matter the income is supplied again or beforehand.

Disposable Income of Urban Households refers to the disposable income of the sample households, including those which can be used for final expenditure and other non-obligation expenditure and savings. It refers to the difference of total income minus income tax, expenditure for social security and subsidies of account. The following formula is used :

Disposable Income of Urban Households= Total Income-Income Tax-Expenditure for Social Security-Survey Subsidies

Expenditure for Consumption of Urban Households refer to total expenditure of the sample households for consumption in daily life. It is classified into 8 categories food, clothing, household facilities and articles service, medicine and medical service, transportation and communication, recreation, education and culture service, residence, miscellaneous commodities services.

Service Expenditure for Consumption of Urban Households refers to total non-commodity expenditure of the sample households for consumption in culture and life. It excludes service expenditure paid for other persons.

Rural Permanent Resident Population refers to population staying at home permanently or for over 6 months during a year and sharing life economically with the household. Members of the household staying away from the household for over 6 months but keeping a close economic life with the household by sending the majority of income to the household are regarded as resident population of the household. Government staff and workers or retirees living as close members of the household are also considered as resident population. However, servicemen, students of secondary technical schools or schools of higher education and persons with stable jobs and residence outside the household (excluding those visiting relatives or seeking medical service) are not included as resident population of the household.

Net Income of Rural Residents refers to the total income of the rural households after the deduction of the expenses for the various cost, which can then be spent for investment in reproduction, expenditure for living consumption, saving, non-productive construction. The formula for calculating is as follows:

Net Income of Rural Households= Total Income-Expenses for Productive Operation-Taxes-Depreciation of Fixed Assets for Production- Gifts to Relatives

Rewards of Labours of Rural Residents refers to income from labor earned by members of rural households employed by other units or individuals. It includes :

(a) Income by members of rural households employed by administration business units and social organizations, including wages (Cash awards and subsidy) of village staff and teachers in schools run by the local people, ages(Cash awards and subsidy) of staff employed by administration business units at township and higher level.

(b) Income earned at local region income from labor earned by members of rural households employed by other units or individuals at local township.

Explanastory Notes on Main Statistical Indicators

(c) Income of permanent residence outside the household income from labor earned by members of rural households employed by other units or individuals at outside local region.

Income of Productive Operation of Rural Households refers to income obtained from family productive operation. Family productive operation cover farming, forestry, animal husbandry, fishery, industry, construction, transport, post, telecommunication, wholesale and retail trade, catering, social services, culture, education, health care and other household operation.

Property Income of Rural Residents refers to the income received as returns by owners of financial assets or tangible non-productive assets by providing capital or tangible non-productive assets to other institutional units. It includes interest income, bonus stock income, rent income, compensatory income of collected land.

Transfer Income of Rural Residents refers to the receipt by rural hou seholds and their members of goods, services, capitals or rights of assets without giving or repaying accordingly, excluding capitals provided to them for the formation of fixed assets. In general, it refers to all income received by rural household through redistribution. It includes income receipt by non-permanent residents, gifts of urban & rural relatives.

Expenditure on Consumption of Rural Residents

That Expenditure was use on matter life and energy life by rural households, including food expenditure, clothing expenditure, residence, household facilities, articles and services, medicines and medical services, transportation and communications, cultural, education and recreation articles and services, other commodity and services.

第9篇
CHAPTER 9

城市建设和环境保护
Urban Construction and Environment Protection

9-1 城市建设用地
CITY CONSTRUCTION LAND-USED

单位：平方公里 (sq. km)

指　标	Item	2004	2005	2006
建成区面积	**Developed Area**	**500.14**	**530.00**	**539.98**
市中心区	Central Districts	257.18	269.05	270.3
滨海新区	Binhai New Area	175.15	188.65	194.78
塘沽地区小计	Tanggu District	117.04	127.26	133.39
塘沽城区和天津港	Central District of Tanggu and Tianjin Port	87.44	93.11	95.37
经济技术开发区	TEDA	24.60	28.86	32.73
天津港保税区	TPFTZ	5.00	5.29	5.29
汉沽区	Han'gu District	16.16	16.16	16.16
大港区	Dagang District	41.95	45.23	45.23
西青区	Xiqing District	15.49	15.49	15.49
津南区	Jinnan District	6.94	6.95	6.95
武清区	Wuqing District	31.14	34.95	37.55
宝坻区	Baodi District	14.24	14.91	14.91
城市建设用地	**City Construction Land-used**	**500.14**	**530.00**	**539.98**
居住用地	Dwelling	159.49	167.56	168.47
公共设施用地	Public Facilities	60.08	65.42	67.20
工业用地	Industry	114.9	119.63	119.05
仓储用地	Warehouse	30.34	27.02	31.44
对外交通用地	Traffic	16.96	18.31	18.51
道路广场用地	Road and Square	41.60	43.00	46.2
市政公用设施用地	Public Facilities of Municipal Administration	16.04	19.13	20.41
绿　地	Green Land	48.71	58.25	57.07
特殊用地	Special Land	12.01	11.67	11.63

资料来源：天津市建委，9-3 表同。
Sources: Tianjin Municipal Urban & Rural Construction Commission, same as following table 9-3.

9-2 城市房屋建筑面积
FLOOR SPACE OF BUILDINGS IN CITY

单位：万平方米 (10 000 sq. m)

项　目	Item	2004	2005	2006
年末实有房屋建筑面积	**Total Floor Space of Buildings (year-end)**	**20902.87**	**22578.12**	**24450.45**
# 房管部门直管产	Under House Management Department	2945.73	2949.64	2924.86
私　产	Private Property	10178.76	11089.9	12328.42
年末实有住宅建筑面积	**Residential Buildings (year-end)**	**13465.32**	**14043.16**	**14875.76**
# 房管部门直管产	Under House Management Department	1713.28	1678.62	1617.52
私　产	Private Property	9050.02	10120.23	11057.48
人均住宅建筑面积(平方米/人)	**Per Capita Floor Space of Residential Buildings (sq. m/person)**	**24.70**	**24.97**	**26.05**

资料来源：天津市国土资源和房屋管理局。
Sources: Bureau of Land Resources and Housing Management of Tianjin.

9-3 城市市政设施情况
MUNICIPAL FACILITIES IN CITY

指　标	Item	单 位	Unit	2005	2006
年末实有道路	**Road (year-end)**				
铺装道路长度	Length of Paved Roads	公　里	km	5460	5991
铺装道路面积	Area of Paved Roads	万平方米	10 000 sq. m	6669	7933
# 人行道面积	Area of Footway	万平方米	10 000 sq. m	1070	1788
人均拥有道路面积	Per Capita Area of Paved Roads	平方米	sq. m	10.4	14.0
年末实有桥梁	**Bridges (year-end)**				
桥梁座数	Number of Bridges	座	unit	563	376
# 立交桥	Flyover	座	unit	66.0	49.0
年末实有路灯盏数	**Number of Road Lamps (year-end)**	**万　盏**	**10 000 units**	**17.57**	**20.3**
排泄污水能力	**Capacity of Sewage Drainage**				
污水年排放量	Annual Volume of Sewage Drainage	万　吨	10 000 tons	59484	63932
排水管道长度	Length of Drainpipes	公　里	km	10889	11939
污水处理厂	Sewage Treatment Works	座	set	9	14
污水处理厂能力	Disposal Capacity of Sewage Treatment Works	万吨/日	10 000 tons/day	157.8	176.1
排水管道密度	Density of Drainpipes	公里/平方公里	km/sq. km		5.45
污水处理率	**Percentage of Sewage Disposed**	**(%)**	**%**	**58.0**	**58.9**

资料来源：天津市市政工程管理局。
Sources: Tianjin Municipal Administration Bureau.

9-4 城市自来水
URBAN TAP WATER

指　标	Item	单 位	Unit	2005	2006
综合生产能力	Production Capacity	万吨／日	10 000 tons/day	359	357.3
供水管道	Length of Water Supply Pipelines	公　里	km	7093	7335
供水总量	Total Annual Volume of Water Supply	万　吨	10 000 tons	68236	68180
售水总量	Total Annual Volume of Water Sold	万　吨	10 000 tons	60173	58680
# 生活用水	For Residential Use	万　吨	10 000 tons	28885	27084
生产用水	For Productive Use	万　吨	10 000 tons	31430	31597
用水人口	Number of Residents With Access to Tap Water	万　人	10 000 persons		567.5
人均日生活用水量	Per Capita Daily Consumption of Tap Water for Residential Use	公　斤	kg	123.6	130.4

资料来源：天津市公共办，9-5、9-9表同。
Sources: Tianjin Municipal Public Department, same following table 9-5 and 9-9.

9-5 城市燃气设备能力、销售量和用气户数
GAS EQUIPMENT CAPACITY, GAS SOLD AND GAS USERS IN CITY

项　目	Item	2004	2005	2006
液化石油气	**Liquefied Petroleum Gas**			
储气能力(吨)	Storage Capacity (ton)	21524	15829	21273
销售量(吨)	Volume of Gas Sold (ton)	69779	61503	23770
工业用	For Industrial Use	42347	37704	4439
民　用	For Residential Use	27432	23799	19331
用气户数(户)	Gas Users (household)	422416	449511	303054
工业用	For Industrial Use	5323	5838	3516
民　用	For Residential Use	417093	443673	309538
天然气	**Natural Gas**			
储气能力(万立方米)	Storage Capacity (10 000 cu. m)	120.6	120.4	130.2
管道长度(公里)	Length of Pipelines (km)	5715	6751	8515
销售量(万立方米)	Volume of Gas Sold (10 000 cu. m)	52710	68966	92561
工业用	For Industrial Use	25147	26190	44723
福利用	For Welfare Use	11839	14568	17468
民　用	For Residential Use	15145	15465	17730
用气户数(户)	Gas Users (household)	1422495	1493271	1760126
工业用	For Industrial Use	242	270	483
福利用	For Welfare Use	7468	7347	9359
民　用	For Residential Use	1414785	1485654	1750274
煤制气	**Coal Gas**			
销售量(万立方米)	Volume of Gas Sold (10 000 cu. m)	23683	26078	24031
# 工业用	For Industrial Use	13978	16246	17009
福利用	For Welfare Use	1782	2052	1452
民　用	For Residential Use	7594	7421	5357
用气普及率	**Percentage of Population with Access to Gas (%)**	98.5	98.5	99.2

注：工业用液化石油气数据含福利、商业和其他用。
Note: Volume of liquefied petroleum gas sold for industrial use include those of welfare,commerce and other use.

9-6 城市园林绿化情况（2006年）
PARKS, GARDENS AND GREEN AREAS IN CITY, 2006

指　标　Item	数量 Amount	指　标　Item	数量 Amount
公　园(含动物园)(个)		年末实有树木(万株)	
Parks (Including Zoos) (unit)	62	Trees (year-end) (10 000 trees)	2221.4
花　圃(个)		#行道树	
Gardens(unit)	16	Roadside Trees	167.7
园林绿地总面积(公顷)		全年植树(万株)	
Total Area of Parks, Gardens and Green Areas (hectare)	16499.3	Trees Planted (10 000 trees)	140.1
#公园面积		建成区绿化覆盖率(%)	
Area of Parks	1100.4	Coverage Rate of Afforestation in Developed Areas (%)	37
花圃面积		建成区绿地率(%)	
Area of Gardens	65.8	Coverage Rate of Green Areas in Developed Areas (%)	29
附属绿地		人均公园面积(平方米)	
Accessarial Green Area	6173.6	Per Capita Area of Parks (sq. m)	6.59

资料来源：天津市园林局。
Sources: Tianjin Municipal Bureau of Parks.

9-7 公园分布（2006年）
DISTRIBUTION OF PARKS, 2006

地　区	Region	公园个数(个) Number of Parks (unit)	地　区	Region	公园面积(公顷) Area of Parks (hectare)
合　计	Total	62	合　计	Total	1100.35
河东区	Hedong District	1	河东区	Hedong District	10
河西区	Hexi District	8	河西区	Hexi District	89.8
南开区	Nankai District	5	南开区	Nankai District	286.67
河北区	Hebei District	3	河北区	Hebei District	58.95
红桥区	Hongqiao District	6	红桥区	Hongqiao District	48.55
塘沽区	Tanggu District	6	塘沽区	Tanggu District	91.82
开发区	TEDA District	7	开发区	TEDA District	62.43
汉沽区	Han'gu District	2	汉沽区	Han'gu District	23.81
大港区	Dagang District	4	大港区	Dagang District	103.52
东丽区	Dongli District	3	东丽区	Dongli District	15.2
津南区	Jinnan District	5	津南区	Jinnan District	190.37
北辰区	Beichen District	3	北辰区	Beichen District	10.3
武清区	Wuqing District	6	武清区	Wuqing District	75.75
宝坻区	Baodi District	3	宝坻区	Baodi District	33.18

9-8 城市集中供热
HEATING IN CITY

项　目	Item	单　位	Unit	2004	2005	2006
供热能力	Heating Capacity					
蒸　汽	Steam	吨/小时	ton/hour	3407	3294	3551
热　水	Hot Water	兆瓦/小时	mega watts/hour	10111	10563	12106
供热总量	Volume Supplied					
蒸　汽	Steam	万吉焦/年	10 000 giga-joules/year	1764	1966	1891
热　水	Hot Water	万吉焦/年	10 000 giga-joules/year	6530	7572	8451
管道长度	Length of Pipelines	公　里	km	8038	8705	9494
供热面积	Heating Area	万平方米	10 000 sq. m	11441	14041	15611.3
#住　宅	Residential Buildings	万平方米	10 000 sq. m	8970	10967	12040.7

资料来源：天津市供热办。
Sources: Tianjin Municipal Heating Department.

9-9 城市公共交通
PUBLIC TRAFFIC IN CITY

指　标	Item	单　位	Unit	2004	2005	2006
公共汽车	**Public Transportation Vehicles**					
营运车辆	Operation Vehicles	辆	unit	6331	6768	7401
线路条数	Number of Routes	条	route	402	432	447
线路长度	Length of Routes	公　里	km	8114	9354	10140
乘客人数	Passengers	万人次	10 000 person-time	78502	89529	94241
日均乘客人数	Average Daily Passengers	万人次	10 000 person-time	218	249	262
每万人拥有公共交通车辆	**Number of Public Transportation Vehicles per 10 000 Persons**	**标　台**	**unit**	**10.7**	**11.2**	**14.2**
营运出租汽车	**Operating Taxis**	**辆**	**unit**	**31939**	**31939**	**31940**

9-10 城市环境卫生事业发展情况
DEVELOPMENT OF URBAN ENVIRONMENTAL SANITATION

指　标	Item	单　位	Unit	2004	2005	2006
清运垃圾粪便工作量	**Volume of Garbage, Excrement and Urine Disposal**					
清扫街道面积	Area Cleaned	万平方米	10 000 sq. m	6090	7357	7998
清运垃圾	Volume of Garbage Disposal	万　吨	10 000 ton	204	167	153.7
清运粪便	Volume of Excrement and Urine Disposal	万　吨	10 000 ton	26.4	27.3	30
垃圾无害化处理量	Volume of Garbage Innocuous Disposal	万　吨	10 000 ton	110.7	119	136
垃圾粪便无害化处理率	**Innocuous Disposal Rate of Garbage, Excrementand Urine**	**%**	**%**	**61**	**80.5**	**85**
环境卫生设施	**Environmental Sanitation Facilities**					
公共厕所	Lavatories	座	unit	2731	2778	2458
垃圾无害化处理厂	Garbage Innocuous Disposal Plant	座	unit	6	6	6
无害化处理厂能力	Capacity of Innocuous Disposal Plant	吨/日	ton/day	5690	6800	7000
环卫职工人数	**Number of Environment Sanitation Staff & Workers**	**人**	**person**	**18477**	**19087**	**20059**

资料来源：天津市市容委。
Sources: Tianjin Municipal Environment Committee.

9-11 水资源情况(2000-2006年) WATER RESOURCES, 2000-2006

年份 Year	水资源总量 (亿立方米) Total Amount of Water Resources (100 million cu. m)	地表水 Surface Water	地下水 Underground Water	地表水与地下水资源重复量 Duplicated Measurement between Surface and Underground	人均水资源量 (立方米/人) Per Capita Water Resources (cu. m/person)
2000	3.15	0.62	2.75	0.22	31.46
2001	5.66	3.53	2.41	0.28	56.37
2002	3.67	1.85	2.09	0.27	36.44
2003	10.60	6.15	4.82	0.37	104.82
2004	14.31	9.79	5.16	0.64	139.79
2005	10.63	7.13	4.44	0.94	101.92
2006	10.11	6.62	4.46	0.97	94.05

9-12 供水用水情况(2000-2006年) WATER SUPPLY AND WATER USE, 2000-2006

单位：万立方米 (10 000 cu. m)

年份 地区	Year Region	供用水总量 Water Supply & Use	地表水 Surface Water	地下水 Underground Water	#农业用水 Agricultural Use
	2000	226345	144164	82181	119469
	2001	188141	111738	76403	99056
	2002	199610	117421	82189	106244
	2003	205118	133713	71405	114072
	2004	219623	148932	70691	121529
	2005	225193	160224	64969	135267
	2006	**224996**	**161001**	**63995**	**133965**
市内六区	Six Urban Districts	53524	53122	402	
塘沽区	Tanggu District	7934	6259	1675	624
汉沽区	Han'gu District	4564	1200	3364	1722
大港区	Dagang District	3488	170	3318	161
东丽区	Dongli District	1981	99	1882	409
西青区	Xiqing District	13682	11195	2487	12000
津南区	Jinnan District	4082	1100	2982	1777
北辰区	Beichen District	5242	2995	2247	3930
武清区	Wuqing District	28259	18671	9588	24200
宝坻区	Baodi District	67075	56589	10486	63776
宁河县	Ninghe County	14331	9001	5330	11157
静海县	Jinghai County	4823		4823	3261
蓟县	Jixian County	15915	600	15315	10937
其他	Others	96		96	11

资料来源：天津市水利局。
Sources: Tianjin Municipal Water Conservancy Bureau.

9-13 工业废水、废气、固体废物排放及处理情况（2003-2006年）
EMISSION AND TREATMENT OF INDUSTRIAL WASTE WATER, WASTE GAS, WASTE RESIDUE AND DUST, 2003-2006

指　标　Item	2003	2004	2005	2006
工业废水　Industrial Waste Water				
工业废水排放量(万吨) Volume of Waste Water Discharged (10 000 tons)	21605	22628	30081	22978
工业废水排放达标率(%) Rate of Reaching the Standard of Industrial Waste Water (%)	100	99	99.6	99.77
工业废气　Industrial Waste Gas				
工业废气排放总量(亿标立方米) Total Volume of Industrial Waste Gas Emission (100 million cu. m)	4360	3058	4602	6512
生产工艺过程中废气排放量 Volume of Waste Gas from the Process of Production	893	835	1222	1945
燃料燃烧过程中废气排放量 Volume of Waste Gas from the Burning Process of Fuel	3467	2223	3380	4567
废气中二氧化硫排放量(万吨) Sulphur Dioxide in Waste Gas (10 000 tons)	26	20	24	23
工业粉尘产生量(万吨) Amount of Industrial Dust Produced (10 000 tons)	21	26	28	44
工业粉尘排放量 Volume of Industrial Dust Emission	2	2	2	1
工业粉尘去除量 Volume of Industrial Dust Removed	19	24	26	43
工业粉尘去除率(%) Rate of Industrial Dust Removed (%)	90	93	93	97.7
工业固体废物　Industrial Waste Residue				
工业固体废物产生量(万吨) Amount of Industrial Waste Residue Produced (10 000 tons)	644	753	1123	1292
# 已处理量 Volume of Treatment	57	21	20	20
已综合利用量 Volume of Comprehensive Utilization	619	782	1153	1271
工业固体废物处置率(%) Disposal Rate of Industrial Waste Residue (%)	8	3	1	1.5
工业固体废物综合利用率(%) Rate of Comprehensive Using Industrial Waste Residue (%)	96	97	98	98.4

9-14 城市水、大气、声、生态环境基本情况（2003-2006年）
URBAN WATER, ATMOSPHERIC, ACOUSTIC AND ECOLOGICAL ENVIRONMENT, 2003-2006

指标 Item	2003	2004	2005	2006
水环境情况 Water Environment Conditions				
城市饮用水源地水质达标率(%) Urban Drinking Water Sources Quality Rate (%)	100	100	100	100
近海海域功能区水质达标率(%) Inshore Area Water Quality Rate (%)	55.0	57.1	59.5	60.0
大气环境情况 Atmospheric Environment Conditions				
可吸入颗粒物(毫克/立方米) (PM_{10}) Paticulate Matters (milligram/cu. m)	0.133	0.111	0.106	0.113
二氧化硫(毫克/立方米) (SO_2) Sulphur Dioxide (milligram/cu. m)	0.073	0.073	0.077	0.065
二氧化氮(毫克/立方米) (NO_2) Nitrogen Dioxide (milligram/cu. m)	0.051	0.052	0.047	0.048
空气质量达到及好于二级的天数(天) Days of Air Quality Equal to or Above Grade II (day)	264	299	298	305
环境空气质量优良率(%) Ambient Air Quality Fine Rate (%)	72.3	81.7	81.6	83.6
声环境情况 Acoustic Environment Conditions				
城市交通噪声等效声级(分贝) Equivalent Sound Level of City Traffic Noise (decibel)	68	68	68	67.7
城市区域环境噪声平均声级(分贝) Urban Area Average Environmental Noise Level (decibel)	55.0	54.9	54.9	54.9
生态环境情况 Ecological Environment Conditions				
自然保护区（个） Nature Reserves (unit)	8	9	8	8
自然保护区面积（万公顷） Nature Reserves Area (10 000 hectare)	15.33	16.45	16.30	16.28

9-15 环境保护系统人员构成（2003-2006年）
COMPOSITION OF ENVIRONMENT PROTECTION PERSONNEL, 2003-2006

指标	Item	2003	2004	2005	2006
年末实有人数(人)	Persons (year-end) (person)	1703	1781	1853	1851
科技人员	Science and Technology Personnel	724	728	839	846
#科研人员	Scientific Research Personnel	176	176	176	171
监测人员	Monitoring Personnel	402	421	688	711
行政干部	Administrative Personnel	438	457	522	484
科技业务人员占全部人员比重(%)	Percentage of Science and Technology Personnel in Total (%)	43	41	45	46

9-16 环境管理"三同时"制度执行情况(2003-2006年)
IMPLEMENTATION OF "THREE MEANTIME" SYSTEM OF ENVIRONMENTAL MANAGEMENT, 2003-2006

指　标	Item	2003	2004	2005	2006
当年建成投产项目数(个)	Projects Putting into Use (unit)	1439	1121	1181	1073
应执行"三同时"项目数(个)	Number of Project Executing "Three Meantime" (unit)	1439	1121	1181	1073
实际执行"三同时"项目(个)	Number of Actual Executing Project (unit)	1439	1121	1181	1073
项目实际投资额(亿元)	Actual Investment of Project (100 million yuan)	93	113	253	274.7
# 环保工程实际投资额	Actual Investment of Protecting Environment	3	4	24	7.9
"三同时"执行率(%)	Rate of Executing "Three Meantime" (%)	100	100	100	100
"三同时"合格率(%)	Qualified Rate of Executing "Three Meantime" (%)	100	100	100	100

注:"三同时"指同时设计、同时施工、同时使用。
Note: "Three Meantime" refers to design,construction,and use at the same time.

9-17 排污费征收、工业污染治理情况(2003-2006年)
COLLECTION OF DISCHARGE FEE AND INDUSTRIAL POLLUTION HARNESSING PROJECTS, 2003-2006

单位：个、万元 (unit, 10 000 yuan)

指　标	Item	2003	2004	2005	2006
排污费收支情况	**Revenue And Expenditure of Discharge Fee**				
排污费交纳单位	Unit of Paying Discharge Fee	6766	6508	5875	6182
排污费征收额	Collection of Discharge Fee	14219	14675	20177	23953
工业污染治理情况	**Industrial Pollution Harnessing Projects**				
本年完成投资	Investment Completed in Current Year	87152	72546	186316	149534
治理废水	Treating Waste Water	28612	20352	28530	26537
治理废气	Treating Waste Gas	45627	42940	101091	68426
治理固体废物	Treating Waste Residue	6587	1560	4328	148
治理噪声	Treating Noise Pollution	719	711	1707	260
其　他	Others	5608	6984	50660	54163
本年安排治理项目	Number of Project of Treating in Current Year	319	262	235	162
本年竣工项目	Number of Project Completed in Current Year	182	194	178	149
治理废水	Treating Waste Water	58	73	60	55
治理废气	Treating Waste Gas	79	72	70	55
治理固体废物	Treating Waste Residue	10	10	20	4
治理噪声	Treating Noise Pollution	3	9	4	3
其　他	Others	32	30	24	32

主要统计指标解释

建成区面积　指城市行政区内实际已成片开发建设、市政公用设施和公共设施基本具备的区域。对核心城市，它包括集中连片的部分以及分散的若干个已经成片建设起来的市政公用设施和公共设施基本具备的地区；对一城多镇来说，它包括由几个连片开发建设起来的市政公用设施和公共设施基本具备的地区组成。因此建成区范围，一般是指建成区外轮廓线所能包括的地区，也就是这个城市实际建设用地所达到的范围。

城市园林绿地面积　指报告期末用作园林和绿化的各种绿地面积。包括公共绿地、居住区绿地、单位附属绿地、防护绿地、生产绿地、道路绿地和风景林地面积。

建成区绿化覆盖率　指报告期末建成区内绿化覆盖面积与建成区面积之比。用百分数表示。计算公式：

建成区绿化覆盖率 =(建成区内绿化覆盖面积 / 建成区面积)×100%

房屋建筑面积　指从房屋外墙线算起的各层平面面积的总和，包括可供使用的有效面积和房屋结构（如柱、墙）占用的面积。多层建筑按各层（包括地下室）面积总和计算。

住宅建筑面积　指施工和竣工房屋建筑面积中供居住用的施工和竣工房屋建筑面积。

工业废水排放量　指经过企业厂区所有排放口排到企业外部的工业废水量。包括生产废水、外排的直接冷却水、超标排放的矿井地下水和与工业废水混排的厂区生活污水，不包括外排的间接冷却水（清污不分流的间接冷却水应计算在内）。

工业废水排放达标率　指工业废水排放达标量占工业废水排放量的百分率，计算公式为：

工业废水排放达标率 =(工业废水排放达标量 / 工业废水排放量) ×100%

工业废气排放量　指报告期内企业厂区内燃料燃烧和生产工艺过程中产生的各种排入大气的含有污染物的气体的总量，以标准状态 (273K，101325Pa) 计算。测算公式为：

工业废气排放量 = 燃料燃烧过程中废气排放量 + 生产工艺过程中废气排放量

工业粉尘排放量　指企业在生产工艺过程中排放的能在空气中悬浮一定时间的固体颗粒物排放量。如钢铁企业的耐火材料粉尘、焦化企业的筛焦系统粉尘、烧结机的粉尘、石灰窑的粉尘、建材企业的水泥粉尘等。不包括电厂排入大气的烟尘。

工业固体废物产生量　指报告期内企业在生产过程中产生的固体状、半固体状和高浓度液体状废弃物的总量，包括危险废物、冶炼废渣、粉煤灰、炉渣、煤矸石、尾矿、放射性废物和其他废物等；不包括矿山开采的剥离废石和掘进废石（煤矸石和呈酸性或碱性的废石除外）。酸性或碱性废石指采掘的废石其流经水、雨淋水的 pH 值小于 4 或 pH 值大于 10.5 者。

工业固体废物综合利用量　指报告期内企业通过回收、加工、循环、交换等方式，从固体废物中提取或者使其转化为可以利用的资源、能源和其他原材料的固体废物量（包括当年利用往年的工业固体废物贮存量），如用作农业肥料、生产建筑材料、筑路等。

工业固体废物综合利用率　指工业固体废物综合利用量占工业固体废物产生量（包括综合利用往年贮存量）的百分率。计算公式为：

工业固体废物综合利用率 =(工业固体废物综合利用量 / 工业固体废物产生量 + 综合利用往年贮存量) ×100%

噪声等效声级（简称 LEQ）　指在规定的时间内，某一连续稳态声的 A〔计权〕声压，具有与时变的噪声相同的均方 A〔计权〕声压，则这一连续稳态声的声级，就是此时变噪声的等效声级。噪声等效声级（分贝）数值越小越好。

Explanastory Notes on Main Statistical Indicators

Developed Areas refer to the land in administrative areas having been developed concentratedly with municipal public facilities. For core city, developed areas include concentrated areas and decentralized areas, having basic perfect municipal public facilities; for the city with several towns, developed areas are composed of several concentrated areas with municipal public facilities. Therefore, the scope of developed areas refers to actual construction land of a city.

Area of Urban Gardens and Green Areas refers to the total area used for gardens and green by the report period, including public green land, residential zone green land, units green land, protection green land, production green land, roadside green land and suburban scenic spots.

The Rate of Green Coverage of the Developed refers to the ratio of gardens and green areas to the developed zones areas, which is often expressed in percentage. The following formula is used:

The Rate of Green Coverage of the Developed Zones= (gardens and green areas) / (the developed zones areas)×100%

Floor Space of Buildings under Construction refers to total floor space of the horizontal section of outer walls above the plinth of the buildings, including the effective area and the area occupied by the structure.

Floor Space of Residential Buildings refers to the floor space of residential buildings among the total space of buildings under construction or completed.

Waste Water Discharged by Industry refers to the volume of waste water discharged by industrial enterprises through all their outlets, including waste water from production process, directly cooled water, groundwater from mining wells which does not meet discharge standards and sewage from households mixed with waste water produced by industrial activities, but excluding indirectly cooled water discharged (It should be included if the discharge is not separated with waste water).

Ratio of Industrial Waste Water Meeting Discharge Standards refers to percentage of industrial waste water meeting discharge standards over total industrial waste water discharge. It is calculated as:

Ratio of industrial waste water meeting discharge standards = industrial waste water meeting discharge standards / total industrial waste water discharge×100%

Industrial Waste Air Emission refers to discharge into atmosphere of waste air containing pollutants generated from fuel burning and production process in enterprises within a given period of time. It is calculated at standard status (273K, 101325Pa) as:

Industrial waste air emission = emission through fuel burning + emission through production process

Industrial Dust Emission refers to volume of dust emitted by production process of enterprises and suspended in the air for a given period of time, including dust from refractory material of iron and steel works, dust from coke-screening systems and sintering machines of coke plants, dust from lime kilns and dust from cement production in building material enterprises, but excluding soot and dust emitted from power plants.

Industrial Solid Wastes Produced refers to total volume of solid, semi-solid and high concentration liquid residues produced by industrial enterprises from production process in a given period of time, including hazardous wastes, slag, coal ash, gangue, tailings, radioactive residues and other wastes, but excluding stones stripped or dug out in mining (gangue and acid or alkaline stones not included). A stone is acid or alkaline depending on the pH value of the water below 4 or above 10.5 when the stone is in, or soaked by, the water.

Industrial Solid Wastes Utilized refers to volume of solid wastes from which useful materials can be extracted or which can be converted into usable resources, energy or other materials by means of reclamation, processing, recycling and exchange (including utilizing in the year the stocks of industrial solid wastes of the previous year). Examples of such utilizations include fertilizers, building materials and road materials.

Ratio of Industrial Solid Wastes Utilized refers to the percentage of industrial solid wastes utilized over industrial solid wastes produced (including stocks of the previous years). It is calculated as:

Ratio of industrial solid wastes utilized = volume of industrial solid wastes utilized / (industrial solid wastes produced + stock of previous years) ×100%

Level of Equivalent Noise (LEQ) In the specified time interval, it refer to the A sound pressure of a continuous steady state sound, with the same mean square A sound pressure as the time variant noise. This sound level of a continuous steady state sound is the equivalent sound level of the time variant noise. The smaller of the value of noise equivalent sound level (dB), the better.

第10篇
CHAPTER 10

农村经济
Rural Economy

10-1 农村经济主要指标
MAJOR INDICATORS OF RURAL ECONOMY

项　目	Item	2004	2005	2006	2006比2005年增长(%) Increase Rate in 2006 over 2005 (%)
农林牧渔业总产值	**Gross Output Value of Farming, Forestry, Animal**				
(亿元)	**Husbandry and Fishery (100 million yuan)**	**221.35**	**238.34**	**250.28**	**3.6**
农　业	Farming	95.29	97.49	105.45	4.0
林　业	Forestry	1.66	1.89	1.98	4.6
牧　业	Animal Husbandry	92.55	102.71	104.15	2.9
渔　业	Fishery	31.85	36.25	38.70	4.8
农业机械及灌溉	**Agricultural Machinery and Irrigation**				
农机总动力(万千瓦)	Total Power of Agricultural Machinery (10 000 kW)	608.13	611.94	603.39	-1.4
大中型拖拉机(台)	Large and Medium-sized Tractors (set)	9400	10260	10700	4.3
小型拖拉机(万台)	Mini-tractors (10 000 sets)	3.64	3.54	3.51	-0.8
年末实有机电井(眼)	Motor-pumped Well (year-end) (unit)	25855	26648	25990	-2.5
有效灌溉面积(万公顷)	Effective Irrigated Areas (10 000 hectares)	35.34	35.52	34.96	-1.6
节水灌溉面积(万公顷)	Water-saving Irrigated Areas (10 000 hectares)	18.57	19.67	19.77	0.5
农作物总播种面积	**Total Sown Areas of Farm Crops (10 000 hectares)**				
(万公顷)		**50.43**	**49.94**	**51.39**	**2.9**
# 粮　食	Grain	26.35	28.77	29.52	2.6
蔬　菜	Vegetables	13.19	12.97	12.04	-7.2
总产量(万吨)	**Yield of Farm Crops (10 000 tons)**				
# 粮　食	Grain	125.27	137.50	143.52	4.4
蔬　菜	Vegetables	585.43	542.74	471.45	-13.1
水果产量(万吨)	**Yield of Fruits (10 000 tons)**	**69.05**	**68.24**	**66.96**	**-1.9**
# 果用瓜	Melon-Fruits	39.47	40.45	36.96	-8.6
年末实有林地面积	**Forest Area (year-end) (10 000 hectares)**				
(万公顷)		**18.75**	**19.05**	**19.35**	**1.6**
# 当年造林面积	Afforested Area in Current Year	0.53	0.36	0.30	-16.7

注：农林牧渔业总产值按当年价格计算，增长速度按可比价格计算（下同）。
Note: Gross output value of farming, forestry, animal husbandry and fishery are calculated at current prices, increase rate based on comparable prices (same as following next).

10-1 续表 Continued

项　目	Item	2004	2005	2006	2006比2005年增长(%) Increase Rate in 2006 over 2005 (%)
畜牧业生产	**Production of Animal Husbandry**				
生猪年末存栏(万头)	Pigs in Hand (year-end) (10 000 heads)	252.42	255.45	262.45	2.7
生猪当年出栏(万头)	Number of Slaughtered Pigs (10 000 heads)	446.61	481.45	503.16	4.5
牛年末存栏(万头)	Cattle in Hand (year-end) (10 000 heads)	43.42	44.40	39.25	-11.6
#乳　牛	Cows	16.14	17.61	18.24	3.6
牛当年出栏(万头)	Number of Slaughtered Cattle (10 000 heads)	33.84	37.83	37.27	-1.5
羊年末存栏(万只)	Sheep & Goats in Hand (year-end) (10 000 heads)	93.61	84.69	73.30	-13.4
羊当年出栏(万只)	Number of Slaughtered Sheep and Goats (10 000 heads)	143.97	140.11	128.31	-8.4
家禽年末存栏(万只)	Poultry in Hand (year-end) (10 000heads)	3218.25	2894.32	2945.73	1.8
#产蛋鸡	Hens	1620.43	1701.35	1490.04	-12.4
家禽当年出栏(万只)	Number of Slaughtered Poultry (10 000 heads)	8500.13	9205.64	9412.25	2.2
畜禽产品产量(万吨)	**Output of Animal and Poultry (10 000 tons)**				
肉类总产量	Output of Meat	53.73	57.78	59.53	3.0
#猪　肉	Pork	33.05	35.63	37.20	4.4
牛羊肉	Beef and Mutton	8.73	9.28	8.95	-3.6
禽　肉	Poultry	11.53	12.49	12.82	2.6
禽蛋产量	Output of Poultry Eggs	24.38	23.47	23.08	-1.7
奶类产量	Output of Milk	54.24	63.41	68.28	7.7
渔业生产	**Production of Fishery**				
水产养殖面积(万公顷)	Cultured Areas of Aquatic Products (10 000 hectares)	4.04	4.17	4.34	4.1
#淡　水	Fresh Water	3.50	3.69	3.79	2.7
水产品产量(万吨)	Output of Aquatic Products (10 000 tons)	31.00	33.81	35.49	5.0
#淡　水	Fresh Water	26.14	28.92	30.18	4.4

10-2 农业生产条件情况(1990-2006年) CONDITIONS OF AGRICULTURAL PRODUCTION, 1990-2006

年份 Year	年末实有常用耕地面积(万公顷) Cultivated Area (year-end) (10 000 hectares)	年末实有林地面积(万公顷) Forest Area (year-end) (10 000 hectares)	#当年造林面积 Afforested Area in Current Year	水产养殖面积(万公顷) Cultured Area of Aquatic Products (10 000 hectares)	有效灌溉面积(万公顷) Effective Irrigated Area (10 000 hectares)
1990	43.15	4.47	0.73	2.68	32.69
1991	43.16	6.40	0.55	2.65	32.88
1992	42.95	7.12	0.72	2.70	32.75
1993	42.87	7.37	0.77	2.73	32.85
1994	42.74	8.32	0.78	2.90	32.96
1995	42.61	8.70	0.48	3.12	33.24
1996	42.58	9.26	0.62	3.41	33.26
1997	42.52	9.85	0.90	3.81	33.28
1998	42.49	11.14	0.91	3.71	33.29
1999	42.46	12.74	0.94	3.76	34.39
2000	42.43	13.69	0.93	3.64	35.32
2001	42.39	14.19	0.50	3.67	35.43
2002	42.28	17.53	0.85	3.82	35.44
2003	41.85	18.21	0.69	3.83	35.41
2004	41.53	18.75	0.53	4.04	35.34
2005	41.45	19.05	0.36	4.17	35.52
2006		19.35	0.30	4.34	34.96

年份 Year	农用机械总动力(万千瓦) Total Power of Agricultural Machinery (10 000 kW)	机耕面积(万公顷) Cultivated Area Using Machinery (10 000 hectares)	机播面积(万公顷) Sown Area Using Machinery (10 000 hectares)	化肥施用量(折纯)(万吨) Consumption of Chemical Fertilizers (Pureness) (10 000 tons)	农村用电量(万千瓦小时) Rural Electricity Consumption (10 000 kWh)
1990	311.27	39.90	13.21	40.99	165331
1991	303.76	40.17	14.53	42.53	180834
1992	308.63	40.65	17.13	41.19	218273
1993	302.22	38.47	15.00	40.13	231072
1994	335.72	39.93	17.22	41.06	250611
1995	364.08	38.08	19.50	45.29	325482
1996	384.22	39.85	22.28	48.82	358184
1997	417.37	39.66	25.00	49.15	330249
1998	440.57	40.13	24.99	51.48	337565
1999	481.54	39.62	24.93	47.24	343667
2000	593.40	39.62	25.73	16.64	354946
2001	603.32	37.26	24.11	17.31	377823
2002	612.72	38.17	23.95	17.59	402785
2003	601.66	37.05	23.57	17.80	423157
2004	608.13	37.35	27.66	22.85	484221
2005	611.94	37.62	28.94	23.29	522492
2006	603.39	37.74	29.91		

注：化肥施用量2000年以前为实物量。

Note: Consumption of chemical fertilizers refered to full-scale quantity before 2000.

10-3 农林牧渔业总产值和增长速度(1990-2006年)
GROSS OUTPUT VALUE AND INCREASE RATE OF FARMING, FORESTRY, ANIMAL HUSBANDRY AND FISHERY, 1990-2006

年 份 Year	合 计 Total	农 业 Farming	林 业 Forestry	牧 业 Animal Husbandry	渔 业 Fishery
总产值(亿元) Gross Output Value (100 million yuan)					
1990	51.72	34.71	0.45	11.54	5.02
1991	54.55	36.68	0.34	12.88	4.65
1992	58.50	39.24	0.45	13.44	5.37
1993	66.32	44.28	0.44	15.82	5.78
1994	88.74	57.71	0.60	22.91	7.52
1995	125.44	85.25	0.85	28.76	10.58
1996	133.53	90.17	0.96	30.27	12.13
1997	140.47	89.77	1.00	33.99	15.71
1998	156.16	98.83	1.19	38.09	18.05
1999	150.11	91.58	1.42	38.95	18.16
2000	156.30	83.42	1.37	51.75	19.76
2001	169.51	86.73	1.46	60.76	20.56
2002	181.07	86.06	1.52	69.21	24.28
2003	193.44	88.20	1.61	77.22	26.41
2004	221.35	95.29	1.66	92.55	31.85
2005	238.34	97.49	1.89	102.71	36.25
2006	250.28	105.45	1.98	104.15	38.70
比上年增长(%) Increase Rate over Preceding Year (%)					
1990	6.7	6.6	17.4	7.4	5.0
1991	6.7	7.0	-16.3	10.2	-0.2
1992	4.1	4.5	21.5	3.0	3.4
1993	4.3	5.6	-12.3	7.8	-9.6
1994	7.3	4.3	4.1	14.3	8.4
1995	13.0	13.5	-1.0	5.1	33.4
1996	7.5	8.5	10.3	3.5	10.6
1997	7.6	5.1	2.6	10.5	15.7
1998	11.8	8.2	39.7	15.4	21.2
1999	0.4	-6.3	15.1	13.7	3.1
2000	4.2	-4.4	-5.7	19.6	6.1
2001	8.0	4.1	7.2	15.9	3.0
2002	6.0	-8.9	13.7	14.9	36.2
2003	6.6	0.0	3.8	13.6	6.7
2004	5.2	3.1	2.6	5.8	10.5
2005	4.8	0.2	13.6	7.5	10.6
2006	3.6	4.0	4.6	2.9	4.8

10-4 农林牧渔业总产值结构(1990-2006年)
STRUCTURE OF GROSS OUTPUT VALUE OF FARMING, FORESTRY, ANIMAL HUSBANDRY AND FISHERY, 1990-2005

单位: % (%)

年 份 Year	合 计 Total	农 业 Farming	林 业 Forestry	牧 业 Animal Husbandry	渔 业 Fishery
1990	100	67.1	0.9	22.3	9.7
1991	100	67.2	0.6	23.6	8.6
1992	100	67.1	0.8	23.0	9.1
1993	100	66.8	0.7	23.9	8.6
1994	100	65.0	0.7	25.8	8.5
1995	100	68.0	0.7	22.9	8.4
1996	100	67.5	0.7	22.7	9.1
1997	100	63.9	0.7	24.2	11.2
1998	100	63.3	0.8	24.4	11.5
1999	100	61.0	0.9	25.9	12.2
2000	100	53.4	0.9	33.1	12.6
2001	100	51.2	0.9	35.8	12.1
2002	100	47.5	0.8	38.3	13.4
2003	100	45.6	0.8	39.9	13.7
2004	100	43.1	0.7	41.8	14.4
2005	100	40.9	0.8	43.1	15.2
2006	100	42.1	0.8	41.6	15.5

10-5 农作物播种面积(1990-2006年)
SOWN AREAS OF FARM CROPS, 1990-2006

单位: 万公顷 (10 000 hectares)

年 份 Year	合 计 Total	粮 食 Grain	棉 花 Cotton	油 料 Oil-bearing Crops	蔬 菜 Vegetables	其他农作物 Others
1990	54.95	45.23	1.04	2.21	5.08	1.39
1991	55.30	45.19	1.74	1.93	5.24	1.20
1992	54.56	44.03	1.67	1.85	5.71	1.30
1993	54.61	44.64	0.57	1.83	6.12	1.45
1994	53.00	41.74	1.33	1.72	7.02	1.19
1995	54.91	43.78	1.00	1.69	7.50	0.94
1996	56.44	45.57	0.38	1.37	8.08	1.04
1997	55.73	43.99	0.28	1.61	8.82	1.03
1998	56.32	44.45	0.35	1.69	8.64	1.19
1999	56.29	43.10	0.60	1.62	9.86	1.11
2000	53.31	34.59	1.51	2.63	12.83	1.75
2001	54.45	32.85	4.50	2.05	12.95	2.10
2002	52.28	31.13	4.48	1.89	12.84	1.94
2003	50.15	25.81	7.06	1.58	13.46	2.24
2004	50.43	26.35	8.69	0.61	13.19	1.59
2005	49.94	28.77	6.12	0.51	12.97	1.57
2006	51.39	29.52	7.89	0.46	12.04	1.48

10-6 主要农产品产量情况（1990-2006年）
YIELD OF MAJOR FARM CROPS, 1990-2006

单位：万吨 (10 000 tons)

年 份 Year	粮 食 Grain	#小 麦 Wheat	#玉 米 Corn	棉 花 Cotton	油 料 Oil-bearing Crops	蔬 菜 Vegetables
1990	188.75	64.74	74.00	1.53	4.68	268.14
1991	198.50	62.00	79.90	2.55	4.50	282.56
1992	198.74	62.00	76.04	1.63	3.96	310.41
1993	199.82	59.07	80.80	0.76	4.45	354.34
1994	190.33	50.76	77.65	0.93	4.03	407.86
1995	207.46	65.40	80.50	1.12	4.01	434.17
1996	207.00	67.35	75.41	0.51	3.13	452.71
1997	206.16	77.41	65.45	0.39	3.01	486.23
1998	210.12	76.06	75.51	0.63	3.76	505.35
1999	174.85	71.60	56.30	0.57	2.34	486.07
2000	124.05	59.91	40.95	1.75	3.31	530.60
2001	143.33	45.09	75.19	6.36	3.90	564.50
2002	137.82	44.11	71.05	6.24	3.40	584.31
2003	119.29	35.91	64.81	9.47	3.08	602.78
2004	125.27	37.81	70.71	12.03	1.55	585.43
2005	137.50	47.42	73.16	8.36	1.29	542.74
2006	143.52	52.04	75.75	10.87	1.20	471.45

年 份 Year	肉 类 Meats	#猪 肉 Pork	#牛羊肉 Beef and Mutton	禽 蛋 Poultry Eggs	奶 类 Milk	水产品 Aquatic Products
1990	9.13	7.07	0.84	13.01	7.40	10.83
1991	9.89	7.19	1.05	15.01	8.41	10.81
1992	11.31	7.43	1.24	14.95	9.10	11.10
1993	11.47	7.26	1.61	15.08	9.14	11.39
1994	13.69	8.32	2.37	17.48	9.43	12.83
1995	15.86	9.59	3.09	16.94	10.47	15.35
1996	16.94	10.50	3.30	16.65	10.69	16.99
1997	18.70	11.77	3.44	17.71	12.13	18.98
1998	21.74	13.88	3.74	22.68	11.69	21.38
1999	23.53	14.59	4.24	23.56	12.94	23.03
2000	29.49	17.96	4.76	25.60	16.52	24.22
2001	36.40	21.92	5.97	26.00	24.06	26.46
2002	44.88	26.09	7.39	24.47	33.59	28.56
2003	52.41	30.56	8.53	24.25	43.23	29.83
2004	53.73	33.05	8.73	24.38	54.24	31.00
2005	57.78	35.63	9.28	23.47	63.41	33.81
2006	59.53	37.20	8.95	23.08	68.28	35.49

10-7 农村居民家庭户均生产性固定资产原值(2003-2006年)
ORIGINAL VALUE OF PRODUCTIVE FIXED ASSETS PER RURAL HOUSEHOLD, 2003-2006

单位：元 (yuan)

项目	Item	2003	2004	2005	2006
年末户均生产性固定资产原值	**Original Value of Productive Fixed Assets (year-end)**	**7051**	**8311**	**10150**	**10837**
1.农、林、牧、渔业	Farming, Forestry, Animal Husbandry and Fishery	4232	4781	5006	5110
#役畜、产品畜	Draught Animals and Commodity Animals	729	469	515	522
大中型铁木农具	Large and Medium-sized Wood & Iron Farm Tools	263	363	162	172
农林牧渔业机械	Machinery for Farming, Forestry, Animal Husbandry and Fishery	1300	1480	1910	1809
2.制造业	Manufacturing	230	286	1151	1478
3.批发和零售业	Wholesale and Retail Trade	289	247	418	724
4.住宿和餐饮业	Accommodation and Catering Services	201	348	33	33
5.文化、体育和娱乐业	Culture, Sports and Recreational Services	30	25		
6.其　他	Others	2069	2624	3512	3492

注：本表数据为农村住户抽样调查数。
Note: The data of this table are collected from sample survey on rural households.

10-8 农村居民家庭每百户生产性固定资产拥有量(2003-2006年)
NUMBER OF PRODUCTIVE FIXED ASSETS PER 100 RURAL HOUSEHOLDS, 2003-2006

项目	Item	2003	2004	2005	2006
汽　车(辆)	Motor Vehicles (set)	5.83	5.50	6.67	6.50
大中型拖拉机(台)	Large and Medium-sized Tractors (set)	1.83	2.50	1.67	1.67
小型和手扶拖拉机(台)	Mini-tractors (set)	22.33	21.67	18.00	17.83
机动脱粒机(台)	Motorized Threshing Machines (set)	2.69	1.67	0.67	1.33
胶轮大车(辆)	Carts with Rubber Tires (set)	7.17	3.83	4.67	5.00
水　泵(台)	Pumps (set)	18.67	19.25	19.00	19.00
役　畜(头)	Draught Animals (head)	17.08	10.50	5.50	5.83
产品畜(头)	Commodity Animals (head)	35.17	22.50	25.00	27.00

注：本表数据为农村住户抽样调查数。
Note: The data of this table are collected from sample survey on rural households.

10-9 各区县农林牧渔业总产值和增加值(2006年)
GROSS OUTPUT VALUE AND VALUE-ADDED OF FARMING, FORESTRY, ANIMAL HUSBANDRY AND FISHERY BY DISTRICT AND COUNTY, 2006

单位：万元 (10 000 yuan)

地　区	Region	合计 Total	农业 Farming	林业 Forestry	牧业 Animal Husbandry	渔业 Fishery
总产值	**Gross Output Value**					
塘沽区	Tanggu District	40144	8025	322	8678	23119
汉沽区	Han'gu District	86304	24358	29	14481	47436
大港区	Dagang District	43336	14227	119	20653	8337
东丽区	Dongli District	92202	43939	1275	25980	21008
西青区	Xiqing District	136063	64145	480	32045	39393
津南区	Jinnan District	61887	22252	253	20835	18547
北辰区	Beichen District	137048	52169	275	71082	13522
武清区	Wuqing District	502835	274835	4109	186284	37607
宝坻区	Baodi District	329224	167013	905	134901	26405
宁河县	Ninghe County	288320	126997	999	133734	26590
静海县	Jinghai County	265880	126366	3051	117448	19015
蓟　县	Jixian County	463516	178131	4286	260226	20873
增加值	**Value-added**					
塘沽区	Tanggu District	14388	2836	142	2800	8610
汉沽区	Han'gu District	35165	13275	18	3372	18500
大港区	Dagang District	17220	4203	57	9233	3727
东丽区	Dongli District	40940	20476	561	9924	9979
西青区	Xiqing District	65658	31878	289	14613	18878
津南区	Jinnan District	29944	10412	103	9772	9657
北辰区	Beichen District	66222	31036	137	29290	5759
武清区	Wuqing District	216717	136347	2466	63261	14643
宝坻区	Baodi District	137839	65253	508	61515	10563
宁河县	Ninghe County	140400	62102	476	64641	13181
静海县	Jinghai County	127153	69380	1800	49606	6367
蓟　县	Jixian County	199530	92895	2805	94333	9497

10-10 各区县主要农作物播种面积（2006年）
SOWN AREAS OF MAJOR FARM CROPS BY DISTRICT AND COUNTY, 2006

单位：公顷 (hectare)

地　区	Region	粮食作物 Grain Crops	#小　麦 Wheat	#稻　谷 Rice	#玉　米 Corn
塘沽区	Tanggu District	833	16	14	508
汉沽区	Han'gu District	505		126	278
大港区	Dagang District	12164	2688		4949
东丽区	Dongli District	1910		180	1400
西青区	Xiqing District	8086	2412	1333	3467
津南区	Jinnan District	3807		267	2739
北辰区	Beichen District	10258	1053	51	7634
武清区	Wuqing District	94093	38873	85	53949
宝坻区	Baodi District	72917	29832	6364	33547
宁河县	Ninghe County	12094	329	3438	6893
静海县	Jinghai County	51746	8654		33395
蓟　县	Jixian County	71136	28246	718	40972

地　区	Region	油料作物 Oil-bearing Crops	#花　生 Peanuts	棉　花 Cotton	蔬　菜 Vegetables
塘沽区	Tanggu District			1907	1359
汉沽区	Han'gu District			804	381
大港区	Dagang District	104	10	1019	813
东丽区	Dongli District			5524	4711
西青区	Xiqing District	173	18	3102	9194
津南区	Jinnan District			4468	3467
北辰区	Beichen District	517	238	3827	6145
武清区	Wuqing District	1241	527	9896	33071
宝坻区	Baodi District	363	176	10833	15646
宁河县	Ninghe County	254	13	20116	9659
静海县	Jinghai County	967	56	16652	5764
蓟　县	Jixian County	916	916	747	12780

10-11 各区县主要农作物产量（2006年）
YIELD OF MAJOR FARM CROPS BY DISTRICT AND COUNTY, 2006

地　区	Region	粮食作物 Grain Crops	#小　麦 Wheat	#稻　谷 Rice	#玉　米 Corn
产　量(吨)	Total Yield (ton)				
塘沽区	Tanggu District	3699	68	74	2705
汉沽区	Han'gu District	3174		953	1778
大港区	Dagang District	41489	3909		26889
东丽区	Dongli District	9676		1284	7301
西青区	Xiqing District	43391	11242	8582	21211
津南区	Jinnan District	19688		1952	14893
北辰区	Beichen District	52388	4903	352	43063
武清区	Wuqing District	609864	226141	758	379193
宝坻区	Baodi District	434937	156036	51434	216197
宁河县	Ninghe County	88914	1706	29201	53531
静海县	Jinghai County	266319	32808		210217
蓟　县	Jixian County	455773	166087	5211	279936
单　产(公斤/公顷)	Unit Yield (kg/hectare)				
塘沽区	Tanggu District	4441	4250	5286	5325
汉沽区	Han'gu District	6285		7563	6396
大港区	Dagang District	3411	1454		5433
东丽区	Dongli District	5066		7133	5215
西青区	Xiqing District	5366	4661	6438	6118
津南区	Jinnan District	5172		7311	5437
北辰区	Beichen District	5107	4656	6902	5641
武清区	Wuqing District	6482	5817	8918	7029
宝坻区	Baodi District	5965	5230	8082	6445
宁河县	Ninghe County	7352	5185	8494	7766
静海县	Jinghai County	5147	3791		6295
蓟　县	Jixian County	6407	5880	7258	6832

10-11 续表 Continued

地　区	Region	油料作物 Oil-bearing Crops	#花　生 Peanuts	棉　花 Cotton	蔬　菜 Vegetables
产　量(吨)	Total Yield (ton)				
塘沽区	Tanggu District			1207	48134
汉沽区	Han'gu District			850	33437
大港区	Dagang District	159	13	764	30230
东丽区	Dongli District			5974	216612
西青区	Xiqing District	389	54	3258	371220
津南区	Jinnan District			4424	122730
北辰区	Beichen District	1170	683	3554	304956
武清区	Wuqing District	3395	1818	11616	1423739
宝坻区	Baodi District	784	488	24347	566296
宁河县	Ninghe County	584	40	23358	377396
静海县	Jinghai County	2042	186	21168	330576
蓟　县	Jixian County	3416	3416	1168	888666
单　产(公斤/公顷)	Unit Yield (kg/hectare)				
塘沽区	Tanggu District			633	35419
汉沽区	Han'gu District			1057	87761
大港区	Dagang District	1529	1300	750	37183
东丽区	Dongli District			1081	45980
西青区	Xiqing District	2249	3000	1050	40376
津南区	Jinnan District			990	35399
北辰区	Beichen District	2263	2870	929	49627
武清区	Wuqing District	2736	3450	1174	43051
宝坻区	Baodi District	2160	2773	2247	36194
宁河县	Ninghe County	2299	3077	1161	39072
静海县	Jinghai County	2112	3321	1271	57352
蓟　县	Jixian County	3729	3729	1564	69536

10-12 各区县畜牧业生产情况（2006年）
PRODUCTION OF ANIMAL HUSBANDRY BY DISTRICT AND COUNTY, 2006

地　区	Region	猪出栏（万头）Slaughtered Pigs (10 000 heads)	牛出栏（万头）Slaughtered Cattle (10 000 heads)	羊出栏（万只）Slaughtered Sheep and Goats (10 000 heads)	家禽出栏（万只）Slaughtered Poultry (10 000 heads)	# 鸡 Cocks and Hens	产蛋鸡存栏（万只）Hens in Hand (10 000 heads)	乳牛存栏（头）Cows in Hand (head)
塘沽区	Tanggu District	8.60	0.12	0.89	18.78	18.45	2.46	217
汉沽区	Han'gu District	9.97	0.08	0.44	113.00	113.00	5.47	578
大港区	Dagang District	6.74	0.27	4.89	263.00	263.00	33.10	2000
东丽区	Dongli District	16.74	0.57	2.99	347.43	346.93	11.88	1361
西青区	Xiqing District	16.65	0.06	1.03	782.74	647.78	33.71	4465
津南区	Jinnan District	9.83	0.17	1.48	1265.77	1265.77	33.42	430
北辰区	Beichen District	22.51	0.90	11.70	605.09	590.09	116.11	28485
武清区	Wuqing District	69.13	4.43	32.56	1903.03	1837.76	215.74	61076
宝坻区	Baodi District	92.73	7.63	14.67	428.58	360.89	215.19	2635
宁河县	Ninghe County	105.54	0.97	4.61	852.00	848.00	112.00	32000
静海县	Jinghai County	48.80	1.75	23.40	1873.78	1867.95	60.47	28430
蓟　县	Jixian County	158.60	18.13	23.62	1209.93	840.40	561.72	2955

地　区	Region	肉类总产量（吨）Output of Meat (ton)	# 猪　肉 Pork	# 牛羊肉 Beef & Mutton	# 禽　肉 Meat of Poultry	禽蛋产量（吨）Output of Poultry Eggs (ton)	# 鸡　蛋 Eggs	牛奶产量（吨）Output of Milk (ton)
塘沽区	Tanggu District	7011	6125	598	287	727	516	619
汉沽区	Han'gu District	10168	7481	101	2246	1083	1083	2679
大港区	Dagang District	10293	5730	1205	3156	3110	3110	5538
东丽区	Dongli District	21839	12509	2297	6948	1645	1645	5099
西青区	Xiqing District	25692	12656	282	12729	6652	4231	12989
津南区	Jinnan District	17430	7371	680	9379	3485	3403	3497
北辰区	Beichen District	29887	15757	5193	8929	18609	18010	118342
武清区	Wuqing District	91071	48388	17967	24604	42868	33539	245988
宝坻区	Baodi District	103361	76666	16674	14759	36902	36652	12396
宁河县	Ninghe County	93485	73878	2716	16865	19000	17890	90000
静海县	Jinghai County	81287	37573	10670	32864	15678	14395	112388
蓟　县	Jixian County	164733	115528	27463	21427	76575	74552	16213

10-13 林业生产、果园面积及产量
FORESTRY PRODUCTION, ORCHARD AREAS AND OUTPUT

项　目	Item	2004	2005	2006
年末实有林地面积(万公顷)	**Forestry Areas (year-end) (10 000 hectares)**	**18.75**	**19.05**	**19.35**
#当年造林面积	Afforested Areas in Current Year	0.53	0.36	0.30
封山育林面积（万公顷）	**Afforested Areas on Sealed Moutain (10 000 hectares)**	**2.21**	**2.20**	**2.60**
育苗面积	Areas Used for Cultivating Sapling	0.89	0.52	0.90
年末实有果园面积(万公顷)	**Areas of Orchards (year-end) (10 000 hectares)**	**3.64**	**3.71**	**3.64**
干果产量(吨)	**Output of Dry Fruits (ton)**	**697**	**754**	**827**
#核　桃	Walnuts	412	442	478
栗　子	Chestnuts	285	312	349
园林水果产量(吨)	**Output of Fruits in Orchards (ton)**	**295819**	**277877**	**300038**
#苹　果	Apples	64721	66039	64076
梨	Pears	25182	22553	25719
桃	Peaches	49006	48997	52399
鲜　枣	Fresh Jujubes	13560	24691	30574
葡　萄	Grapes	132084	93229	104103
柿　子	Persimmons	6301	11402	12456

10-14 各区县渔业生产情况（2006年）
FISHERY PRODUCTION BY DISTRICT AND COUNTY, 2006

地　区	Region	水产品总产量(吨) Total Aquatic Products (ton)	海水产品 Seawater Aquatic Products	淡水产品 Freshwater Aquatic Products	水产养殖面积(公顷) Cultured Areas of Aquatic Products (hectare)	海水养殖 Seawater Cultured	淡水养殖 Freshwater Cultured
塘沽区	Tanggu District	21402	16198	5204	4081	1747	2334
汉沽区	Han'gu District	25863	19538	6325	1434	967	467
大港区	Dagang District	7652	2270	5382	5470	2568	2902
东丽区	Dongli District	21017		21017	2733		2733
西青区	Xiqing District	50789		50789	5169		5169
津南区	Jinnan District	20406		20406	3932		3932
北辰区	Beichen District	13056		13056	2117		2117
武清区	Wuqing District	55522		55522	6334		6334
宝坻区	Baodi District	35788		35788	3521		3521
宁河县	Ninghe County	18382	420	17962	3371	133	3238
静海县	Jinghai County	27929		27929	2661		2661
蓟　县	Jixian County	27876		27876	1800		1800

10-15 农垦集团总公司主要指标（2003-2006年）
MAJOR INDICATORS OF STATE FARMS OF AGRIBUSINESS GROUP CORPORATION, 2003-2006

项　目	Item	2003	2004	2005	2006
直属企事业单位(个)	Number of Units (unit)	40	40	40	41
# 农场个数	Farms	15	15	14	15
工业企业个数	Industrial Enterprises	12	14	12	20
商业企业个数	Commercial Enterprises	2	2	2	2
土地面积(公顷)	Land Areas (hectare)	9025	9269	9077	7874
# 耕地面积	Cultivated Areas	3051	3168	3039	2920
工农业总产值(万元)	Gross Output Value of Agriculture and Industry (10 000 yuan)	173676	183295	236404	242830
# 农业总产值	Gross Agricultural Output Value	27154	28353	32638	33078
增加值 (万元)	Value-added (10 000 yuan)	66910	76605	73001	73624
第一产业	Primary Industry	7380	5859	5825	6693
第二产业	Secondary Industry	50767	59727	56103	56420
第三产业	Tertiary Industry	8763	11019	11073	10511
种植业生产情况	Production of Planting				
农作物播种面积(公顷)	Sown Areas of Farm Crops (hectare)	2513	2911	2997	3021
# 粮　食	Grain	1077	1323	1414	1973
商品蔬菜	Vegetables for Sale	72	6	56	125
农作物总产量(吨)	Total Yield of Farm Crops (ton)				
#粮　食	Grain	5782	8237	7942	17996
商品蔬菜	Vegetables for Sale	3620	255	2712	6888
水果生产情况	Production of Fruits				
果园面积(公顷)	Areas of Orchards (hectare)	184	213	181	178
水果总产量(吨)	Total Yield of Fruits (ton)	1268	1886	853	715
畜牧水产生产情况	Production of Animal Husbandry and Fishery				
奶牛年末存栏(头)	Cows in Hand (year-end) (head)	19979	21157	21469	21865
# 成母牛	Female Cows	11966	12499	11040	12677
牛奶总产量(吨)	Output of Milk (ton)	79455	81741	79585	86787

10-15 续表 Continued

项　　目	Item	2003	2004	2005	2006
鸡年末存栏(万只)	Cocks and Hens in Hand (year-end) (10 000 heads)	22.69	22.74	22.59	27.68
#产蛋鸡	Hens	22.29	22.74	22.59	27.68
鸡蛋总产量(吨)	Total Output of Eggs (ton)	4516	4842	3905	1505
肉类总产量(吨)	Total Output of Meat (ton)	833	673	1054	834
养殖水面(公顷)	Cultured Water Areas (hectare)	516	422	646	687
水产品产量(吨)	Total Aquatic Products (ton)	4077	3754	6877	7511
农业机械总动力(万千瓦)	Total Power of Agricultural Machinery (10 000 kW)	1.05	1.16	1.09	1.06
#大中型拖拉机(台)	Large and Medium-sized Tractors (set)	38	28	31	28
小型拖拉机(台)	Mini-tractors (set)	8	7	4	6
汽　车(辆)	Number of Motor Vehicles (set)	296	276	321	368
#载重汽车(辆)	Trucks (set)	62	57	62	78
用电量(万千瓦小时)	Electricity Consumption (10 000 kWh)	4328	7123	5295	7379
化肥施用量(折纯)(吨)	Consumption of Chemical Fertilizers (pureness) (ton)	758	648	686	884
主要工业产品产量	Output of Major Industrial Products				
葡萄酒(吨)	Wine (ton)	27150	36650	38151	41137
淀　粉(吨)	Starch (ton)	22			
奶　粉(吨)	Milk Powder (ton)	2200	3007	2028	3491
消毒牛奶(吨)	Sterilized Milk (ton)	65157	70011	66125	92123
饲料添加剂(吨)	Added Preparation for Forage (ton)	151	307	288	300
固定资产投资总额(万元)	Total Investment in Fixed Assets (10 000 yuan)	16744	27860	10000	13403
新增固定资产	Newly Increased Fixed Assets	7697	20705	10000	13403
外贸出口总值(万元)	Total Value of Exports (10 000 yuan)	14010	10332	6897	6023
利润总额(万元)	Total Profits (10 000 yuan)	7808	22757	20038	12884
年末职工人数(人)	Number of Staff and Workers (year-end) (person)	7958	7122	6489	6392
工资总额(万元)	Total Wages (10 000 yuan)	10392	11838	12934	15239
职工年平均工资(元)	Annual Average Wage (yuan)	11829	15954	18739	23202
年末固定资产原值(万元)	Original Value of Fixed Assets (year-end) (10 000 yuan)	111067	121421	148534	172586
年末固定资产净值(万元)	Net Value of Fixed Assets (year-end) (10 000 yuan)	76113	84774	107894	127772

10-16 大型水库基本情况（2006年）
LARGE RESERVOIRS OF TIANJIN, 2006

项　目	Item	于桥水库 Yuqiao Reservoir	北大港水库 Beidagang Reservoir	团泊洼水库 Tuanbowa Reservoir
建设地点	Construction Site	蓟　县 Jixian	大港区 Dagang	静海县 Jinghai
所属河系	Location River	蓟运河 Jiyun River	大清河 Daqing River	独流减河 Duliujian River
总库容(万立方米)	Total Capacity of Reservoir (10 000 cu. m)	155900	50000	18000
设计灌溉面积(万公顷)	Designed Irrigated Areas (10 000 hectares)	4.20	1.38	3.00
有效灌溉面积(万公顷)	Effective Irrigated Areas (10 000 hectares)	3.00	0.66	2.60

10-17 中型水库基本情况（2006年）
MEDIUM RESERVOIRS OF TIANJIN, 2006

水库名称 Name of Reservoir	座落地点 Site	所在河系 Location River	总库容(万立方米) Total Capacity of Reservoir (10 000 cu. m)	灌溉面积(万公顷) Irrigated Areas (10 000 hectares) 设计 Designed Areas	有效 Effective Areas	年设计灌溉用水(万立方米) Annual Irrigated Water (10 000 cu. m)
七里海水库 Qilihai Reservoir	宁河县 Ninghe	潮白新河 Chaobaixin River	2400	1.00	0.40	1800
新地河水库 Xindihe Reservoir	东丽区 Dongli	金钟河 Jinzhong River	2200	0.27	0.27	1000
鸭淀水库 Yadian Reservoir	西青区 Xiqing	津港运河 Jingang Canal	3150	0.47	0.47	1997
黄港一库 HuanggangⅠ Reservoir	塘沽区 Tanggu	黑猪河 Heizhu River	1295	0.09	0.06	800
黄港二库 HuanggangⅡ Reservoir	塘沽区 Tanggu	黑猪河 Heizhu River	4615	0.21	0.18	400
北塘水库 Beitang Reservoir	塘沽区 Tanggu	永定新河 Yongdingxin River	1580			
营城水库 Yingcheng Reservoir	汉沽区 Han'gu	蓟运河 Jixian Canal	3000	0.04	0.04	400
钱圈水库 Qianquan Reservoir	大港区 Dagang	马厂减河 Machangjian River	2650	0.20	0.10	
沙井子水库 Shajingzi Reservoir	大港区 Dagang	青县、静海县、黄骅县 Qingxian, Jinghai & Huanghua County	2000	0.07	0.07	300
上马台水库 Shangmatai Reservoir	武清区 Wuqing	北运河 North Canal	2680	0.86	0.86	1900
津南水库 Jinnan Reservoir	津南区 Jinnan	海　河 Haihe River	2966	0.15	0.15	600
尔王庄水库 Erwangzhuang Reservoir	宝坻区 Baodi	潮白新河 Chaobaixin River	4530			

主要统计指标解释

农林牧渔业总产值　指以货币表现的农林牧渔业全部产品总量。它用价值量形式综合说明了一定时期（通常指一年）农林牧渔业生产的总成果和总规模，是观察农林牧渔业生产水平和发展速度；研究农林牧渔业内部比例关系和农林牧渔业在国民经济中的产业布局的一个重要指标，同时，也是计算农林牧渔业劳动生产率和农林牧渔业增加值的基础资料。

农林牧渔业增加值　指各种经济类型的农业生产单位和农户从事农业生产经营活动所提供的社会最终产品的货币表现。其计算方法有两种，一是生产法：农牧渔业增加值=农林牧渔业总产值-农林牧渔业中间消耗；二是分配法：农林牧渔业增加值=固定资产折旧+劳动者报酬+生产税净额（生产税-生产补贴）+营业盈余。

农业机械总动力　指主要用于农、林、牧、渔业的各种动力机械的动力总和。包括耕作机械、收获机械、农产品加工机械、运输机械、植保机械、牧业机械、林业机械、渔业机械和其它农业机械的动力。

有效灌溉面积　指灌溉工程或设备已基本配套，有一定水源，土地比较平整，在一般年景可以进行正常灌溉的耕地面积。在一般情况下，有效灌溉面积应等于灌溉工程或设备已经配套，能够进行灌溉的水田和水浇地面积之和。

造林面积　指报告期内在荒地、荒山、沙丘等一切可造林的土地上，采用人工播种、植苗、飞机播种等方法种植成片的乔木林和灌木林，经过检查验收符合技术规程要求，并按《中华人民共和国森林法实施细则》规定，成活率达 85% 以上的造林面积。包括四旁植树如一侧在四行以上，连续面积 0.066 公顷以上的面积，造林面积不包括补植面积和治沙及沿河种草面积。

当年出栏头数　指农林牧渔企业生产单位饲养的，供屠宰并已出栏的全部牲畜头数。包括交售给国家，集市上出售的部分。

肉类总产量　指当年出栏并已屠宰的猪、牛、羊、马、骡、驴、家禽、兔等肉产量。即屠宰后除去头、蹄、下水后带骨肉的重量，也叫胴体重。

水产品产量　指本年度内捕捞的水产品（包括人工养殖并捕捞的水产品和捕捞天然生长的水产品）产量。不论自食或出售的，都应计算在内。用作继续扩大再生产的水产品（如鱼苗、鱼种、鱼饵及转塘鱼、存塘鱼等）不作水产品产量统计。在淡水生长的各种水生植物，如莲藕、菱角等，因属农作物范畴，均不包括在水产品产量之内。

Explanastory Notes on Main Statistical Indicators

Gross Output Value of Farming, Forestry, Animal Husbandry and Fishery refers to the total volume of products of farming, forestry, animal husbandry and fishery in value terms, which reflects the total scale and total result of agricultural production during a given period of time, which observe development level and speed of farming, forestry, animal husbandry and fishery, study proportional relations of farming, forestry, animal husbandry and fishery and proportional relations in national economic, which is also calculated labor productivity of farming, forestry, animal husbandry and fishery and value-added of farming, forestry, animal husbandry and fishery.

Value-added of Farming, Forestry, Animal Husbandry and Fishery refers to the final results of various agricultural production and trade units in money terms. It is calculated with two approaches. First, production approach, value-added of farming, forestry, animal husbandry and fishery=gross output value of farming, forestry, animal husbandry and fishery intermediate input of farming, forestry, animal husbandry and fishery. Second, distribution approach, value-added of farming, forestry, animal husbandry and fishery=depreciation of fixed assets + laborers remuneration +net taxes on production (taxes on production subsidies production) + operating surplus.

Total Power of Farm Machinery refers to total mechanical power of machinery used in farming, forestry, animal husbandry, and fishery, including cultivating, harvesting, farming products process, transport, plant protection, stock breeding, forestry and fishery and other power of farm machinery.

Effective Irrigated Area refers to areas that are effectively irrigated, i.e. level land which has water source and complete sets of irrigation facilities to lift and move adequate water for irrigation purpose under normal conditions. In general, irrigated area equal sum area of paddy fields and irrigated land for irrigated engineering or complete sets.

Afforested Area refers to the area of forest land where tree and bush by artificially seed, young plant, plane seed on the waste land, barren mountain, dune, during the reference period. Live rate of forest area coverage above 85% in accordance with the Regulation of the People's Republic of China on the Management of Forest Law, including the area of forest land inside farm land and the area of tree planted by the side of farm houses and along the roads, continuing area coverage above 0.066 hectare, excluding the area of sand and planted grass lands along the river.

Number of Livestock Slaughtered refers to the total number of animals for butchering by farming, forestry, animal husbandry and fishery, including parts of selling to country and markets.

Output of Meat refers to output of having butchered of pork, beef, mutton, horse, mule, donkey, fowls, rabbit in the current year, namely the heaviness minus head, hoof, offal.

Output of Aquatic Products Amount of fishing (including artificially cultured, naturally grown) ,in respective consumption by peasants themselves or sold. It excludes aquatic (i.e. fish fry, fish grows, fish bait and transferred fish from piscine, leave fish) for continuing expanded reproduction aquatic. Various fresh water plants (i.e. lotus roots, water chestnut) are not included.

第11篇
CHAPTER 11

工　业
Industry

11-1 工业总产值及增长速度(1990-2006年)
GROSS OUTPUT VALUE AND INCREASE RATE OF INDUSTRY, 1990-2006

年 份 Year	全部工业 Gross Industry			全部国有及规模以上 All State-Owned and Above Designated Size		
	合 计 Total	轻工业 Light Industry	重工业 Heavy Industry	合 计 Total	轻工业 Light Industry	重工业 Heavy Industry
绝对数(亿元) Gross Output Value (100 million yuan)						
1990	679.94	354.50	325.44	543.47	266.27	277.20
1991	786.60	392.29	394.31	599.31	274.65	324.66
1992	997.91	465.48	532.43	722.35	308.34	414.01
1993	1401.84	530.05	871.79	1068.09	354.79	713.30
1994	1754.30	760.80	993.50	1293.80	504.40	789.40
1995	1879.65	752.03	1127.62	1382.43	536.06	816.37
1996	2177.42	1014.46	1162.96	1666.26	678.68	987.58
1997	2450.21	1130.04	1320.17	1782.35	675.23	1107.21
1998	2562.62	1157.09	1405.53	2068.51	767.01	1301.50
1999	2751.37	1128.47	1622.90	2264.55	838.30	1426.25
2000	3080.74	1263.10	1817.64	2606.38	895.24	1711.14
2001	3366.53	1153.73	2212.80	2940.40	942.37	1998.03
2002	3717.72	1207.88	2509.84	3323.12	1012.41	2310.71
2003	4370.76	1254.68	3116.08	4049.61	1095.39	2954.22
2004	6186.04	1398.65	4787.39	5853.72	1265.73	4587.98
2005	7169.62	1569.06	5600.56	6774.10	1372.88	5401.23
2006	8907.45	1664.03	7243.42	8527.70	1475.67	7052.03
比上年增长(%) Increase Rate over Preceding Year (%)						
1990	7.8	5.3	11.2	3.7	3.1	4.4
1991	12.2	7.1	17.8	5.9	2.3	12.3
1992	24.2	22.5	26.3	16.7	12.9	20.1
1993	25.1	8.9	40.5	27.6	8.5	43.6
1994	19.1	33.8	8.2	13.9	30.8	3.1
1995	23.5	11.2	34.8	16.4	11.6	20.3
1996	24.7	31.8	19.5	19.3	20.0	18.8
1997	12.9	13.6	12.2	13.2	8.8	16.5
1998	8.5	9.9	7.2	8.3	5.0	10.6
1999	13.0	5.9	19.4	16.3	21.8	12.7
2000	17.5	19.7	16.0	17.7	15.3	19.3
2001	14.0	-6.6	28.4	17.7	7.6	23.1
2002	19.6	13.3	23.7	22.8	17.1	26.0
2003	24.1	18.5	27.0	26.1	20.8	28.7
2004	31.0	19.4	35.5	31.8	19.2	36.3
2005	19.5	9.3	22.8	20.8	9.6	24.0
2006	25.1	6.1	29.3	25.3	12.4	28.3

注：工业总产值绝对数按当年价格计算，增长速度按可比价格计算(下同)。
Note: Gross output value of industry are calculated at current prices, increase rate are calculated based on comparable prices (same as following next).

11-2 全部国有及规模以上工业总产值
GROSS OUTPUT VALUE OF ALL STATE-OWNED AND ABOVE DESIGNATED SIZE INDUSTRY

单位：亿元 (100 million yuan)

项　目	Item	2005	2006	2006比2005年增长(%) Increase Rate in 2006 over 2005 (%)
全市总计	**Total**	**6774.10**	**8527.70**	**25.3**
#国有及国有控股企业	State-owned and State-holding Enterprises	2628.84	3415.84	28.8
按登记注册类型分	**Grouped by Status of Registration**			
内资企业	Domestic-funded Enterprises	3454.87	4157.15	21.1
国有企业	State-owned Enterprises	532.12	673.18	20.3
集体企业	Collective-owned Enterprises	194.41	148.48	-24.1
股份合作企业	Cooperative Enterprises	65.25	57.84	-11.9
私营企业	Private Enterprises	638.31	891.03	26.6
股份有限公司	Share-holding Corporations Ltd.	979.39	1265.32	23.9
有限责任公司	Limited Liability Corporations	1020.20	1091.23	19.1
#国有独资	Sole State-funded Corporations	205.09	295.50	41.9
联营企业	Joint Ownership Enterprises	17.42	21.91	0.5
#国有与国有联营企业	State Joint Ownership Enterprises	1.73	0.90	-3.4
集体与集体联营企业	Collective Joint Ownership Enterprises	1.51	0.47	-69.1
其他内资企业	Other Domestic-funded Enterprises	7.78	8.16	4.2
港澳台商投资企业	Enterprises with Investment from Hong Kong, Macao and Taiwan	314.85	425.08	23.8
外商投资企业	Foreign Funded Enterprises	3004.38	3945.47	30.4
按经济类型分	**Grouped by Ownership**			
国有经济	State-owned	738.93	969.58	26.1
集体经济	Collective-owned	261.17	206.79	-21.3
私有经济	Private and Individual	638.31	891.03	26.6
港澳台商投资经济	Hong Kong, Macao and Taiwan Funded	314.85	425.08	23.8
外商投资经济	Foreign Funded	3004.38	3945.47	30.4
其　他	Others	1816.46	2089.76	18.7

11-2 续表 1 Continued

单位：亿元 (100 million yuan)

项　目	Item	2005	2006	2006比2005年增长(%) Increase Rate in 2006 over 2005 (%)
按隶属关系分	**Grouped by Administrative Relationship**			
中央工业	Central Industry	1091.57	1409.07	25.5
地方工业	Local Industry	5682.53	7118.63	25.3
#市管工业	City Industry	4012.37	4946.48	15.7
#工业系统	Industry System	2250.36	2816.00	24.3
区县管工业	District & County Industry	285.67	485.34	40.5
街管工业	Neighbour Industry	5.69	9.04	38.8
乡镇管工业	Town and Country Industry	1226.84	1547.47	3.4
按轻重工业分	**Grouped by Light & Heavy Industry**			
轻工业	Light Industry	1372.88	1475.67	12.4
重工业	Heavy Industry	5401.23	7052.03	28.3
按企业规模分	**Grouped by Size of Enterprises**			
大　型	Large-sized	2625.04	3461.16	27.0
中　型	Medium-sized	2366.05	2871.49	20.9
小　型	Small-sized	1783.01	2195.05	28.7
按行业分	**Grouped by Sector**			
煤炭开采和洗选业	Mining and Washing of Coal	16.07	24.49	53.8
石油和天然气开采业	Extraction of Petroleum and Natural Gas	474.76	656.70	38.0
有色金属矿采选业	Mining and Processing of Non-ferrous Metal Ores	39.63	49.36	24.6
非金属矿采选业	Mining and Processing of Nonmetal Ores	10.42	8.14	-3.9
农副食品加工业	Processing of Food from Agricultural Products	130.01	149.92	28.2
食品制造业	Manufacture of Foods	85.17	88.96	14.6
饮料制造业	Manufacture of Beverages	65.35	72.27	11.7
烟草制品业	Manufacture of Tobacco	7.11	11.47	7.9
纺织业	Manufacture of Textile	82.08	70.83	-14.2
纺织服装鞋帽制造业	Manufacture of Textile Wearing Apparel, Footware, and Caps	89.18	71.81	-20.0
皮革毛皮羽毛(绒)及其制品业	Manufacture of Leather, Fur, Feather and Related Products	32.61	29.82	-4.3
木材加工及木、竹、藤棕、草制品	Processing of Timber, Manufacture of Wood, Bamboo, Rattan, Palm, and Straw Products	21.28	20.12	-4.7

11-2 续表 2 Continued

单位：亿元 (100 million yuan)

项　目	Item	2005	2006	2006比2005年增长(%) Increase Rate in 2006 over 2005 (%)
家具制造业	Manufacture of Furniture	41.41	36.94	-6.0
造纸及纸制品业	Manufacture of Paper and Paper Products	50.15	51.51	19.2
印刷业和记录媒介的复制	Printing, Reproduction of Recording Media	17.06	23.17	12.5
文教体育用品制造业	Manufacture of Articles For Culture, Education and Sport Activity	28.85	30.56	9.1
石油加工炼焦及核燃料加工业	Processing of Petroleum, Coking, Processing of Nuclear Fuel	373.94	453.79	20.5
化学原料及化学制品制造业	Manufacture of Raw Chemical Materials and Chemical Products	340.23	400.25	16.8
医药制造业	Manufacture of Medicines	139.70	166.35	9.0
化学纤维制造业	Manufacture of Chemical Fibers	6.67	2.56	-61.9
橡胶制品业	Manufacture of Rubber	48.74	63.10	23.1
塑料制品业	Manufacture of Plastics	110.56	146.36	29.1
非金属矿物制品业	Manufacture of Non-metallic Mineral Products	95.47	100.33	30.2
黑色金属冶炼及压延加工业	Smelting and Pressing of Ferrous Metals	838.93	1159.41	25.0
有色金属冶炼及压延加工业	Smelting and Pressing of Non-Ferrous Metals	96.23	148.44	55.5
金属制品业	Manufacture of Metal Products	241.46	270.80	8.9
通用设备制造业	Manufacture of General Purpose Machinery	232.62	280.81	25.6
专用设备制造业	Manufacture of Special Purpose Machinery	121.36	145.60	27.2
交通运输设备制造业	Manufacture of Transport Equipment	585.79	800.29	44.7
电气机械及器材制造业	Manufacture of Electrical Machinery and Equipment	333.88	456.39	23.4
通信设备计算机及其他电子设备制造业	Manufacture of Communication Equipment, Computers and Other Electronic Equipment	1616.84	2045.26	26.0
仪器仪表及文化办公用机械制造业	Manufacture of Measuring Instruments and Machinery for Cultural Activity and Office Work	51.05	103.20	63.1
工艺品及其他制造业	Manufacture of Artwork and Other Manufacturing	28.09	30.40	28.9
废弃资源和废旧材料回收加工业	Recycling and Disposal of Waste	7.50	11.85	10.5
电力热力的生产和供应业	Production and Supply of Electric Power and Heat Power	288.58	320.53	16.2
燃气生产和供应业	Production and Supply of Gas	14.06	12.48	-3.2
水的生产和供应业	Production and Supply of Water	11.28	13.42	21.9

11-3 地方全部国有及规模以上工业总产值
GROSS OUTPUT VALUE OF ALL STATE-OWNED AND ABOVE DESIGNATED SIZE LOCAL INDUSTRY

单位：亿元 (100 million yuan)

项　目	Item	2005	2006	2006 比2005年增长(%) Increase Rate in 2006 over 2005 (%)
全市总计	**Total**	**5682.53**	**7118.63**	**25.3**
按登记注册类型分	**Grouped by Status of Registration**			
内资企业	Domestic-funded Enterprises	2385.56	2774.19	19.0
国有企业	State-owned Enterprises	319.16	395.88	22.3
集体企业	Collective-owned Enterprises	193.74	148.29	-23.9
股份合作企业	Cooperative Enterprises	65.12	57.84	-11.7
私营企业	Private Enterprises	638.31	891.03	26.6
股份有限公司	Share-holding Corporations Ltd.	241.47	328.32	15.3
有限责任公司	Limited Liability Corporations	903.00	922.79	16.9
# 国有独资	Sole State-funded Corporations	167.24	216.03	27.1
联营企业	Joint Ownership Enterprises	16.98	21.89	0.3
# 国有与国有联营企业	State Joint Ownership Enterprises	1.29	0.88	-18.3
集体与集体联营企业	Collective Joint Ownership Enterprises	1.51	0.47	-69.1
其他内资企业	Other Domestic-funded Enterprises	7.78	8.16	4.2
港澳台商投资企业	Enterprises with Investment from Hong Kong, Macao and Taiwan	314.22	424.36	23.9
外商投资企业	Foreign Funded Enterprises	2982.75	3920.08	30.5
按经济类型分	**Grouped by Ownership**			
国有经济	State-owned	487.69	612.78	23.9
集体经济	Collective-owned	260.38	206.60	-21.1
私有经济	Private and Individual	638.31	891.03	26.6
港澳台商投资经济	Hong Kong, Macao and Taiwan Funded	314.22	424.36	23.9
外商投资经济	Foreign Funded	2982.75	3920.08	30.5
其　他	Others	999.18	1063.78	14.1

11-3 续表 1 Continued

单位：亿元 (100 million yuan)

项　目	Item	2005	2006	2006 比 2005 年增长 (%) Increase Rate in 2006 over 2005 (%)
按隶属关系分	**Grouped by Administrative Relationship**			
# 市管工业	City Industry	4012.37	4946.48	15.7
# 工业系统	Industry System	2250.23	2816.00	24.3
区县管工业	District & County Industry	285.67	485.34	40.5
街管工业	Neighbour Industry	5.69	9.04	38.8
乡镇管工业	Town and Country Industry	1226.84	1547.47	3.4
按轻重工业分	**Grouped by Light & Heavy Industry**			
轻工业	Light Industry	1357.18	1457.17	12.5
重工业	Heavy Industry	4325.36	5661.46	29.0
按企业规模分	**Grouped by Size of Enterprises**			
大　型	Large-sized	1990.57	2663.69	26.9
中　型	Medium-sized	1970.42	2328.06	19.9
小　型	Small-sized	1721.54	2126.88	29.5
按行业分	**Grouped by Sector**			
煤炭开采和洗选业	Mining and Washing of Coal	16.07	24.49	53.8
有色金属矿采选业	Mining and Processing of Non-Ferrous Metal Ores	39.63	49.36	24.6
非金属矿采选业	Mining and Processing of Nonmetal Ores	10.42	8.14	-3.9
农副食品加工业	Processing of Food from Agricultural Products	130.01	149.92	28.2
食品制造业	Manufacture of Foods	84.73	88.31	14.4
饮料制造业	Manufacture of Beverages	65.35	72.27	11.7
纺织业	Manufacture of Textile	81.70	70.81	-13.9
纺织服装鞋帽制造业	Manufacture of Textile Wearing Apparel, Footware, and Caps	89.18	71.81	-20.0
皮革毛皮羽毛(绒)及其制品业	Manufacture of Leather, Fur, Feather and Related Products	32.61	29.82	-4.3
木材加工及木、竹、藤、棕、草制品业	Processing of Timber, Manufacture of Wood, Bamboo, Rattan, Palm, and Straw Products	21.09	19.77	-5.5

11-3 续表 2 Continued

单位：亿元 (100 million yuan)

项目	Item	2005	2006	2006比2005年增长(%) Increase Rate in 2006 over 2005 (%)
家具制造业	Manufacture of Furniture	41.41	36.94	-6.0
造纸及纸制品业	Manufacture of Paper and Paper Products	50.15	51.51	19.2
印刷业和记录媒介的复制	Printing, Reproduction of Recording Media	16.32	22.52	13.1
文教体育用品制造业	Manufacture of Articles For Culture, Education and Sport Activity	28.85	30.56	9.1
石油加工炼焦及核燃料加工业	Processing of Petroleum, Coking, Processing of Nuclear Fuel	63.26	57.41	-9.8
化学原料及化学制品制造业	Manufacture of Raw Chemical Materials and Chemical Products	322.67	381.25	15.4
医药制造业	Manufacture of Medicines	136.59	163.11	9.1
化学纤维制造业	Manufacture of Chemical Fibers	6.67	2.56	-61.9
橡胶制品业	Manufacture of Rubber	48.74	63.10	23.1
塑料制品业	Manufacture of Plastics	109.81	145.60	29.3
非金属矿物制品业	Manufacture of Non-metallic Mineral Products	93.59	99.91	30.5
黑色金属冶炼及压延加工业	Smelting and Pressing of Ferrous Metals	838.93	1159.41	25.7
有色金属冶炼及压延加工业	Smelting and Pressing of Non-Ferrous Metals	96.23	148.44	56.3
金属制品业	Manufacture of Metal Products	220.62	247.85	8.8
通用设备制造业	Manufacture of General Purpose Machinery	232.29	280.70	25.4
专用设备制造业	Manufacture of Special Purpose Machinery	118.33	136.27	29.9
交通运输设备制造业	Manufacture of Transport Equipment	568.27	779.62	45.5
电气机械及器材制造业	Manufacture of Electrical Machinery and Equipment	329.72	451.76	23.5
通信设备计算机及其他电子设备制造业	Manufacture of Communication Equipment, Computers and Other Electronic Equipment	1614.07	2041.96	26.0
仪器仪表及文化办公用机械制造业	Manufacture of Measuring Instruments and Machinery for Cultural Activity and Office Work	50.48	100.37	59.7
工艺品及其他制造业	Manufacture of Artwork and Other Manufacturing	28.09	30.40	28.9
废弃资源和废旧材料回收加工业	Recycling and Disposal of Waste	7.50	11.85	10.5
电力热力的生产和供应业	Production and Supply of Electric Power and Heat Power	63.81	64.91	24.4
燃气生产和供应业	Production and Supply of Gas	14.06	12.48	-3.2
水的生产和供应业	Production and Supply of Water	11.28	13.42	22.4

11-4 主要工业产品产量(1990-2006年) OUTPUT OF MAJOR INDUSTRIAL PRODUCTS, 1990-2006

年 份 Year	布 (万米) Cloth (10 000 m)	纱 (万吨) Yarn (10 000 tons)	机制纸及纸板 (万吨) Machine-made Paper and Paperboards (10 000 tons)	合成洗涤剂 (万吨) Synthetic Detergent (10 000 tons)	饮料酒 (万吨) Alcoholic Beverages (10 000 tons)	家用电冰箱 (万台) Household Refrigerators (10 000 units)	电视机 (万台) Television Sets (10 000 units)	#彩色电视机 Color Television Sets
1990	49194	11.69	26.75	8.54	9.28	23.34	143.93	62.46
1991	46790	11.23	27.18	9.34	10.75	6.71	140.27	72.63
1992	43031	10.86	33.32	10.56	10.88	9.27	140.99	68.29
1993	39259	11.59	36.84	10.00	11.40	2.71	134.88	73.30
1994	41437	13.19	31.01	9.68	11.09	3.95	124.00	80.37
1995	49803	12.35	41.42	11.95	12.34	3.70	160.82	109.54
1996	39662	10.51	45.89	12.07	10.72	0.29	157.34	117.80
1997	49845	13.61	40.56	10.28	13.73	0.69	84.36	59.16
1998	33326	8.37	33.64	9.65	15.25	2.29	82.94	47.87
1999	27308	8.45	25.50	8.75	14.21	9.93	84.67	50.34
2000	29217	8.80	25.18	7.19	15.75	8.42	94.27	72.28
2001	25861	8.13	20.63	5.68	20.71	3.85	66.24	51.42
2002	27082	9.18	27.98	5.41	20.64	19.14	87.06	76.35
2003	25114	7.47	17.76	5.09	24.72	29.17	121.09	112.41
2004	30805	7.51	36.03	5.04	23.65	28.25	110.99	109.42
2005	25850	7.32	18.89	1.40	20.81	19.30	66.01	64.90
2006	28346	7.62	26.71	0.74	29.8	9.34	98.51	98.11

年 份 Year	原 油 (万吨) Crude Oil (10 000 tons)	发电量 (亿千瓦小时) Electricity (100 million kWh)	钢 (万吨) Steel (10 000 tons)	水 泥 (万吨) Cement (10 000 tons)	硫 酸 (万吨) Sulfuric Acid (10 000 tons)	烧 碱 (万吨) Caustic Soda (10 000 tons)	农用化肥 (万吨) Chemical Fertilizer (10 000 tons)	化学农药 (万吨) Chemical Pesticide (10 000 tons)
1990	469.50	94.85	166.74	122.14	7.70	25.23	7.21	1.97
1991	474.90	90.27	175.43	137.24	8.31	27.25	7.85	2.12
1992	491.76	98.62	183.45	144.58	8.15	27.99	7.84	2.01
1993	517.00	126.65	221.98	152.39	7.36	28.27	10.61	2.37
1994	589.00	122.47	188.55	177.00	7.79	29.28	15.75	2.81
1995	620.82	133.65	171.57	200.62	5.58	32.57	9.74	1.69
1996	646.60	146.04	200.99	207.88	8.11	50.75	11.31	2.95
1997	645.90	166.53	236.79	209.00	11.33	44.15	10.91	3.27
1998	691.28	172.51	255.27	250.00	10.36	39.90	10.26	3.38
1999	686.72	182.56	317.69	240.51	11.47	47.04	26.82	3.68
2000	763.99	211.49	356.76	267.81	11.17	49.28	17.04	2.79
2001	970.29	217.43	395.30	338.99	11.27	49.39	14.91	0.71
2002	1215.94	268.83	482.58	377.75	12.15	63.65	16.03	3.30
2003	1316.30	319.95	565.95	449.31	10.96	79.89	16.40	2.10
2004	1446.21	339.76	788.48	520.52	9.99	81.14	15.96	0.44
2005	1782.89	365.70	955.28	519.15	11.95	80.45	16.94	1.26
2006	1943.09	359.24	1285.34	607.33	13.76	88.86	16.33	1.23

11-5 主要工业产品产量
OUTPUT OF MAJOR INDUSTRIAL PRODUCTS

产品名称	Item	单位	Unit	2005	2006
原油	Crude Oil	万吨	10 000 tons	1782.89	1943.09
原油加工量	Crude Oil Processed	万吨	10 000 tons	467.02	528.33
发电量	Electricity	亿千瓦小时	100 million kWh	365.70	359.24
供热量	Heating Supply	万百万千焦	10 000 billion joule	5651.98	5704.33
天然气	Natural Gas	亿立方米	100 million cu. m	8.80	10.50
液化气	Liquefied Petroleum Gas	万吨	10 000 tons	44.78	42.04
原盐	Salt	万吨	10 000 tons	230.10	236.10
食用植物油	Edible Vegetable Oil	万吨	10 000 tons	51.57	111.27
饮料酒	Alcoholic Beverages	万吨	10 000 tons	20.81	29.80
#啤酒	Beer	万吨	10 000 tons	14.49	21.89
方便主食品	Staple Foods	万吨	10 000 tons	10.88	8.74
软饮料	Soft Drinking	万吨	10 000 tons	81.40	123.79
卷烟	Cigarettes	万箱	10 000 cases	26.50	29.20
家具	Furniture	万件	10 000 pieces	403.97	619.47
地毯	Carpet	万元	10 000 yuan	120186.00	125294.40
化学纤维	Chemical Fiber	万吨	10 000 tons	20.54	18.68
纱(混合)	Yarn	万吨	10 000 tons	7.32	7.62
布(混合)	Cloth	万米	10 000 m	25849.89	28346.34
毛线	Knitting Wool	吨	ton	2845.31	4280.00
呢绒	Woolen Piece Goods	万米	10 000 m	770.10	1164.40
服装	Garments	万件	10 000 pieces	17815.94	14531.08
人造板	Artificial Board	万立方米	10 000 cu. m	16.16	13.04
机制纸及纸	Machine-made Paper & Paperboard	万吨	10 000 tons	18.89	26.71
电子琴	Electronic Organ	万架	10 000 units	130.64	129.78
硫酸	Sulfuric Acid	万吨	10 000 tons	11.95	13.76
纯碱	Soda Ash	万吨	10 000 tons	86.87	88.37
烧碱	Caustic Soda	万吨	10 000 tons	80.45	88.86
电石	Calcium Carbide	万吨	10 000 tons		11.04
合成氨	Synthetic Ammonia	万吨	10 000 tons	22.58	24.59
农用化肥	Chemical Fertilizer	万吨	10 000 tons	16.94	16.33
化学农药	Chemical Pesticide	吨	ton	12606.71	12309.77
乙烯	Ethene	万吨	10 000 tons	20.71	23.17

11-5 续表 Continued

产品名称	Item	单 位	Unit	2005	2006
油 漆	Paint	吨	ton	66229	111919
染 料	Dyestuff	吨	ton	62617	52897
轮胎外胎	Tires	万 条	10 000 units	676.01	1215.89
农用塑料薄膜	Plastic Film for Farm Use	吨	ton	16603.87	24908.38
合成洗涤剂	Synthetic Detergents	万 吨	10 000 tons	1.40	0.74
化学原料药	Chemical Raw Medicine	吨	ton	11240.93	13915.23
中成药	Traditional Chinese Medicine	吨	ton	6200.00	6013.44
水 泥	Cement	万 吨	10 000 tons	519.15	607.33
平板玻璃	Plate Glass	万重量箱	10 000 weight cases	379.75	303.78
生 铁	Pig Iron	万 吨	10 000 tons	660.24	1131.51
钢	Steel	万 吨	10 000 tons	955.28	1285.34
钢 材	Steel Products	万 吨	10 000 tons	1664.04	2117.51
黄 金	Gold	千 克	kg	41755	39282
焦 炭	Coke	万 吨	10 000 tons	360.24	376.22
电焊条	Welding Rod	万 吨	10 000 tons	129.10	110.26
内燃机	Internal Combustion Engine	万千瓦	10 000 kW	1839.81	2245.81
金属切削机床	Metal-cutting Machine	台	unit	524	395
升降移动机械	Lift	台	unit	17173	28827
汽 车	Motor Vehicle	辆	unit	327756	414403
# 轿 车	Car	辆	unit	325594	410277
摩托车	Motorcycle	万 辆	10 000 units	111.42	19.40
自行车	Bicycle	万 辆	10 000 units	1306.70	1707.77
家用电冰箱	Household Refrigerator	万 台	10 000 units	19.30	9.34
房间空气调节器	Air Conditioner	万 台	10 000 units	434.43	482.13
微波炉	Microwave Oven	万 台	10 000 units	1431.15	1434.79
移动电话	Mobile Phone	万 部	10 000 units	6319.82	10129.72
微型计算机	Micro-computer	万 部	10 000 units	2.14	3.19
半导体集成电路	Semiconductor Integrated Circuit	亿 块	100 million pieces	5.20	5.76
电视机	Television Sets	万 台	10 000 units	66.01	98.51
# 彩色电视机	Color Television Sets	万 台	10 000 units	64.9	98.11
录像机	Videocorder	万 台	10 000 units	152.28	141.88
吸尘器	Vacuum Cleaners	万 台	10 000 units	322.16	364.87
无缝钢管	Seamless Steel Pipe	万 吨	10 000 tons	174.59	216.59
照相机	Cameras	万 台	10 000 units	74.34	407.37

11-6 主要产品销售量和产销率
SALES VOLUME AND SALES RATIO OF MAJOR INDUSTRIAL PRODUCTS

产品名称	Item	单 位	Unit	2005		2006	
				销售量 Sales Volume	产销率(%) Sales Ratio (%)	销售量 Sales Volume	产销率(%) Sales Ratio (%)
生 铁	Pig Iron	万 吨	10 000 tons	128.79	19.5	125.50	11.1
钢 材	Steel Products	万 吨	10 000 tons	1706.16	100.4	2130.94	100.6
无缝钢管	Seamless Steel Pipe	万 吨	10 000 tons	174.99	100.2	213.39	98.5
硫 酸	Sulfuric Acid	万 吨	10 000 tons	11.68	97.7	13.40	97.4
烧 碱	Caustic Soda	万 吨	10 000 tons	81.31	96.7	86.72	97.6
纯 碱	Soda Ash	万 吨	10 000 tons	83.59	96.2	86.67	98.1
轮胎外胎	Tires	万 吨	10 000 units	676.21	100	1207.22	99.3
水 泥	Cement	万 吨	10 000 tons	512.39	98.7	605.43	99.7
平板玻璃	Plate Glass	万重量箱	10 000 weight cases	370.82	97.6	285.28	93.9
焦 炭	Coke	万 吨	10 000 tons	237.57	66.4	245.96	65.4
原 油	Crude Oil	万 吨	10 000 tons	1770.74	99.3	1913.63	98.5
汽 车	Motor Vehicle	万 辆	10 000 units	32.65	99.6	40.95	98.8
电视机	Television Sets	万 台	10 000 units	66.82	101.2	97.61	99.1
#彩色电视机	Color Television Sets	万 台	10 000 units	65.41	100.8	97.22	99.1
家用电冰箱(柜)	Household Refrigerator	万 台	10 000 units	18.97	98.3	8.00	85.7
吸尘器	Vacuum Cleaners	万 台	10 000 units	321.76	99.9	365.00	100.0
房间空气调节器	Air Conditioner	万 台	10 000 units	434.78	100.1	482.80	100.1
微波炉	Microwave Ovens	万 台	10 000 units	1429.29	99.9	1433.35	99.9
移动电话机	Mobile Phone	万 部	10 000 units	6311.18	99.9	10085.29	99.6
纱(混合)	Yarn	万 吨	10 000 tons	4.85	66.3	4.18	54.8
布(混合)	Cloth	万 米	10 000 m	26022.32	100.7	27688.85	97.7
毛 线	Knitting Wool	吨	ton	3202.31	112.5	4177.00	97.6
呢 绒	Woolen Piece Goods	万 米	10 000 m	773.03	100.4	758.86	65.2
合成洗涤剂	Synthetic Detergents	万 吨	10 000 tons	1.94	102.7	0.77	103.1
录像机	Videocorder	万 部	10 000 units	154.76	101.6	143.80	101.4
照相机	Cameras	万 台	10 000 units	75.49	101.5	408.47	100.3
服 装	Garments	万 件	10 000 pieces	17959.02	99.4	14386.19	99.0
自行车	Bicycle	万 辆	10 000 units	1286.87	99.4	1691.28	99.2
微型计算机	Micro-computer	万 部	10 000 units	2.07	96.8	3.10	97.4
人造板	Artificial Board	万立方米	10 000 cu. m	15.98	98.9	12.43	95.4
摩托车	Motorcycles	万 辆	10 000 units	113.47	101.1	19.39	99.9

11-7 工业企业主要财务指标(1990-2006年)
MAIN FINANCIAL INDICATORS OF INDUSTRIAL ENTERPRISES,1990-2006

单位：亿元 (100 million yuan)

年 份 Year	固定资产原价 Original Value of Fixed Assets	固定资产净值年平均余额 Annual Average Balance of Net Value of Fixed Assets	流动资产年平均余额 Annual Average Balance of Circulating Funds	主营业务收入 Principal Business Revenue	利税总额 Total Pre-tax Profits	从业人员年平均人数(万人) Annual Average Employment Personnel (10 000 persons)
全 市 Total						
1990	329.93	217.17	148.83	465.55	48.36	159.31
1991	379.97	252.86	173.89	538.50	52.61	155.64
1992	458.50	276.80	207.99	646.92	59.40	160.30
1993	611.67	312.14	559.47	1040.49	83.94	178.08
1994	852.75	429.40	756.09	1101.71	109.86	177.93
1995	1273.46	628.11	888.92	1376.70	133.51	173.58
1996	1338.28	892.14	1044.83	1498.67	139.73	165.56
1997	1590.96	1092.54	1232.07	1668.15	139.96	158.52
1998	1899.35	1289.83	1386.17	1943.89	148.69	142.99
1999	2157.03	1446.46	1490.98	2182.17	175.66	128.75
2000	2488.60	1561.39	1488.27	2656.98	274.27	120.19
2001	2763.94	1657.85	1772.75	2983.26	326.55	122.15
2002	2940.21	1729.50	1874.76	3437.46	325.07	120.95
2003	3036.78	1793.13	1991.12	4202.02	401.35	115.28
2004	3415.23	2076.99	2682.47	5861.43	608.91	122.85
2005	3845.17	2155.41	3058.69	7125.93	815.63	122.21
2006	4240.28	2308.49	3425.59	8794.35	1003.39	116.33
#国有经济 State-owned						
1990	273.52	176.86	112.41	356.60	37.35	97.07
1991	314.71	207.30	129.89	407.79	39.01	96.74
1992	376.34	245.69	255.46	459.59	37.32	96.08
1993	467.63	292.18	345.77	663.86	37.91	117.79
1994	612.46	363.96	444.30	584.78	44.50	93.50
1995	942.91	644.15	474.69	625.98	44.91	90.70
1996	910.56	647.65	518.45	594.08	37.06	83.05
1997	1031.89	732.58	577.59	625.22	39.26	78.99
1998	1130.86	773.73	601.69	587.69	29.63	69.34
1999	1261.91	817.29	631.78	594.55	26.88	56.84
2000	1193.87	836.48	648.06	667.84	18.70	48.12
2001	1151.07	699.45	615.11	649.26	17.08	42.99
2002	1087.90	693.21	605.08	629.86	22.63	36.42
2003	1066.98	704.47	576.42	817.42	52.83	30.71
2004	882.16	585.60	575.46	738.40	40.14	23.52
2005	898.32	549.77	627.10	841.32	50.27	20.61
2006	913.23	531.41	658.50	1133.61	78.97	18.20

注：1.本表统计范围1998年以前为街乡及以上工业，以后为全部国有及规模以上工业。2.从业人员年平均人数1998年以前为职工平均人数。

Note: a) Data before 1998 of this table refer to industrial enterprises at township and higher level.Since 1998, data refer to all the enterprises of state-owned and above designated size. b) Annual average employment personnel before 1998 refer to average staff and workers.

11-8 全部国有及规模以上工业企业主要经济指标（2006年）
MAIN ECONOMIC INDICATORS OF ALL STATE-OWNED AND ABOVE DESIGNATED SIZE INDUSTRIAL ENTERPRISES, 2006

项　　目	Item	企业单位数(个) Number of Enterprises (unit)	从业人员年平均人数(人) Annual Average Employment Personnel (person)	工业增加值(万元) Value Added of Industry (10 000 yuan)
全市总计	**Total**	**6301**	**1163264**	**24438360**
#国有及国有控股企业	State-owned and State-holding Enterprises	1225	381608	11777344
按登记注册类型分	**Grouped by Status of Registration**			
内资企业	Domestic-funded Enterprises	4347	708221	13974902
国有企业	State-owned Enterprises	653	102257	1990319
集体企业	Collective-owned Enterprises	486	49404	340392
股份合作企业	Cooperative Enterprises	147	17364	104334
私营企业	Private Enterprises	2042	213778	2347591
股份有限公司	Share-holding Corporations Ltd.	95	74370	5507158
有限责任公司	I imited Liability Corporations	858	243906	3618780
#国有独资	Sole State-funded Corporations	44	79216	784974
联营企业	Joint Ownership Enterprises	32	4241	41925
#国有与国有联营企业	State Joint Ownership Enterprises	7	504	4196
集体与集体联营企业	Collective Joint Ownership Enterprises	4	1044	1633
其他内资企业	Other Domestic-funded Enterprises	34	2901	24403
港澳台商投资企业	Enterprises with Investment from Hong Kong, Macao and Taiwan	403	83751	1231398
外商投资企业	Foreign Funded Enterprises	1551	371292	9232060
按经济类型分	**Grouped by Ownership**			
国有经济	State-owned	704	181977	2779489
集体经济	Collective-owned	637	67812	446358
私有经济	Private and Individual	2042	213778	2347591
港澳台商投资经济	Hong Kong, Macao and Taiwan Funded	403	83751	1231398
外商投资经济	Foreign Funded	1551	371292	9232060
其　他	Others	964	244654	8401464
按隶属关系分	**Grouped by Administrative Relationship**			
中央工业	Central Industry	91	102957	6152827
地方工业	Local Industry	6210	1060307	18285532
#市管工业	City Industry	2852	553467	12882244
#工业系统	Industry System	1031	322211	6294454
区县管工业	District & County Industry	514	70309	1315531
街管工业	Neighbour Industry	40	3570	21692
乡镇管工业	Town and Country Industry	2509	399989	3701841
按轻重工业分	**Grouped by Light & Heavy Industry**			
轻工业	Light Industry	2461	427356	3928482
重工业	Heavy Industry	3840	735908	20509877
按企业规模分	**Grouped by Size of Enterprises**			
大　型	Large-sized	48	279585	9237127
中　型	Medium-sized	514	380722	8879283
小　型	Small-sized	5739	502957	6321949

资产总计 (万元) Total Assets (10 000 yuan)	流动资产年平均余额 (万元) Annual Average Balance of Circulating Funds (10 000 yuan)	固定资产原价 (万元) Original Value of Fixed Assets (10 000 yuan)	固定资产净值年平均余额(万元) Annual Average Balance of Net Value of Fixed Assets (10 000 yuan)	主营业务收入 (万元) Principal Business Revenue (10 000 yuan)	利税总额 (万元) Total Pre-tax Profits (10 000 yuan)	#利润总额 Total Profits
71290174	**34255906**	**42402837**	**23084929**	**87943490**	**10033905**	**6929954**
36568511	13622696	27234771	14010556	35298051	6129411	4030212
43003661	17496516	29242954	15370065	42743759	6292500	4246102
10744492	4300497	5441960	2948002	7741401	340519	42692
910729	574491	342965	199372	1523107	100858	38759
508998	325557	154282	98497	619944	48542	32570
5423322	3122799	1988521	1417318	8838299	521551	338697
9409562	2799330	12311011	5297003	12530841	4105270	3136328
15738774	6209661	8905909	5348630	11191292	1168083	656458
6729358	2277894	3680302	2358921	3589046	449657	251702
188268	128604	59437	35515	218233	5179	165
14526	6564	10044	7168	5683	-466	-1704
2726	1370	1603	794	4473	516	125
79516	35577	38869	25730	80643	2498	434
4579282	2335665	2645569	1476384	4458442	377742	280974
23707231	14423726	10514313	6238481	40741289	3363663	2402877
17488376	6584955	9132305	5314092	11336130	789710	292690
1422454	901418	498851	298662	2147524	149916	71454
5423322	3122799	1988521	1417318	8838299	521551	338697
4579282	2335665	2645569	1476384	4458442	377742	280974
23707231	14423726	10514313	6238481	40741289	3363663	2402877
18669509	6887344	17623277	8339993	20421807	4831323	3543262
12351808	3076942	16536818	7505761	13935645	4390001	3233010
58938366	31178965	25866019	15579168	74007845	5643904	3696944
43417181	22782945	18869991	11015270	51901196	4038543	2591733
26321222	12723863	11038301	6385892	29912763	2449872	1376165
3558438	1839965	1738531	1089783	5150043	304628	202484
70901	43671	29469	15912	82645	7304	3679
11158472	6071720	4915013	3272489	15695538	1219786	863671
16876943	8395010	7557454	4862236	15695293	1248102	739945
54413231	25860896	34845383	18222693	72248197	8785803	6190009
27558627	13049206	15640853	8249633	36688814	3692859	2336848
23869651	10555374	17941654	9093921	30347110	4899516	3722048
19861896	10651326	8820330	5741376	20907565	1441530	871058

11-9 地方全部国有及规模以上工业企业主要经济指标（2006年）
MAIN ECONOMIC INDICATORS OF ALL STATE-OWNED AND ABOVE DESIGNATED SIZE LOCAL INDUSTRIAL ENTERPRISES, 2006

项目	Item	企业单位数(个) Number of Enterprises (unit)	从业人员年平均人数(人) Annual Average Employment Personnel (person)	工业增加值(万元) Value Added of Industry (10 000 yuan)
全市总计	**Total**	**6210**	**1060307**	**18285532**
按登记注册类型分	**Grouped by Status of Registration**			
内资企业	Domestic-funded Enterprises	4266	608050	7885810
国有企业	State-owned Enterprises	607	69351	1332738
集体企业	Collective-owned Enterprises	485	49337	339850
股份合作企业	Cooperative Enterprises	147	17364	104334
私营企业	Private Enterprises	2042	213778	2347591
股份有限公司	Share-holding Corporations Ltd.	87	47715	670861
有限责任公司	Limited Liability Corporations	833	203363	3024348
# 国有独资	Sole State-funded Corporations	41	43050	632060
联营企业	Joint Ownership Enterprises	31	4241	41685
# 国有与国有联营企业	State Joint Ownership Enterprises	6	504	3956
集体与集体联营企业	Collective Joint Ownership Enterprises	4	1044	1633
其他内资企业	Other Domestic-funded Enterprises	34	2901	24403
港澳台商投资企业	Enterprises with Investment from Hong Kong, Macao and Taiwan	399	83441	1226788
外商投资企业	Foreign Funded Enterprises	1545	368816	9172934
按经济类型分	**Grouped by Ownership**			
国有经济	State-owned	654	112905	1968755
集体经济	Collective-owned	636	67745	445816
私有经济	Private and Individual	2042	213778	2347591
港澳台商投资经济	Hong Kong, Macao and Taiwan Funded	399	83441	1226788
外商投资经济	Foreign Funded	1545	368816	9172934
其他	Others	934	213622	3123648
按隶属关系分	**Grouped by Administrative Relationship**			
# 市管工业	City Industry	2852	553467	12882244
# 工业系统	Industry System	1031	322211	6294454
区县管工业	District & County Industry	514	70309	1315531
街管工业	Neighbour Industry	40	3570	21692
乡镇管工业	Town and Country Industry	2509	399989	3701841
按轻重工业分	**Grouped by Light & Heavy Industry**			
轻工业	Light Industry	2444	424651	3836439
重工业	Heavy Industry	3766	635656	14449093
按企业规模分	**Grouped by Size of Enterprises**			
大型	Large-sized	41	203577	7020277
中型	Medium-sized	490	358970	5236785
小型	Small-sized	5679	497760	6028470

资产总计 (万元) Total Assets (10 000 yuan)	流动资产年平均余额 (万元) Annual Average Balance of Circulating Funds (10 000 yuan)	固定资产原价 (万元) Original Value of Fixed Assets (10 000 yuan)	固定资产净值年平均余额(万元) Annual Average Balance of Net Value of Fixed Assets (10 000 yuan)	主营业务收入 (万元) Principal Business Revenue (10 000 yuan)	利税总额 (万元) Total Pre-tax Profits (10 000 yuan)	#利润总额 Total Profits
58938366	**31178965**	**25866019**	**15579168**	**74007845**	**5643904**	**3696944**
30833576	14551727	12755073	7897629	29079870	1939198	1048427
7287390	3391646	2051091	1200429	4908236	139268	33822
910039	573952	342836	199317	1521199	100520	38554
508998	325557	154282	98497	619944	48542	32570
5423322	3122799	1988521	1417318	8838299	521551	338697
3539104	1723039	1832104	943329	3393912	264851	117104
12896940	5250553	6287932	3977496	9499405	856790	487081
5356358	1583513	2921489	1968903	2773243	388723	243347
188268	128604	59437	35515	218233	5179	165
14526	6564	10044	7168	5683	-466	-1704
2726	1370	1603	794	4473	516	125
79516	35577	38869	25730	80643	2498	434
4531607	2301144	2638354	1472477	4447420	369500	273081
23573183	14326094	10472592	6209063	40480555	3335206	2375436
12658274	4981723	4982624	3176500	7687161	527526	275466
1421763	900879	498722	298607	2145616	149577	71249
5423322	3122799	1988521	1417318	8838299	521551	338697
4531607	2301144	2638354	1472477	4447420	369500	273081
23573183	14326094	10472592	6209063	40480555	3335206	2375436
11330217	5546327	5285206	3005204	10408794	740544	363017
43417181	22782945	18869991	11015270	51901196	4038543	2591733
26321222	12723863	11038301	6385892	29912763	2449872	1376165
3558438	1839965	1738531	1089783	5150043	304628	202484
70901	43671	29469	15912	82645	7304	3679
11158472	6071720	4915013	3272489	15695538	1219786	863671
16672027	8301375	7439073	4798359	15505306	1182172	737961
42266339	22877590	18426946	10780809	58502539	4461732	2958983
20356277	10976043	7385795	4147575	28830797	2562824	1702906
19662670	9874714	10464040	6196816	24941681	1808419	1235838
18919419	10328208	8016184	5234777	20235367	1272661	758201

11-10 分行业全部国有及规模以上工业企业主要经济指标（2006年）
MAIN ECONOMIC INDICATORS OF ALL STATE-OWNED AND ABOVE DESIGNATED SIZE INDUSTRIAL ENTERPRISES BY SECTOR, 2006

项　目	Item	企业单位数(个) Number of Enterprises (unit)	从业人员年平均人数(人) Annual Average Employment Personnel (person)	工业增加值(万元) Value Added of Industry (10 000 yuan)
总　计	Total	6301	1163264	24438360
煤炭开采和洗选业	Mining and Washing of Coal	3	83	15761
石油和天然气开采业	Extraction of Petroleum and Natural Gas	6	55607	4708060
有色金属矿采选业	Mining and Processing of Non-Ferrous Metal Ores	1	2761	22469
非金属矿采选业	Mining and Processing of Nonmetal Ores	6	10071	50599
农副食品加工业	Processing of Food from Agricultural Products	155	16862	275090
食品制造业	Manufacture of Foods	149	25351	331060
饮料制造业	Manufacture of Beverages	50	12219	230495
烟草制品业	Manufacture of Tobacco	1	975	74611
纺织业	Manufacture of Textile	261	50788	202140
纺织服装鞋帽制造业	Manufacture of Textile Wearing Apparel, Footware, and Caps	305	74242	221945
皮革毛皮羽毛(绒)及其制品	Manufacture of Leather, Fur, Feather and Related Products	70	17923	59203
木材加工及木、竹、藤、棕、草制品业	Processing of Timber, Manufacture of Wood, Bamboo, Rattan, Palm, and Straw Products	68	6219	25765
家具制造业	Manufacture of Furniture	95	20218	84806
造纸及纸制品业	Manufacture of Paper and Paper Products	173	16777	129486
印刷业和记录媒介的复制	Printing, Reproduction of Recording Media	118	8945	63383
文教体育用品制造业	Manufacture of Articles For Culture, Education and Sport Activity	63	11921	78438
石油加工炼焦及核燃料加工业	Processing of Petroleum, Coking, Processing of Nuclear Fuel	46	17027	433726
化学原料及化学制品制造业	Manufacture of Raw Chemical Materials and Chemical Products	581	66415	999232
医药制造业	Manufacture of Medicines	115	39565	691889
化学纤维制造业	Manufacture of Chemical Fibers	18	1691	5657
橡胶制品业	Manufacture of Rubber	102	21603	148802
塑料制品业	Manufacture of Plastics	288	41799	452786
非金属矿物制品业	Manufacture of Non-metallic Mineral Products	230	27083	306270
黑色金属冶炼及压延加工业	Smelting and Pressing of Ferrous Metals	267	77841	4081782
有色金属冶炼及压延加工业	Smelting and Pressing of Non-Ferrous Metals	85	7056	233308
金属制品业	Manufacture of Metal Products	562	63478	540879
通用设备制造业	Manufacture of General Purpose Machinery	483	63449	672403
专用设备制造业	Manufacture of Special Purpose Machinery	313	39955	476815
交通运输设备制造业	Manufacture of Transport Equipment	482	102425	1533621
电气机械及器材制造业	Manufacture of Electrical Machinery and Equipment	366	53796	784272
通信设备计算机及其他电子设备制造业	Manufacture of Communication Equipment, Computers and Other Electronic Equipment	415	134311	5094443
仪器仪表及文化办公用机械制造业	Manufacture of Measuring Instruments and Machinery for Cultural Activity and Office Work	155	17311	222918
工艺品及其他制造业	Manufacture of Artwork and Other Manufacturing	143	20596	68664
废弃资源和废旧材料回收加工业	Recycling and Disposal of Waste	30	2297	26144
电力热力的生产和供应业	Production and Supply of Electric Power and Heat Power	62	24112	991566
燃气生产和供应业	Production and Supply of Gas	14	6775	31948
水的生产和供应业	Production and Supply of Water	20	3717	67923

资产总计(万元) Total Assets (10 000 yuan)	流动资产年平均余额(万元) Annual Average Balance of Circulating Funds (10 000 yuan)	固定资产原价(万元) Original Value of Fixed Assets (10 000 yuan)	固定资产净值年平均余额(万元) Annual Average Balance of Net Value of Fixed Assets (10 000 yuan)	主营业务收入(万元) Principal Business Revenue (10 000 yuan)	利税总额(万元) Total Pre-tax Profits (10 000 yuan)	#利润总额 Total Profits
71290174	**34255906**	**42402837**	**23084929**	**87943490**	**10033905**	**6929954**
328127	274270	12465	10157	369295	7375	5999
5657645	1222980	9258369	3713846	6357952	4003598	3279164
144480	59479	51942	28810	476320	19991	17474
326299	130385	154079	88189	79112	13809	591
975196	615427	472017	299490	1611249	38415	26912
974642	454167	619549	359996	872971	71019	31811
764916	345758	456973	252139	813079	124829	50212
104388	49724	74347	36291	116310	59729	240
1243530	499213	655824	528928	717093	26346	13004
537225	313792	248640	164999	653426	39790	17849
210246	141457	81660	53033	287477	14943	11966
154702	101393	53690	33033	206569	9882	7504
464060	177973	181723	128867	350922	29331	20115
535425	227746	311146	222594	439415	21995	6973
728920	557433	191291	114548	223001	17361	6683
185619	109955	108240	57224	284020	16786	14487
2427566	988397	2516999	1389716	4741211	-83060	-257230
3901922	1739978	2411613	1345416	4030239	315742	181433
4016464	1824489	1166386	756878	2167833	291236	173407
46771	16024	29519	23227	26167	627	-413
826802	357486	525831	327407	698549	13588	-4665
1487851	736341	715180	471278	1366647	110741	74764
1410171	681082	854370	538369	965599	71228	30833
10408721	5010180	3666255	2226806	11861738	874979	583904
514977	364086	151480	122825	1554416	58768	15624
1922097	1158958	610042	395144	2948854	166465	121753
2725362	1535775	1098493	696888	2816877	372011	275206
1723126	1109109	591370	348593	1674307	200058	150857
5919278	2909389	2928802	1656294	8504350	1000318	484005
3618604	2323478	1341594	837608	4780291	254862	180163
9881528	6587247	3985808	2091423	20732654	1375449	1184797
722803	431400	234621	148590	1162832	57758	36402
292837	154043	133670	107567	321291	19488	12713
90327	47525	28623	13602	116257	6289	4079
4832931	739301	5566163	2891796	3229612	405735	182830
455968	150035	340274	197907	235724	-3576	-12398
728651	110432	573789	405453	149830	10003	908

11-11 分行业国有大中型工业企业主要经济指标（2006年）
MAIN ECONOMIC INDICATORS OF LARGE AND MEDIUM-SIZED STATE-OWNED ENTERPRISES BY SECTOR, 2006

项 目	Item	企业单位数(个) Number of Enterprises (unit)	从业人员年平均人数(人) Annual Average Employment Personnel (person)	工业总产值(万元) Gross Industrial Output Value (10 000 yuan)
总 计	**Total**	**73**	**142446**	**8037091**
石油和天然气开采业	Extraction of Petroleum and Natural Gas	3	41243	868238
非金属矿采选业	Mining and Processing of Nonmetal Ores	3	9691	77778
农副食品加工业	Processing of Food from Agricultural Products	1	785	26994
食品制造业	Manufacture of Foods	1	431	9804
饮料制造业	Manufacture of Beverages	4	2404	142487
烟草制品业	Manufacture of Tobacco	1	975	114712
纺织业	Manufacture of Textile	1	5481	76591
纺织服装鞋帽制造业	Manufacture of Textile Wearing Apparel, Footware, and Caps	1	590	5260
石油加工炼焦及核燃料加工业	Processing of Petroleum, Coking, Processing of Nuclear Fuel	2	1409	252694
化学原料及化学制品制造业	Manufacture of Raw Chemical Materials and Chemical Products	8	8934	391356
医药制造业	Manufacture of Medicines	2	4595	156132
塑料制品业	Manufacture of Plastics	2	1815	53981
非金属矿物制品业	Manufacture of Non-metallic Mineral Products	2	1216	12479
黑色金属冶炼及压延加工业	Smelting and Pressing of Ferrous Metals	6	22041	3069976
有色金属冶炼及压延加工业	Smelting and Pressing of Non-Ferrous Metals	1	339	6610
金属制品业	Manufacture of Metal Products	4	1777	126856
通用设备制造业	Manufacture of General Purpose Machinery	2	1724	30864
专用设备制造业	Manufacture of Special Purpose Machinery	3	1874	29768
交通运输设备制造业	Manufacture of Transport Equipment	7	8360	234581
电气机械及器材制造业	Manufacture of Electrical Machinery and Equipment	1	1363	12367
通信设备计算机及其他电子设备制造业	Manufacture of Communication Equipment, Computers and Other Electronic Equipment	1	397	39037
仪器仪表及文化、办公用机械制造业	Manufacture of Measuring Instruments and Machinery for Cultural Activity and Office Work	1	605	20241
电力热力的生产和供应	Production and Supply of Electric Power and Heat Power	12	16396	2123563
燃气生产和供应业	Production and Supply of Gas	3	6103	86476
水的生产和供应业	Production and Supply of Water	1	1898	68246

工业增加值(万元) Value Added of Industry (10 000 yuan)	资产总计(万元) Total Assets (10 000 yuan)	流动资产年平均余额(万元) Annual Average Balance of Circulating Funds (10 000 yuan)	固定资产原价(万元) Original Value of Fixed Assets (10 000 yuan)	固定资产净值年平均余额(万元) Annual Average Balance of Net Value of Fixed Assets (10 000 yuan)	主营业务收入(万元) Principal Business Revenue (10 000 yuan)	利税总额(万元) Total Pre-tax Profits (10 000 yuan)	#利润总额 Total Profits
1783962	**14727502**	**5478117**	**8034977**	**4573333**	**10421382**	**810256**	**335340**
143810	1525690	783622	905826	484329	921187	34282	-21916
49452	319649	127790	147237	84194	75657	13620	575
3748	18168	11510	10699	7074	29589	355	138
3151	12681	6058	4365	2456	8673	438	29
38227	85679	43163	57165	32081	132872	16661	4251
74611	104388	49724	74347	36291	116310	59729	240
12850	326281	95501	86178	158198	73520	1615	184
694	4853	1884	1743	541	5051	134	-4
25845	185017	72475	106601	87754	260848	5952	2604
75389	663633	263756	389866	220985	443168	-5799	-14131
6159	1144278	481327	217585	159423	394595	57669	44342
3227	170736	25947	42057	33681	55719	-1202	-1304
1264	26851	8816	20978	19085	12211	-2299	-2521
664913	5853396	2502453	1961589	1173878	4865282	453019	295940
2040	42918	32831	3635	2876	62036	1630	1358
2608	131059	88233	23108	14866	199057	-2366	-3328
8330	45644	19895	31312	12226	29046	2290	365
9916	51436	34328	34622	15403	35336	1124	195
58128	439022	292263	151017	56717	217031	10066	2645
7012	23194	11063	12214	8569	15026	1535	741
2801	33478	9299	21007	13155	40690	578	300
6167	33895	22604	10409	6863	18732	3239	2555
522823	2625807	330625	3043217	1513158	2142218	169273	45155
15855	385992	123718	278988	158440	197963	-6443	-13821
44944	473758	39233	399213	271092	69566	-4845	-9252

11-12 各区县工业企业主要指标（2006年）
MAIN INDICATORS OF INDUSTRIAL ENTERPRISES BY DISTRICT AND COUNTY, 2006

单位：亿元 (100 million yuan)

地 区	Region	企业单位数（个）Number of Enterprises (unit)	资产总计 Total Assets	固定资产原价 Original Value of Fixed Assets	固定资产净值年平均余额 Annual Average Balance of Net Value of Fixed Assets	流动资产年平均余额 Annual Average Balance of Circulating Funds
全市总计	Total	6301	7129.02	4240.28	2308.49	3425.59
和平区	Heping District	70	200.40	124.67	70.44	70.93
河东区	Hedong District	160	530.65	124.32	75.97	240.82
河西区	Hexi District	222	395.76	121.71	64.76	220.68
南开区	Nankai District	392	204.37	73.96	43.76	106.36
河北区	Hebei District	172	292.61	248.95	146.59	67.80
红桥区	Hongqiao District	90	41.78	16.28	9.44	22.72
塘沽区	Tanggu District	623	1744.87	1158.15	563.17	927.00
汉沽区	Han'gu District	125	84.56	57.96	33.06	33.27
大港区	Dagang District	240	602.34	697.87	324.78	224.78
东丽区	Dongli District	549	595.03	355.87	217.01	231.05
西青区	Xiqing District	962	972.53	525.83	304.22	508.49
津南区	Jinnan District	549	225.31	94.59	66.56	128.97
北辰区	Beichen District	624	594.55	211.01	134.50	347.48
武清区	Wuqing District	478	248.14	169.90	96.77	126.08
宝坻区	Baodi District	370	67.89	39.45	30.56	31.95
宁河县	Ninghe County	167	56.92	29.71	18.15	31.22
静海县	Jinghai County	333	172.80	68.46	37.57	83.90
蓟 县	Jixian County	175	98.51	121.60	71.19	22.09

地 区	Region	主营业务收入 Principal Business Revenue	主营业务税金及附加 Sales Tax and Extra Charge of Principal Business	利税总额 Total Pre-tax Profits	#利润总额 Total Profits	工业总产值 Gross Industrial Output Value	工业增加值 Value Added of Industry
全市总计	Total	8794.35	89.68	1003.39	693.00	8527.70	2443.84
和平区	Heping District	127.02	0.56	10.08	3.59	216.45	124.22
河东区	Hedong District	298.27	0.86	20.37	12.72	237.92	38.56
河西区	Hexi District	350.92	0.67	21.75	13.97	275.95	106.36
南开区	Nankai District	171.05	0.44	16.78	9.91	150.75	45.04
河北区	Hebei District	232.11	0.94	15.78	5.13	225.02	49.98
红桥区	Hongqiao District	33.26	0.38	3.85	2.45	27.15	7.05
塘沽区	Tanggu District	2857.03	53.21	499.07	386.45	2788.94	911.53
汉沽区	Han'gu District	80.52	0.42	5.73	2.26	78.69	19.97
大港区	Dagang District	769.13	13.91	108.64	64.44	775.24	208.63
东丽区	Dongli District	574.90	6.46	63.92	35.63	527.80	143.48
西青区	Xiqing District	1450.82	5.05	92.04	61.63	1395.82	316.90
津南区	Jinnan District	324.62	0.76	29.14	20.08	325.32	65.65
北辰区	Beichen District	712.75	3.06	48.34	28.79	650.88	125.39
武清区	Wuqing District	257.97	0.43	21.37	16.31	259.58	71.40
宝坻区	Baodi District	79.64	0.35	5.32	2.45	86.93	26.94
宁河县	Ninghe County	74.78	0.86	5.63	3.47	81.10	15.42
静海县	Jinghai County	328.48	0.28	18.11	13.21	348.19	132.87
蓟 县	Jixian County	71.08	1.05	17.47	10.51	75.99	34.45

11-13 全部国有及规模以上工业企业主要经济效益指标(1990-2006年)
MAIN INDICATORS ON ECONOMIC BENEFIT OF ALL STATE-OWNED AND DESIGNATED SIZE INDUSTRIAL ENTERPRISES, 1990-2006

年 份 Year	产销率(%) Sales Ratio (%)	资金利税率 (%) Ratio of Pre-tax Profits to Total Assets(%)	总资产贡献率 (%) Ratio of Total Assets to Industrial Output Value (%)	成本费用利润率(%) Ratio of Profits to Industrial Cost(%)	万元产值耗能源 (现价、吨标准煤) Energy Consumption per 10 000 yuan Output Value (tons of SCE)	工 业 增加值率(%) Ratio of Value Added to Gross Industrial Output Value (%)	全员劳动生产率 (元/人) Overall Labor Productivity (yuan/person)
全市合计 Total							
1990	88.8	10.7			1.99		
1991	93.1	9.6			1.65	22.5	8574
1992	92.7	9.2			1.44	22.7	9864
1993	97.6	9.6	9.1	3.5	1.12	20.8	11814
1994	85.2	9.3			0.94	20.9	15214
1995	86.4	8.8	9.6	4.5	0.91	21.9	20084
1996	91.6	7.2	8.3	5.0	0.83	21.3	20993
1997	96.4	6.0	7.1	3.7	0.69	20.4	23073
1998	97.9	5.6	6.6	2.9	0.66	20.1	29055
1999	98.6	6.0	6.5	3.6	0.58	20.7	35730
2000	98.4	9.0	8.9	6.5	0.58	24.2	52425
2001	96.7	9.5	9.3	6.6	0.55	24.8	59605
2002	99.1	9.0	8.7	5.8	0.53	25.4	69728
2003	98.9	10.6	9.9	6.0	0.48	26.5	93235
2004	99.0	12.8	12.8	7.5	0.39	26.1	124367
2005	100.6	15.6	14.5	8.5	0.38	27.1	150260
2006	99.2	17.5	15.9	8.7	0.34	28.7	210084
# 国有经济 State-owned							
1990	92.1	10.7					
1991	97.6	7.3				22.9	10126
1992	98.2	7.9				23.2	11371
1993	100.8	6.7	7.0	0.7		20.3	10813
1994	97.9	6.3				23.0	15910
1995	107.5	5.6	6.5	0.5		27.3	20536
1996	98.2	3.3	5.0	0.3		27.3	18365
1997	95.8	3.2	4.7			25.0	19587
1998	99.2	2.2	4.1			25.8	21340
1999	101.0	1.9	3.2			28.4	26743
2000	100.0	1.3	1.3			28.0	32545
2001	99.0	1.3	2.4			23.2	29470
2002	100.5	1.7	2.4			22.5	32058
2003	100.2	4.1	4.2	1.6		28.9	56402
2004	101.0	3.5	3.3	0.4		28.0	85329
2005	102.0	4.3	3.7	1.5		22.3	80057
2006	99.9	6.6	7.1	2.6		28.7	152738

11-14 全部国有及规模以上工业企业主要经济效益指标（2006年）
MAIN INDICATORS ON ECONOMIC BENEFIT OF ALL STATE-OWNED AND ABOVE DESIGNATED SIZE INDUSTRIAL ENTERPRISES, 2006

项 目	Item	单 位	Unit	全 市 Total	#地 方 Local
全 市	Total				
总资产贡献率	Ratio of Total Assets to Industrial Output Value	%		15.9	10.7
增加值率	Ratio of Value Added to Gross Industrial Output Value	%		28.7	25.7
全员劳动生产率	Overall Labor Productivity	元/人	yuan/person	210084	172455
流动资产周转次	Number of Times of Turnover of Circulating Funds	次	times	2.6	2.4
亏损企业个数	Number of Loss-suffering Enterprises	个	unit	1439	1419
亏损企业亏损额	Total Loss of Loss-suffering Enterprises	亿元	100 million yuan	91.11	55.84
国有及国有控股经济	State-owned and State-holding				
总资产贡献率	Ratio of Total Assets to Industrial Output Value	%		21.7	10.0
增加值率	Ratio of Value Added to Gross Industrial Output Value	%		34.5	28.0
全员劳动生产率	Overall Labor Productivity	元/人	yuan/person	308624	202213
流动资产周转次	Number of Times of Turnover of Circulating Funds	次	times	2.6	2.0
亏损企业个数	Number of Loss-suffering Enterprises	个	unit	502	483
亏损企业亏损额	Total Loss of Loss-suffering Enterprises	亿元	100 million yuan	53.44	18.20
国有经济	State-owned				
总资产贡献率	Ratio of Total Assets to Industrial Output Value	%		7.1	6.9
增加值率	Ratio of Value Added to Gross Industrial Output Value	%		28.7	32.1
全员劳动生产率	Overall Labor Productivity	元/人	yuan/person	152738	174373
流动资产周转次	Number of Times of Turnover of Circulating Funds	次	times	1.7	1.5
亏损企业个数	Number of Loss-suffering Enterprises	个	unit	368	354
亏损企业亏损额	Total Loss of Loss-suffering Enterprises	亿元	100 million yuan	16.65	10.27
集体经济	Collective-owned				
总资产贡献率	Ratio of Total Assets to Industrial Output Value	%		8.3	8.3
增加值率	Ratio of Value Added to Gross Industrial Output Value	%		21.6	21.6
全员劳动生产率	Overall Labor Productivity	元/人	yuan/person	65823	65808
流动资产周转次	Number of Times of Turnover of Circulating Funds	次	times	2.4	2.4
亏损企业个数	Number of Loss-suffering Enterprises	个	unit	103	103
亏损企业亏损额	Total Loss of Loss-suffering Enterprises	亿元	100 million yuan	1.22	1.22
"三资" 经济	Foreign, Hong Kong, Macao and Taiwan Funded				
总资产贡献率	Ratio of Total Assets to Industrial Output Value	%		13.2	13.1
增加值率	Ratio of Value Added to Gross Industrial Output Value	%		23.9	23.9
全员劳动生产率	Overall Labor Productivity	元/人	yuan/person	229944	229952
流动资产周转次	Number of Times of Turnover of Circulating Funds	次	times	2.7	2.7
亏损企业个数	Number of Loss-suffering Enterprises	个	unit	491	491
亏损企业亏损额	Total Loss of Loss-suffering Enterprises	亿元	100 million yuan	31.41	31.41
股份制经济	Share-holding				
总资产贡献率	Ratio of Total Assets to Industrial Output Value	%		31.0	8.5
增加值率	Ratio of Value Added to Gross Industrial Output Value	%		40.5	29.6
全员劳动生产率	Overall Labor Productivity	元/人	yuan/person	348907	147247
流动资产周转次	Number of Times of Turnover of Circulating Funds	次	times	3.0	1.9
亏损企业个数	Number of Loss-suffering Enterprises	个	unit	202	196
亏损企业亏损额	Total Loss of Loss-suffering Enterprises	亿元	100 million yuan	37.73	8.83

11-15 国有及国有控股大中型工业企业主要经济指标
MAIN ECONOMIC INDICATORS OF LARGE & MEDIUM-SIZED STATE-OWNED AND STATE-HOLDING ENTERPRISES

单位：亿元 (100 million yuan)

指 标	Item	全市工业 Total	国有及国有控股大中型 Large & Medium-sized State-owned and State-holding 绝对数 Number	占全市比重(%) As Percentage of Whole Industry (%)
2005 年				
企业单位数(个)	Number of Enterprises (unit)	6144	174	2.8
从业人员年平均人数(万人)	Annual Average Employment Personnel (10 000 persons)	122.21	29.49	24.1
工业总产值	Gross Industrial Output Value	6774.10	2312.13	34.1
工业增加值	Value Added of Industry	1836.30	780.37	42.5
资产总计	Total Assets	6347.92	2539.74	40.0
# 流动资产年平均余额	Annual Average Balance of Circulating Funds	3058.69	911.52	29.8
固定资产净值年平均余额	Annual Average Balance of Net Value of Fixed Assets	2155.41	1104.77	51.3
主营业务收入	Principal Business Revenue	7125.93	2401.95	33.7
# 主营业务成本	Cost of Principal Business	6039.33	1959.80	32.5
主营业务税金及附加	Tax and Extra Charges of Principal Business	77.74	55.50	71.4
利税总额	Total Pre-tax Profits	815.63	403.74	49.5
总资产贡献率(%)	Ratio of Total Assets to Industrial Output Value (%)	14.5	18.5	
全员劳动生产率(元/人)	Overall Labor Productivity (yuan/person)	150260	264587	
亏损企业个数(个)	Number of Loss-suffering Enterprises (unit)	1599	39	2.4
亏损企业亏损额	Total Loss of Loss-suffering Enterprises	74.49	30.86	41.4
2006 年				
企业单位数(个)	Number of Enterprises (unit)	6301	179	2.8
从业人员年平均人数(万人)	Annual Average Employment Personnel (10 000 persons)	116.33	29.99	25.8
工业总产值	Gross Industrial Output Value	8527.70	2999.98	35.2
工业增加值	Value Added of Industry	2443.84	1006.84	41.2
资产总计	Total Assets	7129.02	3079.85	43.2
# 流动资产年平均余额	Annual Average Balance of Circulating Funds	3425.59	1116.80	32.6
固定资产净值年平均余额	Annual Average Balance of Net Value of Fixed Assets	2308.49	1208.12	52.3
主营业务收入	Principal Business Revenue	8794.35	3171.00	36.1
# 主营业务成本	Cost of Principal Business	7400.42	2542.41	34.4
主营业务税金及附加	Tax and Extra Charges of Principal Business	89.68	80.14	89.4
利税总额	Total Pre-tax Profits	1003.39	587.64	58.6
总资产贡献率(%)	Ratio of Total Assets to Industrial Output Value (%)	15.9	24.3	
全员劳动生产率(元/人)	Overall Labor Productivity (yuan/person)	210084	335771	
亏损企业个数(个)	Number of Loss-suffering Enterprises (unit)	1439	47	3.3
亏损企业亏损额	Total Loss of Loss-suffering Enterprises	91.11	42.39	46.5

11-16 大中型工业企业主要经济指标及占全市比重
MAIN ECONOMIC INDICATORS OF LARGE & MEDIUM-SIZED INDUSTRIAL ENTERPRISES AND AS PERCENTAGE OF WHOLE INDUSTRY

单位：亿元 (100 million yuan)

指　　标	Item	大中型 Large & Medium-sized		#国有大中型 State-owned	
		绝对数 Number	占全市比重(%) As Percentage of Whole Industry (%)	绝对数 Number	占全市比重(%) As Percentage of Whole Industry (%)
2005年					
企业单位数(个)	Number of Enterprises (unit)	549	8.9	73	1.2
从业人员年平均人数(万人)	Annual Average Employment Personnel (10 000 persons)	64.58	52.8	14.08	11.5
工业总产值	Gross Industrial Output Value	4991.10	73.7	646.61	9.5
工业增加值	Value Added of Industry	1372.29	74.7	145.27	7.9
资产总计	Total Assets	4360.80	68.7	1131.19	17.8
#流动资产年平均余额	Annual Average Balance of Circulating Funds	2033.32	66.5	418.34	13.7
固定资产净值年平均余额	Annual Average Balance of Net Value of Fixed Assets	1578.83	73.2	413.66	19.2
主营业务收入	Principal Business Revenue	5233.00	73.4	742.93	10.4
#主营业务成本	Cost of Principal Business	4384.02	72.6	676.81	11.2
主营业务税金及附加	Tax and Extra Charges of Principal Business	64.83	83.4	8.35	10.7
利税总额	Total Pre-tax Profits	667.48	81.8	51.61	6.3
总资产贡献率(%)	Ratio of Total Assets to Industrial Output Value (%)	17.8		5.8	
全员劳动生产率(元/人)	Overall Labor Productivity (yuan/person)	212499		103204	
亏损企业个数(个)	Number of Loss-suffering Enterprises (unit)	94	5.9	25	1.6
亏损企业亏损额	Total Loss of Loss-suffering Enterprises	45.79	61.5	6.50	8.7
2006年					
企业单位数(个)	Number of Enterprises (unit)	562	8.9	73	1.2
从业人员年平均人数(万人)	Annual Average Employment Personnel (10 000 persons)	66.03	56.8	14.24	12.2
工业总产值	Gross Industrial Output Value	6332.65	74.3	803.71	9.4
工业增加值	Value Added of Industry	1811.64	74.1	178.40	7.3
资产总计	Total Assets	5142.83	72.1	1472.75	20.7
#流动资产年平均余额	Annual Average Balance of Circulating Funds	2360.46	68.9	547.81	16.0
固定资产净值年平均余额	Annual Average Balance of Net Value of Fixed Assets	1734.36	75.1	457.33	19.8
主营业务收入	Principal Business Revenue	6703.59	76.2	1042.14	11.9
#主营业务成本	Cost of Principal Business	5565.91	75.2	953.00	12.9
主营业务税金及附加	Tax and Extra Charges of Principal Business	84.30	94.0	10.03	11.2
利税总额	Total Pre-tax Profits	859.24	85.6	81.03	8.1
总资产贡献率(%)	Ratio of Total Assets to Industrial Output Value (%)	18.7		8.5	
全员劳动生产率(元/人)	Overall Labor Productivity (yuan/person)	274363		125238	
亏损企业个数(个)	Number of Loss-suffering Enterprises (unit)	112	7.8	27	1.9
亏损企业亏损额	Total Loss of Loss-suffering Enterprises	57.76	63.4	9.70	10.6

11-17 主要工业集团（总公司）部分经济指标（2006年）
PARTIAL ECONOMIC INDICATORS OF MAIN INDUSTRIAL GROUP CORPORATION, 2006

单位：万元 (10 000 yuan)

集团名称 Name of Group Corporation	企业单位数(个) Number of Enterprises (unit)	资产总计 Total Assets	固定资产原价 Original Value of Fixed Assets	固定资产值年平均余额 Annual Average Balance of Net Value of Fixed Assets	流动资产年平均余额 Annual Average Balance of Circulating Funds	主营业务收入 Principal Business Revenue
冶金集团(控股)有限公司 Tianjin Metallurgical Group (Holding) Corporation	43	2065802	490192	288251	1084911	2181011
渤海化工集团公司 Tianjin Bohai Chemical Industry Group Corporation	213	2592124	1720402	871421	863819	2131984
机电工业控股集团公司 Tianjin Machinery & Electric Industry Holding Group Company	157	1929159	724153	414925	1107743	2134372
中环电子信息集团有限公司 Tianjin Zhonghuan Electronics & Information Group	151	3165700	1388775	659526	1920853	7560416
纺织集团(控股)有限公司 Tianjin Textile Industrial General Corporation	347	1333377	627280	544942	452749	411000
一轻集团(控股)有限公司 The First Light Industry Group (Holding) Co., Ltd.	222	1380516	530571	322348	734082	1330506
二轻集团(控股)有限公司 The Second Light Industry Group (Holding) Co., Ltd.	196	1108833	465115	268496	661503	1387814
医药集团有限公司 Tianjin Pharmaceutical Holdings	49	943770	389159	226558	426119	679625
建筑材料集团(控股)有限公司 Tianjin Building Materials Group (Holding) Co., Ltd.	32	433563	341578	197857	207445	200834
汽车工业(集团)有限公司 Tianjin Automobile Industry Group Co., Ltd.	38	2802737	1442865	742604	1364347	5256984
飞鸽集团有限公司 Tianjin Flying Pigeon Group Co., Ltd.	46	106752	37091	23421	52959	61703
钢管集团有限公司 Tianjin Pipe Group Co., Ltd	27	2564355	1741400	1163339	827352	2820474
有色金属集团有限公司 Tianjin Non-ferrous Metals Group Co., Ltd.	21	198794	36777	19119	138767	454540
天铁冶金集团有限公司 Tianjin Tian Tie Metallurgical Group Co., Ltd.	10	1707738	836510	457077	848024	2316251
塑料集团 Tianjin Plastics Group	12	195286	55881	53174	38809	69785

11-17 续表 Continued

单位：万元 (10 000 yuan)

集团名称 Name of Group Corporation	主营业务税金及附加 Tax and Extra Charge of Principal Business	利税总额 Total Pre-tax Profits	利润总额 Total Profits	工业总产值 Gross Industrial Output Value	工业总产值比上年增长(%) Increase Rate of Gross Industrial Output Value Over Preceding Year (%)	工业增加值 Value Added of Industry
冶金集团(控股)有限公司 Tianjin Metallurgical Group (Holding) Corporation	2399	47860	20628	1532128	20.0	91123
渤海化工集团公司 Tianjin Bohai Chemical Industry Group Corporation	9634	99325	26666	2094990	15.6	431204
机电工业控股集团公司 Tianjin Machinery & Electric Industry Holding Group Company	3527	197430	125547	1898343	20.3	364683
中环电子信息集团有限公司 Tianjin Zhonghuan Electronics & Information Group	1731	458923	361896	7395772	20.0	1104175
纺织集团(控股)有限公司 Tianjin Textile Industrial General Corporation	929	13927	4679	402377	6.0	86659
一轻集团(控股)有限公司 The First Light Industry Group (Holding) Co., Ltd.	8344	91764	54762	1156658	44.1	183823
二轻集团(控股)有限公司 The Second Light Industry Group (Holding) Co., Ltd.	262	8149	2040	1349332	12.3	132610
医药集团有限公司 Tianjin Pharmaceutical Holdings	2261	91880	33213	527680	4.5	214996
建筑材料集团(控股)有限公司 Tianjin Building Materials Group (Holding) Co., Ltd.	919	2019	-8348	232479	10.1	42072
汽车工业(集团)有限公司 Tianjin Automobile Industry Group Co., Ltd.	272889	732737	308640	5128360	48.8	753832
飞鸽集团有限公司 Tianjin Flying Pigeon Group Co., Ltd.	39	1386	460	69688	20.3	7030
钢管集团有限公司 Tianjin Pipe Group Co.,Ltd	9971	388199	261736	2005369	32.6	369768
有色金属集团有限公司 Tianjin Non-ferrous Metals Group Co., Ltd.	182	15069	5564	412560	61.9	70657
天铁冶金集团有限公司 Tianjin Tian Tie Metallurgical Group Co., Ltd.	6180	124642	58286	1955095	11.0	270473
塑料集团 Tianjin Plastics Group	88	-496	-1220	69037	-2.5	8951

11-18 高新技术产业主要经济指标
MAIN ECONOMIC INDICATORS OF HIGH & NEW TECHNOLOGY INDUSTRY

单位：亿元 (100 million yuan)

项　目 Item	工业总产值 Gross Industrial Output Value		主营业务收入 Principal Business Revenue		利税总额 Total Pre-tax Profits	
	2005	2006	2005	2006	2005	2006
全市总计 Total	**2141.37**	**2713.01**	**2238.35**	**2802.67**	**214.30**	**218.70**
按企业规模分 Grouped by Size of Enterprises						
大型企业 Large-sized	943.19	1235.24	1045.52	1316.25	124.05	108.07
中型企业 Medium-sized	917.35	1186.62	885.18	1190.10	67.05	89.80
小型企业 Small-sized	280.83	291.15	307.65	296.32	23.20	20.83
按经济类型分 Grouped by Ownership						
国有经济 State-owned	21.64	18.03	39.59	17.54	3.43	1.39
集体经济 Collective-owned	14.06	13.71	34.25	13.63	3.03	1.07
私有经济 Private and Individual	10.53	40.35	26.64	39.54	3.74	3.99
外商及港澳台商投资经济 Foreign, Hong Kong, Macao and Taiwan Funded	1850.20	2395.78	1935.18	2435.67	180.25	183.61
其他经济 Others	244.94	245.14	202.69	296.29	23.85	28.64
按技术领域分 Grouped by Technical Field						
电子信息 Electronics and Information	1682.37	2149.35	1728.45	2182.54	157.13	149.04
航空航天 Aviation and Spaceflight	2.20	3.47	2.30	3.22	0.51	0.81
光机电一体化 Photoeletric Mechanical Electron Incorporated	172.86	235.91	177.85	252.96	16.77	27.52
生物技术和医药 Biology Technology and Pharmaceutical	163.85	167.65	207.25	209.40	33.52	31.60
新材料 New Materials	61.44	81.78	64.74	82.67	2.35	4.95
新能源和节能材料 New Energy and Energy Saving Materials	58.41	74.15	57.54	71.13	4.00	4.71
环境保护 Environmental Protection	0.24	0.70	0.22	0.75	0.02	0.07

11-19 电子信息产品制造业主要经济指标（2006年）
MAIN ECONOMIC INDICATORS OF ELECTRONIC AND INFORMATION PRODUCTS MANUFACTURING, 2006

单位：亿元 (100 million yuan)

项　目 Item	工业总产值 Gross Industrial Output Value	主营业务收入 Principal Business Revenue	利税总额 Total Pre-tax Profits
全市总计 Total	**2333.33**	**2368.07**	**159.31**
按企业规模分 Grouped by Size of Enterprises			
大型企业 Large-sized	1221.20	1245.20	95.27
中型企业 Medium-sized	883.67	880.98	49.85
小型企业 Small-sized	228.46	241.89	14.19
按经济类型分 Grouped by Ownership			
国有经济 State-owned	8.81	9.65	-0.85
集体经济 Collective-owned	12.28	18.59	1.33
私有经济 Private and Individual	27.99	30.55	2.05
外商及港澳台商投资经济 Foreign, Hong Kong, Macao and Taiwan Funded	2130.56	2158.73	144.20
其他经济 Others	153.69	150.55	12.58
按行业分 Grouped by Sector			
雷达业 Radar	0.03	0.19	-0.18
通信设备业 Telecommunications Equipment	1154.42	1182.82	93.98
广播电视设备业 Equipment of Radio and Television	3.02	2.88	0.05
电子计算机业 Electronic Computer	135.93	131.04	4.68
家电业 Home Appliances	98.18	102.28	14.01
电子测量仪器业 Instruments of Electronic Survey	4.91	5.04	0.34
电子工业专用设备业 Industrial Electronic Equipment for Special Use	32.70	40.67	4.89
电子元件业 Electronic Element	472.41	458.77	24.32
电子器件业 Electronic Implements	220.96	226.27	4.07
电子信息机电产品业 Machinery & Electric Products	206.34	214.07	10.86
电子信息专用材料业 Electronic and Information Materials for Special Use	4.31	4.02	0.99

11-20 主营业务收入百强工业企业（2006年） TOP 100 INDUSTRIAL ENTERPRISES ON BUSINESS REVENUE, 2006

名 次 Position	企业名称 Name of Enterprises	名 次 Position	企业名称 Name of Enterprises
1	摩托罗拉（中国）电子有限公司	51	天津三美电机有限公司
2	中海石油（中国）有限公司天津分公司	52	鹏思特(天津)实业有限公司
3	天津一汽丰田汽车有限公司	53	天津荣程祥矿产有限公司
4	天津三星通信技术有限公司	54	天津中集北洋集装箱有限公司
5	中国石油化工股份有限公司天津分公司	55	天津乐金大沽化学有限公司
6	天津天钢集团有限公司	56	天津大唐国际盘山发电有限责任公司
7	天津市电力公司	57	天津英泰汽车饰件有限公司
8	中国石油天然气股份有限公司大港油田公司	58	天津市华北电缆厂
9	天津津亚电子有限公司	59	天津国华盘山发电有限责任公司
10	天津市轧一制钢有限公司	60	天津顶津食品有限公司
11	天津钢管集团有限公司	61	蓝星石化有限公司天津石油化工厂
12	中国石油天然气股份公司大港石化分公司	62	天津顶益国际食品有限公司
13	乐金电子（天津）电器有限公司	63	赫比（天津）电子有限公司
14	飞思卡尔半导体（中国）有限公司	64	天津市轧三金属材料科技有限公司
15	天津三星电子显示器有限公司	65	天津市万达轮胎集团有限公司
16	天津天铁冶金集团有限公司	66	亚光耐普罗精密注塑(天津)有限公司
17	大港油田集团有限责任公司	67	天津渤海化工有限公司天津碱厂
18	奥的斯电梯（中国）投资有限公司	68	天津市飞龙制管有限公司
19	天津一汽夏利股份有限公司	69	诺和诺德（中国）制药有限公司
20	天津友发钢管集团有限公司	70	SEW-传动设备（天津）有限公司
21	天津市荣程联合钢铁集团有限公司	71	天津电装电子有限公司
22	天津新利钢铁有限公司	72	天津市力神电池股份有限公司
23	天津三星光电子有限公司	73	罗姆半导体（中国）有限公司
24	天津大沽化工股份有限公司	74	天津大桥焊材集团有限公司
25	天津三星电子有限公司	75	大成万达（天津）有限公司
26	天津塑力线缆集团有限公司	76	中国石化集团天津石油化工公司
27	中金黄金股份有限公司	77	天津军粮城发电有限公司
28	天津天士力集团有限公司	78	天津丰津汽车传动部件有限公司
29	天津金耀集团有限公司	79	天津市轧一岐丰制钢有限公司
30	天津通广三星电子有限公司	80	天津新港船厂
31	天津市天铁轧二制钢有限公司	81	天津市冷轧薄板厂
32	天津三星视界有限公司	82	西门子电气传动有限公司
33	天津三星视界移动有限公司	83	PPG涂料（天津）有限公司
34	天津大通铜业有限公司	84	天津市燃气集团有限公司
35	天津大无缝铜材有限公司	85	天津市东益钢铁有限公司
36	天津渤天化工有限责任公司	86	天津利金粮油股份有限公司
37	三星高新电机(天津)有限公司	87	天津里碑冷轧板材有限公司
38	天津丰田发动机有限公司	88	天津俊安煤焦化工有限公司
39	天津中新药业集团股份有限公司	89	天津市达亿钢铁有限公司
40	天津市静海县宝来工贸有限公司	90	中法合营王朝葡萄酿酒有限公司
41	天津市金桥焊材集团有限公司	91	天津三洋通信设备有限公司
42	日新（天津）塑胶有限公司	92	天津丰田合成有限公司
43	俊安（天津）实业有限公司	93	壳牌（天津）石油化工有限公司
44	天津富士通天电子有限公司	94	天津天铁炼焦化工有限公司
45	天津钢管还原铁厂	95	天津富士达自行车有限公司
46	富士能（天津）光学有限公司	96	上海烟草集团公司天津卷烟厂
47	天津惠鑫大豆科技开发有限公司	97	天津可口可乐饮料有限公司
48	嘉里粮油（天津）有限公司	98	天津市无缝钢管厂
49	天津三星电机有限公司	99	天津矢崎汽车配件有限公司
50	北海粮油工业（天津）有限公司	100	天津津住汽车线束有限公司

11-21 实现利税百强工业企业（2006年）
TOP 100 INDUSTRIAL ENTERPRISES ON TOTAL PRE-TAX PROFITS, 2006

名 次 Position	企业名称 Name of Enterprises	名 次 Position	企业名称 Name of Enterprises
1	中海石油（中国）有限公司天津分公司	51	天津华丰汽车装饰有限公司
2	中国石油天然气股份有限公司大港油田公司	52	天津渤天化工有限责任公司
3	摩托罗拉（中国）电子有限公司	53	喜来健医疗器械有限公司
4	天津一汽丰田汽车有限公司	54	天津军粮城发电有限公司
5	天津钢管集团有限公司	55	诺和诺德（中国）制药有限公司
6	天津市电力公司	56	天津华能杨柳青热电有限责任公司
7	奥的斯电梯（中国）投资有限公司	57	中金黄金股份有限公司
8	天津三星通信技术有限公司	58	天津中集北洋集装箱有限公司
9	天津天铁冶金集团有限公司	59	天津大港广安津能发电有限责任公司
10	天津天钢集团有限公司	60	西门子电气传动有限公司
11	天津一汽夏利股份有限公司	61	丹佛斯（天津）有限公司
12	天津通广三星电子有限公司	62	因塔思天津电子有限公司
13	天津大唐国际盘山发电有限责任公司	63	天津力生制药股份有限公司
14	天津国华盘山发电有限责任公司	64	天津赛象电气自动化技术有限公司
15	天津市荣程联合钢铁集团有限公司	65	赫比（天津）电子有限公司
16	天津天士力集团有限公司	66	天津大通铜业有限公司
17	上海烟草集团公司天津卷烟厂	67	天津三星光电子有限公司
18	大港油田集团有限责任公司	68	世讯工业（天津）有限公司
19	天津金耀集团有限公司	69	约翰迪尔天拖有限公司
20	天津三星电子有限公司	70	天津天管特钻具有限公司
21	天津荣程祥矿产有限公司	71	天津富奥电装空调有限公司
22	天津市轧一制钢有限公司	72	斯必克冷却技术（天津）有限公司
23	中法合营王朝葡萄酿酒有限公司	73	天津三星电机有限公司
24	飞思卡尔半导体（中国）有限公司	74	天津新伟祥工业有限公司
25	天津友发钢管集团有限公司	75	飞比达电子元器件（天津）有限公司
26	天津津亚电子有限公司	76	天津阿尔斯通水电设备有限公司
27	天津大沽化工股份有限公司	77	天津三星视界有限公司
28	中美天津史克制药有限公司	78	SEW-工业减速机（天津）有限公司
29	SEW-传动设备（天津）有限公司	79	天津三五汽车部件有限公司
30	天津英泰汽车饰件有限公司	80	天津丰铁汽车部件有限公司
31	施耐德电气低压（天津）有限公司	81	天津津住汽车线束有限公司
32	天津三星电子显示器有限公司	82	天津东海理化汽车部件有限公司
33	天津丰田发动机有限公司	83	天津可口可乐饮料有限公司
34	天津市力神电池股份有限公司	84	天津双协机械工业有限公司
35	日新（天津）塑胶有限公司	85	罗姆半导体（中国）有限公司
36	天津天狮生物发展有限公司	86	天津顶益国际食品有限公司
37	天津市静海县宝来工贸有限公司	87	亚实履带（天津）有限公司
38	天津电装电子有限公司	88	中国大冢制药有限公司
39	爱信（天津）车身零部件有限公司	89	天津塑力线缆集团有限公司
40	诺维信（中国）生物技术有限公司	90	申克（天津）矿业设备有限公司
41	阿克苏诺贝尔涂料（天津）有限公司	91	天津三星视界移动有限公司
42	天津悦泰石化科技有限公司	92	博福-益普生（天津）制药有限公司
43	天津丰田合成有限公司	93	天津赛瑞机器设备有限公司
44	三星高新电机（天津）有限公司	94	天津南玻工程玻璃有限公司
45	PPG涂料（天津）有限公司	95	洛伊热工工程（天津）有限公司
46	天津新利钢铁有限公司	96	天津市中环半导体股份有限公司
47	亚光耐普罗精密注塑(天津)有限公司	97	天津双叶协展机械有限公司
48	天津顶津食品有限公司	98	天津市环欧半导体材料技术有限公司
49	天津市金桥焊材集团有限公司	99	埃克森美孚（天津）石油有限公司
50	天津大港华实发电有限责任公司	100	天津南辰钢铁有限公司

主要统计指标解释

工业总产值 是以货币表现的工业企业在报告期内生产的工业产品总量。它是反映一定时间内工业生产总规模和总水平的重要指标。工业总产值采用"工厂法"计算。1995年全国第三次工业普查对工业总产值的范围和计算方法作出新规定。工业总产值包括本年生产成品价值，对外加工费收入，自制半成品、在产品期末期初差额价值。新规定与原规定的变化：一是对工业产值中凡自备原材料，不论其加工繁简程度如何，一律按全价计算产值。凡来料加工，一律按加工费计算总产值；二是自制半成品、在产品期末期初差额价值的计算改变了生产周期六个月以上的原则，而以当期会计是否将其计入成本核算作为是否计入产值的依据；三是现价产值按不含增值税的价格计算。1995年以后各年工业总产值均是按新规定计算的。

规模以上工业企业 包括全部国有(含国有联营、国有独资)工业企业和年主营业务收入在500万元及以上的非国有工业企业。

工业行业类别 根据新颁布的行业分类标准《国民经济行业分类》GB/T 4754-2002)"工业"包括"采矿业"、"制造业"和"电力、燃气及水的生产和供应业"三个门类。

轻工业 一般指提供生活消费品和制作手工工具的工业。

重工业 一般指生产生产资料为国民经济各部门提供物质技术基础的工业。

大、中、小型企业 根据2003年国家统计局制定的《统计上大中小型企业划分办法(暂行)》，以从业人员数、销售额和资产总额三项指标为依据，将工业企业划分为大、中、小型，而不再按照企业产品的年生产能力和生产用固定资产原值划分。划分标准如下：

指标名称	单位	大型	中型	小型
从业人员数	人	2000及以上	300-2000以下	300以下
销售额	万元	30000及以上	3000-30000以下	3000以下
资产总额	万元	40000及以上	4000-40000以下	4000以下

主营业务收入 指企业在销售商品、提供劳务及让渡资产使用权等日常活动中所发生的收入。

主营业务成本 指企业因销售商品、提供劳务或让渡资产使用权等日常活动而发生的实际成本。

主营业务税金及附加 反映企业经营主营业务应负担的营业税、消费税、城市维护建设税、资源税、土地增值税和教育费附加等。

利润总额 指企业在生产经营过程中各种收入扣除各种耗费后的盈余，反映企业在报告期内实现的亏盈总额，包括营业利润、补贴收入、投资净收益和营业外收支净额。

利税总额 指利润总额、产品销售税金及附加和本期应交增值税之和。

固定资产净值年平均余额 固定资产净值指固定资产原价减去累计折旧后的净额，其平均余额指报告期内余额的平均数。计算公式为：

固定资产净值年平均余额=1至12月各月月初、月末固定资产净值之和/24

或：固定资产净值年平均余额=1至12月各月固定资产净值平均余额/12

总资产贡献率 反映企业全部资产的获利能力，是企业经营业绩和管理水平的集中体现，是评价和考核企业盈利能力的核心指标。计算公式为：

总资产贡献率(%)=[(利润总额+税金总额+利息支出)/平均资金总额]×100%

公式中：税金总额为产品销售税金及附加与应交增值税之和；平均资产总额为期初期末资产之和的算术平均值。

资产负债率 该指标既反映企业经营风险的大小，也反映企业利用债权人提供的资金从事经营活动的能力。计算公式为：

资产负债率(%)=(负债总额/资产总额)×100%

主要统计指标解释

流动资产周转次数 指一定时期内流动资产完成的周转次数，反映投入工业企业流动资金的周转速度。计算公式为:

流动资产周转次数 = 产品销售收入 / 全部流动资产平均余额

公式中：全部流动资产平均余额为期初和期末的流动资产之和的算术平均值。

成本费用利润率 反映企业投入的生产成本及费用的经济效益，同时也反映企业降低成本所取得的经济效益。计算公式为:

成本费用利润（%）=（利润总额 / 成本费用总额）×100%

公式中: 成本费用总额为产品销售成本、销售费用、管理费用、财务费用之和。

全员劳动生产率 该指标反映企业的生产效率和劳动投入的经济效益。计算公式为:

全员劳动生产率（元 / 人）= 工业增加值 / 全部从业人员平均人数

Explanastory Notes on Main Statistical Indicators

Gross Industrial Output Value is the total volume of industrial products sold or available for sale in value terms which reflect the total achievements and overall scale of industrial production during a given period. The gross industrial output value is calculated with "factory method". Data of the gross industrial output value were adjusted in accordance with the 1995 industrial census. It includes the value of the finished products, the value of industrial services rendered to other units, and the changes in the value of the semi-finished products and products in process between the beginning and end of the period. The changes between the new regulation and the old regulation: the first, calculating output value as whole price for ready source materials by themselves, calculating output value as cost for processed with imported materials; the second, the changes producing circulation above six months for the value of the semi-finished products and products in process between the beginning and end of the period, calculating output value in accordance with financial accounting in current period; the third, output value of current price excluded value added tax. It is not comparable with the data before 1995.

Industrial Enterprises above Designated Size refer to all state-owned (including sole state-funded, state-owned joint ownership) industrial enterprises, and other non-state-owned industrial enterprises with annual business revenue of over 5 million yuan.

Industrial Sector Classification According to the new industrial classification of China Industrial Classification by Sector of the National Economy (GB/T4754-2002) in 2003, industry is classified into three categories: minerals mining, manufacturing, production & supply of power, gas & water.

Light Industry refers to the industry that produces consumer goods and hand tools.

Heavy Industry refers to the industry which produces capital goods, and provides various sectors of the national economy with necessary material and technical basis.

Large, Medium, Small-sized Enterprises Industrial enterprises are classified into large, medium, small-sized enterprises according to employment personnel, sales revenue and total assets in accordance with the regulation of Classification (temporary) of Large, Medium, Small-sized Enterprises on Statistics, are not classified according to production capacity and original value of fixed assets. The standard of classification as following:

Indicator	Unit	Large-sized	Medium-sized	Small-sized
Employment personnel	person	2 000 and over	300-2000	below 300
Sales Revenue	10 000 yuan	30000 and over	3000-30000	below 3000
Total assets	10 000 yuan	40000 and over	4000-40000	below 4000

Principal Business Revenue refers to revenues from the sales of products, labor services provided, alienation of using asset right and etc.

Cost of Principal Business refers to real costs from the sales of products, labor services provided, alienation of using asset right and etc.

Tax and Extra Charges of Principal Business refer to the tax and charges including the business tax, consumption tax, city maintenance and construction tax, resources tax, land increasing value tax and extra charges for education and etc.

Total Profits refer to the profits gained from the revenues after deducting the costs, which means the final achievements in the reference period, including business profit, subsidies, net income of investment and net income of other business.

Total Value of Profit and Tax (Pre-tax) refers to the sum of the total net profits, products sales tax & surcharges and the value added tax payable of industrial enterprises, namely pre-tax profits.

Annual Average of Net Value of Fixed Assets Net value of fixed assets refers to the original value of fixed assets minus depreciation over the years. And the annual average of it refers to average of the net value of fixed assets during the reference period.

Annual Average of Net Value of Fixed Assets = sum of net value of fixed assets at the beginning and at the end of each month from January to December / 24;

Or Annual Average of Net Value of Fixed Assets = sum of average of net value of fixed assets of each month from January to December / 12.

Ratio of Total Assets to Industrial Output Value reflects the profit-making capability of all assets of the enterprise and is a key indicator manifesting the performance and management and evaluating the profit-making potential of the enterprise. It is calculated as follows:

Ratio of Total Assets to Industrial Output Value (%) = [(total profits + total taxes + interest payment) / average assets]× 100%

Explanastory Notes on Main Statistical Indicators

In the above formula, total taxes is the sum of tax and extra charges on the sales of products and value-added tax payable; and average assets is the arithmetic mean of the sum of beginning assets and ending assets.

Ratio of Debts to Assets reflect both the operation risk and the capability of the enterprise in making use of the capital from the creditors. It is calculated as follows:
Ratio of Debts to Assets (%) = (total debts / total assets)× 100%

Turnover of Circulating Fands refers to the number of times of turnover of circulating fands in a given period of time, which reflects the speed of the turnover of circulating fands of industrial enterprises, and is calculated as follows:
Turnover of circulating fands=sales revenue of products / average balance of total working capital
In the above formula, average balance of total circulating fands refers to the arithmetic mean of the sum of circulating fands at the beginning and at the end of the reference period.

Ratio of Profits to Total Industrial Costs refers to the ratio of profits realized in a given period to the total costs in the same period, which reflects the economic efficiency of input cost and is calculated as follows:
Ratio of Profits to Total Industrial Cost (%)=(total profits/ total costs)×100%

Total costs in the above formula is the sum of cost of products sold, marketing cost, management cost and financial cost.

Overall Labour Productivity is an indicator reflecting the production efficiency of an enterprise and the economic efficiency of its labour input, calculated by the formula:
Overall Labour Productivity (yuan/person) = industrial value-added / average of all persons engaged

第12篇
CHAPTER 12

建筑业
Construction

12-1 建筑企业基本情况（1990-2006年）
BASIC STATISTICS ON CONSTRUCTION ENTERPRISES, 1990-2006

年 份 Year	企业个数 (个) Number of Enterprises (unit)	从业人员平均人数 (万人) Annual Average Employed Personnel (10 000 persons)	建筑业总产值 (万元) Gross Output Value of Construction (10 000 yuan)	房屋建筑施工面积 (万平方米) Floor Space of Building Under Construction (10 000 sq. m)	房屋建筑竣工面积 (万平方米) Floor Space of Building Completed (10 000 sq. m)	#住 宅 Residential Buildings
1990	82	18.71	317009	675.46	333.60	
1991	83	18.95	361739	582.73	295.41	
1992	96	18.76	484293	721.50	344.70	158.50
1993	237	25.87	826585	1210.94	505.02	270.70
1994	482	36.28	1305160	1359.96	600.15	376.97
1995	693	31.53	1656748	1604.10	640.25	328.40
1996	461	29.06	1735679	1579.53	567.98	285.82
1997	477	29.26	1909999	1752.13	727.61	398.82
1998	500	29.34	2111208	2059.23	868.00	527.98
1999	491	28.71	2227406	2087.01	901.88	637.85
2000	456	27.44	2380991	2253.99	1056.40	658.85
2001	420	25.96	2886808	2140.04	924.92	562.40
2002	925	34.56	4061628	2817.84	1332.10	726.87
2003	900	35.55	5208402	3395.94	1465.75	797.72
2004	1155	38.27	6551996	3547.76	1644.90	758.00
2005	1108	39.10	7543702	3940.56	1484.38	728.58
2006	1103	38.57	9839320	4555.08	1735.58	815.52

12-2 建筑企业主要经济效益指标和工程质量（1990-2006年）
MAIN INDICATORS OF ECONOMIC EFFICIENCY AND ENGINEERING QUALITY OF CONSTRUCTION ENTERPRISES, 1990-2006

年 份 Year	全员劳动生产率 (元/人) Overall Labor Productivity (yuan/person)	平均每一从业人员竣工面积 (平方米) Per Capita Floor Space of Building Completed (sq. m)	产值利润率 (%) Ratio of Profit to Gross Output Value (%)	产值利税率 (%) Ratio of Pre-tax Profit to Gross Output Value (%)	按面积计算竣工率 (%) Percentage of Building Completed in terms of Floor Space (%)
1990	15874	16.7	-0.3	2.7	49.4
1991	17952	14.7	0.8	3.4	50.7
1992	23578	16.8	1.0	3.5	38.2
1993	33126	18.6	2.9	5.5	38.7
1994	36762	16.0	0.5	3.2	42.3
1995	52545	19.6	0.6	3.4	37.2
1996	59724	19.5	1.0	3.6	36.0
1997	65274	24.9	1.1	3.7	41.5
1998	71958	29.6	1.4	3.9	42.2
1999	77583	31.4	1.0	3.6	43.2
2000	86771	38.5	1.1	4.0	46.9
2001	111194	35.6	1.3	4.2	43.2
2002	117536	38.5	1.8	4.7	47.3
2003	146499	41.2	1.9	4.8	43.2
2004	171190	43.0	1.9	4.9	46.4
2005	192931	38.0	2.3	5.3	37.7
2006	255108	45.0	2.6	5.8	38.1

12-3 建筑企业基本情况（2006年）（按登记注册类型和经济类型分）

BASIC STATISTICS ON CONSTRUCTION ENTERPRISES, 2006 (Grouped by Status of Registration and Ownership)

项 目 Item	企业个数（个）Number of Enterprise (unit)		从业人员平均人数（万人）Average Employed Personnel (10 000 persons)		从业人员劳动报酬（万元）Earnings of Employed Personnel (10 000 yuan)		建筑业总产值（万元）Gross Output Value of Construction (10 000 yuan)	
	2005	2006	2005	2006	2005	2006	2005	2006
总 计 Total	1108	1103	39.10	38.57	561648	615132	7543702	9839320
按登记注册类型分 Grouped by Status of Registration								
内资企业 Domestic-funded Enterprises	1070	1067	38.55	38.21	552390	606788	7397444	9673835
国有企业 State-owned Enterprises	131	117	10.22	9.13	206102	135894	2462821	2001217
集体企业 Collective-owned Enterprises	105	88	3.09	2.22	36881	34685	331891	286117
股份合作企业 Cooperative Enterprises	27	9	0.56	0.28	11032	5875	73496	38238
私营企业 Private Enterprises	444	457	4.37	3.72	41279	46123	550388	674745
股份有限公司 Share-holding Corporations Ltd.	34	34	1.21	1.40	26252	39635	426483	652356
有限责任公司 Limited Liability Corporations	300	339	18.52	20.81	222799	337737	3469667	5951438
# 国有独资 Sole State-funded Corporations	8	12	2.16	1.36	22147	46701	364435	1073032
联营企业 Joint Ownership Enterprises	8	8	0.13	0.39	2615	5314	12534	32449
# 国有与国有联营企业 State Joint Ownership Enterprises	1	1	0.01	0.01	96	95	474	1040
集体与集体联营企业 Collective Joint Ownership Enterprises	4	5	0.07	0.38	895	5176	4920	31075
其他内资企业 Other Domestic-funded Enterprises	21	15	0.45	0.26	5430	1525	70164	37275
港澳台商投资企业 Enterprises with Investment from Hong Kong, Macao and Taiwan	20	17	0.24	0.16	6312	2293	79607	44401
外商投资企业 Foreign Funded Enterprises	18	19	0.31	0.20	2946	6051	66651	121084
按经济类型分 Grouped by Ownership								
国有经济 State-owned	140	130	12.38	10.50	228345	182690	2827729	3075289
集体经济 Collective-owned	136	102	3.72	2.88	48807	45736	410307	355430
私有经济 Private and Individual	444	457	4.37	3.72	41279	46123	550388	674745
港澳台商投资经济 Hong Kong, Macao and Taiwan Funded	20	17	0.24	0.16	6312	2293	79607	44401
外商投资经济 Foreign Funded	18	19	0.31	0.20	2947	6051	66651	121084
其 他 Other	350	378	18.08	21.11	233958	332239	3609020	5568371

12-3 续表 Continued

项　目 Item	竣工产值（万元）Gross Output Value Completed (10 000 yuan)		房屋建筑施工面积（万平方米）Floor Space of Building Under Construction (10 000 sq. m)		房屋建筑竣工面积（万平方米）Floor Space of Building Completed (10 000 sq. m)		#住　宅 Residential Buildings	
	2005	2006	2005	2006	2005	2006	2005	2006
总　计 Total	**4596374**	**6808347**	**3940.56**	**4555.08**	**1484.38**	**1735.58**	**728.58**	**815.52**
按登记注册类型分 Grouped by Status of Registration								
内资企业 Domestic-funded Enterprises	4549337	6728103	3872.55	4469.64	1464.78	1698.28	728.58	815.52
国有企业 State-owned Enterprises	1616346	1265300	1080.09	1182.20	296.78	281.86	135.45	117.02
集体企业 Collective-owned Enterprises	289006	258113	313.15	216.25	208.81	140.02	101.52	90.58
股份合作企业 Cooperative Enterprises	62454	38238	7.08	4.91	2.10	4.91	0.26	
私营企业 Private Enterprises	400499	444385	245.30	185.86	138.33	93.85	51.79	35.37
股份有限公司 Share-holding Corporations Ltd.	160619	472721	126.60	114.09	45.48	52.49	21.03	33.07
有限责任公司 Limited Liability Corporations	1951460	4196711	2084.57	2712.26	762.33	1081.70	412.39	512.19
#国有独资 Sole State-funded Corporations	220172	556942	216.29	21.89	69.19	6.32	50.66	1.02
联营企业 Joint Ownership Enterprises	10808	29016	4.32	35.18	3.87	28.55	0.56	18.87
#国有与国有联营企业 State Joint Ownership Enterprises		1040						
集体与集体联营企业 Collective Joint Ownership Enterprises	4920	27642	3.75	35.18	3.75	28.55	0.56	18.87
其他内资企业 Other Domestic-funded Enterprises	58145	23619	11.44	18.89	7.08	14.90	5.58	8.42
港澳台商投资企业 Enterprises with Investment from Hong Kong, Macao and Taiwan	22313	32650						
外商投资企业 Foreign Funded Enterprises	24724	47594	68.01	85.44	19.60	37.30		
按经济类型分 Grouped by Ownership								
国有经济 State-owned	1836518	1823282	1296.39	1204.09	365.97	288.18	186.11	118.04
集体经济 Collective-owned	356380	323993	323.97	256.34	214.66	173.48	102.34	109.45
私有经济 Private and Individual	400499	444385	245.30	185.86	138.33	93.85	51.79	35.37
港澳台商投资经济 Hong Kong, Macao and Taiwan Funded	22313	32650						
外商投资经济 Foreign Funded	24724	47594	68.01	85.44	19.60	37.30		
其　他 Other	1955940	4136443	2006.89	2823.35	745.82	1142.77	388.34	552.66

12-4 建筑企业基本情况(2006年)(按行业和资质等级分)
BASIC STATISTICS ON CONSTRUCTION ENTERPRISES, 2006 (Grouped by Sector and Qualification Grade)

指 标 Item	企业个数(个) Number of Enterprises (unit)		从业人员平均人数(万人) Average Employed Personnel (10 000 persons)		从业人员劳动报酬(万元) Remuneration of Employed Personnel (10 000 yuan)		建筑业总产值(万元) Gross Output Value of Construction (10 000 yuan)	
	2005	2006	2005	2006	2005	2006	2005	2006
按行业类别分 Grouped by Sector								
房屋工程建筑业 Building Engineering	167	165	17.03	15.12	142014	154638	2614781	2964217
土木工程建筑业 Civil Engineering	159	171	12.70	15.33	270762	297287	3485805	5149847
建筑安装业 Building Installation	363	370	6.51	5.49	122029	132750	1046200	1217482
建筑装饰业 Building Decoration	278	251	1.63	1.57	14468	15352	229701	244791
其他建筑业 Others	141	146	1.23	1.06	12375	15105	167215	262983
按资质等级分 Grouped by Qualification Grade								
施工总承包 General Contractor	**245**	**247**	**28.44**	**29.25**	**402607**	**440212**	**5606342**	**7477512**
特 级 Super Grade	4	8	4.55	8.62	71782	108277	1151948	2556176
一 级 First Grade	49	49	15.16	13.03	238421	215644	3355988	3666096
二 级 Second Grade	77	82	6.18	4.91	64786	78483	776658	918354
三 级 Third Grade	115	108	2.55	2.69	27618	37808	321748	336886
专业承包 Specialized Contractor	**863**	**856**	**10.66**	**9.32**	**159041**	**174920**	**1937360**	**2361808**
一 级 First Grade	51	60	2.93	2.72	51738	55752	976958	1187548
二 级 Second Grade	135	154	3.07	2.55	43256	48295	361103	454718
三 级 Third Grade	662	637	4.60	4.04	63494	70719	586351	718672
不分等级 No Grade	15	5	0.06	0.01	553	154	12948	870

12-4 续表 Continued

指 标 Item	竣工产值(万元) Gross Output Value Completed (10 000 yuan)		房屋建筑施工面积(万平方米) Floor Space of Building Under Construction (10 000 sq. m)		房屋建筑竣工面积(万平方米) Floor Space of Building Completed (10 000 sq. m)		#住 宅 Residential Buildings	
	2005	2006	2005	2006	2005	2006	2005	2006
按行业类别分								
Grouped by Sector								
房屋工程建筑业								
Building Engineering	1754038	2014209	3587.42	3612.81	1361.34	1455.42	694.50	746.70
土木工程建筑业								
Civil Engineering	1883397	3596385	235.62	787.30	75.12	217.72	28.17	57.22
建筑安装业								
Building Installation	662644	838935	105.10	137.86	45.78	61.09	5.91	11.60
建筑装饰业								
Building Decoration	187503	206687		2.46				
其他建筑业								
Others	108792	152131	12.42	14.65	2.14	1.35		
按资质等级分								
Grouped by Qualification Grade								
施工总承包								
General Contractor	**3343088**	**5235883**	**3750.23**	**4272.02**	**1387.07**	**1630.68**	**715.34**	**795.50**
特 级								
Super Grade	368203	1544661	325.79	1073.92	80.86	224.15	34.03	83.54
一 级								
First Grade	2171502	2903175	2367.24	2295.11	760.55	874.41	375.78	379.10
二 级								
Second Grade	530416	538887	780.79	637.72	343.57	355.31	192.70	238.08
三 级								
Third Grade	272967	249160	276.41	265.27	202.09	176.81	112.83	94.78
专业承包								
Specialized Contractor	**1253286**	**1572464**	**190.33**	**283.06**	**97.31**	**104.90**	**13.24**	**20.02**
一 级								
First Grade	494146	715558	98.98	150.76	51.57	49.82		1.57
二 级								
Second Grade	300193	320402	52.79	80.75	28.64	37.98	8.12	4.75
三 级								
Third Grade	454586	535647	38.56	51.55	17.10	17.10	5.12	13.70
不分等级								
No Grade	4361	857						

12-5 建筑企业主要财务指标（2006年）
MAIN FINANCIAL INDICATORS OF CONSTRUCTION ENTERPRISES, 2006

单位：万元 (10 000 yuan)

指　标	Item	全市总计 Total	#国有经济 State-owned	#地　方 Local
资本金	**Capital**			
资本金合计	Total Capital	1996471	604163	147766
年末资产负债	**Assets and Liabilities at Year-end**			
流动资产合计	Total Circulating Funds	6605356	1743618	631695
固定资产合计	Total Fixed Assets	1834812	408582	138955
固定资产原价	Original Value of Fixed Assets	2613919	659630	189927
#生产经营用	Used in Production and Management	2038513	568182	151645
累计折旧	Accumulative Depreciation	993034	279438	63317
资产总计	Total Assets	9190087	2458953	805616
损益及分配	**Profit, Loss and Distribution**			
工程结算收入	Revenue of Project Settle Accounts	10207405	3056034	685651
工程结算成本	Costs of Project Settle Accounts	9188099	2824322	623008
工程结算税金及附加	Taxes & Extra Charges of Project Settle Accounts	296735	90738	21242
工程结算利润	Profits of Project Settle Accounts	694290	139294	40245
其他业务收入	Other Revenue from Business	262099	68549	40591
其他业务利润	Other Profits from Business	24202	8350	3776
管理费用	Management Expenses	448480	113699	41946
#税　金	Taxes	12368	2545	1306
利润总额	Total Profits	257432	49814	2045
应交所得税	Income Taxes Payable	64643	8222	2338
应付利润	Profits Payable	86361	37336	1085
利税总额	Total Pre-tax Profits	566535	143097	24594
工资、福利费	**Wage and Welfare Expenses**			
应付工资总额	Total Wage Payable	555819	166203	42365
应付福利费总额	Total Welfare Expenses Payable	59314	16488	4969

注：本表按原经济类型分组，下同。
Note: Data is grouped by original ownership in this table, same as following tables.

12-5 续表 Continued

单位：万元 (10 000 yuan)

指　　标	Item	# 集体经济 Collective -owned	# 私有经济 Private	# 港澳台投资经济 Hong Kong, Macao and Taiwan Funded	# 外商投资经济 Foreign Funded
资本金	**Capital**				
资本金合计	Total Capital	76186	303267	20696	22495
年末资产负债	**Assets and Liabilities at Year-end**				
流动资产合计	Total Circulating Funds	324507	482167	61918	105265
固定资产合计	Total Fixed Assets	40760	149303	11455	9818
固定资产原价	Original Value of Fixed Assets	62870	189064	16982	12926
# 生产经营用	Used in Production and Management	47396	125379	6766	7445
累计折旧	Accumulative Depreciation	25268	56678	6705	4948
资产总计	Total Assets	382223	672071	79443	117540
损益及分配	**Profit, Loss and Distribution**				
工程结算收入	Revenue of Project Settle Accounts	375396	676453	46842	99728
工程结算成本	Costs of Project Settle Accounts	325920	580229	43066	79824
工程结算税金及附加	Taxes & Extra Charges of Project Settle Accounts	14554	20102	1280	1137
工程结算利润	Profits of Project Settle Accounts	32757	69245	2375	9069
其他业务收入	Other Revenue from Business	4626	13601	17634	911
其他业务利润	Other Profits from Business	1170	2693	-926	478
管理费用	Management Expenses	25479	42901	2983	13065
# 税　金	Taxes	1365	1648	80	42
利润总额	Total Profits	9215	20910	-3430	-2572
应交所得税	Income Taxes Payable	6067	6373	43	101
应付利润	Profits Payable	5202	8255	89	95
利税总额	Total Pre-tax Profits	25134	42660	-2070	-1393
工资、福利费	**Wage and Welfare Expenses**				
应付工资总额	Total Wage Payable	42052	41389	2135	5927
应付福利费总额	Total Welfare Expenses Payable	3684	4734	159	124

12-6 建筑企业年末自有机械设备总功率和净值（1990-2006年）
TOTAL POWER AND NET VALUE OF MACHINERY AND EQUIPMENT OWNED BY CONSTRUCTION ENTERPRISES (YEAR-END), 1990-2006

年 份 Year	年末自有机械设备总功率(万千瓦) Total Power of Machinery and Equipment Owned (year-end) (10 000 kW)	# 国有经济 State-owned	# 地 方 Local	年末自有机械设备净值(万元) Net Value of Machinery and Equipment Owned (year-end) (10 000 yuan)	# 国有经济 State-owned	# 地 方 Local
1990	91.70	86.70	41.40	79168	77633	28493
1991	89.74	85.46	42.95	76234	74526	27722
1992	94.60	89.90	42.60	76234	74252	29646
1993	98.92	89.57	41.20	116608	108817	55009
1994	116.58	103.91	37.47	172348	153207	47757
1995	138.36	110.17	43.77	179888	164162	60526
1996	137.98	109.22	40.47	384677	178790	47006
1997	151.18	119.22	43.87	207571	173245	54521
1998	173.03	111.19	39.28	206033	163854	49153
1999	185.54	146.77	38.00	214052	174687	67470
2000	157.27	102.26	36.14	217748	122519	45433
2001	168.83	87.31	32.16	231546	126407	51157
2002	221.56	85.37	33.03	529838	166556	83098
2003	227.81	86.32	34.65	582022	208634	79305
2004	258.80	96.86	42.66	622763	223307	63141
2005	246.33	93.87	29.07	694990	230140	53538
2006	297.62	97.08	50.98	782820	195335	52195

12-7 建筑企业技术装备率和动力装备率（1990-2006年）
VALUE AND POWER OF MACHINES PER LABORER OF CONSTRUCTION ENTERPRISES, 1990-2006

年 份 Year	全部职工技术装备率(元/人) Value of Machines per Labor (yuan/person)	# 国有经济 State-owned	# 地 方 Local	全部职工动力装备率(千瓦/人) Power of Machines per Labor (kW/person)	# 国有经济 State-owned	# 地 方 Local
1990	4231	4480	2893	4.90	5.00	4.20
1991	4023	4259	2697	4.70	4.90	4.10
1992	4063	4279	2878	5.00	5.20	4.10
1993	4507	5490	4461	3.80	4.50	3.30
1994	5114	5075	2350	3.46	3.44	1.84
1995	6281	6622	4299	4.83	4.44	3.11
1996	13237	7677	3647	4.75	4.69	3.14
1997	7094	7680	4300	5.17	5.28	3.46
1998	7022	7908	4134	5.90	5.37	3.30
1999	8774	11542	10233	7.61	9.70	5.76
2000	10714	9483	9008	7.74	7.92	7.17
2001	12881	14697	11768	9.39	10.15	7.40
2002	19423	18366	16571	8.12	9.41	6.59
2003	24203	27824	24187	9.47	11.51	10.57
2004	27354	33064	25506	11.37	14.34	17.23
2005	26064	26376	16793	9.24	10.76	9.12
2006	25420	21640	22518	9.66	10.75	22.00

12-8 建筑企业机械设备情况及经济效益指标
MACHINERY & EQUIPMENT AND ECONOMIC EFFICIENCY INDICATORS OF CONSTRUCTION ENTERPRISES

指　标　Item	全市 Total	#国有经济 State-owned	#地方 Local
2005年			
建筑业机械设备情况			
Machinery and Equipment of Construction Enterprises			
自有机械设备总台数(台) Number of Machinery and Equipment Owned (set)	100040	28704	13146
自有机械设备总功率(万千瓦) Power of Machinery and Equipment Owned (10 000 kW)	246.33	93.87	29.07
自有机械设备净值(万元) Net Value of Machinery and Equipment Owned (10 000 yuan)	694990	230140	53538
技术装备率(元/人) Value of Machines per Labor (yuan/person)	26064	26376	16793
动力装备率(千瓦/人) Power of Machines per Labor (kW/person)	9.24	10.76	9.12
建筑业经济效益指标			
Economic Efficiency Indicators of Construction Enterprises			
全员劳动生产率(元/人) Overall Labor Productivity (yuan/person)	192931	228354	172133
房屋竣工率(%) Percentage of Buildings Completed (%)	37.7	28.2	40.0
平均每一从业人员竣工面积(平方米/人) Per Capita Floor Space of Buildings Completed (sq. m/person)	38.0	29.6	30.7
每百元产值实现利税(元) Ratio of Pre-tax Profit to Gross Output Value (yuan)	5.3	4.4	4.4
百元产值占用流动资产(元) Ratio of Circulating Funds to Gross Output Value (yuan)	72.0	73.8	106.5
全员资金占有率(元/人) Per Capita Owned Capital (yuan/person)	175392	207821	222012
2006年			
建筑业机械设备情况			
Machinery and Equipment of Construction Enterprises			
自有机械设备总台数(台) Number of Machinery and Equipment Owned (set)	97767	23902	10237
自有机械设备总功率(万千瓦) Power of Machinery and Equipment Owned (10 000 kW)	297.62	97.08	50.98
自有机械设备净值(万元) Net Value of Machinery and Equipment Owned (10 000 yuan)	782820	195335	52195
技术装备率(元/人) Value of Machines per Labor (yuan/person)	25420	21640	22518
动力装备率(千瓦/人) Power of Machines per Labor (kW/person)	9.66	10.75	22.00
建筑业经济效益指标			
Economic Efficiency Indicators of Construction Enterprises			
全员劳动生产率(元/人) Overall Labor Productivity (yuan/person)	255108	293052	224185
房屋竣工率(%) Percentage of Buildings Completed (%)	38.1	23.9	35.7
平均每一从业人员竣工面积(平方米/人) Per Capita Floor Space of Buildings Completed (sq. m/person)	45.0	27.5	20.1
每百元产值实现利税(元) Ratio of Pre-tax Profit to Per 100 yuan Output Value (yuan)	5.8	4.7	3.5
百元产值占用流动资产(元) Ratio of Circulating Funds to per 100 yuan Output Value (yuan)	67.1	56.7	91.3
全员资金占有率(元/人) Per Capita Owned Capital (yuan/person)	218831	205089	249636

12-9 全市建筑企业建筑业总产值、利税总额五十强（2006年）
TOP 50 CONSTRUCTION ENTERPRISES BY GROSS OUTPUT VALUE AND TOTAL PRE-TAX PROFITS OF CONSTRUCTION, 2006

总产值名次 Position of Output Value	单位名称 Name of Enterprise	利税总额名次 Position of Total Pre-tax Profits	单位名称 Name of Enterprise
1	中铁十八局集团有限公司	1	海洋石油工程股份有限公司
2	中冶天工建设有限公司	2	中铁十八局集团有限公司
3	海洋石油工程股份有限公司	3	中交天津航道局有限公司
4	中交一航局第一工程有限公司	4	中交第一航务工程局有限公司
5	中交第一航务工程局有限公司	5	中交一航局第一工程有限公司
6	天津电力建设公司	6	中冶天工建设有限公司
7	天津二十冶金建设有限公司	7	天津二十冶金建设有限公司
8	中交天津航道局有限公司	8	天津电力建设公司
9	中国建筑第六工程局	9	中交一航局第四工程有限公司
10	天津市建工工程总承包有限公司	10	天津送变电工程公司
11	中交一航局第四工程有限公司	11	中国水电基础局有限公司
12	中国建筑第六工程局土木工程公司	12	中国建筑第六工程局
13	天津三建建筑工程有限公司	13	中国建筑第六工程局土木工程公司
14	天津第二市政工程有限公司	14	天津滨电电力工程公司
15	中国建筑第六工程局第四建筑工程公司	15	天津三建建筑工程有限公司
16	天津二建建筑工程有限公司	16	天津市津南区北闸口建筑工程公司
17	天津第一市政公路工程有限公司	17	天津第二市政工程有限公司
18	中国建筑第六工程局第二建筑工程公司	18	中交一公局第六工程有限公司
19	天津城建集团有限公司	19	天津城建集团有限公司
20	中国石化集团第四建设公司	20	中国建筑第六工程局第四建筑工程公司
21	天津六建建筑工程有限公司	21	中国建筑第六工程局第二建筑工程公司
22	天津一建建筑工程有限公司	22	天津市建工工程总承包有限公司
23	天津五市政公路工程有限公司	23	天津第一市政公路工程有限公司
24	渤海石油航务建筑工程公司	24	天津二建建筑工程有限公司
25	中交一公局第六工程有限公司	25	天津五市政公路工程有限公司
26	天津第三市政公路工程有限公司	26	天津蓝巢电力检修有限公司
27	中铁建工集团北方工程有限公司	27	天津市青龙建筑安装工程有限公司
28	中国建筑第六工程局第三建筑工程公司	28	天津市建城地基基础工程有限公司
29	天津路桥建设工程有限公司	29	天津武清建筑建材集团
30	中铁六局集团天津铁路建设有限公司	30	中国建筑第六工程局第三建筑工程公司
31	天津送变电工程公司	31	天津市光达电力有限责任公司
32	中国水电基础局有限公司	32	天津第三市政公路工程有限公司
33	中国建筑第六工程局第五建筑工程公司	33	天津六建建筑工程有限公司
34	西门子楼宇科技（天津）有限公司	34	中铁六局集团天津铁路建设有限公司
35	天津港航工程有限公司	35	中国石化集团第四建设公司
36	天津四建建筑工程有限公司	36	天津市蓟县光源电力有限公司
37	天津市青龙建筑安装工程有限公司	37	中国建筑第六工程局第五建筑工程公司
38	天津电信建设工程有限公司	38	天津市西青区光源电力工程有限公司
39	天津市管道工程集团有限公司	39	天津一建建筑工程有限公司
40	天津第六市政公路工程有限公司	40	中铁建工集团北方工程有限公司
41	天津市河东区房屋建筑工程公司	41	天津市三通市政工程有限公司
42	天津市龙祥建材建设工程有限公司	42	天津市城南电力工程安装有限公司
43	天津市水利工程有限公司	43	天津市管道工程集团有限公司
44	天津振津工程集团有限公司	44	天津市建设发展总公司
45	天津市机电设备安装公司	45	天津市水利工程有限公司
46	天津大港油田集团工程建设有限公司	46	天津新宇建筑工程有限公司
47	天津市宝地建筑工程有限公司	47	天津第六市政公路工程有限公司
48	天津富凯建设集团有限公司	48	天津蓝巢特种吊装工程有限公司
49	天津市建城地基基础工程有限公司	49	天津德丰电力开发有限责任公司
50	天津第四市政建筑工程有限公司	50	天津市四通通讯工程安装公司

主要统计指标解释

建筑业总产值 是以货币表现的建筑安装企业在一定时期内生产的建筑业产品的总和。

建筑工程产值 指列入建筑工程预算内的各种工程价值，主要包括：各种用途的房屋、构筑物的建筑工程和暖气、卫生、通风、照明、煤气等设备安装价值；设备基础、支柱、操作台、梯子、烟囱、凉水塔的砌筑工程；各种锅炉炉体砌筑和金属结构安装工程；施工现场布置、场地平整、施工临时用水、电、道路的铺筑与架设；矿井的开凿、井巷掘进延伸、露天矿的剥离、石油、天然气钻井工程；铁路、公路、港口、桥梁的建筑工程；水利工程；防空、地下建筑等特殊工程。和对建筑物内部或外部进行装饰、装修的价值。

设备安装工程产值 指设备安装工程价值，主要包括生产、动力、起重、运输、传动、医疗、实验、电讯、光纤、电话、计算机和电子设备等各种需要安装设备的装配与安装，与设备相联接的工作台、梯子、栏杆等装设工程；附属于被安装设备的管线敷设工程；被安装设备的绝缘、防腐保温、油漆等工作；为测定安装工作质量，对单个设备、系统设备进行单机试车和系统联动无负荷试运转工作，但产值中不包括被安装设备的价值。

其他产值 建筑业总产值中除建筑工程、安装工程以外的产值。包括房屋、构筑物修理产值、非标准设备制造产值、总包企业向分包企业收取的管理费以及不能明确划分的施工活动所完成的产值。

房屋、构筑物修理产值 指房屋和构筑物修理所完成的产值，但不包括被修理房屋、构筑物本身产值和生产设备的修理产值。

非标准设备制造产值 指加工制造没有定型的非标准生产设备的加工费和原材料价值。

年末自有机械设备总功率 指本企业自有施工机械、生产设备、运输设备以及其他设备等列为在册固定资产的生产性机械设备年末总功率，按设定能力或查定能力计算。包括机械本身的动力和为该机械服务的单独动力设备，如电动机等。计算单位用千瓦，动力换算可按 1 马力= 0.735 千瓦折合成千瓦数。电焊机、变压器、锅炉不计算动力。

Explanastory Notes on Main Statistical Indicators

Gross Output Value of Construction refers to the total of construction products, expressed in money terms, completed by construction and installation enterprises during a given period of time.

Output Value of Construction Projects refers to the value of projects covered by the project budgets, including the value of various buildings and structures, the value of the installation projects of central heating, public health, ventilation, lighting, gas, etc., the building of the base of equipment, pillar, operation desk, ladder, funnel, water tower, the building boiler room and installation of metals construction, arrange construction site, level the land, temporary expenses of water, electrical, pave the way, cutting mine, well drilling construction of oil, gas, the building engineering of railways, highways, port and bridges, water engineering, output value of building decoration, air defense, underground.

Output Value of Installation Projects refers to the value of the installation of equipment, (excluding the value of the equipment to be installed), mainly including production, power, lifting, transportation, medical treatment, experimentation, telecommunications, fiber optics, telephone, computer, electronic equipment, working desk, ladder, banisters, insulation, heat preservation, paint, etc.

Other Output Value refers to the output value outside of output value of construction projects and installation projects. It includes output value of repair of buildings and structures, output value of manufactured non-standard equipment, management fee of chief contractor received from subcontractor, other output value of construction.

Output value of repair of buildings and structures refer to the value created through the repairs of buildings or structures, but does not include the value of buildings or structures being repaired and the value of the repair of production equipment.

Output value of manufactured non-standard equipment refer to the value of non-standard production equipment (including raw materials and manufacturing cost)made for the construction projects.

Total Capacity of Machinery and Equipment Owned by the End of Year refers to the total power of machinery and equipment owned by the enterprises, and listed as the fixed assets of the enterprises by the end of the year, including machinery and equipment for construction, production and transportation. The power of the machinery is calculated on basis of the designed or verified capacity, covering the power of the machinery/equipment and the separate power equipment serving the machinery/equipment (such as electric motors), but excluding welders, transformers and boilers. The unit used for the calculation of power is kilowatt, with horsepower converted to kilowatt by 1 horsepower = 0.735 kilowatt.

第13篇
CHAPTER 13

交通运输和邮电
Transportation, Post and Telecommunications

13-1 社会客、货运输量和周转量(1990-2006年)
PASSENGER & FREIGHT TRAFFIC AND THE TURNOVER VOLUME OF PASSENGER & FREIGHT TRAFFIC, 1990-2006

年份 Year	客运量(万人) Passenger Traffic (10 000 persons)	#铁路 Railways	#公路 Highways	#水运 Waterways	旅客周转量(百万人公里) Turnover Volume of Passenger Traffic (million passenger-km)	#铁路 Railways	#公路 Highways	#水运 Waterways
1990	2175	1722	447			5409	307	
1991	2922	1718	1196			4974	941	
1992	2662	1731	897			6242	819	
1993	3225	1812	1380	4	8825	6584	1463	92
1994	3373	1863	1463	6	8299	5778	1639	49
1995	3308	1802	1464	5	7927	5437	1680	41
1996	3125	1580	1496	5	7599	4917	1772	43
1997	3136	1449	1640	5	7921	5050	2017	41
1998	3207	1511	1651	4	7950	5280	1914	33
1999	3259	1546	1671	3	8277	5780	1782	25
2000	3474	1594	1820	2	8845	6022	1864	26
2001	3302	1456	1780	6	9197	5996	2205	34
2002	3457	1498	1870	5	9255	5782	2272	33
2003	3507	1281	2109	2	9274	5526	2158	23
2004	4103	1491	2457	2.5	11713	7112	2404	30
2005	4679	1550	2961	3.2	14210	9070	2646	36
2006	5670	1632	3807	3.5	16341	9651	3564	38

年份 Year	货运量(万吨) Freight Traffic (10 000 tons)	#铁路 Railways	#公路 Highways	#水运 Waterways	货物周转量(亿吨公里) Turnover Volume of Freight Traffic (100 million ton-km)	#铁路 Railways	#公路 Highways	#水运 Waterways
1990	15929	2228	12329	1046	1139	234	52	852
1991	18308	2290	14537	1163	1216	204	37	973
1992	17522	2392	13562	1248	1321	217	37	1067
1993	21640	2618	17244	1347	1341	264	46	1030
1994	23783	2634	19270	1421	1325	225	46	1053
1995	24040	2722	19323	1517	1412	230	41	1139
1996	24133	2668	19491	1489	1052	224	41	784
1997	25090	2548	20515	1390	1031	219	44	765
1998	24505	2467	18584	2867	3710	198	60	3449
1999	27052	2380	20049	3884	4759	200	60	4497
2000	26400	3079	18764	4165	4674	275	63	4334
2001	28608	3727	19382	5037	5166	230	65	4870
2002	31016	4519	19554	6452	6484	228	66	6188
2003	35252	5662	20072	8944	8169	259	68	7840
2004	37934	6108	19560	11613	11473	286	72	11112
2005	40263	7241	19850	12375	12461	353	74	12031
2006	42863	8409	20290	13313	12184	353	76	11751

13-2 社会客、货运输量和周转量
PASSENGER & FREIGHT TRAFFIC AND THE TURNOVER VOLUME OF PASSENGER & FREIGHT TRAFFIC

指标	Item	2004	2005	2006	2006比2005年增长(%) Increase Rate in 2006 over 2005 (%)
客运量(万人)	**Passenger Traffic (10 000 persons)**	**4103**	**4679**	**5670**	**21.2**
铁路	Railways	1491	1550	1632	5.3
公路	Highways	2457	2961	3807	28.6
水运	Waterways	2.5	3.2	3.5	9.4
民航	Civil Aviation	153	165	227	37.6
旅客周转量	**Turnover Volume of Passenger Traffic**				
(百万人公里)	**(million passenger-km)**	**11713**	**14210**	**16341**	**15.0**
铁路	Railways	7112	9070	9651	6.4
公路	Highways	2404	2646	3564	34.7
水运	Waterways	30	36	38	5.6
民航	Civil Aviation	2166	2458	3088	25.6
货运量(万吨)	**Freight Traffic (10 000 tons)**	**37934**	**40263**	**42863**	**6.5**
铁路	Railways	6108	7241	8409	16.1
公路	Highways	19560	19850	20290	2.2
水运	Waterways	11613	12375	13313	7.6
民航	Civil Aviation	1.7	1.9	2.4	26.3
管道输油气量	Traffic of Petroleum & Gas Pipelines	651	795	848	6.7
货物周转量	**Turnover Volume of Freight Traffic**				
(亿吨公里)	**(100 million ton-km)**	**11473**	**12461**	**12184**	**-2.2**
铁路	Railways	286	353	353	
公路	Highways	72	74	76	2.7
水运	Waterways	11112	12031	11751	-2.3
民航	Civil Aviation	0.26	0.3	0.35	16.7
管道输油气量	Traffic of Petroleum & Gas Pipelines	2.6	3.1	3.8	22.6

13-3 运输线路长度
LENGTH OF TRANSPORT ROUTES

单位：公里 (km)

指标	Item	2004	2005	2006	2006比2005年增长(%) Increase Rate in 2006 over 2005 (%)
公路通车里程	Length of Highways Having Transport Service	10514	10836	11316	4.4
等级公路	Expressway and Class I to IV Highway	10420	10791	11306	4.8
#高速公路	Expressway	517	593	682	15.0
等外公路	Highway Below Class IV	94	44	10	-77.3
内河航道里程	Length of Navigable Inland Waterways	412	412	412	
民航航线里程	Length of Civil Aviation Routes	22802	19504	20297	4.1
输油气管道里程	Length of Petroleum & Gas Pipelines	613	503	545	8.3

注：内河航道里程为内河清淤里程。民用航空航线里程为国航天津分公司在天津机场起降飞机的里程。

Note: Length of navigable inland waterways refer to length of cleaning up the silt inland waterways. Length of civil aviation refer to the length of Air China Tianjin Company flights at Tianjin Airport.

13-4 港口客、货吞吐量(1990-2006年)
VOLUME OF PASSENGER & FREIGHT HANDLED IN PORTS, 1990-2006

年 份 Year	港口旅客吞吐量 (万人次) Volume of Passenger Handled in Ports (10 000 person-times)	港口货物吞吐量 (万吨) Volume of Freight Handled in Ports (10 000 tons)	出 港 Out-port	比 重(%) Proportion (%)	进 港 In-port	比 重(%) Proportion (%)	集装箱吞吐量 (万国际标准箱) Handled Containers (10 000 TEU)
1990	37.0	2063	1195	57.9	868	42.1	29
1991	47.7	2378	1488	62.6	890	37.4	34
1992	61.2	2929	1915	65.4	1014	34.6	39
1993	57.6	3719	2527	68	1192	32	48
1994	51.9	4652	3507	75.4	1145	24.6	63
1995	50.4	5787	4551	78.6	1236	21.4	70
1996	58.7	6188	4839	78.2	1349	21.8	82
1997	52.7	6789	5198	76.6	1591	23.4	94
1998	45.3	6818	5124	75.2	1694	24.8	102
1999	48.7	7298	5280	72.4	2018	27.6	130
2000	40.2	9582	6936	72.4	2646	27.6	171
2001	37.1	11369	8086	71.1	3283	28.9	201
2002	33.0	12906	8802	68.2	4104	31.8	241
2003	22.7	16182	10912	67.4	5270	32.6	302
2004	32.5	20619	13217	64.1	7402	35.9	382
2005	31.6	24069	14700	61.1	9369	38.9	480
2006	34.0	25760	15285	59.3	10475	40.7	595

注：货物吞吐量是全港数据，即包括货主码头数据。
Note: Volume of freight handled in ports refer to the figure of ports, including those of docks.

13-5 港口设施
PORTS FACILITIES

指 标	Item	2004	2005	2006	2006 比2005年 增长(%) Increase Rate in 2006 over 2005 (%)
码头长度(米)	Length of Quay Line (m)	20324	20906	24584	17.6
港口泊位(个)	Number of Berths (unit)	114	116	132	13.8
天津港(集团)有限公司	Tianjin Port Group Corporation Ltd.	74	76	85	11.8
货主码头	Docks	40	40	47	17.5
# 万吨级泊位	10 000 Ton Class	53	55	66	20.0
# 天津港(集团)有限公司	Tianjin Port Group Corporation Ltd.	52	54	63	16.7
铁路专用线长度(米)	Length of Railways (m)	100037	120665	128115	6.2
仓库总面积(平方米)	Areas of Store Houses (sq. m)	273777	282868	403541	42.7
堆场总面积(平方米)	Areas of Goods Pile (sq. m)	3743714	4636202	5973896	28.9
集装箱堆场堆存能力(TEU)	Capacity of Piling Containers (TEU)	143809	140644	238718	69.7
装卸机械台数(台)	Number of Loading & Unloading Machines (unit)	1422	1932	2179	12.8

注：本表除港口泊位含货主码头数据外，其余设施均为天津港(集团)有限公司数据。
Note: Number of berths include docks, other ports facilities refer to those owned by Tianjin Port Group Corporation Ltd.

13-6 港口分货类吞吐量
VOLUME OF FREIGHT HANDLED IN PORTS BY CATEGORY

单位：万吨 (10 000 tons)

指 标 Item	合 计 Total		出港量 Out-port		进港量 In-port	
	2005	2006	2005	2006	2005	2006
港口货物吞吐量 Volume of Freight Handled in Ports	**24069**	**25760**	**14700**	**15285**	**9369**	**10475**
国 外 Abroad	12310	13967	5591	6695	6719	7272
国 内 Domestic	11759	11793	9109	8590	2650	3203
分品种货物吞吐量 Volume of Freight Handled by Category						
煤炭及制品 Coal and Related Products	7990	7189	7948	7163	42	26
石油、天然气及制品 Petroleum, Natural Gas and Related Products	2614	2889	1336	1271	1278	1618
金属矿石 Metal Ores	4072	4456	54	45	4018	4411
钢 铁 Steel and Iron	2030	2723	1790	2570	240	153
矿建材料 Mineral Building Materials	1244	1508	149	152	1095	1356
水 泥 Cement	5	10	5	10	0	0
木 材 Timber	34	47	20	28	14	19
非金属矿石 Nonmetal Ores	263	311	225	276	37	35
化学肥料及农药 Chemical Fertilizers and Pesticides	77	59	3	9	74	51
盐 Salt	39	8	4	4	35	4
粮 食 Grain	251	248	41	33	210	215
机械、电器、设备 Machine, Electric Machinary, Equipment	1441	2000	795	1150	646	850
化工原料及制品 Chemical Materials and Related Products	931	882	603	529	328	353
有色金属 Nonferrous Metals	168	143	87	62	81	81
轻工、医药产品 Light Industry, Medical and Pharmaceutical Products	1130	1466	849	1131	281	335
农林牧渔产品 Agricultural Products	416	377	184	157	232	219
其 他 Others	1365	1444	607	695	758	749
集装箱吞吐量(万国际标准箱) Handled Containers (10 000 TEU)	**480**	**595**	**245**	**308**	**235**	**287**

13-7 公路及民航运输主要技术经济指标
MAIN TECHNICAL AND ECONOMIC INDICATORS OF HIGHWAY AND CIVIL AVIATION TRANSPORT

指　标	Item	2004	2005	2006
公　路	**Highways**			
载货汽车里程利用率(%)	Utilization Rate of Length of Trucks in Operation (%)	52.7	53.8	52
载客汽车里程利用率(%)	Utilization Rate of Length of Passenger Vehicles in Operation (%)	99.6	95.6	96.0
载货汽车每百吨公里耗汽油(升)	Gasoline Consumption of Trucks (L/100 ton-km)	7.4	6.7	6.7
载客汽车每百吨公里耗汽油(升)	Gasoline Consumption of Passenger Vehicles (L/100 ton-km)	23.1	25.1	25.1
载货汽车每百吨公里耗柴油(升)	Diesel Oil Consumption of Trucks (L/100 ton-km)	4.7	4.5	4.5
载客汽车每百吨公里耗柴油(升)	Diesel Oil Consumption of Passenger Vehicles (L/100 ton-km)	29.4	28.6	28.6
载货汽车实载率(%)	Utilization Rate of Capacity of Freight Trucks (%)	60.9	63.4	54.0
载客汽车实载率(%)	Utilization Rate of Capcity of Passenger Vehicles (%)	34.9	47.2	55.0
民　航	**Civil Aviation**			
飞行小时(小时)	Flying Time (hour)	39398	43939	55422
平均每可用机飞行小时(小时)	Flying Time per Avaliable Aircraft (hour)	3796	3881	3854
正班飞行距离(万公里)	Distance under Normal Conditions (10 000 km)	2272.6	2530.2	3192.2
平均每可用机日生产飞行小时(小时)	Average Daily Flying Time per Avaliable Aircraft (hour)	10.3	10.6	10.5
正班平均载运率(%)	Average Utilization Rate of Capacity under Normal Conditions (%)	71.8	72.4	72.4

注：本表民航数据为国航天津分公司数据。
Note: In this table, the data of civil aviation is provided by Air China Tianjin Company.

13-8 民用航空机场主要指标
MAIN INDICATORS OF CIVIL AVIATION AIRPORT

指　标	Item	2005	2006	2006比2005年增长(%) Increase Rate in 2006 over 2005 (%)
旅客吞吐量(万人)	**Passenger Traffic (10 000 Persons)**	**219.4**	**276.7**	**26.1**
国内旅客	Domestic Passenger Traffic	172.2	228.1	32.5
国际旅客	International Passenger Traffic	41	39.9	-2.7
港、澳、台地区旅客	Hong Kong, Macao & Taiwan Passenger Traffic	6.2	8.7	40.3
货(邮)吞吐量(万吨)	**Freight Traffic (10 000 tons)**	**8**	**9.7**	**21.3**
国内货邮	Domestic Routes	2.4	3.2	33.3
国际货邮	International Routes	5.5	6.3	14.5
港、澳、台地区货邮	Hong Kong, Macao & Taiwan Regional Routes	0.1	0.1	
起、降架次(万架次)	**Times of Ascend and Descend (10 000 times)**	**4.8**	**5.5**	**14.6**

13-9 民用车辆拥有量(2006年) NUMBER OF CIVIL MOTOR VEHICLES OWNED, 2006

单位：辆 (unit)

指 标	Item	合 计 Total	#个 人 Private-owned	#当年新注册 Registered in 2006
总 计	**Total**	**1195995**	**932517**	**135275**
民用汽车	Civil Motor Vehicles	816576	572104	129347
1. 载客汽车	Passenger Vehicles	648211	477325	115154
#轿 车	cars	431881	325658	93959
大 型	Large-sized	15227	1040	1825
中 型	Medium-sized	26002	11383	1284
小 型	Small-sized	504198	371384	111400
微 型	Minisize	102784	93518	645
2. 载货汽车	Trucks	128240	68666	12574
#普通载货	Ordinary Trucks	95676	53497	7857
重 型	Heavy Trucks	18516	5695	531
中 型	Medium-sized Trucks	17757	7618	1146
轻 型	Light Trucks	85226	49590	10647
微 型	Minisize Trucks	6741	5763	250
3. 其他汽车	Other Civil Motor Vehicles	40125	26113	1619
摩托车	Motorcycles	332923	323716	5313
拖拉机	Tractor	32619	32619	
挂 车	Trailer	11664	3816	574
其他类型车	Other Vehicles	1576	262	41

13-10 邮电业基本情况(1990-2006年) BASIC STATISTICS ON POST AND TELECOMMUNICATIONS, 1990-2006

年 份 Year	邮电业务总量(万元) Business Value of Post and Telecommunications (10 000 yuan)	邮电局所数(处) Number of Post and Telecommunications Offices (unit)	局用电话交换机容量(门) Capacity of Office Telephone Exchanges (line)	电话机(含移动、小灵通)(万部) Telephone (Include Mobile) (10 000)	平均每百人拥有电话机数(含移动)(部/百人) Popularization Rate of Telephone (Include Mobile) (unit/100 persons)
1990	32735	281	230586	31.78	3.7
1991	44527	280	271356	34.28	3.9
1992	61063	273	359932	42.27	4.8
1993	97062	277	532118	63.91	7.2
1994	132464	297	1137748	96.03	10.8
1995	187195	300	1522493	135.61	15.2
1996	256978	314	1694092	174.65	19.4
1997	342848	328	1945020	207.82	23.1
1998	474067	399	2447630	259.58	28.7
1999	567242	470	2761633	329.30	36.2
2000	753669	563	3182465	431.28	46.6
2001	702206	543	3645600	511.57	56.0
2002	903296	597	3865700	601.45	65.4
2003	1157060	619	4024500	761.91	82.3
2004	1467836	700	4237700	835.01	89.5
2005	1763477	827	6288300	939.82	90.1
2006	2277902	818	6190300	1147.17	106.7

13-11 邮电通信业务基本情况
BASIC STATISTICS ON POST AND TELECOMMUNICATION SERVICES

指标 Item	单位 Unit	2004	2005	2006	2006比2005年增长(%) Increase Rate in 2006 over 2005 (%)
一、通信业务量 Business Value of Communication Services					
邮电业务总量 Business Value of Post and Telecommunication Services	万元 10 000 yuan	1467836	1763477	2277902	29.2
函件 Letters	万件 10 000 pcs	10591.27	8384.81	8889	6.0
特快专递 Pieces of Express Mail Services	万件 10 000 pcs	372.67	410.24	489	19.2
订销报刊期发数 Number of Newspapers and Magazines Subscibed	万份 10 000 pcs	374.21	353	404	14.4
集邮业务 Philately	万枚 10 000 pcs	5352.98	5000.22	3129	-37.4
邮政储蓄年末余额 Balance of Post Deposits at Year-end	亿元 100 million yuan	161.04	235.14	287.2	22.1
长途电话通话量 Long Distance Calls	万次 10 000 times	88049.05	86002.92	85656.98	-0.4
国内长途电话 Domestic	万次 10 000 times	86403.18	83792.83	83205.23	-0.7
国际电话及港澳台电话 International and Hong Kong, Macao & Taiwan	万次 10 000 times	1645.87	2210.09	2451.75	10.9
短信业务发送量 Number of Messages Send Out	万条 10 000 pcs		450791.82	585055	29.8
移动电话年末用户 Number of Mobile Telephone Subscribers at Year-end	万户 10 000 subscribers	423	502.9	601.59	19.6
固定电话年末用户 Number of Fixed Telephone Subscribers at Year-end	万户 10 000 subscribers	413.3	436.92	435.8	-0.3
住宅电话年末用户 Number of Residential Telephone Subscribers at Year-end	万户 10 000 subscribers	241.17	351.59	338.4	-3.8
公用电话 Number of Public Telephone Sets	万部 10 000 sets	33.64	34.01	33.95	-0.2
数字数据用户 Digital and Data Users	户 Subscriber	6600	6054	5274	-12.9
国际互联网络用户 Number of Subscriber of Internet Services	万户 10 000 subscriber	267.49	207.36	228.85	10.4
二、邮政及通信网络 Post & Communication Facilities					
邮电局所数 Number of Post & Telecommunications Offices	处 unit	700	827	818	-1.1
#邮政局所数 Number of Post Offices	处 unit	460	454	464	2.2
信筒信箱 Number of Post Boxes	处 unit	1656	1728	1474	-14.7
邮路总长度 Length of Postal Routes	公里 km	21705	21996	23902	8.7
#汽车邮路长度 Length of Postal Routes by Highway	公里 km	11114	10671	11444	7.2
铁路邮路长度 Length of Postal Routes by Railway	公里 km	5071	5754	5754	
邮政汽车 Automobile for Post Bussiness	辆 unit	812	1104	1125	1.9
农村投递线路长度 Rural Delivery Routes	公里 km	16172	16144	16436	1.8

注：本表邮政数据取自天津市邮政公司。
Note: The data of post in this sheet are provided by Tianjin Post Office.

13-12 电信主要通信能力
MAIN COMMUNICATION CAPACITY OF TELECOMMUNICATIONS

指　标　Item	2004	2005	2006
长途电话业务电路(2M) Number of Long-distance Telephones (2M)	3555	3846	6623
数据通信网长途电路(2M) Digital Long-distance Communication (2M)	13299	77962	77930
长途电话交换机容量(路端) Capacity of Long-distance Telephone Exchanges (circuit)	270160	267869	263668
局用电话交换机容量(万门) Capacity of Office Telephone Exchanges (10 000 lines)	423.8	628.8	619.03
移动电话交换机容量(万户) Capacity of Mobile Telephone Exchanges (10 000 subscribers)	559	619	845
长途光缆线路长度(公里) Length of Long-distance Optical Cable Lines (km)	1873	2244	2884.59

13-13 邮政电信服务水平
LEVEL OF POST AND TELECOMMUNICATION SERVICES

指　标　Item	2004	2005	2006
平均每一邮电局所服务面积（平方公里） Average Area Served by Every Post Telecommunications Office (sq. km)	17.03	14.41	14.57
# 平均每一邮政局所服务面积 Average Area Served by Every Post Office	29.36	26.25	25.69
平均每一邮电局所服务人口（万人） Average People Served by Every Post Office Telecommunications (10 000 persons)	1.33	1.26	1.31
# 平均每一邮政局所服务人口 Average People Served by Every Post Office	2.3	2.3	2.3
平均每人每年发函件数（件） Annual Average Number of Letters Mailed per Capita (piece)	11.4	8.11	8.27
平均每百人每年订报刊数（件） Annual Average Number of Newspaper and Magazine Subscribed per 100 Persons (piece)	40.3	34.2	37.6
平均每百人拥有电话机（含移动）（部） Popularization Rate of Telephone (include mobil telephone) (set)	89.5	90.1	93.7
平均每百人拥有移动电话（部） Popularization Rate of Mobile Telephone (set)	45.4	48.2	56
平均每千人拥有公用电话（部） Per 1 000 Person Public Telephone (set)	36.2	32.9	31.6

13-14 邮政、电信局（所、厅）数
NUMBER OF POST AND TELECOMMUNICATIONS OFFICES BY REGION

单位：处 (unit)

地　区	Region	2004	2005	2006
全　市	**Total**	**700**	**827**	**81**
#邮政局	Post Offices	460	454	464
市辖区	**Districts Under City Administration**	**556**	**679**	**664**
#市内六区	Six Urban Districts	241	320	314
滨海三区	Three Coastal Districts	122	141	134
和平区	Heping District	37	53	48
河东区	Hedong District	47	59	59
河西区	Hexi District	46	55	54
南开区	Nankai District	49	62	60
河北区	Hebei District	38	52	55
红桥区	Hongqiao District	24	39	38
塘沽区	Tanggu District	53	64	59
汉沽区	Han'gu District	23	26	25
大港区	Dagang District	46	51	50
东丽区	Dongli District	22	26	28
西青区	Xiqing District	26	33	30
津南区	Jinnan District	23	23	22
北辰区	Beichen District	20	27	26
武清区	Wuqing District	57	58	61
宝坻区	Baodi District	45	51	49
市辖县	**Counties Under City Administration**	**144**	**148**	**154**
宁河县	Ninghe County	46	49	51
静海县	Jinghai County	56	59	61
蓟　县	Jixian County	42	40	42

主要统计指标解释

货运量 指在一定时期内，以重量单位（吨）计算的由各种运输工具实际完成运送过程的货物数量。

货物周转量 指在一定时期内，由各种运输工具实际完成运送过程的以综合货物运量和运送距离的乘积之和。

客运量 指在一定时期内，各运输部门实际运送的旅客人数，计算单位为人。

旅客周转量 指在一定时期内，实际运送的旅客人数与其相应的旅客运输距离乘积之和。

港口货物吞吐量 又称港口吞吐量，指经由水路运进、出港区范围，并经过装卸的货物数量。按货物流向分为进港吞吐量和出港吞吐量；按货物的贸易性质分为内贸和外贸吞吐量；按货物的类别分，可根据现行的交通行业标准《运输货物分类和代码》分类。

邮电业务总量 指以价值量形式表现的邮电通信企业为社会提供各类邮电通信服务的总数量。邮电业务量按专业分类包括函件、包件、汇票、报刊发行、邮政快件、特快专递、邮政储蓄、集邮、公众电报、用户电报、传真、长途电话、出租电路、无线寻呼、移动电话、分组交换数据通信、出租代维等。计算方法为各类产品乘以相应的平均单价（不变价）之和，再加上出租电路和设备、代用户维护电话交换机和线路等的服务收入。该指标综合反映了一定时期邮电业务发展的总成果，是研究邮电业务量构成和发展趋势的重要指标。计算公式为：

邮电业务总量 = ∑（各类邮电业务量 × 不变单价）+ 出租代维及其他业务收入 = 邮政业务总量 + 电信业务总量

民用汽车拥有量 指报告期末，在公安交通管理部门按照《机动车注册登记工作规范》，已注册登记领有民用车辆牌照的全部汽车数量。汽车拥有量统计的主要分类：根据汽车结构分为载客汽车、载货汽车及其他汽车；根据汽车所有者不同分为个人（私人）汽车、单位汽车；根据汽车的使用性质分为营运汽车、非营运汽车和特种汽车；根据汽车大小规格不同载客汽车分为大型、中型、小型和微型，载货汽车分为重型、中型、轻型和微型。

长途电话交换机容量 指用于接入长途电话网的电话交换机设备的额定容量，包括国际电话交换机容量。

局用交换机容量 指安装在电信运营企业内用于接续本地固定电话的电话交换机容量，包括现用和备用的人工或自动交换机的全部容量。不包括用户交换机容量。

移动电话交换机容量 指移动电话交换机根据一定话务模型和交换机处理能力计算出来的最大同时服务用户的数量。

Explanastory Notes on Main Statistical Indicators

Freight Traffic refers to the volume (tons) of freight transported with various traffic facilities in a given period.

Turnover Volume of Freight Traffic refers to the sum of the volume of transported cargo multiplying by the transport distance in a given period.

Passengers Traffic refers to the sum of the passengers transported in some time in a given period.

Turnover Volume of Passengers Traffic refers to the sum of the volume of transported passengers multiplied by the transport distance in a given period.

Ports Cargo Handled Capacity refers to the volume of cargo passing in and out the harbor area and having been loaded and unloaded. The volume of freight handled may be classified as in-port & out-port. It can also be classified as national trade and international trade by the attribute of trade or be classified by the classification of cargo according to the standard of traffic in use "The Classification and Code of Transported Cargo".

Business Volume of Post and Telecommunications refers to the total amount of post and telecommunication services, expressed in value terms, provided by the post and telecommunications departments for the society. Post and telecommunication services can be classified as letters, parcels, remittance, issue of newspapers and magazines, fast mail service, express mail service, savings deposits, stamps for collection, public and individual telegraph service, facsimiles, long-distance telephone service, leasing of telephone lines, urban paging service, mobile telephone service, data transfer and transmission, etc. The accounting approach is to multiply the service products of all types with their average unit price (constant price) to get sum of business value, plus income from other services such as leasing of telephone lines and equipment, maintenance of telephone switchboards and lines on behalf of customers. This indicator reflects the overall results of post and telecommunications service during a given period, and is important to study the composition of business service and the development of post and telecommunications service.

The formula is as follows:

Business volume of post and telecommunications = ∑ *(Transaction of post and telecommunication service×constant price) + Income from leasing, maintenance and other services = Business volume of post + Business volume of telecommunication*

Possession of Civil Motor Vehicles refers to the total number of vehicles that are registered and received vehicles license tags according to the Work Standard for Motor Vehicles Registration formulated by transport management office under department of public security at the end of reference period. They are divided into following categories according to the structure of motor vehicles: passenger vehicles, trucks and others; and private vehicles and vehicles for units use according to ownerships; working vehicles, non-working vehicles and special motor vehicles according to kind of usage; large passenger vehicles, medium passenger vehicles, small passenger vehicles and mini passenger vehicle, heavy trucks, light-heavy trucks, light trucks and mini trucks according to sizes of vehicles.

Capacity of Long Distance Telephone Exchanges refers to the rated capacity of telephone exchanges to connect long distance telephone network, including capacity of international telephone exchanges.

Capacity of Office Telephone Exchanges refers to the capacity (measured in gate) of telephone exchanges installed in the offices of telecommunication service providers for communication between fixed telephones. It includes the capacity of both manual and automatic exchanges in use and for stand-by purpose, excluding the capacity of subscribers' exchanges.

Capacity of Mobile Telephone Exchanges refers to the capacity of the maximum services provided to subscribers at one time basing on a certain model and transacting capacity of the mobile telephone exchanges.

第14篇
CHAPTER 14

国内贸易
Domestic Trade

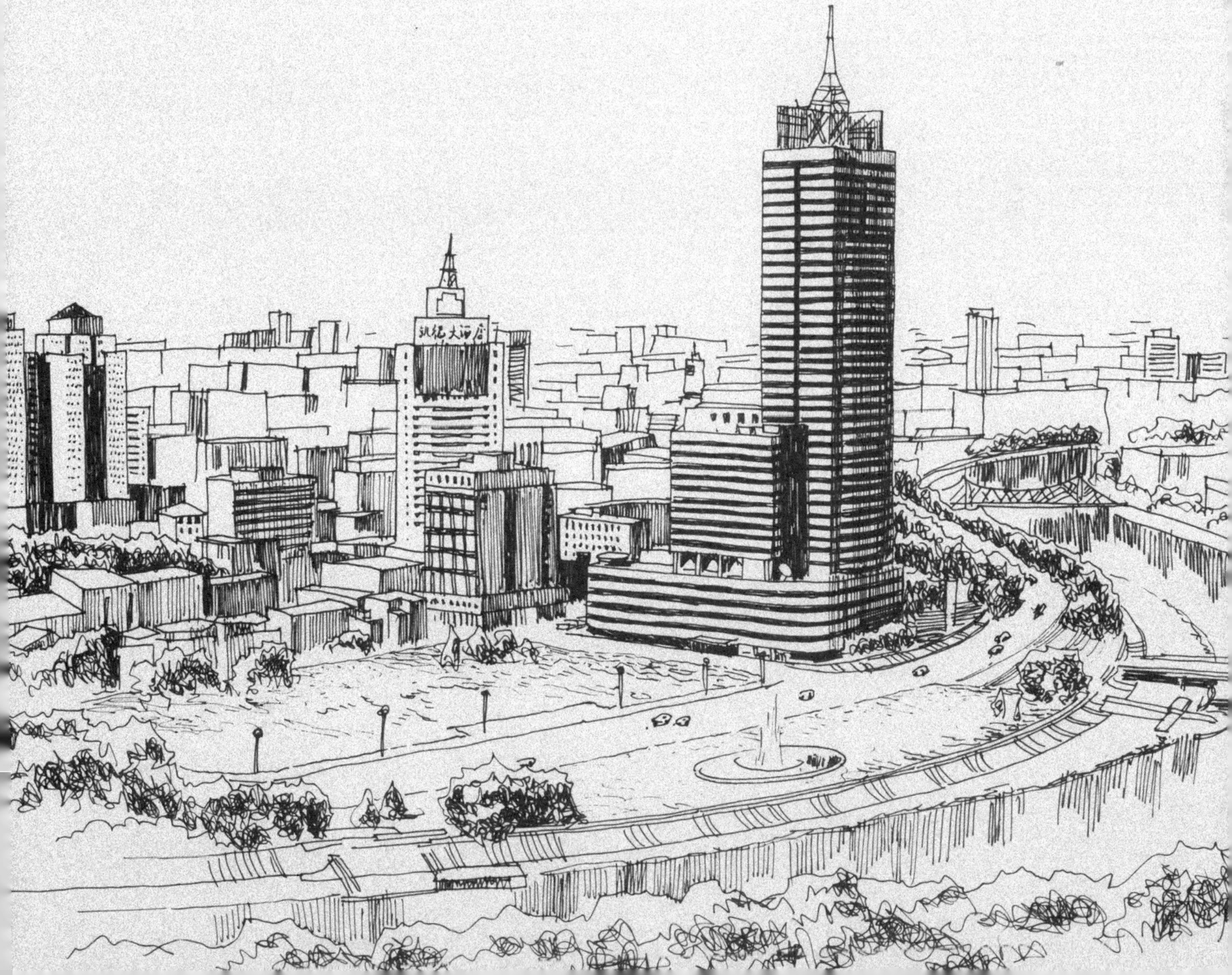

14-1 社会消费品零售总额
TOTAL RETAIL SALES OF CONSUMER GOODS

单位：万元 (10 000 yuan)

指　　标	Item	2005	2006	2006比2005年增长(%) Increase Rate in 2006 over 2005 (%)
社会消费品零售总额	**Total Retail Sales of Consumer Goods**	**11900636**	**13567865**	**14.0**
按销售地区分	**Grouped by Region**			
市	City	11191741	12753806	14.0
县	County	388490	442718	14.0
县以下	Under County Level	320405	371341	15.9
按行业分	**Grouped by Sector**			
批发和零售业	Wholesale and Retail Trade	10073447	11430362	13.5
住宿和餐饮业	Catering Trade	1788980	2099656	17.4
其他行业	Others	38209	37847	-0.9

14-2 批发和零售业商品销售总额(2006年)
TOTAL SALES OF WHOLESALE AND RETAIL TRADE, 2006

单位：万元 (10 000 yuan)

项　　目	Item	商品销售总额 Total Sales	#批　发 Wholesale
总　　计	**Total**	**67738678**	**55847083**
批发业	**Wholesale Trade**	**55661698**	**53441671**
农畜产品批发	Farm & Livestock Products	632378	600558
食品、饮料及烟草制品批发	Food, Beverages and Tobacco	1804018	1624082
纺织、服装及日用品批发	Textile, Garments and Daily Articles	1730013	1672434
文化、体育用品及器材批发	Cultural and Sports Goods & Equipments	452656	419726
医药及医疗器械批发	Medicine and Medical Appliances	1872593	1645492
矿产品、建材及化工产品批发	Mineral Products, Building Material and Chemical Products	38398916	37510765
机械设备、五金交电及电子产品批发	Machinery Equipment, Hardware, Transport, Electric and Electronic Products	8666077	7966222
贸易经纪与代理	Trade Broker and Agent	503623	481034
其他批发	Others	1601425	1521358
零售业	**Retail Trade**	**12076980**	**2405412**
综合零售	Comprehensive Retail	2441480	437459
食品、饮料及烟草制品专门零售	Special Retail of Food, Beverages and Tobacco	442945	61117
纺织、服装及日用品专门零售	Special Retail of Textile, Garments and Daily Articles	519176	110243
文化、体育用品及器材专门零售	Special Retail of Cultural and Sports Goods & Equipments	484912	78094
医药及医疗器械专门零售	Special Retail of Medicine and Medical Appliances	483054	199922
汽车、摩托车、燃料及零配件专门零售	Special Retail of Motor Vehicles, Motorcycles, Parts and Fuel	2699842	432531
家用电器及电子产品专门零售	Special Retail of Household Appliances and Electronic Products	1869981	364813
五金、家具及室内装修材料专门零售	Special Retail of Hardware, Furniture and Decoration Materials for Indoors	1448364	271087
无店铺及其他零售	Non-shop and Other Retail	1687227	450146

14-3 限额以上批发和零售业商品购进总额
TOTAL PURCHASES OF WHOLESALE AND RETAIL TRADE ABOVE DESIGNATED SIZE

单位：万元 (10 000 yuan)

项　目 Item	商品购进总额 Total Goods Purchases		#进　口 Imports	
	2005	2006	2005	2006
总　计 Total	**41923855**	**49120941**	**1974435**	**2675563**
#国有及国有控股企业 State-owned and State-holding Enterprises	27652039	33751393	839668	1140816
按登记注册类型分 Grouped by Registered Status				
内资企业 Domestic-funded Enterprises	39848073	46147407	1260697	1769110
国有企业 State-owned Enterprises	15937343	21405317	222305	624786
集体企业 Collective-owned Enterprises	736553	578692	23607	542
股份合作企业 Cooperative Enterprises	130483	74433		
私营企业 Private Enterprises	7452351	8361591	429419	488898
股份有限公司 Share-holding Corporations Ltd.	4769702	3387651	84630	104664
有限责任公司 Limited Liability Corporations	10350407	11763215	490877	542378
#国有独资 Sole State-funded Corporations	2062914	2020832	222300	23773
联营企业 Joint Ownership Enterprises	293572	480890	995	134
#国有与国有联营企业 State Joint Ownership Enterprises	115437	323294		29
集体与集体联营企业 Collective Joint Ownership Enterprises	9824	6435		
其他内资企业 Other Domestic-funded Enterprises	177663	95619	8866	7708
港澳台商投资企业 Enterprises with Investment from Hong Kong, Macao and Taiwan	492790	886556	234267	130363
外商投资企业 Foreign Funded Enterprises	1582993	2086978	479471	776089
按经济类型分 Grouped by Ownership				
国有经济 State-owned	18115694	23749442	444605	648589
集体经济 Collective-owned	876859	659560	23607	542
股份制经济 Share-holding	13057195	13130034	353206	623269
私有经济 Private and individual	7452351	8361591	429419	488898
"三资"经济 Hong Kong, Macao, Taiwan and Foreign Funded	2075782	2973534	713738	906453
其　他 Others	345974	246780	9860	7812

14-3 续表 Continued

单位：万元 (10 000 yuan)

项目 Item	商品购进总额 Total Goods Purchases		#进口 Imports	
	2005	2006	2005	2006
按国民经济行业分 Grouped by Sector				
批发业 Wholesale Trade	**38288382**	**45075246**	**1954908**	**2645549**
农畜产品批发 Farm & Livestock Products	505316	375488	36787	48177
食品、饮料及烟草制品批发 Food, Beverages and Tobacco	927238	927890	64706	62294
纺织、服装及日用品批发 Textile, Garments and Daily Articles	1069760	1024946	133528	93640
文化、体育用品及器材批发 Cultural and Sports Goods & Equipments	176509	215752	10048	27228
医药及医疗器械批发 Medicine and Medical Appliances	1428967	1673215	78755	30747
矿产品、建材及化工产品批发 Mineral Products, Building Material and Chemical Products	28522177	33343723	576532	1185949
机械设备、五金交电及电子产品批发 Machinery Equipment, Hardware, Transport, Electric and Electronic Products	4540129	6189488	886501	995154
贸易经纪与代理 Trade Broker and Agent	381679	476065	122414	136310
其他批发 Others	736607	848679	45638	66051
零售业 Retail Trade	**3635473**	**4045695**	**19527**	**30014**
综合零售 Comprehensive Retail	1500896	1602587		356
食品、饮料及烟草制品专门零售 Special Retail of Food, Beverages and Tobacco	57613	49710	2723	
纺织、服装及日用品专门零售 Special Retail of Textile, Garments and Daily Articles	107301	192309		
文化、体育用品及器材专门零售 Special Retail of Cultural and Sports Goods & Equipments	75756	109928		
医药及医疗器械专门零售 Special Retail of Medicine and Medical Appliances	48889	29423		
汽车、摩托车、燃料及零配件专门零售 Special Retail of Motor Vehicles, Motorcycles, Parts and Fuel	1214679	1335536	16804	27684
家用电器及电子产品专门零售 Special Retail of Household Appliances and Electronic Products	465557	549247		
五金、家具及室内装修材料专门零售 Special Retail of Hardware, Furniture and Decoration Materials for Indoors	85027	83422		
无店铺及其他零售 Non-shop and Other Retail	79755	93532		1974

14-4 限额以上批发和零售业商品销售和库存总额
TOTAL SALES AND INVENTORY OF WHOLESALE AND RETAIL TRADE ABOVE DESIGNATED SIZE

单位：万元 (10 000 yuan)

项　目 Item	商品销售总额 Total Sales		#批　发 Wholes Sale		年末库存总额 Inventory (year-end)	
	2005	2006	2005	2006	2005	2006
总　计 Total	**43160074**	**51089993**	**38977967**	**46402472**	**2045196**	**2458739**
#国有及国有控股企业 State-owned and State-holding Enterprises	27652039	35242442	26812853	33559304	1117987	1112578
按登记注册类型分 Grouped by Registered Status						
内资企业 Domestic-funded Enterprises	40834674	47978894	36971279	43808843	1834703	2083136
国有企业 State-owned Enterprises	16287685	22279634	15735382	22052844	415084	501877
集体企业 Collective-owned Enterprises	753898	597750	643765	508385	46988	48029
股份合作企业 Cooperative Enterprises	134528	76293	109399	54352	13093	9414
私营企业 Private Enterprises	7707232	8705188	6448187	7279005	439239	669177
股份有限公司 Share-holding Corporations Ltd.	5073521	3716386	4461573	2971281	172835	155270
有限责任公司 Limited Liability Corporations	10392851	12010879	9209300	10416432	713920	684345
#国有独资 Sole State-funded Corporations	1966664	2111002	1963887	1936207	232201	239630
联营企业 Joint Ownership Enterprises	308520	492762	225045	468913	6170	9867
#国有与国有联营企业 State Joint Ownership Enterprises	117007	323332	86088	299482	3387	2470
集体与集体联营企业 Collective Joint Ownership Enterprises	9870	7259	9870	7259	304	
其他内资企业 Other Domestic-funded Enterprises	176440	100002	138628	57632	27375	5157
港澳台商投资企业 Enterprises with Investment from Hong Kong, Macao and Taiwan	505481	775609	431653	661284	65620	126765
外商投资企业 Foreign Funded Enterprises	1819919	2335490	1575034	1932345	144873	248838
按经济类型分 Grouped by Ownership						
国有经济 State-owned	18371355	24713968	17785357	24288533	650671	743978
集体经济 Collective-owned	898296	681301	763034	569996	60385	57443
股份制经济 Share-holding	13499708	13616263	11706987	11451506	654554	599985
私有经济 Private and individual	7707232	8705188	6448187	7279005	439239	669177
"三资"经济 Hong Kong, Macao, Taiwan and Foreign Funded	2325400	3111099	2006687	2593629	210493	375603
其　他 Others	358084	262174	267715	219803	29854	12554

14-4 续表 Continued

单位：万元 (10 000 yuan)

项　目 Item	商品销售总额 Total Sales		#批　发 Wholes Sale		年末库存总额 Inventory (year-end)	
	2005	2006	2005	2006	2005	2006
按国民经济行业分 Grouped by Sector						
批发业 Wholesale Trade	**39313949**	**46858833**	**38265676**	**45759411**	**1758245**	**2035116**
农畜产品批发 Farm & Livestock Products	440823	419171	440752	416651	194292	176109
食品、饮料及烟草制品批发 Food, Beverages and Tobacco	977114	945506	960417	937275	62779	61019
纺织、服装及日用品批发 Textile, Garments and Daily Articles	1227178	1093598	1221894	1083634	58031	52731
文化、体育用品及器材批发 Cultural and Sports Goods & Equipments	190335	218382	180247	208448	21029	51964
医药及医疗器械批发 Medicine and Medical Appliances	1516993	1678845	1293161	1477804	123704	142476
矿产品、建材及化工产品批发 Mineral Products, Building Material and Chemical Products	29015012	34831717	28557469	34416755	827593	1024073
机械设备、五金交电及电子产品批发 Machinery Equipment, Hardware, Transport, Electric and Electronic Products	4809084	6380353	4505294	5954075	417363	476427
贸易经纪与代理 Trade Broker and Agent	391042	388464	391042	370105	19070	21539
其他批发 Others	746369	902798	715401	894663	34385	28779
零售业 Retail Trade	**3846125**	**4231160**	**712290**	**643061**	**286951**	**423623**
综合零售 Comprehensive Retail	1705054	1859103	232145	228233	87189	116267
食品、饮料及烟草制品专门零售 Special Retail of Food, Beverages and Tobacco	66557	64112	5551	3384	6579	19497
纺织、服装及日用品专门零售 Special Retail of Textile, Garments and Daily Articles	131524	96057	32603	7149	33013	52193
文化、体育用品及器材专门零售 Special Retail of Cultural and Sports Goods & Equipments	80113	89856	9670	14640	16994	21795
医药及医疗器械专门零售 Special Retail of Medicine and Medical Appliances	49591	30946	12902	159	3689	5148
汽车、摩托车、燃料及零配件专门零售 Special Retail of Motor Vehicles, Motorcycles, Parts and Fuel	1195336	1394844	331084	267701	74666	141412
家用电器及电子产品专门零售 Special Retail of Household Appliances and Electronic Products	440964	511694	38691	39235	42134	48745
五金、家具及室内装修材料专门零售 Special Retail of Hardware, Furniture and Decoration Materials for Indoors	89454	83397	12092	3484	11431	11312
无店铺及其他零售 Non-shop and Other Retail	87534	101151	37553	79078	11254	7255

14-5 限额以上国有及国有控股批发和零售业主要指标（2006年）
MAIN INDICATORS OF STATE-OWNED & STATE-HOLDING WHOLESALE AND RETAIL TRADE ABOVE DESIGNATED SIZE, 2006

项目 Item	机构（个）Organization (unit)	商品购进总额（万元）Total Purchases (10 000 yuan)	商品销售总额（万元）Total Sales (10 000 yuan)
总计 Total	**369**	**33751393**	**35242442**
批发业 Wholesale Trade	**285**	**32488839**	**33808629**
农畜产品批发 Farm & Livestock Products	11	224724	259748
食品、饮料及烟草制品批发 Food, Beverages and Tobacco	24	665167	681809
纺织、服装及日用品批发 Textile, Garments and Daily Articles	28	594533	659998
文化、体育用品及器材批发 Cultural and Sports Goods & Equipments	8	104231	107391
医药及医疗器械批发 Medicine and Medical Appliances	24	1335658	1403474
矿产品、建材及化工产品批发 Mineral Products, Building Material and Chemical Products	125	26437267	27575529
机械设备、五金交电及电子产品批发 Machinery Equipment, Hardware, Transport, Electric and Electronic Products	42	2714770	2787805
贸易经纪与代理 Trade Broker and Agent	10	157405	73116
其他批发 Others	13	255086	259759
零售业 Retail Trade	**84**	**1262553**	**1433814**
综合零售 Comprehensive Retail	20	678611	839406
食品、饮料及烟草制品专门零售 Special Retail of Food, Beverages and Tobacco	10	12308	14597
纺织、服装及日用品专门零售 Special Retail of Textile, Garments and Daily Articles	2	10676	13605
文化、体育用品及器材专门零售 Special Retail of Cultural and Sports Goods & Equipments	27	83662	62258
医药及医疗器械专门零售 Special Retail of Medicine and Medical Appliances	2	3940	3547
汽车、摩托车、燃料及零配件专门零售 Special Retail of Motor Vehicles, Motorcycles, Parts and Fuel	17	463885	488165
家用电器及电子产品专门零售 Special Retail of Household Appliances and Electronic Products	2	4318	4144
五金、家具及室内装修材料专门零售 Special Retail of Hardware, Furniture and Decoration Materials for Indoors	2	1206	1316
无店铺及其他零售 Non-shop and Other Retail	2	3948	6776

14-6 限额以上住宿业基本情况（2006年）
BASIC STATISTICS ON ACCOMMODATION SERVICES ABOVE DESIGNATED SIZE, 2006

项目	Item	门店总数(个) Number of Stores (unit)	从业人员(人) Employed Persons (person)	餐饮营业面积(平方米) Operational Area of Catering Services(sq. m)	床位数(个) Number of Beds (unit)
总计	**Total**	**133**	**20961**	**279192**	**32965**
#国有及国有控股企业	State-owned and State-holding Enterprises	68	11848	152721	17590
按登记注册类型分	**Grouped by Status of Registration**				
内资企业	Domestic-funded Enterprises	111	16031	241262	27131
国有企业	State-owned Enterprises	48	7217	122575	11592
集体企业	Collective-owned Enterprises	14	996	10213	2938
联营企业	Joint Ownership Enterprises	1	68	700	114
有限责任公司	Limited Liability Corporations	19	3771	57716	5644
股份有限公司	Share-holding Corporations Ltd.	2	161	4300	1020
私营企业	Private Enterprises	26	3688	43758	5664
私营独资	Private-funded Enterprises	4	195	2672	896
私营有限责任公司	Private Limited Liability Corporations	22	3493	41086	4768
其他内资企业	Other Enterprises	1	130	2000	159
港澳台商投资企业	Enterprises with Funds from Hong Kong, Macao and Taiwan	7	2219	10856	1853
合资经营	Joint-venture Enterprises	4	1595	6258	1174
合作经营	Cooperative Enterprises	1	467	3818	329
独资经营企业	Enterprises with Sole Investment	1	42	500	222
投资股份有限公司	Share-holding Corporations Ltd. with Investment	1	115	280	128
外商投资企业	Foreign Funded Enterprises	15	2711	27074	3981
中外合资经营	Joint-venture Enterprises	10	2126	18989	2718
中外合作经营	Cooperative Enterprises	5	578	8085	1263
按行业分	**Grouped by Sector**				
旅游饭店	Tourism Restaurant	87	16133	199400	24595
一般旅馆	Hotel	39	3962	68358	7404
其他住宿服务	Other Accommodation Services	7	866	11434	966

14-6 续表 Continued

单位：万元 (10 000 yuan)

项　目	Item	资产总计 Total Assets	负债合计 Total Liabilities	营业收入 Revenue of Sale	主营业务成本 Cost of Principal Business
总　计	**Total**	**833582.7**	**503710.2**	**209728.6**	**51118.6**
#国有及国有控股企业	State-owned and State-holding Enterprises	597524	379557.9	134147.7	32640.9
按登记注册类型分	**Grouped by Status of Registration**				
内资企业	Domestic-funded Enterprises	606306.3	281490.4	144762.6	37733.4
国有企业	State-owned Enterprises	286655.8	110916.4	59671.7	19332.1
集体企业	Collective-owned Enterprises	18119.1	7513	6762.2	2445.1
联营企业	Joint Ownership Enterprises	341.2	1768.3	285.2	100
有限责任公司	Limited Liability Corporations	146518.1	98116.1	37795.1	6488.3
股份有限公司	Share-holding Corporations Ltd.	26497.2	12770.8	4117.7	597
私营企业	Private Enterprises	127755.9	49988.3	35143.7	8648.5
私营独资	Private-funded Enterprises	2960.2	2519.3	1360	866.6
私营有限责任公司	Private Limited Liability Corporations	124795.7	47469	33783.7	7781.9
其他内资企业	Other Enterprises	419	417.5	987	122.4
港澳台商投资企业	Enterprises with Funds from Hong Kong, Macao and Taiwan	65853.5	65900.8	19404.1	2491.3
合资经营	Joint-venture Enterprises	37321.9	43438.7	12544.8	1324.2
合作经营	Cooperative Enterprises	22561	19946.9	4933.1	524.1
独资经营企业	Enterprises with Sole Investment	3419.5	842.2	1171.7	508.5
投资股份有限公司	Share-holding Corporations Ltd. with Investment	2551.1	1673	754.5	134.5
外商投资企业	Foreign Funded Enterprises	161422.9	156319	45561.9	10893.9
中外合资经营	Joint-venture Enterprises	146641.7	144431.8	39435.6	10098.3
中外合作经营	Cooperative Enterprises	14781.2	11887.2	6126.3	795.6
按行业分	**Grouped by Sector**				
旅游饭店	Tourism Restaurant	671256.6	373367.7	171709.5	41125.8
一般旅馆	Hotel	129840.6	106769	29418.7	8418.5
其他住宿服务	Other Accommodation Services	32485.5	23573.5	8600.4	1574.3

14-7 天津市三星级以上饭店一览表（2006年）
LIST OF THREE, FOUR, FIVE-STAR HOTELS, 2006

宾馆名称 Name of Hotel	星 级 Star Level	客房数（间） Number of Guest Rooms (unit)	床位数（个） Number of Beds (nuit)	地 址 Address
喜来登大酒店	五 星			河西区紫金山路
SHERATON TIANJIN HOTEL	Five-star	300	380	Zijinshan Road, Hexi Dist.
泰达国际酒店暨会馆	五 星			天津经济技术开发区第二大街
TEDA INTERNATIONAL HOTEL	Five-star	235	329	Second Avenue of TEDA
天津泰达国际会馆	五 星			南开区复康路7号增2号
TEDA INTERNATIONAL CLUB TIANJIN	Five-star	115	278	No. 7-2, Fukang Road, Nankai Dist.
天津天保国际酒店	五 星			天津港保税区京门大道368号
TIANJIN TIANBAO INTERNATIONAL HOTEL	Five-star	145	232	No. 368, Jingmen Avenue, TFTZ
天津金皇大酒店	五 星			河西区南京路18号
TIANJIN GOLDEN CROWN HOTEL	Five-star	259	415	No. 18, Nanjing Road, Hexi Dist.
天津万丽泰达酒店及会议中心	五 星			天津经济技术开发区第二大街29号
RENAISSANCE TIANJIN TEDA HOTEL & CONVENTION CENTRE	Five-star	543	735	No. 29, Second Avenue of TEDA
凯悦饭店	四 星			和平区解放北路219号
HYATT TIANJIN	Four-star	360	720	No. 219, North Jiefang Road, Heping Dist.
水晶宫饭店	四 星			河西区友谊路28号
THE CRYSTAL PALACE HOTEL	Four-star	287	421	No. 28, Youyi Road, Hexi Dist.
利顺德大饭店	四 星			和平区台儿庄路33号
ASTOR HOTEL	Four-star	203	295	No. 33, Tai'erzhuang Road, Heping Dist.
津利华大酒店	四 星			河西区友谊路32号
GENEVA HOTEL	Four-star	259	480	No. 32, Youyi Road, Hexi Dist.
天宇大酒店	四 星			和平区电台道19号
TIANJIN TIANYU HOTEL	Four-star	134	234	No. 19, Diantai Road,Heping Dist.
天津假日饭店	四 星			河北区中山路288号
HOLIDAY INN TIANJIN	Four-star	248	343	No. 288, Zhongshan Road, Hebei Dist.
美都大酒店	四 星			河西区围堤道117号
MEIDU HOTEL	Four-star	158	250	No. 117, Weidi Road, Hexi Dist.
泰达中心酒店	四 星			天津经济技术开发区第三大街16号
TEDA CENTRAL HOTEL	Four-star	238	342	No. 16, Third Avenue of TEDA
君悦酒店	四 星			和平区贵州路16号
JUNYUE HOTEL	Four-star	195	247	No. 16, Guizhou Road, Heping Dist.
天鹅湖温泉度假村	四 星			武清开发区福源道20号
SWAN LAKE SPRING VACATION VILLAGE	Four-star	500	980	No. 20, Fuyuan Road, Wuqing Development Area
天津利顺德大厦	四 星			和平区台儿庄路32号
ASTOR PLAZA	Four-star	85	125	No. 32, Tai'erzhuang Road, Heping Dist.
舒泊花园大酒店	四 星			和平区荣业大街2号
SUPER GARDEN HOTEL TIANJIN	Four-star	128	258	No. 2, Rongye Avenue, Heping Dist.
胜利宾馆	四 星			塘沽区津塘公路11号
VICTORY HOTEL TIANJIN CHINA	Four-star	313	497	No. 11, Jintang Highway, Tanggu Dist.
凯德大酒店	四 星			河北区自由道15号
KIND HOTEL	Four-star	195	344	No. 15, Ziyou Road, Hebei Dist.
天津世纪酒店	四 星			河西区黑牛城道179号
CENTURY HOTEL TIANJIN	Four-star	115	151	No. 179, Heiniucheng Road, Hexi Dist.
天津惠中酒店	四 星			天津经济技术开发区第三大街芳林泰达园A座
TIANJIN ELEGANCE HOTEL	Three-star	151	193	Building A, TEDA Fanglin Garden, Third Avenue of TEDA
友谊宾馆	三 星			和平区南京路94号
TIANJIN FRIENDSHIP HOTEL	Three-star	346	692	No. 94, Nanjing Road, Heping Dist.
凯撒皇宫大酒店	三 星			河西区气象台路46号
CAESAR PALACE HOTEL	Three-star	96	168	No. 46, Qixiangtai Road, Hexi Dist.

14-7 续表 1 Continued

宾馆名称 Name of Hotel	星 级 Star Level	客房数（间） Number of Guest Rooms (unit)	床位数个） Number of Beds (nuit)	地 址 Address
天津市皇宫饭店 TIANJIN IMPERIAC HOTEL	三 星 Three-star	50	75	和平区解放北路177号 No. 177, North Jiefang Road, Heping Dist.
东亚大酒店 EAST ASIA HOTEL CO.LTD	三 星 Three-star	114	213	和平区昆明路86号 No. 86, Kunming Road, Heping Dist.
华富宫大饭店 GHA FU PALACE GRAND HOTEL	三 星 Three-star	475	940	和平区南市旅馆街 Nanshi Hotel Mall, Heping Dist.
金禧国际大酒店 CAIRNHILL INTERNATIONAL HOTEL	三 星 Three-star	320	438	南开区南开三马路2号 No. 2, Third Road, Nankai Dist.
双鹿大厦 SHUANGLU HOTEL	三 星 Three-star	144	260	南开区南开三马路165号 No. 165, Third Road, Nankai Dist.
金帆酒店 GOLDEN SAIL HOTEL	三 星 Three-star	98	135	天津经济技术开发区第一大街49号 NO. 49, First Avenue of TEDA
夏日酒店 SUMMER HOTEL	三 星 Three-star	76	140	塘沽区滨海游乐城内 Binhai Entertainment City, Tanggu Dist.
天大天财酒店 TIANCAI HOTEL	三 星 Three-star	150	286	华苑新技术产业园区榕苑路1号 No. 1, Rongyuan Road, THIP, Huayuan
柳林宾馆 LIULIN HOTEL	三 星 Three-star	100	180	河西区柳林东 East of Liulin, Hexi Dist.
津华饭店(天津第一饭店) JINHUA HOTEL	三 星 Three-star	99	128	和平区解放北路158号 No. 158, North Jiefang Road, Heping Dist.
月坛酒店 MOON HOTEL	三 星 Three-star	115	216	津南区咸水沽为民路4号 No. 4, Weimin Road, Xianshuigu Town, Jinnan Dist.
新业国际饭店 XINYE INTERNATIONAL HOTEL	三 星 Three-star	46	92	塘沽区新港路129号 No. 129, Xingang Road, Tanggu Dist.
银河大酒店 YINHE HOTEL	三 星 Three-star	176	330	东丽区津塘公路十号桥 No. 10 Bridge, Jintang Highway, Dongli Dist.
升云大酒店 SHENGYUN HOTEL	三 星 Three-star	50	100	大港区上古林东环海鲜街88号 No. 88, Haixian Street, Shanggulin, Dagang Dist.
正达酒店 ZHENGDA HOTEL	三 星 Three-star	84	140	河北区万柳村大街6号 No. 6, Wanliucun Street, Hebei Dist.
贵达酒店 GUIDA HOTEL	三 星 Three-star	75	147	宁河县苗庄镇刘庄村 Liuzhuang Village, Miaozhuang Town, Ninghe County
津海大酒店 JINHAI RESTAURANT	三 星 Three-star	130	260	静海县大邱庄镇黄山路8号 No. 8, Huangshan Road, Daqiuzhuang Town, Jinghai County
尧舜大酒店 TIANJIN YAOSHUN HOTEL	三 星 Three-star	78	120	静海县大邱庄镇尧舜街 Yaoshun Street, Daqiuzhuang Town, Jinghai County
石化天华宾馆 TIANHUA HOTEL	三 星 Three-star	106	194	大港区北围堤路(西)68号 No. 68, North Weidi Road, Dagang Dist.
和平宾馆 PEACE HOTEL	三 星 Three-star	102	126	和平区大理道66号 No. 66, Dali Road, Heping Dist.
天津金世界酒店 TIANJIN JINSHIJIE HOTEL	三 星 Three-star	84	134	塘沽区新港二号路2169号 No. 2169, Xin'gang No.2 Road, Tanggu Dist.
天津市中泰大酒店 TIANJIN ZHONGTAI HOTEL	三 星 Three-star	165	307	塘沽区和平路588号 No. 588, Heping Road, Tanggu Dist.
大通会馆酒店 TIANJIN DATONG CLUB	三 星 Three-star	82	185	河东区中环线红星路东 East of Hongxing Road, Middle of Ring Road, Hedong Dist.
华海大酒店 HUAHAI HOTEL	三 星 Three-star	117	149	天津经济技术开发区第三大街9号 No. 9, Third Avenue of TEDA

14-7 续表 2 Continued

宾馆名称 Name of Hotel	星 级 Star Level	客房数(间) Number of Guest Rooms (unit)	床位数(个) Number of Beds (nuit)	地 址 Address
天波大酒店	三 星			河东区六经路11号
TIANBO HOTEL	Three-star	173	307	No. 11, Liujing Road, Hedong Dist.
建设大厦	三 星			蓟县中昌北路
JIANSHE BUILDING TIANJIN	Three-star	50	100	North Zhongchang Road, Jixian County
水上会宾园饭店	三 星			南开区水上公园路46号
HUIBINYUAN HOTEL	Three-star	161	272	No. 46, Water Park Road, Nankai Dist.
体育宾馆	三 星			南开区宾水道延长线
SPORTS HOTEL	Three-star	101	156	Continuation of Binshui Road, Nankai Dist.
红楼大酒店	三 星			南开区卫津南路38号
RED BUILDING HOTEL	Three-star	98	182	No. 38, South Weijin Road, Nankai Dist.
长青温泉宾馆	三 星			河西区小围堤道
HOT SPRING HOTEL TIANJIN	Three-star	260	520	Xiaoweidi Road, Hexi Dist.
天津远洋宾馆	三 星			河北区远洋广场5号
OCEAN HOTEL TIANJIN	Three-star	122	301	No. 5, Ocean Square, Hebei Dist.
渔阳宾馆	三 星			蓟县城内迎宾路12号
YUYANG HOTEL	Three-star	161	322	No. 12, Yingbin Road of County, Jixian County
大港油田宾馆	三 星			大港油田三号院团结西路
DAGANG OIL FIELD HOTEL	Three-star	183	350	No. 3 yard, Tuanjie West Road, Dagang Oil Field
东丽湖度假村	三 星			东丽区东丽湖北侧
DONGLI LAKE HOLIDAY VILLAGE	Three-star	110	241	North of Dongli Lake, Dongli Dist.
宝坻宾馆	三 星			宝坻区城关镇广川路23号
BAODI HOTEL	Three-star	208	460	No. 23, Guangchuan Road, Chengguan Town, Baodi Dist.
雍阳宾馆	三 星			武清区杨村镇雍阳东道16号
YONGYANG HOTEL	Three-star	130	300	No. 16, East Yongyang Road, Yangcun Town, Wuqing Dist.
枫林宾馆	三 星			南开区宾水西道2号
FENGLIN HOTEL	Three-star	84	89	No. 2, West Binshui Road, Nankai Dist.
鸿发大厦	三 星			天津经济技术开发区洞庭路41号
HONGFA BUILDING	Three-star	67	134	No. 41, Dongting Road, TEDA
富蓝特大酒店	三 星			和平区新华路231号
TIANJIN FRIEND HOTEL	Three-star	97	173	No. 231, Xinhua Road, Heping Dist.
憩园山庄	三 星			蓟县官庄镇营房村北
QIYUAN HOTEL	Three-star	99	203	North of Yingfang Village, Guanzhuang Town, Jixian County
天水大酒店	三 星			河西区平山道25号
NARCISSUS HOTEL	Three-star	120	150	No. 25, Pingshan Road, Hexi Dist.
麓琳宾馆	三 星			东丽区卫国道216号(余门)
LULIN HOTEL	Three-star	102	151	No. 216, Weiguo Road, Dongli Dist.
太阳雨大酒店	三 星			天津经济技术开发区第一大街明园路渤化小区
SUNNYRAIN HOTEL	Three-star	152	212	Bohua Area, Mingyuan Road, First Avenue of TEDA
天城度假村	三 星			蓟县逯庄子乡东大屯北
TIANCHENG VACATION VILLAGE	Three-star	90	170	North of Dongdatun, Daizhuangzi Township, Jixian County
海得润滋酒店	三 星			大港区津岐公路千米桥北侧
HYDRUS HOTEL	Three-star	138	236	North of Qianmi Bridge, Jinqi Road, Dagang Dist.
天津市华城宾馆	三 星			南开区红旗路253号
TIANJIN HUACHENG HOTEL	Three-star	97	190	No. 253, Hongqi Road, Nankai Dist.

14-8 限额以上餐饮业基本情况(2006年)
BASIC STATISTICS ON CATERING SERVICES ENTERPRISES ABOVE DESIGNATED SIZE, 2006

单位：万元 (10 000 yuan)

项目	Item	门店总数(个) Number of Stores (unit)	从业人员(人) Employed Persons (person)	营业面积(平方米) Operational Area (sq. m)	餐位数(位) Number of Beds (unit)
总计	**Total**	**180**	**25963**	**538646**	**103228**
#国有及国有控股企业	State-owned and State-holding Enterprise	19	2519	77770	8998
按登记注册类型分	**Grouped by Status of Registration**				
内资企业	Domestic-funded Enterprises	156	16046	447016	79490
国有企业	State-owned Enterprises	10	1343	33888	5296
集体企业	Collective-owned Enterprises	8	550	8685	2804
股份合作企业	Cooperative Enterprises	2	130	3300	780
有限责任公司	Limited Liability Corporations	32	3848	172018	13193
股份有限公司	Share-holding Corporations Ltd.	5	372	6435	1594
私营企业	Private Enterprises	87	8474	202345	50759
私营独资	Private-funded Enterprises	17	961	17921	4982
私营合伙	Private Limited Liability Corporations	5	540	10551	1726
私营有限责任公司	Private Share-holding Corporations Ltd.	63	6693	167473	41855
私营股份有限公司	Private Share-holding Corporations Ltd.	2	280	6400	2196
其他内资企业	Other Enterprises	12	1329	20345	5064
港澳台商投资企业	Enterprises with Funds from Hong Kong, Macao and Taiwan	6	449	6402	2079
合资经营企业	Joint-venture Enterprises	5	422	5758	1925
独资经营企业	Enterprises with Sole Investment	1	27	644	154
外商投资企业	Foreign Funded Enterprises	18	9468	85228	21659
中外合资经营	Joint-venture Enterprises	5	420	18046	1877
外资企业	Enterprises with Sole Foreign Investment	12	9009	49676	18924
外商投资股份有限公司	Share-holding Corporations Ltd. with Foreign Investment	1	39	17506	858
按行业分	**Grouped by Sector**				
正餐服务业	Restaurant	153	15155	446279	74771
快餐服务业	Snack Counter	17	9739	58104	25993
饮料及冷饮服务业	Cafe	1	119	500	0
其他餐饮服务业	Others	9	950	33763	2464

14-8 续表　Continued

单位：万元 (10 000 yuan)

项　目	Item	资产总计 Total Assets	负债合计 Total Liabilities	营业收入 Revenue of Sale	主营业务成本 Cost of Principal Business
总　计	**Total**	**289707**	**196291**	**338463**	**161180**
# 国有及国有控股企业	State-owned and State-holding Enterprise	46827	25366	33535	17966
按登记注册类型分	**Grouped by Status of Registration**				
内资企业	Domestic-funded Enterprises	205692	141083	182892	104612
国有企业	State-owned Enterprises	20105	15280	11784	5712
集体企业	Collective-owned Enterprises	8871	5139	3050	1766
股份合作企业	Cooperative Enterprises	418	349	1339	763
有限责任公司	Limited Liability Corporations	57013	31527	58803	33218
股份有限公司	Share-holding Corporations Ltd.	1664	1223	3727	2153
私营企业	Private Enterprises	109767	84091	96397	56262
私营独资	Private-funded Enterprises	3054	2264	8251	4523
私营合伙	Private Limited Liability Corporations	4367	2964	4404	2088
私营有限责任公司	Private Share-holding Corporations Ltd.	100678	77603	80374	47757
私营股份有限公司	Private Share-holding Corporations Ltd.	1668	1261	3368	1894
其他内资企业	Other Enterprises	7854	3473	7794	4739
港澳台商投资企业	Enterprises with Funds from Hong Kong, Macao and Taiwan	4593	1800	4748	2030
合资经营企业	Joint-venture Enterprises	4176	1499	4391	1870
独资经营企业	Enterprises with Sole Investment	416	301	358	161
外商投资企业	Foreign Funded Enterprises	79423	53407	150822	54538
中外合资经营	Joint-venture Enterprises	2190	2309	2309	983
外资企业	Enterprises with Sole Foreign Investment	76326	50403	146011	52226
外商投资股份有限公司	Share-holding Corporations Ltd. with Foreign Investment	907	695	2502	1329
按行业分	**Grouped by Sector**				
正餐服务业	Restaurant	176959	127163	162516	92378
快餐服务业	Snack Counter	82836	54670	151759	54741
饮料及冷饮服务业	Cafe	1771	947	1592	929
其他餐饮服务业	Others	28140	13511	22596	13133

14-9 按登记注册类型分限额以上批发和零售企业财务状况(2006年)
MAIN FINANCIAL INDICATORS OF ENTERPRISES ABOVE DESIGNATED SIZE OF WHOLESALE AND RETAIL TRADES BY STATUS OF REGISTRATION, 2006

单位：万元 (10 000 yuan)

项　目	Item	主营业务收入 Revenue from Principal Business	主营业务成本 Cost of Principal Business	主营业务税金及附加 Taxes and Other Charge on Principal Business
总　计	**Total**	**44985172**	**42754771**	**31488**
批发企业合计	**Wholesale Trade**	**40961691**	**39216183**	**23295**
#国有及国有控股企业	State-owned and State-holding Enterprises	28804435	27671042	13243
内资企业	Domestic-funded Enterprises	38587041	37044879	22485
国有企业	State-owned Enterprises	19322679	18536574	7594
集体企业	Collective-owned Enterprises	488029	473195	288
股份合作企业	Cooperative Enterprises	53258	50178	59
联营企业	Joint Ownership Enterprises	407911	394776	869
有限责任公司	Limited Liability Corporations	8961512	8658253	4174
股份有限公司	Share-holding Corporations Ltd.	2506071	2378607	1793
私营企业	Private Enterprises	6787228	6495150	7665
其他企业	Others	60353	58146	44
港澳台商投资企业	Enterprises with Investment from Hong Kong, Macao and Taiwan	588751	565407	15
外商投资企业	Foreign Funded Enterprises	1785898	1605897	795
零售企业合计	**Retail Trade**	**4023482**	**3538588**	**8194**
内资企业	Domestic-funded Enterprises	3327916	3044993	7577
国有企业	State-owned Enterprises	152550	124217	549
集体企业	Collective-owned Enterprises	72096	63936	224
股份合作企业	Cooperative Enterprises	16635	14541	45
联营企业	Joint Ownership Enterprises	27427	26534	9
有限责任公司	Limited Liability Corporations	1071587	966959	2649
股份有限公司	Share-holding Corporations Ltd.	712313	663167	1317
私营企业	Private Enterprises	1245561	1156691	2773
其他企业	Others	29748	28948	12
港澳台商投资企业	Enterprises with Investment from Hong Kong, Macao and Taiwan	336702	176242	278
外商投资企业	Foreign Funded Enterprises	358864	317354	338

14-9 续表 1 Contiued

单位：万元 (10 000 yuan)

项　目	Item	主营业务利润 Profits from Principal Business	资产总计 Total Assets	# 流动资产 Working Capitals
总　　计	**Total**	**1939345**	**13568523**	**10880750**
批发企业合计	**Wholesale Trade**	**1532380**	**11225541**	**9473063**
# 国有及国有控股企业	State-owned and State-holding Enterprises	1009965	6816418	5503384
内资企业	Domestic-funded Enterprises	1339757	10324899	8643922
国有企业	State-owned Enterprises	741410	3634316	2856360
集体企业	Collective-owned Enterprises	9495	177641	145302
股份合作企业	Cooperative Enterprises	2302	22835	19510
联营企业	Joint Ownership Enterprises	11087	87029	78021
有限责任公司	Limited Liability Corporations	214997	3454794	3074409
股份有限公司	Share-holding Corporations Ltd.	121608	642465	363998
私营企业	Private Enterprises	236777	2290325	2092401
其他企业	Others	2082	15495	13921
港澳台商投资企业	Enterprises with Investment from Hong Kong, Macao and Taiwan	23300	233668	223085
外商投资企业	Foreign Funded Enterprises	169323	666974	606056
零售企业合计	**Retail Trade**	**406965**	**2342983**	**1407686**
内资企业	Domestic-funded Enterprises	215792	1938585	1121863
国有企业	State-owned Enterprises	19804	291088	151179
集体企业	Collective-owned Enterprises	4103	42809	32839
股份合作企业	Cooperative Enterprises	1744	8933	7415
联营企业	Joint Ownership Enterprises	7	9139	8772
有限责任公司	Limited Liability Corporations	77581	639364	323715
股份有限公司	Share-holding Corporations Ltd.	43929	406750	179598
私营企业	Private Enterprises	67944	538062	416961
其他企业	Others	680	2441	1385
港澳台商投资企业	Enterprises with Investment from Hong Kong, Macao and Taiwan	154079	224581	206078
外商投资企业	Foreign Funded Enterprises	37094	179817	79746

14-9 续表 2 Contiued

单位：万元 (10 000 yuan)

项　目	Item	负债合计 Total Liabilities	所有者权益合计 Total Owners' Equities
总　计	**Total**	**10026981**	**3541542**
批发企业合计	**Wholesale Trade**	**8379365**	**2846176**
#国有及国有控股企业	State-owned and State-holding Enterprises	5092333	1724085
内资企业	Domestic-funded Enterprises	7707878	2617021
国有企业	State-owned Enterprises	2716378	917937
集体企业	Collective-owned Enterprises	143093	34548
股份合作企业	Cooperative Enterprises	17200	5635
联营企业	Joint Ownership Enterprises	66518	20511
有限责任公司	Limited Liability Corporations	2708652	746142
股份有限公司	Share-holding Corporations Ltd.	374587	267878
私营企业	Private Enterprises	1668218	622107
其他企业	Others	13233	2262
港澳台商投资企业	Enterprises with Investment from Hong Kong, Macao and Taiwan	200521	33147
外商投资企业	Foreign Funded Enterprises	470966	196008
零售企业合计	**Retail Trade**	**1647616**	**695367**
内资企业	Domestic-funded Enterprises	1423788	514797
国有企业	State-owned Enterprises	208042	83046
集体企业	Collective-owned Enterprises	34485	8324
股份合作企业	Cooperative Enterprises	7167	1766
联营企业	Joint Ownership Enterprises	8067	1072
有限责任公司	Limited Liability Corporations	521131	118233
股份有限公司	Share-holding Corporations Ltd.	212769	193981
私营企业	Private Enterprises	431240	106821
其他企业	Others	889	1552
港澳台商投资企业	Enterprises with Investment from Hong Kong, Macao and Taiwan	89671	134910
外商投资企业	Foreign Funded Enterprises	134157	45660

14-10 按国民经济行业分限额以上批发和零售业财务状况（2006年）
MAIN FINANCIAL INDICATORS OF ENTERPRISES ABOVE DESIGNATED SIZE OF WHOLESALE AND RETAIL TRADES BY SECTOR, 2006

项　目	Item	主营业务收入 Revenue from Principal Business	主营业务成本 Cost of Principal Business
总　计	**Total**	**44985172**	**42754771**
批发企业合计	**Wholesale Trade**	**40961691**	**39216183**
农畜产品批发业	Wholesale of Farm & Livestock Product	393901	381700
食品、饮料及烟草制品批发业	Wholesale of Food, Beverages and Tobacco	1211318	1060978
纺织、服装及日用品批发业	Wholesale of Textiles, Garments and Daily Consumer Articles	1111868	1046285
文化、体育用品及器材批发业	Wholesale of Culture, Sports Appliances and Equipments	196375	184984
医药及医疗器材批发业	Wholesale of Medicines and Medical Appliances	1235104	1167463
矿产品、建材及化工产品批发业	Wholesale of Mineral Products, Building Material and Chemical Products	30594788	29459433
机械设备、五金交电及电子产品批发	Wholesale of Machinery, Hardware and Electronic Equipments	4970262	4724218
贸易经纪与代理	Trade Broker and Agency	409731	378136
其他批发业	Other Wholesales	838344	812985
零售企业合计	**Retail Trade**	**4023482**	**3538588**
综合零售业	Comprehensive Retail	1629326	1442625
食品、饮料及烟草制品专门零售业	Retail of Food, Beverages and Tobacco	57111	48973
纺织、服装及日用品专门零售业	Special Retail of Textiles, Garments and Daily Consumer Articles	325141	160822
文化、体育用品及器材专门零售业	Retail of Culture, Sports Appliances and Equipments	79888	60803
医药及医疗器材专门零售业	Retail of Medicines and Medical Appliances	35198	29489
汽车、摩托车、燃料及零配件专门零售业	Retail of Motor Vehicles, Motorcycles, Fuel and Parts	1295708	1235349
家用电器及电子产品专门零售业	Special Retail of Household Electric Appliances and Electronic Products	429961	409510
五金、家具及室内装修材料专门零售业	Special Retail of Hardware, Furniture and Decoration Materials	72090	58593
无店铺及其他零售业	Non-shop and Other Retails	99058	92424

单位：万元（10 000 yuan）

主营业务税金及附加 Taxes and Other Charge on Principal Business	主营业务利润 Profits from Principal Business	资产总计 Total Assets	#流动资产 Working Capitals	负债合计 Total Liabilities	所有者权益合计 Total Owners' Equities
31488	**1939345**	**13568523**	**10880750**	**10026981**	**3541542**
23295	**1532380**	**6816418**	**5503384**	**5092333**	**1724085**
74	-2475	394484	318413	238487	155997
3242	129506	537618	420770	304111	233507
533	51582	372995	306523	264184	108811
83	9228	80967	67015	101099	-20132
909	46934	517283	457785	405405	111878
12028	1034248	6978564	5808349	5223141	1755423
5834	222684	1953255	1753011	1542494	410762
183	23409	120964	109135	90084	30879
409	17266	269411	232061	210360	59051
8194	**406965**	**2342983**	**1407686**	**1647616**	**695367**
4208	144080	1202600	569432	934320	268279
221	5170	39503	23387	32881	6622
304	162836	287245	241248	104349	182895
534	9429	79116	47579	38329	40787
138	4432	20644	11896	10325	10319
1069	50284	456311	294402	316352	139959
1396	15166	186272	171185	157763	28509
198	13063	35331	22778	32022	3309
126	2506	35961	25781	21275	14686

14-11 天津市主要亿元商品交易市场情况（2006年）
TIANJIN MAIN MARKET WITH TRANSACTION VOLUME OF 100 MILLION YUAN, 2006

市场名称	Name of Market
天津储宝钢材现货交易市场	Tianjin Chubao Steel Spot Exchange Market
金钟蔬菜批发市场	Jinzhong Vegetable Wholesale Market
天津市宝钢储菱钢材交易市场	Tianjin Baogang Chuling Steel Exchange Market
天津万隆大胡同置业有限公司万隆大胡同商业中心	Tianjin Wanlong Dahutong Development Co., Ltd.
天津市大胡同天奕商城	Tianjin Dahutong Tianyi Shopping Center
天津石化交易中心市场有限责任公司	Tianjin Petroleum Chemical Products Exchange Market Co., Ltd.
天津市金地商贸发展有限责任公司	Tianjin Jindi Bussiness & Commerce Development Co., Ltd.
天津市宁河县贸易开发区综合批发市场	Tianjin Ninghe County Trade Development Zone Comprehensive Wholesale Market
天津轻纺万象城有限责任公司	Tianjin Wanxiang Light Industry Products and Textile Goods Market Co., Ltd.
天津市大胡同集团有限公司大胡同百货批发市场	Tianjin Dahutong Group Co., Ltd., Grocery Wholesale Market
天津滨海国际汽车城	Tianjin Coastal International Auto City
何庄子蔬菜批发市场	Hezhuangzi Vegetables Wholesale Market
中国(天津)粮油批发交易市场	China (Tianjin) Grain & Oil Wholesale Market
天津市食品公司冷冻厂	Tianjin Freezing Food Factory
天津市南开区王顶堤水产批发市场	Tianjin Nankai Wangdingdi Aquatic Product Wholesale Market
天津钢铁炉料交易市场	Tianjin Steel & Iron Materials Exchange Market
天津市卞兴钢材批发市场	Tianjin Bianxing Steel Wholesale Market
天津市兴耀消费品综合批发市场	Tianjin Xingyao Comprehensive Wholesale Market
天津市静海县范庄子蔬菜批发市场	Tianjin Jinghai County Fanzhuangzi Vegetable Wholesale Market
天津市环渤海家居购物广场	Tianjin Bohai Area living Shopping Center
天津市棉花交易市场	Tianjin Cotton Exchange Market
天津泰丰工业园区置业有限公司都行商城市场	Tianjin Taifeng Industry Zone Co., Ltd., Duxing Shopping Market
天津空港二手车交易市场	Tianjin Airport Second-hand Car Exchange Market
天津市碧城农产品批发市场	Tianjin Bicheng Agriculture Products Wholesale Market
天津市兴华市场	Tianjin Xinghua Market
天津市南马路五金城	Tianjin Nanmalu Metal Hardware Center
天津市红旗农贸综合批发市场	Tianjin Hongqi Farm Product Wholesale Market
天津市登发实业发展有限公司	Tianjin Dengfa Co., Ltd.
天津市运达旧机动车交易市场有限公司	Tianjin Yunda Second-hand Motor Vehicle Exchange Market Co., Ltd.
天津市隆海葛沽农产品市场	Tianjin Longhai Gegu Farm Product Market
天津市津海商城有限公司	Tianjin Jinhai Shopping Center Co., Ltd.
天津市金三角农贸批发市场	Tianjin Jinsanjiao Farm Product Wholesale Market
天津津都轻工商贸城有限公司	Tianjin Jindu Light Industry Product Market Co., Ltd.

交易场所面积(平方米) Area of the Transaction Place (sq. m)	交易额(万元) Transaction Value (10 000 yuan)	市场类别 Market Type	地 址 Address
7500	4026700	金属材料	天津市北辰区顺义道
260000	580900	蔬 菜	天津市东丽区金钟河大街与外环线交口
2500	423116	金属材料	天津市北辰区顺义道
80782	370163	服 装	红桥区南运河南路
57300	306729	纺织品、服装、鞋帽	天津市红桥区南运河南路9号
2500	250966	化工材料及制品	天津市河西区珠江道58号
18146	161794	金属材料	天津市南开区黄河道481号
183631	152306	农产品综合	天津市宁河县贸易开发区
52200	150169	纺织品	天津市河北区天纬路
17000	143467	服装、小百货、鞋帽	天津市红桥区金钟里大街2号
2800	139954	机动车	天津保税区天保大道86号
84000	139467	蔬 菜	津南区双港镇何庄子南
2000	137281	粮 油	河西区台儿庄路39号
5000	136000	食 品	天津市南开区保山道18号
26000	127000	水产品	天津市南开区富康路立交桥南侧
400	126510	金属材料	河西区马场道103号
120000	120000	金属材料	天津市西青区中北大卞庄
90000	117953	农产品综合	河北区建昌道与外环线交口
115606	115400	蔬 菜	天津市静海县范庄子
50000	110000	建材装饰材料	天津市塘沽区建材路18号
1000	98780	棉麻类	天津市保税区管委会大楼首层
19000	87386	服装、小百货、鞋帽	天津市红桥区金钟桥大街
22000	84710	机动车	天津空港物流加工区汽车园中路8号
80000	81665	蔬 菜	天津市西青区辛口镇当成村
60000	69386	综合市场	天津市蓟县
17573	55900	五 金	天津市南开区南马路与西马路交口
60000	55293	蔬菜、水果、水产品	南开区王顶堤复康路立交桥北
45074	53400	建筑及装潢材料	天津市解放南路与大沽南路交口
63765	52946	机动车	天津市河东区
45000	52504	食品、饮料、烟酒	天津市津南区葛沽镇津沽路旁
40000	48113	工业品综合	天津市静海县津海商城
19200	46440	农产品综合	天津市杨柳青津静公路与柳口路交口东侧
73739	46100	五金电料	天津市东丽区大毕庄镇政府对过(金钟公路3699号)

14-11 续表 Continued

市场名称	Name of Market
天津建工集团物资供应中心钢材交易市场	Tianjin Jiangong Group Supply Center Steel Exchange Market
北方日用工业品中心批发市场	Beifang Industry Product Center Wholesale Market
天津市环渤海建材中心批发市场	Tianjin Bohai Area Construction and Decoration Material Center Wholesale Market
中国天津粮油批发交易市场宝坻分市场	China (Tianjin) Grain & Oil Wholesale Market, Baodi Sub-market
天津市塘沽区蔬菜交易市场	Tianjin Tanggu District Vegetable Exchange Market
天津市河北区王串场街道幸福道商业街	Xingfu Road Business Street
天津市宝坻区蔬菜水果批发市场	Tianjin Baodi District Vegetable & Fruit Wholesale Market
兴业鞋帽批发市场	Xingye Shoes and Hats Market
天津市塘沽区美家装饰商城	Tianjin Tanggu District Meijia Decoration Shopping Center
天津市塘沽区巨川家饰广场、巨川金海岸	Tianjin Tanggu District Juchuan Living Decoration Center
天津市西青区宏旨木材交易市场	Tianjin Xiqing District Hongzhi Wood Exchange Market
天津市塘沽区新洋世纪商厦	Tianjin Tanggu District Xinyang Century Shopping Center
天津市津南区耀华市场服务中心	Tianjin Jinnan District Yaohua Market Service Center
天津市塘沽区盛洋商城	Tianjin Tanggu District Shengyang Shopping Center
天津市华北建材陶瓷批发市场	Tianjin North China Construction Material
天津市宁河县芦台新市场	Tianjin Ninghe County Lutai New Market
天津市王顶堤汽车城有限责任公司	Tianjin Wangdingdi Car Center Co., Ltd.
天津市塘沽区新洋市场	Tianjin Tanggu District Xinyang Market
天津市汉沽区寨上工业品市场	Tianjin Han'gu District Zhaishang Industry Product Market
天津市武清区大沙河蔬菜批发市场	Tianjin Wuqing District Dashahe Vegetable Wholesale Market
天津市武清区河西务镇综合集贸市场	Tianjin Wuqing District Hexiwu Town Comprehensive Market
天津市河西区友谊菜市场	Tianjin Hexi District Youyi Vegetalbe Market
天津市北辰区集贤市场	Tianjin Beichen District Jixian Market
天津市塘沽区新港街濒开里市场	Tianjin Tanggu District Xingang Street Binkaili Market
天津市汉沽区五阳里商贸市场	Tianjin Han'gu District Wuyangli Commercial Market
天津市北辰区引河桥市场	Tianjin Beichen District Yinhe Bridge Market
天津市温州城	Tianjin Wenzhou Market
天津市东丽区商贸城	Tianjin Dongli District Commercial Market
天津市五矿钢铁天津钢材交易市场	Tianjin Minmetal Steel Exchange Market
天津市静海县连荣农贸市场	Tianjin Jinghai County Lianrong Agriculture Product Market
天津市武清区运来农副产品市场有限公司	Tianjin Wuqing District Yunlai Agriculture & By-product Market Co., Ltd.
天津市静海县静宏旧货市场	Tianjin Jinghai County Jinghong Second-hand Market

交易场所面积(平方米) Area of the Transaction Place(sq. m)	交易额(万元) Transaction Value (10 000 yuan)	市场类别 Market Type	地 址 Address
90000	45684	金属材料	天津市东丽区张贵庄外环线京山立交桥东侧
45000	39080	灯具、花卉及其它	天津市河东区张贵庄路160号
175000	32581	建筑及装潢材料	天津市河西区解放南路
69308	31400	粮 油	天津市宝坻区
130000	29091	农产品综合	天津市塘沽区韶山道3号
3000	28950	农产品综合	河北区幸福道1号路
6666	25066	蔬 菜	天津市宝坻区
11400	24000	鞋	南开区西湖道78号
8000	24000	建材装饰材料	天津市塘沽区杭州道4号
51370	22990	工业品综合	天津市塘沽区
9500	22294	木 材	天津市西青区杨柳青西青道
28000	21565	家 具	天津市塘沽区
12717	20545	农产品综合	天津市津南区咸水沽镇八米路
5018	20060	纺织品、服装、鞋帽	天津市塘沽区抚顺道
118000	18449	建筑及装潢材料	天津市塘沽区津塘公路7-189号
13950	18000	纺织品、服装、鞋帽	天津市宁河县芦台镇
2000	18000	汽 车	天津市南开区复康路196号
3320	17294	工业品综合	天津市塘沽区抚顺道570号
7000	15711	农产品综合	天津市汉沽区
68000	13250	蔬 菜	天津市武清区河西务镇大沙河村
80000	12749	综合市场	天津市武清区河西务镇肖庄村
2380	12738	农产品综合	天津市紫金山路与黑牛城道交口
8353	12464	农产品综合	天津市北辰区延吉道
6967	11829	农产品综合	天津市塘沽新港街
8170	11653	农产品综合	天津市汉沽区河西街三经路
40000	11135	农产品综合	天津市北辰区引河桥
6000	11050	服装、鞋帽、针纺织品	东丽区大毕庄常青村
4300	10619	农产品综合	天津市东丽区顾庄村
3400	10380	金属材料	天津市东丽区合兴路698号
15000	10300	食品、饮料、烟酒	天津市静海县连荣农贸市场
20000	10041	农产品综合	天津市武清区杨村镇七街
23951	10020	旧 货	天津市静海县静宏旧货市场

14-12　营业收入五十强餐饮业企业（2006年）
TOP 50 CATERING TRADE ENTERPRISES BY BUSINESS REVENUE, 2006

单位：万元 (10 000 yuan)

名次 Position	单位名称 Name of Enterprise	名次 Position	单位名称 Name of Enterprise
1	天津肯德基有限公司	26	天津狗不理餐饮有限公司
2	天津麦当劳食品有限公司	27	天津全聚德餐饮有限公司
3	天津市桂发祥十八街麻花总店有限公司	28	天津市森泰贵宾楼餐饮有限公司
4	天津市瀚金佰餐饮有限公司	29	天津市康德劳动服务有限公司
5	天津绿色时代有限公司	30	浙江老板娘食品有限公司天津大酒店
6	天津市鹏天阁时代酒楼	31	天津白金宫大酒楼有限公司
7	天津德克士食品开发有限公司	32	泰达津菜城（天津）美食有限公司
8	天津泰达标准食品有限公司	33	天津市双街新家园海鲜餐饮有限公司
9	天津开发区海港世家餐饮有限公司	34	天津市凯德龙园美食有限责任公司
10	天津大岛餐饮有限公司	35	天津市康乐饮料有限公司
11	天津市桂发祥麻花饮食集团有限公司	36	天津市松江酒店管理有限公司
12	天津森纳尔餐饮有限公司	37	宴宾美食娱乐城有限公司
13	天津海都世纪酒楼有限公司	38	天津市天府饮食文化有限公司
14	天津市津南宝德福酒家	39	天津市鸿起顺餐饮有限责任公司
15	天津市森泰餐饮有限公司	40	天津市月坛酒店有限公司
16	天津狗不理大酒店有限公司	41	天津市楚云天餐饮有限责任公司
17	天津市丁香餐饮发展有限公司	42	天津市粤唯鲜娱乐苑集团有限公司
18	天津市食为天粮油便民连锁有限责任公司	43	天津市峰光大酒楼有限公司
19	天津市天麟娱乐有限公司	44	天津市集贤大酒家有限公司
20	天津市集贤佰悦海鲜酒楼有限公司	45	天津市起士林大饭店
21	天津市皇冠明珠餐饮娱乐有限公司	46	天津市河东区鸿起顺饭庄有限公司
22	天津市翠亨邨餐饮娱乐有限公司	47	天津市运河渔村餐饮发展有限公司
23	天津开发区北塘周记餐饮服务有限公司	48	天津津卫一九二八餐饮有限公司
24	天津快客利餐饮管理服务有限公司	49	天津市河西区富祥酒楼
25	天津市大圆碗食品有限公司	50	天津市中山美食林快餐有限责任公司

14-13 销售总额百强批发贸易企业(2006年)
TOP 100 WHOLESALE TRADE ENTERPRISES BY TOTAL SALES, 2006

名 次 Position	单位名称 Name of Enterprise	名 次 Position	单位名称 Name of Enterprise
1	中国石化销售有限公司华北分公司	51	天津钢管工程设备材料公司
2	中国石油化工股份有限公司天津石油分公司	52	天津经济技术开发区机电设备公司
3	天津宝钢北方贸易有限公司	53	天津市英驰不锈钢有限公司
4	中国石油天燃气股份有限公司华北销售大港分公司	54	京瓷(天津)商贸有限公司
5	天津一汽汽车销售有限公司	55	天津开发区嘉诚钢材贸易有限公司
6	天津市金属材料总公司	56	天津本钢钢铁贸易有限公司
7	天津市咸通生产资料有限责任公司	57	天津市正泰实业总公司
8	中国铁路物资天津公司	58	中冀斯巴鲁(天津)汽车销售有限公司
9	中钢集团天津公司	59	天津市化工轻工材料总公司
10	天津国能投资有限公司	60	天津中邮普泰移动通信设备有限责任公司
11	天津市亚益成工贸有限责任公司	61	天津市福浩实业有限公司
12	国药控股天津有限公司	62	天津市浩物机电汽车贸易有限公司
13	天津钢管国际经济贸易有限公司	63	天津市润飞贸易有限公司
14	天津天铁冶金集团商贸有限公司	64	天津世盛投资集团有限公司
15	天津市浩通物产有限公司	65	天津机电进出口有限公司
16	天津市化轻贸易有限公司	66	永立建机(天津)国际贸易有限公司
17	天津市丽兴京津钢铁贸易有限公司	67	天津辰晔实业有限公司
18	丰田通商(天津)有限公司	68	天津市博通华信科技发展有限公司
19	天津市盈通物资有限公司	69	三星爱商(天津)国际物流有限公司
20	天津太平(集团)有限公司	70	天津开发区福源商贸有限公司
21	天津中联进出口贸易有限公司	71	天津市北辰区北方实业发展有限公司
22	中国烟草总公司天津市公司	72	中石化中海船舶燃料供应有限公司天津分公司
23	天津港保税区瀚通国际贸易有限公司	73	天津物资招商有限公司
24	天津市燃料油公司	74	天津海尔工贸有限公司
25	天津轧三物流有限公司	75	天津港保税区和昌物资回收有限公司
26	天津大桥集团电焊条供销有限公司	76	渤海石油物资供应公司
27	天津中新药业集团股份有限公司	77	天津市京津工贸开发有限公司
28	天津市物资集团总公司	78	天津市瑞通矿业贸易有限责任公司
29	天津荣程祥国际贸易有限公司	79	天津市润德中天机电设备有限公司
30	天津市大港区蓝盾商贸有限公司	80	天津市惠天承运商贸有限公司
31	天津市基建物资总公司	81	天津市电力燃料公司
32	天津纺织集团进出口股份有限公司	82	天津立业钢铁贸易有限公司
33	天津市顺鑫进出口贸易有限公司	83	天津港保税区四辟国际贸易有限公司
34	天津住友商事有限公司	84	中国农业机械华北集团有限公司
35	天津晟达石化有限公司	85	天津市物资实业发展中心
36	天津服装进出口股份有限公司	86	天津盈通国际贸易有限公司
37	五矿钢铁天津有限公司	87	天津市盈博商贸有限公司
38	中化物产股份有限公司天津分公司	88	天津裕华经济贸易总公司
39	天津太钢销售有限公司	89	天津市城区电力物资公司
40	天津天士力医药营销集团有限公司	90	天津港保税区亨运国际贸易有限公司
41	天津大沽贸易有限公司	91	天津英之杰国际物流有限公司
42	天津市方正延中信息系统有限公司	92	上海大众汽车有限公司天津分公司
43	大众进口汽车销售有限公司	93	华利行(天津)国际贸易有限公司
44	中化天津公司	94	天津开发区四达石化产品经销有限公司
45	天津浩安矿产有限公司	95	天津机械进出口有限公司
46	天津天资棉纺织品物流有限公司	96	天津市轻化实业进出口公司
47	天津市浩瑞矿产有限公司	97	天津万隆金属有限公司
48	天津里碑冷轧板材有限公司	98	天津汽车工业华北销售有限公司
49	天津市中煤进出口有限公司	99	北方国际集团天津同鑫进出口有限公司
50	中国有色金属进出口天津公司	100	天津鸿浩进出口贸易有限公司

14-14 销售总额百强零售贸易企业(2006年)
TOP 100 RETAIL TRADE ENTERPRISES BY TOTAL SALES, 2006

名次 Position	单位名称 Name of Enterprise	名次 Position	单位名称 Name of Enterprise
1	中国石油天然气股份有限公司天津销售分公司	51	天津市大唐通信有限公司
2	天津国美电器有限公司	52	天津市新中国现代文化用品有限责任公司
3	天津家世界连锁超市有限公司	53	天津开发区蜂星通信设备有限公司
4	天津一商友谊股份有限公司	54	上海汽车工业天津销售有限公司
5	天津劝业场(集团)股份有限公司	55	天津捷通汽车销售有限公司
6	中原百货集团股份有限公司	56	天津市冀东汽车贸易有限公司
7	天津壳牌石油有限公司	57	天津劝宝超市有限责任公司
8	天津金元宝商厦集团有限公司	58	天津津南区华润万家超级市场有限公司
9	天津苏宁电器连锁加盟有限公司	59	天津市佳成汽车贸易有限公司
10	天津市津工超市有限责任公司	60	天津月坛商厦集团股份有限公司
11	天津家世界家居建材超市有限公司	61	天津市贸顺汽车销售有限公司
12	天津精典汽车销售咨讯有限公司	62	天津世宏远东国际贸易有限公司
13	天津金升冶金产品有限公司	63	天津欧尚超市有限公司峰汇广场店
14	天津劝业家乐福超市有限公司	64	天津开发区乐购生活购物有限公司
15	天津伊势丹有限公司	65	天津路金汽车销售有限公司
16	天津市大中电器有限公司	66	天津一商世纪联华商贸有限公司
17	天津华润超级市场有限公司	67	天津市宝通汽车销售服务有限公司
18	天津通和汽车销售有限公司	68	天津凯达丰田汽车销售服务有限公司
19	天津滨江商厦有限公司	69	天津远百百货有限公司
20	天津东方集团有限公司	70	武清区海隆商贸有限公司
21	天津福业商业有限公司	71	天津市鹏峰汽车贸易有限公司
22	天津市大港滨城商贸有限责任公司	72	天津市好利来食品有限公司
23	天津市鑫海达汽车贸易有限公司	73	天津中原百货滨海有限公司
24	天津市人人乐商业有限公司	74	天津日报社报刊发行部
25	天津泰达易买得超市有限公司	75	天津一商世纪联华购物广场有限公司
26	天津新濠汽车贸易有限公司	76	天津北创机电设备有限公司
27	沃尔玛深国投百货有限公司天津和平路分店	77	天津市班尼路服饰有限公司
28	天津易初莲花连锁超市有限公司	78	天津市环宇福星汽车销售有限公司
29	天津时尚新世界购物广场有限公司	79	天津金文图书城股份有限公司
30	天津市新濠汽车销售有限公司	80	天津市文物公司
31	天津华苑丰田汽车销售服务有限公司	81	天津银诺威臣汽车销售服务有限公司
32	天津柳林丰田汽车销售服务有限公司	82	天津蓟县家乐商贸有限公司
33	天津开发区四联汽车贸易有限公司	83	天津市大港区迎宾超市
34	天津凯通汽车服务发展有限公司	84	米盖尔(天津)发展有限公司
35	天津滨江购物中心	85	天津开发区鑫兴物资贸易有限公司
36	天津市风神汽车销售有限公司	86	天津市国际商场有限公司
37	天津市中乒汽车服务有限公司	87	天津津泰石油有限公司
38	天津东联丰田汽车销售服务有限公司	88	天津市中乒北骏汽车销售有限公司
39	天津塘沽乐购生活购物有限公司	89	天津凯旋门百货有限公司
40	天津一商联华超市有限公司	90	绫致时装天津有限公司
41	天津津日汽车销售服务有限公司	91	天津市津物发商贸有限公司
42	锦江麦德龙现购自运有限公司天津红桥商场	92	天津市亨得利钟表眼镜有限公司
43	天津百盛商业发展有限公司	93	天津重汽恒业汽车销售有限公司
44	天津开发区晟陆汽车销售服务有限公司	94	天津开发区新雅特电子城有限公司
45	天津汽车工业交通出租车销售有限公司	95	宁河县家乐超市有限责任公司
46	天津市中油航汽车贸易有限公司	96	天津市飞亚汽车销售有限公司
47	上海金瑶贸易发展有限公司天津分公司	97	天津市西青区百顺商贸有限公司
48	天津一商友谊名都店有限公司	98	天津石油集团红桥石油有限公司
49	天津物美未来商贸发展有限公司	99	天津骏华汽车销售服务有限公司
50	天津金钟乐购生活有限公司	100	天津市大港油田炼达超市有限公司

14-15 实际利用内资额(2003-2006年) DOMESTIC CAPITAL ACTUALLY USED, 2003-2006

单位：万元 (10 000 yuan)

地　区	Region	2003	2004	2005	2006
总　计	**Total**	**1122103**	**2387495**	**3399285**	**4318546**
各区县	**Districts and Counties**	**603411**	**1796824**	**3042565**	**3840778**
和平区	Heping District	92099	195000	311013	426028
河东区	Hedong District	28180	72374	117794	187906
河西区	Hexi District	32650	92800	158764	205425
南开区	Nankai District	24690	114500	293522	399244
河北区	Hebei District	32400	82000	126100	192616
红桥区	Hongqiao District	35000	120660	180990	275218
塘沽区	Tanggu District	82862	181897	290000	150537
汉沽区	Han'gu District	10900	26100	36800	50000
大港区	Dagang District	22365	55000	182850	281678
东丽区	Dongli District	42176	96370	183686	231269
西青区	Xiqing District	38863	110000	154049	190198
津南区	Jinnan District	21210	91569	155822	185830
北辰区	Beichen District	35101	74601	104441	118772
武清区	Wuqing District	19121	120273	183810	267032
宝坻区	Baodi District	18390	183860	307651	388684
宁河县	Ninghe County	6650	42300	62735	75200
静海县	Jinghai County	39229	67520	94528	104700
蓟　县	Jixian County	21525	70000	98010	110441
"三　区"	**"Three Districts"**	**167230**	**271081**	**356720**	**477768**
天津经济技术开发区	TEDA	43568	90567	117738	149900
天津保税区	TFTZ	56151	93000	124600	187965
天津新技术产业园区	THIP	67511	87514	114382	139903

14-16 外省市在津投资情况
DOMESTIC CAPITAL FROM OTHER PROVINCES AND MUNICIPALITIES

地 区	Region	项目数(个) Number of Contracts (unit)		实际利用内资额 (万元) Total Capital Actually Used (10 000 yuan)	
		2005	2006	2005	2006
总 计	**Total**	**2343**	**1840**	**3399285**	**4318546**
北京市	Beijing	459	370	1331377	1615910
河北省	Hebei	493	380	403296	434227
山西省	Shanxi	90	44	42618	31643
内蒙古自治区	Inner Mongolia	64	49	29191	19853
辽宁省	Liaoning	78	83	61426	60985
吉林省	Jilin	90	57	25859	12115
黑龙江省	Heilongjiang	127	85	45353	72296
上海市	Shanghai	72	62	357274	521291
江苏省	Jiangsu	76	74	100485	44755
浙江省	Zhejiang	118	113	262336	550103
安徽省	Anhui	31	37	11150	31395
福建省	Fujian	71	68	68163	148615
江西省	Jiangxi	22	14	18771	5025
山东省	Shandong	151	111	34508	49685
河南省	Henan	87	59	18120	16233
湖北省	Hubei	40	19	6487	1909
湖南省	Hunan	15	23	2030	6668
广东省	Guangdong	120	96	510021	605480
广西壮族自治区	Guangxi	4	2	100	80
海南省	Hainan	4	4	10804	55224
重庆市	Chongqing	10	7	1695	785
四川省	Sichuan	41	23	34202	8063
贵州省	Guizhou	1	3	100	2065
云南省	Yunnan	3	2	130	1028
陕西省	Shannxi	25	20	11337	7015
甘肃省	Gansu	18	12	1563	10195
青海省	Qinghai	7	4	3440	419
宁夏回族自治区	Ningxia	8	7	465	3174
新疆维吾尔自治区	Xinjiang	18	12	6984	2310

主要统计指标解释

批发和零售业 根据新颁布的行业分类标准《国民经济行业分类》(GB/T4754-2002)，将原批发零售贸易、餐饮业门类中的餐饮业调出，且不含原“金属和非金属废料和碎屑的加工处理”部分。

社会消费品零售总额 各种经济类型的批发和零售业、餐饮业和其他行业对城乡居民和社会集团的消费品零售额总和。

商品购进总额 指从本企业以外的单位和个人购进（包括从国外直接进口）作为转卖或加工后转卖的商品金额。包括从工农业生产者购进额，从批发和零售业购进额，进口额和其他购进组成。这个指标反映批发和零售企业从国内外市场上购进商品的总量。

商品销售总额 指售予本企业以外的单位和个人的商品金额（含增值税）。销售总额包括零售额和批发额两部分，其中零售额包括：售予居民和社会集团商品的金额；批发额包括：售予生产经营单位商品的金额和商品的金额。这个指标反映批发零售业在国内市场上销售商品以及出口商品的总量。

营业收入 指企业(单位)在生产经营活动中通过销售商品或提供劳务等取得的收入。营业收入包括主营业务收入和其他业务收入。主营业务收入是指企业在销售商品、提供劳务等主要业务活动所产生的收入总额。其他业务收入是指各类企业主营业务以外其他业务或不独立核算的附营业务所发生的收入。

限额以上批发和零售业、餐饮业企业划分标准
批发业是指年销售额2000万元及以上，年末从业人员20人及以上；零售业是指年销售额500万元及以上，年末从业人员60人及以上；餐饮业是指年销售额200万元及以上，年末从业人员40人及以上。

Explanastory Notes on Main Statistical Indicators

Wholesale and Retail Trade refers to original wholesale, retail trade and catering deducting catering according to the new classification of "national economic classification and code" (GB T4754-2002),excluding original "metal and non-metal waste materials processing".

Total Retail Sales of Consumer Goods refers to the sum of retail sales of consumer goods to urban and rural residents and social groups by the establishments in wholesale, retail, catering and other industries of various ownerships.

Total Purchases of Commodities refers to the total value of purchases of commodities by the establishments from other establishments or individuals (including direct import from abroad) for the purpose of reselling, either with or without further processing of the commodities purchased. The total purchases include agricultural and industrial products purchased from producers, commodities purchased from wholesale and retail trades, commodities directly imported from abroad, commodities purchased from other units. This indicator issued to show the total value of purchases of commodities by wholesale and retail establishments from domestic and overseas markets.

Total Sales of Commodities refers to value of commodities sold by the establishments to other establishments and individuals (including added-value tax). Total sales of commodities include retail sales and wholesale sales. Retail sales include value sold to individuals and social groups. Wholesale sales include value sold to productive units and exports value. The indicator reflects the sum of commodities sold in domestic markets and export commodities by retail and wholesale track.

Business Revenue refers to revenue of enterprises through selling commodities or providing services. It includes income of principal business and other business income. Income of principal business refers to income of main business activities. Other business income refers to income of other business or attached business not including main business.

Classified Standard of Wholesale, Retail Trade and Catering Enterprises above Designated Size
Wholesale enterprises refer to enterprises with sales over 20 million yuan, with laborers over 20 persons. Retail enterprises refer to enterprises with sales over 5 million yuan, with laborers over 60 persons. Catering enterprises refer to enterprises with sales over 2 million yuan, with laborers over 40 persons.

第15篇
CHAPTER 15

对外经济贸易和旅游
Foreign Economy Trade and Tourism

15-1 对外贸易进出口商品总值(1990-2006年)
TOTAL VALUE OF IMPORTS AND EXPORTS, 1990-2006

年 份 Year	绝对数(万美元) Absolute Value (USD 10 000)			增长速度(%) (比上年) Increase Rate (%) (Over Preceding Year)		
	进出口总值 Imports & Exports	出口总值 Exports	进口总值 Imports	进出口总值 Imports & Exports	出口总值 Exports	进口总值 Imports
1990	220979	178555	42424	-0.2	5.9	-19.7
1991	202013	160636	41377	-8.6	-10.0	-2.5
1992	237577	175234	62343	17.6	9.1	50.7
1993	277666	194234	83432	16.9	10.8	33.8
1994	331232	239978	91254	19.3	23.6	9.4
1995	654556	299841	354715	97.6	24.9	288.7
1996	829743	404913	424830	26.8	35.0	19.8
1997	1002286	501818	500468	20.8	23.9	17.8
1998	1061595	549856	511739	5.9	9.6	2.3
1999	1260465	633199	627265	18.7	15.2	22.6
2000	1715741	862906	852835	36.1	36.3	36.0
2001	1818636	950177	868459	6.0	10.1	1.8
2002	2282658	1159490	1123168	25.5	22.0	29.3
2003	2937141	1437396	1499745	28.7	24.0	33.5
2004	4201948	2086544	2115404	43.2	45.4	41.4
2005	5338661	2741476	2597186	27.1	31.4	22.8
2006	6457292	3353985	3103307	21.0	22.3	19.5

注：自1998年始，用海关数据。
Note: Since 1998, the data of this table are gotten from Tianjin Customs.

15-2 天津口岸进出口商品总值(1990-2006年)
TOTAL VALUE OF IMPORTS AND EXPORTS IN TIANJIN PORT, 1990-2006

年 份 Year	按美元计算(亿美元) Calculated by USD (USD 100 million)			按人民币计算(亿元) Calculated by RMB (100 million yuan)		
	进出口总值 Imports & Exports	出口总值 Exports	进口总值 Imports	进出口总值 Imports & Exports	出口总值 Exports	进口总值 Imports
1990	85.95	42.53	43.42	410.84	203.29	207.55
1991	91.37	46.48	44.89	486.98	239.59	247.39
1992	104.61	54.6	50.01	572.23	298.68	273.55
1993	125.04	66.03	59.01	726.48	383.63	342.85
1994	161.67	86.81	74.86	1397.96	750.65	647.31
1995	217.46	127.81	89.65	1821.23	1070.41	750.82
1996	216.85	122.89	93.96	1804.19	1022.44	781.75
1997	215.62	131.24	84.38	1787.55	1088.02	699.53
1998	223.19	134.84	88.35	1852.48	1119.17	733.31
1999	248.29	139.18	109.11	2055.34	1152.13	903.21
2000	298.03	165.29	132.74	2479.60	1375.20	1104.40
2001	323.71	178.13	145.58	2679.30	1474.40	1204.90
2002	365.35	190.55	174.80	3025.46	1577.94	1447.52
2003	461.67	259.57	202.10	3831.86	2154.43	1677.43
2004	677.66	384.80	292.86	5608.66	3184.80	2423.86
2005	819.29	446.83	372.46	6711.38	3660.30	3051.08
2006	1018.85	571.24	447.61	8122.07	4553.81	3568.26

15-3 利用外资情况(1990-2006年)
UTILIZATION OF FOREIGN CAPITAL, 1990-2006

年 份 Year	绝对数(万美元) Absolute Value (USD 10 000)		增长速度(%) (比上年) Increase Rate (%) (Over Preceding Year)	
	直接利用外资 Foreign Direct Investment	借用国外资金 Foreign Loans	直接利用外资 Foreign Direct Investment	借用国外资金 Foreign Loans
合同额 **Foreign Investment Contracted**				
1990	16367	2000	93.6	-87.3
1991	19656	4100	20.1	87.0
1992	121927	12100	520.3	195.1
1993	225567	9154	85.0	-24.3
1994	350234	52000	55.3	468.1
1995	385053	35600	9.9	-31.5
1996	392431	120400	1.9	238.2
1997	385066	202100	-1.9	67.9
1998	363729	132989	-5.5	-34.2
1999	362034	102545	-0.5	-22.9
2000	460000		27.1	
2001	463000		0.7	
2002	581220		25.5	
2003	351297		74.3	
2004	558855		59.1	
2005	732281		31.0	
2006	811156		10.8	
实际利用外资 **Foreign Capital Actually Used**				
1990	8315	25122	2.7	-28.6
1991	9388	38711	12.9	54.1
1992	23138	59922	146.5	54.8
1993	54120	39112	133.9	-34.7
1994	101499	75985	87.5	94.3
1995	152064	58924	49.8	-22.5
1996	200587	97771	31.9	65.9
1997	251135	91166	25.2	-6.8
1998	251803	53984	0.3	-40.8
1999	253203	21332	0.6	-60.5
2000	256000	26467	1.1	24.1
2001	322000	7688	25.8	-71.0
2002	380591	6310	18.2	-17.9
2003	163325	7225	62.9	14.5
2004	247243	22993	51.4	218.2
2005	332885	31688	34.6	37.8
2006	413077	23819	24.1	-24.8

注：自2003年开始，直接利用外资额采用商务部新口径，速度为可比口径；15-8、15-9、15-11表同。

Note: Foreign direct investment since 2003 refers to new coverage of Ministry of Commerce, and its increase rate is calculated on the basis of comparable coverage; same as following table 15-8, 15-9 and 15-11.

15-4 对外贸易进出口商品总值(2006年)
TOTAL VALUE OF IMPORTS AND EXPORTS IN FOREIGN TRADE, 2006

单位：万美元 (USD 10 000)

项　目	Item	进出口总值 Imports & Exports	出口总值 Exports	进口总值 Imports
合　计	**Total**	**6457292**	**3353985**	**3103307**
按口岸分	**By Port**			
本口岸	Local Port	4616028	2157933	2458095
外口岸	Outside Port	1841264	1196052	645212
按经营单位分	**By Managing Unit**			
# 国有企业	State-owned Enterprises	709321	401420	307900
中外合资企业	Joint Venture Enterprises	2016485	1010273	1006212
中外合作企业	Cooperative Operation Enterprises	76012	36045	39967
外商独资企业	Foreign-funded Sole Enterprises	3181183	1637562	1543621
按贸易性质分	**By Way of Trade**			
# 一般贸易	General Trade	2194480	1107132	1087348
进料加工	Processing Using Import Material	3087107	2016207	1070899
外商投资企业进口设备	Equipments of Foreign-funded Enterprises Import	144561		144561
来料加工	Processing Using Provided Material	203140	123640	79500
易货贸易	Dicker Trade			
捐　赠	Donation	708	646	62
保税区仓储进出境货物	Goods Passed in and out TFTZ	24279	996	23283
保税区仓储转口货物	Goods Transited in TFTZ	773738	96029	677709
按商品类别分	**By Category of Commodities**			
# 食品及活动物	Food and Live Animals	34999	32147	2853
饮料及烟类	Beverages and Tobacco	6196	4908	1288
非食用原料(燃料油除外)	Non-edible Raw Materials (exclude Fuel Oil)	64067	27123	36944
矿物燃料、润滑油及有关原料	Mineral Fuels, Lubricants and Related Materials	299755	243691	56064
动植物油、脂及蜡	Animal and Vegetable Oils, Fats and Wax	62317	621	61696
化学成品及有关产品	Chemicals and Related Products	301418	125170	176249
按原料分类的制成品	Related Products By Raw Materials	809138	425407	383732
机械及运输设备	Machinery and Transport Equipment	4140942	2155409	1985531
杂项制品	Miscellaneous Products	72199	66261	5938

15-5 对外贸易分国别、地区进出口商品总值
TOTAL VALUE OF IMPORTS AND EXPORTS IN FOREIGN TRADE BY COUNTRY AND REGION

单位：万美元 (USD 10 000)

国别、地区 Country, Region		2005			2006		
		进出口总值 Imports & Exports	出口总值 Exports	进口总值 Imports	进出口总值 Imports & Exports	出口总值 Exports	进口总值 Imports
合　计	**Total**	**5338661**	**2741476**	**2597185**	**6457292**	**3353985**	**3103307**
亚　洲	**Asia**	**3102793**	**1160556**	**1942237**	**3920600**	**1570390**	**2350209**
#中国香港	Hong Kong, China	252677	148670	104007	300178	219830	80348
中国澳门	Macao, China	649	467	182	304	291	13
朝　鲜	Democratic People's Republic of Korea	534	448	86	452	188	264
韩　国	Republic of Korea	867484	234554	632930	1095604	324078	771526
日　本	Japan	815729	284909	530820	972898	314597	658302
菲律宾	Philippines	32741	11043	21698	51407	14972	36435
缅　甸	Burma	5180	5083	97	3121	2955	165
泰　国	Thailand	54098	31514	22584	65023	35884	29140
马来西亚	Malaysia	119000	52470	66530	142188	72828	69359
新加坡	Singapore	312068	156245	155823	450765	266117	184648
巴基斯坦	Pakistan	9609	8992	617	21962	21196	767
伊　朗	Iran	11275	7861	3414	24077	13370	10706
叙利亚	Syria	1208	1208		5172	5025	147
中国台湾	Taiwan, China	153385	29894	123491	197247	34937	162309
黎巴嫩	Lebanon	685	627	58	594	594	
约　旦	Jordan	1615	1599	16	1688	1688	
也　门	Yeman	932	918	14	2004	1961	44
沙　特	Saudi Arabia	11435	7600	3835	19307	14087	5220
科威特	Koweit	1300	1042	258	2559	2154	405
巴　林	Bahrein	308	308		639	632	8
非　洲	**Africa**	**46877**	**36342**	**10535**	**70820**	**58057**	**12764**
#埃　及	Egypt	4199	3229	970	5017	4445	572
苏　丹	Sudan	6194	6064	130	4622	4012	610
利比亚	Libya	672	672		1288	1288	
肯尼亚	Kenya	1893	1797	96	1714	1617	97
坦桑尼亚	Tanzania	1258	998	260	1780	1390	390
欧　洲	**Europe**	**914403**	**614182**	**300221**	**995858**	**676673**	**319184**
#波　兰	Poland	3910	3014	896	9322	8328	994
俄罗斯	Russia	79104	54737	24367	63193	36961	26232
爱沙尼亚	Esthonia	438	320	118	687	607	80
拉托维亚	Latvia	541	509	32	818	803	15
立陶宛	Lithuania	907	792	115	1660	1315	345
斯洛文尼亚	Slovenia	679	624	55	2350	1224	1127
斯洛伐克	Slovakia	3771	1182	2589	4903	2501	2403

15-5 续表 Continued

单位：万美元 (USD 10 000)

国别、地区	Country, Region	2005			2006		
		进出口总值 Imports & Exports	出口总值 Exports	进口总值 Imports	进出口总值 Imports & Exports	出口总值 Exports	进口总值 Imports
匈牙利	Hungary	13434	12789	645	19280	17976	1304
捷　克	Czech	4475	2501	1974	4822	2968	1855
保加利亚	Bulgaria	1569	931	638	1665	1550	115
阿尔巴尼亚	Albania	80	80		38	38	
罗马尼亚	Roumania	3425	2055	1370	4517	3410	1107
德　国	Germany	375027	263558	111469	370310	252107	118203
南斯拉夫	Yugoslavia	171	171		654	650	4
法　国	France	69542	33534	36008	76896	41172	35724
意大利	Italy	41075	22129	18946	58920	37194	21726
荷　兰	Netherlands	61364	52007	9357	57428	48733	8696
比利时	Belgium	21033	10812	10221	27155	18094	9061
英　国	United Kingdom	86633	57328	29305	90953	59846	31107
爱尔兰	Ireland	4497	2417	2080	6524	4221	2303
丹　麦	Danmark	23307	9838	13469	27315	12036	15279
芬　兰	Finland	37520	31865	5655	53662	46364	7298
瑞　典	Sweden	12284	7481	4803	15491	9512	5979
挪　威	Norway	6542	1966	4576	4548	2989	1559
瑞　士	Switzerland	11775	5632	6143	18850	12045	6805
奥地利	Austria	7177	915	6262	6875	2771	4104
西班牙	Spain	24597	17769	6828	41324	27749	13575
希　腊	Greece	2256	2127	129	3830	3654	177
葡萄牙	Portugal	2610	2440	170	4500	4419	81
塞普路斯	Cyprus	307	271	36	469	467	2
马耳他	Malta	290	49	241	295	63	232
拉丁美洲及北美洲	**Latin and North America**	**1191239**	**888696**	**302543**	**1376027**	**999404**	**376623**
# 墨西哥	Mexico	43018	32791	10227	43652	36469	7183
古　巴	Cuba	17146	4871	12275	3537	3484	53
智　利	Chile	1161	848	313	10500	7804	2696
加拿大	Canada	53849	35479	18370	70975	49810	21165
美　国	United States	974340	761476	212864	1119933	825526	294407
大洋洲及太平洋地区	**Oceania and Pacific Region**	**82248**	**41498**	**40750**	**107284**	**54807**	**52476**
# 澳大利亚	Australia	71773	36844	34929	80691	44114	36577
新西兰	New Zealand	9779	3229	6550	12107	4435	7672

15-6 天津口岸进出口商品检验情况(2003-2006年)
INSPECTION OF IMPORTS AND EXPORTS COMMODITIES IN TIANJIN PORT, 2003-2006

单位：批、万美元 (batch, USD 10 000)

项　目	Item	2003	2004	2005	2006
进口商品检验	Imports Inspection				
批　数	Batches	105340	133767	153949	141241
#不合格	Disqualification	602	1420	2330	3223
金　额	Value	1035630	1481248	1713168	2063952
#不合格	Disqualification	24721	125877	220364	268275
出口商品检验	Exports Inspection				
批　数	Batches	171394	166023	185513	213002
#不合格	Disqualification	163	675	766	663
金　额	Value	1030159	1624435	1848814	2153408
#不合格	Disqualification	355	16106	16123	16142

15-7 本市在境外设立企业和机构情况
MUNICIPAL OVERSEAS ENTERPRISES AND AGENCIES

项　目	Item	2005	2006	至2006年底累计 Accumulated at the End of 2006
企业和机构总计(个)	Total (unit)	75	72	689.0
企　业	Enterprises	54	39	518.0
机　构	Agencies	21	33	171.0
投资总额(万美元)	Total Investment (USD 10000)	5049	7545	57233.0
#中方投资额	Chinese Investment	4372	5983	42034.0
中方投资占比重(%)	Proportion of Chinese Investment (%)	86.6	79.3	73.4
投资国家和地区(个)	Number of Countries Regions (unit)	31	35	123.0

15-8 直接利用外资签约情况
UTILIZATION OF FOREIGN DIRECT INVESTMENT

单位：个、万美元 (batch, USD 10 000)

项　目	Item	2004	2005	2006	2006比2005年增长(%) Increased Rate in 2006 over 2005 (%)
合同数	**Number of Contracts**	**1102**	**1309**	**1050**	**-19.8**
合资企业	Joint Venture Enterprises	328	357	317	-11.2
合作企业	Cooperative Operation Enterprises	30	16	25	56.3
独资企业	Sole Foreign-funded Enterprises	744	936	708	-24.4
合同投资总额	**Total Investment Contracted**	**959300**	**1297272**	**1443631**	**11.3**
合资企业	Joint Venture Enterprises	261910	461763	486187	5.3
合作企业	Cooperative Operation Enterprises	34529	51663	59324	14.8
独资企业	Sole Foreign-funded Enterprises	662861	783846	898121	14.6
合同外资金额	**Foreign Investment Contracted**	**558855**	**732281**	**811156**	**10.8**
合资企业	Joint Venture Enterprises	92537	170925	176709	3.4
合作企业	Cooperative Operation Enterprises	20916	21408	31935	49.2
独资企业	Sole Foreign-funded Enterprises	445402	539948	602512	11.6

15-9 实际利用外资情况
FOREIGN CAPITAL ACTUALLY USED

单位：万美元 (USD 10 000)

项　目	Item	2004	2005	2006	2006比2005年增长(%) Increased Rate in 2006 over 2005 (%)
总　计	**Total**	**270236**	**364573**	**436896**	**19.8**
借用国外资金	**Foreign Loans**	**22993**	**31688**	**23819**	**-24.8**
外国政府贷款	Foreign Government Loans	2835	1925	43	-97.7
国际金融组织贷款	Loans from International Financial Organizations	7130	15000		
出口信贷	Export Loans				
外国银行商业贷款	Commercial Loans from Foreign Banks	13028	14763	23776	61.1
对外发行债券、股票	External Bonds, Stocks				
直接利用外资	**Foreign Direct Investment**	**247243**	**332885**	**413077**	**24.1**
合资企业	Joint Venture Enterprises	83566	91370	118795	30.0
合作企业	Cooperative Operation Enterprises	10002	14303	37226	160.3
独资企业	Sole Foreign-funded Enterprises	153676	227213	257057	13.1

15-10 借用国外资金情况
BORROWING FOREIGN CAPITAL

单位：万美元 (USD 10 000)

项 目 Item	上年结转资金 Capital Carried From Last Year		当年新增借款 New Increased Loans		偿还本金 Repaid Principals	
	2005	2006	2005	2006	2005	2006
国外贷款合计						
Total Loans	**98367**	**47004**	**31688**	**23819**	**34531**	**24967**
按债务期限分						
By Period of Debt						
中长期						
Long-term & Medium-term	93421	38446	16929	3106	24871	10428
短 期						
Short-term	4946	8558	14763	20713	9660	14539
按借款方式分						
By Mode of Borrowing						
外国政府贷款						
Government Loans	42891	23139	1925	43	6919	4388
国际金融组织贷款						
Loans from International Financial Organization	19637	856	15000		1221	
出口信贷						
Export Loans	17250	12959			3089	2277
外国银行商业贷款						
Commercial Loans of Foreign Banks	18589	10050	14763	23776	9660	18302

项 目 Item	外汇汇率差额 Margin of Foreign Exchange Rate		期末借款余额 Loaned Balance of Year-end		偿还利息 Repaid Interests	
	2005	2006	2005	2006	2005	2006
国外贷款合计						
Total Loans	**-2828**	**622**	**92756**	**46478**	**1741**	**801**
按债务期限分						
By Period of Debt						
中长期						
Long-term & Medium-term	-2828	622	82707	31746	1740	801
短 期						
Short-term			10049	14732	1	
按借款方式分						
By Mode of Borrowing						
外国政府贷款						
Government Loans	-178	85	37719	18879	530	148
国际金融组织贷款						
Loans from International Financial Organization	-1448		32028	856	175	
出口信贷						
Export Loans	-1202	536	12950	11218	809	652
外国银行商业贷款						
Commercial Loans of Foreign Banks			10050	15524	227	

15-11 外商及港澳台商投资企业投资情况（2006年）
INVESTMENT OF FOREIGN-FUNDED AND HONG KONG, MACAO AND TAIWAN FUNDED ENTERPRISES, 2006

项　目	Item	签订合同项目(个) Number of Contracts Signed (item)		签订合同投资总额(亿美元) Total Capital of Contracted Investment (100 million USD)	
		2006	至2006年底累计 Total by the End of 2006	2006	至2006年底累计 Total by the End of 2006
总　计	**Total**	**1050**	**19451**	**1443631**	**9349892**
按投资方式分	**By Mode of Investment**				
合资企业	Joint Venture Enterprises	317	6950	486187	3630636
合作企业	Cooperative Operation Enterprises	25	629	59324	699561
独资企业	Foreign-funded Sole Enterprises	708	11872	898121	5019695
按行业分	**By Sector**				
农　业	Agriculture	8	143	6626	58508
制造业	Manufacturing	557	10876	645282	5255084
建筑业	Construction	8	358	12850	143705
交通运输及仓储业	Transportation and Storage	28	198	189454	473018
批发零售贸易及餐饮业	Wholesale, Retail Trade and Catering	186	5509	133348	1142635
房地产业	Real Estate	76	778	274765	1624739
社会服务业	Social Services	187	1550	181308	624345
其他行业	Others		39		27858
按国别(地区)分	**By Country (Region)**				
#中国香港	Hong Kong, China	192	5950	314403	2970801
中国台湾	Taiwan, China	54	1792	22492	310396
韩　国	Republic of Korea	241	2576	131625	831501
日　本	Japan	72	1814	56187	749775
美　国	United States	113	2984	134253	1297823
新加坡	Singapore	47	604	132252	406307
英　国	United Kingdom	13	205	40341	178700
德　国	Germany	31	270	31072	176187
法　国	France	8	157	9973	80736
意大利	Italy	15	105	26281	75690
英属维尔京群岛	Virgin Islands of United Kingdom	87	458	269085	967443

15-11 续表 *Continued*

项　目	Item	# 外资合同额(亿美元) Foreign Investment Contracted (100 million USD)		实际直接利用外资(亿美元) Foreign Investment Actually Used (100 million USD)	
		2006	至2006年底累计 Accumulated at the End of 2006	2006	至2006年底累计 Accumulated at the End of 2006
总　计	**Total**	**811156**	**6632437**	**413077**	**3447208**
按投资方式分	**By Mode of Investment**				
合资企业	Joint Venture Enterprises	176709	1976947	118795	1334842
合作企业	Cooperative Operation Enterprises	31935	543446	37226	232347
独资企业	Foreign-funded Sole Enterprises	602512	4112044	257057	1880019
按行业分	**By Sector**				
农　业	Agriculture	5455	34579	1096	8656
制造业	Manufacturing	369556	3732179	264999	2199732
建筑业	Construction	10230	105388	2710	54389
交通运输及仓储业	Transportation and Storage	45950	244228	37553	155018
批发零售贸易及餐饮业	Wholesale, Retail Trade and Catering	105072	903903	36002	572202
房地产业	Real Estate	157951	1164241	53376	252303
社会服务业	Social Services	116944	423545	16132	191631
其他行业	Others		24374	1209	13277
按国别(地区)分	**By Country (Region)**				
# 中国香港	Hong Kong, China	211030	2197232	87570	1087754
中国台湾	Taiwan, China	16185	224955	5045	104138
韩　国	Republic of Korea	79205	482539	28129	274292
日　本	Japan	31955	473198	57245	431336
美　国	United States	100141	1039944	23201	415000
新加坡	Singapore	46165	176675	16195	118789
英　国	United Kingdom	13368	73156	6790	55373
德　国	Germany	19401	120942	3870	65335
法　国	France	7056	58167	3817	26006
意大利	Italy	20970	58793	8238	21846
英属维尔京群岛	Virgin Islands of United Kingdom	119865	543531	75813	304235

15-12 外商及港澳台商投资企业生产经营情况（2006年）
PRODUCTION AND OPERATION OF FOREIGN-FUNDED AND HONG KONG, MACAO AND TAIWAN FUNDED ENTERPRISES, 2006

单位：万元 (10 000 yuan)

项　目 Item	企业个数(个) Number of Enterprises (unit)	全部从业人员数(人) Number of Employment Personnel (person)	全部从业人员劳动报酬 Total Remuneration of Employment Personnel	销售(营业)收入 Sales (Business) Revenue	利润总额 Total Profits
合　计 Total	5810	571625	1575983	50775093	2995517
按投资方式分 By Mode of Investment					
港澳台合资 Hong Kong, Macao and Taiwan Joint Venture	818	74345	176333	4272442	219180
港澳台合作 Hong Kong, Macao and Taiwan Cooperative Operation	55	6202	11566	234537	55760
港澳台独资 Hong Kong, Macao and Taiwan Sole Funded	1103	74861	180547	3343121	232841
中外合资 Joint Venture	1162	161704	470764	21013636	1037613
中外合作 Cooperative Operation	109	10108	28640	472204	38586
外商独资 Foreign-funded Sole	2563	244405	708133	21439153	1411537
按国民经济行业分 By Sector					
农、林、牧、渔业 Farming, Forestry, Animal Husbandry and Fishery	20	474	625	10660	877
采矿业 Minerals Mining	12	801	2148	290517	1746
制造业 Manufacturing	3586	496150	1325702	45224770	2513338
# 食品制造业 Manufacture of Foods	120	13486	30557	528186	27254
饮料制造业 Manufacture of Beverages	58	7427	22545	574085	41927
纺织业 Manufacture of Textile	103	9582	17519	222253	12731
纺织服装、鞋、帽制造业 Manufacture of Textile, Wearing Apparel, Footwear and Caps	200	28967	41229	340844	6924
家具制造业 Manufacture of Furniture	60	9381	14990	203028	9824
化学原料及化学制品制造业 Manufacture of Chemical Raw Materials and Chemical Products	192	10108	46914	1165295	87097
医药制造业 Manufacture of Medicines	80	11161	57559	703476	80954
塑料制品业 Manufacture of Plastic	526	47232	103993	2383544	93152
非金属矿物制品业 Manufacture of Non-metallic Mineral Products	109	7344	23967	717539	18404

15-12 续表 1 Continued

单位：万元 (10 000 yuan)

项　目 Item	企业个数(个) Number of Enterprises (unit)	全部从业人员数(人) Number of Employment Personnel (person)	全部从业人员劳动报酬 Total Remuneration of Employment Personnel	销售(营业)收　入 Sales (Business) Revenue	利润总额 Total Profits
黑色金属冶炼及压延加工业 Smelting and Pressing of Ferrous Metals	23	3793	9075	293977	6211
通用设备制造业 Manufacture of General Purpose Machinery	172	25263	95128	2175114	257643
专用设备制造业 Manufacture of Special Machinery	233	20908	49233	912999	110775
交通运输设备制造业 Manufacture of Transport Equipment	239	53413	122089	6237218	330958
电气机械及器材制造业 Manufacture of Electric Machinery and Equipment	125	16793	40646	949245	65368
通信设备、计算机及其他电子设备制造业 Manufacture of Communications Equipment, Computers and Other Electronic Equipment	427	129577	426619	21653817	1199651
电力、燃气及水的生产和供应业 Production & Supply of Power, Gas and Water	16	2594	12045	247126	9203
建筑业 Construction	121	1829	3926	147828	-1201
交通运输、仓储及邮政业 Transportation, Storage and Post Services	227	11122	56464	829759	119221
信息传输、计算机服务和软件业 Information Transmitting, Computer Services and Software	69	2682	14997	55520	6534
批发和零售业 Wholesale and Retail Trade	1152	21176	68396	3039818	219411
住宿和餐饮业 Accommodation and Catering Services	71	13073	21601	206394	16460
金融业 Finance Intermediation	20	535	6541	161594	26204
房地产业 Real Estate	191	4549	14035	289657	22264
租赁和商务服务业 Leasing and Business Services	144	1753	8273	47142	5100
科学研究、技术服务和地质勘察业 Scientific Research, Technical Services and Geological Prospecting	111	3645	24567	179702	55696
水利、环境和公共设施管理业 Management for Water Conservancy, Environment and Public Facilities	8	104	229	1465	56
居民服务和社会服务业 Resident Services and Other Social Services	43	9871	13207	30073	-163
文化、体育和娱乐业 Culture, Sports and Recreational Services	12	1001	1904	9028	560
其　他 Others	7	266	1323	4040	211

15-12 续表 2 Continued

单位：万元 (10 000 yuan)

项　目	Item	企业个数(个) Number of Enterprises (unit)	全部从业人员数(人) Number of Employment Personnel (person)	全部从业人员劳动报酬 Total Remuneration of Employment Personnel	销售(营业)收　入 Sales (Business) Revenue	利润总额 Total Profits
按坐落地点分	**By Site of Location**					
和平区	Heping District	427	10543	39204	1501773	72632
河东区	Hedong District	214	11966	29146	874796	22243
河西区	Hexi District	611	34771	120239	2421082	151592
南开区	Nankai District	599	33929	109138	2085557	117007
河北区	Hebei District	144	9011	21063	288306	28678
红桥区	Hongqiao District	47	1501	2717	54399	6771
塘沽区	Tanggu District	1554	163886	546928	21165898	1520971
汉沽区	Han'gu District	49	3478	7520	246447	2436
大港区	Dagang District	59	7022	16192	377075	5648
东丽区	Dongli District	453	42704	87882	2303763	121499
西青区	Xiqing District	528	99450	269726	12067550	488941
津南区	Jinnan District	304	34063	68815	1027410	70295
北辰区	Beichen District	352	32737	96063	3166504	97581
武清区	Wuqing District	208	47361	95845	1900054	215283
宝坻区	Baodi District	63	14985	21067	259533	32059
宁河县	Ninghe County	29	2588	6578	77545	4757
静海县	Jinghai County	132	17772	29669	642655	13415
蓟　县	Jixian County	37	3858	8191	314746	23709
按国别(地区)分	**by Country (Region)**					
亚　洲	**Asia**	**3995**	**414176**	**998238**	**32013765**	**1482328**
#孟加拉国	Bangladesh	4	86	113	4055	-621
中国香港	Hong Kong, China	1523	113077	280532	5936884	408708
印度尼西亚	Indonesia	6	46	312	35485	-232
日　本	Japan	840	116744	296872	12276846	533460
中国澳门	Macao, China	29	1432	3626	188371	5751
马来西亚	Malaysia	32	3694	5823	63259	-5802
新加坡	Singapore	185	22878	56428	945824	73753
韩　国	Republic of Korea	845	107280	250508	10449187	368204
泰　国	Thailand	16	2516	6623	176562	-3626
中国台湾	Taiwan, China	424	40899	84288	1724845	93322

15-12 续表 3 Continued

单位：万元 (10 000 yuan)

项　　目	Item	企业个数(个) Number of Enterprises (unit)	全部从业人员数(人) Number of Employment Personnel (person)	全部从业人员劳动报酬 Total Remuneration of Employment Personnel	销售(营业)收　入 Sales (Business) Revenue	利润总额 Total Profits
非　洲	**Africa**	**34**	**954**	**3913**	**135110**	**18821**
欧　洲	**Europe**	**498**	**37054**	**168654**	**3587653**	**407889**
# 比利时	Belgium	9	162	508	7336	537
丹　麦	Danmark	14	2832	20735	396811	53237
英　国	United Kingdom	101	8891	31730	584193	80140
德　国	Germany	104	7029	31723	930573	115101
法　国	France	60	7042	37084	644077	77569
意大利	Italy	37	2429	7318	193010	-2612
荷　兰	Netherlands	35	1874	12495	308398	40659
西班牙	Spain	21	1734	3727	48366	-1834
芬　兰	Finland	9	282	1695	43379	6732
匈牙利	Hungary	7	176	360	1816	255
挪　威	Norway	2	120	669	3838	896
罗马尼亚	Roumania	6	84	153	2644	103
瑞　典	Sweden	21	873	2969	118848	12040
瑞　士	Switzerland	28	1908	10263	185811	21937
俄罗斯	Russia	7	110	706	9422	478
拉丁美洲	**Latin**	**174**	**29366**	**91969**	**2264756**	**59294**
# 巴　西	Brazil	44	5223	10760	185641	12489
凯曼群岛	Cayman	12	6378	14173	326784	-61386
巴拿马	Panama	8	121	296	1532	-43
英属维尔京群岛	Virgin Islands	96	16303	63338	1723464	111098
北美洲	**North America**	**1002**	**80677**	**295624**	**11977763**	**993371**
# 加拿大	Canada	121	5284	12325	181311	3250
美　国	United States	875	74915	282166	11785567	990348
大洋洲	**Oceania**	**107**	**9398**	**17585**	**796046**	**33814**
# 澳大利亚	Australia	72	5812	10744	518137	21290

15-13 新批准外商及港澳台商投资企业投资情况（2006年）
INVESTMENT OF NEW APPROVED FOREIGN-FUNDED AND HONG KONG, MACAO AND TAIWAN FUNDED ENTERPRISES, 2006

企业名称 Name of Enterprise	投资国别（地区） Investment Country (Region)	合同投资总额（万美元） Value of Investment Contracted (USD 10 000)	# 合同外资额 Foreign Capital Contracted
天津港太平洋国际集装箱码头有限公司 Tianjin Port Pacific International Container Terminal Co., Ltd.	新加坡 Singapore	81841	14036
中国远洋控股股份有限公司 China COSCO Holdings Company Limited	中国香港 Hong Kong, China	77162	27906
国中（天津）水务有限公司 Interchina (Tianjin) Water Treatment Co., Ltd.	中国香港 Hong Kong, China	11579	3680
比克国际（天津）有限公司 Bak International (Tianjin) Limited	中国香港 Hong Kong, China	9999	9999
天津彩虹发展有限公司 Tianjin Rainbow Development Co., Ltd.	英属维尔京群岛 Virgin Islands	9998	6000
安暨房地产发展（天津）有限公司 Anji Real Estate Development Co., Ltd.	中国香港 Hong Kong, China	9998	9980
元利源（天津）投资管理有限公司 Yuanliyuan (Tianjin) Investment Management Co., Ltd.	中国香港 Hong Kong, China	9998	9998
菲特置业（天津）有限公司 Feite Bideti (Tianjin) Co., Ltd.	巴巴多斯 Barbados	9910	5610
莱纳（天津）投资管理有限公司 Liners (Tianjin) Investment Management Co., Ltd.	马来西亚 Malaysia	9900	8415
华元半导体（天津）有限公司 Columbia Semiconductor (Tianjin) Co., Ltd.	英属维尔京群岛 Virgin Islands	9900	9900
盛世埃萨（天津）投资管理有限公司 Century Asie (Tianjin) Private Co., Ltd.	马来西亚 Malaysia	9800	6860
海神（天津）投资管理有限公司 Triton (Tianjin) Investment And Management Co., Ltd.	马来西亚 Malaysia	9800	3750
天津中远航运有限公司 Tianjin Cosco Shipping Co., Ltd.	中国香港 Hong Kong, China	9800	1500
天津国际创新科技城有限公司 International InnoXity (Tianjin) Co., Ltd.	中国香港 Hong Kong, China	9800	4000
天津立中车轮有限公司 Tianjin Lizhong Wheel Co., Ltd.	新加坡 Singapore	9682	3227
大陆汽车系统（天津）有限公司 Continental Automotive Systems (Tianjin) Co., Ltd.	德　国 Germany	9000	6000
卡利亚（天津）投资管理有限公司 Kadiah (Tianjin) Investment Management Co., Ltd.	马来西亚 Malaysia	9000	2100
未来创辉（天津）实业发展有限公司 Future (Tianjin) International Corp.	中国香港 Hong Kong, China	9000	6000
天津市路驰科技有限公司 Tianjin Luchi Technology Co., Ltd.	中国香港 Hong Kong, China	9000	5800
天津复地浦和发展有限公司 Tianjin Forte Puhe Development Co., Ltd.	英属维尔京群岛 Virgin Islands	8954	746
天津合生滨海房地产开发有限公司 Tianjin Hopson Binhai Real Estate Development Co., Ltd.	中国香港 Hong Kong, China	8705	4624
鑫山（天津）置业有限公司 Xinshan (Tianjin) Properties Co., Ltd.	意大利 Italy	8600	8600
天津再生能科技发展有限公司 Tianjin InfoSkill Technology Corp.	美　国 United States	8500	2900

注：本表为合同投资总额在2500万美元以上的企业。
Note: This table includes new approved foreign-funded and Hong Kong, Macao and Taiwan funded enterprises with contracted investment of over 25 million USD.

15-13 续表 1 Continued

企业名称 Name of Enterprise	投资国别(地区) Investment Country (Region)	合同投资总额(万美元) Value of Investment Contracted (USD 10 000)	# 合同外资额 Foreign Capital Contracted
天津宝沃实业有限公司 Baowall Enterprise Co., Ltd.	英属维尔京群岛 Virgin Islands	8000	3000
英博特（天津）科技有限公司 Yingbote (Tianjin) Technology Co., Ltd.	美　国 United States	8000	5476
天津奥的斯电梯有限公司 Tianjin Otis Elevator Company Limited	中国香港 Hong Kong, China	7398	2466
林军万国（天津）置业发展有限公司 Linjun Mutinational (Tianjin) Real Estate Co., Ltd.	新加坡 Singapore	6900	3000
天津全新能科技发展有限公司 Tianjin InfoPower Technology Corp.	中国台湾省 Taiwan, China	6500	2600
天津港财务有限公司 Tianjin Port Finance Co., Ltd.	中国香港 Hong Kong, China	6218	1243
天津万泰时尚置业有限责任公司 Tianjin Wantai Cisang Real Estate Co., Ltd.	中国香港 Hong Kong, China	6207	1266
苏司兰能源（天津）有限公司 Suzlon Enegry （Tianjin） Limited	印　度 India	6000	2120
天津空港华宇航空货运站有限公司 Tianjin Airport Hua Yu Air Cargo Terminal Co., Ltd.	毛里求斯 Mauritius	6000	1900
天津恩吉吉国际贸易有限公司 Tianjin NGG International Trade Co., Ltd.	意大利 Italy	6000	6000
天津比亚迪电子有限公司 BYD (Tianjin) Co., Ltd.	英属维尔京群岛 Virgin Islands	6000	2000
天津澳巴克科技发展有限公司 Tianjin Aobake Technology Development Co., Ltd.	澳大利亚 Australia	6000	6000
奕霖四海（天津）置业有限公司 Dynasty Two Ocean (Tianjin) Real Estate Co., Ltd.	中国香港 Hong Kong, China	6000	3000
天津临港思多而特码头有限公司 Tianjin Lingang Stolthaven Jetty Company	荷　兰 Netherlands	6000	800
天津盖世理和新物流设施发展有限公司 Tianjin Gazeley Hexin Logistics Facilities Development Co., Ltd.	英属维尔京群岛 Virgin Islands	6000	2044
天津新润房地产开发有限公司 Tianjin Xinrun Real Estate Development Co., Ltd.	英属维尔京群岛 Virgin Islands	5969	2985
天津万科新里程房地产有限公司 Tianjin Vanke Milestone Real Estate Co., Ltd.	中国香港 Hong Kong,China	5721	1287
天津药明康德新药开发有限公司 Tianjin PharmaTech Co., Ltd.	英属维尔京群岛 Virgin Islands	5700	900
天津大田集团有限公司 Tianjin Da Tian W.Group Co. Limited	中国香港 Hong Kong, China	5302	1988
中粮包装（天津）有限公司 Cofco Packaging Tianjin Company Limited	英属维尔京群岛 Virgin Islands	5000	2000
EKC工业（天津）有限公司 EKC Industries (Tianjin) Co., Ltd.	印　度 India	5000	1667
前景源（天津）置业有限公司 Qianjingyuan (Tianjin) Co., Ltd.	韩　国 Republic of Korea	5000	5000
天津元洲置业有限公司 Tianjin Yuanzhou RealEstate Co., Ltd.	英属维尔京群岛 Virgin Islands	5000	5000
天津考利亚投资管理有限公司 Tianjin KOREA Investment Co., Ltd.	韩　国 Republic of Korea	5000	5000
天津汇丰利实业发展有限公司 Tianjin Goodprofit Industrial Development Co., Ltd.	中国香港 Hong Kong, China	5000	5000
天津优恩耐房地产开发有限公司 Tianjin UNID&C Real Estate Development Co., Ltd.	韩　国 Republic of Korea	5000	3000

15-13 续表 2 Continued

企业名称 Name of Enterprise	投资国别(地区) Investment Country (Region)	合同投资总额(万美元) Value of Investment Contracted (USD 10 000)	# 合同外资额 Foreign Capital Contracted
天津华鹰航空科技发展有限公司 Tianjin Huaying Aircraft Science & Technology Development Co., Ltd.	中国澳门 Macao, China	5000	1800
天津威林格瑞材料科技有限公司 Tianjin Greenwell Materials Technology Co., Ltd.	中国香港 Hong Kong, China	4980	4980
盛捷友谊(天津)置业有限公司 Somerset Youyi (Tianjin) Property Co., Ltd.	新加坡 Singapore	4950	2500
天津萨贝克房地产经营管理有限公司 Tianjin Sabex Real Estate Management Co., Ltd.	巴巴多斯 Barbados	4950	2500
天津卓著房地产经营管理有限公司 Tianjin Excel Real Fstate Management Co., Ltd.	巴巴多斯 Barbados	4950	2500
大津赛瑞克房地产经营管理有限公司 Tianjin Seric Real Estate Management Co., Ltd.	巴巴多斯 Barbados	4950	2500
天津南玻节能玻璃有限公司 Tianjin CSG Energy Conservation Glass Co., Ltd.	英属维尔京群岛 Virgin Islands	4775	398
GAD(天津)实业发展有限公司 GAD (Tianjin) Industrial Development Co., Ltd.	巴拉圭 Paraguay	4500	3000
天津创博实业有限公司 Tianjin Chuangbo Industry Co., Ltd.	美　国 United States	4500	4500
新进电子(天津)有限公司 Surface Mount Technology (Tianjin) Co., Ltd.	英属维尔京群岛 Virgin Islands	4500	1500
天元四海(天津)置业有限公司 Dynasty Three Ocean (Tianjin) Real Estate Co., Ltd.	中国香港 Hong Kong, China	4500	2250
通邮(中国)科技有限公司 ATMU (China) Technology Co., Ltd.	开曼群岛 Cayman Island	4500	1500
天津安琪尔普睿司曼电缆有限公司 Prysmian Angel Tianjin Cable Co., Ltd.	荷　兰 Netherlands	4200	1400
新盛特(天津)国际贸易有限公司 SHINSUNG TECH (Tianjin) International Trade Co., Ltd.	韩　国 Republic of Korea	4020	4020
天津联发精密钢铁有限公司 Tianjin Lianfa Precision Steel Corporation	大洋洲其他 Others of Oceania	4000	1350
天津思多而特临港仓储有限公司 Tianjin Stolthaven Lingang Terminal Company	荷　兰 Netherlands	4000	1495
蜡笔小新(天津)有限公司 Labixiaoxin (Tianjin) Co., Ltd.	英属维尔京群岛 Virgin Islands	3987	2573
天津鸿富房地产开发有限公司 Tianjin Prominence Real Estate Development Co., Ltd.	英属维尔京群岛 Virgin Islands	3731	1306
天津立中合金有限公司 Tianjin Lizhong Alloy Co., Ltd.	英属维尔京群岛 Virgin Islands	3724	497
天津市雅禄线缆有限公司 Tianjin Yalu Cable Co., Ltd.	中国香港 Hong Kong, China	3625	906
康师傅(天津)饮品有限公司 Master Kong (Tianjin) Beverage Co., Ltd.	开曼群岛 Cayman Islands	3600	300
天津德盛镁汽车部件有限公司 GMA German Metal Automotive Accessories (Tianjin) Co., Ltd.	英属维尔京群岛 Virgin Islands	3600	1200
天津日进汽车系统有限公司 Tianjin Iljin Automotive Systems	韩　国 Republic of Korea	3600	1200

15-13 续表 3 Continued

企业名称 Name of Enterprise	投资国别(地区) Investment Country (Region)	合同投资总额(万美元) Value of Investment Contracted (USD 10 000)	# 合同外资额 Foreign Capital Contracted
天津和昇塑料制品有限公司 Tianjin Hesheng Plastic Products Co., Ltd.	英属维尔京群岛 Virgin Islands	3600	1200
比尔姆发展(天津)有限公司 Bierman Development (Tianjin) Co., Ltd.	美　国 United States	3500	3500
天津应大国际服饰有限公司 Tianjin Ying Da International Garments Co., Ltd.	中国台湾 Taiwan, China	3300	500
掌信彩通信息科技(中国)有限公司 Palm Commerce Information Technology (China) Co., Ltd.	英属维尔京群岛 Virgin Islands	3000	1200
飞模(天津)进出口有限公司 Fimor (Tianjin) Export and Import Co.	埃　及 Egypt	3000	1200
天达悦晖(天津)生物制药有限责任公司 TianDaYueHui (Tianjin) Biology Pharmacy Co., Ltd.	中国香港 Hong Kong, China	3000	1200
天津白头山实业有限公司 Tianjin Baitoushan Investment Co., Ltd.	韩　国 Republic of Korea	3000	900
天津金谷亨通实业发展有限公司 Tianjin Golden Growth Co., Ltd.	韩　国 Republic of Korea	3000	1500
凯赫威(天津)精密制造有限公司 KHV (Tianjin) Precision Manufacturing Co., Ltd.	韩　国 Republic of Korea	2999	1500
旗舰超导磁浮轨道(天津)有限公司 Flagship Super Conductivity Meglev Railway (Tianjin) Co., Ltd.	新加坡 Singapore	2999	2999
明星(中国)置业发展有限公司 Star (China) Real Estate Development Co., Ltd.	韩　国 Republic of Korea	2999	2999
天津星富置业有限公司 Tianjin Star Property Co., Ltd.	中国台湾省 Taiwan, China	2999	2800
天津羽吉创世置业有限公司 Tianjin Yujichuangshi Cooperation Co., Ltd.	英属维尔京群岛 Virgin Islands	2998	1200
摩天(天津)文化发展有限公司 Superlands(Tianjin) Hi-Tech Theme Park Co., Ltd.	英属维尔京群岛 Virgin Islands	2998	2998
万控(天津)电气有限公司 Wankong (Tianjin) Electric Co., Ltd.	中国香港 Hong Kong, China	2998	800
天津灿特电子有限公司 Tianjin Chaarmtech Electronic Co., Ltd.	韩　国 Republic of Korea	2990	1400
利菲斯(天津)置业有限公司 Lifeisi (Tianjin) Co., Ltd.	菲律宾 Philippines	2990	2990
佳利(天津)置业有限公司 JiaLi(Tianjin)Industrial Co., Ltd.	英属维尔京群岛 Virgin Islands	2989	572
爱洁世环保材料(天津)有限公司 Ajisco Paint (Tianjin) Co., Ltd.	日　本 Japan	2988	1350
天津荣程联合金属制品有限公司 Tianjin Rockcheck Metalwork Co., Ltd.	中国香港 Hong Kong, China	2985	469
天津卡菱房地产开发有限公司 Carpe Diem Investment Management Inc.	美　国 United States	2980	2980
爱琴(天津)燃料油进出口服务有限公司 Aegean (Tianjin) Petroleum Trading Service S. A.	利比里亚 Liberia	2980	2980
天津香唐房地产开发有限公司 Tianjin Xiangtang Real Estate Development Co., Ltd.	中国香港 Hong Kong, China	2980	2980
天津老板娘水产食品物流有限公司 Tianjin Lebanner Seafood Logistics Co., Ltd.	新西兰 New Zealand	2980	313
中信津达(天津)房地产开发有限公司 CITIC Jin Da (Tianjin) Property Development Co., Ltd.	英属维尔京群岛 Virgin Islands	2980	660
斯帝尔(天津)机械设备有限公司 Still (Tianjin) Machinery Equipment Co., Ltd.	美　国 United States	2960	2100

15-13 续表 4 Continued

企业名称 Name of Enterprise	投资国别(地区) Investment Country (Region)	合同投资总额(万美元) Value of Investment Contracted (USD 10 000)	# 合同外资额 Foreign Capital Contracted
天津莎丽隆服装有限公司 Tianjin Salilong Garment Co., Ltd.	中国香港 Hong Kong, China	2960	2960
天津联合电气有限公司 Tianjin United Electric Co., Ltd.	中国香港 Hong Kong, China	2950	2360
迅通储运发展（天津）有限公司 CWT Tianjin Logistics HUB Co., Ltd.	新加坡 Singapore	2950	1200
海凯铭（天津）医药化学有限公司 Haikanming (Tianjin) Pharm & Chem Co., Ltd.	英属维尔京群岛 Virgin Islands	2900	2900
松汇（天津）电子有限公司 Songhui (Tianjin) Electron Co., Ltd.	萨摩亚 Samoa	2900	2900
天津仕友林汽车部件有限公司 Tianjin Shiyoulin Automotive Components Co., Ltd.	中国香港 Hong Kong, China	2900	2900
天津兰松德管理咨询有限公司 Tianjin Lansongde Management Consultants Co., Ltd.	德　国 Germany	2900	1750
天津德华石油装备制造有限公司 Tianjin Dehua Petroleum Equipment Manufacturing Co.,Ltd.	美　国 United States	2900	1200
天津黄埔福盛电子有限公司 Tianjin Huangpufusheng Electron Co., Ltd.	中国香港 Hong Kong, China	2900	1600
天津华威华商包装材料有限公司 Tianjin Huawei Huashang Packing Material Co., Ltd.	中国香港 Hong Kong, China	2900	2450
天津中新水城置地有限公司 Tianjin Zhongxin Shuicheng Land Co., Ltd.	英属维尔京群岛 Virgin Islands	2900	1500
天津耀皮工程玻璃有限公司 Tianjin SYP Engineering Glass Co., Ltd.	中国香港 Hong Kong, China	2873	497
亚斯风都（天津）空调设备有限公司 Yasifengdu (Tianjin) Air-conditioning Co., Ltd.	美　国 United States	2860	1660
中钢国际广场（天津）有限公司 SINOSTEEL International Plaza(Tianjin) Co., Ltd.	中国香港 Hong Kong, China	2855	1241
温耐斯电机（天津）有限公司 Wennaisi Electric Appliances (Tianjin) Co., Ltd.	中国香港 Hong Kong, China	2850	2700
旭达斯（天津）工程管理有限公司 Xudasi (Tianjin) Engineering Project Management Co., Ltd.	开曼群岛 Cayman Islands	2850	2300
天津联亚泰环保设备有限公司 Tianjin Lianyatai Environment Protection Equipment Co., Ltd.	中国香港 Hong Kong, China	2800	2800
天津凯莱房地产开发有限公司 Tianjin Kailai Real Estate Co., Ltd.	中国香港 Hong Kong, China	2800	2800
天津市韩兴科技发展有限公司 Tianjin Hanxing Tech Development Co., Ltd.	韩　国 Republic of Korea	2800	2800
天津大中光电子有限公司 Tianjin Dazhong Photo Electron Co., Ltd.	韩　国 Republic of Korea	2800	2800
天津华璟金属材料有限公司 Splendor Metal Material Co., Ltd.	英属维尔京群岛 Virgin Islands	2800	1200
法西努高（天津）污水处理设备有限公司 Faxinugao (Tianjin) Polluted Water Treatment Equipment Co., Ltd.	丹　麦 Danmark	2760	1990
嘉吉食品（天津）有限公司 Cargill Food (Tianjin) Co., Ltd.	美　国 United States	2750	1100
天津斯沃莱特汽车仪表有限公司 Tianjin Swalet Automobile Instrument Co., Ltd.	美　国 United States	2700	2700
贝努（天津）涂料有限公司 Beinu (Tianjin) Painting Co., Ltd.	美　国 United States	2690	1460
天怡置业（天津）有限公司 Tiley Realestate (Tianjin) Co., Ltd.	中国香港 Hong Kong, China	2668	1353

15-13 续表 5 Continued

企业名称 Name of Enterprise	投资国别(地区) Investment Country (Region)	合同投资总额(万美元) Value of Investment Contracted (USD 10 000)	# 合同外资额 Foreign Capital Contracted
天津凯泰福风电设备零部件有限公司 Tianjin Kantaifu Windpower Equipment Parts Co., Ltd.	丹 麦 Danmark	2660	1660
天津木洛达家具配件有限公司 Tianjin Muluoda Furniture Parts Co., Ltd	新西兰 New Zealand	2650	1150
天津东峰日工程管理有限公司 Tianjin Dongfengri Engineering Project Management Co., Ltd.	新加坡 Singapore	2650	2650
天津丰益汽车配件有限公司 Tianjin Fengyi Instrument Parts Co., Ltd	日 本 Japan	2650	2650
玛多兹液压技术(天津)有限公司 Maduozi Hydraulics Tech (Tianjin) Co., Ltd	法 国 France	2650	2350
GMPT(天津)发展有限公司 GMPT (Tianjin) Development Co., Ltd.	瑞 士 Switzerland	2649	1060
歌美飒叶片(天津)有限公司 Gamesa Blade(Tianjin) Co., Ltd.	西班牙 Spain	2643	1436
意浦(天津)金属配件有限公司 Yipu (Tianjin) Metal Parts Co., Ltd.	意大利 Italy	2600	1400
福尼亚(天津)国际贸易有限公司 Fornia (Tianjin) International Co., Ltd.	美 国 United States	2600	2600
天津美成电子有限公司 Tianjin Meicheng Electron Co., Ltd.	美 国 United States	2500	1250
天津日信日达科技有限公司 Tianjin Rixinrida Tech Co., Ltd.	日 本 Japan	2500	2500
中联电(天津)集成电路有限公司 China United Electric (Tianjin) Integrated Circuit Co., Ltd.	美 国 United States	2500	1000
天津柯能佳顿电子有限公司 Tianjin Kenengjiadun Electron Co., Ltd.	法 国 France	2500	2500
天津长辉商贸发展有限公司 Tianjin Changhui Commerce Developmeng Co., Ltd.	中国香港 Hong Kong, China	2500	1000
天津建昌不锈钢有限公司 Tianjin Chain Chon Stainless Steel Co., Ltd.	毛里求斯 Mauritius	2500	1000
中基汉斯食品有限公司 Hunt's Chalkis Company Limited	毛里求斯 Mauritius	2500	500
天津春保钨钢精密工业有限公司 Chun Bao (Tianjin) Carbide Industrial Co., Ltd.	英属维尔京群岛 Virgin Islands	2500	1000
天津威斯修尔房地产开发有限公司 Tianjin Weisixiuer Realestate Co., Ltd.	中国香港 Hong Kong, China	2500	2500
天津朝光自动化技术有限公司 Tianjin Chaoguang Automation Tech. Co., Ltd.	新加坡 Singapore	2500	2000
凯发新泉水务(天津)有限公司 HYFLUX New Spring (Tianjin) Co., Ltd.	英属维尔京群岛 Virgin Islands	2500	1500
优爱特(天津)电子有限公司 USER Interface Technology Co., Ltd.	韩 国 Republic of Korea	2500	1000
普洛斯(天津)实业发展有限公司 Prologis (Tianjin) Industry Development Co., Ltd.	巴巴多斯 Barbados	2500	1250
碧珍(中国)日用品有限公司 Pigeon (China) Corporation	韩 国 Republic of Korea	2500	1010
天津威达科技有限公司 VegaTech Company Limited	英属维尔京群岛 Virgin Islands	2500	1000

15-14 接待入境旅游人数和居住天数（2003-2006年）
NUMBER OF INTERNATIONAL TOURISTS AND DWELLING DAYS, 2003-2006

单位：人次、天 (person-times, day)

项　目	Item	2003	2004	2005	2006
接待人数总计(含不过夜)	**Total Tourists (include not stay for night)**	**489017**	**615900**	**740071**	**880588**
接待人数(过夜)	Accommodated Tourists (stay for night)	172104	275753	309789	422227
外国人	Foreigners	144087	236004	266672	392437
#日　本	Japan	45268	80015	89648	110420
韩　国	Republic of Korea	51753	69606	72655	72787
菲律宾	Philippines	438	1029	1356	1876
新加坡	Singapore	4198	7194	9004	10831
泰　国	Thailand	425	958	853	1175
印　尼	Indonesia	510	832	1166	1386
美　国	United States	10705	19271	21427	35383
加拿大	Canada	1651	2981	3624	5000
英　国	United Kingdom	2754	5897	6571	10021
法　国	France	2030	4421	4970	7552
德　国	Germany	3409	6198	8112	13259
意大利	Italy	1277	2093	3547	5784
俄罗斯	Russia	3337	3846	2782	2312
澳大利亚	Australia	1875	3556	4447	6356
港澳台同胞	Hong Kong, Macao & Taiwan Compatriots	28017	39749	43117	49790
平均每人居住天数	**Per Capita Staying Days in Tianjin**	**9.6**	**8.3**	**8.9**	**7.7**

15-15 接待入境旅游外汇收入（2003-2006年）
FOREIGN EXCHANGE EARNING FROM INTERNATIONAL TOURISTS, 2003-2006

单位：万美元 (USD 10 000)

项　目	Item	2003	2004	2005	2006
总　计	**Total**	**32947**	**41253**	**50930**	**62590**
长途交通	Long-distance Transportation	12403	12012	21526	26484
飞　机	Civil Aviation	10047	10030	13636	16786
火　车	Railway	1326	1174	1147	1415
汽　车	Motor Vehicles	447	324	1043	1283
海　运	Sea Transportation	583	484	5700	7000
游　览	Tour	1916	2179	1435	1671
住　宿	Accommodation	4333	4841	5166	6362
餐　饮	Catering Service	2394	2172	4428	5509
娱　乐	Entertainment	2427	2077	2090	2460
购　物	Shopping	5266	11714	10046	12558
邮电通讯	Posts and Telecommunications	1177	1655	933	999
市内交通	Local Transportation	1117	1102	1160	1556
其　他	Others	1913	3501	4146	4991

15-16 天津与国外结成友好城市一览表
LIST OF FOREIGN SISTER CITIES WITH TIANJIN

友好城市 Sister City	国　别 Country of Origin	缔结时间 Time of Conclusion	友好城市 Sister City	国　别 Country of Origin	缔结时间 Time of Conclusion
神户市	日　本	1973年6月24日	乌兰巴托市	蒙　古	1992年9月27日
Kobe	Japan	June 24, 1973	Ulan Bator	Mongolia	Sept. 27, 1992
费　城	美　国	1980年2月10日	哈尔科夫市	乌克兰	1993年6月14日
Philadephia	U.S.A	Feb. 10, 1980	Kharkov	Ukraine	June 14, 1993
墨尔本市	澳大利亚	1980年5月5日	延雪坪市	瑞　典	1993年9月23日
Melbourne	Australia	May 5, 1980	Jon Koping	Sweden	Sept. 23, 1993
四日市	日　本	1980年10月28日	仁川市	韩　国	1993年12月7日
Yokkaichi	Japan	Oct. 28, 1980	Inchon	Republic of Korea	Dec. 7, 1993
萨拉热窝市	波黑共和国	1980年5月28日	萨尔州	德　国	1994年9月27日
Sarajevo	Bosnia Herzegovina	May 28, 1980	State of Saarland	Germany	Sept. 27, 1994
北加莱海峡大区	法　国	1984年10月10日	罗兹市	波　兰	1994年10月11日
Region Nord Pas de Clais	France	Oct. 10, 1984	Lodz	Poland	Oct. 11, 1994
伦巴第大区	意大利	1985年5月9日	里约热内卢市	巴　西	1995年4月18日
Lombardia Region	Italy	May 9, 1985	Rio de Janeiro	Brazil	Apr. 18, 1995
格罗宁根市	荷　兰	1985年9月12日	橘郡	美　国	1997年8月1日
Groningen	Netherlands	Sept. 12, 1985	Orange County	U.S.A	Aug. 1, 1997
千叶市	日　本	1989年5月7日	亚马逊州	巴　西	1997年10月21日
Chiba	Japan	May 7, 1989	State of Amazon	Brazil	Oct. 21, 1997
普罗夫迪夫大区	保加利亚	1989年10月15日	海防市	越　南	1999年1月8日
Plovdiv	Bulgaria	Oct. 15, 1989	Haiphong City	Vietnam	Jan. 8, 1999
伊兹密尔市	土耳其	1991年9月25日	南蒲市	朝　鲜	2002年8月11日
Izmir	Turkey	Sept. 25, 1991	Nampo City	DPRK	Aug. 11, 2002
阿比让市	科特迪瓦	1992年9月26日			
La Ville D'abidjan	Cote Divoire	Sept. 26, 1992			

15-17 对外承包工程和劳务合作（2003-2006年）
CONTRACTED FOREIGN PROJECTS AND LABOR COOPERATION, 2003-2006

项　目	Item	2003	2004	2005	2006
签订合同份数(个)	Number of Contracts (unit)	1107	777	907	1098
#对外承包工程	Contracted Foreign Projects	633	159	68	130
劳务合作	Labor Cooperation	461	598	828	928
签订合同金额(万美元)	Contracted Value (USD 10 000)	40419	54709	43230	124737
#对外承包工程	Contracted Foreign Projects	31227	44087	32563	112097
劳务合作	Labor Cooperation	8746	9125	10003	9516
实际营业额(万美元)	Fulfilling Value (USD 10 000)	40515	52688	32017	60895
#对外承包工程	Contracted Foreign Projects	28863	40597	18013	45930
劳务合作	Labor Cooperation	11161	11581	13630	13719
年末在外劳动人数(人)	Number of Outside Labors of Year-end (person)	11320	12485	13140	11975
#对外承包工程	Contracted Foreign Projects	768	1241	1091	1287
劳务合作	Labor Cooperation	10544	11190	11990	10611

15-18 按国别(地区)分对外承包工程、劳务合作(2006年)
CONTRACTED FOREIGN PROJECTS AND LABOR COOPERATION BY COUNTRY (REGION), 2006

国 别、地 区	Country, Region	对外承包工程 Contracted Foreign Projects		劳务合作 Labor Cooperation	
		合同个数(个) Number of Projects (unit)	合同金额(万美元) Contracted Value (USD 10 000)	合同个数(个) Number of Projects (unit)	合同金额(万美元) Contracted Value (USD 10 000)
合　计	**Total**	**130**	**112097**	**928**	**9516**
亚　洲	**Asia**	**48**	**66754**	**329**	**8015**
缅　甸	Myanmar	5	2013		
柬埔寨	Cambodia			45	670
中国香港	Hong Kong, China			44	1542
印　度	India	10	6463		
印度尼西亚	Indonesia	2	19793		
巴基斯坦	Pakistan	3	831		
阿　曼	Oman	2	1571		
日　本	Japan			123	2345
中国台湾	Taiwan, China			36	890
越　南	Vietnam	13	13842	2	19
土耳其	Turkey	6	11160		
泰　国	Thailand	1	7800		
韩　国	Republic of Korea			8	2022
新加坡	Singapore			57	306
卡塔尔	Katar			4	4
菲律宾	Philippine	1	173		
阿联酋	United Arab Emirates	5	3108	10	217
非　洲	**Africa**	**52**	**9383**	**10**	**120**
尼日利亚	Nigeria	1	341		
苏　丹	Sudan	42	4147		
加　蓬	Gabon	1	899		
埃　及	Egypt	2	286		
科特迪瓦	Cote d'ivoire	3	3451		
几内亚	Guinea	1	1		
莱索托	Lesotho			10	120
厄立特里亚	Eritrea	2	258		
欧　洲	**Europe**	**7**	**8919**	**1**	**18**
英　国	United Kingdom			1	18
哈萨克斯坦	Kazakhstan	5	7800		
俄罗斯	Russia	2	1119		
拉丁美洲	**Latin America**	**21**	**22000**	**9**	**90**
委内瑞拉	Venezuela	20			
巴拿马	Panama			2	55
尼加拉瓜	Nicaragua			7	35
墨西哥	Mexico	1	22000		
北美洲	**North America**	**1**	**3000**	**27**	**794**
美　国	United States	1	3000	27	794
大洋洲	**Oceania**	**1**	**2041**		
澳大利亚	Australia	1	2041		
国　内	**Domestic**			**552**	**479**

15-19 外商及港澳台商投资企业利润总额百强企业(2006年)
TOP 100 FOREIGN-FUNDED AND HONG KONG, MACAO AND TAIWAN FUNDED ENTERPRISES BY PROFITS, 2006

名 次 Position	企业名称 Name of Enterprise	名 次 Position	企业名称 Name of Enterprise
1	摩托罗拉(中国)电子有限公司	51	西门子电气传动有限公司
2	天津丰田汽车有限公司	52	天津三五汽车部件有限公司
3	绫致时装(天津)有限公司	53	天津三星视界移动有限公司
4	奥的斯电梯中国投资有限公司	54	天津天惠船务企业有限公司
5	天津通广三星电子有限公司	55	天津三星视界有限公司
6	天津三星通信技术有限公司	56	天津天昂高速公路有限公司
7	飞思卡尔半导体(中国)有限公司	57	天津富奥电装空调有限公司
8	天津三星电子有限公司	58	申克(天津)矿业设备有限公司
9	天津津亚电子有限公司	59	天津丰铁汽车部件有限公司
10	SEW传动设备(天津)有限公司	60	天津三星光电子有限公司
11	施耐德电气低压(天津)有限公司	61	天津津住汽车线束有限公司
12	天津天狮生物发展有限公司	62	天津五洲国际集装箱码头有限公司
13	日新(天津)塑胶有限公司	63	天津塑力线缆集团有限公司
14	天津英泰汽车饰件有限公司	64	亚实履带(天津)有限公司
15	华利行(天津)国际贸易有限公司	65	天津三星电子显示器有限公司
16	天津丰田汽车发动机有限公司	66	天津双叶协展机械有限公司
17	诺维信(中国)生物技术有限公司	67	罗姆半导体(中国)有限公司
18	天津合生珠江房地产开发有限公司	68	天津东方海陆集装箱码头有限公司
19	天津港集装箱码头有限公司	69	丰田通商(天津)有限公司
20	三星高新电机(天津)有限公司	70	天津嘉里粮油工业有限公司
21	中美天津史克制药有限公司	72	美卓矿机(天津)有限公司
22	天津电装电子有限公司	73	天津天利航空机电有限公司
23	爱信(天津)车身零部件有限公司	74	天津双协机械工业有限公司
24	阿克苏诺贝尔涂料(天津)有限公司	75	天津雅马哈电子乐器有限公司
25	亚光耐普罗精密注塑(天津)有限公司	76	天津住友商事有限公司
26	天津中集北洋集装箱有限公司	77	天津阿尔斯通水电设备有限公司
27	中法合营王朝葡萄酿酒有限公司	78	永立建机(天津)国际贸易有限公司
28	PPG涂料(天津)有限公司	79	中国大冢制药有限公司
29	天津新展高速公路有限公司	80	京瓷商贸(天津)有限公司
30	天津华丰汽车装饰有限公司	81	弗兰德机电传动(天津)有限公司
31	丹佛斯(天津)有限公司	82	天津大通铜业有限公司
32	天津丰田合成有限公司	83	美孚石油(天津)有限公司
33	天津肯德基有限公司	84	劲量(中国)有限公司
34	因塔思(天津)电子有限公司	85	天津天永高速公路有限公司
35	天津顶津食品有限公司	86	博福-益普生(天津)制药有限公司
36	世讯工业(天津)有限公司	87	天津东洋油墨有限公司
37	赫比(天津)电子有限公司	88	天津正大饲料科技有限公司
38	天津三星电机有限公司	89	天津可口可乐饮料有限公司
39	诺和诺德(中国)制药有限公司	90	天津美和工业发展有限公司
40	天津新伟祥工业有限公司	91	美克国际家私(天津)制造有限公司
41	约翰·迪尔天拖有限公司	92	洛伊热工工程(天津)有限公司
42	天津赛象电气自动化技术有限公司	92	西湖(天津)橡塑制品有限公司
43	天津天管特钻具有限公司	93	麦格昆磁(天津)有限公司
44	德芬工业减速机(天津)有限公司	94	天津丰田物流有限公司
45	飞比达电子元器件(天津)有限公司	95	大众进口汽车销售有限公司
46	德国马克斯.博格建筑有限责任及两合公司	96	高丘六和(天津)有限公司
47	天津南玻工程玻璃有限公司	97	天津阿克苏诺贝尔过氧化物有限公司
48	天津喜来健医疗器械有限公司	98	3M(天津)国际贸易有限公司
49	天津港远航矿石码头有限公司	99	东海橡塑(天津)有限公司
50	天津东海理化汽车部件有限公司	100	天津金皇房地产有限公司

15-20 外商及港澳台商投资企业出口创汇百强企业(2006年)
TOP 100 FOREIGN-FUNDED AND HONG KONG, MACAO AND TAIWAN FUNDED ENTERPRISES BY EXPORTS, 2006

名 次 Position	企业名称 Name of Enterprise	名 次 Position	企业名称 Name of Enterprise
1	摩托罗拉(中国)电子有限公司	51	英保达资讯(天津)有限公司
2	天津三星通信技术有限公司	52	汤浅(天津)实业有限公司
3	飞思卡尔半导体(中国)有限公司	53	天津北方之星运动器材有限公司
4	乐金电子(天津)电器有限公司	54	天津国际联合轮胎橡胶有限公司
5	天津津亚电子有限公司	55	功学社
6	天津三星电子显示器有限公司	56	现代电子(天津)多媒体有限公司
7	天津三星电子有限公司	57	天津矢崎汽车配件有限公司
8	天津通广三星电子有限公司	58	天津汇宇实业有限公司
9	天津三星光电子有限公司	59	天津中远关西涂料化工有限公司
10	天津三星视界移动有限公司	60	天津三和电机有限公司
11	三星高新电机(天津)有限公司	61	大宇空调(天津)有限公司
12	天津富士光机有限公司	62	天津三王风展轮胎有限公司
13	天津富士通天电子有限公司	63	天津松下电子部品有限公司
14	天津三美电机有限公司	64	天津佳利福铸铁搪瓷制品有限公司
15	天津中集北洋集装箱有限公司	65	亚实履带(天津)有限公司
16	天津三星电机有限公司	66	天津富川电机有限公司
17	天津三星视界有限公司	67	安施电子(天津)有限公司
18	罗姆半导体(中国)有限公司	68	西迪斯(天津)电子有限公司
19	奥的斯电梯中国投资有限公司	69	天津伸和有限公司
20	天津三洋通信设备有限公司	70	诺维信(中国)生物技术有限公司
21	大宇微波炉(天津)有限公司	72	天津进平电子有限公司
22	天津富士达自行车有限公司	73	新大洲本田摩托有限公司天津分公司
23	通用半导体(中国)有限公司	74	天津天狮生物发展有限公司
24	天津爱普生有限公司	75	天津新午星机电有限公司
25	日新(天津)塑胶有限公司	76	天津沃茨阀门有限公司
26	三洋能源(天津)有限公司	77	天津星湖实业有限公司
27	中芯国际集成电路制造(天津)有限公司	78	霍尼韦尔(天津)有限公司
28	鹏思特(天津)实业有限公司	79	东海橡塑(天津)有限公司
29	赫比(天津)电子有限公司	80	天津中集物流装备有限公司
30	天津雅马哈电子乐器有限公司	81	诺曼地橡胶有限公司
31	世讯工业(天津)有限公司	82	麦格昆磁(天津)有限公司
32	天津太平货柜有限公司	83	雅士佳(天津)汽车零件有限公司
33	美克国际家私(天津)制造有限公司	84	天津新伟祥工业有限公司
34	富士康(天津)精密工业有限公司	85	天津高力预一预应力钢绞线有限公司
35	天津泰达津联电力有限公司	86	天津科林自行车有限公司
36	天津阿尔卑斯电子有限公司	87	九维机电(天津)有限公司
37	丹佛斯(天津)有限公司	88	天星科生皮革制品有限公司
38	照光电视(天津)有限公司	89	劲量(中国)有限公司
39	可立新电子(天津)有限公司	90	锦湖轮胎(天津)有限公司
40	天津乐金大沽化学有限公司	91	天津安费诺凯翼电子科技有限公司
41	京瓷太阳能有限公司	92	天津大星电子有限公司
42	亚光耐普罗精密注塑(天津)有限公司	92	天津长威科技有限公司
43	天津盛日通讯电子有限公司	93	科莱恩颜料(天津)有限公司
44	村田电子贸易(天津)有限公司	94	天津莱尔德电子材料有限公司
45	天津彼恩特通信有限公司	95	天津天一食品有限公司
46	大真空有限公司	96	天禧(天津)餐具有限公司
47	天津中辰番茄制品有限公司	97	波海航空复合材料部件有限公司
48	天津鑫山家具有限公司	98	天津磁化电子有限公司
49	因塔思(天津)电子有限公司	99	天津渤油船舶工程有限公司
50	天津津住汽车线束有限公司	100	天津华住金属制品有限公司

15-21　外商及港澳台商投资企业实缴税金总额百强企业（2006年）
TOP 100 FOREIGN-FUNDED AND HONG KONG, MACAO AND TAIWAN FUNDED ENTERPRISES BY PAID-UP TAXES, 2006

名次 Position	企业名称 Name of Enterprise
1	摩托罗拉（中国）电子有限公司
2	天津丰田汽车有限公司
3	天津三星通信技术有限公司
4	天津津亚电子有限公司
5	奥的斯电梯中国投资有限公司
6	丰田通商（天津）有限公司
7	天津三星光电子有限公司
8	绫致时装（天津）有限公司
9	天津惠鑫大豆科技开发有限公司
10	天津三星电子显示器有限公司
11	中法合营王朝葡萄酿酒有限公司
12	诺和诺德（中国）制药有限公司
13	天津丰田汽车发动机有限公司
14	PPG涂料（天津）有限公司
15	中美天津史克制药有限公司
16	乐金电子（天津）电器有限公司
17	新大洲本田摩托有限公司
18	天津三星电子有限公司
19	天津三星视界有限公司
20	天津泰瑞房地产开发有限公司
21	罗姆半导体（中国）有限公司
22	天津通广三星电子有限公司
23	SEW传动设备（天津）有限公司
24	俊安（天津）实业有限公司
25	天津嘉里粮油工业有限公司
26	天津华润超级市场有限公司
27	西门子电气传动有限公司
28	正大集团（天津）实业有限公司
29	天津电装电子有限公司
30	斯必克冷却技术（天津）有限公司
31	爱信（天津）车身零部件有限公司
32	天津丰田合成有限公司
33	施耐德电气低压（天津）有限公司
34	天津英泰汽车饰件有限公司
35	天津三五汽车部件有限公司
36	永立建机（天津）国际贸易有限公司
37	天津肯德基有限公司
38	北海粮油工业（天津）有限公司
39	天津富奥电装空调有限公司
40	天津顶益国际食品有限公司
41	壳牌润滑油有限公司
42	天津太平货柜有限公司
43	亚光耐普罗精密注塑（天津）有限公司
44	天津日石润滑油脂有限公司
45	天津大通铜业有限公司
46	加德士润滑油有限公司
47	天津顶津食品有限公司
48	普利司通（天津）轮胎有限公司
49	天津中集北洋集装箱有限公司
50	天津华丰汽车装饰有限公司
51	日新（天津）塑胶有限公司
52	天津三星视界移动有限公司
53	天津罗升企业有限公司
54	天津阿尔斯通水电设备有限公司
55	中国大冢制药有限公司
56	天津天寰聚氨酯有限公司
57	诺维信（中国）生物技术有限公司
58	天津可口可乐饮料有限公司
59	天津华润啤酒有限公司
60	天津住友商事有限公司
61	天津矢崎汽车配件有限公司
62	天津双协机械工业有限公司
63	阿克苏诺贝尔涂料（天津）有限公司
64	天津津住汽车线束有限公司
65	天津电装空调有限公司
66	天津丰铁汽车部件有限公司
67	世讯工业（天津）有限公司
68	天津宝洁工业有限公司
69	赛威工业设备（天津）有限公司
70	天津港集装箱码头有限公司
72	天津星运（集团）有限公司
73	3M（天津）国际贸易有限公司
74	美孚石油（天津）有限公司
75	三星高新电机（天津）有限公司
76	天津天狮生物发展有限公司
77	欧姆龙贸易（天津）有限公司
78	天津丰田钢材加工有限公司
79	弗兰德机电传动（天津）有限公司
80	三星爱商（天津）国际物流有限公司
81	丹佛斯（天津）有限公司
82	飞比达电子元器件（天津）有限公司
83	天津乐金大沽化学有限公司
84	葛兰素史克（天津）有限公司
85	博福 益普生（天津）制药有限公司
86	天津东海理化汽车部件有限公司
87	洛伊热工工程（天津）有限公司
88	天津雀巢有限公司
89	天津天昂高速公路有限公司
90	天津南侨油脂有限公司
91	巴特勒（天津）有限公司
92	威娜化妆品（中国）有限公司
92	天津统一工业有限公司
93	天津华住金属制品有限公司
94	哈里伯顿（天津）能源服务有限公司
95	德芬工业减速机（天津）有限公司
96	现代高新电子（天津）有限公司
97	天津天管特钻具有限公司
98	施维雅（天津）制药有限公司
99	天津盛祥塑料制品有限公司
100	天津电装汽车电机有限公司

主要统计指标解释

外贸进出口总值 指所有天津进出口经营单位经天津口岸和其他省市口岸进出口货物的总金额。自1999年1月开始使用海关统计数据。

口岸进出口总值 指天津口岸实际进出的货物总金额。包括天津经营单位和其他省市经营单位经天津口岸实现的进出口货物总额。按海关监管的贸易方式分为：一般贸易实际进出口货物，来料加工装配进出口货物，国家间、联合国及国际组织无偿援助物资和赠送品，华侨、港澳台同胞和外籍华人捐赠品，租赁期满归承租人所有的租赁货物，进料加工进出口货物，边境地方贸易及边境地区小额贸易进出口货物（边民互市贸易除外），中外合资企业、中外合作经营企业、外商独资经营企业进出口货物和公用物品，到、离岸价格在规定限额以上的进出口货样和广告品（无商业价值、无使用价值和免费提供出口的除外），从保税仓库提取在中国境内销售的进口货物，以及其他进出口货物。进出口总额用以观察一个国家在对外贸易方面的总规模。我国规定出口货物按离岸价格统计，进口货物按到岸价格统计。

利用外资 包括三部分，一是借用国外资金；二是直接利用投资；三是其他利用投资。外资包括现金、实物、工业产权或专有技术等。凡是本年内实际投资（不论是执行本年签订的协议或是执行过去几年签订的协议）均应计算在内。

借用国外资金 指由我国政府、部门、企业或其他经济组织从境外借入的资金或在境外发行的外币债券。按借款类别不同划分为：外国政府贷款、国际金融组织贷款、外国银行商业贷款、出口信贷和其他：包括对外发行债券、股票等。本年鉴公布的我市的对外借款统计数据中，不含外国及港、澳、台在津投资企业的对外借款。

直接利用投资 指国外及港澳台地区的法人和自然人按照我国有关政策、法规在中国大陆地区以现金、实物、无形资产等各种方式投资于非上市公司中的全部投资及在单个外国投资者所占股权比例不低于10%的上市公司中的投资。

其他利用投资 凡是国外及港澳台地区的法人和自然人按照我国有关政策、法规在中国大陆地区以现金、实物、无形资产等各种方式进行的投资中不属于客商直接投资的部分，均列入本类。

直接利用外资合同外资额 是根据外商投资企业合同（章程）规定，外方投资者应缴付的注册资本。包括外方从企业获得的利润对企业的再投资以及批准的企业投资总额内的外方股东贷款（2002年以前还包括以企业名义从境内外借入的其他外资）。

实际利用外资 包括借用国外资金、直接利用投资和其他利用投资三部分实际到位的外资。借用国外资金按实际提取或拨交的使用数、直接利用投资按外方实际到位资金统计（以会计师事务所出具的验资报告为准）、其他利用投资按到位数计算。

Explanastory Notes on Main Statistical Indicators

Foreign Trade Imports & Exports include imports and exports of business units of Tianjin at Tianjin Port and other ports. The data of custom statistics has been used since January, 1999.

Total Imports and Exports in Port refer to the value of commodities imported into and exported from Tianjin Port. It includes the value of commodities imported into and exported from Tianjin Port of Tianjin business units and business units of other provinces (municipalities). Imports and exports trade are the base on custom supervision, being divided into the actual imports and exports from common trade, imported and exported goods under the processing and assembling trades and materials, supplies and gifts as aid given gratis between governments and by the United Nations and other international organizations, and contributions donated by overseas Chinese, compatriots in Hong Kong and Macao and Chinese with foreign citizenship, leasing commodities owned by tenant at the expiration of leasing period, imported and exported commodities processed with imported materials, commodities trading in border areas (excluding mutual exchange goods) , the imported and exported commodities and articles for public use of the Sino-foreign joint ventures, cooperative enterprises and ventures exclusively with foreign own investment. Also included are import and export of samples and advertising goods for whose CIF or FOB value are beyond the permitted ceiling (excluding goods of no trading or use value and free commodities for export), imported goods sold in China from bonded warehouses and other imported or exported goods. The indicator of the total imports and exports at custom can be used to observe the total size of external trade in a country. In accordance with the stipulation of the Chinese government, imports are calculated at CIF, while exports are calculated at FOB.

Utilization of Foreign Capital includes foreign borrowing, foreign direct investment, and other foreign investment. Foreign capital includes cash, foods, industrial property right, special technique, etc. It includes actual investment in current year or signed in previous years.

Foreign Borrowing refer to funds borrowed from abroad by the Chinese government, departments, enterprises and other economic units, foreign currency bond issued abroad. Grouped by the category of borrowing, it includes (a) loans of foreign governments, (b) loans of international financial institutions, (c) commercial loans of foreign banks, (d) export credit of foreign banks, (e) bonds, shares issued abroad, etc. The data in this yearbook excludes foreign borrowing of foreign funded and Hong Kong, Macao and Taiwan funded enterprises.

Foreign Direct Investment refers to the investment inside China by foreign funded and Hong Kong, Macao and Taiwan funded enterprises, economic organizations or individuals, following the relevant policies and laws of China and using cash, practicalities technology, for the investment of corporations that are not listed in stock market, share ownership of single foreign investor is not lower than 10%.

Other Foreign Investment refers to the investment except foreign direct investment inside China by foreign funded and Hong Kong, Macao and Taiwan funded enterprises, economic organizations or individuals, following the relevant policies and laws of China and using cash, practicalities technology.

Foreign Direct Investment Contracted refer to the total registered capital that according to the contract, foreign investor should provide. It includes re-investment of foreign investor using the profits obtained from enterprise, loans of foreign shareholder among the total investment (also includes other investment of enterprise borrowed from China and abroad before 2002).

Foreign Capital Actually Used refers to the actual investment of foreign borrowing, foreign direct investment and other investment by foreign enterprises. It includes actual withdraw of foreign borrowing, actual capital of foreign direct investment (in accordance with the capital report of Accountant Services), actual capital of other investment by foreign enterprises.

第16篇
CHAPTER 16

金融业
Financial Intermediation

16-1 各类金融机构
FINANCIAL INSTITUTIONS

单位：个 (unit)

项　目	Item	2005	2006
各类金融机构总计	**Financial Institutions**	**2874**	**2981**
银行类机构	**Banking Institutions**	**1552**	**2094**
中央银行	Central Banks	2	2
政策性银行	Policy Banks	10	10
商业银行	Commercial Banks	1526	2065
国有独资商业银行	State-owned Sole Commercial Banks	1215	1287
股份制商业银行	Share-holding Commercial Banks	129	80
天津市商业银行	Bank of Tianjin	180	182
中德住房储蓄银行	Sino-German Bausparkasse	1	1
农村合作金融机构	Rural Cooperative Financial Institutions	1	515
外资银行	Foreign Funded Banks	14	17
非银行类机构	**Non-banking Institutions**	**1322**	**887**
保险公司	Insurance Companies	371	367
信托投资公司	Trust Investment Companies	2	2
证券经营公司	Securities Business Companies	79	74
农村信用社	Rural Credit Cooperatives	516	
财务公司	Financial Affairs Companies	1	2
邮局储蓄所	Savings Deposit Offices of Postal Offices	349	362
金融资产管理公司	Finance Assets Supervision Corporation	4	4

16-2 中资金融机构人民币各项存贷款余额(1990-2006年)
RMB SAVING DEPOSITS AND LOANS OF CHINESE FINANCIAL INSTITUTIONS, 1990-2006

单位：亿元 (100 million yuan)

年份 Year	存款合计 Total Deposits	企业存款 Deposits of Enterprises	财政性存款 Treasury Deposits	储蓄存款 Savings Deposits	农业存款 Agricultural Deposits	信托及其他类存款 Trust Deposits and Others	贷款合计 Total Loans	#工业贷款 Industrial Loans
1990	263.21	86.66	19.15	126.92	9.42	21.07	415.91	136.49
1991	336.56	106.84	24.73	163.18	13.15	28.67	487.43	158.14
1992	467.81	157.39	23.50	202.66	18.51	65.75	624.82	182.23
1993	586.12	193.71	23.78	269.70	21.75	77.19	768.57	223.91
1994	800.56	301.12	24.26	394.50	18.26	62.43	927.05	248.74
1995	1079.97	385.21	37.59	549.97	22.87	84.33	1113.95	289.50
1996	1399.06	527.68	28.54	724.91	25.82	98.64	1357.38	340.91
1997	1634.95	638.88	26.22	863.36	28.76	77.73	1502.91	379.86
1998	1860.84	655.38	12.53	1020.14	34.28	138.50	1629.12	407.52
1999	2060.02	736.03	45.78	1130.19	37.94	110.08	1825.26	429.22
2000	2281.55	871.31	53.97	1172.40	44.10	139.76	1863.60	369.25
2001	2562.55	946.89	63.82	1284.95	56.32	210.56	2159.86	433.16
2002	3018.26	1115.35	102.30	1486.38	73.86	240.37	2519.04	450.32
2003	4033.51	1542.75	136.89	1825.32	164.72	363.83	3426.02	429.13
2004	4729.61	1823.00	182.03	2116.73	157.14	450.71	3821.38	405.46
2005	5684.40	2185.23	234.75	2462.41	163.66	638.35	4417.45	425.74
2006	6531.94	2661.96	250.26	2811.02	189.50	619.20	5106.94	550.21

年份 Year	#商业贷款 Commercial Loans	#建筑业贷款 Construction Loans	#私营及个体贷款 Loans to Private and Individuals	#乡镇企业贷款 Loans to Township Enterprises	#农业贷款 Agricultural Loans	#中长期贷款 Medium-term & Long-term Loans	#信托类贷款及其他 Trust Loans and Others
1990	162.49	8.23	0.09	10.75	27.29	50.00	20.57
1991	173.04	8.86	0.11	12.20	36.26	73.88	24.95
1992	196.20	9.75	0.14	13.50	49.78	105.67	67.56
1993	223.91	10.76	0.80	16.18	65.83	143.93	83.25
1994	219.58	13.06	1.44	67.29	16.58	210.87	71.98
1995	242.71	16.18	3.47	85.70	22.46	262.01	85.70
1996	278.76	31.82	11.48	106.12	29.66	305.50	116.22
1997	297.74	36.28	8.63	125.32	41.46	298.81	67.61
1998	295.91	37.38	10.11	147.17	50.65	302.69	94.42
1999	292.08	36.00	10.15	163.59	51.33	405.04	113.77
2000	235.64	44.85	15.64	163.14	42.65	431.27	113.89
2001	249.95	60.84	38.96	174.28	47.55	637.76	137.91
2002	240.68	77.45	34.76	192.22	74.99	846.93	179.49
2003	275.22	95.23	31.50	239.98	132.30	1468.35	283.53
2004	261.13	80.47	26.89	278.72	175.25	1789.78	278.48
2005	255.02	80.85	36.15	311.35	172.37	2203.93	302.80
2006	267.43	95.39	31.13	270.92	159.48	2756.82	278.11

注：1. 中长期贷款1994年以前为固定资产贷款，1998年起中长期贷款中含中期流动资金贷款。2. 农业存款1996年以前为农村存款。3. 信托类贷款及其他含票据融资贷款及垫款。4. 16-3表同。

Note: a) Before 1994, medium-term & long-term loans refered to fixed assets loans, they had included medium-term circulating capital loans since 1998.
b) Agricultural deposits refered to rural deposits before 1996. c) Trust loans and others include bill financing and all advanced money. d) Same as following table 16-3.

16-3 银行机构人民币存贷款余额(1990-2006年)
RMB SAVING DEPOSITS AND LOANS OF BANKING INSTITUTIONS, 1990-2006

单位：亿元 (100 million yuan)

年份 Year	存款合计 Total Deposits	企业存款 Deposits of Enterprises	财政性存款 Treasury Deposits	储蓄存款 Savings Deposits	农业存款 Agricultural Deposits	信托及其他类存款 Trust Deposits and Others	贷款合计 Total Loans	#工业贷款 Industrial Loans
1990	236.31	83.78	19.15	101.88	18.58	12.92	387.72	134.42
1991	297.65	103.33	24.73	130.31	22.86	16.43	449.95	155.69
1992	376.19	141.99	23.50	160.47	24.27	25.96	539.53	178.32
1993	461.52	158.42	23.77	215.28	28.74	35.29	655.99	218.90
1994	596.96	250.75	24.26	317.46	2.31	2.18	788.51	243.47
1995	812.45	321.99	37.59	445.14	2.89	4.83	898.43	283.26
1996	1071.75	443.35	28.54	593.35	2.59	3.93	1147.90	332.65
1997	1415.43	630.45	26.22	741.43	2.70	14.62	1334.79	379.27
1998	1605.63	648.00	12.53	880.82	2.78	61.50	1427.53	406.79
1999	1801.79	728.74	45.69	975.06	2.89	49.41	1606.22	428.54
2000	2000.58	861.62	53.88	1011.47	2.54	71.07	1635.99	368.86
2001	2255.95	934.36	63.67	1117.34	3.76	136.83	1918.86	432.23
2002	2672.47	1090.57	102.16	1308.25	3.69	167.80	2233.48	448.66
2003	3482.63	1466.20	136.63	1593.74	4.33	281.73	2973.90	427.43
2004	4096.92	1763.90	175.18	1815.25	7.60	334.99	3301.60	403.82
2005	5006.21	2118.82	234.58	2117.56	5.06	530.19	3887.17	423.95
2006	6022.91	2624.63	249.77	2528.18	88.08	532.25	4776.70	547.43

年份 Year	#商业贷款 Commercial Loans	#建筑业贷款 Construction Loans	#私营及个体贷款 Loans to Private and Individuals	#乡镇企业贷款 Loans to Township Enterprises	#农业贷款 Agricultural Loans	#中长期贷款 Medium-term & Long-term Loans	#信托类贷款及其他 Trust Loans and Others
1990	160.99	8.23	0.04	10.75	7.86	50.00	15.43
1991	171.22	8.86	0.03	12.20	9.74	73.88	18.34
1992	190.01	9.75	0.03	13.50	11.16	105.67	31.09
1993	210.73	10.76	0.05	16.18	14.20	143.93	41.23
1994	214.48	13.06	0.14	21.00	12.31	203.97	18.82
1995	237.52	16.18	0.10	25.42	16.37	257.00	21.28
1996	271.66	31.82	0.29	35.78	22.66	303.03	37.28
1997	297.74	36.28	8.63	41.29	30.43	297.02	12.53
1998	295.91	37.38	10.11	51.22	35.08	301.56	19.02
1999	292.08	35.99	10.15	57.22	31.64	404.36	34.23
2000	235.64	44.85	15.64	47.34	21.57	430.05	36.89
2001	249.93	60.81	38.96	49.35	19.92	634.26	66.47
2002	240.66	77.45	34.76	53.41	20.35	841.14	109.68
2003	275.20	95.23	31.50	59.10	16.52	1460.80	167.50
2004	261.11	80.47	22.29	67.62	15.53	1782.72	167.16
2005	255.02	80.85	32.21	66.89	14.62	2198.34	211.45
2006	267.22	95.39	25.73	98.95	48.48	2744.97	276.66

注：自2001年起，银行机构没有信托类存贷款。
Note: Since 2001, banking institutions have no Trust loans or deposits.

16-4 中资金融机构现金投放与回笼（1990-2006年）
CASH STATISTICS OF CHINESE FINANCIAL INSTITUTIONS, 1990-2006

单位：亿元 (100 million yuan)

年 份 Year	现金收入 Cash Income	现金支出 Cash Expenditures	投 放 Currency Issuance
1990	239.92	242.00	2.08
1991	287.09	295.37	8.28
1992	407.75	418.72	10.97
1993	646.66	656.34	9.68
1994	892.28	893.48	1.20
1995	1285.46	1275.46	-10.00
1996	1696.42	1704.67	8.25
1997	2637.49	2636.20	-1.29
1998	3209.96	3218.63	8.67
1999	3673.32	3689.52	16.20
2000	4277.52	4268.38	-9.14
2001	4782.14	4793.23	11.09
2002	5081.47	5126.79	45.32
2003	6561.94	6651.99	90.05
2004	8689.80	8779.70	89.90
2005	9675.45	9779.48	104.03
2006	11120.24	11267.11	146.87

16-5 中外资金融机构存贷款余额（2003-2006年）
SAVING DEPOSITS AND LOANS BALANCE OF CHINESE & FOREIGN FINANCIAL INSTITUTIONS, 2003-2006

单位：亿元、亿美元 (100 million yuan, USD 100 million)

项 目		2003	2004	2005	2006
存款余额(折人民币)	**Saving Deposits Balance (as RMB)**	**4362.60**	**5139.72**	**6090.50**	**6839.20**
中资金融机构	Chinese Financial Institutions	4317.98	5044.07	5990.37	6762.39
人民币	RMB	4033.51	4729.61	5684.40	6531.94
外 汇	Foreign Exchange	34.37	37.99	37.91	29.51
外资金融机构	Foreign-funded Financial Institutions	44.63	95.65	100.13	76.81
外 汇	Foreign Exchange	4.26	9.06	8.48	5.67
人民币	RMB	9.37	20.67	31.69	32.52
贷款余额(折人民币)	**Loans Balance (as RMB)**	**3791.22**	**4146.49**	**4722.38**	**5415.72**
中资金融机构	Chinese Financial Institutions	3679.61	4010.17	4571.40	5243.71
人民币	RMB	3426.02	3821.38	4417.45	5106.94
外 汇	Foreign Exchange	30.64	22.81	19.08	17.52
外资金融机构	Foreign-funded Financial Institutions	112.76	136.32	150.98	172.02
外 汇	Foreign Exchange	12.77	14.39	13.73	12.32
人民币	RMB	7.06	17.21	40.18	75.82
汇 率（1美元折合人民币元）	**Exchange Rate (1 USD as RMB yuan)**	**8.2772**	**8.2765**	**8.0702**	**7.8087**

16-6 中外资金融机构本外币信贷资金平衡表
RMB & FOREIGN CURRENCY CREDIT FUNDS BALANCE SHEET OF CHINESE & FOREIGN FINANCIAL INSTITUTIONS

单位：亿元 (100 million yuan)

项　目	Item	2005	2006	2006比2005年增长(%) Increase Rate in 2006 over 2005 (%)
资金来源合计	**All Sources**	**5993.72**	**5775.89**	**12.2**
各项存款余额总计	Total Deposits Balance	6090.50	6839.20	12.2
企事业存款	Deposits of Enterprises and Institutions	2448.99	2834.82	15.8
活期存款	Current Deposits	1721.98	2117.64	23.0
定期存款	Fixed Deposits	727.01	717.18	-1.4
储蓄存款	Savings Deposits	2584.40	2922.70	13.1
活期存款	Current Deposits	791.54	926.52	17.1
定期存款	Fixed Deposits	1792.86	1996.18	11.3
信托存款	Trust Deposits	0.16		-100.0
委托存款	Entrust Deposits	105.70	9.10	-91.7
其他存款	Other Deposits	951.25	1072.58	12.8
境外联行存放	External Inter-bank Deposits	44.17		-100.0
所有者权益	Owner's Equity	189.52	213.95	12.9
其　他	Others	-330.47	-1277.26	-20.2
资金运用合计	**All Uses**	**5993.72**	**5775.89**	**14.8**
各项贷款余额总计	Total Loans Balance	4722.38	5415.72	14.2
短期贷款	Short-term Loans	2077.95	2239.24	7.7
中长期贷款	Medium-term and Long-term Loans	2255.23	2800.89	23.7
信托贷款	Trust Loans	6.72		-100.0
委托贷款	Entrust Loans	82.94	0.32	-99.6
其他贷款	Other Loans	71.52	79.02	10.1
票据融资	Bill Financing	225.02	286.83	27.5
各项垫款	Money Advanced for sb. to be Paid Back Later	3.00	9.42	43.4
存放境内联行	Internal Inter-bank Deposits	979.44		-100.0
有价证券及投资	Securities & Investment	291.90	360.17	23.4

注：表中增长速度按可比口径计算。16-7、16-8、16-9、16-14表同。
Note: The increase rates are calculated at comparable coverage. Same as following table 16-7, 16-8, 16-9, 16-14.

16-7 中资金融机构人民币各项存贷款余额
RMB SAVING DEPOSITS AND LOANS BALANCE OF CHINESE FINANCIAL INSTITUTIONS

单位：亿元 (100 million yuan)

项　目	Item	2005	2006	2006 比2005年 增长(%) Increase Rate in 2006 over 2005 (%)
各项存款总计	**Total Deposits**	**5684.40**	**6531.94**	**14.8**
企业存款	Deposits of Enterprises	2185.23	2661.96	21.8
财政性存款	Treasury Deposits	234.75	250.26	6.6
储蓄存款	Savings Deposits	2462.41	2811.02	14.2
# 定期储蓄	Fixed Deposits	1697.42	1911.81	12.6
农业存款	Agricultural Deposits	163.66	189.50	15.8
信托类存款	Trust Deposits	106.45	9.10	-91.5
其他类存款	Other Deposits	531.90	610.10	12.8
各项贷款总计	**Total Loans**	**4417.45**	**5106.94**	**15.3**
短期贷款	Short-term Loans	1910.72	2072.01	8.4
工业贷款	Industrial Loans	425.74	550.21	26.0
商业贷款	Commercial Loans	255.02	267.43	4.1
建筑业贷款	Construction Loans	80.85	95.39	15.7
私营及个体贷款	Loans to Private and Individuals	36.15	31.13	-13.9
乡镇企业贷款	Loans to Township Enterprises	311.35	270.92	-11.7
农业贷款	Agricultural Loans	172.37	159.48	-4.7
三资企业贷款	Loans to Hong Kong, Macao, Taiwan and Foreign-funded Enterprises	38.86	34.97	-6.7
其他短期贷款	Other Short-term Loans	590.38	662.48	12.4
中长期贷款	Medium-term and Long-term Loans	2203.93	2756.82	24.9
# 技术改造贷款	Loans to Technical Innovation	15.27	12.93	-10.9
基本建设贷款	Loans to Capital Construction	1229.95	1551.10	25.9
信托类贷款	Trust Loans	90.61	1.43	-98.4
票据融资	Bill Financing	209.54	268.18	28.0
各项垫款	Money Advanced for sb. to be Paid Back Late	2.65	8.50	66.2

16-8 银行机构人民币各项存贷款余额
RMB SAVING DEPOSITS AND LOANS BALANCE OF BANKING INSTITUTIONS

单位：亿元 (100 million yuan)

项　目	Item	2005	2006	2006比2005年增长(%) Increase Rate in 2006 over 2005 (%)
各项存款总计	**Total Deposits**	**5006.21**	**6022.91**	**20.3**
企业存款	Deposits of Enterprises	2118.82	2624.63	23.9
财政性存款	Treasury Deposits	234.58	249.77	6.5
储蓄存款	Savings Deposits	2117.56	2528.18	19.4
# 定期储蓄	Fixed Deposits	1463.19	1719.22	17.5
农业存款	Agricultural Deposits	5.06	88.08	1640.7
其他类存款	Other Deposits	530.19	532.25	0.4
各项贷款总计	**Total Loans**	**3887.17**	**4776.70**	**22.9**
短期贷款	Short-term Loans	1477.38	1755.07	18.8
工业贷款	Industrial Loans	423.95	547.43	29.1
商业贷款	Commercial Loans	255.02	267.22	4.8
建筑业贷款	Construction Loans	80.85	95.39	18.0
私营及个体贷款	Loans to Private and Individuals	32.21	25.73	-20.1
乡镇企业贷款	Loans to Township Enterprises	66.89	98.95	47.9
农业贷款	Agricultural Loans	14.62	48.48	231.6
三资企业贷款	Loans to Hong Kong, Macao, Taiwan and Foreign-funded Enterprises	38.83	34.92	-10.1
其他短期贷款	Other Short-term Loans	565.01	636.95	12.7
中期流动资金贷款	Medium-term Circulating Capital Loans			
中长期贷款	Medium-term and Long-term Loans	2198.34	2744.97	24.9
# 技术改造贷款	Loans to Technical Innovation	15.27	12.93	-15.3
基本建设贷款	Loans to Capital Construction	1229.95	1549.22	26.0
票据融资	Bill Financing	208.80	268.16	28.4
各项垫款	Money Advanced for sb. to be Paid Back Later	2.65	8.50	220.8

16-9 中资金融机构现金收入和支出
CASH INCOME AND EXPENDITURES OF CHINESE FINANCIAL INSTITUTIONS

单位：亿元 (100 million yuan)

项　目	Item	2005	2006	2006比2005年增长(%) Increase Rate in 2006 over 2005 (%)
现金收入总计	**Total Cash Income**	**9675.45**	**11120.24**	**14.9**
商品销售收入	Income from Commodity Sales	1464.86	1579.95	7.9
服务事业收入	Income from Service Trade	379.40	379.60	0.1
税款收入	Income from Taxes	53.74	64.95	20.9
城乡个体经营收入	Income from Urban and Rural Individual Business	433.90	451.88	4.1
储蓄存款收入	Income from Savings Deposits	6640.71	7870.70	18.5
其他金融机构收入	Income from Other Financial Institutions	93.09	104.73	12.5
居民归还贷款收入	Income from Repayment of Loans by Residents	192.10	211.61	10.2
汇兑收入	Income from Remittances	42.02	68.44	62.9
有价证券收入	Income from Securities	11.35	10.93	-3.7
其他收入	Others	364.28	377.45	3.6
现金支出总计	**Total Cash Expenditures**	**9779.48**	**11267.11**	**15.2**
工资性支出	Wages	676.52	788.79	16.6
# 国家职工工资奖金	Wages and Bonuses to the Staff and Workers from Government	300.72	375.94	25.0
国家对个人其他支出	Other Payments to Individuals from Government	114.27	129.55	13.4
其他单位工资性支出	Wages from Other Units	243.73	261.43	7.3
农副产品采购支出	Purchases of Agricultural and Sideline Products	157.82	173.00	9.6
工矿及其他产品采购支出	Expenditure for Purchases of Industrial and Mineral Products	167.37	182.11	8.8
行政企事业管理费支出	Government and Enterprises Overhead	451.35	455.44	0.9
城乡个体经营支出	Expenditure for Individual Business	688.30	694.30	0.9
储蓄存款支出	Expenditure for Savings Deposits	6981.65	8377.56	20.0
其他金融机构支出	Expenditure for Other Financial Institutions	71.04	68.34	-3.8
居民提取贷款支出	Expenditure for Loans by Residents	163.15	130.46	-20.0
汇兑支出	Expenditure for Remittances	22.51	36.22	60.9
有价证券支出	Expenditure for Securities	20.78	7.16	-65.5
其他支出	Others	378.99	353.73	-6.7
货币投放(+)或回笼(–)	**Currency Issuance (+) and Cash Withdrawal (–)**	**+104.03**	**+146.87**	**41.2**

16-10 金融机构法定存款利率表(1998-2006年)
NOMINAL INTEREST RATES ON DEPOSITS OF FINANCIAL INSTITUTIONS, 1998-2006

单位：年利率% (annual interest rate %)

项　目	Item	1998年3月25日 Mar 25, 1998	1998年7月1日 July 1, 1998	1998年12月7日 Dec. 7, 1998	1999年6月10日 June 10, 1999
个人人民币储蓄存款	RMB Household Deposits				
活　期	Current Deposits	1.71	1.44	1.44	0.99
定　期	Fixed Deposits				
三个月	3 Months	2.88	2.79	2.79	1.98
半　年	6 Months	4.14	3.96	3.33	2.16
一　年	1 Year	5.22	4.77	3.78	2.25
二　年	2 Years	5.58	4.86	3.96	2.43
三　年	3 Years	6.21	4.95	4.14	2.70
五　年	5 Years	6.66	5.22	4.50	2.88
存本取息、零存整取、整存零取	Three Convenients & Flexible Ways of Savings Deposits				
一　年	1 Year	4.14	3.96	3.33	1.98
三　年	3 Years	5.22	4.77	3.78	2.16
五　年	5 Years	6.21	4.95	4.14	2.25
企业单位存款	Enterprises Deposits				
活　期	Current Deposits	1.71	1.44	1.44	0.99
定　期	Fixed Deposits				
三个月	3 Months	2.88	2.79	2.79	1.98
半　年	6 Months	4.14	3.96	3.33	2.16
一　年	1 Year	5.22	4.77	3.78	2.25
二　年	2 Years	5.58	4.86	3.96	2.43
三　年	3 Years	6.21	4.95	4.14	2.70
五　年	5 Years	6.66	5.22	4.50	2.88

项　目	Item	2002年2月21日 Feb. 21, 2002	2004年10月29日 Oct. 29, 2004	2006年8月19日 Aug. 19, 2006
个人人民币储蓄存款	RMB Household Deposits			
活　期	Current Deposits	0.72	0.72	0.72
定　期	Fixed Deposits			
三个月	3 Months	1.71	1.71	1.80
半　年	6 Months	1.89	2.07	2.25
一　年	1 Year	1.98	2.25	2.52
二　年	2 Years	2.25	2.70	3.06
三　年	3 Years	2.52	3.24	3.69
五　年	5 Years	2.79	3.60	4.14
存本取息、零存整取、整存零取	Three Convenients & Flexible Ways of Savings Deposits			
一　年	1 Year	1.71	1.71	1.80
三　年	3 Years	1.89	2.07	2.25
五　年	5 Years	1.98	2.25	2.52
企业单位存款	Enterprises Deposits			
活　期	Current Deposits	0.72	0.72	0.72
定　期	Fixed Deposits			
三个月	3 Months	1.71	1.71	1.80
半　年	6 Months	1.89	2.07	2.25
一　年	1 Year	1.98	2.25	2.52
二　年	2 Years	2.25	2.70	3.06
三　年	3 Years	2.52	3.24	3.69
五　年	5 Years	2.79	3.60	4.14

16-11 金融机构法定贷款利率表(1999-2006年)
NOMINAL INTEREST RATES ON LOANS OF FINANCIAL INSTITUTIONS, 1999-2006

单位: 年利率% (annual interest rate %)

项　目	Item	1999年6月10日 June 10, 1999	2002年2月21日 Feb. 21, 2002	2004年10月29日 Otc. 29, 2004
短期贷款	Short-term Loans			
一般流动资金	General Circulating Funds			
半年以内	Less than 6 Months	5.58	5.04	5.22
一年(六个月至一年)	1 Year (6 months to 1 year)	5.85	5.31	5.58
长期贷款	Long-term Loans			
基本建设贷款	Loans to Capital Construction			
一年以上至三年	1-3 Years	5.94	5.49	5.76
三年以上至五年	3-5 Years	6.03	5.58	5.85
五年以上至十年	5-10 Years	6.21	5.76	6.12
住房贷款	Housing Loans			
个人住房公积金贷款	Accumulation Fund Loans			
五年以内	Less than 5 Years	4.14	3.60	3.78
五年以上	More than 5 Years	4.59	4.05	4.23
商业银行自营性住房贷款	Self-supported by Commercial Banks			
半年以内	Less than 6 Months			
一年(六个月至一年)	1 Year (6 months to 1 year)			
一年以上至三年	1-3 Years			
五年以内	Less than 5 Years	5.31	4.77	4.95
五年以上	More than 5 Years	5.58	5.04	5.31

项　目	Item	2005年3月17日 Mar. 17, 2005	2006年4月28日 Apr. 28, 2006	2006年8月19日 Aug. 19, 2006
短期贷款	Short-term Loans			
一般流动资金	General Circulating Funds			
半年以内	Less than 6 Months	5.22	5.40	5.58
一年(六个月至一年)	1 Year (6 months to 1 year)	5.58	5.85	6.12
长期贷款	Long-term Loans			
基本建设贷款	Loans to Capital Construction			
一年以上至三年	1-3 Years	5.76	6.03	6.30
三年以上至五年	3-5 Years	5.85	6.12	6.48
五年以上至十年	5-10 Years	6.12	6.39	6.84
住房贷款	Housing Loans			
个人住房公积金贷款	Accumulation Fund Loans			
五年以内	Less than 5 Years	3.96	4.14	
五年以上	More than 5 Years	4.41	4.59	

注: 1. 从1999年9月起，金融机构对中小企业贷款利率可在法定贷款利率基础上上浮30%，对大型企业贷款最高上浮10%；金融机构贷款贷款最低下浮10%。2. 从2005年3月17日起，自营性个人住房贷款利率改按商业性贷款利率执行，上限放开，实行下限管理，下限利率水平为相应期限档次贷款基准利率的0.9倍。3. 从2006年8月19日起，个人住房贷款利率下限由基准利率的0.9倍扩大到0.85倍。

Note: a) As of September 1999, the loan interest rate for medium-and small-sized enterprises could be 30% higher than nominal interest rates; for large-sized enterprises, the lending rate could be as much as 10% higher than nominal interest rates. For all financial institutions, the lending rate could be 10% lower than nominal interest rates. b) As of March 17 2005, the loan interest rate of self-supported by Commercial Banks is running as commercial loan interest rates with upper limit opened and lower limit controlled, the lower limit loan interest rate is 0.9 times of nominal interest rates at the same time grouping. c) As of August 19 2006, the lower limit loan interest rate of self-supported was changed from 0.9 times of benchmark interest rate to 0.85 times of benchmark interest rate.

16-12 保险机构
INSURANCE INSTITUTIONS

单位：个 (unit)

项　目	Item	2005	2006
保险机构	**Insurance Institutions**	**431**	**443**
保险公司机构	**Insurance Companies**	**371**	**367**
#总公司	Parent Companies	3	3
#中外合资、外资公司	Joint-venture and Sole Foreign Investment	2	2
分公司	Divisions	17	23
支公司	Sub-divisions	99	102
营销服务部	Operation & Service Offices	233	239
专业保险中介机构	**Professional Insurance Intermediary Institutions**	**56**	**72**
保险代理公司	Insurance Agent Companies	43	51
保险公估公司	Insurance Assessment Companies	4	5
保险经纪公司	Insurance Broker Companies	9	16
外资保险公司代表处	**Agencies of Foreign-founded Insurance Companies**	**4**	**4**

注：本表中支公司包含中心支公司。
Note: In this table, sub-divisions insurance companies include center sub-divisions insurance companies.

16-13 保险业务主要指标（1990-2006年）
MAIN INDICATORS OF INSURANCE BUSINESS, 1990-2006

年份 Year	保险金额（亿元）Amount Insured (100 million yuan)	保费（万元）Premium (10 000 yuan)	人身险 Personal Insurance	财产险 Property Insurance	赔款及给付（万元）Claim and Payment (10 000 yuan)	人身险 Personal Insurance	财产险 Property Insurance
1990	918.00	34327	4384	17896	9827	334	5237
1991	1009.18	39474	5832	20222	14715	894	8651
1992	1136.06	49624	10185	23639	22843	1637	12963
1993	1514.16	67412	14492	32496	34689	4866	17885
1994	2434.06	100561	24628	47147	47434	6642	27405
1995	2274.74	123655	31588	61338	52985	6545	30973
1996	2488.21	171768	63373	74399	62613	10186	33257
1997	3306.04	243377	125327	112401	83528	18334	61900
1998	3949.15	271654	161097	110557	70075	14206	55869
1999	4848.10	291382	175804	115578	69163	14703	54460
2000	3696.19	314663	191786	122877	71950	7714	64236
2001	5176.91	417049	276050	140999	119062	56364	62698
2002	5632.35	649698	505966	143732	114818	46513	68305
2003	6497.87	753098	597450	155648	173608	72493	101115
2004	9852.79	809874	622284	187590	174178	77905	96273
2005	12141.02	906391	688629	217762	174637	67284	107353
2006	16690.02	1051842	785664	266178	218608	92220	126388

16-14 保险业务情况
BASIC INDICATORS OF INSURANCE BUSINESS

项　目	Item	2005	2006	2006比2005年增长(%) Increase Rate in 2006 over 2005 (%)
保险金额(亿元)	**Amount Insured (100 million yuan)**	**12141.02**	**16690.02**	**37.5**
财产保险	Property Insurance	8078.20	11331.53	40.3
人身保险	Personal Insurance	4062.82	5358.49	31.9
保　费(万元)	**Premium (10 000 yuan)**	**906390.56**	**1051842.47**	**16.0**
财产保险	Property Insurance	217762.09	266178.46	22.2
# 机动车辆保险	Motor Vehicle Insurance	128986.50	167419.47	29.8
人寿保险	Life Insurance	585604.88	678610.29	15.9
人身意外伤害保险	Unforeseen Human Injury Insurance	17864.63	20096.06	12.5
健康保险	Health Insurance	85158.95	86957.67	2.1
赔款及给付额(万元)	**Claim and Payment (10 000 yuan)**	**174637.17**	**218608.15**	**25.2**
财产保险	Property Insurance	107353.40	126387.88	17.7
# 机动车辆保险	Motor Vehicle Insurance	80132.57	89643.21	11.9
人寿保险	Life Insurance	37163.21	64523.96	73.6
人身意外伤害保险	Unforeseen Human Injury Insurance	4935.27	5421.30	9.8
健康保险	Health Insurance	25185.29	22275.01	-11.6
保险密度(元)	**Insurance Density (yuan)**	**869.02**	**978.45**	**12.6**
财产保险	Property Insurance	209.20	247.61	18.4
人身保险	Personal Insurance	654.54	730.85	11.7
保险深度(%)	**Insurance Depth (%)**	**2.47**	**2.42**	
财产保险	Property Insurance	0.61	0.61	
人身保险	Personal Insurance	1.86	1.58	
赔付率(%)	**Claim and Payment Rate (%)**	**19.27**	**20.78**	
财产保险	Property Insurance	48.88	47.48	
人身保险	Personal Insurance	9.58	53.54	

注：人身保险金额为期末有效保险金额。
Note: Amount insured of personal insurance is the efficiency amount insured at the end of term.

16-15 外资(合资)银行、保险公司在津分行、代表处一览(2006年)
BRANCHES OR OFFICES OF FOREIGN INVESTMENT (JOINT VENTURE) BANKS AND INSURANCE COMPANIES IN TIANJIN, 2006

名　称 Name	行长、首席代表 Director	办公地址 Address
渣打银行(中国)有限公司天津分行	石新宇	天津津汇广场20层
Standard Chartered Bank (China) Limited Tianjin Branch	Edward	20 Floor, Exchange Office Tower of Tianjin
法国巴黎银行有限公司天津分行	宋宝成	天津国际大厦16层
BNP Paribas Tianjin Branch	Victor Song	16 Floor, International Building of Tianjin
汇丰银行(中国)有限公司天津分行	孙伟发	天津远洋广场1层
HSBC Bank (China) Company Limited Tianjin Branch	Freddy Suen	1 Floor, Ocean Shipping Plaza of Tianjin
法国东方汇理银行股份有限公司天津分行	张家麟	天津国际大厦710室
Corporate and Investment Bank Tianjin Branch	Charles Chang	Rm. 710, International Building of Tianjin
法国兴业银行有限公司天津分行	刘德凤	天津河川大厦22层
Societe Generale Tianjin Branch	Luce Liu	22 Floor, Innotec Tower of Tianjin
新加坡华侨银行有限公司天津分行	杨伟义	天津国际大厦511室
Oversea Chinese Banking Corporation Limited Tianjin Branch	Yeo Wee Ghee	Rm. 511, International Building of Tianjin
美国摩根大通银行有限公司天津分行	佟静星	天津国际大厦14层
JPMorgan Chase Bank Tianjin Branch	Charles Tong	14 Floor, International Building of Tianjin
韩国外换银行股份有限公司天津分行	李光铉	天津利顺德饭店1层
Korea Exchange Bank Tianjin Branch	Lee Kwang Hyun	1 Floor, Astor Hotel of Tianjin
韩国新韩银行股份有限公司天津分行	朴成根	天津国际大厦1901室
Shinhan Bank Tianjin Branch	Park Sung Geun	Rm. 1901, International Building of Tianjin
日本三井住友银行股份有限公司天津分行	田中隆一	天津国际大厦1210室
Sumitomo Mitsui Banking Corporation Tianjin Branch	Ryuichi Tanaka	Rm. 1210, International Building of Tianjin
日本三菱东京日联银行股份有限公司天津分行	山内一英	天津国际大厦811室
Bank of Tokyo-Mitsubishi UFJ. Ltd., Tianjin Branch	Yamauchi Kazuhide	Rm. 811, International Building of Tianjin
韩国中小企业银行有限公司天津分行	金龙满	天津国际大厦911室
Industrial Bank of Korea Tianjin Branch	Kim Yong Man	Rm. 911, International Building of Tianjin

16-15 续表 Continued

名　称 Name	行长、首席代表 Director	办公地址 Address
日本瑞穗实业银行股份有限公司天津分行	唐沢武彦	天津国际大厦2202室
Mizuho Corporate Bank Ltd., Tianjin Branch	Karasawa Takehiko	Rm. 2202, International Building of Tianjin
花旗银行(中国)有限公司天津分行	陆　烜	天津津汇广场1801室
Citibank (China) Co., Ltd., Tianjin Branch	Luke	Rm. 1801, Exchange Office Tower of Tianjin
中德住房储蓄银行	岳慕礼	天津河西区南京路19号增1号
Sino-German Bausparkasse	Joachim Dumitsch	19-1 Nanjing Road, Hexi District, Tianjin
星展银行(香港)有限公司天津代表处	李　虹	天津津汇广场1902室
DBS Bank (Hong Kong) Limited, Tianjin Representative Office	Lillian H li	Rm. 1902, Exchange Tower of Tianjin
荷兰银行有限公司天津代表处	许　燕	天津国际大厦718室
ABN AMRO Bank N. V., Tianjin Rep. Office	Jennifer Xu	Rm. 718, International Building of Tianjin
东亚银行有限公司天津代表处	栗艳冰	天津国际大厦907室
The Bank of East Asia Limited, Tianjin Representative Office	Judy	Rm. 907, International Building of Tianjin
日本三井住友海上火灾保险公司天津代表处	山本猛志	天津国际大厦2408室
Mitsui Sumitomo Insurance Co., Ltd., Tianjin Representative Office	Yama Moto Takeshi	Rm. 2408, International Building of Tianjin
日本东京海上日动火灾保险公司天津代表处	唐金才	天津国际大厦2201室
The Tokio Marine and Nichido Fire Insurance Co., Ltd. Tianjin Representative Office	Tang Jincai	Rm. 2201, International Building of Tianjin
爱和谊保险公司天津代表处	宫崎守	天津国际大厦1609室
Aioi Insurance Co., Ltd., Tianjin Representative Office	Miyazaki Mamoru	Rm. 1609, International Building of Tianjin
裕利安宜信用保险股份公司天津代表处	王　洁	天津津汇广场905室
Euler Hermes Kreditversicherungs-AG Tianjin Representative Office	John Wang	Rm. 905, Exchange Office Tower of Tianjin

主要统计指标解释

存款 指企业、机关、团体或居民根据资金必须收回的原则，把货币资金存入金融机构保管并取得一定利息的一种信用活动形式。根据存款对象的不同可划分为企业存款、财政性存款、城乡储蓄存款、农村存款、信托及其他存款等，它是银行信贷资金的主要来源。

贷款 指金融机构根据资金必须归还的原则，按一定利率，为企业、个人等提供资金的一种信用活动形式。我国银行贷款分为工业贷款、农业贷款、商业贷款、建筑业贷款、私营和个体贷款、乡镇企业贷款、中长期贷款、信托及其他贷款等。

保险金额 指保险人承担赔偿或者给付保险金责任的最高限额。

保费 指投保人为取得保险人在约定范围内所承担赔偿责任而支付给保险人的费用。

赔款 指保险人根据保险合同的规定，向被保险人支付的赔偿保险责任损失的金额。

给付 包括死伤医疗给付和满期给付。死伤医疗给付是指保险人根据人寿保险及长期健康保险合同的规定，因被保险人在保险期内发生保险责任范围内的保险事故支付给被保险人（或受益人）的金额。满期给付是指被保险人生存期满，保险人按人寿保险合同规定支付给被保险人的满期保险金额。

保险密度 为按常住人口计算的人均保费收入。

保险深度 指保费收入相当于国内生产总值的比例。

Explanastory Notes on Main Statistical Indicators

Deposit is a form of credit by which enterprises, institutions, organizations or households can put money into banks and other credit institutions for safekeeping and interest earning under the principle of free withdrawal. According to different depositors, deposits are divided into enterprise deposits, treasury deposits, urban and rural savings deposits, rural deposits, entrust and other deposits. Deposits are major sources of credit funds of banks.

Loan is a form of credit by which banks and other credit institutions provide funds at certain interest rate to enterprises and individuals in the light of the principle of unconditional repayment. Loans from Chinese banks include industry loans, agriculture loans, commerce loans, construction loans, loans to private and individuals, township enterprises loans, medium & long term loans, entrust and other loans.

Amount Insured refers to the maximum that the insurant will get for the claim of the case insured.

Premium is the fee paid by the insurant to the insurer to obtain the obligation of compensation from the insurance within the agreed terms.

Settled Claim is the compensation paid by the insurer to insurant in accordance with the insurance contract.

Payment includes payment for death, injury or medical treatment and mature payment. Payment for death, injury or medical treatment refers to the money paid to insurant (or the beneficiary) in accordance with the life or health insurance contract when the insurant encounters accidents within the insured period covered in the contract. Mature payment refers to the mature payment to the insurant in accordance with the life insurance contract at the end of the insured period.

Insurance Density refers to per capita premiums which is based on permanent resident population.

Insurance Depth refers to the proportion of premiums to gross domestic product.

第17篇
CHAPTER 17

教育和科技
Education and Science & Technology

17-1 各级各类学校基本情况（1990-2006年）
BASIC STATISTICS BY LEVEL AND TYPE OF SCHOOL, 1990-2006

单位：人 (person)

年 份 Year	学校数(所) Number of Schools (unit)			毕业生数 Graduates			招生数 New Students Enrollment		
	高等学校 Institutions of Higher Education	中等学校 Secondary Schools	小 学 Primary Schools	高等学校 Institutions of Higher Education	中等学校 Secondary Schools	小 学 Primary Schools	高等学校 Institutions of Higher Education	中等学校 Secondary Schools	小 学 Primary Schools
1990	28	1013	3259	15200	119401	101398	13856	151254	147349
1991	27	1003	3232	15059	129497	117856	14523	171048	132025
1992	26	981	3238	14857	130538	119529	17320	173291	132209
1993	26	975	3243	13494	132538	121237	21678	180770	143268
1994	26	991	3219	14661	143373	138344	21422	203277	152941
1995	25	1059	3216	20203	151024	156641	22055	229589	148922
1996	20	1098	3185	18429	156924	145705	22664	227918	144438
1997	20	1108	3030	19535	191798	133616	22016	230692	133012
1998	20	1091	2841	18342	219593	166618	23678	273472	115988
1999	21	1041	2642	19292	216950	156584	31670	254033	104452
2000	21	1006	2323	19022	220099	155253	45468	251777	100453
2001	33	1012	1307	19103	233427	147639	56066	249761	95492
2002	37	978	1208	27295	234711	133301	69453	244181	92955
2003	37	897	1136	40221	244398	132022	86115	259174	84963
2004	40	848	1099	51666	252596	114771	96182	250591	81603
2005	42	803	1062	69211	243305	106447	103616	234837	78373
2006	45	746	1023	81983	247421	106075	107920	230246	82102

年 份 Year	在校学生数 Students Enrollment			教职工数 Teachers, Staff and Workers			# 专任教师数 Full-time Teachers		
	高等学校 Institutions of Higher Education	中等学校 Secondary Schools	小 学 Primary Schools	高等学校 Institutions of Higher Education	中等学校 Secondary Schools	小 学 Primary Schools	高等学校 Institutions of Higher Education	中等学校 Secondary Schools	小 学 Primary Schools
1990	51039	443400	855319	28821	73855	56773	11121	47056	47110
1991	49900	464700	865500	28686	73052	58307	10704	46460	47762
1992	52127	483238	872412	22338	73563	59781	10391	46935	49030
1993	60247	504963	887412	21907	73092	61377	10160	46688	50448
1994	66672	533908	896174				10170	46591	51616
1995	68080	600243	884476	27421	74887	62499	10490	47196	51401
1996	71354	662873	879772	26203	76640	62207	9811	48771	51202
1997	73630	692918	877554	20775	77045	62054	9589	51309	51048
1998	78651	735764	826732	20349	77569	60500	9496	51643	49420
1999	90450	761741	773064	21001	79345	59002	9647	53012	48293
2000	117690	712762	717146	25952	80321	56948	10137	53844	46697
2001	153998	785891	665495	29953	77277	55311	12552	52732	45651
2002	196892	792772	627242	32019	76590	54237	14175	53386	44922
2003	245213	801680	585446	33371	75531	52603	15553	53706	43829
2004	286145	775673	554844	36400	73720	50989	18973	52270	42122
2005	331553	755915	533003	39434	72009	49629	21670	51835	41076
2006	357382	714146	516823	42229	70815	47916	24464	51920	39951

17-2 各级各类学校数、学生数和教职工数
SCHOOLS, STUDENTS AND TEACHERS BY LEVEL AND TYPE OF SCHOOL

单位：人 (person)

学校类别	Item	学校数(所) Number of Schools (unit)		毕业生数 Graduates		招生数 New Students Enrollment	
		2005	2006	2005	2006	2005	2006
合　计	Total	1907	1814	418963	435479	416826	420268
高等学校	Institutions of Higher Education	42	45	69211	81983	103616	107920
中等专业学校	Specialized Secondary Schools	40	37	17250	21416	25526	24006
技工学校	Secondary Technical Schools	57	52	13550	14406	17228	17408
农业、职业中学	Rural, Vocational Secondary Schools	66	50	18430	17383	17854	16556
普通中学	Regular Secondary Schools	640	607	194075	194216	174229	172276
高　中	Senior Secondary Schools	232	231	57263	69891	74449	68023
初　中	Junior Secondary Schools	408	376	136812	124325	99780	104253
小　学	Primary Schools	1062	1023	106447	106075	78373	82102

学校类别	Item	在校学生数 Students Enrollment		教职工数 Teachers,Staff and Workers		# 专任教师数 Full-time Teachers	
		2005	2006	2005	2006	2005	2006
合　计	Total	1620471	1608521	161072	160960	114581	116335
高等学校	Institutions of Higher Education	331553	357382	39434	42229	21670	24464
中等专业学校	Specialized Secondary Schools	76994	77404	5707	5301	3369	3263
技工学校	Secondary Technical Schools	47104	47878	5420	5249	3278	3515
农业、职业中学	Rural, Vocational Secondary Schools	55527	56970	5560	5414	3651	3508
普通中学	Regular Secondary Schools	576290	552064	55322	54851	41537	41634
高　中	Senior Secondary Schools	217180	216281			14207	15101
初　中	Junior Secondary Schools	359110	335783			27330	26533
小　学	Primary Schools	533003	516823	49629	47916	41076	39951

17-3 平均每万人口拥有学生数（2003-2006年）
NUMBER OF STUDENT ENROLLMENT PER 10 000 PERSONS, 2003-2006

单位：人 (person)

项　目	Item	2003	2004	2005	2006
合　计	**Total**	**1617**	**1589**	**1615**	**1519**
高等学校	Institutions of Higher Education	243	281	330	337
中等学校	Secondary Schools	794	762	712	674
中等专业学校	Specialized Secondary Schools	73	68	77	73
技工学校	Secondary Technical Schools	52	46	47	45
农业、职业中学	Rural, Vocational Schools	61	59	55	54
普通中学	Regular Secondary Schools	609	589	574	521
高　中	Senior Secondary Schools	181	195	216	204
初　中	Junior Secondary Schools	429	394	358	317
小　学	Primary Schools	580	545	531	488

17-4 平均每一教师负担学生数（2003-2006年）
STUDENT-TEACHER RATIO, 2003-2006

单位：人 (person)

项　目	Item	2003	2004	2005	2006
合　计	**Total**	**14**	**14**	**14**	**14**
高等学校	Institutions of Higher Education	16	15	15	15
中等学校	Secondary Schools	15	15	14	13
中等专业学校	Specialized Secondary Schools	20	21	20	24
技工学校	Secondary Technical Schools	13	14	14	14
农业、职业中学	Rural, Vocational Schools	13	15	10	16
普通中学	Regular Secondary Schools	15	15	14	13
高　中	Senior Secondary Schools	15	15	15	14
初　中	Junior Secondary Schools	15	14	13	12
小　学	Primary Schools	13	13	13	13

17-5 各级学校学生升入学率（2003-2006年）
PERCENTAGE OF GRADUATE STUDENTS AND ENROLLMENT IN ALL SCHOOLS BY LEVEL, 2003-2006

单位：% (%)

指　标　Item	2003	2004	2005	2006
初中毕业生升学率 Percentage of Graduates in Junior Secondary Schools Entering Senior Secondary School	93.1	94	99.28	99.75
初中净入学率 Percentage of Graduates in Primary Schools Entering Junior Secondary Schools	98.97	99.89	99.83	98.41
学龄儿童毛入学率 Percentage of School-age Children Enrolled	99.97	99.97	99.97	101.08

17-6 研究生在校、毕业、招生及指导教师人数（2003-2006年）
ENROLLED,GRADUATED AND RECRUITED STUDENTS FOR MASTER & DOCTOR DEGREE AND THEIR TEACHERS, 2003-2006

单位：人 (person)

指标	Item	2003	2004	2005	2006
总计	Total				
在校生数	Students Enrollment	20657	24543	28470	30614
毕业生数	Graduates	3252	4995	6142	9165
招生人数	New Students Enrollment	8506	9259	10169	10880
指导教师	Teachers	3273	3699	4271	4761
攻读博士学位	Postgraduate for Doctor Degree				
在校生数	Students Enrollment	4304	4940	5766	6732
毕业生数	Graduates	585	982	944	1320
招生人数	New Students Enrollment	1680	1717	1787	1740
攻读硕士学位	Postgraduate for Master Degree				
在校生数	Students Enrollment	16353	19603	22704	23882
毕业生数	Graduates	2667	4013	5198	7845
招生人数	New Students Enrollment	6826	7542	8382	9140

17-7 分学科在校研究生人数
NUMBER OF ENROLLED STUDENTS FOR MASTER & DOCTOR DEGREE BY SUBJECT

单位：人 (person)

学科	Item	博士生 Doctor			硕士生 Master		
		2004	2005	2006	2004	2005	2006
总计	**Total**	**4940**	**5766**	**6732**	**19603**	**22704**	**23882**
哲学	Philosophy	84	98	164	196	217	168
经济学	Economics	1441	616	717	4859	2161	1670
法学	Law	189	232	291	852	1016	882
教育学	Education	21	24	31	802	792	701
文学	Literature	172	209	263	1353	1770	1963
历史学	History	245	270	301	316	371	312
理学	Science	627	769	940	1900	2149	2215
工学	Engineering	1752	2153	2471	7695	8663	9627
医学	Medicine	387	454	433	1606	2138	2504
农学	Agriculture	22	25	22	24	22	21
管理学	Management	877	916	1099	2859	3405	3819

17-8 各类高等学校基本情况 BASIC STATISTICS ON INSTITUTIONS OF HIGHER EDUCATION

单位：人 (person)

项　目	Item	学校数(所) Number of Schools (unit)		在校学生数 Students Enrollment		毕业生数 Graduates	
		2005	2006	2005	2006	2005	2006
总　计	Total	42	45	331553	357382	69211	81983
综合大学	Comprehensive Universities	11	12	74615	84066	16416	20073
理工院校	Science and Engineering	14	15	135758	142490	30104	35177
农林院校	Agriculture and Forestry	1	1	10005	11043	1600	2261
医药院校	Medicine	3	4	18841	20779	3001	3525
师范院校	Teacher Training	2	2	29551	31973	5166	6007
语文院校	Linguistics and Literary	2	2	12047	13730	2162	2482
财经院校	Economics and Finance	3	3	36207	37158	7888	9190
政法院校	Political Science And law	1	1	2174	2694	1025	732
体育院校	Physical Culture	1	1	5145	5708	922	851
艺术院校	Art Institutes	4	4	7210	7741	927	1685

项　目	Item	招生数 New Students Enrollment		教职工数 Teachers, Staff and Workers		# 专任教师数 Full-time Teachers	
		2005	2006	2005	2006	2005	2006
总　计	Total	103616	107920	39434	42229	21670	24464
综合大学	Comprehensive Universities	27672	28225	9308	10384	4857	5817
理工院校	Science and Engineering	41120	43444	16391	16850	8826	9376
农林院校	Agriculture and Forestry	2918	3299	877	951	472	530
医药院校	Medicine	6055	5635	3085	3771	1846	2390
师范院校	Teacher Training	8245	8856	3273	3393	1761	2067
语文院校	Linguistics and Literary	3995	4214	995	1223	701	851
政法院校	Political Science and law	9427	9601	3254	3440	149	2076
财经院校	Economics and Finance	740	1187	271	295	1908	155
体育院校	Physical Culture	1419	1277	655	652	406	404
艺术院校	Art Institutes	2025	2182	1325	1270	744	798

17-9 高等学校分科学生数
NUMBER OF STUDENTS ENROLLMENT IN INSTITUTIONS OF HIGHER EDUCATION BY SUBJECT

单位：人 (person)

学科	Item	在校学生数 Students Enrollment			
		本科 Undergraduate		专科 Junior Collage	
		2005	2006	2005	2006
总计	**Total**	**190629**	**212526**	**140924**	**144856**
#师范	Teacher Training	12675	13328	679	52
哲学	Philosophy	208	206		
经济学	Economics	13432	15681	9164	8041
法学	Law	7104	7835	5447	5006
教育学	Education	9056	9857	793	1027
文学	Literature	32221	37291	15781	14848
历史学	History	605	662		
理学	Science	16849	18678		
工学	Engineering	62554	68753	66572	73545
农学	Agriculture	2658	2927	948	879
医学	Medicine	11344	12108	6873	7013
管理学	Management	34598	38528	35346	34497

学科	Item	毕业生数 Graduates			
		本科 Undergraduate		专科 Junior Collage	
		2005	2006	2005	2006
总计	**Total**	**33759**	**39279**	**35452**	**42704**
#师范	Teacher Training	2761	1346	139	18
哲学	Philosophy	54	49		
经济学	Economics	2617	3025	2915	3624
法学	Law	1205	1496	1924	1759
教育学	Education	1753	1597	139	256
文学	Literature	4736	6369	4664	5278
历史学	History	112	110		
理学	Science	2685	3256		
工学	Engineering	12615	13363	16212	19590
农学	Agriculture	363	446	287	346
医学	Medicine	1450	1673	1600	1898
管理学	Management	6169	7895	7711	9953

学科	Item	招生数 New Students Enrollment			
		本科 Undergraduate		专科 Junior Collage	
		2005	2006	2005	2006
总计	**Total**	**53013**	**61831**	**50603**	**46089**
#师范	Teacher Training	3143	3284	343	34
哲学	Philosophy	35	53		
经济学	Economics	3538	4975	2787	2214
法学	Law	2028	2214	1935	1524
教育学	Education	2326	2158	379	448
文学	Literature	10177	11316	4799	4336
历史学	History	205	174		
理学	Science	4760	5304		
工学	Engineering	16932	20772	24940	24920
农学	Agriculture	757	742	375	283
医学	Medicine	3156	2786	2609	1975
管理学	Management	9099	11337	12779	10389

17-10 高等学校分科专任教师数（按职称分）
NUMBER OF FULL-TIME TEACHERS IN INSTITUTIONS OF HIGHER EDUCATION (by Subject)

单位：人 (person)

学科	Item	合计 Total		正高级 Senior Title		副高级 Asso. Senior Title	
		2005	2006	2005	2006	2005	2006
总计	**Total**	**21670**	**24464**	**2827**	**3279**	**7148**	**8001**
哲学	Philosophy	599	678	80	89	240	271
经济学	Economics	1443	1629	197	241	429	507
法学	Law	678	744	83	81	203	211
教育学	Education	1643	1539	116	106	523	506
文学	Literature	4283	4906	414	506	1229	1289
历史学	History	264	292	68	74	95	112
理学	Science	2649	2873	539	527	934	1000
工学	Engineering	6882	7696	816	906	2397	2708
农学	Agriculture	203	228	34	39	71	75
医学	Medicine	1517	1923	325	494	567	693
管理学	Management	1509	1956	155	216	460	629

学科	Item	中级 Middle Title		初级 Junior Title		无职称 No Title	
		2005	2006	2005	2006	2005	2006
总计	**Total**	**6481**	**7453**	**4187**	**4887**	**1027**	**844**
哲学	Philosophy	214	200	62	108	3	10
经济学	Economics	480	482	266	316	71	83
法学	Law	202	229	150	180	40	43
教育学	Education	530	530	387	330	87	67
文学	Literature	1346	1503	1076	1402	218	206
历史学	History	67	79	24	20	10	7
理学	Science	741	872	360	405	75	69
工学	Engineering	1966	2366	1326	1429	377	287
农学	Agriculture	46	95	52	18		1
医学	Medicine	427	493	179	233	19	10
管理学	Management	462	604	305	446	127	61

17-11 中等专业学校基本情况
BASIC STATISTICS ON SPECIALIZED SECONDARY SCHOOLS

单位：人 (person)

学　科	Item	在校学生数 Students Enrollment		毕业生数 Graduates	
		2005	2006	2005	2006
总　计	**Total**	**76994**	**77404**	**17250**	**21416**
农林类	Agriculture and Forestry	1093	202	274	125
资源与环境类	Resources and Environment	674	1060	294	186
能源类	Energy	100	165	45	
土木水利工程类	Civil and Hydraulic Engineering	5090	5162	1512	1718
加工制造类	Processing and Manufacturing	18550	24175	2949	4954
交通运输类	Communication and Transportation	3026	4011	656	608
信息技术类	Information Technology	22769	21400	4911	7028
医药卫生类	Medicine and Health	3890	4625	723	1014
商贸与旅游类	Trade and Tourism	11997	10382	3638	3864
财经类	Finance and Economics	2196	1859	377	578
文化艺术与体育类	Culture, Arts and Physical Education	1996	2444	445	438
社会公共事业类	Public Affairs	2982	380	1063	370
师范类	Teacher Training	1006	1140	173	274
其　他	Others	1625	399	190	259

学　科	Item	招生数 New Students Enrollment		专业课教师数 Special Course Teachers	
		2005	2006	2005	2006
总　计	**Total**	**25526**	**24006**	**1641**	**1628**
农林类	Agriculture and Forestry	541	46	56	19
资源与环境类	Resources and Environment	254	597	20	25
能源类	Energy	27	165	25	4
土木水利工程类	Civil and Hydraulic Engineering	1450	1556	142	141
加工制造类	Processing and Manufacturing	6484	8882	232	229
交通运输类	Communication and Transportation	798	1294	40	159
信息技术类	Information Technology	7147	5451	334	361
医药卫生类	Medicine and Health	1223	1049	82	95
商贸与旅游类	Trade and Tourism	3914	2993	81	83
财经类	Finance and Economics	874	675	186	179
文化艺术与体育类	Culture, Arts and Physical Education	815	964	201	152
社会公共事业类	Public Affairs	1347	35	79	4
师范类	Teacher Training	232	294	52	68
其　他	Others	420	5	111	109

17-12 普通中学基本情况（2006年）
BASIC STATISTICS OF REGULAR SECONDARY SCHOOLS, 2006

单位：人（person）

项　目	Item	学校数（所）Number of Schools (unit)	在校学生数 Students Enrollment	毕业生数 Graduates	招生数 New Students Enrollment	专任教师数 Full-time Teachers
总　计	**Total**	**607**	**552064**	**194216**	**172276**	**41634**
按城乡分组	**By Urban and Rural**					
城　市	City	265	239786	83941	71886	18064
县　镇	County	207	201914	68634	65136	15024
农　村	Rural	135	110364	41641	35254	8546
按部门分	**By Basic Statistics**					
教育部门	Education Department	532	490187	171201	154079	39161
其他部门	Other Departments	55	15724	6826	4564	1804
民　办	Private Units	20	46153	16189	13633	669
按学校性质分组	**By School Type**					
完全中学	Whole Secondary Schools	151	203979	68320	63827	16407
#高　中	Senior		85345	30376	36284	15101
高级中学	Senior Secondary Schools	80	97334	31500	31614	6691
初级中学	Junior Secondary Schools	343	236558	88300	73104	17565
九年一贯制学校	Whole Primary and Junior Secondary Schools	33	10136	2495	3480	969
其他学校附设中学班	Appendent Secondary School of Other Institutions		4057	3601	251	2
#初　中	Junior		3744	3154	126	

注：本表不含民办公助和公办民助学校。
Note: This table exclude private units supported by state and state-owned units supported by private units.

17-13 幼儿园基本情况（2003-2006年）
BASIC STATISTICS ON KINDERGARTENS, 2003-2006

指　标	Item	2003	2004	2005	2006
幼儿园所数（所）	Number of Kindergartens	1778	1636	1657	1617
入园儿童数(人)	Children Enrollment (person)	199551	198558	204722	193838
三岁及以上儿童	Children over Three Age	192552	191828	198461	184690
三岁以下儿童	Children under Three Age	6999	6730	6261	9148
教职工数(人)	Teachers, Staff and Workers (person)	15309	15378	15686	14721
#教养员	Teachers and Health Workers	10046	10040	10020	9706

17-14 普通中小学分布情况（2006年）
DISTRIBUTION OF REGULAR SECONDARY SCHOOLS AND PRIMARY SCHOOLS, 2006

地 区	Region	学校数(所) Number of Schools (unit)		在校学生数(人) Students Enrollment (persons)		专任教师(人) Full-time Teachers (person)	
		普通中学 Regular Middle Schools	小 学 Primary Schools	普通中学 Regular Middle Schools	小 学 Primary Schools	普通中学 Regular Middle Schools	小 学 Primary Schools
全 市	**Total**	**607**	**1023**	**552064**	**516823**	**41634**	**39951**
市辖区	**Districts Under City Administration**	**460**	**736**	**414682**	**399136**	**31781**	**31732**
和平区	Heping District	29	32	32459	27162	2401	2111
河东区	Hedong District	23	23	26874	19260	2000	1975
河西区	Hexi District	42	46	35777	29891	2587	2093
南开区	Nankai District	39	36	32743	26334	2657	2227
河北区	Hebei District	34	29	30479	23641	1920	1633
红桥区	Hongqiao District	29	31	24124	15656	1717	1979
塘沽区	Tanggu District	38	53	27028	35958	2222	2495
汉沽区	Han'gu District	15	21	10325	9488	898	1019
大港区	Dagang District	38	29	28915	25709	2430	1930
东丽区	Dongli District	23	40	16431	25342	1340	1830
西青区	Xiqing District	13	38	15899	16650	1272	1924
津南区	Jinnan District	18	43	19153	24232	1209	1553
北辰区	Beichen District	20	42	15894	17097	1329	1647
武清区	Wuqing District	49	134	46453	56846	3650	3643
宝坻区	Baodi District	48	134	50402	44451	3998	3479
天津铁厂	Tianjin Iron Works	2	5	1726	1419	151	194
市辖县	**Counties Under City Administration**	**147**	**287**	**137382**	**117687**	**9853**	**8219**
宁河县	Ninghe County	30	61	28383	25381	2250	1864
静海县	Jinghai County	52	96	42597	40478	2820	2671
蓟 县	Jixian County	65	130	66402	51828	4783	3684

注：专任教师数中不包括民办教师数。
Note: Number of full-time teachers exclude civilian teachers.

17-15 普通中学、小学及幼儿园校舍情况(2006年)
STATISTICS FOR SCHOOLHOUSES OF REGULAR SECONDARY SCHOOLS, PRIMARY SCHOOLS AND KINDERGARTENS, 2006

单位：平方米 (sq. m)

地区	Region	占地面积 Areas	校舍建筑面积 Floor Space of Schoolhouses			学生人均建筑面积 Average Floor Space of Students		
			普通中学 Regular Middle Schools	小学 Primary Schools	幼儿园 Kindergartens	普通中学 Regular Middle Schools	小学 Primary Schools	幼儿园 Kindergartens
全市	**Total**	**31485457**	**5633777**	**3457043**	**874949**	**10.20**	**6.69**	**4.51**
市辖区	**Districts Under City Administration**	**22594911**	**4538759**	**2658044**	**731017**	**10.95**	**6.66**	**5.23**
和平区	Heping District	521794	313239	129601	45568	9.65	4.77	8.40
河东区	Hedong District	841166	249161	137993	56894	9.27	7.16	7.34
河西区	Hexi District	980880	405403	171784	71918	11.33	5.75	7.79
南开区	Nankai District	1221954	464905	214674	76574	14.20	8.15	8.49
河北区	Hebei District	925610	302005	139007	50759	9.91	5.88	8.18
红桥区	Hongqiao District	553233	209171	123565	35085	8.67	7.89	6.83
塘沽区	Tanggu District	1599734	409319	245781	65798	15.14	6.84	5.69
汉沽区	Han'gu District	502630	76163	56976	10557	7.38	6.01	3.98
大港区	Dagang District	2772158	400316	167881	72493	13.84	6.53	8.64
东丽区	Dongli District	1556647	292923	170963	29343	17.83	6.75	3.56
西青区	Xiqing District	1128747	172302	160843	26981	10.84	9.66	2.95
津南区	Jinnan District	1203810	194124	167004	19285	10.14	6.89	1.80
北辰区	Beichen District	1303227	205149	178317	52411	12.91	10.43	4.55
武清区	Wuqing District	4246402	461782	355723	77504	9.94	6.26	3.11
宝坻区	Baodi District	3167682	364462	225683	32192	7.23	5.08	3.55
天津铁厂	Tianjin Iron Works	69237	18335	12249	7655	10.62	8.63	9.08
市辖县	**Counties Under City Administration**	**8890546**	**1095018**	**798999**	**143932**	**7.97**	**6.79**	**2.66**
宁河县	Ninghe County	1515673	197401	161940	9278	6.95	6.38	1.22
静海县	Jinghai County	3431485	331353	286402	68904	7.78	7.08	3.24
蓟县	Jixian County	3943388	566264	350657	65750	8.53	6.77	2.62

注：占地面积包括中等师范学校、幼儿园教师进修学校、特殊教育学校及其他。
Note: Areas of schools include middle teacher training,kindergarten teacher training,special education and other schools.

17-16 其他教育基本情况（2003-2006年）
BASIC STATISTICS ON OTHER EDUCATION, 2003-2006

单位：所、人 (unit, person)

指　标	Item	2003	2004	2005	2006
成人教育	**Adult Education**				
成人高等学校	Adult Higher Education Schools				
学校数	Number of Schools	22	20	20	16
在校学生数	Students Enrollment	115770	78486	84420	91758
成人中等学校	Secondary Schools for Adults				
学校数	Number of Schools	29	25	15	16
在校学生数	Students Enrollment	7619	5367	2905	2405
特殊教育	**Specific Education**				
盲聋哑学校	**Blind and Deaf-Mute Schools**				
学校数	Number of Schools	8	8	8	7
在校学生数	Students Enrollment	751	694	651	589
初　中	Junior Middle Schools	249	220	180	150
小　学	Primary Schools	502	474	471	439
教职工人数	Teachers, Staff and Workers	402	399	407	316
# 专任教师数	Full-time Teachers	254	256	269	235
弱智学校	**Schools for Low Intelligence Student**				
学校数	Number of Schools	13	13	14	14
在校学生数	Students Enrollment	2416	1937	1957	1915
初　中	Junior Middle Schools	451	414	394	386
小　学	Primary Schools	1965	1523	1563	1529
教职工人数	Teachers, Staff and Workers	304	286	293	287
# 专任教师数	Full-time teachers	200	200	215	201
工读学校	**Schools for Mistaken Students**				
学校数	Number of Schools	3	3	3	3
在校学生数	Students Enrollment	82	62	41	10
教职工人数	Teachers, Staff and Workers	113	107	88	107
# 专任教师数	Full-time Teachers	28	27	25	20

17-17 专业技术人员
SPECIAL TECHNICAL PERSONNEL

单位：人 (person)

项目 Item	全市 Total 2004	2005	2006	平均每万人口有科技人员 Scientific and Technological Personnel per 10 000 Persons (2006)	平均每万名城镇单位从业人员有科技人员 Scientific and Technological Personnel per 10 000 Persons Employed In Urban Units (2006)
合计 Total	**439578**	**424845**	**421065**	**392**	**2159**
自然科学专业技术人员 Natural Science	**212049**	**206222**	**207958**	**193**	**1066**
#工程技术人员 Engineering	114331	107745	109984	102	564
农业技术人员 Agriculture	2973	2951	3073	3	16
科学研究人员 Scientific Research	3693	3887	4042	4	21
卫生技术人员 Health Care	59920	59604	58338	54	299
教学人员 Teaching	31132	32035	32521	30	167
社会科学专业技术人员 Social Science	**227529**	**218623**	**213107**	**198**	**1093**
#科学研究人员 Scientific Research	878	1002	906	1	5
教学人员 Teaching	99838	99029	96615	90	495
经济人员 Economics	46409	43682	41117	38	211
财会人员 Accountant	37418	34913	35179	33	180
统计人员 Statistician	4126	3787	3307	3	17
翻译人员 Translator	675	606	631	1	3
图书、档案、资料人员 Librarian and Archivist	5605	5461	5280	5	27
编辑、记者、播音员 Editor, Reporter and Broadcasting	2800	2656	2664	3	14
体育教练人员 Coach	529	546	619	1	3
工艺美术人员 Arts and Craft	330	295	253		1
文艺人员 Literature and Art	2205	2184	2102	2	11

注：专业技术人员统计范围为公有制企事业单位。
Note: The coverage of special technical personnel refer to public-owned units.

17-18 专业技术人员构成（2006年）
COMPOSITION OF SPECIAL TECHNICAL PERSONNEL, 2006

单位：人 (person)

项 目 Item	按性别分 By Sex	按受教育程度分 By Education Status		按职称分 By Title	
	#女专业技术人员数 Female	#受过高等专业教育人数 Having Higher Special Education Background	#受过中等专业教育人数 Having Special Secondary School Background	#高 级 职称人数 Senior Professional Certification	#中 级 职称人数 Medium Professional Certification
合 计 Total	**209084**	**304251**	**86247**	**60462**	**148490**
自然科学专业技术人员 Natural Science	**92457**	**152324**	**45860**	**34121**	**66071**
#工程技术人员 Engineering	31073	82230	21170	17236	32508
农业技术人员 Agriculture	998	1754	1098	432	859
科学研究人员 Scientific Research	1605	3965	60	1651	1297
卫生技术人员 Health Care	40342	35054	20749	5801	18259
教学人员 Teaching	18439	29321	2783	9001	13148
社会科学专业技术人员 Social Science	**116627**	**151927**	**40387**	**26341**	**82419**
#科学研究人员 Scientific Research	401	853	27	299	399
教学人员 Teaching	62008	78357	15684	15601	51380
经济人员 Economics	14951	23585	9007	1848	7770
财会人员 Accountant	22258	21175	9767	909	6585
统计人员 Statistician	2360	1782	843	188	814
翻译人员 Translator	348	620	10	186	213
图书、档案、资料人员 Librarian and Archivist	3777	4090	678	809	2285
编辑、记者、播音员 Editor, Reporter and Broadcasting	1217	2495	77	934	873
体育教练人员 Coach	172	548	46	181	172
工艺美术人员 Arts and Craft	71	161	64	47	92
文艺人员 Literature and Art	781	752	975	731	885

17-19 自然科学专业技术人员构成(2006年)(按国民经济行业分)
COMPOSITION OF SPECIAL TECHNICAL PERSONNEL OF NATURAL SCIENCE, 2006
(Grouped by Sector)

单位：人 (person)

行业 Sector	合计 Total	#工程技术人员 Engineering	#卫生技术人员 Health Care	#教学人员 Teaching
总计 Total	**207958**	**109984**	**58338**	**32521**
农、林、牧、渔业 Farming, Forestry, Animal Husbandry and Fishery	3147	990	44	7
采矿业 Minerals Mining	6951	6859	31	27
制造业 Manufacturing	31160	29450	1560	111
电力、燃气及水的生产和供应业 Production & Supply of Power, Gas and Water	5072	4999	70	3
建筑业 Construction	15954	15569	349	33
交通运输、仓储及邮政业 Transportation, Storage and Post Services	8015	7769	235	11
信息传输、计算机服务和软件业 Information Transmitting, Computer Services & Software	3046	3037	6	2
批发和零售业 Wholesale and Retail Trade	2487	1300	1175	2
住宿和餐饮业 Accommodation and Catering Services	82	70	12	
金融业 Finance Intermediation	1294	1270	6	
房地产业 Real Estate	2620	2565	40	3
租赁和商务服务业 Leasing and Business Services	1613	1533	17	5
科学研究、技术服务和地质勘察业 Scientific Research, Technical Services and Geological Prospecting	23802	20865	423	30
水利、环境和公共设施管理业 Management for Water Conservancy, Environment and Public Facilities	5926	5766	66	5
居民服务和其他服务业 Resident Services and Other Social Services	421	401	7	1
教育 Education	40824	5771	1011	32104
卫生、社会保障和社会福利业 Health Care, Social Security and Social Welfare	54757	1066	53244	162
文化、体育和娱乐业 Culture, Sports and Recreational Services	732	673	41	15
公共管理和社会组织 Public Management and Social Organizations	55	31	1	

17-20 社会科学专业技术人员构成(2006年)(按国民经济行业分)
COMPOSITION OF SPECIAL TECHNICAL PERSONNEL OF SOCIAL SCIENCE, 2006
(Grouped by Sector)

单位：人 (person)

行业 Sector	合计 Total	#教学人员 Teaching	#经济人员 Economics	#财会人员 Accountant	#图书、档案、资料人员 Librarian and Archivist
总计 Total	**213107**	**96615**	**41117**	**35179**	**5280**
农、林、牧、渔业 Farming, Forestry, Animal Husbandry and Fishery	1067	100	240	434	9
采矿业 Minerals Mining	4605	610	1357	995	164
制造业 Manufacturing	21863	1173	7844	5523	370
电力、燃气及水的生产和供应业 Production & Supply of Power, Gas and Water	3147	32	962	926	70
建筑业 Construction	6396	155	1840	2481	84
交通运输、仓储及邮政业 Transportation, Storage and Post Services	8049	53	3956	1813	78
信息传输、计算机服务和软件业 Information Transmitting, Computer Services & Software	894	2	351	228	20
批发和零售业 Wholesale and Retail Trade	8337	27	4336	2361	73
住宿和餐饮业 Accommodation and Catering Services	385	2	88	175	4
金融业 Finance Intermediation	27010	19	15906	9817	60
房地产业 Real Estate	2765	13	1077	926	49
租赁和商务服务业 Leasing and Business Services	2930	94	998	833	50
科学研究、技术服务和地质勘察业 Scientific Research, Technical Services and Geological Prospecting	4228	120	665	1355	363
水利、环境和公共设施管理业 Management for Water Conservancy, Environment and Public Facilities	2329	6	330	935	61
居民服务和其他服务业 Resident Services and Other Social Services	692	105	136	244	5
教育 Education	104853	93809	331	2738	1643
卫生、社会保障和社会福利业 Health Care, Social Security and Social Welfare	5761	262	562	2783	289
文化、体育和娱乐业 Culture, Sports and Recreational Services	7707	33	106	593	1888
公共管理和社会组织 Public Management and Social Organizations	89		32	19	

17-21 独立科学研究和技术开发机构情况
BASIC STATISTICS OF INDEPENDENT INSTITUTIONS OF SCIENTIFIC RESEARCH AND TECHNOLOGICAL DEVELOPMENT

指　标 Indicator	自然科学研究与技术开发机构 Institutions of Natural Scientific Research and Technical Development		社会、人文科研与开发机构 Institutions of Social Science and Humanities of Research and Development		科学技术情报和文献机构 Institutions of Scientific and Technological Information and Documents	
	2005	2006	2005	2006	2005	2006
机构数(个) Number of Institutions (unit)	128	127	3	3	11	11
科技活动人员(人) Number of Persons Engaged in Scientific and Technological Activities (person)	10309	10546	299	306	612	609
高级职称 Senior Professional Certification	3421	3428	140	144	220	206
中级职称 Medium Professional Certification	3038	3048	87	93	221	216
初级职称 Junior Professional Certification	2504	2579	51	60	125	142
其　他 Others	1346	1491	21	9	46	45
经费支出总额(万元) Total Expenditures of Operating Expense (10 000 yuan)	150918	171783	2301	2793	8280	9944

17-22 独立自然科学研究机构课题开展和投入(按课题类型分)
PROJECTS AND INPUT OF INDEPENDENT INSTITUTIONS OF NATURAL SCIENCE RESEARCH (Grouped by Type of Projects)

项　目 Item	课题数(项) Number of Projects (item)		投入人力(人年) Labor Force Input (person-year)		投入经费(万元) Funds Input (10 000 yuan)	
	2005	2006	2005	2006	2005	2006
合　计 Total	1552	1637	4796	5145	63290	66708
基础研究 Basic Research	49	59	135	135	946	1354
应用研究 Application Research	152	195	467	617	3884	5770
试验发展 Experiment Development	545	528	2147	2287	32449	27725
R&D成果应用 R&D Achievements Used	390	415	1040	1059	18292	22221
科技服务 Services of Science and Technology	386	421	913	1000	6536	9227
生产性活动 Activities of Production	30	19	94	47	1183	411

17-23 专利申请受理量和授权量
PATENT APPLICATIONS EXAMINED AND GRANTED

单位：项 (item)

项　目	Item	申请受理量 Patent Applications Examined			申请授权量 Patent Applications Granted		
		2004	2005	2006	2004	2005	2006
合　计	**Total**	**8406**	**11657**	**13299**	**2578**	**3045**	**4159**
按种类分	**Grouped by Type**						
发　明	Inventions	4013	4470	4981	432	763	967
实用新型	Utility Models	3142	4690	4184	1587	1543	2164
外观设计	Designs	1251	2497	4134	559	739	1028
按对象分	**Grouped by Applicator**						
职务发明	**Service Inventions**	**4703**	**6956**	**8915**	**1213**	**1675**	**2873**
# 工矿企业	Industrial and Mineral Enterprises	3812	5600	7039	810	1240	2237
大专院校	Universities and Colleges	674	1008	1140	267	317	460
科研单位	Scientific Research Institutions	183	303	362	105	103	142
机关团体	Government Agencies and Organizations	34	45	374	31	15	34
非职务发明	**Non-service Inventions**	**3703**	**4701**	**4384**	**1365**	**1370**	**1286**

17-24 科学技术成果（2003-2006年）
ACHIEVEMENTS IN SCIENCE AND TECHNOLOGY, 2003-2006

单位：项 (item)

项　目	Item	2003	2004	2005	2006
市级科学技术成果登记数	**Number of City Level Major Achievements in Science and Technology**	**1203**	**1408**	**1508**	**1559**
国际领先	Leading Level in the World	59	75	75	69
国际先进	Advanced World Standard	311	282	321	397
国内领先	Leading Level in China	559	697	732	719
国内先进	Advanced National Standard	236	306	321	328
其　他	Others	38	48	59	46
获天津市科学技术奖	**Number of Tianjin Scientific and Technological Prizes Awarded**	**218**	**215**	**210**	**205**
# 自然科学奖	Awards for Natural Science	17	15	14	14
技术发明奖	Invention Prizes Awarded	5	10	17	12
科技进步奖	Scientific and Technological Progress Prize	195	190	179	179
获国家科学技术奖	**Number of National Scientific and Technological Prizes Awarded**	**14**	**9**	**14**	**12**
# 自然科学奖	Awards for Natural Science	3	1	2	1
技术发明奖	Invention Prizes Awarded		2	1	
科技进步奖	Scientific and Technological Progress Prize	11	6	11	11

17-25 天津市获国家科学技术奖科技成果一览(2006年)
LIST OF NATIONAL SCIENTIFIC AND TECHNOLOGICAL PRIZES AWARDED IN TIANJIN, 2006

获奖项目和等级 Project and Grade Awarded	完成单位和个人 Name of Unit and Individual
自然科学二等奖(1项) **Second Class of National Awards for Natural Science (one item)**	
神经元N受体及其失敏态的药理毒理和病理生理学特征的系列研究 Researches on Characteristics of Netron N Receptors and Its Desensitization on Pharmacology & Toxicology and Pathology & Physiology	汪海、吴杰、刘传缵、陈汝筑、崔文玉 Wang Hai, Wu Jie, Liu Chuanhui, Chen Ruzhu, Cui Wenyu
科技进步二等奖(11项) **Second Class of National Scientific and Technological Progress Award (eleven items)**	
1. 高浓缩倍率工业冷却水处理及智能化在线(远程)监控技术 Highly Concentrated Industrial Cooling Water Treatment and The Intelligentized Online (long-range) Monitoring Technology	郑书忠、严泽生、张世忠、周红慧、程峰 郭亚新、梅春晓、王鼎、李春国、李晨光 天津化工研究设计院、天津钢管集团有限公司 中国石油化工股份有限公司天津分公司 Zhen Shuzhong, Yan Zesheng, Zhang Shizhong, Zhou Honghui, Cheng Feng, Guo Yaxin, Mei Chunxiao, Wang Ding, Li Chunguo, Li Chenguang Tianjin Research &Design Institute of Chemical Industry Tianjin Steel Pipe Group Co., Ltd. Tianjin Petrochemical Co., Sinopec Group
2. 恶性肿瘤流行趋势分析及预防的研究 Researches on The Prevention of Sarcomata and The Analysis of Its Epidemic Trend	郝希山、陈可欣、钱碧云、宋丰举、李海欣 何敏、董淑芬、孙保存、只向成、王培忠 天津医科大学附属肿瘤医院、天津市肿瘤研究所 Hao Xishan, Chen Kexin, Qian Biyun, Song Fengjiu, Li Haixin He Min, Dong Shufeng, Sun Baocun, Zhi Xiangcheng, Wang Peizhong Tianjin Medical University Cancer Institute and Hospital Tianjin Cancer Research Institute
3. 原油管道泄漏检测与定位技术 Monitoring and Orientation Technologies of The Crude Oil Pipelines Leakage	靳世久、钱建华、杨祖佩、李健、卜文平 崔涛、王立坤、夏于飞、谭东杰、曾周末 天津大学、…… Jin Shijiu, Qian Jianhua, Yang Zupei, Li Jian, Bu Wenping Cui Tao, Wang Likun, Xia Yufei, Tan Dongjie, Zeng Zhoumo Tianjin University
4. 渤海海域复杂油气藏勘探 Exploration of Complex Oil and Gas Accumulation In The Bo Sea Areas	邓运华、茹克、夏庆龙、项华、薛永安 朱伟林、刘春成、米立军、周心怀、田立新 中海石油(中国)有限公司天津分公司 Deng Yunhua, Ru Ke, Xia Qinglong, Xiang Hua, Xue Yongan Zhu Weilin, Liu Chuncheng, Mi Lijun, Zhou Xinhuai, Tian Lixin China National Offshore Oil Corporation (China) Ltd. Tianjin Filiale
5. 苯酚烷基化清洁催化技术及工业应用 The Phenol Alkylation Clean-Catalyzed Technology and Its Application in Industry	陈群、何明阳、秦金来、朱洪涛、程立明 白忻平、郭驯宙、尹芳华、郭一、钱锡平 天津双孚精细化工有限公司 Chen Qun, He Mingyang, Qin Jinlai, Zhu Hongtao, Cheng Liming Bai Xinping, Guo Xunzhou, Yin Fanghua, Guo Yi, Qian Xiping Tianjin Shuangfu Speciality Chemicals Ltd.
6. 2000国家大地控制网 National 2000 Geodetic Control Network	陈俊勇、杨元喜、王敏、张燕平、唐颖哲 李辉、程鹏飞、孙凤华、张鹏、郭春喜 中国地震局第一监测中心 Chen Jiuyong, Yang Yuanxi, Wang Mi, Zhang Yanping, Tang Yinzhe Li Hui, Cheng Pengfei, Sun Fenghua, Zhang Peng, Guo Chunxi China Earthquake Administraton No.1 Center
7. 气体钻井技术研究与应用 The Research and Application of Air Drilling Technology	陈星元、吴仕荣、陈光、伍贤柱、孟英峰 陈刚、屈建省、魏武、刘德胜、郑有成 中国石油集团工程技术研究院 Chen Xingyuan, Wu Shirong, Chen Guang, Wu Xianzhu, Meng Yingfeng, Chen Gang, Qu Jianxing, Wei Wu, Liu Desheng, Zheng Youcheng PetroChina Group Engineering Technology Research Institute
8. 年产20万吨聚酯四釜流程工艺和装备研发暨国产化聚酯装置系列化 Development of The Flow Technics and Equipments producing Polyester 200 Thousand Tons per Year-Nationalized Polyesterequipment Systemization	罗文德、周华堂、刘金宝、张莼、洪学立 梅兆林、张慧书、万网胜、顾爱军、黄家琪 天津大学 Luo Wende, Zhou Huatang, Liu Jinbao, Zhang Chun, Hong Xueli Mei Zhaolin, Zhang Huishu, Wan Wangsheng, Gui Aijun, Huang Jiaqi Tianjin University
9. 火电厂厂级运行性能在线诊断及优化控制系统 Online Diagnoses and Optimized Controlling System of Function Performance in The Plant Level of Fossil Fuel Power Plant	刘吉臻、蒋敏华、何新、牛玉广、杨东 曾德良、张永年、张春发、沈治、吴克河 天津大唐国际盘山发电有限责任公司 Liu Jizhen, Jiang Mihua, He Xin , Niu Yuguang, Yang Dong Zeng Deliang, Zhang Yongnian, Zhang Chunfa, Shen Zhi, Wu Kehe Tianjin Datang International Panshan Power Generation Ltd.
另有两项为专用项目。 Besides, There Are Two Special Projects.	

17-26 高等学校科研课题开展与投入(2006年)(理、工、农、医类)
PROJECTS OF DEVELOPMENT AND INPUT OF SCIENTIFIC RESEARCH IN UNIVERSITIES AND COLLEGES, 2006 (Science, Engineering, Agriculture and Medicine)

项　　目	Item	课题数(项) Number of Projects (item)	投入人力(人年) Labor Force Input (person/year)	#科学家和工程师 Scientists and Engineers	投入经费(万元) Funds Input (10 000 yuan)
总　计	**Total**	**5282**	**5321**	**4465**	**83600**
按课题活动类型分	**Grouped by Type of Projects**				
基础研究	Basic Research	1622	1601	1365	17767
应用研究	Application Research	2709	2623	2189	35363
试验发展	Experiment Development	559	654	577	18500
R&D成果应用	R&D Achievement Used	131	171	132	3118
科技服务	Service of Science and Technology	261	272	202	8852
按(课题)项目类别分	**Grouped by Project**				
国家"973"项目	State "973" Project	40	68	60	2382
国家科技攻关项目	State S&T Strategical Project	14	27	22	422
国家"863"项目	State "863" Project	26	47	40	1438
国家自然科学基金项目	State Natural Scientific Fund Project	840	852	753	8964
主管部门科技项目	S&T Project from Administrative Department	611	635	521	5037
国家部委其他科技项目	S&T Project from Ministry	233	279	238	7668
省、市、自治区科技项目	S&T Project from Province, Municipality, Autonomous Region	1037	1126	947	13776
企事业单位委托科技项目	S&T Project from Enterprise, Institution	1563	1597	1307	41118
国际合作项目	International Cooperate Project	38	33	27	956
自选项目	Self-choosing Project	857	635	534	1798
其他项目	Other Project	23	22	16	41

17-27 高等学校科技专著和论文(2003-2006年)(理、工、农、医类)
S&T WORKS AND PAPERS IN UNIVERSITIES AND COLLEGES, 2003-2006 (Science, Engineering, Agriculture and Medicine)

项　目	Item	单 位 Unit	2003	2004	2005	2006
科技专著	**Scientific and Technological Work**	**部 copy**	**135**	**60**	**88**	**85**
		万字10 000 words	**4056**	**1524**	**1635**	**1800**
#自然科学	Natural Science	部 copy	26	7	10	6
		万字10 000 words	910	200	272	172
工程科学	Engineering	部 copy	65	23	23	27
		万字10 000 words	1957	630	556	538
医学科学	Medicine	部 copy	43	30	45	45
		万字10 000 words	1186	695	709	1007
农业科学	Agriculture	部 copy	1		10	7
		万字10 000 words	3		98	83
科学论文	**Scientific Papers**	**篇 piece**	**9540**	**11460**	**13077**	**14361**
#国外发表	Published Abroad	篇 piece	1312	1968	2293	3299

17-28 新技术产业园区主要经济指标
MAIN INDICATORS OF HI-TECH INDUSTRIAL PARK

单位：亿元 (100 million yuan)

指标	Item	2005	2006	2006比2005年增长(%) Increase Rate in 2006 over 2005 (%)
新技术产业园区	Hi-tech Industrial Park			
地区生产总值	Gross Domestic Product	188.62	257.46	36.5
技工贸总收入	Total Income from Technology, Industry and Trade	751.29	1187	42.5
#华苑产业区	Huayuan Industry Development Area			
地区生产总值	Gross Domestic Product	57.7	83.5	40.1
#第二产业	Secondary Industry	40.5	61.5	45.9
#工　业	Industry	39	59.4	46.3
第三产业	Tertiary Industry	17.2	22	26.5
技工贸总产值	Gross Output Value of Technology, Industry and Trade	211.4	296.2	40.1
技工贸总收入	Total Income from Technology, Industry and Trade	284.5	399.1	40.3
财政收入	Government Revenue	14.7	18.4	25.2
固定资产投资额	Investment in Fixed Assets	23.2	31.5	36.0
软件著作权申请量(件)	Software Copyright Applications (item)	179	237	32.4
软件著作权登记量(件)	Software Copyright Registrations (item)	125	186	48.8
认定高新技术企业数(个)	Certificated High & New Technology Enterprises (unit)		591	
房屋施工面积(万平方米)	Floor Space of Buildings Under Construction (10 000 sq. m)		63.3	
房屋竣工面积(万平方米)	Floor Space of Buildings Completed (10 000 sq. m)		71.3	

17-29 技术监督机构人员、行政执法情况
PERSONNEL, EXECUTING LAW OF ADMINISTRATION OF PRODUCT QUALITY & TECHNIQUE SUPERVISION AGENCIES

项目	Item	2005 全市 Total	#市级单位 City Level	2006 全市 Total	#市级单位 City Level
机构人员情况	Agencies and Personnel				
机构数(个)	Number of Agencies (unit)	79	12	78	11
职工人数(人)	Number of Employees (person)	2007	797	1980	772
行政机构人员	Administrative Agencies	640	105	632	103
事业机构人员	Institutions	1367	692	1348	669
#执法人员	Staff of Executing Law	853	223	1015	269
行政执法情况	Administrative Cases				
受理案件数(件)	Number of Accepted and Heared Cases (case)	5811	305	6410	310
万元以上案件	Cases over 10 000 yuan	378	111	385	85
12365接待投诉、咨询	"12365" Accepting Lawsuit & Consulting	27570		29113	
罚没金额(万元)	Total Value of Punishment (10 000 yuan)	2868		2996	832

资料来源：天津市质量技术监督局，17-31-33表同。
Sources: Tianjin Municipal Quality & Technology Supervision Bureau, same as table 17-31-33.

17-30 计量仪器检定情况(2003-2006年)
STATISTICS OF MEASURING IMPLEMENTS TEST, 2003-2006

单位：台、件 (set, piece)

类　别	Sort	2003	2004	2005	2006
总　计	**Total**	**1325488**	**1481652**	**1027813**	**644101**
长　度	Length	30525	59322	40536	53648
温　度	Temperature	41102	39325	63081	45378
力　学	Mechanics	447634	767458	347050	404901
#衡　器	Weighing Apparatus	87179	77320	69384	109229
电　学	Electrology	105670	590594	541682	86597
光　学	Optics	254	1596	426	2471
声　学	Acoustics	385	455	576	838
化　学	Chemistry	3018	2351	2126	3567
电离辐射	Ionization Radiation	460	349	390	461
无线电	Radio	598194	491	455	989
时间频率	Time Frequency	1341	1070	1265	1973
其　他	Others	96905	18641	30226	43278

17-31 产品质量专项监督检验情况
RESULTS OF SPECIALIZED CHECK ON THE QUALITY OF PRODUCTS UNDER STATE SUPERVISION

项　目	Item	检查商业企业数(个) Number of Commercial Enterprises Checked (unit)	检查商品批次(批次) Batch-times Checked (batch/time)	合格批次(批次) Batch-times with Qualified Quality (batch/times)	批次合格率(%) Rate of Batch-times Qualified (%)
2005年					
合　计	**Total**	**207**	**352**	**254**	**72.16**
#农用产品	Agricultural Products	17	30	20	66.67
加工食品和饮料	Food and Beverages	78	115	57	49.57
纺织、鞋类产品	Textile and Shoes	16	30	30	100.00
化工产品	Chemical Products	40	75	65	86.67
建材产品	Building Raw Materials	34	60	47	78.33
机电产品	Mechanical and Electrical Products	22	42	35	83.33
2006年					
合　计	**Total**	**628**	**1198**	**878**	**73.29**
#农用产品	Agricultural Products	36	42	33	78.57
加工食品和饮料	Food and Beverages	147	230	161	70.00
家用电器	Household Electrical Appliances	20	20	7	35.00
轻工产品	Light Industry Products	100	321	207	64.49
纺织、鞋类产品	Textile and Shoes	10	20	8	40.00
化工产品	Chemical Products	74	115	86	74.78
建材产品	Building Raw Materials	25	36	29	80.56
能源产品	Energy Products	216	414	347	83.82

17-32 定期监督检验情况（2006年）
RESULTS OF FIXED-PERIOD CHECK ON THE QUALITY OF PRODUCTS UNDER STATE SUPERVISION, 2006

项　目	Item	检查企业（个）Number of Enterprises Checked (unit)	检查批次（批次）Checked-times (batch/times)	批次合格率（%）Rate of Batch-times Qualified (%)
合　计	**Total**	**4220**	**5269**	**89.37**
农副食品加工业	Processing of Food from Agricultural Products	100	119	78.15
食品制造业	Manufacture of Foods	1129	1367	85.30
饮料制造业	Manufacture of Beverages	232	256	89.06
纺织服装鞋帽制造业	Manufacture of Textile Wearing Apparel, Footware, and Caps	87	119	93.28
皮革毛皮羽毛(绒)及其制品业	Manufacture of Leather, Fur, Feather and Related Products	5	5	80.00
家具制造业	Manufacture of Furniture	115	116	87.07
造纸及纸制品业	Manufacture of Paper and Paper Products	99	114	89.47
印刷业和记录媒介的复制	Printing, Reproduction of Recording Media	42	43	76.74
文教体育用品制造业	Manufacture of Articles For Culture, Education and Sport Activity	8	14	100.00
石油加工炼焦及核燃料加工业	Processing of Petroleum, Coking, Processing of Nuclear Fuel	35	72	95.83
化学原料及化学制品制造业	Manufacture of Raw Chemical Materials and Chemical Products	383	586	93.69
橡胶制品业	Manufacture of Rubber	106	130	100.00
塑料制品业	Manufacture of Plastics	61	77	92.21
非金属矿物制品业	Manufacture of Non-metallic Mineral Products	249	351	97.15
黑色金属冶炼及压延加工业	Smelting and Pressing of Ferrous Metals	32	29	100.00
有色金属冶炼及压延加工业	Smelting and Pressing of Non-Ferrous Metals	3	3	66.67
金属制品业	Manufacture of Metal Products	258	305	85.57
通用设备制造业	Manufacture of General Purpose Machinery	168	227	96.92
专用设备制造业	Manufacture of Special Purpose Machinery	14	21	71.43
交通运输设备制造业	Manufacture of Transport Equipment	548	648	94.29
电气机械及器材制造业	Manufacture of Electrical Machinery and Equipment	203	260	82.69
通信设备计算机及其他电子设备制造业	Manufacture of Communication Equipment, Computers and Other Electronic Equipment	18	19	100.00
工艺品及其他制造业	Manufacture of Artwork and Other Manufacturing	325	388	83.76

17-33 天津市科学技术协会和所属学会科技活动（2006年）
SCIENTIFIC AND TECHNOLOGICAL ACTIVITIES OF TIANJIN SCIENCE AND TECHNOLOGY ASSOCIATIONS AND AFFILIATED INSTITUTION SOCIETIES, 2006

项　目	Item	合 计 Total	市及区、县科协 Science Association of City, District and County	市级学会 Institution of City Level
机构与人员	Institutions and Personnel			
机　构(个)	Institutions (unit)	473	19	454
人　员(人)	Personnel (person)	131932	196	131736
学术交流情况	Academic Activities of Exchange			
学术会议(次)	Academic Meetings (time)	468	3	465
国　内	Domestic	458	3	455
国　际	International	10		10
参加人数(人次)	Number of Participants (person-time)	57998	700	57298
国　内	Domestic	56236	700	55536
国　际	International	1762		1762
交流论文(篇)	Number of Papers Presented (piece)	12326	237	12089
国　内	Domestic	11475	237	11238
国　际	International	851		851
科技交流(个)	Exchange of Science and Technological (unit)	69	12	57
接　待	Received	37	7	30
外　派	Sent Abroad	32	5	27
交流人数(人次)	Number of Exchange (person-time)	392	61	331
接　待	Received	163	25	138
外　派	Sent Abroad	229	36	193
科学普及	Activities for Popular Science			
科普讲座(次)	Lectures of Popular Science (time)	2999	2287	712
参加人数(万人次)	Number of Participants (10 000 person-times)	91	72	19
科普展览(次)	Exhibitions of Popular Science (time)	1232	999	233
参加人数(万人次)	Number of Participants (10 000 person-times)	109	71	38
科技培训	Science and Technological Training			
培训班数(个(期))	Number of Training Classes (unit (period))	616	342	274
培训人数(人次)	Number of Persons in Training Classes (person-time)	62362	33595	28767
科技咨询服务(项)	Service of Consultative Activities (item)			
无偿咨询项目	Gratis Consultative Projects	957	201	756
完成技术合同数	Number of Consultative Contracts Completed	1294	639	655
青少年科技活动	Scientific and Technological Activities of Teenagers			
科技夏(冬)令营(次)	Scientific and Technological Summer (Winter) Camp (time)	131	119	12
参加人数(人次)	Number of Participants (person-time)	10148	9316	832
青少年科技竞赛(次)	Number of Teenagers Participating in Science and Technology Competition (time)	305	293	12
科技出版物	Science and Technology Publication			
出版科技期刊(种)	Science and Technology Magazine (kind)	39	1	38
年发行总数(万册)	Number of Issue (10 000 volumes)	75		75
年发表学术论文(篇)	Number of Papers Presented (piece)	5137		5137

17-34 大中型工业企业科技活动基本情况（2006年）（按企业类型和经济类型分）
S&T ACTIVITIES IN LARGE AND MEDIUM-SIZED ENTERPRISES, 2006
(Grouped By Type And Ownership)

项 目 Item	合 计 Total	按企业类型分 Grouped by Type of Enterprises	
		大 型 Large	中 型 Medium
1. 有科技活动企业数(个)			
Number of Enterprises with Scientific and Technological Activities (unit)	218	33	185
2. 从事科技活动人员(人)			
Employees Engaged in Scientific and Technological Activities (person)	35458	17483	17975
# 科学家和工程师			
Scientists and Engineers	23035	11695	11340
研究与试验发展人员			
Personnel of R&D	15604	7131	8473
3. 科技活动经费筹集(万元)			
Funding for Scientific and Technological Activities (10 000 yuan)	1052432	520454	531978
4. 科技活动经费支出(万元)			
Expenditures of Scientific and Technological Activities (10 000 yuan)	1259039	570137	688902
# 研究与试验发展经费支出			
Expenditures of R&D	491091	318741	172350
新产品开发经费支出			
Expenditures of New Product Development	528234	233841	294393
5. 科技活动项目数(项)			
Number of Scientific and Technological Activities (item)	1765	899	866
# 研究与试验发展项目数			
Number of R&D	1149	516	633
6. 科技机构数(个)			
Number of Scientific and Technological Institutions (unit)	205	64	141
科技机构人员数(人)			
Persons in Scientific and Technological Institutions (person)	15979	8979	7000
科技机构经费支出(万元)			
Expenditures of Scientific and Technological Institutions (10 000 yuan)	434959	319189	115770
# 仪器设备经费支出			
Expenditures of Instruments and Equipment	461241	291625	169616
7. 新产品产值(万元)			
Output Value of New Products (10 000 yuan)	19757200	13003012	6754188
新产品销售收入(万元)			
Sales Revenue of New Products (10 000 yuan)	18865124	12690548	6174576
# 出口销售收入(万元)			
Sales Revenue of Exports (10 000 yuan)	4848496	1692344	3156152
8. 专利申请数(件)			
Number of Patent Applications (piece)	1920	1036	884
拥有发明专利数(件)			
Number of Patent Granted (piece)	611	424	187
9. 技术改造经费支出(万元)			
Expenditures of Technical Innovation (10 000 yuan)	1083551	982797	100754
10. 技术引进经费支出(万元)			
Expenditures of Technical Introduction (10 000 yuan)	351848	56358	295490

17-34 续表 Continued

项　目　Item	按经济类型分 Grouped by Ownership			
	国有经济 State-owned	集体经济 Collective-owned	"三资"经济 Hong Kong, Macao, Taiwan and Foreign Funded	其他经济 Others
1. 有科技活动企业数(个) Number of Enterprises with Scientific and Technological Activities (unit)	42	3	72	101
2. 从事科技活动人员(人) Employees Engaged in Scientific and Technological Activities (person)	10760	766	8840	15092
# 科学家和工程师 Scientists and Engineers	6586	249	6532	9668
研究与发展人员 Personnel of R&D	3328	113	4825	7338
3. 企业科技活动经费筹集(万元) Funding for Scientific and Technological Activities (10 000 yuan)	223410	4040	418358	406624
4. 企业科技活动经费支出(万元) Expenditures of Scientific and Technological Activities (10 000 yuan)	245153	5435	572681	435770
# 研究与试验发展经费支出 Expenditures of R&D	110281	721	194646	185443
新产品开发经费支出 Expenditures of New Product Development	101852	2003	267926	156453
5. 企业科技活动项目数(项) Number of Scientific and Technological Activities (item)	630	6	333	796
# 研究与试验发展项目数 Number of R&D	277	3	290	579
6. 科技机构数(个) Scientific and Technological Institutions (unit)	58	1	46	100
科技机构人员数(人) Persons in Scientific and Technological Institutions (person)	3143	265	3814	8757
科技机构经费支出(万元) Expenditures of Scientific and Technological Institutions (10 000 yuan)	137845	2150	146197	148767
# 仪器设备经费支出 Expenditures of Instruments and Equipment	114286	2365	154779	189811
7. 新产品产值(万元) Output Value of New Products (10 000 yuan)	1538522	14854	16115104	2088720
新产品销售收入(万元) Sales Revenue of New Products (10 000 yuan)	1515454	13747	15089734	2246189
# 出口销售收入 Sales Revenue of Exports (10 000 yuan)	676798	80	3942227	229391
8. 专利申请数(件) Number of Patent Applications (piece)	292	18	764	846
拥有发明专利数(件) Number of Patent Granted (piece)	63	2	360	186
9. 技术改造经费支出(万元) Expenditures of Technical Innovation (10 000 yuan)	279335	1264	239477	563475
10. 技术引进经费支出(万元) Expenditures of Technical Introduction(10 000 yuan)	9796		293677	48375

17-35 大中型工业企业科技活动基本情况(2006年)(按国民经济行业分)
S&T ACTIVITIES IN LARGE AND MEDIUM-SIZED ENTERPRISES, 2006 (Grouped By Sector)

项目	Item	有科技活动企业数(个) Number of Enterprises with Scientific Technological Activities (unit)	从事科技活动人员(人) Employees Engaged in Scientific and Technological Activities (person)	#科学家和工程师 Scientists and Engineers	#研究与试验发展人员 Personnel of R&D
总计	**Total**	**218**	**35458**	**23035**	**15604**
#石油和天然气开采业	Extraction of Petroleum and Natural Gas	5	2694	1976	1092
非金属矿采选业	Mining and Processing of Nonmetal Ores	3	1198	431	725
农副食品加工业	Processing of Food from Agricultural Products	1	50	38	
食品制造业	Manufacture of Foods	4	323	253	134
饮料制造业	Manufacture of Beverages	5	245	196	156
烟草制品业	Manufacture of Tobacco				
纺织业	Manufacture of Textile	6	648	295	411
纺织服装、鞋、帽制造业	Manufacture of Textile Wearing Apparel, Footware and Caps	3	196	161	16
皮革、毛皮、羽毛(绒)及其制品业	Manufacture of Leather, Fur, Feather and Related Products	1	32		9
木材加工及木、竹、藤、棕、草制品业	Processing of Timber, Manufacture of Wood, Bamboo, Rattan, Palm, and Straw Products				
家具制造业	Manufacture of Furniture	1	16	16	7
造纸及纸制品业	Manufacture of Paper and Paper Products				
印刷业和记录媒介的复制	Printing, Reproduction of Recording Media	1	92	73	74
文教体育用品制造业	Manufacture of Articles For Culture, Education and Sport Activity	3	117	99	71
石油加工、炼焦及核燃料加工业	Processing of Petroleum, Coking, Processing of Nuclear Fuel	4	1281	939	817
化学原料及化学制品制造业	Manufacture of Raw Chemical Materials and Chemical Products	15	1716	1036	975
医药制造业	Manufacture of Medicines	18	2808	2022	1545
化学纤维制造业	Manufacture of Chemical Fibers				
橡胶制品业	Manufacture of Rubber	8	727	379	348
塑料制品业	Manufacture of Plastics	3	164	60	49
非金属矿物制品业	Manufacture of Non-metallic Mineral Products	4	244	129	77
黑色金属冶炼及压延加工业	Smelting and Pressing of Ferrous Metals	7	5253	3123	1014
有色金属冶炼及压延加工业	Smelting and Pressing of Non-Ferrous Metals				
金属制品业	Manufacture of Metal Products	9	418	182	97
通用设备制造业	Manufacture of General Purpose Machinery	23	3077	1892	1702
专用设备制造业	Manufacture of Special Purpose Machinery	14	1498	913	795
交通运输设备制造业	Manufacture of Transport Equipment	21	3004	1897	1098
电气机械及器材制造业	Manufacture of Electrical Machinery and Equipment	20	2707	1827	1783
通信设备、计算机及其他电子设备制造业	Manufacture of Communication Equipment, Computers and Other Electronic Equipment	30	5545	3977	2188
仪器仪表及文化、办公用机械制造业	Manufacture of Measuring Instruments and Machinery for Cultural Activity and Office Work	2	212	174	82
电力、热力的生产和供应业	Production and Supply of Electric Power and Heat Power	4	774	670	27
煤气生产和供应业	Production and Supply of Gas	1	28	24	28
水的生产和供应业	Production and Supply of Water	1	258	172	258

17-35 续表 1 Continued

项　目	Item	科技活动经费支出(万元) Expenditures of Scientific and Technological Activities (10 000 yuan)	#研究与试验发展经费支出 Expenditu-res of R&D	科技活动项目数(项) Number of Scientific and Activities (item)	新产品销售收入(万元) Sales Revenue of New Products (10 000 yuan)
总　计	**Total**	**1259039**	**491091**	**1765**	**18865124**
#石油和天然气开采业	Extraction of Petroleum and Natural Gas	90042	18629	285	75571
非金属矿采选业	Mining and Processing of Nonmetal Ores	5513	2280	32	18412
农副食品加工业	Processing of Food from Agricultural Products	600		1	205666
食品制造业	Manufacture of Foods	9861	8447	13	69021
饮料制造业	Manufacture of Beverages	11529	8321	19	57359
烟草制品业	Manufacture of Tobacco				
纺织业	Manufacture of Textile	5718	1322	22	43402
纺织服装、鞋、帽制造业	Manufacture of Textile Wearing Apparel, Footware and Caps	363	25	3	446
皮革、毛皮、羽毛(绒)及其制品业	Manufacture of Leather, Fur, Feather and Related Products	86	86		2893
造纸及纸制品业	Manufacture of Paper and Paper Products				
印刷业和记录媒介的复制	Printing, Reproduction of Recording Media	821	810	11	6374
文教体育用品制造业	Manufacture of Articles For Culture, Education and Sport Activity	661	491	1	26252
石油加工、炼焦及核燃料加工业	Processing of Petroleum, Coking, Processing of Nuclear Fuel	40072	9787	69	223382
化学原料及化学制品制造业	Manufacture of Raw Chemical Materials and Chemical Products	64488	29547	83	263392
医药制造业	Manufacture of Medicines	73901	44765	241	270606
化学纤维制造业	Manufacture of Chemical Fibers				
橡胶制品业	Manufacture of Rubber	10001	3458	55	112902
塑料制品业	Manufacture of Plastics	1187	761	6	18054
非金属矿物制品业	Manufacture of Non-metallic Mineral Products	8368	1074	7	57281
黑色金属冶炼及压延加工业	Smelting and Pressing of Ferrous Metals	227407	113739	269	1263336
有色金属冶炼及压延加工业	Smelting and Pressing of Non-Ferrous Metals				
金属制品业	Manufacture of Metal Products	14282	9201	10	163921
通用设备制造业	Manufacture of General Purpose Machinery	77855	39796	179	488628
专用设备制造业	Manufacture of Special Purpose Machinery	22925	12346	68	83718
交通运输设备制造业	Manufacture of Transport Equipment	187193	18059	99	4070975
电气机械及器材制造业	Manufacture of Electrical Machinery and Equipment	90088	78055	86	1441497
通信设备、计算机及其他电子设备制造业	Manufacture of Communication Equipment, Computers and Other Electronic Equipment	301289	87438	124	9484212
仪器仪表及文化、办公用机械制造业	Manufacture of Measuring Instruments and Machinery for Cultural Activity and Office Work	2666	760	3	412540
电力、热力的生产和供应业	Production and Supply of Electric Power and Heat Power	9834	275	55	
煤气生产和供应业	Production and Supply of Gas	77	77	3	
水的生产和供应业	Production and Supply of Water	1199	1026	16	

17-35 续表 2 Continued

项　目	Item	科技机构数(个) Number of Scientific and Technological Research Institutions (unit)	科技机构经费支出(万元) Expenditures of Scientific and Technological Research Institutions (10 000 yuan)	专利申请数(件) Number of Patent Applications (piece)	拥有发明专利数(件) Number of Invention Patent Owned (piece)
总　计	**Total**	**205**	**434959**	**1920**	**611**
#石油天然气开采业	Extraction of Petroleum and Natural Gas	26	29058	80	14
非金属矿采选业	Mining and Processing of Nonmetal Ores	2	1950	7	3
农副食品加工业	Processing of Food from Agricultural Products				
食品制造业	Manufacture of Foods	3	1703	8	12
饮料制造业	Manufacture of Beverages	3	7676	36	4
烟草制品业	Manufacture of Tobacco				
纺织业	Manufacture of Textile	6	1653	38	1
纺织服装、鞋、帽制造业	Manufacture of Textile Wearing Apparel, Footware and Caps				
皮革、毛皮、羽毛(绒)及其制品业	Manufacture of Leather, Fur, Feather and Related Products				
造纸及纸制品业	Manufacture of Paper and Paper Products				
印刷业和记录媒介的复制	Printing, Reproduction of Recording Media	6	735	6	2
文教体育用品制造业	Manufacture of Articles For Culture, Education and Sport Activity	2	31	25	
石油加工、炼焦及核燃料加工业	Processing of Petroleum, Coking, Processing of Nuclear Fuel	2	4505	4	12
化学原料及化学制品制造业	Manufacture of Raw Chemical Materials and Chemical Products	14	49670	156	16
医药制造业	Manufacture of Medicines	27	36240	336	90
化学纤维制造业	Manufacture of Chemical Fibers				
橡胶制品业	Manufacture of Rubber	5	3432	13	6
塑料制品业	Manufacture of Plastics	2	1031	2	
非金属矿物制品业	Manufacture of Non-metallic Mineral Products	2	862	6	
黑色金属冶炼及压延加工业	Smelting and Pressing of Ferrous Metals	5	111296	98	31
有色金属冶炼及压延加工业	Smelting and Pressing of Non-Ferrous Metals				
金属制品业	Manufacture of Metal Products	5	81	10	14
通用设备制造业	Manufacture of General Purpose Machinery	19	20046	128	12
专用设备制造业	Manufacture of Special Purpose Machinery	11	6194	43	17
交通运输设备制造业	Manufacture of Transport Equipment	15	16992	25	30
电气机械及器材制造业	Manufacture of Electrical Machinery and Equipment	16	72515	625	313
通信设备、计算机及其他电子设备制造业	Manufacture of Communication Equipment, Computers and Other Electronic Equipment	27	64561	195	25
仪器仪表及文化、办公用机械制造业	Manufacture of Measuring Instruments and Machinery for Cultural Activity and Office Work	2	743	69	1
电力、热力的生产和供应业	Production and Supply of Electric Power and Heat Power	1.	3864	6	5
煤气生产和供应业	Production and Supply of Gas				
水的生产和供应业	Production and Supply of Water	3	10	4	2

17-36 技术市场基本情况(2006年) BASIC STATISTICS ON TECHNICAL MARKET, 2006

项　目	Item	签订合同数(项) Number of Contracts Signed (item)	合同金额(万元) Value of Contracts Signed (10 000 yuan)	# 技术交易额 Technology Volume
合　计	Total	10181	588625	450179
按技术合同类别分	Grouped by the Type of Technical Contract			
技术开发合同	Technology Development Contracts	2759	299360	208987
技术转让合同	Technology Transfer Contracts	626	35373	31970
技术咨询合同	Technology Inquiry Contracts	1869	51763	31645
技术服务合同	Technology Services Contracts	4927	202129	177577
按合同卖方类别分	Grouped by the Type of Sellers			
机关法人	Agencies as Legal Persons	17	62070	51792
事业法人	Institutions as Legal Persons	3089	187284	119746
社团法人	Social Organizations as Legal Persons	395	4869	4436
企业法人	Enterprises as Legal Persons	6502	326633	266473
自然人	Persons	25	4569	4569
其他组织	Other Organizations	153	3200	3163
按合同买方类别分	Grouped by the Type of Buyers			
机关法人	Agencies as Legal Persons	972	34746	30680
事业法人	Institutions as Legal Persons	1247	92421	52760
社团法人	Social Organizations as Legal Persons	38	433	397
企业法人	Enterprises as Legal Persons	7696	432653	351504
自然人	Persons	34	1333	1075
其他组织	Other Organizations	194	27039	13763
按社会经济目标分	Grouped by the Social and Economic Activities			
农业、林业与渔业的发展	Development of Farming, Forestry & Fishery	148	9303	9133
促进工业的发展	Promoting the Development of Industry	3742	216058	192618
能源的生产和合理利用	Energy Production & Rational Use	878	36703	26791
基础设施的发展	Development of Basic facilities	1131	89894	65727
环境治理与保护	Environmental Inprovement & Protection	798	11847	10988
卫生(不包括污染)	Health (Excluded Pollutions)	364	24785	20109
社会发展和社会服务	Social Development & Social Service	1695	58485	49429
知识的发展	Development of Knowledge	83	6044	5436
其　他	Others	1342	135506	69948
按技术流向分类	Grouped by the Buyer's Region			
天　津	Tianjin	6335	299809	
外　地	Others	3846	288816	

主要统计指标解释

学校(机构) 是按国家规定的设置标准和审批程序批准设立的，招收适龄人口实施各级各类教育活动的教育机构。

普通高等学校 是按国家规定的设置标准和审批程序批准举办的，通过全国普通高等教育统一招生考试，招收高中毕业生为主要培养对象，实施高等学历教育的全日制大学、独立设置的学院和高等专科学校、高等职业学校和其他机构。大学、独立设置的学院主要实施本科及本科层次以上的教育。高等专科学校、高等职业学校实施专科层次教育。

成人高等学校 是按国家规定的设置标准和审批程序批准举办的，通过全国成人高等教育统一招生考试，招收高中毕业或同等学历的人员为主要培养对象，利用函授、业余、脱产的多种形式对其实施高等学历教育的学校。包括：职工高等学校、农民高等学校、管理干部学院、教育学院、独立函授学院、广播电视大学、其他机构。

中等职业学校 是按国家规定的设置标准和审批程序批准成立的实施中等职业教育的学校(机构)。调整后的中等职业学校是指将普通中等专业学校(中等技术学校、中等师范学校)、成人中等专业学校、职业高中学校等各种实施中等职业教育的办学类型，通过合并、共建、联办、划转等形式调整为统一的办学类型，即中等职业学校。

职业中学(职业高中、职业初中) 职业中学是指经县或县以上教育行政部门批准设立，招收小学或初中毕业生实施中等职业技术教育的教学机构。职业中学按学校性质类别可分为：独立设置的职业中学(包括：职业初中、职业高中、职业初高中合设学校)；附设有普通中学班的职业中学。

普通中等学校(普通高中、普通初中) 普通中等学校通常称普通中学，分为普通高级中学和普通初级中学两个阶段。普通初级中学是指独立设置的招收小学毕业的适龄人口进行初级中等基础教育的机构；普通高级中学是指独立设置的招收初中毕业的适龄人口进行高级中等基础教育的机构；完全中学是指普通初、高中合设的教育机构；一贯制学校是指在一所学校连续实施中小学教育的机构。其中包括实施九年义务教育的九年一贯制学校和实施高中教育的十二年一贯制学校。(说明：一贯制学校的办学条件如能划分为小学、初中、高中，则分开填报；如不能划分清楚，可按就高不就低的方法填入初中、高中报表中，不能重复填写。)

初等教育(普通小学) 普通小学是指由县或县以上教育行政部门批准，招收学龄儿童实施初等教育的教学机构。

学前教育 (幼儿园) 幼儿园是指招收三周岁以上(含三周岁)学龄前幼儿，对其进行保育和教育的单位，包括全市各幼儿教学点；幼儿园以游戏为基本活动形式，寓教于乐、寓教于动。

工读学校 指由教育和公安部门联合举办的，对有轻微违法行为的中学生进行挽救教育的教学机构。

特殊教育学校 指某地独立设置的招收盲聋哑和智残儿童，以及其他特殊需要的儿童、青少年进行普通或职业初、中等教育的教学机构。

毕业生数 指上学年，具有学籍的学生学完教学计划规定的全部课程，考试及格，取得毕业证书，实际毕业的学生数。

招生数 指通过国家统一招生考试，按照国家招生计划实际招收入学的新生数。(高等教育包括春秋两季招收的学生。)

在校生数 指本学年初，具有学籍的注册学生总数。

教职工数 指在学校(机构)工作并由学校(机构)支付劳动报酬的教职工，人员包括在编人员，即根据原人事管理制度，人事关系和档案均在学校的人员；聘任制人员，即人事制度改革后，高校(机构)招聘录用的长期、全时工作人员。聘任制人员的人事关系在学校但档案不在学校。教职工数包括校本部教职工、科

主要统计指标解释

研机构人员、校办企业职工、其他附设机构人员。

专任教师　指具有教师资格，专门从事教学工作的人员。

科技活动　指在自然科学、农业科学、医药科学、工程与技术科学、人文与社会科学领域（简称科学技术领域）中与科技知识的产生、发展、传播和应用密切相关的有组织的活动。为核算科技投入的需要，科技活动可分为科学研究与试验发展（R&D）、科学研究与试验发展成果应用及相关的科技服务三类活动。

科学研究与试验发展　指在科学技术领域，为增加知识总量、以及运用这些知识去创造新的应用进行的系统的创造性的活动，包括基础研究、应用研究、试验发展三类活动。在工业企业开展的科学研究与试验发展（R&D）活动中，较为普遍的和大量的活动属于试验发展活动。

基础研究　指为了获得关于现象和可观察事实的基本原理的新知识（揭示客观事物的本质、运动规律，获得新发现、新学说）而进行的实验性或理论性研究，它不以任何专门或特定的应用或使用为目的。其成果以科学论文和科学著作为主要形式。

应用研究　指为获得新知识而进行的创造性研究，主要针对某一特定的目的或目标。应用研究是为了确定基础研究成果可能的用途，或是为达到预定的目标探索应采取的新方法（原理性）或新途径。其成果形式以科学论文、专著、原理性模型或发明专利为主。

试验发展　指利用从基础研究、应用研究和实际经验所获得的现有知识，为产生新的产品、材料和装置，建立新的工艺、系统和服务，以及对已生产和建立的上述各项作实质性的改进而进行的系统性工作。其成果形式主要是专利、专有技术、新产品原型或样机样件等。

研究与试验发展成果应用　指为使试验发展阶段产生的新产品、材料和装置，建立的新工艺、系统和服务以及作实质性改进后的上述各项能够投入生产或实际应用，解决所存在的技术问题而进行的系统性的工作。这类活动的成果形式大多是可供生产和实际操作的带有技术和工艺参数的图纸、技术标准和操作规范。

科技服务　与科学研究与试验发展有关并有助于科学技术知识的产生、传播和应用的活动，包括为扩大科技成果的使用范围而进行的示范性推广工作；为用户提供科技信息和文献服务的系统性工作；为用户提供可行性报告、技术方案、建议及进行技术论证等技术咨询工作；自然、生物现象的日常观测、监测，资源的考察和勘探；有关社会、人文、经济现象的通用资料的收集，如统计、市场调查等，以及这些资料的常规分析与整理；为社会和公众提供的测试、标准化、计量、计算、质量控制和专利服务，不包括工商企业为进行正常生产而开展的上述活动。

技术市场　从狭义看，是指在一定时间、地点进行技术转让和技术商品交易的场所。目前统计反映的是企业购买技术开发、技术转让、技术咨询、技术服务项目的合同数和成交额。

Explanastory Notes on Main Statistical Indicators

Schools (Institutions) refer to educational establishments at different levels set up according to the government evaluation and approval procedures, enrolling school-age population.

Regular Institutions of Higher Learning refer to educational establishments set up according to the government evaluation and approval procedures, enrolling graduates from senior secondary schools and providing higher education courses and training for senior professionals. They include full-time universities, colleges, high professional schools, high professional vocational schools and others. Universities and colleges are mainly providing undergraduate courses; those high professional schools and high professional vocational schools are mainly providing professional trainings.

Institutions of Higher Learning for Adults refer to educational establishments, set up in line with relevant rules approved by the government, enrolling staff and workers with senior secondary school or equivalent education, and providing higher education courses in many forms of correspondence, spare time, or full time for adults. Professionals thus trained receive a qualification equivalent to graduates studying regular courses at regular universities, colleges and professional colleges. Institutions of higher learning for adults include schools of high education for staff and workers, schools of high education for peasants, colleges for management cadres, pedagogical colleges, independent correspondence colleges, Radio and TV universities and other educational establishments.

Secondary Professional Schools refer to educational establishments, set up in line with relevant rules approved by the government, implementing secondary professional education. Secondary professional schools are original specialized secondary schools (secondary technical schools, secondary teacher training schools) , specialized secondary schools for adults, vocational secondary schools, which are named secondary professional schools after they are merged, constructed together and adjusted to be a kind of education type.

Vocational Secondary Schools (vocational senior secondary schools, vocational junior secondary schools) refer to educational establishments approved by county or above education administrative department, enrolling graduates from primary schools and junior secondary schools and providing vocational secondary education courses. They include vocational secondary schools (including vocational senior secondary schools, vocational junior secondary schools, vocational junior & senior secondary schools), vocational secondary schools with regular secondary school classes.

Regular Secondary Schools (regular senior secondary schools, regular junior secondary schools) are divided into regular senior secondary schools and regular junior secondary schools. Regular junior secondary schools refer to educational establishments enrolling graduates from primary schools and providing junior secondary education courses. Regular senior secondary schools refer to educational establishments enrolling graduates from junior secondary schools and providing senior secondary education courses. Whole secondary schools refer to educational establishments including senior secondary school and junior secondary school. Successive schools refer to educational establishments providing successive primary and secondary education courses including nine-year successive schools and twelve-year successive schools. (Note: If successive schools can be divided into primary school, junior secondary school and senior secondary school, should fill in respectively, otherwise, should fill in junior secondary school or senior secondary school and have no repetition.)

Primary Education (Regular Primary Schools) refer to educational establishments approved by county or above education administrative department, enrolling school-age children and providing primary education courses.

Baby Education (Kindergartens) refer to educational units enrolling children aged 3-6, including all baby education units. Kindergartens take games as basic activities.

Schools for Juvenile Delinquents refer to educational establishments founded by education department and public security department, enrolling students of secondary schools with slight illegal behavior.

Special Education Schools refer to educational establishments, enrolling blind, deaf, dumb children, weak-minded children and providing regular or vocational primary and secondary education courses.

Graduates refer to the number of students who have student status, learn over all education courses, pass the graduate examination and receive diploma.

New Students Enrollment refer to number of new students who have passed enrollment examination (Higher Learning include students enrolled in spring and autumn).

Students Enrollment refers to number of students with student status at the beginning of the school year.

Explanastory Notes on Main Statistical Indicators

Number of Teachers, Officers and Workers refer to persons work at schools (institutions) and receive wages from schools (institutions). They include personnel whose personal connections and files put in schools, engaged personnel, i.e. full-time personnel engaged by higher learning (institutions). The personal connections of personnel engaged are put in schools but files are not put in schools. Number of teachers, officers and workers include staff, personnel of science research institutions, staff and workers of enterprises founded by schools and personnel of other subordinated institutions.

Full-time Teachers refer to personnel who have qualifications of teacher and undertake educational working.

Science and Technology Activities refer to organizational activity aimed at developing, spreading and applying the scientific technology about natural science, agriculture science, medicine science, engineering and technology science, human and social science. In order to calculate the input of science and technology, science and technology activities are divided into R&D, Achievements Applying on Researches & Experiments Developing and Science and Technique Services.

Research and Experimental Development(R&D) refers to systematic and creative endeavor aimed at expanding the overall volume of knowledge and applying the knowledge in inventing new uses. It includes basic studies, application research and experimental development. For industrial enterprises, their R&D mainly belongs to experimental development activities.

Basic Research refers to empirical or theoretical research aiming at obtaining new knowledge on the fundamental principles of phenomena of observable facts to reveal the nature and law of movement of objects and to acquire new discoveries or new theories. Basic research takes no specific or designated application as the aim of the research. Results of basic research are mainly released or disseminated in the form of scientific papers or monographs.

Applied Research refers to creative research aiming at obtaining new knowledge on a specific objective or target. Purpose of the applied research is to identify the possible use of results from basic research, or to explore new (fundamental) methods or new approaches. Results of applied research are expressed in the form of scientific papers, monographs, fundamental models or invention patents.

Experiments and Development refer to systematic activities aiming at using the knowledge from basic and applied researches or from practical experience to develop new products, materials and equipment, to establish new production process, system and service, or to make substantial improvement on the existing products, process and services. Results of experiment and development activities are embodied in patents, exclusive technology and monotype of new products or equipment.

Achievements Applying on Researches & Experiments Developing It means that a lot of work is systematically taken to find solutions applicable both/either to technological problems in products, materials and devices put into production and in skills, systems and services into practical use. This kind of achievements include blueprint, technical standard and operating rules with technology and technological parameter for the purpose of production and practical operation.

Science and Technique Services A forward movement in research of the science and development of experiment is a help in creation, spread and application of scientific and technological knowledge, including seven principal matters: (a) extending application, on scope, of an achievement in science and technique by setting an example related there to in popularization, (b) furnishing users with the systematic information on sciences and value-lasting documents as a study, (c) making technique- inquiring business available to users for requirement of technologies either by way of a suggestion or of a scheme, either analysis or feasibility report, (d) people observing day by day and/or listening and reporting on or testing, by apparatus, things appearing in or changes brought about by the nature and living beings, (e) inspecting and/or searching for resources, (f) collecting, analyzing routinely and sorting out the general-purpose information on societies, humanities and economics, e.g. statistics and on-the-spot investigation on markets, (g) providing a test, standardization, measure, calculation, quality control and patent-related services to the society and the public, not to industrial enterprises and/or firms engaged in the above items-developing dealings made available to their normal production and/or operation.

Technique Market It can be regarded narrowly as technical-dealings office where technique transfer is made or technology-related good traded at certain time. As shown in statistical datum presently, turnovers are resulting either from purchase or from transfer of techniques, together with numbers related to the inquiry or services involved in technologies.

第18篇
CHAPTER 18

文化和体育
Culture and Sports

18-1 文化事业机构和人员情况（2001-2006年）
BASIC STATISTICS OF CULTURAL INSTITUTIONS AND PERSONNEL, 2001-2006

单位：个、人（unit, person）

年 份 Year	艺术机构 Art	公 共 图书馆 Public Library	档案机构 Archives Institution	群众文化 活动机构 Mass Culture	文 物 保护机构 Agency of Historic Relics Preservation	博物馆 Museums
机构数 Institutions						
2001	49	31	494	19	8	14
2002	49	31	508	19	8	15
2003	49	31	497	19	8	17
2004	70	32	481	19	8	17
2005	61	32	410	19	8	18
2006	61	32	329	19	8	19
人员数 Personnel						
2001	2562	1014	1044	752	116	672
2002	2483	974	1046	755	127	689
2003	2322	1095	999	750	131	629
2004	2937	1082	1144	706	117	658
2005	2663	1057	913	710	133	679
2006	2686	1086	784	707	132	724

18-2 图书报纸杂志出版情况
BOOK, NEWSPAPERS AND MAGAZINES PUBLICATION

项 目	Item	种 类(种) Number of Publications (kind)			总印数(万册) Total Copies (10 000 volumes)		
		2004	2005	2006	2004	2005	2006
图书出版总计	**Total Publication of Books**	**4356**	**4434**	**3691**	**8299**	**5917**	**5106**
#本 版	Local Publications	4028	4213	3461	8263	4574	3803
#书 籍	Books	3403	3600	2993	4897	3713	3030
课 本	Textbooks	898	794	677	3366	2133	2040
图 片	Pictures	55	40	21	36	71	36
报纸出版总计	**Total Publication of Newspapers**	**41**	**44**	**44**	**86687**	**87557**	**94821**
综合报	Comprehensive Newspapers	28	26	26	81064	76539	84356
专业报	Professional Newspapers	13	14	18	5623	11018	10465
省、直辖市级报纸合计	Newspapers at Provincial or Municipal Level	25	28	28	86556	87409	94664
区(市)级报纸合计	Newspapers at District (City) Level	16	16	16	131	148	157
杂志出版总计	**Total Publication of Magazines**	**244**	**243**	**243**	**4493**	**4192**	**4060**
综 合	Comprehensive	21	28	17	654	584	501
哲学、社会科学	Philosophy and Social Sciences	40	34	39	819	730	802
自然科学、技术	Natural Sciences and Technology	136	133	139	825	852	811
文化、教育	Culture and Education	29	28	26	1304	964	786
文学、艺术	Literature and Art	16	16	13	861	832	735
少年儿童读物	Juvenile and Children's Book	1	3	8	49	229	424
画 刊	Pictorial	2	1	1	30	1	1

18-3 书籍和课本分类出版情况 PUBLICATION OF BOOKS AND TEXTBOOKS BY CATEGORY

类别 Item	种类(种) Number of Publication (kind)			总印数(万册) Total Copies (10 000 volumes)		
	2004	2005	2006	2004	2005	2006
总计 Total	**4301**	**4394**	**3691**	**8263**	**5842**	**5106**
马列主义、毛泽东思想 Marxism-Leninism, Mao Zedong Thought	4	13	3	10	8	3
哲学 Philosophy	79	72	47	55	33	23
社会科学总论 General Social Sciences	42	59	21	33	46	7
政治、法律 Politics and Law	57	69	70	44	34	22
军事 Military Affairs		3	2		1	1
经济 Economics	231	270	246	118	131	107
文化、科学、教育、体育 Culture, Science, Education and Sports	1507	1521	1388	5267	3902	3957
语言、文字 Languages	339	317	290	234	195	137
文学 Literature	401	465	410	348	379	269
艺术 Art	809	680	524	1774	721	241
历史、地理 History and Geography	84	121	115	47	57	50
自然科学总论 General Natural Sciences	8	6	6	8	5	7
数理科学、化学 Mathematics and Chemistry	113	106	80	75	65	34
天文学、地球科学 Astronomy and Geology	3	8	8	1	3	3
生物科学 Biology	9	11	6	5	7	4
医药、卫生 Medicine and Health Care	214	238	136	68	63	44
农业科学 Agricultural Science	39	36	5	9	8	1
工业技术 Industrial Technology	348	376	294	162	175	152
交通运输 Transportation	6	8	10	3	2	5
环境科学 Environmental Science	3	11	7	1	3	2
综合性图书 Comprehensive Books	5	4	2	1	4	1
其他 Others			21			36

18-4 录像和录音制品出版情况 PUBLICATION OF VIDEO PRODUCTS

项目	Item	种数(种) kind			数量(万盒、万张) Volume (10 000 cassettes、10 000pieces)		
		2004	2005	2006	2004	2005	2006
数码激光视盘	VCD	132	50	73	91.48	140	120
高密度激光视盘	DVD	12	19	28	18.70	41	67
录音带	Audio-tapes	89	95	48	155.38	83.7	128
激光唱盘	CD	59	48	96	68.90	39.3	108

18-5 广播和电视节目制作情况(2006年) PRODUCTION OF BROADCASTING AND TELEVISION, 2006

单位：小时 (hour)

项 目 Item	全年制作节目时间 Annual Production of Programs	新闻资讯类 News	专题服务类 Special Topic Service	综艺益智类 Integrative Art and Improve Wise	广播/影视剧类 Broadcasting Film and Teleplay	广告类 Advertisement	其他类 Others
广播电台 Broadcasting Stations	**64422**	**11466**	**9764**	**27042**	**185**	**13170**	**2795**
电视台 Television Stations	**28248**	**4082**	**7309**	**6193**	**8819**	**1209**	**636**
天津电视台 Tianjin	9376	1642	6053	1429	158	94	
塘沽区电视台 Tanggu District	1172	396	60	486		200	30
汉沽区电视台 Han'gu District	996	54	17	864		61	
大港区电视台 Dagang District	1333	73	73	913		123	151
武清区电视台 Wuqing District	823	164	279	220		130	30
宝坻区电视台 Baodi District	586	92	182	130		182	
宁河县电视台 Ninghe County	310	95	110			105	
静海县电视台 Jinghai County	1590	87	98	1308		79	18
蓟县电视台 Jixian County	1035	110	150	395		140	240

18-6 广播和电视节目播出情况(2006年) PROGRAMS OF BROADCASTING AND TELEVISION, 2006

单位：小时：分 (hour : minute)

项 目 Item	全年播出节目时间 Annual Production of Programs	新闻资讯类 News	专题服务类 Special Topic Service	综艺益智类 Integrative Art and Improve Wise	广播/影视剧类 Broadcasting Film and Teleplay	广告类 Advertisement	其他类 Others
广播电台 Broadcasting Stations	**77957:55**	**15482:05**	**9946:15**	**35557:05**	**365:00**	**13170:25**	**3437:05**
电视台 Television Stations	**127175:05**	**9688:30**	**32684:22**	**12417:41**	**48961:23**	**18303:58**	**5119:11**
天津电视台 Tianjin	68096:06	4176:40	29341:53	3888:31	15804:53	14884:09	
塘沽区电视台 Tanggu District	12997:54	2227:00	734:54	1884:00	5182:00	830:04	2139:56
汉沽区电视台 Han'gu District	12410:00	274:00	65:00	2180:00	8411:00	1297:00	183:00
大港区电视台 Dagang District	6205:00	274:00	292:00	913:00	3382:00	123:00	1221:00
武清区电视台 Wuqing District	4840:00	289:00	1030:00	707:00	1650:00	398:00	766:00
宝坻区电视台 Baodi District	3726:00	274:00	365:00	260:00	2280:00	183:00	364:00
宁河县电视台 Ninghe County	715:15	220:00	135:00		245:00	115:15	
静海县电视台 Jinghai County	5104:10	464:35	165:35	1399:10	2977:30	79:05	18:15
蓟县电视台 Jixian County	4335:00	110:00	150:00	395:00	3300:00	140:00	240:00

18-7 广播电台和电视台情况（2003-2006年）
STATISTICS OF BROADCASTING AND TELEVISION STATIONS, 2003-2006

单位：套、时：分、%(set, hour : minute, %)

项目	Item	2003	2004	2005	2006
广播电台	**Broadcasting Stations**				
节目套数	Number of Programs	7	7	9	10
平均每日播音时间	Broadcasting Hours per Day	148:32	158:15	190:58	213:35
广播覆盖率	Listener Rating	100	100	100	100
电视台	**Television Stations**				
节目套数	Number of Programs	16	17	18	26
平均每周播出时间	Program Hours per Week	1509:51	1545:38	1911:05	2445:40
电视覆盖率	Viewer Rating	99	99	99.83	99.83

18-8 有线电视基本情况（2003-2006年）
BASIC STATISTICS ON CABLE TELEVISION, 2003-2006

指标 Item	2003	2004	2005	2006
有线电视总用户数（万户） Subscribers (10 000 households)	150	180	194	200
有线电视入户率（%） Popularity Rate (%)	50.23	59.39	61.47	61.98
有线广播电视传输网络干线总长（公里） Lines Total (kilometer)	2074	2074	25095	21884

18-9 电影放映单位基本情况（2003-2006年）
BASIC STATISTICS ON FILM PROJECTING UNITS, 2003-2006

单位：个 (unit)

指标	Item	2003	2004	2005	2006
电影院	Cinema	12	13	11	11
影剧院	Theater	11	12	12	12
开放礼堂俱乐部	Opening Auditorium	8	8	7	7
电影放映队	Projecting Team	139	139	139	139
对内俱乐部	Internal Club	15	15	15	15
电影放映单位拥有座席数	Seats	31718	34469	30576	30576
放映场次(场次)	Projecting Performances (times)	41970	51515	34751	26305
观众人次(万人次)	Audience (10 000 person-times)	103	117	65	37

18-10 艺术事业基本情况（2003-2006年） BASIC STATISTICS ON ART, 2003-2006

指 标	Item	2003	2004	2005	2006
艺术表演团体	Art Performance Troupes				
机构数(个)	Institutions (unit)	15	16	16	16
话剧团、儿童剧团	Drama and Children Troupes	2	2	3	3
歌舞剧团	Song and Dance Troupes	1	1	1	1
文工团、文宣队	Culturaland Performance Troupe	1	2	1	1
戏曲剧团	Local Opera Troupes	7	7	7	7
#京 剧	Local Beijing Opera Troupes	2	2	2	2
曲剧团、杂技团、木偶团	Recitation and Ballad Troupes, Acrobatic and Circus Troupes, Puppet Show Troup	3	3	3	3
乐团、合唱团	Philharmonic Troupes and Chorus	1	1	1	1
工作人员数(人)	Employment (person)	1769	1831	1803	1821
演出场次(场)	Number of Performances (times)	2191	2500	2332	2343
#到农村演出	Shows In Rural Areas	433	400	444	490
观众人次(万人次)	Number of Spectators (10 000 person-times)	260	212	159	186
艺术表演场所	Art Performance Places				
机构数(个)	Institutions (unit)	32	29	28	28
剧场、音乐厅	Theatre and Concert Hall	31	28	27	27
书场、曲艺厅	Storytelling Places, Rectation and Ballad Places	1	1	1	1
座席数(个)	Seats (unit)	15792	17233	15529	14609
工作人员数(人)	Employment (person)	537	500	395	420
演出场次(场)	Number of Performances (times)	30336	28600	20025	25908
观众人次(万人次)	Number of Spectators (10 000 person-times)	73	76	64	102

18-11 档案事业基本情况（2003-2006年）
BASIC STATISTICS ON ARCHIVES, 2003-2006

单位：个、人 (unit, person)

项　目	Item	2003	2004	2005	2006
机构数	**Number of Institutions**	**497**	**481**	**410**	**329**
# 档案馆	Archives	32	35	34	35
机关事业单位档案室	Archives in Government and Institutions	186	158	153	125
大型工业企业档案馆	Archives in Large Industrial Enterprises	279	288	223	169
专职工作人员	**Full-time Personnel**	**999**	**1144**	**913**	**784**
# 档案馆	Archives	410	425	434	435
机关事业单位档案室	Archives in Government and Institutions	218	200	176	135
大型工业企业档案馆	Archives in Large Industrial Enterprises	371	519	303	214
兼职工作人员	**Part-time Personnel**	**2466**	**3746**	**2000**	**1011**
# 机关事业单位档案室	Archives in Government and Institutions	1003	1017	856	221
大型工业企业档案馆	Archives in Large Industrial Enterprises	1463	2729	1144	790

18-12 档案馆档案资料馆藏与开发利用情况（2003-2006年）
COLLECTION,DEVELOPMENT AND UTILIZATION OF MATERIALS IN ARCHIVES, 2003-2006

项　目	Item	2003	2004	2005	2006
馆藏档案	**Collection of Archives**				
全　宗(个)	Full-Records (unit)	2713	2851	2799	2856
案　卷(万卷)	Files (10 000 volumes)	393	419	434	472.31
录音、录像、影片(盘)	Sounds and Movies Files (cassette)	6900	7300	30000	9500
照　片(张)	Photo Files (picture)	253600	315900	304200	344500
保存资料	**Collection of Materials**				
资料数量(万册)	Materials (10 000 volumes)	26	30	27	28
利用档案资料	**Utilization**				
利用人次(万人次)	Users (10 000 person-times)	3	3	4	5
利用档案(万卷次)	Access to Files (10 000 volume-times)	11	13	13	16
利用资料(册次)	Materials (volume-times)	6700	13700	8000	8700
利用档案资料(万页)	Copy Materials (10 000 pages)	8	8	10	55
编研档案资料	**Editing Materials**				
公开出版 (种)	Public Publication (kind)	2	9	14	18
(万字)	(10 000 words)	11	330	208	151
内部参考 (种)	Internal Reference (kind)	55	79	85	72
(万字)	(10 000 words)	278	819	456	435

18-13 机关事业单位档案资料保存与开发利用情况（2003-2006年）
KEEPING, DEVELOPMENT AND UTILIZATION OF GOVERNMENT AND INSTITUTION ARCHIVES AND MATERIALS, 2003-2006

项　目	Item	2003	2004	2005	2006
保存档案	Keeping Archives				
全　宗(个)	Full-Records (unit)	263	232	191	173
案　卷(万卷)	Files (10 000 volumes)	125	96	82	63
底　图(万张)	Chart (10 000 pictures)	83	140	132	0.59
微缩胶片(万张)	Compressed Film (10 000 pictures)				
保存资料	Keeping Materials				
保存数量(万册)	Number of Materials (10 000 volumes)	5	5	5	4
借阅利用档案资料	Lending				
利用人次(万人次)	Users (10 000 person-times)	5	6	5	5
利用档案资料数量(万卷册数)	Access to Files (10 000 volumes)	12	10	9	8
编研档案资料	Editing Materials and Archives				
公开出版(种)	Public Publication (kind)	28	30	27	14
(万字)	(10 000 words)	1247	394	1400	380
内部参考(种)	Internal Reference (kind)	139	108	91	177
(万字)	(10 000 words)	1335	5499	1207	1263

18-14 大型工业企业档案资料保存与开发利用情况（2003-2006年）
KEEPING, DEVELOPMENT AND UTILIZATION OF ARCHIVES MATERIALS IN LARGE-SIZED INDUSTRIAL ENTERPRISES, 2003-2006

项　目	Item	2003	2004	2005	2006
保存档案	Keeping Archives				
全　宗(个)	Full-Records (unit)	444	673	429	363
案　卷(万卷)	Files (10 000 volumes)	167	311	201	117
底　图(万张)	Chart (10 000 pictures)	333	339	114	52
缩微胶片(万张)	Compressed Film (10 000 pictures)	8			
保存资料数量(万册)	Number of Keeping Materials (10 000 volumes)	13	10	3	7
借阅利用人次(万人次)	Lenders (10 000 person-times)	8	11	6	3
借阅利用数量(万卷册数)	Access to Files (10 000 volumes)	19	23	11	7
编辑档案资料	Editing Materials and Archives				
公开出版（种）	Public Publication (kind)		1	1	
(万字)	(10 000 words)		50	40	
内部参考（种）	Internal Reference (kind)	266	468	739	184
(万字)	(10 000 words)	725	9093	1462	320

18-15 公共图书馆情况（2003-2006年）
BASIC STATISTICS ON PUBLIC LIBRARIES, 2003-2006

项　目	Item	单　位	Unit	2003	2004	2005	2006
工作人员	Employment	个	person	1095	1082	1057	1086
藏　书	Collections	万　册	10 000 volumes	840	827	869	945
借阅人次	Person-times of Borrowing	万人次	10 000 person-times	187	170	212	180
借阅册次	Number of Books Borrowed	万册次	10 000 volume-times	339	263	380	359
建筑面积	Floor Space of Buildings	平方米	sq. m	100444	170000	168685	125942
阅览室座席	Seating Capacity of Reading Room	次	unit	7467	7959	9747	9090

18-16 博物馆和文物保护单位基本情况（2003-2006年）
BASIC STATISTICS ON MUSEUMS AND CULTURAL RELIC PROTECTION UNITS, 2003-2006

项　目	Item	单　位	Unit	2003	2004	2005	2006
博物馆	**Museums**						
单位数	Number of Units	个	unit	17	17	18	19
工作人员数	Employment	人	person	629	658	679	724
文物藏品	Number of Collection	万　件	10 000 pieces	55	57	57	57
举办陈列	Number of Displays	个	unit	11			
举办展览	Number of Exhibitions	个	unit	46	31	68	76
参观人次	Numbers of Visitors	万人次	10 000 person-times	58	88	102	126
文物保护单位	**Cultural Relic Protection Units**						
单位数	Number of Units	个	unit	8	8	8	8
工作人员数	Employment	人	person	131	117	133	132
藏　品	Number of Collection	件	piece	2975	2239	2995	3042

18-17 群众文化事业基本情况（2003-2006年）
BASIC STATISTICS ON MASS ART, 2003-2006

项　目	Item	单　位	Unit	2003	2004	2005	2006
单位数	**Number of Units**	**个**	**unit**	**19**	**19**	**19**	**19**
群众艺术馆	Mass Art Centers	个	unit	1	1	1	1
文化馆	Cultural Centers	个	unit	18	18	18	18
工作人员数	**Employment**	**人**	**person**	**750**	**706**	**710**	**707**
文化活动情况	**Cultural Activity**						
举办展览	Number of Exhibitions	次	time	144	220	177	160
组织文艺活动次数	Number of Art Performances	次	time	1097	1143	1345	709
举办训练班	Training Courses						
班　次	Number of Classes	班	class	595	603	660	594
结业人数	Number of Persons Completing Course	人	person	10000	10491	9699	45945

18-18 县及县以上举办运动会情况（2003-2006年）
SPORTS MEETINGS HELD BY COUNTY AND ABOVE, 2003-2006

单位：次、万人 (times, 10 000 persons)

指　标	Item	2003	2004	2005	2006
举办运动会次数	Sports Meetings	367	386	378	428
参加运动会人数	Athletes Attending Sports Meetings	25	28	33	35
体委系统	Physical Culture and Sports Commissions				
运动会次数	Times	82	96	108	84
参加人数	Persons	12	14	18	16
其他系统	Other Departments				
运动会次数	Times	285	290	270	292
参加人数	Persons	13	14	15	16

18-19 体委系统体育工作者（2003-2006年）
PERSONNEL IN SPORTS COMMISSIONS SYSTEM, 2003-2006

单位：人 (person)

指　标　Item	2003	2004	2005	2006
体育工作者人数 Personnel of Sports	4100	4080	3920	4042
专职教练员 Full-time Coaches	512	524	531	551
国家级教练员 National Coaches	6	5	8	8
每十万人口中有体育工作者 Number of Physical Personnel in per 100 000 Persons	41	46	46	45

18-20 等级裁判员和运动员人数
NUMBER OF ATHLETES AND REFEREES IN GRADES

单位：人 (person)

指　标	Item	裁判员 Referees			运动员 Athletes		
		2004	2005	2006	2004	2005	2006
总人数	**Total**	**424**	**436**	**397**	**1250**	**1132**	**638**
一　级	First Grade	82	88	77	86	62	74
二　级	Second Grade	342	348	320	1164	1070	564
#女　性	**Female**	**178**	**184**	**165**	**533**	**490**	**246**
一　级	First Grade	47	50	40	37	30	26
二　级	Second Grade	131	134	125	496	460	220

主要统计指标解释

电视人口覆盖率 指用普通的电视接收机，室外天线在离地面4米高处能在晚上正常收看电视节目的人数与全市总人口数之比。

广播人口覆盖率 指用普通的收音机在中午能正常收听广播节目的人数与全市总人口数之比。

文化事业机构 指从事专业文化工作和为专业文化工作服务的单独核算、独立建制的单位，不包括文化主管部门直属单位举办的其他行业和各部门的业余文化组织。

艺术表演团体 指从事戏曲、音乐、舞蹈、杂技等专业艺术表演有独立帐户、实行单独核算的团体。

电影放映单位 指具有放映机器设备，固定或不固定的放映场所与专职或兼职的放映技术人员，经文化部门登记批准，经常为一定的观众对象映出电影的机构。包括经批准对外开放进行营业、并与电影发行放映管理机构分帐的专用放映单位或军委系统租片在内。

等级运动员人数 指经考核正式批准授予等级运动员称号的人数。分为国际级运动健将、运动健将、一、二、三级运动员和少年级运动员。

等级裁判员人数 指经考核正式批准授予等级裁判员称号的人数。分为国际裁判、国家级裁判、一级裁判、二级裁判、三级裁判。

Explanastory Notes on Main Statistical Indicators

Viewer Rate refers to the ratio of the number of watching TV to the total population using normal television sets with outdoor antenna four meters apart from ground in the evening.

Listener Rate refers to the ratio of the number of listening radio to the total population using normal radiogram at noon.

Cultural Institutions refer to units which have their own organizational system and independent accounting system and specialize in or serve cultural development. They exclude other establishments run by these cultural institutions and amateur cultural groups established by various departments.

Art Troupe refers to the troupe which is engaged in drama, opera, music, dance, acrobatics or other art performance, opens independent accounts with banks and has self-supporting accounting system.

Film Projection Units refer to these units with film projection equipment, full or part-time projectionists, permanent or non-permanent places, approved by related administrative departments to show films regularly for certain groups of audience, including those film projection units which have been approved to give commercial shows and run business with independent accounting system as well as those film-renting units of the military system.

Number of Athletes in Grades refers to the number of athletes who have been given titles through examination. The titles of athletes include international masters of sports, masters of sports, first-grade, second-grade and third-grade sportsmen and young athletes.

Number of Referees in Grades refers to the number of referees who have been given titles after examination. They are classified as international referees, national referees and referees of the first, second and third grades.

第19篇
CHAPTER 19
卫生、社会保障和社会福利
Public Health, Social Security and Social Welfare

19-1 卫生事业基本情况(1990-2006年)
STATISTICS ON PUBLIC HEALTH, 1990-2006

年 份 Year	卫生事业机构(个) Number of Health Care Institutions (unit)	#医院、卫生院 Hospitals and Health Care Centers	卫生机构床位数(张) Beds (unit)	#医院、卫生院 Hospitals and Health Care Centers	卫生技术人员数(人) Medical Technical Personnel (person)	#执业及助理医师 Certified And Assistant Doctors	#注册护士 Registered Nurses
1990	3 392	293	35 581	33 382	67 485	32 034	21 228
1991	3 397	300	37 504	35 124	68 887	32 385	22 086
1992	3 287	301	38 137	36 035	69 815	32 320	22 804
1993	3 182	304	39 023	36 724	70 920	33 026	22 884
1994	3 182	419	38 986	37 157	71 217	33 373	22 936
1995	3 182	416	39 092	37 280	71 806	33 693	23 177
1996	4 171	476	39 612	38 284	71 014	32 975	23 156
1997	3 571	483	40 758	39 467	70 431	32 475	23 045
1998	3 190	482	40 471	39 134	68 070	31 482	22 209
1999	2 969	487	39 779	38 579	65 901	30 273	21 977
2000	2 983	488	40 039	38 842	65 145	30 031	21 667
2001	2 665	495	41 637	40 394	63 475	29 215	21 298
2002	2 636	486	40 090	38 837	56 705	23 888	19 257
2003	2 671	485	40 194	38 074	55 629	22 780	19 173
2004	2 577	474	40 994	38 876	60 722	25 299	19 602
2005	2 489	461	41 556	39 491	61 284	25 088	19 624
2006	2 384	401	43 643	38 893	62 258	25 358	20 030

19-2 卫生事业机构数(2003-2006年)
NUMBER OF HEALTH CARE INSTITUTIONS, 2003-2006

单位：个 (unit)

名 称	Item	2003	2004	2005	2006
总 计	**Total**	**2671**	**2577**	**2489**	**2384**
医院、卫生院	Hospitals and Health Care Centers	485	474	461	401
疗养院	Sanatoriums	3	3	3	3
门诊部、诊所、医务室、社区服务站	Clinics	2051	1965	1892	1847
专科疾病防治院(所、站)	Specialized Prevention Stations	17	18	17	16
卫生防疫站	Sanitation and Antiepidemic Stations	25	24	24	24
妇幼保健院(所、站)	Maternity and Children Care Centers	22	23	23	23
卫生监督所	Health Offices	3	3	3	4
医学科学研究机构	Research Institutes of Medical Science	8	8	8	8
高等医学教育机构	High Education Institutions of Medicine	3	3	3	3
其他卫生事业机构	Other Health Care Institutions	54	56	55	55
平均每个医院负担人口(人)	Average Burden Population of Each Hospital (person)	19021	19605	22615	26409

19-3 卫生事业基本情况（2006年）
STATISTICS ON PUBLIC HEALTH, 2006

项　目	Item	卫生机构(个) Health Care Institutions (unit)	卫生机构床位(张) Number of Institutions Beds (unit)	卫生技术人员(人) Medical Technical Personnel (person)	#执业及助理医师 Certified And Assistant Doctors
总　计	**Total**	**2384**	**43643**	**62258**	**25358**
按市县分	Grouped by City & County				
市	City	1952	40431	55237	22094
县	County	432	3212	7021	3264
按经济类型分	Grouped by Ownership				
国有经济	State-owned	1136	39798	55184	21858
集体经济	Collective-owned	226	1612	2368	1481
联营、私营经济	Joint Ownership Enterprises and Private	903	1408	3483	1420
其　他	Others	119	825	1223	599
按设置主办单位分	Grouped by Management				
政府办	Run by Government	512	34534	49209	19157
#卫生部门	Health sector	480	34381	49074	19076
企业办	Run by Enterprises	494	3186	5073	2598
其　他	Others	1379	5923	7976	3603

项　目	Item	注册护士 Registered Nurses	药剂人员 Pharmacists	检验人员 Laboratory Technicians	其他人员 Others
总　计	**Total**	**20030**	**4596**	**3140**	**9134**
按市县分	Grouped by City & County				
市	City	18741	4181	2873	7348
县	County	1289	415	267	1786
按经济类型分	Grouped by Ownership				
国有经济	State-owned	19154	4044	2945	7183
集体经济	Collective-owned	254	236	86	311
联营、私营经济	Joint Ownership Enterprises and Private	414	191	64	1394
其　他	Others	208	125	45	246
按设置主办单位分	Grouped by Management				
政府办	Run by Government	17156	3665	2738	6493
#卫生部门	Health sector	17140	3656	2728	6474
企业办	Run by Enterprises	1559	370	187	359
其　他	Others	1315	561	215	2282

19-4 卫生技术人员数(2006年)
NUMBER OF MEDICAL TECHNICAL PERSONNEL, 2006

单位：人 (person)

项　目	Item	总计 Total	#执业及助理医师 Certified And Assistant Doctors	#注册护士 Registered Nurses	#药剂人员 Pharmacists	#检验人员 Laboratory Technicians
总　计	**Total**	**62258**	**25358**	**20030**	**4596**	**3140**
医　院	Hospitals	43744	15901	16893	3282	2142
#综合医院	Comprehensive Hospitals	26807	9726	10488	1880	1387
专科医院	Special Hospitals	10109	3277	4215	626	462
# 口腔医院	Stomatitis Hospitals	684	338	180	20	7
眼科医院	Eye Hospitals	309	127	129	24	14
耳鼻喉科医院	E. N. T. Hospitals	47	9	10	2	2
肿瘤医院	Tumour Hospitals	1200	373	514	62	32
胸科医院	Chest Hospitals	749	263	351	41	24
血液病医院	Blood Disease Hospitals	515	139	187	25	58
妇产科医院	Gynecology Hospitals	1091	337	527	67	74
儿童医院	Children Hospitals	1082	339	500	82	46
精神病医院	Mental Disease Hospitals	1279	294	526	71	34
传染病医院	Infectious Disease Hospitals	497	126	208	48	38
皮肤病医院	Skin Disease Hospitals	17	11	3	2	1
骨科医院	Orthopaedics Hospitals	1134	373	474	84	50
疗养院	Sanatoriums	203	54	95	10	3
社区卫生服务中心	Community Health Care Centers	3529	1501	1072	455	166
卫生院	Health Care Centers	4253	2420	581	401	197
门诊部	Clinics	1096	622	148	93	32
急救中心(站)	First-aid Centers	49	30	13	1	
采供血机构	Blood Collection and Supplying Institutions	159	26	51	1	42
妇幼保健院(所、站)	Maternity and Children Care Centers	1569	728	487	87	103
专科疾病防治院(所、站)	Specialized Prevention Stations	473	188	141	38	44
疾病预防控制中心(防疫站)	Disease Prevention and Control Centers	1854	1066	88	9	326
卫生监督所	Sanitation Supervision Institutions	166	97	5	2	8
其他卫生机构	Other Health Care Institutions	5163	2725	456	217	77

19-5 卫生机构的床位数（2003-2006年）
NUMBER OF BEDS IN HEALTH CARE INSTITUTIONS, 2003-2006

单位：张 (unit)

名　称	Item	2003	2004	2005	2006
总　计	**Total**	**40194**	**40994**	**41556**	**43643**
医　院	Hospitals	35896	36645	37255	36662
疗养院	Sanatoriums	633	643	643	643
卫生院	Health Care Centers	2178	2231	2236	2231
门诊部	Clinics	114	111	201	156
社区卫生服务中心	Community Health Care Centers				2696
妇幼保健院(所、站)	Maternity and Children Care Centers	837	839	818	852
专科疾病防治院(所、站)	Specialized Prevention Stations	499	500	360	360
其他卫生机构	Other Health Care Institutions	37	25	43	43
平均每千人口有医院床位	Hospital Beds per 1000 Population	3.56	3.60	3.71	3.46

19-6 医疗机构诊疗和病床使用情况（2003-2006年）
DIAGNOSIS, TREATMENT AND BEDS USED OF MEDICAL INSTITUTIONS, 2003-2006

项　目	Item	2003	2004	2005	2006
诊疗情况(万人次)	**Diagnosis and Treatment (10 000 person-times)**				
诊疗人数	Patients Treated	2226	2455	2704	3855
#门　诊	Out-patients	1910	2176	2411	3530
入院人数	In-patients	45	52	57	71
平均每月门诊诊疗人数	Number of Out-patients per Month	159	205	225	294
平均每月入院诊疗人数	Number of In-patients per Month	4	4	5	6
病床使用情况	**Sickbeds Used**				
病人治愈率(%)	Recovering Rate (%)	37	37	36	43
病床周转次数(次)	Turnover Beds (times)	13	14	16	17
病床使用率(%)	Utilization Rate (%)	62	65	68	67
病床工作日(日)	Working Days of Beds (day)	227	238	247	245
出院者平均 住院日数(日)	Average Hospitalization Period (day)	16	15	16	13

19-7 医院、卫生院、门诊部运营情况(2006年)
OPERATION OF HOSPITALS, HEALTH CLINICS AND OUT-PATIENT, 2006

指　标	Item	医　院 Hospitals	卫生院 Hospitals in Township	门诊部 Clinics
机构数(个)	Number of Institutions (unit)	218	183	135
总诊疗人次数(万人次)	Patients Treated (10 000 person-times)	2488	470	314
#门诊人次数	Out-patients	2230	463	311
急　诊	Emergency	222	7	
观察室收容人数(人)	Observation Room (person)	930734	17903	2800
健康检查人数(人)	Health Check (person)	843678	47935	96152
入院人数(人)	In-patients (person)	593572	71714	140
出院人数(人)	Leaving Hospital (person)	590059	71707	143
住院病人手术人次(万人次)	In-patients Surgery Trips (10 000 person-times)	20.33	1.24	
治愈率(%)	Rate of Fully Recovery (%)	36.47	86.73	29.37
好转率(%)	Rate of Taking a Turn for the Better (%)	51.88	8	70.63

19-8 社区卫生服务站基本情况(2003-2006年)
BASIC INFORMATION OF HEALTH SERVICE STATIONS, 2003-2006

项　目	Item	2003	2004	2005	2006
机构总数(个)	Number of Institutions (unit)	151	151	143	143
总人员数(人)	Total Personnel (person)	685	685	1023	1016
执业医师	Certified Doctors	1	1	2	2
执业助理医师	Certified Assistant Doctors	4	5	11	11
药剂人员	Pharmacists	49	62	28	28
检验人员	Laboratory Technicians	1	9	10	10
其　他	Others	630	608	972	965
诊疗人次数(人次)	Number of Hospital Patients (person-times)	700392	895324	784029	808254
#出诊人次数	Home Visits	111890	208171	189618	219859

19-9 村卫生室基本情况(2003-2006年)
BASIC INFORMATION OF VILLAGE HEALTH ROOM, 2003-2006

项　目	Item	2003	2004	2005	2006
机构总数(个)	Number of Institutions (unit)	2266	2252	2322	2380
执业助理医师(人)	Certified Assistant Doctors (person)	196	331	253	295
乡村医生和卫生员(人)	Village Health Room & Hygienists (person)	4037	3859	4932	5178
乡村医生	Village Health Room	3978	3805	4862	5123
卫生员	Hygienists	59	54	70	55
诊疗人次数(万人次)	Number of Hospital Patients (10 000 person-times)	642.23	697.02	722.94	819.89
#孕产妇检查人次数	Number of Checked Pregnant Women	1.41	0.67	0.28	0.25
儿童疫苗接种人次数	Number of Vaccinated Children	29.31	20.96	12.69	11.48

19-10 妇女儿童卫生保健状况（2003-2006年）
BASIC STATISTICS OF MATERNITY AND CHILD CARE, 2003-2006

指　标	Item	2003	2004	2005	2006
妇幼保健经费(万元)	Expenses for maternity and children care (10 000 yuan)	1156	1858	1718	11272
计划生育事业费(万元)	Operating Expenses for Children Planning (10 000 yuan)	5802	7676	9974	14434
户籍人口(万人)	Registered Population (10 000 persons)	926	932.6	939.3	948.9
#女　性	Female	458.7	462	465.5	470.6
0-4岁人口	Age 0-4	28.9	29.7	30.8	32.1
#女　性	Female	13.5	13.9	14.4	15.1
0-17岁人口	Age 0-17	171.2	165	156.9	151.1
#女　性	Female	81.8	78.7	74.7	71.8
育龄妇女人口(15-49岁)	Women of Child-bearing Age (Age 15-49)	268.3	268.1	266.9	265.1
婴儿死亡率 (‰)	Death Rate of Infant (‰)	8.5	7.3	6.2	5.2
5岁以下儿童死亡率(‰)	Death Rate of Children at Age 5 and below (‰)	9.9	8.3	7.1	6.0
孕产妇死亡率(1/10万)	Death Rate of Pregnant and Lying-in Woman (1/100 000)	11.3	12.2	14.7	6.6
卡介苗接种率(%)	BCG Vaccination Rate (%)	97.9	99.8	99.4	99.7
脊灰疫苗接种率(%)	Poliovirus Vaccination Rate (%)	98.3	100	99.4	99.7
白百破三联制剂接种率(%)	Pertussis, Diphtheria & Tetanus Vaccination Rate (%)	98.4	99.1	99.4	99.7
麻疹疫苗接种率(%)	Measles Virus Vaccination Rate (%)	98.1	99.3	97.7	99.5
乙肝疫苗接种率(%)	Hepatitis B Vaccination Rate (%)	96.9	99.8	99.8	99.8
5岁以下儿童中、重度营养不良患病率(%)	Incidence Disease Rate from Medium and Serious Malnutrition of Children at Age 5 and below (%)	0.3	0.3	0.16	0.17
7岁以下儿童保健管理率(%)	Management Rate of Children Health Care System at Age 7 and below (%)	87.9	86.3	83.4	85.4

19-11 全市居民前十位死亡原因、死亡专率
CAUSE OF DEATH AND DEATH RATE OF 10 MAJOR DISEASES

序位及死因	Position and Cause of Death	死亡专率 Death Rate (1/100 000)		占全部死亡人数的% Proportion (%)	
		2005	2006	2005	2006
1. 心脏病	Heart Trouble	164.72	162.96	27.01	25.90
2. 脑血管病	Cerebrovascular Disease	147.78	159.02	24.23	25.27
3. 恶性肿瘤	Malignant Tumour	125.86	136.77	20.64	21.73
4. 呼吸系统疾病	Respiratory Disease	67.56	65.37	11.08	10.39
5. 损伤和中毒外部原因	Trauma and Toxicosis	29.56	30.72	4.85	4.88
6. 内分泌、营养和代谢的其他疾病	Internal System, Nutrition, Metabolive and Immunity Diseas	18.69	18.8	3.06	2.99
7. 消化系统疾病	Digestive Disease	12.57	12.5	2.06	1.99
8. 神经系统疾病	Neuropathy	8.27	9.52	1.36	1.51
9. 泌尿生殖系统病	Urinary Disease	8.74	7.72	1.43	1.23
10. 起源于围生期的某些情况	Causes in Perinatal Period	2.59	2.82	0.46	0.45

19-12 社会保障事业发展情况（2003-2006年）
BASIC STATISTICS ON SOCIAL SECURITY, 2003-2006

指　标　Item	单　位　Unit	2003	2004	2005	2006
医疗保险参保人员情况　Medical Insurance					
参加基本医疗保险人数	万　人				
Personnel Participated in Medical Insurance	10 000 persons	242.92	263.03	299.10	344.20
职工人数	万　人				
Staff and Workers	10 000 persons	165.17	158.24	180.80	218.22
退休人数	万　人				
Retired Personnel	10 000 persons	77.75	104.79	118.30	125.98
基本医疗保险基金收入	亿　元				
Revenue of Basic Medical Insurance Funds	100 million yuan	19.53	25.03	38.80	52.10
基本医疗保险基金支出	亿　元				
Expenditure of Basic Medical Insurance Funds	100 million yuan	20.40	27.17	35.90	42.80
基本医疗保险基金累计结余	亿　元				
Balance of Basic Medical Insurance Funds	100 million yuan	1.39	3.72	10.00	19.30
失业保险参保人员情况　Unemployment Insurance					
参加失业保险职工人数	万　人				
Personnel Participated in Unemployment Insurance	10 000 persons	193.45	195.06	197.50	216.66
领取失业保险金人数	万　人				
Drawing Unemployment Insurance Funds	10 000 persons	9.50	5.13	3.80	3.62
# 本年新增	万　人				
Newly Increased This Year	10 000 persons	3.40	3.23	2.30	2.67
失业保险基金收入	亿　元				
Revenue of Unemployment Insurance Funds	100 million yuan	5.66	6.45	8.24	10.68
失业保险基金支出	亿　元				
Expenditure of Unemployment Insurance Funds	100 million yuan	4.43	3.06	2.27	3.44
失业保险基金累计结余	亿　元				
Balance of Unemployment Insurance Funds	100 million yuan	3.34	6.73	12.69	19.94
基本养老保险参保人员情况　Pension Insurance					
参加基本养老保险职工人数	万　人				
Personnel Participated in Pension Insurance	10 000 persons	185.67	194.20	200.60	215.54
基本养老保险实际缴费人数	万　人				
Paying Expense for Pension Insurance	10 000 persons	175.80	185.80	198.60	202.14
基本养老保险基金收入	亿　元				
Revenue of Pension Insurance Funds	100 million yuan	85.33	104.27	126.80	157.71
基本养老保险基金支出	亿　元				
Expenditure of Pension Insurance Funds	100 million yuan	81.78	94.20	102.20	130.25
基本养老保险基金累计结余	亿　元				
Balance of Pension Insurance	100 million yuan	22.10	32.18	60.00	87.42
社会保障标准　Social Security Standard					
职工工资最低标准	元/月				
Minimum Standard of Wages of Staff and Workers	yuan per month	480	530	590	670
城镇居民生活保障最低标准	元/月				
Minimum Standard of Living Security	yuan per month	241	241	265	320

19-13 社会福利事业、企业单位和工作人员数
NUMBER OF SOCIAL WELFARE INSTITUTIONS, ENTERPRISES, PERSONS ENGAGED

部门	Department	机构(个) Institutions or Enterprises (unit) 2005	2006	职工人数(人) Staff and Workers (person) 2005	2006
收养性事业单位	Adopting Social Welfare Institutions	277	287	3974	4422
# 优抚事业单位	Subsidy Institutions	9	9	398	405
民政部门办	Run by Civil Adminstration	23	22	1444	1480
社会办	Run by Society	254	265	2530	2942
福利企业单位	Social Welfare Enterprises	781	692	32204	27612
民政部门办	Run by Civil Adminstration	35	29	3931	1881
社会办	Run by Society	746	663	28273	25731
烈士纪念建筑物管理单位	Martyr Memorial Building Management Units	10	11	176	198
救助管理单位	Collecting and Repatriation Units	9	10	183	204
殡仪服务单位	Funeral and Interment Units	25	26	1003	1008
慈善团体	Lottery & Collecting Purse Units	4	9	22	27
福利彩票发行单位	Welfare Lottery Issuing Units	6	6	42	44
城镇社区服务中心	Urban Community Service Institutions	111	111	920	888

19-14 收养性社会福利事业单位基本情况（2006年）
BASIC STATISTICS ON SOCIAL WELFARE INSTITUTIONS, 2006

指标	Item	单位数(个) Institutions (unit)	床位数(张) Number of Beds (unit)	职工人数(人) Staff and Workers (person)	年末在院收养人员(人) Adopted Personnel at the Year-end (person)	# 女性 Female
总计	**Total**	**278**	**18080**	**4017**	**12844**	**5045**
民政部门办	Run by Civil Administration	9	2546	878	2469	630
社会福利机构	Social Welfare Homes	5	1040	359	997	133
儿童福利机构	Welfare Homes for Children	2	906	149	862	331
社会福利医院	Social Welfare Hospital	2	600	370	610	166
社会办	Run by Society	269	15534	3139	10375	4415
城镇老年福利机构	Urban Seni Welfare	145	12158	2592	8248	3960
农村老年福利机构	Rural Homes	124	3376	547	2127	455

19-15 社会救济情况(2003-2006年) BASIC STATISTICS OF SOCIAL RELIEF FUNDS, 2003-2006

指标 Item	2003	2004	2005	2006
社会救济总人数(人)				
Total Persons Receiving Relief Funds (person)	**273627**	**239834**	**182696**	**192916**
#城镇居民最低生活保障人数				
Urban Persons Receiving Lowest Cost-of-living	241308	205118	150821	151275
#在职人员				
On-post Staff and Workers	10933	6038	4246	3875
下岗人员				
Laid-off Staff and Workers	37381	18618	11442	10052
退休人员				
Retired	4768	2886	2486	2133
失业人员				
Unemployed	61121	43107	37464	39511
“三无人员”				
"Non-Three" persons	2205	2816	3857	5219
农村居民最低生活保障人数				
Rural Persons Receiving Lowest Cost-of-living	26140	28954	31875	37280
临时救济人次数(人次)				
Total Persons Receiving Temporary Almsgiving (person-times)	**118987**	**84624**	**88700**	**44472**
城市临时救济人次数				
Urban Persons Receiving Temporary Almsgiving	76577	38667	44244	7113
农村临时救济人次数				
Rural Persons Receiving Temporary Almsgiving	42410	45957	44456	37359
社会救济费(万元)				
Relief Funds (10 000 yuan)	**33499**	**36128**	**47176**	**69244**
#农村低保费				
Rural Relief Funds	1036	1310	1336	1751
城镇低保费				
Urban Relief Funds	22187	24743	26680	32914
精简退职老职工救济费				
Relief for Old Staff and Workers Reduced and Discharged	487	505	696	839
自然灾害救济费(万元)				
Relief for Natural Disasters (10 000 yuan)	**1745**	**1721**	**1170**	**1203**

19-16 优抚事业单位情况(2003-2006)
SITUATION OF ADMINISTRATION AGENCIES FOR MARTYRS, 2003-2006

指　标	Item	2003	2004	2005	2006
优抚对象(人)	**Martyrs and Disabled Veterans (person)**	**25413**	**24582**	**24521**	**24653**
烈　属	Members of Revolutionary Martyr's Family	882	830	799	757
因公牺牲病故军人家属	Families of Soldiers Sacrificed or Died of Illness	454	444	450	435
革命伤残人员	Revolutionary Disabled	7106	7094	7251	7032
在乡红军老战士	Demobilized Old Red Army Men in Hometown	2	2	2	1
在乡复员军人	Demobilized Soldiers in Hometown	7927	7621	7436	6982
在乡退伍军人	Veterans in Hometown	4669	4758	4693	5642
城镇义务兵	Urban Voluntary Soldiers	4373	3833	3890	3804
优抚对象补助金额(万元)	**Funds for Family Members of Martyrs and Disabled Veterans (10 000 yuan)**	**5715**	**5757**	**5878**	**8756**
国家支出	Government Funds	3809	4014	4232	6764
集体供给	Collective Funds	1906	1743	1646	1992
抚恤事业费(万元)	Pensions (10 000 yuan)	8472	9068	12879	15326

19-17 城镇社区服务情况(2003-2006年)
BASIC STATISTICS ON URBAN COMMUNITY SERVICE, 2003-2006

指　标	Item	2003	2004	2005	2006
城镇社区服务设施数(个)	Number of Urban Welfare Facilities (unit)	1913	1976	2139	2166
#星光老年之家	to Agedness	342	445	482	483
社区从业人员(万人)	Persons Employed in Community (10 000 persons)	2	10	10	10
#安置下岗人员	Placement of Laid-off Staff and Workers	1	1	2	2
社区服务志愿者人数(万人)	Number of Service Volunteers in Community (10 000 persons)	30	33	36	34
便民利民服务网点(个)	Urban Service Points for Civilian (unit)	8373	9476	8907	8833
城镇社区服务中心	Urban Community Service Centers				
单位数(个)	Number of Units (unit)	105	108	111	101
年末职工人数(人)	Number of Staff and Workers Year-end (person)	792	821	920	888
活动项目数(个)	Number of Project Activities (unit)	797	867	918	978
#老年人活动	Senile	183	213	238	366
家务劳动服务	Housework Service	312	325	324	228
活动人次(人次)	Number of Persons Coming to Center (person-times)	594781	673304	568796	519504
#老年人活动	Senile	268925	368844	368467	395740

19-18 老年事业基本情况(2004-2006年) SENILE CITIZEN UNDERTAKINGS 2004-2006

指　标	Item	2004	2005	2006
老年法律援助中心(个)	Senial legal aid Center (unit)			188
涉老案件数(件)	Senial Case (case)	1330	4906	5549
维权协调组织数(个)	Safeguard and Mediation Organization (unit)			2097
老年活动站、中心、室(个)	Senial Activity Station, Center, Room (unit)	2522	2570	2514
老年人参与活动人数(万人)	Senial Activity Participant (10 000 person)			36.91
老年医院(个)	Hospital for Senile (unit)	108	88	29
老年医院病床数(张)	Senile Sick Beds in Hospital (bed)			1578
老年人协会个数(个)	Senile Union (unit)	3710	3643	3741
老年基金会个数(个)	Senile Fund (unit)	6	6	4
老年事业投入经费(万元)	Expenditures for Senile (10 000 yuan)	11	10	967
老年学校个数(个)	Senile School (unit)	600	635	372
老年学校在校人数(万人)	Students Enrollment in Senile School (10 000 person)	7.84	1055	12.96
享受高龄补贴的老年人数(人)	Citizen with Senial subsidy (person)			11182

资料来源：天津市民政局。
Sources: Tianjin Civil Affairs Bureau.

19-19 残疾人事业基本情况(2006年) BASIC INFORMATION OF PEOPLE WITH DISABILITIES, 2006

单位：人、个 (person, unit)

项　目	Item	2006
白内障复明手术(例)	Sight-Rrestoring Cataract Surgeries (case)	5800
低视力配用助视器	Vision-aids Provided for Individuals with Low-vision	313
综合防治康复精神病人数	Prevention and Treatment of Psychiatric Diseases	58487
监护率(%)	Guardianship Rate of Psychiatric Diseases (%)	98.3
显好率(%)	Significant Improvement Rate of Psychiatric Diseases (%)	76.3
参与率(%)	Social Involvement Rate of Psychiatric Diseases (%)	65.9
肢体残疾康复训练数	Function Training Provided to Persons with Physical Disabiligy	1416
#肢体残疾儿童机构康复训练数	# Rehabilitation Training Provided to Physical Disabled Children	223
肢体残疾人社区、家庭康复训练数	Rehabilitation Training Provided to Handicappeds in Communities and Families	1193
贫困智力残疾儿童训练数	Rehabilitation Training Provided to Poor Children with Intellectual Disability	288
残疾人中等职业教育机构数	Handicappeds Middle Vocational Education Facilities	3
残疾人中等职业教育在校学生数	Students Enrollment in Handicappeds Middle Vocational Education Facilities	90
残疾人职业技术培训机构数	Handicappeds Vocational Education and Training Facilities	3
残疾人职业培训人数(人次)	Number of Handicappeds Educated and Trained (person-times)	5052
当年安排城镇残疾人就业	Employment of Urban Handicappeds in the Year	7998
集中安排就业	Employed at Welfare Enterprises	418
按比例安排就业	Employed by Quota Scheme	6788
个体就业	Self-employed	792
农村残疾人就业人数	Employment of Rural Handicapped	47862
残疾人就业服务机构	Employment Placement Service Facilities for Disabled Jobseekers	19
享受城乡低保的残疾人数	Enjoy the Urban Lowest Cost-of-living Subsidizes of Handicapped	29047
各级残联实有人员数	Staff and Workers of Disabled Persons Federations	776

资料来源：天津市残疾人联合会。
Sources: Tianjin Disabled Persons Federation.

主要统计指标解释

卫生技术人员　指卫生事业机构支付工资的全部固定职工和合同制职工中现任职务为卫生技术工作的人员。包括中医师、西医师、中西医结合高级医师、护师、中药师、西药师、检验师、其他技师、中医士、西医士、护士、助产士、中药剂士、西药剂士、检验士、其他技士、其他中医、护理员、中药剂员、西药剂员、检验员和其他初级卫生技术人员。不包括从事管理工作的卫生技术人员。

执业（助理）医师　指持有执业（助理）医师证书，并从事医疗卫生工作的人员。

妇幼保健经费　包括妇幼保健机构经费、业务费、妇幼医疗减免费等。

计划生育事业费　包括九个部分，即计划生育手术减免经费、避孕药具经费、基层计划生育专职干部经费、独生子女保健费、宣传经费、服务站经费、流动人口计划生育管理费、干部培训费、其他计划生育事业费。

婴儿死亡率　指一年内未满周岁死亡的婴儿数与当年活产数之比。计算公式为：

婴儿死亡率 =（一年内未满周岁的婴儿死亡数 / 当年活产数）×1000‰

5岁以下儿童死亡率　指一年内未满5岁儿童死亡人数与当年活产数之比。计算公式为：

5岁以下儿童死亡率 =（一年内未满5岁儿童死亡数 / 当年活产数）×1000‰

孕产妇死亡率　指年内孕产妇死亡人数与活产数之比。孕产妇死亡一般指从妊娠开始至产后42天内死亡者，包括外科原因、计划生育手术、宫外孕、葡萄胎死亡者，但不包括意外原因死亡者。

卡介苗、脊灰疫苗、百白破三联制剂、麻疹疫苗接种率　指按照儿童免疫程度进行合格接种的人数占全部应接种人数的百分比。应接种人数包括禁忌症人数和外地寄居3个月及以上的适龄人数，不包括外出3个月及以上的适龄人数。计算公式为：

单项疫苗接种率 =（合格接种该疫苗人数 / 应接种人数）×100%

分子：按"合格接种判断"标准，判定当年实际完成合格接种的儿童数。

分母：按免疫程序规定当年应在12月龄内完成该项疫苗接种的儿童数。

5岁以下儿童中、重度营养不良患病率　指年内5岁以下儿童中，患中度和重度营养不良的儿童数与全部5岁以下儿童数之比。

7岁以下儿童保健管理率　指年内7岁以下儿童中当年实际接受1次及以上儿童保健服务的人数与当地7岁以下儿童数之比。

监护率　指通过各种方式得到有效监护的精神病人数占全部精神病人总数的比重，计算公式为：

监护率 (%) =（监护人数 / 精神病人数）×100%

显好率　指经过采取有效的治疗康复措施，病情稳定，症状缓解的精神病人数占监护精神病人数的比重，计算公式为：

精神病人显好率 (%) =（显好人数 / 监护人数）×100%

参与率　指生活能自理、参加家务劳动、社会生产和社会活动的精神病人数占监护精神病人数的比重，计算公式为：

参与率 (%) =（参与社会人数 / 监护人数）×100%

Explanastory Notes on Main Statistical Indicators

Medical Technical Personnel refer to all medical staff and workers employed by medical institutions, including doctors of Chinese and Western medicine, senior doctors who integrate traditional Chinese therapeutics with Western therapeutics in practice, senior nurses, pharmacists of Chinese and Western medicine, laboratory specialists, other specialists, paramedics of Chinese and Western medicine, nurses, midwives, druggists in Chinese and Western medicine, laboratory technicians, other technicians, other practitioners of Chinese medicine, nursing attendants, pharmacological workers of Chinese and Western medicine, laboratory workers, and other primary medical personnel, excluding management personnel.

Certified Physician (certified assistant physician) refer to personnel with certifications working in health care institutions.

Expenses for Maternity and Child Care include expenses for maternity and child care institutions, business cost, relief or free medicine for maternity and child, etc..

Operating Expenses for Family Planning include nine components: namely, expenses for relief or free family planning operation, expenses for birth control medicine & tools, expenses for family planning employee, health care expenses for only son and daughter, expenses for publicity, expenses for service station, expenses for family planning management of fluid population, expenses for personnel training, other operation expenses for family planning.

The Death Rate of Infant refers to the ratio of the number of dead infant below 1 year to the number of living in one year. The following formula is used:

The death rate of infant=(number of dead infant/number of living)×1000‰

The Death Rate of Baby Below 5 year-old refers to the ratio of the number of dead baby below 5 to the living number. The following formula is used:

The death rate of baby below 5 year-old=(number of dead baby bellow 5 /number of living)×1000‰

The Death Rate of Pregnant Woman refers to the ratio of the number of dead pregnant woman to the living number. The death of pregnant woman usually refers from gestation to die after give birth to child in 42 days, including surgery reason, family planning operation, pregnancy outside the womb, grape embryo dead women, excluding die due to accident trouble.

The Rate of Vaccine Inoculation of Bcg Vaccine, Poliomyelitis, Pertussis and Measles refers to the ratio of the number of children inoculating vaccine to the children on the age to inoculate vaccine. The children on the age to inoculate vaccine include the children avoiding inoculating vaccine and living in some other place for 3 and more than 3 months, but exclude the children on age going out for 3 months. The following formula is used:

The rate of vaccine inoculation=(the number of children inoculating vaccine / the children on the age to inoculate vaccine)×100%

The molecule: the actual number of children inoculating vaccine according to the standard of vaccine inoculation.

The denominator: the number of children according to the process of immunity should inoculate the vaccine in 12 months.

The Ratio of Innutritious Child below 5 year-old refers to the ratio of the number of children below five-year old have modest and heavy innutrition to the total number of children below 5.

The Ratio of Health Care and Management of Child below 7 year-old refers to the ratio of the number of children below 7 year-old who take child health care serves more than 1 time to the total number of local children below 7 year-old.

Guardianship Rate refers to the ratio of psychiatric patients under effective guardianship through various ways to total psychiatric patients.

Guardianship Rate=(psychiatric patients under effective guardianship / total psychiatric patients)×100%

Significant Improvement Rate refers to the ratio of psychiatric patients with significant improvement after treatments to psychiatric patients under effective guardianship.

Significant Improvement Rate=(psychiatric patients with significant improvement / psychiatric patients under guardianship) ×100%

Social Involvement Rate refers to the ratio of psychiatric patients who are self-sufficiency and are able to participate in the housework and social activities to psychiatric patients under effective guardianship.

Social Involvement Rate = (psychiatric patients with social involvement / psychiatric patients under guardianship) × 100%

第20篇
CHAPTER 20

公共管理和社会组织
Public Management and Social Organizations

20-1 检察机关立案侦察经济案件情况（2006年）
ECONOMIC CASES UNDER INVESTIGATION BY PROCURATORIAL OFFICES, 2006

项目 Item	侦查经济案件 Economic Cases Investigated	#贪污 Corruption	#挪用公款 Misappropriate Public Funds	#贿赂案 Bribery	#受贿 Accepting Bribe
立案(件)					
Cases Registered (case)	**385**	**193**	**84**	**98**	**74**
#5万元至10万元					
50-100 thousand yuan	145	96	3	46	36
10万元至50万元					
100-500 thousand yuan	127	46	53	28	17
50万元至100万元					
500-1000 thousand yuan	32	15	11	3	3
100万元以上					
Over 1000 thousand yuan	33	5	15	6	3
犯罪嫌疑人(人)					
Criminal in Cases Registered (person)	**413**	**209**	**90**	**104**	**76**
机关工作人员					
Civil Servant	48	15	9	20	18
国有公司企业工作人员					
Personnel of State-owned Enterprises	223	128	50	40	38
国有事业单位工作人员					
Personnel of State-owned Institutions	53	31	7	14	12
委派到非国有单位从事公务人员					
Functionary Appointed to Non-state Units					
人民团体从事公务人员					
Functionary Appointed to Mass Organizations					
其他依法从事公务人员					
Other Personnel Line of Duty	54	25	21	8	8
其他					
Others	35	10	3	22	
结案					
Cases Settled					
件数(件)					
Number of Cases (case)	350	174	86	86	70
人数(人)					
Number of Persons (person)	369	185	91	89	72
#移送起诉					
Hand over to Suit					
件数(件)					
Number of Cases (case)	322	165	78	76	65
人数(人)					
Number of Persons (person)	341	176	83	79	67
撤销案件					
Cases Withdrawed					
件数(件)					
Number of Cases (case)	22	7	8	6	1
人数(人)					
Number of Persons (person)	22	7	8	6	1
侦结认定金额(万元)					
Value Approved by Procuratorial Organs in Cases Settled (10 000 yuan)	54033.51	7130.35	45659.89	956.47	732.3
挽回经济损失(万元)					
Retrieve Pecuniary Losses (10 000 yuan)	7531.53	3334.23	3677	520.3	496.7

20-2 法院民事案件收案和结案情况（2006年）
CASES ACCEPTED & SETTLED BY COURTS, 2006

单位：件 (case)

项目	Item	收案 Cases Accepted	结案 Cases Settled	#调解 Mediation	#判决 Judgement
合同纠纷案件	**Contracts Disputes**	**43697**	**44906**	**8509**	**21419**
#买卖合同纠纷	Buying and Selling Contracts	8583	8763	2015	4151
房地产合同纠纷	Real Estate Contracts	1289	1381	203	877
借款合同纠纷	Debts Contracts	7869	8041	1701	4505
建设工程合同纠纷	Construction Project Contracts	1339	1348	321	666
运输合同纠纷	Transportation Contracts	419	418	99	207
婚姻家庭案件	**Marriages and Family Affairs**	**12454**	**12559**	**4717**	**5060**
#离婚	Divorce	10093	10169	3902	4031
抚育	Foster	655	677	222	301
赡养	Support	610	612	150	290
继承纠纷案件	**Inheritance Disputes**	**388**	**403**	**112**	**191**
继承	Inheritance	190	204	54	103
遗嘱	Testaments	11	8	2	5
继承权	Inheritance Right	12	14	3	8
抚养	Bring-up	2	3	1	1
其他	Others	173	174	52	74

20-3 法院行政案件收案和结案情况（2006年）
ADMINISTRATIVE CASES ACCEPTED AND SETTLED BY COURTS, 2006

单位：件 (case)

项目	Item	收案 Cases Accepted	结案 Cases Settled	#维持 Affirmation of Original Judgement	#撤消 Cancel Settled	#撤诉 Withdraw	未结 Cases Unsettled
合计	**Total**	**1437**	**1302**	**402**	**44**	**362**	**277**
公安	Public Security	118	115	43	8	33	18
资源	Resources	88	81	25	5	18	23
城建	City Construction	923	786	272	9	208	200
工商	Industry and Commerce	18	18	2	4	6	6
技术监督	Technology Supervision	5	5		2	2	
计划生育	Family Planning	7	6	1			1
卫生	Health Care	6	10	5		2	1
药品	Medicine	1	2			1	
农业	Agriculture	1	1		1		
环保	Environment Protection	9	9			5	
交通	Transportation	22	24	3		8	1
税务	Tax	3	3	3			
金融	Finance	1	1			1	
外贸	Commerce	1	1			1	
劳动和社会保险	Labour & Social Security	81	83	24	10	24	3
烟草专卖	Tobacco	4	4			2	
司法行政	Judicature		2				
民政	Civil Affairs	10	10	2		5	1
教育	Education	8	8	6		1	
文化	Culture	1					1
乡政府	Township Government	4	4		2		
其他	Others	126	129	16	3	45	22

20-4 调解工作基本情况（2003-2006年）
BASIC STATISTICS ON MEDIATION, 2003-2006

项 目 Item	单 位 Unit	2003	2004	2005	2006
司法助理员 Judicial Assistants	人 person	585	645	589	551
人民调解委员会 People's Mediation Committees	个 unit	6136	6428	5984	5837
调解民间纠纷 Civil Disputes	件 case	25377	29785	30647	30000
调解成功 Success	件 case	24583	28814	29699	28650
防止民事案件转化为刑事案件	件 case	57	84	127	168
Prevent Intensification of Civil Disputes	人 person	243	316	787	898
防止非正常死亡案件	件 case	27	45	34	29
Avoid Injuries and Deaths	人 person	34	55	42	40

20-5 律师工作基本情况（2003-2006年）
BASIC STATISTICS ON LAWYERS, 2003-2006

项 目 Item	单 位 Unit	2003	2004	2005	2006
律师事务所 Law Offices	所 unit	210	223	239	242
职业律师 Lawyers	人 person	1729	1816	1856	1967
# 专职律师 Full-time Lawyers	人 person	1618	1705	1722	1821
兼职律师 Part-time Lawyers	人 person	111	111	134	146
聘请常年法律顾问的单位 Units with Permanent Legal Advisers	个 unit	6026	4582	4657	4625
民事代理 Civil Case	件 case	10632	12011	13156	12766
经济代理 Economic Case	件 case	6084	5454	5641	5713
刑事辩护 Criminal Defense	件 case	3619	3380	4040	3518
行政诉讼代理 Agent of Administrative Action	件 case	372	634	539	409
非诉讼事务 Off-court Case	件 case	17621	24396	20277	12552
解答法律咨询 Legal Advisory Services	人次 person-times	23774	27900	22718	35561
代写法律文书 Legal Document Written on Behalf of Clients	件 case	7966	8144	8463	9457

20-6 主要年份公证工作基本情况
BASIC STATISTICS ON NOTARIZATION IN MAIN YEARS

单位：件 (case)

项目	Item	1995	2000	2005	2006
公证机构(个)	**Notary Offices (unit)**	**20**	**20**	**21**	**21**
公证员(人)	**Notarial Personnel (person)**	**286**	**278**	**267**	**245**
办理公证(件)	**Notarized Documents (case)**	**111811**	**175486**	**149483**	**145171**
国内公证总计	**Domestic Affairs Total**	**82316**	**107198**	**91454**	**80532**
民事公证	**Civil Legal Relations Notarized**	**35055**	**37249**	**46455**	**50627**
#收 养	Children Adoption	398	172	57	58
解除收养	Adoption Renouncements	44	3	1	2
继承权	Rights of Inheritance	2378	3526	6228	5688
遗 嘱	Testaments	804	1606	906	1109
亲属关系	Kinship Confirmation	252	429	812	2763
房屋买卖	Purchases and Sales of House	660	2926	3420	3051
房屋租赁	House Leases	198	12	428	113
委托书	Certificate of Entrustment	874	1463	16534	14750
赠予书	Presentation Documents	3334	2453	1072	1555
声明书	Declarations	642	2390	2440	3844
经济公证	**Business Notarized**	**47261**	**69949**	**44999**	**29905**
#购 销	Purchases and Sales of Contracts	485	38	74	164
联 营	Joint Ownership Contracts	42	3	450	
贷 款	Loans Contracts	16572	44570	15564	5398
招标投标	Bidding	227	385	915	951
劳务合同	Labour Contracts	1660	426		11
建筑工程承包	Construction Project Contracts	521	178	475	409
农林牧副渔业承包	Farming, Forestry, Animal Husbandry, Sideline	492	783	60	41
财产租赁	Property Leases	2831	620	2056	1761
法人资格	Legal Person Identification	782	153	19	101
法人委托书	Legal Person Certificate of Entrustment	303	401	3094	1177
涉外公证总计	**Foreign Affairs Total**	**29495**	**67803**	**58029**	**64639**
#出 生	Births	4254	11308	7703	8770
学 历	Schooling	5632	11919	6393	7305
经 历	Personal Histories	1845	2517	660	770
生存、居住	Survial and Residence		89	41	326
死 亡	Deaths		120	112	147
亲属关系	Kinship	2011	5313	5023	5768
婚姻状况	Marriages	3056	5067	2360	2460
继承权	Rights of Inheritance		3		
委托书	Trust Deeds		244	539	670
声明书	Declarations		450	980	1089
受、未受刑事处分	Criminal Reords & Uncriminal Records	3444	9131	7014	6707
文本相符	Confirmation of Copies and Photo-Offset Copies to Originals	581	7445	3971	3966
其 他	Others	2241	3411	10734	12120

20-7 基层工会组织情况(2003-2006年) STATISTICS ON GRASSROOTS UNIONS, 2003-2006

项　目	Item	2003	2004	2005	2006
机构数(个)	**Institutions (unit)**	**12440**	**15980**	**16199**	**20917**
# 国有企业	State-owned Enterprises	2278	2377	2112	1961
集体企业	Collective-owned Enterprises	1862	1933	1722	1496
私营企业	Private Enterprises	1726	4456	4542	6318
港澳台商投资企业	Enterprises with Investment from Hong Kong, Macao and Taiwan	162	236	219	493
外商投资企业	Foreign Funded Enterprises	1215	528	555	2211
事　业	Institutions	2979	3353	3505	3623
机　关	Agencies	902	909	1055	1134
# 建立职代会制度的单位	Unit of Founding Employee Congress System	5415	5682	5216	5434
职工人数(人)	**Staff and Workers (person)**	**1984048**	**2612680**	**2766620**	**3104406**
# 女职工	Female	798939	905524	921897	1053061
# 工会专职干部	Full-time Personnel	970	930	915	1285
# 国有企业	State-owned Enterprises	805061	857775	869485	826318
集体企业	Collective-owned Enterprises	251563	306914	236108	239074
私营企业	Private Enterprises	125662	311062	366225	452517
港澳台商投资企业	Enterprises with Investment from Hong Kong, Macao and Taiwan	16026	41656	41802	56746
外商投资企业	Foreign Funded Enterprises	119011	142305	163375	383654
事　业	Institutions	321334	364608	394196	431024
机　关	Agencies	85860	94330	98276	103016

20-8 妇联组织情况(2003-2006年) STATISTICS FOR WOMEN'S FEDERATION ORGANIZATIONS, 2003-2006

项　目	Item	2003	2004	2005	2006
妇联组织机构(个)	**Woman Organizations (unit)**	**253**	**248**	**246**	**275**
区妇联	District Woman Organizations	15	15	15	15
县妇联	County Woman Organizations	3	3	3	3
乡妇联	Township Woman Organizations	140	141	140	140
街妇联	Street Woman Organizations	95	89	88	117
妇联干部总数(人)	**Cadres in Woman Organizations (person)**	**484**	**544**	**510**	**502**
市妇联	Municipal Woman Organizations	66	64	60	61
区妇联	District Woman Organizations	119	115	110	121
县妇联	County Woman Organizations	22	23	20	17
乡镇、街道妇联	Township and Street Woman Organizations	277	342	320	303

20-9 妇联工作情况（2003-2006年）WOMEN'S FEDERATION WORK, 2003-2006

项目 Item	单位 Unit	2003	2004	2005	2006
双学双比活动					
Double Study And Double Compare Activity					
实用技术培训情况					
Training of Practical Technology					
接受技术培训的妇女数					
Women Received Technology Training	人 person	152426	136421	210049	190019
女农民技术员					
Female Peasant Technicians	人 person	3010	3307	2195	3597
获绿色证书人数					
Persons Obtaining Green Certificate	人 person	4166	3669	18958	20389
扶贫情况					
Poverty Helping					
"三八"绿色基地个数					
Number of "3.8" Green Base	个 unit	88	43	17	50
脱贫户数					
Number of Female of Escaping from Poverty	人 person	3086	3180	1144	1690
巾帼建功活动					
Activity of Women Making Contribution					
岗位建功成才					
Making Professional Contribution					
评选巾帼文明示范岗数					
Number of Civilization Post Chosen	个 unit	132	91	144	246
表彰标兵数					
Number of Prised Pacesetter	人 person	2325	2345	225	211
下岗女工再就业情况					
Reemployment of Laid-off Female Workers					
培训下岗女工人数					
Laid-off Trained	人 person	19431	25707	21734	21066
介绍下岗女工就业人数					
Laid-off Introduced to Employ	人 person	5835	21944	19750	11766
"三八"红旗手					
3.8 Advanced Individual	人 person	554	1314	624	1067
"三八"红旗集体					
3.8 Advanced Collectivity	个 unit	140	284	212	262
五好文明家庭					
Five Good Families	户 household	41256	38167	41858	2057
家庭教育场所					
Families Educational Places					
家长学校					
Householder School	个 unit	2034	2187	2513	2782
广播电视父母学校					
Broadcasting Parents School	个 unit	162	98	188	193
实施春蕾计划					
Actualizing Spring Bud Project					
资助女童入学或返校数					
Supporting Female Children Entering School	人 person	1278	1367	1925	1157
社会捐资总额					
Total of Social Donation	万元 10 000 yuan	80	226	143	84

20-10 受理消费者投诉情况(2006)
BASIC STATISTICS ON ACCEPTED CASES OF CONSUMER INSTITUTION, 2006

项　目	Item	总计 Total	质量 Quality	安全 Safety	价格 Price	计量 Measure
受理投诉件数总计(件)	**Total Number of Accepted Cases (item)**	**4247**	**3455**	**95**	**142**	**20**
家用电子电器类	Household Electric Appliance	1545	1435	2	18	
电视机	Television Set	215	200	1	1	
家庭影院	Household Cinema	13	10			
空调器类产品	Air-conditioner	140	128	1	2	
洗衣机类产品	Washing Machine	31	27			
电冰箱(冰柜)	Refrigerator (Freezer)	78	77			
厨房电器及相关产品	Kitchen Electric Appliances and Relative Products	103	93		2	
照摄像产品	Camera and DV	25	22			
通讯类产品	Telecommunications Products	816	773		10	
计算机类产品	Computer Series	53	48			
#计算机	Computer	42	39			
其　他	Others	71	57		3	
家用机械类	Household Machinery	335	296	6	6	
汽　车	Car	71	57		3	
摩托车	Motorcycle	36	35			
热水器	Water Heater	126	118	1	1	
其　他	Others	102	86	5	2	
百货类	Daily Using Commodities	1237	1050	34	40	8
#化妆用品	Cosmetic	24	19	1		
保健用品	Health Care Goods	37	29	2	1	
家俱类产品	Furniture	183	145	1	19	3
服装鞋帽	Garments, Shoes & Hats	530	511		5	
保健食品	Health Care Food Stuff	18	11	2	1	
药　品	Medicine	20	9	5	1	
医疗辅助用品	Medical Treatment Articles	8	4		1	
房屋及装修建材	House and Decoration Materials	273	214	2	2	7
#房　屋	House	73	48	2		1
装饰材料	Decoration Materials	175	152		2	3
农用生产资料类	Agricultural Production Materials	44	42			
#种子苗木、化肥	Seed, Young Plant, Chemical Fertilizer	22	22			
服务类	Service	756	391	46	72	3
#美容、美发、洗浴	Hairdressing and Wash	83	53	8	12	
电　信	Telecommunications	113	59		41	2
邮　政	Posts	16	5	2		
洗衣业	Laundry	110	90	9	1	
旅　游	Tourism	18	10	3	1	
房屋装修与物业管理	Building Decoration and Property Management	53	33	4	2	
咨询中介	Consulting Agent	56	17		6	
其他商品类	Other Commodities	57	27	5	4	2
解决件数总计(件)	**Total Cases Solved (item)**	**4247**				
为消费者挽回损失(万元)	**Exempting Expense for Consumers (10 000 yuan)**	**493.9**				

注：本资料为天津市消费者协会系统的统计数据，不含各监测站的统计资料。
Note: The data of this table are provided by Tianjin Municipal Consumer Institution, exclude those data calculated by each monitor station.

20-10 续表 Continued

项　　目	Item	广　告 Advertise-ment	假　冒 Counter-feit	营销合同 Business Contract	其　他 Others
受理投诉件数总计(件)	**Total Number of Accepted Cases (item)**	**31**	**23**	**187**	**294**
家用电子电器类	Household Electric Appliance	7	10	19	54
电视机	Television Set			5	8
家庭影院	Household Cinema	1			2
空调器类产品	Air-conditioner	1		2	6
洗衣机类产品	Washing Machine				4
电冰箱(冰柜)	Refrigerator (Freezer)				1
厨房电器及相关产品	Kitchen Electric Appliances and Relative Products	1		2	5
照摄像产品	Camera and DV	1			2
通讯类产品	Telecommunications Products	1	8	9	15
计算机类产品	Computer Series	1		1	3
# 计算机	Computer			1	2
其　他	Others	1	2		8
家用机械类	Household Machinery	1	1	6	19
汽　车	Car			2	9
摩托车	Motorcycle				1
热水器	Water Heater			3	3
其　他	Others	1	1	1	6
百货类	Daily Using Commodities	9	10	19	67
# 化妆用品	Cosmetic			2	2
保健用品	Health Care Goods		4		1
家俱类产品	Furniture		1	8	6
服装鞋帽	Garments, Shoes & Hat		3		11
保健食品	Health Care Food Stuff	2		1	1
药　品	Medicine	1			4
医疗辅助用品	Medical Treatment Articles		1	1	1
房屋及装修建材	House and Decoration Materials	1	1	29	17
# 房　屋	House			16	6
装饰材料	Decoration Materials	1	1	9	7
农用生产资料类	Agricultural Production Materials				2
# 种子苗木、化肥	Seed, Young Plant, Chemical Fertilizer				
服务类	Service	12	1	112	119
# 美容、美发、洗浴	Hairdressing and Wash			3	7
电　信	Telecommunications	1		10	
邮　政	Posts			7	2
洗衣业	Laundry			4	6
旅　游	Tourism			3	1
房屋装修与物业管理	Building Decoration and Property Management			8	6
咨询中介	Consulting Agent	7		21	5
其他商品类	Other Commodities	1		2	16
解决件数总计(件)	**Total Cases Solved (item)**				
为消费者挽回损失(万元)	**Exempting Expense for Consumers (10 000 yuan)**				

20-11 劳动争议处理情况
THE DISPOSAL OF LABOR DISPUTES

单位：件 (case)

项　目　Item	2005	2006
上期未结案数　Number of Cases Left Over from Last Period	**244**	**596**
案件受理情况　Cases Accepted		
当期案件受理数 Number of Cases	4210	5682
#集体劳动争议数 Number of Collective Labor Disputes	82	109
#劳动者申诉案件数 Number of Cases Appealed by Laborers	4139	5628
劳动者当事人数(人) Number of Persons Involved (person)	6096	8188
#集体争议劳动者当事人数 Number of Persons Involved in Collective Disputes	1942	2549
争议原因 Cause of the Disputes		
变更劳动合同 Change the Labor Contract	7	55
解除劳动合同 Relieve the Labor Contract	310	401
终止劳动合同 End the Labor Contract	128	303
其　他 Others	3765	4923
案件处理情况　Cases Settled		
结案数 Number of Cases Settled	3858	5360
按处理方式分 by Manners of Settlement		
仲裁调解 by Mediation	757	1307
仲裁裁决 by Arbitration Lawsuit	1530	2133
其他方式 Others	1571	1920
按处理结果分 by Results of Settlement		
用人单位胜诉 Won by Units	1730	1861
劳动者胜诉 Won by Labors	1532	2449
双方部分胜诉 Partly by Both Parties	596	1050
本期未结案数　Number of Cases Dissettled	**596**	**918**

资料来源：天津市劳动和社会保障局、民政局。
Sources: Tianjin Municipal Labour & Social Insurance Bureau and Civil Affairs Bureau.

20-12 天津市历届人代会代表人数性别构成及议案、批评建议数

NUMBER OF DELEGACY AND PROPOSAL AND SUGGESTION BY TIANJIN DEMOTIC CONGRESS

届 别	Mark Fall Due	代表人数(人) Number of Delegate (person)			性别比例 Sex Proportion (%)		议案立案数(件) Number of Cases Registered of Proposal (unit)	建议批评和意见(件) Given Criticism and Advice (unit)
		总 计 Total	女 性 Female	男 性 Male	女 性 Female	男 性 Male		
第一届	First Congress	519	109	410	21	79	1614	
第二届	Second Congress	568	122	446	21.48	78.52	1201	
第三届	Third Congress	535	110	425	20.56	79.44		
第四届	Fouth Congress	845	208	637	24.62	75.38	133	
第五届	Fifth Congress	675	169	506	25.04	74.96	104	
第六届	Sixth Congress	698	171	527	24.5	75.5	27	
第七届	Seventh Congress							
第八届	Eighth Congress	959	224	735	23.36	76.64		
第九届	Ninth Congress	960	175	785	18.23	81.77	1958	
第十届	Tenth Congress	800	179	621	22.38	77.62	26	5337
第十一届	Eleventh Congress	719	134	585	18.64	81.36	65	3762
第十二届	Twelveth Congress	719	130	589	18.08	81.92	34	1924
第十三届	Thirteenth Congress	710	141	569	19.86	80.14	80	3597
第十四届	Fourteenth Congress	710	150	560	21.13	78.87	83	3147

注：1. 资料来源天津市人民代表大会常务委员会。2. 天津市第一届至第九届人民代表大会期间代表所提出的议案、建议统称为"提案"。

Note: a) Sources:Tianjin Municipal People's Congress(BMPC) Standing Committee. b) The Registered Cases and Advice Proposed from Tianjin First Congress until Ninth Congress are calculated to Proposals as total.

20-13 天津市历届政协委员会委员人数及提案立案数

NUMBER OF DELEGACY, PROPOSAL AND PUT ON RECORD BY TIANJIN POLITICAL CONSULTATIVE CONFERENCE

单位：人、件 (person, unit)

届 别	Mark Fall Due	起止年月 The Time of Inaugural and Concluding	委员人数 Number of Commissary			提案立案数 Number of Resolution Put on Record
			总 计 Total	女 性 Female	男 性 Male	
第一届	First Congress	1955.3-1960.3	188	42	146	
第二届	Second Congress	1960.3-1963.12	498	76	422	
第三届	Third Congress	1963.12-1965.11	432	73	359	
第四届	Fouth Congress	1965.11-1977.11	457	81	376	
第五届	Fifth Congress	1977.11-1980.6	615	132	483	
第六届	Sixth Congress	1980.6-1983.3	723	142	581	5028
第七届	Seventh Congress	1983.3-1988.4	739	162	577	4410
第八届	Eighth Congress	1988.4-1993.5	743	177	566	4869
第九届	Ninth Congress	1993.5-1998.5	757	179	578	3800
第十届	Tenth Congress	1998.5-2003.1	780	185	595	4563
第十一届	Eleventh Congress	2003.1-至今	780	200	580	5181

资料来源：中国人民政治协商会议天津市委员会。

Sources: The Chinese People's Political Consultative Conference Tianjin Committee.

主要统计指标解释

律师 指依法取得律师执业证书，担任法律顾问，民事（刑事、行政）案件代理人、刑事案件辩护人、办理非诉讼业务，解答法律询问，代写法律事务文书等，为社会提供法律服务的人员。

公证人员 指在公证处工作的人员总称，包括公证处主任、副主任、公证员、公证员助理（助理公证员）和其他从事辅助性工作的人员。

办理公证文书 指公证处根据当事人申请，依照事实和法律，按照法定程序制作的，具有法律效力的司法证明文书。根据公证书用途和使用地，公证书分为国内公证书、国内经济公证书、涉外民事公证书、涉外经济公证书四类。

调解人员 指在人民调解委员会担负调解民间纠纷工作的人员，包括调解委员会的委员和调解小组的调解员。

调解民间纠纷 指调解委员会按照法律规定，根据自愿原则，用说服教育的方法调解民间发生的有关民事权利和义务争执的件数，包括调解成功数和调解未成功数。

Explanastory Notes on Main Statistical Indicators

Lawyers are certified legal workers according to law, and who are employed by legal counseling firms to act as legal advisers, agents in criminal or civil lawsuits, or defenders in criminal lawsuits, or to handle non-litigious legal affairs, to advise on matters of law or to write legal papers for others, and provide service to the public.

Notary Personnel refers to people working for notary offices including: directors, deputy director, notaries, assistant notaries, and other people providing assistance.

Notary Documents refer to the judicatory notary documents drawn up by the request of the party and are in accordance with facts and laws and following certain legal proceedings. According to usage and locality, the notary documents are divided into following 4 types: domestic notary documents, domestic economic notary documents, foreign-related civil notary documents and foreign-related economic notary documents.

Mediators refer to workers on people mediation committees responsible for mediating in civil disputes and cases of slight infraction of the law. They include members of the mediation committees and mediators of mediation groups.

Mediation of Civil Disputes refers to number of cases made by mediation committees in mediating in civil disputes concerning civil rights and duties through persuasion and education in accordance with the provisions of law on a voluntary basis, so as to solve disputes by helping the parties involved come to an agreement and understanding, including those unsuccessful ones.

第21篇
CHAPTER 21

企业及企业集团
Enterprises and Enterprise Groups

21-1 企业集团主要财务指标（2006年）
MAIN FINANCIAL INDICATORS OF ENTERPRISE GROUPS, 2006

项　目	Item	企业数（个）Number of Enterprises (unit)	从业人员（人）Employment Personnel (person)	从业人员劳动报酬总额（亿元）Total Remuneration of Employ-ment Personnel (100 million yuan)
总　计	Total	166	502229	145.54
按集团审批部门分	**Grouped by Examining Department**			
国务院	The State Council	1	50414	12.31
国务院主管部门	Governing Departments of the State Council	2	53538	15.77
省级人民政府	Provincial People's Government	77	253227	73.76
省级人民政府主管部门	Governing Departments of the Provincial People's Government	31	84631	26.44
其　他	Others	55	60419	17.25
按控股情况分	**Grouped by Controlling Shares**			
国有控股	State-owned Holding	72	399338	127.17
集体控股	Collective-owned Holding	34	26822	3.83
私人控股	Personal-owned Holding	58	69484	13.80
外商控股	Foreign-owned Holding	2	6585	0.74
按主营行业分	**Grouped by Sector**			
第一产业	Primary Industry	2	5247	1.31
第二产业	Secondary Industry	84	346194	102.24
工　业	Industry	73	300388	91.26
#制造业	Manufacturing	70	251646	76.30
电力、燃气及水的生产和供应业	Production & Supply of Power, Gas and Water	2	12505	3.18
建筑业	Construction	11	45806	10.98
第三产业	Tertiary Industry	80	150788	41.99
交通运输、仓储和邮政业	Transportation, Storage and Post Services	9	45116	16.85
批发和零售业	Wholesale and Retail Trade	26	70103	12.66
住宿和餐饮业	Accommodation and Catering Services	3	3291	0.75
金融业	Finance Intermediation	1	116	0.03
房地产业	Real Estate	31	12938	2.82
租赁和商务服务业	Leasing and Business Services	8	17535	8.51
科学研究、技术服务和地质勘查业	Scientific Research, Technical Service and Geological Prospecting	1	1455	0.33
公共管理和社会组织	Public Management and Social Organizations	1	234	0.04
按登记注册类型分	**Grouped by Registered Categories**			
国有企业	State-owned Enterprises	7	16088	3.63
公司制企业	Sub-total	152	473882	139.36
国有独资企业	Sole State-funded Enterprises	51	311900	104.05
其他有限责任公司	Other Limited Liability Corporations	87	145088	32.82
股份有限公司	Share Holding Corporations Ltd.	9	8432	1.47
中外合资企业	Chinese-foreign Joint Venture Enterprise	2	6585	0.74
外商投资股份有限公司	Foreign Funded Share Holding Corporations Ltd.	1	251	0.08
港澳台合资企业	Hong Kong, Macao and Taiwan Joint Capital Enterprise	2	1626	0.19
其　他	Others	7	12259	2.55

注：本表统计范围为资产总计亿元以上企业集团。
Note: The data of this table refer to those enterprise groups with total assets of over 100 million yuan.

21-1 续表 1 Continued

单位：亿元 (100 million yuan)

项　目	Item	资产总计 Total Assets	固定资产净值 Net Value of Fixed Assets	流动资产年平均余额 Annual Average Balance of Circulating Funds
总　计	**Total**	**5793.26**	**1849.40**	**2515.97**
按集团审批部门分	**Grouped by Examining Department**			
国务院	The State Council	365.30	213.51	118.32
国务院主管部门	Governing Departments of the State Council	205.43	97.07	122.75
省级人民政府	Provincial People's Government	2764.80	764.23	1124.88
省级人民政府主管部门	Governing Departments of the Provincial People's Government	866.93	369.72	362.58
其　他	Others	1590.79	404.87	787.45
按控股情况分	**Grouped by Controlling Shares**			
国有控股	State-owned Holding	4833.71	1639.71	2099.97
集体控股	Collective-owned Holding	185.09	34.08	99.42
私人控股	Personal-owned Holding	708.58	143.48	316.59
外商控股	Foreign-owned Holding	65.87	32.13	0.00
按主营行业分	**Grouped by Sector**			
第一产业	Primary Industry	66.25	19.96	36.91
第二产业	Secondary Industry	2906.65	1117.72	1191.20
工　业	Industry	2654.04	1054.18	1030.43
# 制造业	Manufacturing	2394.82	903.30	924.68
电力、燃气及水的生产和供应业	Production & Supply of Power, Gas and Water	128.37	76.53	37.91
建筑业	Construction	252.61	63.54	160.78
第三产业	Tertiary Industry	2820.36	711.72	1287.86
交通运输、仓储和邮政业	Transportation, Storage and Post Services	390.61	209.29	80.20
批发和零售业	Wholesale and Retail Trade	622.98	146.74	357.01
住宿和餐饮业	Accommodation and Catering Services	11.14	7.40	4.64
金融业	Finance Intermediation	3.13	0.07	2.43
房地产业	Real Estate	599.78	35.88	285.38
租赁和商务服务业	Leasing and Business Services	1140.56	306.53	542.14
科学研究、技术服务和地质勘查业	Scientific Research, Technical Service and Geological Prospecting	45.50	4.92	11.33
公共管理和社会组织	Public Management and Social Organizations	6.66	0.89	4.73
按登记注册类型分	**Grouped by Registered Categories**			
国有企业	State-owned Enterprises	302.07	40.05	201.01
公司制企业	Sub-total	5224.62	1756.25	2284.23
国有独资企业	Sole State-funded Enterprises	3933.14	1395.15	1667.25
其他有限责任公司	Other Limited Liability Corporations	1152.46	312.23	579.19
股份有限公司	Share Holding Corporations Ltd.	53.11	11.97	26.53
中外合资企业	Chinese-foreign Joint Venture Enterprise	65.87	32.13	0.00
外商投资股份有限公司	Foreign Funded Share Holding Corporations Ltd.	11.25	2.26	8.82
港澳台合资企业	Hong Kong, Macao and Taiwan Joint Capital Enterprise	8.79	2.52	2.43
其　他	Others	266.56	53.10	30.73

21-1 续表 2 Continued

单位：亿元 (100 million yuan)

项目	Item	主营业务收入 Principal Business Revenue	利税总额 Total Pre-tax Profits	#利润总额 Total Profits
总计	**Total**	**3944.22**	**261.99**	**164.17**
按集团审批部门分	**Grouped by Examining Department**			
国务院	The State Council	254.10	10.76	2.73
国务院主管部门	Governing Departments of the State Council	214.57	10.39	0.19
省级人民政府	Provincial People's Government	1952.24	122.58	80.50
省级人民政府主管部门	Governing Departments of the Provincial People's Government	910.92	66.79	42.06
其他	Others	612.40	51.48	38.70
按控股情况分	**Grouped by Controlling Shares**			
国有控股	State-owned Holding	3235.11	204.47	126.16
集体控股	Collective-owned Holding	115.11	7.66	5.31
私人控股	Personal-owned Holding	562.96	48.75	31.78
外商控股	Foreign-owned Holding	31.03	1.11	0.92
按主营行业分	**Grouped by Sector**			
第一产业	Primary Industry	21.94	3.85	1.05
第二产业	Secondary Industry	2524.75	191.36	116.45
工业	Industry	2230.94	181.27	115.74
# 制造业	Manufacturing	2106.90	178.12	119.62
电力、燃气及水的生产和供应业	Production & Supply of Power, Gas and Water	43.66	-2.28	-4.06
建筑业	Construction	293.81	10.09	0.71
第三产业	Tertiary Industry	1397.54	66.78	46.68
交通运输、仓储和邮政业	Transportation, Storage and Post Services	131.89	14.93	11.65
批发和零售业	Wholesale and Retail Trade	900.93	4.87	-2.32
住宿和餐饮业	Accommodation and Catering Services	8.37	0.97	0.60
金融业	Finance Intermediation	0.12	-0.02	-0.02
房地产业	Real Estate	107.66	16.57	10.90
租赁和商务服务业	Leasing and Business Services	244.89	29.12	25.72
科学研究、技术服务和地质勘查业	Scientific Research, Technical Service and Geological Prospecting	1.90	-0.44	-0.51
公共管理和社会组织	Public Management and Social Organizations	1.78	0.78	0.67
按登记注册类型分	**Grouped by Registered Categories**			
国有企业	State-owned Enterprises	557.34	3.63	1.54
公司制企业	Sub-total	3162.95	252.13	159.44
国有独资企业	Sole State-funded Enterprises	2012.92	171.63	113.07
其他有限责任公司	Other Limited Liability Corporations	1088.39	76.22	43.13
股份有限公司	Share Holding Corporations Ltd.	26.01	2.58	1.89
中外合资企业	Chinese-foreign Joint Venture Enterprise	31.03	1.11	0.92
外商投资股份有限公司	Foreign Funded Share Holding Corporations Ltd.	2.65	0.42	0.28
港澳台合资企业	Hong Kong, Macao and Taiwan Joint Capital Enterprise	1.94	0.17	0.15
其他	Others	223.93	6.24	3.20

21-2 企业集团主要经济效益指标（2006年）
MAIN INDICATORS ON ECONOMIC EFFICIENCY OF ENTERPRISE GROUPS, 2006

单位：%（%）

项目	Item	资产负债率 Assets-Liability Ratio	净资产收益率 Earning Rate of Net Assets	资本保值增值率 Ratio of Maintenance or Addition of the Value of Assets
总计	**Total**	**65.5**	**6.3**	**131.5**
按集团审批部门分	**Grouped by Examining Department**			
国务院	The State Council	60.6	1.2	115.0
国务院主管部门	Governing Departments of the State Council	59.2	0.0	123.8
省级人民政府	Provincial People's Government	65.9	7.3	126.4
省级人民政府主管部门	Governing Departments of the Provincial People's Government	62.5	9.0	123.7
其他	Others	68.4	5.0	157.8
按控股情况分	**Grouped by Controlling Shares**			
国有控股	State-owned Holding	66.2	5.9	135.6
集体控股	Collective-owned Holding	60.5	5.4	114.4
私人控股	Personal-owned Holding	60.6	8.6	117.9
外商控股	Foreign-owned Holding	75.8	3.7	91.1
按主营行业分	**Grouped by Sector**			
第一产业	Primary Industry	49.7	1.6	105.8
第二产业	Secondary Industry	64.9	9.4	113.8
工业	Industry	63.5	9.8	114.4
#制造业	Manufacturing	64.6	11.7	114.2
电力、燃气及水的生产和供应业	Production & Supply of Power, Gas and Water	62.9	-8.7	100.1
建筑业	Construction	79.5	0.1	104.4
第三产业	Tertiary Industry	66.4	3.1	159.4
交通运输、仓储和邮政业	Transportation, Storage and Post Services	53.1	4.6	472.8
批发和零售业	Wholesale and Retail Trade	78.2	-2.4	113.1
住宿和餐饮业	Accommodation and Catering Services	80.4	20.6	111.4
金融业	Finance Intermediation	56.6	-2.1	98.3
房地产业	Real Estate	68.8	4.2	108.9
租赁和商务服务业	Leasing and Business Services	62.8	3.8	166.9
科学研究、技术服务和地质勘查业	Scientific Research, Technical Service and Geological Prospecting	78.0	-5.3	226.9
公共管理和社会组织	Public Management and Social Organizations	55.0	18.4	217.4
按登记注册类型分	**Grouped by Registered Categories**			
国有企业	State-owned Enterprises	77.8	1.1	104.4
公司制企业	Sub-total	63.8	6.4	132.4
国有独资企业	Sole State-funded Enterprises	64.2	6.1	140.1
其他有限责任公司	Other Limited Liability Corporations	62.6	7.6	116.2
股份有限公司	Share Holding Corporations Ltd.	53.6	6.3	107.3
中外合资企业	Chinese-foreign Joint Venture Enterprise	75.8	3.7	91.1
外商投资股份有限公司	Foreign Funded Share Holding Corporations Ltd.	71.7	8.0	85.7
港澳台合资企业	Hong Kong, Macao and Taiwan Joint Capital Enterprise	32.6	1.4	99.0
其他	Others	83.9	6.8	142.4

21-2 续表 1 Continued

单位：% (%)

项　目	Item	总资产报酬率 Rate of Return on Total Assets	资产利税率 Ratio of Pre-tax Profits to Assets	资金利润率 Fund-Profit Ratio
总　计	**Total**	**3.8**	**4.5**	**4.3**
按集团审批部门分	**Grouped by Examining Department**			
国务院	The State Council	1.6	2.9	1.1
国务院主管部门	Governing Departments of the State Council	0.3	5.1	0.1
省级人民政府	Provincial People's Government	3.6	4.4	4.9
省级人民政府主管部门	Governing Departments of the Provincial People's Government	5.9	7.7	6.8
其　他	Others	4.0	3.2	3.5
按控股情况分	**Grouped by Controlling Shares**			
国有控股	State-owned Holding	3.6	4.2	3.9
集体控股	Collective-owned Holding	3.6	4.1	4.4
私人控股	Personal-owned Holding	5.3	6.9	7.5
外商控股	Foreign-owned Holding	1.4	1.7	2.9
按主营行业分	**Grouped by Sector**			
第一产业	Primary Industry	1.9	5.8	2.1
第二产业	Secondary Industry	4.8	6.6	6.1
工　业	Industry	5.1	6.8	6.8
#制造业	Manufacturing	5.8	7.4	7.9
电力、燃气及水的生产和供应业	Production & Supply of Power, Gas and Water	-2.8	-1.8	-4.7
建筑业	Construction	1.0	4.0	0.4
第三产业	Tertiary Industry	2.9	2.4	2.6
交通运输、仓储和邮政业	Transportation, Storage and Post Services	3.5	3.8	5.3
批发和零售业	Wholesale and Retail Trade	0.7	0.8	-0.5
住宿和餐饮业	Accommodation and Catering Services	6.3	8.7	7.3
金融业	Finance Intermediation	-0.8	-0.6	-1.0
房地产业	Real Estate	2.5	2.8	3.5
租赁和商务服务业	Leasing and Business Services	4.1	2.6	3.3
科学研究、技术服务和地质勘查业	Scientific Research, Technical Service and Geological Prospecting	-0.3	-1.0	-3.4
公共管理和社会组织	Public Management and Social Organizations	11.4	11.7	12.4
按登记注册类型分	**Grouped by Registered Categories**			
国有企业	State-owned Enterprises	2.0	1.2	0.7
公司制企业	Sub-total	4.1	4.8	4.6
国有独资企业	Sole State-funded Enterprises	3.9	4.4	4.3
其他有限责任公司	Other Limited Liability Corporations	4.6	6.6	5.5
股份有限公司	Share Holding Corporations Ltd.	4.3	4.9	5.7
中外合资企业	Chinese-foreign Joint Venture Enterprise	1.4	1.7	2.9
外商投资股份有限公司	Foreign Funded Share Holding Corporations Ltd.	5.5	3.7	2.7
港澳台合资企业	Hong Kong, Macao and Taiwan Joint Capital Enterprise	2.0	1.9	3.7
其　他	Others	1.0	2.3	4.6

21-2 续表 2 Continued

项　　目	Item	销售利润率(%) Sales Profit Rate (%)	成本费用利润率(%) Ratio of Profits to Cost (%)	劳动生产率(万元/人) Labour Productivity (10 000 yuan/ person)
总　　计	**Total**	**4.1**	**4.3**	**80.0**
按集团审批部门分	**Grouped by Examining Department**			
国务院	The State Council	1.0	1.1	51.7
国务院主管部门	Governing Departments of the State Council	0.1	0.1	40.9
省级人民政府	Provincial People's Government	4.1	4.2	78.3
省级人民政府主管部门	Governing Departments of the Provincial People's Government	4.5	4.8	111.1
其　他	Others	6.3	6.7	101.7
按控股情况分	**Grouped by Controlling Shares**			
国有控股	State-owned Holding	3.8	4.0	82.4
集体控股	Collective-owned Holding	4.5	5.5	44.5
私人控股	Personal-owned Holding	5.5	5.9	83.3
外商控股	Foreign-owned Holding	3.0	3.0	47.2
按主营行业分	**Grouped by Sector**			
第一产业	Primary Industry	4.6	5.2	44.0
第二产业	Secondary Industry	4.5	4.8	74.7
工　业	Industry	5.1	5.4	76.2
# 制造业	Manufacturing	5.5	5.9	85.9
电力、燃气及水的生产和供应业	Production & Supply of Power, Gas and Water	-9.2	-8.8	35.2
建筑业	Construction	0.2	0.2	64.4
第三产业	Tertiary Industry	3.3	3.4	93.6
交通运输、仓储和邮政业	Transportation, Storage and Post Services	8.7	9.6	29.8
批发和零售业	Wholesale and Retail Trade	-0.3	-0.3	129.9
住宿和餐饮业	Accommodation and Catering Services	7.2	7.9	25.5
金融业	Finance Intermediation	-21.0	-18.2	10.2
房地产业	Real Estate	10.0	12.0	84.3
租赁和商务服务业	Leasing and Business Services	10.5	11.3	139.4
科学研究、技术服务和地质勘查业	Scientific Research, Technical Service and Geological Prospecting	-26.9	-22.3	13.1
公共管理和社会组织	Public Management and Social Organizations	31.3	39.8	91.3
按登记注册类型分	**Grouped by Registered Categories**			
国有企业	State-owned Enterprises	0.3	0.3	347.2
公司制企业	Sub-total	4.9	5.2	68.3
国有独资企业	Sole State-funded Enterprises	5.5	5.8	66.0
其他有限责任公司	Other Limited Liability Corporations	3.9	4.2	76.9
股份有限公司	Share Holding Corporations Ltd.	7.2	9.1	31.0
中外合资企业	Chinese-foreign Joint Venture Enterprise	3.0	3.0	47.2
外商投资股份有限公司	Foreign Funded Share Holding Corporations Ltd.	10.4	12.4	105.7
港澳台合资企业	Hong Kong, Macao and Taiwan Joint Capital Enterprise	7.4	8.3	12.7
其　他	Others	1.4	1.4	182.7

21-3 企业家信心指数（2006年）
CONFIDENCE INDEX OF ENTREPRENEUR, 2006

指　标	Item	一季度 First Quarter	二季度 Second Quarter	三季度 Third Quarter	四季度 Fourth Quarter
总体状况	**Overall Confidence Index**	**130.38**	**134.00**	**132.17**	**133.18**
按行业门类分	**Grouped by Sector**				
工　业	Industry	128.00	134.50	132.91	138.50
采矿业	Minerals Mining	176.61	186.55	174.05	174.05
制造业	Manufacturing	123.82	130.92	129.42	135.32
电力、燃气及水的生产和供应业	Production & Supply of Electric Power, Gas & Water	146.81	149.33	149.33	166.24
建筑业	Construction	130.19	125.36	118.32	115.76
# 房屋和土木工程建筑业	House & Civil Engineering	121.05	116.84	112.15	110.13
建筑安装业	Construction Installation	140.00	133.33	144.44	171.43
交通运输、仓储和邮政业	Transportation, Storage and Post Services	126.89	121.87	123.88	124.44
# 铁路运输业	Railway Transport	100.00	100.00	100.00	100.00
公路运输业	Highway Transport	114.29	100.00	93.33	100.00
水上运输业	Waterway Transport	117.46	117.46	112.90	158.60
航空运输业	Civil Aviation Transport	100.00	100.00	200.00	200.00
邮政业	Post Services	200.00	200.00	200.00	200.00
批发和零售业	Wholesale and Retail Trade	137.15	138.08	132.95	121.74
批发业	Wholesale	134.67	145.28	137.87	117.86
零售业	Retail	122.91	88.23	84.60	123.76
房地产业	Real Estate Trade	145.29	139.25	144.97	144.55
社会服务业	Social Services	140.54	143.03	140.09	121.48
租赁业	Leasing	180.00	150.00	125.00	100.00
商务服务业	Business Services	142.11	138.89	138.89	135.29
居民服务业	Resident Services	112.50	100.00	100.00	33.33
其他服务业	Other Social Services	50.00	166.67	166.67	100.00
信息传输和计算机服务及软件业	Information Transmitting, Computer Services and Software	132.54	142.09	142.09	127.57
信息传输业	Information Transmitting	125.25	125.25	125.25	125.25

21-3 续表 Continued

指　标	Item	一季度 First Quarter	二季度 Second Quarter	三季度 Third Quarter	四季度 Fourth Quarter
计算机服务业	Computer Services	112.50	125.00	125.00	100.00
软件业	Software	146.15	157.14	157.14	150.00
住宿和餐饮业	Accommodation and Catering Services	130.48	131.39	128.26	126.15
住宿业	Accommodation	127.47	128.36	125.62	120.90
餐饮业	Catering Services	141.67	144.44	136.36	150.00
按企业登记注册类型分	**Grouped By Status of Registration**				
国有企业	State-owned Enterprises	127.94	122.79	121.02	123.39
集体企业	Collective-owned Enterprises	110.11	107.59	101.99	106.05
股份合作企业	Cooperative Enterprises	119.96	119.96	127.65	113.29
联营企业	Joint Ownership Enterprises	116.67	133.33	133.33	120.00
有限责任公司	Limited Liability Corporations	133.40	140.64	138.30	127.06
股份有限公司	Share-holding Corporations Ltd.	134.03	131.70	123.40	146.15
私营企业	Private Enterprises	130.43	138.10	136.36	146.15
外商及港澳台商投资企业	Enterprises with Investment from Foreign, Hong Kong, Macao and Taiwan	147.58	149.02	150.75	151.11
按企业规模分	**Grouped By Size of Enterprises**				
大型及特大型	Large and Super-sized	152.43	155.80	155.68	155.69
# 特大型	Super-sized	165.79	177.77	171.95	176.40
大　型	Large-sized	146.20	145.47	148.03	145.79
中小型	Medium and Small-sized	124.75	125.59	123.01	118.97
# 中　型	Medium-sized	130.80	130.26	129.33	127.75
小　型	Small-sized	120.56	122.32	118.65	112.32
其他分组	**Others**				
国家重点联系企业	State Key Enterprises	110.62	167.41	162.99	161.72
国家试点企业集团成员	State Experimental Enterprises Groups	143.08	140.18	112.09	140.08
乡镇企业	Township Enterprises	123.35	112.50	87.50	137.50
上市公司	Corporations Listed in the Stock Market	178.78	158.59	141.70	162.61

21-4 企业景气指数（2006年）
CLIMATE INDEX OF ENTERPRISES, 2006

指　标	Item	一季度 First Quarter	二季度 Second Quarter	三季度 Third Quarter	四季度 Fourth Quarter
总体状况	**Overall Confidence Index**	**128.95**	**127.28**	**124.73**	**141.96**
按行业门类分	**Grouped by Sector**				
工　业	Industry	132.72	125.92	122.21	145.21
采矿业	Minerals Mining	176.61	174.51	165.96	174.05
制造业	Manufacturing	129.79	121.37	118.72	143.07
电力、燃气及水的生产和供应业	Production & Supply of Electric Power, Gas & Water	138.03	143.74	146.53	159.57
建筑业	Construction	126.57	129.24	129.11	136.07
#房屋和土木工程建筑业	House & Civil Engineering	119.05	122.38	126.65	135.99
建筑安装业	Construction Installation	120.00	133.33	155.56	157.14
交通运输、仓储和邮政业	Transportation, Storage and Post Services	111.59	125.73	124.37	123.11
#铁路运输业	Railway Transport	100.00	100.00	100.00	100.00
公路运输业	Highway Transport	80.95	80.00	80.00	85.71
水上运输业	Waterway Transport	127.71	155.99	151.42	154.03
航空运输业	Civil Aviation Transport	100.00	200.00	200.00	200.00
邮政业	Post Services	100.00	200.00	200.00	200.00
批发和零售业	Wholesale and Retail Trade	127.60	137.99	135.14	146.42
批发业	Wholesale Trade	124.73	139.49	137.10	144.11
零售业	Retail Trade	117.62	98.89	95.66	104.74
房地产业	Real Estate Trade	127.17	118.17	124.30	146.95
社会服务业	Social Services	116.52	114.12	111.18	129.65
租赁业	Leasing	120.00	100.00	100.00	150.00
商务服务业	Business Services	121.05	122.22	116.67	129.41
居民服务业	Resident Services	75.00	33.33	33.33	66.67
其他服务业	Other Social Services	50.00	133.33	133.33	100.00
信息传输和计算机服务及软件业	Information Transmitting, Computer Services and Software	136.24	142.48	142.48	135.14
信息传输业	Information Transmitting	125.25	125.25	125.25	125.25

21-4 续表 Continued

指　标	Item	一季度 First Quarter	二季度 Second Quarter	三季度 Third Quarter	四季度 Fourth Quarter
计算机服务业	Computer Services	137.50	150.00	150.00	128.57
软件业	Software	138.46	150.00	150.00	141.67
住宿和餐饮业	Accommodation and Catering Services	108.50	115.53	118.73	119.90
住宿业	Accommodation	104.69	111.92	116.03	113.76
餐饮业	Catering Services	125.00	133.33	127.27	150.00
按企业登记注册类型分	**Grouped By Status of Registration**				
国有企业	State-owned Enterprises	117.50	118.00	118.47	123.85
集体企业	Collective-owned Enterprises	96.82	97.73	97.70	93.55
股份合作企业	Cooperative Enterprises	127.65	127.65	112.27	154.95
联营企业	Joint Ownership Enterprises	116.67	166.67	166.67	120.00
有限责任公司	Limited Liability Corporations	134.73	139.88	137.52	146.41
股份有限公司	Share-holding Corporations Ltd.	118.85	123.82	110.45	156.71
私营企业	Private Enterprises	130.43	123.81	127.27	153.85
外商及港澳台商投资企业	Enterprises with Investment from Foreign, Hong Kong, Macao and Taiwan	145.88	131.78	131.17	157.49
按企业规模分	**Grouped By Size of Enterprises**				
大型及特大型	Large and Super-sized	161.38	150.25	148.44	174.70
# 特大型	Super-sized	176.56	133.21	120.28	181.00
大　型	Large-sized	154.30	158.27	161.69	171.69
中小型	Medium and Small-sized	113.14	116.40	114.67	123.51
# 中　型	Medium-sized	122.80	120.61	117.78	132.06
小　型	Small-sized	106.41	113.46	112.54	117.03
其他分组	**Others**				
国家重点联系企业	State Key Enterprises	194.73	167.41	163.50	162.99
国家试点企业集团成员	State Experimental Enterprises Groups	130.60	147.69	117.01	170.79
乡镇企业	Township Enterprises	125.00	114.15	101.65	137.50
上市公司	Corporations Listed in the Stock Market	178.39	178.71	157.24	166.55

21-5 工业行业企业家信心指数（2006年）
CONFIDENCE INDEX OF INDUSTRIAL ENTREPRENEUR, 2006

指　标	Item	一季度 First Quarter	二季度 Second Quarter	三季度 Third Quarter	四季度 Fourth Quarter
工业行业整体状况	**Overall Industrial Confidence Index**	**128.00**	**134.50**	**132.91**	**138.50**
按企业登记注册类型分	**Grouped By Status of Registration**				
国有企业	State-owned Enterprises	125.71	132.65	132.96	132.34
集体企业	Collective-owned Enterprises	96.15	92.31	80.00	100.00
有限责任公司	Limited Liability Corporations	106.07	126.02	122.08	129.92
股份有限公司	Share-holding Corporations Ltd.	130.85	132.60	123.34	150.56
私营企业	Private Enterprises	140.00	160.00	160.00	140.00
外商及港澳台商投资企	Enterprises with Investment from Foreign, Hong Kong, Macao and Taiwan	149.88	150.97	153.09	151.56
按行业门类分	**Grouped By Sector**				
采矿业	Minerals Mining	176.61	186.55	174.05	174.05
#石油和天然气开采业	Extraction of Petroleum and Natural Gas	199.05	200.00	200.00	200.00
制造业	Manufacturing	123.82	130.92	129.42	135.32
#饮料制造业	Manufacture of Beverages	189.62	180.52	166.88	167.46
纺织业	Manufacture of Textile	104.09	122.22	98.76	94.44
纺织服装鞋帽制造业	Manufacture of Textile Wearing Apparel, Footware, and Caps	100.00	108.33	109.09	90.91
造纸及纸制品业	Manufacture of Paper and Paper Products	100.00	124.52	124.52	124.52
化学原料及化学制品制造业	Manufacture of Raw Chemical Materials and Chemical Products	108.68	113.09	114.15	117.27
医药制造业	Manufacture of Plastics	122.80	108.09	108.77	119.29
化学纤维制造业	Manufacture of Chemical Fibers	100.00	100.00	100.00	100.00
塑料制品业	Manufacture of Plastics	115.48	109.49	113.33	119.21
黑色金属冶炼及压延加工业	Smelting and Pressing of Ferrous Metals	98.67	153.10	153.10	162.58
交通运输设备制造业	Manufacture of Transport Equipment	134.84	136.91	130.57	135.56
电气机械及器材制造	Manufacture of Electrical Machinery and Equipment	142.74	138.41	165.83	157.12
通信设备、计算机及其他电子设备制造业	Manufacture of Communication Equipment, Computers and Other Electronic Equipment	161.58	173.19	169.45	173.80
电力、燃气及水的生产供应业	Production & Supply of Electric Power, Gas & Water	146.81	149.33	149.33	166.24
按企业规模分	**Grouped By Size of Enterprises**				
大型及特大型	Large and Super-size	146.87	157.80	156.78	169.09
中小型	Medium and Small-sized	114.53	117.75	115.49	115.67
#中　型	Medium-sized	120.37	123.36	122.12	124.51
小　型	Small-sized	109.52	112.90	109.84	107.83
其他分组	**Others**				
国家重点联系企业	State Key Enterprises	100.56	163.74	163.74	163.74
国家试点企业集团成员	State Experimental Enterprises Groups	139.28	142.86	112.89	142.75
乡镇企业	Township Enterprises	137.36	120.00	80.00	140.00
上市公司	Corporations Listed in the Stock Market	181.90	176.03	130.62	166.03

21-6 工业企业景气指数（2006年）
CLIMATE INDEX OF INDUSTRIAL ENTERPRISES, 2006

指　标	Item	一季度 First Quarter	二季度 Second Quarter	三季度 Third Quarter	四季度 Fourth Quarter
工业行业整体状况	**Overall Industrial Climate Index**	**132.72**	**125.92**	**122.21**	**145.21**
按企业登记注册类型分	**Grouped By Status of Registration**				
国有企业	State-owned Enterprises	123.32	132.76	131.18	133.26
集体企业	Collective-owned Enterprises	80.77	76.92	80.00	82.61
有限责任公司	Limited Liability Corporations	129.05	135.06	130.56	140.24
股份有限公司	Share-holding Corporations Ltd.	123.12	119.99	102.74	160.21
私营企业	Private Enterprises	160.00	160.00	160.00	140.00
外商及港澳台商投资企业	Enterprises with Investment from Foreign, Hong Kong, Macao and Taiwan	152.54	132.54	131.76	159.20
按行业门类分	**Grouped By Sector**				
采矿业	Minerals Mining	176.61	174.51	165.96	174.05
制造业	Manufacturing	129.79	121.37	118.72	143.07
电力、燃气及水的生产供应业	Production & Supply of Electric Power, Gas & Water	138.03	143.74	146.53	159.57
按企业规模分	**Grouped By Size of Enterprises**				
大型及特大型	Large and Super-size	160.60	140.92	138.70	177.98
中小型	Medium and Small-sized	112.82	115.15	110.18	120.74
#中　型	Medium-sized	119.44	114.02	109.62	123.53
小　型	Small-sized	107.14	116.13	110.66	118.26
不同观察指标景气指数	**Climate Index on Different Indicators**				
生产成本	Cost	68.49	80.36	74.07	85.33
生产总量	Gross Output	118.05	110.57	106.07	126.48
产品订货情况	Order for Product	118.07	126.36	114.48	114.14
产品销售量	Total Volume of Sales	111.07	111.22	105.94	124.20
产品销售价格	Price of Sales	96.17	103.27	101.61	93.35
产成品库存	Inventory of Product	121.64	137.04	130.91	135.73
税后利润	Profits after Tax	99.92	103.60	100.22	114.76
劳动力需求	Labour Demand	117.39	109.42	110.95	120.40
固定资产投资情况	Investment in Fixed Assets	120.61	117.83	115.87	117.73
科技开发情况	Science and Technology Development	117.25	117.15	105.95	109.81
其他分组	**Others**				
国家重点联系企业	State Key Enterprises	199.05	163.74	164.31	163.74
国家试点企业集团	State Experimental Enterprises Groups	125.98	144.20	118.14	168.85
乡镇企业	Township Enterprises	160.00	122.64	102.64	140.00
上市公司	Corporations Listed in the Stock Market	191.90	191.90	156.49	174.49

主要统计指标解释

企业家信心指数 是根据企业家对企业外部市场经济环境与宏观政策的认识、看法、判断与预期而编制的指数，用以综合反映企业家对宏观经济环境的感受与信心。分行业企业家信心指数为各行业企业家对本行业企业外部市场经济环境与宏观政策的认识、看法、判断与预期。其表现形式为纯正数，以100作为景气指数的临界值，其数值范围在0-200之间。

企业景气指数 是根据企业家对本企业综合生产经营情况的判断和预期而编制的指数，用以综合反映企业的生产经营状况。分行业企业景气指数用以反映各行业企业的生产经营状况。其表现形式为纯正数，以100作为景气指数的临界值，其数值范围在0-200之间。

Explanastory Notes on Main Statistical Indicators

Entrepreneur Confidence Index is an index made according to the entrepreneur's understanding, view, judgment and forecast of the market economic environment out of the enterprise and macroscopic policy. It reflects the entrepreneur's feeling and confidence in macroeconomic environment comprehensively. The enterprise confidence index by sectors is a reflection of the entrepreneur's understanding, view, judgment and forecast of the market economic environment out of his own sector. It is expressed by a pure positive number between 0 and 200 with 100 as the boundary value of climate index.

Climate Index of Enterprise is an index made according to the entrepreneur's judgment and forecast of the comprehensive production and management. The climate index by sectors reflects the production and management of each sector comprehensively. It is expressed by a pure positive number between 0 and 200 with 100 as the boundary value.

第22篇
CHAPTER 22

滨海新区
Binhai New Area

22-1 滨海新区行政建制（2006年）
ADMINISTRATIVE DIVISIONS OF BINHAI NEW AREA,2006

单位：个 (Unit)

项　目	Item	街道办事处 Subdistrict Offices	居民委员会 Residents' Committees	镇政府 Town Governments	村民委员 Village Committees
合　计	**Total**	**21**	**219**	**9**	**204**
塘沽区	Tanggu District	11	83	1	32
汉沽区	Han'gu District	4	44	4	58
大港区	Dagang District	5	81	3	74
东丽区无瑕街	Wuxia Subdistrict, Dongli District	1	5	0	15
津南区葛沽镇	Gegu Town, Jinnan District	0	6	1	25

22-2 滨海新区建成区面积
DEVELOPED AREA OF BINHAI NEW AREA

单位：平方公里 (sq. km)

项　目	Item	2004	2005	2006
合　计	**Total**	**175.15**	**188.65**	**194.78**
塘沽地区小计	Subtotal in Tanggu District	117.04	127.26	133.39
塘沽城区和天津港	Central District of Tanggu and Tianjin Port	87.44	93.11	95.37
经济技术开发区	TEDA	24.60	28.86	32.73
天津港保税区	TPFTZ	5.00	5.29	5.29
汉沽区	Han'gu District	16.16	16.16	16.16
大港区	Dagang District	41.95	45.23	45.23

22-3 滨海新区主要年份户籍人口主要指标
MAJOR REGISTERED POPULATION STATISTICS OF BINHAI NEW AREA IN MAIN YEARS

指　标	Item	单　位	Unit	1993	1995	2000	2006
户籍人口	Registered Population	万　人	10 000 persons	99.18	100.7	104.58	112.39
人口密度	Population Density	人/平方公里	person/sq. km	437	444	462	
户籍户数	Registered Households	万　户	10 000 households	31.55	32.32	35.8	30.88
户规模	Family Size	人/户	person/household	3.14	3.12	2.91	3.64
按户口性质分	By Registered Character						
非农业	Non-agricultural	万　人	10 000 persons	68.55	70.74	78.03	86.28
农　业	Agricultural	万　人	10 000 persons	30.63	29.96	26.55	26.11
按性别分	By Sex						
男　性	Male	万　人	10 000 persons	51.89	52.56	54.25	57.85
女　性	Female	万　人	10 000 persons	47.29	48.14	50.34	54.54
性别比	Sex Ratio	女=100	female=100	109.74	109.17	107.78	106.07

22-4 滨海新区主要经济指标
MAIN STATISTICS ON BINHAI NEW AREA

单位：亿元 (100 million yuan)

项　目	Item	2005	2006	2006比2005年增长(%) Increase Rate in 2006 over 2005 (%)
户籍人口(万人)	Registered Population (10 000 persons)	109.39	112.39	2.7
#非农业人口	Non-agricultural Population	83.38	86.28	3.5
从业人员劳动报酬	Total Remuneration of Persons Employed	177.36	220.27	24.2
从业人员人均劳动报酬(元)	Per Capita Remuneration of Persons Employed (yuan)	27209	31416	15.5
地区生产总值	Gross Domestic Product	1623.26	1960.49	20.2
第一产业	Primary Industry	7.28	7.51	0.9
第二产业	Secondary Industry	1098.86	1370.77	24.4
第三产业	Tertiary Industry	517.12	582.21	11.5
农业总产值	Gross Output Value of Agriculture	18.02	17.92	-0.6
工业总产值	Gross Output Value of Industry	3996.73	5200.52	30.1
全社会固定资产投资	Total Investment In Fixed Assets	693.31	864.29	24.7
#基础设施	Infrastructure	175.01	218.11	24.6
市重点项目	Key Projects	99.75	190.76	91.2
财政收入	General Budgetary Government Revenue	288.33	379.73	31.7
财政支出	General Budgetary Government Expenditures	100.92	122.29	21.2
社会消费品零售总额	Total Retail Sales of Consumer Goods	183.55	213.83	16.5
外贸出口总额(亿美元)	Exports (USD 100 million)	184.69	226.20	22.5
直接利用外资合同数(个)	Number of Foreign Direct Investment Contracts (unit)	625	500	-20.0
直接利用外资合同额(亿美元)	Foreign Direct Investment Contracted (USD 100 million)	49.86	61.80	23.9
实际直接利用外资额(亿美元)	Actual Direct Utilization of Foreign Capital (USD 100 million)	25.31	33.45	32.2
内联资金到位项目数(个)	Number of Actual Utilization Capital Projects (unit)	797	647	-18.8
外地在津投资实际到位额	Total Domestic Investment Actually Used in Tianjin	89.83	103.25	14.9

22-5 滨海新区生产总值
GROSS DOMESTIC PRODUCT OF BINHAI NEW AREA

项　目	Item	2005	2006	2006比2005年增长(%) Increase Rate in 2006 over 2005 (%)
绝对数(亿元)	**Value (100 million yuan)**			
地区生产总值	Gross Domestic Product	1623.26	1960.49	20.2
第一产业	Primary Industry	7.28	7.51	0.9
第二产业	Secondary Industry	1098.86	1370.77	24.4
#工　业	Industry	1045.44	1310.52	25.0
第三产业	Tertiary Industry	517.12	582.21	11.5
#交通运输、仓储和邮政业	Transportion, Storage and Post Services	125.16	133.17	5.1
批发和零售业	Wholesale and Retail Trade	210.11	240.36	13.9
住宿和餐饮业	Accommodation and Catering Services	16.88	18.96	10.0
金融业	Finance Intermediation	11.00	13.34	19.9
房地产业	Real Estate	29.80	33.85	11.9
构　成(%)	**Composition (%)**			
地区生产总值	Gross Domestic Product	100	100	
第一产业	Primary Industry	0.45	0.38	-0.07
第二产业	Secondary Industry	67.69	69.92	2.23
#工　业	Industry	64.40	66.85	2.45
第三产业	Tertiary Industry	31.86	29.70	-2.16
#交通运输、仓储和邮政业	Transportion, Storage and Post Services	7.71	6.79	-0.92
批发和零售业	Wholesale and Retail Trade	12.94	12.26	-0.68
住宿和餐饮业	Accommodation and Catering Services	1.04	0.97	-0.07
金融业	Finance Intermediation	0.68	0.68	0.00
房地产业	Real Estate	1.84	1.73	-0.11
占全市比重(%)	**As Percentage of The City's GDP (%)**			
地区生产总值	Gross Domestic Product	43.90	45.00	1.10
第一产业	Primary Industry	6.48	6.35	-0.13
第二产业	Secondary Industry	53.57	55.09	1.52
#工　业	Industry	55.46	57.16	1.70
第三产业	Tertiary Industry	33.71	33.22	-0.49
#交通运输、仓储和邮政业	Transportion, Storage and Post Services	55.10	52.67	-2.43
批发和零售业	Wholesale and Retail Trade	48.17	51.35	3.18
住宿和餐饮业	Accommodation and Catering Services	24.06	23.88	-0.18
金融业	Finance Intermediation	6.91	7.14	0.23
房地产业	Real Estate	23.14	21.06	-2.08

22-6 滨海新区固定资产投资
INVESTMENT IN FIXED ASSETS OF BINHAI NEW AREA

单位：万元 (10 000 yuan)

项　目	Item	2005	2006	2006比2005年增长(%) Increase Rate in 2006 over 2005 (%)
总　计	**Total**	**5349906**	**7475899**	**39.7**
按三次产业分	**Grouped by Industries**			
第一产业	Primary Industry	9490	17475	84.1
第二产业	Secondary Industry	3042056	4561802	50.0
第三产业	Tertiary Industry	2298360	2896622	26.0
按隶属关系分	**Grouped by Administrative Relationship**			
中　央	Central Government	1417176	2046597	44.4
地　方	Local Government	3932730	5429302	38.1
按建设性质分	**Grouped by Type of Construction**			
新　建	New Construction	2057382	3631052	76.5
改、扩建及其他	Expansion, Reconstruction and Others	3292524	3844847	16.8
按构成分	**Grouped by Use of Funds**			
建筑工程	Construction	3493970	4394972	25.8
安装工程	Installation	222938	326688	46.5
设备工器具购置	Purchases of Equipment and Instruments	1111086	1942335	74.8
其他费用	Others	521912	811904	55.6
按登记注册类型分	**Grouped by Registered Categories**			
内资企业	Domestic-funded Enterprises	4369293	5708040	30.6
国有企业	State-owned Enterprises	1272933	1926521	51.3
集体企业	Collective-owned Enterprises	12098	44635	268.9
股份合作企业	Cooperative Enterprises	108153	125887	16.4
私营企业	Private Enterprises	386186	473347	22.6
股份有限公司	Share Holding Corporations Ltd.	1236971	1648296	33.3
有限责任公司	Limited Liability Corporations	1324007	1466868	10.8
# 国有独资	Sole State-funded Corporations	962079	684623	-28.8
联营企业	Joint Ownership Enterprises	3913	2560	-34.6
# 国有与国有联营企业	State Joint Ownership Enterprises	900	2200	144.4
集体与集体联营企业	Collective Joint Ownership Enterprise	3013		-100.0
其他内资企业	Other Domestic-funded Enterprises	25032	19926	-20.4
港澳台商投资企业	Enterprises with Investment from Hong Kong, Macao and Taiwan	156100	269722	72.8
外商投资企业	Foreign Funded Enterprises	824513	1498137	81.7

注：本表数据不含农村非农户和农户投资。
Note: The data in this table exclude rural non-agricultural and agricultural investment.

22-6 续表 Continued

单位：万元 (10 000 yuan)

项　目 Item	2005	2006	2006比2005年增长(%) Increase Rate in 2006 over 2005 (%)
按行业分 Grouped by Sectors			
农、林、牧、渔业 Farming, Forestry, Animal Husbandry and Fishery	9490	17475	84.1
采矿业 Minerals Mining	1240463	1825021	47.1
制造业 Manufacturing	1655401	2619315	58.2
电力、燃气及水的生产和供应业 Production & Supply of Power, Gas and Water	109673	102827	-6.2
建筑业 Construction	36519	14639	-59.9
交通运输、仓储和邮政业 Transportation, Storage, Post Services	716861	930964	29.9
批发和零售业 Wholesale and Retail Trade	31252	82408	163.7
住宿和餐饮业 Accommodation and Catering Services	17444	21593	23.8
金融业 Finance		500	
房地产业 Real Estate	794846	998484	25.6
租赁和商务服务业 Leasing and Business Services	14595	49606	239.9
科学研究、技术服务和地质勘查业 Scientific Research, Technical Services and Geological Prospecting	8477	5607	-33.9
水利、环境和公共设施管理业 Management for Water Conservancy, Environment and Public Facilities	486503	565213	16.2
居民服务和其他服务业 Resident Services and Other Social Services	2335	9089	289.3
教　育 Education	53426	48158	-9.9
卫生、社会保障和社会福利业 Health Care, Social Security and Social Welfare	12033	21735	80.6
文化、体育和娱乐业 Culture, Sports and Recreational Services	60774	55174	-9.2
公共管理和社会组织 Public Management and Social Organizations	99814	108091	8.3

22-7 滨海新区直接利用外资情况（2006年）
DIRECT UTILIZATION OF FOREIGN CAPITAL OF BINHAI NEW AREA, 2006

项　目	Item	直接利用外资合同数(个) Number of Contracts (unit)	直接利用外资合同金额(万美元) Foreign Investment Contracted (USD 10 000)	实际直接利用外资金额(万美元) Actual Direct Utilization of Foreign Capital (USD 10 000)
合　计	**Total**	**500**	**618043**	**334493**
按投资方式分	**By Mode of Investment**			
合资企业	Joint Venture Enterprises	133	138009	71832
合作企业	Cooperative Operation Enterprises	11	12963	89771
独资企业	Foreign-funded Sole Enterprises	356	467071	172890
按行业分	**By Sector**			
#农、林、牧、渔业	Farming, Forestry, Animal Husbandry and Fishery	1	4399	136
采矿业	Minerals Mining	1	10	63929
制造业	Manufacturing	198	271736	168262
电力、燃气及水的生产和供应业	Production and Supply of Electric Power, Gas and Water	3	6890	6262
建筑业	Construction	1	9427	2232
交通运输、仓储和邮政业	Transportation, Storage and Post Services	22	45242	36877
信息传输、计算机服务和软件业	Information Transmitting, Computer Services and Software	13	13114	104
批发和零售业	Wholesale and Retail Trade	145	93814	33440
住宿和餐饮业	Accommodation and Catering Services	4	246	
金融业	Finance Intermediation	2	1309	20
房地产业	Real Estate	37	91404	17410
租赁和商务服务业	Leasing and Business Services	52	58824	1708
科学研究、技术服务与地质勘查业	Scientific Research, Technical Services and Geological Prospecting	15	15648	1256
水利、环境和公共设施管理业	Management for Water Conservancy, Environment and Public Facilities	1	600	410
居民服务和其他服务	Resident Services and Other Social Services	5	2587	626
文化、体育与娱乐业	Culture, Sports and Recreational Services		2793	1821
按国别、地区分	**By Country (Region)**			
#中国香港	Hong Kong, China	93	147349	58813
中国台湾	Taiwan, China	17	13410	1099
韩　国	Republic of Korea	60	56405	13185
日　本	Japan	33	22876	38410
美　国	United States	64	79107	15033
新加坡	Singapore	30	39529	10150
英　国	United Kingdom	10	12837	6458
德　国	Germany	20	19817	2175
法　国	France	6	6827	1272
意大利	Italy	9	20209	7716
英属维尔京群岛	Virgin Islands of United Kingdom	46	47910	41968

22-8 滨海新区全部国有及规模以上工业企业主要财务指标(2006年) MAIN FINANCIAL INDICATORS OF ALL STATE-OWENED AND ABOVE DESIGNATED SIZE INDUSTRIAL ENTERPRISES OF BINHAI NEW AREA, 2006

单位：万元 (10 000 yuan)

项　目	Item	从业人员年平均人数(人) Annual Average Employment Personnel (person)	工业增加值 Value Added of Industry	实收资本 Total Capital Hold
总　计	**Total**	**401440**	**14333123**	**10863444**
按登记注册类型分	**Grouped by Status of Registration**			
内资企业	Domestic-funded Enterprises	181561	6609945	4912795
国有企业	State-owned Enterprises	16270	145852	431267
集体企业	Collective-owned Enterprise	10170	54099	29551
股份合作企业	Cooperative Enterprises	3329	26526	22367
私营企业	Private Enterprises	24750	253838	188557
股份有限公司	Share-holding Corporations Ltd.	35441	4988662	2153877
有限责任公司	Limited Liability Corporations	90702	1130861	2072054
# 国有独资	Sole State-funded Corporations	61997	670782	4190725
联营企业	Joint Ownership Enterprises	639	6884	9120
其他内资企业	Other Domestic-funded Enterprises	260	3223	6002
港澳台商投资企业	Enterprises with Investment from Hong Kong, Macao and Taiwan	42572	814018	1089341
外商投资企业	Foreign Funded Enterprises	177307	6909160	4861308
按经济类型分	**Grouped by Ownership**			
国有经济	State-owned	78267	816668	2087126
集体经济	Collective-owned	13499	80625	51918
私有经济	Private and Individual	24750	253838	188557
港澳台商投资经济	Hong Kong, Macao and Taiwan Funded	42572	814018	1089341
外商投资经济	Foreign Funded	177307	6909161	4861309
其　他	Others	65045	5458813	2585193
按隶属关系分	**Grouped by Administrative Relationship**			
中央工业	Central Industry	77558	5185012	3211638
地方工业	Local Industry	323882	9148111	7651806
# 市管工业	City Industry	129011	2649528	3007899
按轻重工业分	**Grouped by Light & Heavy Industy**			
轻工业	Light Industry	103515	1423857	2018096
重工业	Heavy Industry	297925	12909266	8845348
按企业规模分	**Grouped by Size of Enterprises**			
大　型	Large-sized	174514	6880114	3102809
中　型	Medium-sized	126772	5614811	5243285
小　型	Small-sized	100154	1838198	2517350

单位：万元 (10 000 yuan)

资产总计 Total Assets	流动资产年平均余额 Annual Average Balance of Circulating Funds	固定资产原价 Original Value of Fixed Assets	固定资产净值年平均余额 Annual Average Balance of Net Value of Fixed Assets	主营业务收入 Principal Business Revenue	利税总额 Total Pre-tax Profits	#利润总额 Total Profits
33823490	**16484441**	**24520777**	**12517599**	**51636875**	**7241845**	**5299600**
15154371	5146011	16069967	7673979	18227254	4541013	3361984
1099740	576618	774349	375236	842544	-31370	-57284
219078	156766	66663	36225	362028	13450	4059
104720	65633	38765	26795	159586	10974	6910
1048919	620498	407408	298091	1803043	109433	57126
6618399	1320924	11044739	4629314	10220590	3900374	3049122
6021988	2383843	3718915	2294854	4790173	533666	299607
4190725	1491721	2607298	1646345	2764386	384449	218934
28084	12770	15579	11776	39230	4137	2294
13443	8959	3549	1688	10060	349	150
3287518	1655991	1992192	1073530	3160921	229213	168050
15381601	9682439	6458618	3770090	30248700	2471619	1769566
5290465	2068340	3381647	2021581	3606929	353080	161650
323798	222399	105428	63020	521615	24424	10969
1048919	620498	407408	298091	1803043	109433	57126
3287518	1655991	1992192	1073530	3160921	229213	168050
15381601	9682438	6458618	3770091	30248700	2471619	1769566
8491189	2234775	12175484	5291286	12295667	4054076	3132239
8299796	2359734	12134538	5153434	10914287	3943552	3039084
25523694	14124707	12386239	7364165	40722588	3298293	2260516
10646589	4892685	5887749	3528160	17234587	1676007	981815
5411995	2805011	2618613	1607851	6424823	458645	317843
28411495	13679430	21902164	10909748	45212052	6783200	4981757
15825553	8025157	10845488	5512073	26452934	3033954	1992324
10991438	4550871	10423152	4933921	17702776	3776917	3050482
8006499	3908413	3252137	2071605	7481165	430974	25694

22-9 滨海新区财政收支（2006年）
GOVERNMENT REVENUE AND EXPENDITURE OF BINHAI NEW AREA, 2006

单位：亿元 (100 million yuan)

项 目	Item	合 计 Total	# 塘沽区 Tanggu District	# 汉沽区 Han'gu District	# 大港区 Dagang District	# 经济技术开发区 TEDA	# 天津保税区 TFTZ
财政收入合计	**Total Government Revenue**	**379.73**	**32.55**	**6.27**	**16.05**	**180.67**	**34.83**
# 区县级财政收入	**Government Revenue at District & County Level**	**107.88**	**16.60**	**2.44**	**7.38**	**61.33**	**16.07**
一般预算收入	**General Budgetary Government Revenue**	**91.53**	**15.99**	**2.30**	**6.14**	**52.89**	**10.16**
增值税	Value-added Tax	25.93	1.60	0.64	1.08	19.71	1.70
营业税	Business Tax	19.83	3.97	0.40	1.21	10.43	3.52
企业所得税	Income Tax of Enterprises	17.95	1.37	0.14	0.68	13.00	2.33
个人所得税	Private Income Tax	3.79	2.89	0.04	0.19	2.66	0.55
其他收入	Other Income	24.03	6.16	1.08	2.98	7.09	2.06
基金预算收入	**Budgetary Fund Revenue**	**16.35**	**0.61**	**0.14**	**1.24**	**8.44**	**5.91**
财政支出合计	**Total Government Expenditure**	**122.29**	**20.90**	**4.65**	**11.33**	**68.07**	**16.09**
一般预算支出	**General Budgetary Government Expenditure**	**109.57**	**20.26**	**4.62**	**10.26**	**59.84**	**13.34**
# 基本建设支出	Capital Construction	43.88	1.15	0.00	0.97	33.56	8.01
城市维护费	Expenditure for City Maintenance	6.03	1.37	0.69	0.62	2.91	0.44
企业挖潜改造资金	Innovation Funds of Enterprises	17.19	1.12	0.06	0.00	12.91	3.09
行政管理费	Administrative Expenses	7.42	2.29	0.58	1.25	2.38	0.84
公检法司支出	Expenditure for Public Security Agency, Procuratorial Agency and Court of Justice	3.80	2.00	0.40	0.70	0.56	0.14
教育支出	Operating Expenses of Education	10.86	4.46	1.22	4.01	0.93	0.00
医疗卫生支出	Expenditure for Health Care	2.23	0.64	0.49	0.44	0.61	0.00
科学和科技支出	Operating Expense of Science & Technology	2.58	0.29	0.07	0.02	2.20	0.00
文体广播事业费	Operating Expenses of Culture, Sports and Broadcasting	1.90	0.27	0.19	0.28	1.13	0.00
社会保障和救济支出	Social Security and Pensions, Relief	1.94	1.11	0.30	0.29	0.14	0.08
农林水利气象支出	Expenditure of Agriculture, Forestry, Water Conservancy and Meteorology	0.96	0.37	0.22	0.32	0.00	0.00
其他各项支出	Other Expenditure	10.78	5.19	0.40	1.36	2.51	0.74
基金预算支出	**Budgetary Fund Expenditure**	**12.72**	**0.64**	**0.03**	**1.07**	**8.23**	**2.75**

注：财政收入包括滨海新区地域内的三级财政收入及街镇财政收入（不含海关关税等中央级固定收入），还包括滨海新区地域内市级财政固定收入企业上缴的各项税收；财政支出包括滨海新区地域内各区级及街镇财政实际支出。

Note: Government revenue refer to the three grades government revenue from Binhai New Area(excluded the fixed revenue of central government such as custom tariffs etc.) and the taxes from the municipal enterprises with fixed government revenue in Binhai New area; Government expenditure refer to real government expenditure of districts in Binhai New Area.

22-10 滨海新区金融机构现金收入和支出
CASH INCOME AND EXPENDITURES OF FINANCIAL INSTITUTIONS OF BINHAI NEW AREA

单位：万元 (10 000 yuan)

项　目	Item	2005	2006	2006比2005年增长(%) Increase Rate in 2006 over 2005 (%)
现金收入总计	**Total Cash Income**	**15450691**	**17653856**	**14.3**
商品销售收入	Income from Commodity Sales	2273818	2197382	-3.4
服务事业收入	Income from Service Trade	585938	730956	24.7
税款收入	Income from Taxes	141564	149374	5.5
城乡个体经营收	Income from Urban and Rural Individual Business	649560	844750	30.0
储蓄存款收入	Income from Savings Deposits	10677980	12463365	16.7
其他金融机构收入	Income from Other Financial Institutions	84867	136876	61.3
居民归还贷款收入	Income from Repayment of Loans by Residents	303539	359445	18.4
汇兑收入	Income from Remittances	87992	95800	8.9
有价证券收入	Income from Securities	28826	22441	-22.1
其他收入	Other Income	616607	653466	6.0
现金支出总计	**Total Cash Expenditures**	**16339477**	**18709559**	**14.5**
工资性支出	Wages	1012231	1035511	2.3
#国家职工工资奖金	Wages and Bonuses to the Staff and Workers from Government	372074	412244	10.8
国家对个人其他支出	Other Payments to Individuals from Government	116355	115214	-1.0
其他单位工资性支出	Wages from Other Units	513174	498145	-2.9
农副产品采购支出	Expenditure for Purchases of Agricultural and Sideline Products	275088	249916	-9.2
工矿及其他产品采购支出	Expenditure for Purchases of Industrial and Mineral Products	453651	473793	4.4
行政企事业管理费支出	Government and Enterprises Overhead	992362	915188	-7.8
城乡个体经营支出	Expenditure for Individual Business	1168534	1297762	11.1
储蓄存款支出	Expenditure for Savings Deposits	11583636	13760281	18.8
其他金融机构支出	Expenditure for Other Financial Institutions	76654	128174	67.2
居民提取贷款支出	Expenditure for Loans by Residents	256350	266639	4.0
汇兑支出	Expenditure for Remittances	24482	28877	18.0
有价证券支出	Expenditure for Securities	19346	27363	41.4
其他支出	Others	477142	526053	10.3
货币投放(+)或回笼(-)	**Currency Issuance (+) and Cash Withdrawal (-)**	**888787**	**1055703**	**18.8**

资料来源：中国银行业监督管理委员会滨海监管分局。22-11表同。
Sources: China Banking Regulatory Commission Tianjin Binhai Field Office.Same as table 21-11.

22-11 滨海新区金融机构人民币信贷收支情况
RMB CREDIT INCOME & EXPENDITURES OF BANKING INSTITUTIONS OF BINHAI NEW AREA

单位：万元 (10 000 yuan)

项 目	Item	2005	2006	2006比2005年增长(%) Increase Rate in 2006 over 2005 (%)
各项存款总计	**Total Deposits**	**10260836**	**12929999**	**26.0**
企业存款	Deposits of Enterprises	5306792	6939837	30.8
财政性存款	Treasury Deposits	59878	127172	112.4
储蓄存款	Savings Deposits	3810519	4467885	17.3
#定期储蓄	Fixed Deposits	2522297	2891585	14.6
农业存款	Agricultural Deposits	221765	302005	36.2
其他类存款	Other Deposits	861882	1093100	26.8
各项贷款总计	**Total Loans**	**8696799**	**10950479**	**25.9**
短期贷款	Short-term Loans	4484335	5660588	26.2
#工业贷款	Industrial Loans	1160433	1413321	21.8
商业贷款	Commercial Loans	239084	320533	34.1
建筑业贷款	Construction Loans	110442	115234	4.3
私营及个体贷款	Loans to Private and Individuals	146480	64979	-55.6
乡镇企业贷款	Loans to Township Enterprises	105711	398927	277.4
农业贷款	Agricultural Loans	504050	256663	-49.1
三资企业贷款	Loans to Hong Kong, Macao, Taiwan and Foreign Funded Enterprises	179809	153163	-14.8
其他短期贷款	Other Short-term Loans	2038326	2937769	44.1
中长期贷款	Medium-term and Long-term Loans	4019109	5006382	24.6
#技术改造贷款	Loans to Technical Innovation	41936	19560	-53.4
基本建设贷款	Loans to Capital Construction	2443073	3367155	37.8
票据融资	Bill Financing	190855	262049	37.3
各项垫款	Money Advanced to be Paid Back	2500	21460	758.4

22-12 滨海新区工业废水、废气、固体废物排放及处理情况（2003-2006年）
EMISSION AND TREATMENT OF INDUSTRIAL WASTE WATER, WASTE GAS, WASTE RESIDUE AND DUST OF BINHAI NEW AREA, 2003-2006

指　标　Item	2003	2004	2005	2006
工业废水　Industrial Waste Water				
工业废水排放量(万吨) Volume of Waste Water Discharged (10 000 tons)	6768.00	8310.27	16027.10	10935.22
工业废水排放达标率(%) Rate of Reaching the Standard of Industrial Waste Water (%)	99.59	98.97	99.74	99.86
工业废气　Industrial Waste Gas				
工业废气排放总量(亿标立方米) Total Volume of Industrial Waste Gas Emission (100 million st. cu. m)	1688.80	872.97	1414.02	1928.83
生产工艺过程中废气排放量 Volume of Waste Gas from the Process of Production	160.11	681.82	380.27	255.08
燃料燃烧过程中废气排放量 Volume of Waste Gas from the Burning Process of Fuel	1528.69	191.15	1033.75	1674.75
工业粉尘产生量(万吨) Amount of Industrial Dust Produced (10 000 tons)	1.04	1.21	3.83	2.19
工业粉尘排放量 Volume of Industrial Dust Emission	0.15	0.12	0.35	0.30
工业粉尘去除量 Volume of Industrial Dust Removed	0.89	1.09	3.48	1.89
工业粉尘去除率(%) Rate of Industrial Dust Removed (%)	86.02	90.06	90.91	86.36
工业固体废物　Industrial Waste Residue				
工业固体废物产生量(万吨) Amount of Industrial Waste Residue Produced (10 000 tons)	236.09	261.11	447.41	509.67
#已处理量 Volume of Treatment	56.84	20.14	19.08	18.91
已综合利用量 Volume of Comprehensive Utilization	211.63	291.76	480.06	490.65
工业固体废物综合利用率(%) Rate of Comprehensive Using Industrial Waste Residue (%)	89.64	93.50	96.30	96.30

22-13 滨海新区基础设施投资和城市市政设施（2003-2006年）
INFRASTRUCTURE INVESTMENT AND MUNICIPAL INFRASTRUCTURE OF BINHAI NEW AREA, 2003-2006

项　目	Item	2003	2004	2005	2006
基础设施投资(万元)	**Infrastructure Investment (10 000 yuan)**	**1225676**	**1571691**	**1750143**	**2181119**
铁路和轨道交通	Railway and Track Transportation	247176	165780	143812	216766
道路桥梁	Road and Bridge	230354	190142	152897	335742
港　口	Port	146713	292177	459018	730551
排　水	Drainage	25622	7375	2175	4649
供　水	Water Supply	2333	11128	6006	20889
供电供热	Power and Heat Supply	25255	40166	86723	89215
通　讯	Telecommunication	1500	15733	56304	23796
绿化和环境工程	Afforest & Environment Engineering	110983	146290	64269	41123
其　他	Others	435740	702900	778939	718388
市政设施	**Municipal Infrastructure**				
铺装道路长度(公里)	Length of Paved Roads (km)	1135.56	1183.45	1231.35	945.39
铺装道路面积(万平米)	Area of Paved Roads (10 000 sq. m)	1333.49	1415.85	1508.31	1657.64
桥梁座数(座)	Number of Bridges (unit)	153	157	139	83
#立交桥(座)	Flyover (unit)	23	21	25	27
排水水泵站(座)	Pumping Station (unit)	136	136	136	94
排水管道长度(公里)	Length of Drainpipes (km)	1684.14	1738.67	1885.47	1796.1

22-14 经济技术开发区主要年份国民经济主要指标
MAIN STATISTICS ON ECONOMIC-TECHNOLOGICAL DEVELOPMENT AREA IN MAIN YEARS

年　份 Year	地区生产总值 (万元) Gross Domestic Product (10 000 yuan)	工业总产值 (万元) Gross Output Value of Industry (10 000 yuan)	# 外商及港澳台商投资企业 Foreign and Hong Kong, Macao, Taiwan Funded Enterprises	工业产品销售收入 (万元) Sales Revenue of Industrial Product (10 000 yuan)	# 外商及港澳台商投资企业 Foreign and Hong Kong, Macao, Taiwan Funded Enterprises
1985					
1990	25011	78060	68859	73767	60546
1995	801102	2664551	2621361	2526011	2483428
1996	1310135	3701106	3646558	3617960	3563872
1997	1536270	4702422	4590240	4630014	4519091
1998	1801056	5402180	5203573	5337354	5141130
1999	2084516	6085483	5863637	6018543	5802137
2000	2564432	7318248	7089316	7274338	7049651
2001	3120259	8651050	8394351	8633748	8378463
2002	3800899	10312373	10016307	10291748	9996025
2003	4452278	12513994	12158648	12494722	12143923
2004	5302181	18221439	17749893	18476539	17998392
2005	6422936	23051921	22471809	23521464	22908165
2006	7805585	30301617	29522301	30744021	29821700

年　份 Year	直接利用外资合同数 (个) Number of Foreign Direct Investment Contracts (unit)	直接利用外资项目合同投资总额(万美元) Foreign Direct Investment Contracted (USD 10 000)	出口总额 (万美元) Exports (USD 10 000)	从业人员 (人) Employment Personnel (person)	# 外商及港澳台商投资企业 Foreign and Hong Kong, Macao, Taiwan Funded Enterprises
1985	14	3192		823	137
1990	54	12237	6370	14462	8115
1995	361	181129	90103	112874	79682
1996	187	191604	145020	140150	99853
1997	172	149576	200415	157934	113473
1998	194	148207	208135	171604	121093
1999	106	142884	255380	180466	127156
2000	99	277902	326691	191058	134496
2001	94	248779	403531	195012	137702
2002	111	260676	570563	205884	146808
2003	167	233952	688617	231957	159666
2004	164	321112	1117503	258064	179747
2005	225	436305	1397066	288264	201334
2006	232	512046	1714478	315678	221674

22-15 经济技术开发区国民经济主要指标
MAIN STATISTICS ON ECONOMIC-TECHNOLOGICAL DEVELOPMENT AREA

项　目	Item	2005	2006	2006比2005年增长(%) Increase Rate in 2006 over 2005 (%)
地区生产总值(万元)	Gross Domestic Product (10 000 yuan)	6420489	7805585	28.8
第二产业	Secondary Industry	5394349	6546179	30.2
#工　业	Industry	5345029	6485859	30.3
第三产业	Tertiary Industry	1026140	1259406	21.6
#交通运输、仓储和邮政业	Transportation, Storage and Post Services	44898	69896	47.5
批发和零售业	Wholesale and Retail Trade	686988	873107	26.6
住宿和餐饮业	Accommodation and Catering Services	47848	34578	-29.2
金融业	Finance Intermediation			
房地产业	Real Estate	167835	195988	15.1
工业产品销售收入(万元)	Sales Revenue of Industrial Products (10 000 yuan)	23521464	30744021	26.2
#外商及港澳台商投资企业	Foreign and Hong Kong, Macao, Taiwan Funded Enterprises	22908165	29821700	26.3
工业总产值(万元)	Gross Output Value of Industry (10 000 yuan)	23051921	30301617	26.2
#外商及港澳台商投资企业	Foreign and Hong Kong, Macao, Taiwan Funded Enterprises	22471809	29522301	26.3
出口总额(万美元)	Exports (USD 10 000)	1397066	1714478	22.7
直接利用外资合同数(个)	Number of Foreign Direct Investment Contracts (unit)	225	232	3.1
直接利用外资合同额(万美元)	Foreign Direct Investment Contracted (USD 10 000)	259510	325081	25.3
实际直接利用外资金额(万美元)	Actual Direct Utilization of Foreign Capital (USD 10 000)	128510	160029	24.5
单位从业人员期末人数(人)	Number of Year-end Employment Personnel (person)	288264	315678	9.5
外商及港澳台商投资企业	Foreign and Hong Kong, Macao, Taiwan Funded Enterprises	201334	221674	10.1
内资企业	Domestic Funded Enterprises	86930	94004	8.1
按产业分组	Grouped by Industry			
第二产业	Secondary Industry	208530	233029	11.7
第三产业	Tertiary Industry	79734	82649	3.7
单位从业人员人均劳动报酬(元)	Per Capita Remuneration of Employment Personnel (yuan)	28111	31395	11.7

22-16 经济技术开发区小区主要经济指标（2006年）
MAIN STATISTICS ON SUBSIDIARIES AREAS OF TEDA, 2006

项　目	Item	西　区 West Area	微电子工业区 MIP	逸仙科学工业区 YSP	化　学工业区 CIP
工业总产值(万元)	Gross Output Value of Industry (10 000 yuan)	244059	5432451	645453	132741
外贸出口总额(万美元)	Exports (USD 10 000)	2745	415930	29482	3507
固定资产投资(万元)	Total Investment In Fixed Assets (10 000 yuan)	236143	223229	28718	70090
#基础设施	Infrastructure	51414	960	1276	12981
单位从业人员期末人数(人)	Number of Year-end Employment Personnel (person)	4142	25862	6441	1702
直接利用外资项目数(个)	Number of Foreign Direct Investment Contracts (unit)	34	57	30	31
直接利用外资合同额(万美元)	Foreign Direct Investment Contracted (USD 10 000)	104551	78469	48484	46031

注：微电子工业区坐落于西青区、逸仙科学工业区坐落于武清区、化学工业区坐落于汉沽区。
Note: MIP is located at Xiqing district. YSP is located at Wuqing district. CIP is located at Han'gu district.

22-17 经济技术开发区城市建设情况（截止2006年底）
URBAN CONSTRUCTION OF THE ECONOMIC-TECHNOLOGICAL DEVELOPMENT AREA (By the End of 2006)

项　目	Item	单　位	Unit	数 量 Amount
累计房屋开工面积	Total Floor Space Under Construction	万平方米	10 000 sq. m	1757.0
#2006年	in 2006	万平方米	10 000 sq. m	250.8
累计房屋竣工面积	Total Floor Space Completed	万平方米	10 000 sq. m	1123.3
#2006年	in 2006	万平方米	10 000 sq. m	196.3
已开发土地面积	Developed Area	平方公里	sq. km	42
桥　梁	Bridge	座	unit	8
路　灯	Street Lamp	盏	unit	15995
污水处理量	Volume of Sewage Treatment	万立方米	10 000 cu. m	1963.56
绿化面积	Area of Green Land	万平方米	10 000 sq. m	921.66
绿化覆盖率	Coverage Rate of Urban Green Areas	%	%	31.10
出租车辆	Number of Taxis	辆	unit	745
客运总量	Passenger Traffic	万人次	10 000 person-times	3390.96
#轻　轨	Light Railway	万人次	10 000 person-times	882.96

22-18 经济技术开发区利用外资情况（1985-2006年）
FOREIGN INVESTMENT OF ECONOMIC-TECHNOLOGICAL DEVELOPMENT AREA, 1985-2006

单位：万美元 (USD 10 000)

年　份 Year	直接利用外资合同数(个) Number of Foreign Direct Investment Constracts (unit)	直接利用外资合同金额 Foreign Direct Investment Constracted	实际直接利用外资金额 Actual Direct Utilization of Foreign Capital
1985-2006年累计 Total of 1985-2006	**4308**	**2462100**	**1341129**
1985	14	1436	568
1986	27	1693	1231
1987	34	844	1099
1988	48	4835	1298
1989	40	6764	4071
1990	54	10034	3950
1991	121	12653	11006
1992	462	50685	24243
1993	909	75853	34460
1994	487	119908	65546
1995	361	158959	72216
1996	187	158846	75706
1997	172	130815	75558
1998	194	122845	101318
1999	106	127987	100071
2000	99	264034	101003
2001	94	220008	180072
2002	111	89324	41000
2003	167	127751	63251
2004	164	192235	94923
2005	225	259510	128510
2006	232	325081	160029

注：表中数字以核发批准证书为准。
Note: The figures of this table are calculated according to the certificate of agreement.

22-19 经济技术开发区外商及港澳台商投资企业按投资方式及国别(地区)分类(截至2006年底)
TEDA'S FOREIGN AND HONG KONG, MACAO, TAIWAN FUNDED ENTERPRISES BY INVESTING WAY AND COUNTRY (REGION) (By the End of 2006)

国 别 (地 区)	Country (Region)	企业个数(个) Number of Enterprises (unit)	直接利用外资项目合同投资总额(万美元) Total Volume of Contract (USD 10 000)	# 直接利用外资合同金额 Foreign Capital
合 计	Total	1791	2133197	880453
按投资方式分	Grouped by Investing Way			
合资企业	Joint Ventures	725	779237	285413
合作企业	Cooperative Enterprises	29	68199	23329
独资企业	Sole-foreign Enterprises	1037	1285760	571711
按国别、地区分	Grouped by Country, Region			
美 国	United State	286	431433	130986
中国香港	Hong Kong, China	479	346103	136847
韩 国	Republic of Korea	127	175477	68251
英属维尔京	Virgin Islands of United Kingdom	108	281315	126451
日 本	Japan	239	264822	114450
英 国	United Kingdom	40	39395	15693
新加坡	Singapore	87	57660	22547
中国台湾	Taiwan, China	110	24880	11462
开曼群岛	Qaman Islands	26	193506	105993
丹 麦	Denmark	6	40513	16928
德 国	Germany	39	45391	21565
荷 兰	Netherlands	15	29446	15333
瑞 士	Swiss	10	18249	11484
加拿大	Canada	46	36107	17724
中国澳门	Macao, China	11	11002	4055
法 国	France	21	18656	6803
西萨摩亚	Samoa Western	12	22411	11418
泰 国	Thailand	5	3987	1960
澳大利亚	Australia	16	4285	2088
马来西亚	Malaysia	9	5246	3176
芬 兰	Finland	5	1788	1055
比利时	Belgium	12	4294	2402
印度尼西亚	Indonesia	3	365	221

注：表中数字以核发营业执照的企业为准，21-20表同。
Note: The figures of this table refer to enterprises which have gotten business license,same as following table 21-20.

22-19 续表 Continued

国别（地区）	Country (Region)	企业个数(个) Number of Enterprises (unit)	直接利用外资项目合同投资总额(万美元) Total Volume of Contract (USD 10 000)	# 直接利用外资合同金额 Foreign Capital
巴哈马	Bahama	1	885	500
以色列	Israel	1	556	186
新西兰	New Zealand	5	3441	1498
意大利	Italy	3	207	109
毛里求斯	Mauritius	9	14841	8405
菲律宾	Philippines	2	1338	760
匈牙利	Hungary	5	263	215
罗马尼亚	Romania	1	50	35
巴拿马	Panama	3	208	171
捷　克	Czech	2	104	153
波　兰	Poland	1	150	105
西班牙	Spain	4	248	171
俄罗斯	Russia	2	83	42
挪　威	Norway	1	50	35
塞浦路斯	Cyprus	2	25	18
乌拉圭	Uruguay	1	68	24
奥地利	Austria	1	20	20
巴基斯坦	Pakistan	3	58	26
柬埔寨	Cambodia	1	30	30
百慕大群岛	Bermuda	3	3582	1852
巴巴多斯	Barbados	5	25050	10800
卢森堡	Luxembourg	1	1137	337
哥斯达黎加	Costa Rica	1	200	180
美属萨摩亚	American Samoa	2	1500	750
也　门	Yemen	1	28	20
乌克兰	Ukraine	1	1809	338
爱尔兰	Ireland	1	30	27
英属印度洋群岛	British Indian Ocean Territory	1	20	20

22-20 经济技术开发区外商及港澳台商投资企业按行业分类(截至2006年底)
TEDA'S FOREIGN AND HONG KONG, MACAO, TAIWAN FUNDED ENTERPRISES BY SECTOR (By the End of 2006)

行 业	Sector	企业个数(个) Number of Enterprises (unit)	直接利用外资项目合同投资总额(万美元) Total Volume of Contract (USD 10 000)	# 直接利用外资合同金额 Foreign Capital
合 计	Total	1791	2133197	880453
农 业	Agriculture	1	170	30
渔 业	Fishery	1	20	20
农、林、牧、渔服务业	FFAF Services	1	172	155
煤炭开采和洗选业	Mining and Washing of Coal	3	6449	3017
有色金属矿采选业	Mining and Processing of Non-Ferrous Metal Ores	1	77	60
其他矿采选业	Processing of Other Minerals Mining	1	70	70
农副食品加工业	Processing of Food from Agricultural Products	52	53299	27798
食品制造业	Manufacture of Foods	50	73377	32261
饮料制造业	Manufacture of Beverages	24	37877	13555
纺织业	Manufacture of Textile	27	17713	5235
纺织服装、鞋、帽制造业	Manufacture of Textile Wearing Apparel, Footware and Caps	55	8216	3645
皮革、毛皮、羽毛(绒)及其制品业	Manufacture of Leather, Fur, Feather and Related Products	17	3640	1526
木材加工及木竹藤棕草制品业	Processing of Timber, Manufacture of Wood, Bamboo, Rattan, Palm, and Straw Products	13	1248	852
家具制造业	Manufacture of Furniture	24	19017	7259
造纸及纸制品业	Manufacture of Paper and Paper Products	15	9181	3332
印刷业和记录媒介的复制	Printing, Reproduction of Recording Media	21	7402	4222
文教体育用品制造业	Manufacture of Articles For Culture, Education and Sport Activity	18	7522	1939
石油加工、炼焦及核燃料加工业	Processing of Petroleum, Coking, Processing of Nuclear Fuel	9	4965	2523
化学原料及化学制品制造	Manufacture of Raw Chemical Materials and Chemical Products	93	134085	53771
医药制造业	Manufacture of Medicines	41	71269	31517
化学纤维制造业	Manufacture of Chemical Fibers	4	3713	1619
橡胶制品业	Manufacture of Rubber	16	37417	14870
塑料制品业	Manufacture of Plastics	64	40165	16143
非金属矿物制品业	Manufacture of Non-metallic Mineral Products	64	36777	14929
黑色金属冶炼及压延加工	Smelting and Pressing of Ferrous Metals	10	22058	8275
有色金属冶炼及压延加工	Smelting and Pressing of Non-Ferrous Metals	9	15496	5113
金属制品业	Manufacture of Metal Products	43	14693	6184
通用设备制造业	Manufacture of General Purpose Machinery	71	52752	25437

22-20 续表 Continued

行业	Sector	企业个数(个) Number of Enterprises (unit)	直接利用外资项目合同投资总额(万美元) Total Volume of Contract (USD 10 000)	# 直接利用外资合同金额 Foreign Capital
专用设备制造业	Manufacture of Special Purpose Machinery	104	52124	18876
交通运输设备制造业	Manufacture of Transport Equipment	75	145214	62545
电气机械及器材制造业	Manufacture of Electrical Machinery and Equipment	72	66059	34237
通信设备、计算机及其他电子设备制造业	Manufacture of Communication Equipment, Computers and Other Electronic Equipment	160	784002	296856
仪器仪表及文化办公用机械制造业	Manufacture of Measuring Instruments and Machinery for Cultural Activity and Office Work	55	25989	10194
工艺品及其他制造业	Manufacture of Artwork and Other Manufacturing	27	3066	1936
废弃资源和废旧材料回收加工业	Recycling and Disposal of Waste	3	789	165
电力、热力的生产和供应业	Production and Supply of Electric Power and Heat Power	4	12545	6871
燃气生产和供应业	Production and Supply of Gas	2	1689	698
水的生产和供应业	Production and Supply of Water	2	7691	4046
房屋和土木工程建筑业	Buildings and Civil Engineering Construction	14	17951	7110
建筑安装业	Equipment Installation	4	139	67
建筑装饰业	Building Decoration	30	2094	1329
其他建筑业	Other Construction	4	202	119
道路运输业	Road Transportation	5	10681	2853
城市公共交通业	Urban Public Transportation	1	48	24
水上运输业	Water Transportation	6	379	196
装卸搬运和其他运输服务业	Loading, Transportation and Other Transportation Services	22	7398	2524
仓储业	Storage	20	17768	6677
电信和其他信息传输服务业	Telecommunication and Other Information Transmitting Services	17	4182	2532
计算机服务业	Computer Services	1	28	10
软件业	Software	36	2971	2267
批发业	Wholesale	27	13405	5833
零售业	Retail	6	3410	1575
餐饮业	Catering	10	346	281
其他金融活动	Other Finance	2	6151	1326
房地产业	Real Estate	102	93272	37556
租赁业	Leasing Serving	2	1670	800
商务服务业	Commercial Services	101	50816	31729
研究与试验发展	R & D	8	7282	2550
专业技术服务业	Professional Technology Services	35	16043	7888
科技交流和推广服务业	Scientific and Technological Exchange and Promotion Services	50	35692	17424
水利管理业	Water Conservancy	2	183	83
环境管理业	Management for Environment	4	573	515
公共设施管理业	Public Facilities Services	9	42714	12078
居民服务业	Resident Services	2	29	11
其他服务业	Other Services	5	124	45
教　育	Education	1	500	250
体　育	Sports	3	125	101
娱乐业	Entertainment	8	18658	12839
其他业	Others	2	355	80

22-21 建区以来天津保税区国民经济主要指标（1992-2006年）
MAIN STATISTICS ON TIANJIN FREE TRADE ZONE SINCE ITS ESTABLISHMENT, 1992-2006

年 份 Year	地区生产总值 (万元) Gross Domestic Product (10 000 yuan)	工业总产值 (万元) Gross Output Value of Industry (10 000 yuan)	固定资产投资 (亿元) Investment in Fixed Assets (100 million yuan)	进出区货物总值 (亿美元) Total Value of Goods from and to The Zone (USD 100 million)
1992	300		2.56	1.60
1993	6500	800	15.09	8.60
1994	16940	15000	7.18	6.77
1995	33930	46800	2.51	12.78
1996	77498	70010	1.56	27.01
1997	121687	69706	2.32	40.97
1998	231839	48479	10.61	46.97
1999	284363	41436	14.66	46.48
2000	346214	112921	12.22	47.00
2001	443845	169446	12.57	50.01
2002	615109	225396	15.50	65.00
2003	830186	418136	31.20	92.31
2004	1151502	910035	52.82	131.25
2005	1535838	1622752	62.06	187.61
2006	2025573	2550138	71.56	254.25

年 份 Year	直接利用外资合同数(个) Number of Foreign Direct Investment Contracts (unit)	直接利用外资合同金额 (万美元) Foreign Direct Investment Contracted (USD 10 000)	实际直接利用外资金额 (万美元) Foreign Direct Investment Actually Used (USD 10 000)	企业进出口总额 (万美元) Foreign Trade of Enterprises (USD 10 000)	#进 口 Import
1992	508	35253	6500		
1993	1169	53208	15330	6587	3507
1994	390	22179	11011	7413	3985
1995	336	27362	18027	31263	20473
1996	370	35906	20310	39281	23962
1997	413	70375	30044	60744	38970
1998	427	50213	30511	71190	45438
1999	212	55149	35331	74271	55450
2000	168	33779	35497	99284	76873
2001	134	47539	55084	121482	92580
2002	188	52549	23500	212003	173978
2003	218	96662	40177	361912	311927
2004	257	152384	56361	543963	473052
2005	338	206978	76663	814751	702335
2006	200	249044	92422	946841	758064

22-22 天津保税区主要经济指标
MAIN STATISTICS ON TIANJIN FREE TRADE ZONE

单位：万元 (10 000 yuan)

项　目	Item	2005	2006	2006比2005年增长(%) Increase Rete in 2006 over 2005 (%)
地区生产总值	Gross Domestic Product	1535838	2025573	31.9
第二产业	Secondary Industry	156276	337181	115.8
第三产业	Tertiary Industry	1379562	1688392	22.4
工业总产值	Gross Output Value of Industry	1622750	2550138	57.1
进出区货物总值（亿美元）	Total Value of Goods from and to The Zone (USD 100 million)	188	254	35.4
企业进出口额（亿美元）	Foreign Trade of The Enterprises (USD 100 million)	81	95	16.2
#进　口	Imports	70	76	7.9
各项税收总额	Various Taxes	1175749	710711	-39.6
#工商税及所得税	Industrial, Commercial and Income Tax	208377	286689	37.6
海关关税	Tariffs	408772	96403	-76 .4
海关代征税	Tax Levied by The Customs as An Agent	558600	327619	-41.3
企业销售(营业)收入	Sales (Operating) Revenue of Enterprise	1060	1201	13.3
固定资产投资总额	Investment in Fixed Assets	620573	715555	15.3
#基础设施投资	Infrastructure Investment	91713	152409	66.2

22-23 天津保税区基础设施形成能力（截至2006年底）
CAPACITY OF INFRASTRUCTURE ON TIANJIN FREE TRADE ZONE (By the End of 2006)

项　目	Item	单　位	Unit	天津港保税区 Tianjin Port Tree Trade Zone	天津空港加工区 Tianjin Air Port Industrial Park
建成道路长度	Length of Completed Roads	公　里	km	33.12	86.00
建成道路面积	Area of Completed Roads	万平方米	10 000 sq. m	39.69	157.44
绿地面积	Area of Green Areas	万平方米	10 000 sq. m	104.7	429.62
供水能力	Capacity of Water Supply	万立方米/日	10 000 cu. m/day	2.50	5.30
排水管道长度	Length of Drainpipes	公　里	km	67.25	246.00
#污水管道	Sewage Drainpipes	公　里	km	18.45	93.40
供电能力	Capacity of Electricity Supply	千伏安	kVA	127500	173692.00
供气能力	Capacity of Gas Supply	万立方米/日	10 000 cu. m/day	1.40	1.00
供热能力	Heating Supply	吨/小时	ton/hour	250	133.00
局用电话交换机容量	Capacity of Office Telephone Exchanges	万　门	10 000 lines	5.50	6.20

第23篇
CHAPTER 23

区县基本情况
Basic Statistics On Districts and Counties

23-1 和平区基本情况
BASIC STATISTICS OF HEPING DISTRICT

指　标	Item	2005	2006
*户籍户数(万户)	Registered Households (10 000 households)	12.95	12.99
*户籍人口(万人)	Registered Population (10 000 persons)	38.41	38.51
男	Male	18.56	18.59
女	Female	19.85	19.92
*人口出生率(‰)	Birth Rate of Population (‰)	4.0	2.7
*人口自然增长率(‰)	Natural Growth Rate of Population (‰)	-1.5	-1.2
城镇单位从业人员(万人)	Persons Employed in Urban Units (10 000 persons)	3.13	3.13
#在岗职工	On-post Staff and Workers	2.74	2.80
*区县生产总值(亿元)	Gross Domestic Product (100 million yuan)	283.09	313.86
第二产业	Secondary Industry	50.05	58.35
#工　业	Industry	41.13	44.72
第三产业	Tertiary Industry	233.04	255.51
区县生产总值增速(%)	Increase Rate of Gross Domestic Product (%)		8.2
区县增加值(亿元)	Value Added of District (100 million yuan)	59.35	70.21
区县增加值增速(%)	Increase Rate of Value Added of District (%)	20.6	16.7
一般预算区级财政收入(万元)	General Budgetary Government Revenue at District Level (10 000 yuan)	102253	120385
一般预算区级财政支出(万元)	General Budgetary Government Expenditure at District Level (10 000 yuan)	110159	130816
#教育经费支出	Operating Expenses for Education	27717	33240
*固定资产投资(万元)	Investment in Fixed Assets (10 000 yuan)	1782316	1238494
规模以上工业企业	Industrial Enterprises above Designated Size		
单位数(个)	Number of Units (unit)	22	20
从业人员(万人)	Employment (10 000 persons)	0.11	0.12
总产值(万元)	Gross Output Value (10 000 yuan)	16755	31618
主营业务收入(万元)	Principal Business Revenue (10 000 yuan)	18460	32923
利润总额(万元)	Total Profits (10 000 yuan)	1853	2039
资产总值(万元)	Total Assets (10 000 yuan)	16513	27803
负债总额(万元)	Liabilities (10 000 yuan)	9765	17844
社会消费品零售总额(万元)	Retail Sales of Consumer Goods (10 000 yuan)	1127010	1199757

注：1. "*"为全区(县)数据，其余为区(县)属数。2. 区县在地口径生产总值称为区县生产总值，考核口径生产总值称为区县增加值。3. 固定资产投资不含农村非农户和农户投资。4. 23-2至23-18表同。

Note: a) The data with "*" of this table refer to the whole district(county)data, others refer to that of units under the leadership of this district(county). b) GDP of districts and counties refers to the coverage of location, and value added of districts and counties refer to the coverage of examination. c) The investment in fixed assets exclude rural non-agricultrual and agricultrual households. d) Same as following table 23-2 to 23-18.

23-1 续表 Continued

指　标	Item	2005	2006
* 私营工商企业	Private Industrial and Commercial Enterprises		
户　数（户）	Number of Enterprises (unit)	4887	4540
从业人员（人）	Employees (person)	20295	17781
注册资本（万元）	Registered Capital (10 000 yuan)	487802	670154
总产值（万元）	Gross Output Value (10 000 yuan)		
营业收入（万元）	Business Revenue (10 000 yuan)	1022393	
* 个体工商业	Individual Industrial and Commercial Enterprises		
户　数（户）	Number of Enterprises (unit)	4390	4531
从业人员（人）	Employment (person)	6158	5501
资　金（万元）	Fund (10 000 yuan)	13436	14452
营业额（万元）	Turnover (10 000 yuan)	171761	
实际直接利用外资（万美元）	Foreign Direct Capital Actually Used (USD 10 000)	9003	10604
吸引内资到位额（万元）	Actual Domestic Investment (10 000 yuan)	465000	480600
工业企业出口交货值（万元）	Delivery Value of Industrial Enterprises (10 000 yuan)	11490	18093
* 小学校数（所）	Number of Primary Schools (unit)	31	32
* 小学在校学生数（人）	Students Enrollment of Primary Schools (person)	27758	27162
* 普通中学校数（所）	Number of Regular Secondary Schools (unit)	30	30
* 普通中学在校学生数（人）	Students Enrollment of Regular Secondary Schools (person)	34508	32459
幼儿园数（所）	Number of Kindergartens (unit)	28	25
卫生机构数（个）	Health Care Institutions (unit)	22	27
# 医院、卫生院	Hospital and Health Care Center	10	9
卫生机构床位数（张）	Beds (unit)	663	723
# 医院、卫生院	Hospital and Health Care Center	643	723
新增再就业人员（人）	Newly Re-employment Person (person)	3100	1422
享受低保户数（户）	Number of Households Receiving Lowest Cost-of-Living (household)	3053	3036
发放低保金额（万元）	Cost of Lowest Cost-of-Living (10000 yuan)	796.6	880.6
* 人均公共绿地面积（平方米）	Per Capita Public Green Areas (sq. m)	1.84	2.12

23-2 河东区基本情况
BASIC STATISTICS OF HEDONG DISTRICT

指　标	Item	2005	2006
* 户籍户数（万户）	Registered Households (10 000 households)	25.35	25.65
* 户籍人口（万人）	Registered Population (10 000 persons)	69.23	69.94
男	Male	34.89	35.22
女	Female	34.34	34.72
* 人口出生率 (‰)	Birth Rate of Population (‰)	4.3	4.4
* 人口自然增长率 (‰)	Natural Growth Rate of Population (‰)	-1.2	-0.6
城镇单位从业人员（万人）	Persons Employed in Urban Units (10 000 persons)	2.30	2.33
# 在岗职工	On-post Staff and Workers	1.79	1.85
* 区县生产总值（亿元）	Gross Domestic Product (100 million yuan)	129.42	148.98
第二产业	Secondary Industry	59.52	66.98
# 工　业	Industry	37.48	43.00
第三产业	Tertiary Industry	69.90	82.00
区县生产总值增速 (%)	Increase Rate of Gross Domestic Product (%)		10.1
区县增加值（亿元）	Value Added of District (100 million yuan)	50.74	61.45
区县增加值增速 (%)	Increase Rate of Value Added of District (%)	19.5	19.1
一般预算区级财政收入（万元）	General Budgetary Government Revenue at District Level (10 000 yuan)	77253	93880
一般预算区级财政支出（万元）	General Budgetary Government Expenditure at District Level (10 000 yuan)	89493	107843
# 教育经费支出	Operating Expenses for Education	28300	33059
* 固定资产投资（万元）	Investment in Fixed Assets (10 000 yuan)	487782	800217
规模以上工业企业	Industrial Enterprises above Designated Size		
单位数（个）	Number of Units (unit)	56	53
从业人员（万人）	Employment (10 000 persons)	0.38	0.38
总产值（万元）	Gross Output Value (10 000 yuan)	157743	184241
主营业务收入（万元）	Principal Business Revenue (10 000 yuan)	163391	182064
利润总额（万元）	Total Profits (10 000 yuan)	3427	7596
资产总值（万元）	Total Assets (10 000 yuan)	89853	119973
负债总额（万元）	Liabilities (10 000 yuan)	63613	86076
社会消费品零售总额（万元）	Retail Sales of Consumer Goods (10 000 yuan)	626136	753870

23-2 续表 Continued

指　标	Item	2005	2006
* 私营工商企业	Private Industrial and Commercial Enterprises		
户　数（户）	Number of Enterprises (unit)	3815	4732
从业人员（人）	Employees (person)	28895	36464
注册资本（万元）	Registered Capital (10 000 yuan)	414335	586679
总产值（万元）	Gross Output Value (10 000 yuan)	202270	358300
营业收入（万元）	Business Revenue (10 000 yuan)	683269	800850
* 个体工商业	Individual Industrial and Commercial Enterprises		
户　数（户）	Number of Enterprises (unit)	11572	12581
从业人员（人）	Employment (person)	11572	12581
资　金（万元）	Fund (10 000 yuan)	43927	56275
营业额（万元）	Turnover (10 000 yuan)	275005	212400
实际直接利用外资（万美元）	Foreign Direct Capital Actually Used (USD 10 000)	879	1490
吸引内资到位额（万元）	Actual Domestic Investment (10 000 yuan)	117799	187906
工业企业出口交货值（万元）	Delivery Value of Industrial Enterprises (10 000 yuan)	14155	13316
* 小学校数（所）	Number of Primary Schools (unit)	27	23
* 小学在校学生数（人）	Students Enrollment of Primary Schools (person)	20594	19260
* 普通中学校数（所）	Number of Regular Secondary Schools (unit)	30	23
* 普通中学在校学生数（人）	Students Enrollment of Regular Secondary Schools (person)	27535	26874
幼儿园数（所）	Number of Kindergartens (unit)	52	52
卫生机构数（个）	Health Care Institutions (unit)	18	18
# 医院、卫生院	Hospital and Health Care Center	15	15
卫生机构床位数（张）	Beds (unit)	1288	978
# 医院、卫生院	Hospital and Health Care Center	1028	978
新增再就业人员（人）	Newly Re-employment Person (person)	19526	20347
享受低保户数（户）	Number of Households Receiving Lowest Cost-of-Living (household)	11330	11867
发放低保金额（万元）	Cost of Lowest Cost-of-Living (10000 yuan)	4726	4951
* 人均公共绿地面积（平方米）	Per Capita Public Green Areas (sq. m)	6.74	7.34

23-3 河西区基本情况
BASIC STATISTICS OF HEXI DISTRICT

指　标	Item	2005	2006
* 户籍户数（万户）	Registered Households (10 000 households)	26.02	26.34
* 户籍人口（万人）	Registered Population (10 000 persons)	73.96	75.45
男	Male	36.62	37.21
女	Female	37.34	38.23
* 人口出生率 (‰)	Birth Rate of Population (‰)	4.1	4.2
* 人口自然增长率 (‰)	Natural Growth Rate of Population (‰)	-0.8	-0.6
城镇单位从业人员（万人）	Persons Employed in Urban Units (10 000 persons)	3.47	3.46
# 在岗职工	On-post Staff and Workers	2.99	3.00
* 区县生产总值（亿元）	Gross Domestic Product (100 million yuan)	285.99	314.42
第二产业	Secondary Industry	102.40	105.66
# 工　业	Industry	81.97	83.95
第三产业	Tertiary Industry	183.58	208.76
区县生产总值增速 (%)	Increase Rate of Gross Domestic Product (%)		6.4
区县增加值（亿元）	Value Added of District (100 million yuan)	60.99	78.57
区县增加值增速 (%)	Increase Rate of Value Added of District (%)	18.2	26.6
一般预算区级财政收入（万元）	General Budgetary Government Revenue at District Level (10 000 yuan)	113046	136078
一般预算区级财政支出（万元）	General Budgetary Government Expenditure at District Level (10 000 yuan)	98196	130336
# 教育经费支出	Operating Expenses for Education	30344	36075
* 固定资产投资（万元）	Investment in Fixed Assets (10 000 yuan)	445645	746040
规模以上工业企业	Industrial Enterprises above Designated Size		
单位数（个）	Number of Units (unit)	75	64
从业人员（万人）	Employment (10 000 persons)	0.41	0.34
总产值（万元）	Gross Output Value (10 000 yuan)	70926	73486
主营业务收入（万元）	Principal Business Revenue (10 000 yuan)	80133	74903
利润总额（万元）	Total Profits (10 000 yuan)	785	2195
资产总值（万元）	Total Assets (10 000 yuan)	90539	85037
负债总额（万元）	Liabilities (10 000 yuan)	48994	44368
社会消费品零售总额（万元）	Retail Sales of Consumer Goods (10 000 yuan)	1161949	1247481

23-3 续表 Continued

指　标	Item	2005	2006
*私营工商企业	Private Industrial and Commercial Enterprises		
户　数(户)	Number of Enterprises (unit)	6589	8042
从业人员(人)	Employees (person)	52671	64053
注册资本(万元)	Registered Capital (10 000 yuan)	611032	911958
总产值(万元)	Gross Output Value (10 000 yuan)	71550	112240
营业收入(万元)	Business Revenue (10 000 yuan)	262900	322830
*个体工商业	Individual Industrial and Commercial Enterprises		
户　数(户)	Number of Enterprises (unit)	16480	18406
从业人员(人)	Employment (person)	20984	24356
资　金(万元)	Fund (10 000 yuan)	45130	51230
营业额(万元)	Turnover (10 000 yuan)	591500	717150
实际直接利用外资(万美元)	Foreign Direct Capital Actually Used (USD 10 000)	3597	4310
吸引内资到位额(万元)	Actual Domestic Investment (10 000 yuan)	158764	205425
工业企业出口交货值(万元)	Delivery Value of Industrial Enterprises (10 000 yuan)	16020	11108
*小学校数(所)	Number of Primary Schools (unit)	47	46
*小学在校学生数(人)	Students Enrollment of Primary Schools (person)	30661	29891
*普通中学校数(所)	Number of Regular Secondary Schools (unit)	44	42
*普通中学在校学生数(人)	Students Enrollment of Regular Secondary Schools (person)	39186	35777
幼儿园数(所)	Number of Kindergartens (unit)	41	40
卫生机构数(个)	Health Care Institutions (unit)	24	24
#医院、卫生院	Hospital and Health Care Center	18	18
卫生机构床位数(张)	Beds (unit)	1285	1285
#医院、卫生院	Hospital and Health Care Center	1285	1285
新增再就业人员(人)	Newly Re-employment Person (person)	17803	21894
享受低保户数(户)	Number of Households Receiving Lowest Cost-of-Living (household)	7632	7842
发放低保金额(万元)	Cost of Lowest Cost-of-Living (10000 yuan)	1967	2179
*人均公共绿地面积(平方米)	Per Capita Public Green Areas (sq. m)	5.78	6.50

23-4 南开区基本情况
BASIC STATISTICS OF NANKAI DISTRICT

指　标	Item	2005	2006
* 户籍户数（万户）	Registered Households (10 000 households)	27.79	28.05
* 户籍人口（万人）	Registered Population (10 000 persons)	79.73	81.08
男	Male	40.36	41.09
女	Female	39.37	39.99
* 人口出生率 (‰)	Birth Rate of Population (‰)	3.9	4.0
* 人口自然增长率 (‰)	Natural Growth Rate of Population (‰)	-0.6	-0.6
城镇单位从业人员（万人）	Persons Employed in Urban Units (10 000 persons)	3.60	4.08
# 在岗职工	On-post Staff and Workers	2.59	2.82
* 区县生产总值（亿元）	Gross Domestic Product (100 million yuan)	195.29	220.45
第二产业	Secondary Industry	66.89	73.01
# 工　业	Industry	59.38	63.08
第三产业	Tertiary Industry	128.40	147.43
区县生产总值增速 (%)	Increase Rate of Gross Domestic Product (%)		9.9
区县增加值（亿元）	Value Added of District (100 million yuan)	62.04	72.68
区县增加值增速 (%)	Increase Rate of Value Added of District (%)	18.0	15.3
一般预算区级财政收入（万元）	General Budgetary Government Revenue at District Level (10 000 yuan)	102657	139702
一般预算区级财政支出（万元）	General Budgetary Government Expenditure at District Level (10 000 yuan)	103337	123600
# 教育经费支出	Operating Expenses for Education	27807	34749
* 固定资产投资（万元）	Investment in Fixed Assets (10 000 yuan)	1061892	1323923
规模以上工业企业	Industrial Enterprises above Designated Size		
单位数（个）	Number of Units (unit)	128	135
从业人员（万人）	Employment (10 000 persons)	0.83	0.89
总产值（万元）	Gross Output Value (10 000 yuan)	293000	2559223
主营业务收入（万元）	Principal Business Revenue (10 000 yuan)	229041	241747
利润总额（万元）	Total Profits (10 000 yuan)	13303	11931
资产总值（万元）	Total Assets (10 000 yuan)	202317	218731
负债总额（万元）	Liabilities (10 000 yuan)	111284	121215
社会消费品零售总额（万元）	Retail Sales of Consumer Goods (10 000 yuan)	1056231	1332704

23-4 续表 Continued

指　　标	Item	2005	2006
* 私营工商企业	Private Industrial and Commercial Enterprises		
户　数（户）	Number of Enterprises (unit)	8219	9314
从业人员（人）	Employees (person)	62873	69770
注册资本（万元）	Registered Capital (10 000 yuan)	677666	838009
总产值（万元）	Gross Output Value (10 000 yuan)	197482	222745
营业收入（万元）	Business Revenue (10 000 yuan)	679627	811965
* 个体工商业	Individual Industrial and Commercial Enterprises		
户　数（户）	Number of Enterprises (unit)	9177	9007
从业人员（人）	Employment (person)	10667	10159
资　金（万元）	Fund (10 000 yuan)	51472	34650
营业额（万元）	Turnover (10 000 yuan)	378848	526881
实际直接利用外资（万美元）	Foreign Direct Capital Actually Used (USD 10 000)	4628	10941
吸引内资到位额（万元）	Actual Domestic Investment (10 000 yuan)	293522	401140
工业企业出口交货值（万元）	Delivery Value of Industrial Enterprises (10 000 yuan)	170977	196998
* 小学校数（所）	Number of Primary Schools (unit)	38	36
* 小学在校学生数（人）	Students Enrollment of Primary Schools (person)	26949	26334
* 普通中学校数（所）	Number of Regular Secondary Schools (unit)	42	39
* 普通中学在校学生数（人）	Students Enrollment of Regular Secondary Schools (person)	34011	32743
幼儿园数（所）	Number of Kindergartens (unit)	47	48
卫生机构数（个）	Health Care Institutions (unit)	27	27
# 医院、卫生院	Hospital and Health Care Center	19	19
卫生机构床位数（张）	Beds (unit)	1423	1489
# 医院、卫生院	Hospital and Health Care Center	1423	1489
新增再就业人员（人）	Newly Re-employment Person (person)	24694	19249
享受低保户数（户）	Number of Households Receiving Lowest Cost-of-Living (household)	8841	7722
发放低保金额（万元）	Cost of Lowest Cost-of-Living (10000 yuan)	3000	2266
* 人均公共绿地面积（平方米）	Per Capita Public Green Areas (sq. m)	8.6	9.3

23-5 河北区基本情况
BASIC STATISTICS OF HEBEI DISTRICT

指　标	Item	2005	2006
* 户籍户数（万户）	Registered Households (10 000 households)	22.85	23.16
* 户籍人口（万人）	Registered Population (10 000 persons)	62.65	63.44
男	Male	31.61	32.00
女	Female	31.04	31.44
* 人口出生率 (‰)	Birth Rate of Population (‰)	4.3	4.4
* 人口自然增长率 (‰)	Natural Growth Rate of Population (‰)	-2.1	-1.1
城镇单位从业人员（万人）	Persons Employed in Urban Units (10 000 persons)	2.5	2.2
# 在岗职工	On-post Staff and Workers	2.00	1.85
* 区县生产总值（亿元）	Gross Domestic Product (100 million yuan)	139.10	155.66
第二产业	Secondary Industry	40.68	44.99
# 工　业	Industry	37.39	40.43
第三产业	Tertiary Industry	98.42	110.67
区县生产总值增速 (%)	Increase Rate of Gross Domestic Product (%)		8.6
区县增加值（亿元）	Value Added of District (100 million yuan)	41.3	52.76
区县增加值增速 (%)	Increase Rate of Value Added of District (%)	21.0	26.0
一般预算区级财政收入（万元）	General Budgetary Government Revenue at District Level (10 000 yuan)	49676	57421
一般预算区级财政支出（万元）	General Budgetary Government Expenditure at District Level (10 000 yuan)	80487	83270
# 教育经费支出	Operating Expenses for Education	26395	32705
* 固定资产投资（万元）	Investment in Fixed Assets (10 000 yuan)	389750	1124857
规模以上工业企业	Industrial Enterprises above Designated Size		
单位数（个）	Number of Units (unit)	58	47
从业人员（万人）	Employment (10 000 persons)	0.36	0.33
总产值（万元）	Gross Output Value (10 000 yuan)	68702	61339
主营业务收入（万元）	Principal Business Revenue (10 000 yuan)	67684	61208
利润总额（万元）	Total Profits (10 000 yuan)	1269	-146
资产总值（万元）	Total Assets (10 000 yuan)	80991	67527
负债总额（万元）	Liabilities (10 000 yuan)	54679	39596
社会消费品零售总额（万元）	Retail Sales of Consumer Goods (10 000 yuan)	445930	569656

23-5 续表 Continued

指　　标	Item	2005	2006
* 私营工商企业	Private Industrial and Commercial Enterprises		
户　数（户）	Number of Enterprises (unit)	3190	3373
从业人员（人）	Employees (person)	35352	36156
注册资本（万元）	Registered Capital (10 000 yuan)	299452	460454
总产值（万元）	Gross Output Value (10 000 yuan)	162348	161979
营业收入（万元）	Business Revenue (10 000 yuan)	480813	480744
* 个体工商业	Individual Industrial and Commercial Enterprises		
户　数（户）	Number of Enterprises (unit)	6236	6221
从业人员（人）	Employment (person)	6851	6732
资　金（万元）	Fund (10 000 yuan)	21626	24074
营业额（万元）	Turnover (10 000 yuan)	262620	262572
实际直接利用外资（万美元）	Foreign Direct Capital Actually Used (USD 10 000)	2789	5074
吸引内资到位额（万元）	Actual Domestic Investment (10 000 yuan)	126100	265000
工业企业出口交货值（万元）	Delivery Value of Industrial Enterprises (10 000 yuan)	11812	22847
* 小学校数（所）	Number of Primary Schools (unit)	36	29
* 小学在校学生数（人）	Students Enrollment of Primary Schools (person)	24711	23641
* 普通中学校数（所）	Number of Regular Secondary Schools (unit)	40	34
* 普通中学在校学生数（人）	Students Enrollment of Regular Secondary Schools (person)	33418	30479
幼儿园数（所）	Number of Kindergartens (unit)	37	37
卫生机构数（个）	Health Care Institutions (unit)	22	22
# 医院、卫生院	Hospital and Health Care Center	18	17
卫生机构床位数（张）	Beds (unit)	1535	1535
# 医院、卫生院	Hospital and Health Care Center	1535	1535
新增再就业人员（人）	Newly Re-employment Person (person)	23328	17979
享受低保户数（户）	Number of Households Receiving Lowest Cost-of-Living (household)	9942	10230
发放低保金额（万元）	Cost of Lowest Cost-of-Living (10000 yuan)	2751	3230
* 人均公共绿地面积（平方米）	Per Capita Public Green Areas (sq. m)	7.5	3.8

23-6 红桥区基本情况
BASIC STATISTICS OF HONGQIAO DISTRICT

指　标	Item	2005	2006
* 户籍户数（万户）	Registered Households (10 000 households)	20.23	20.42
* 户籍人口（万人）	Registered Population (10 000 persons)	55.16	55.76
男	Male	27.88	28.27
女	Female	27.28	27.49
* 人口出生率 (‰)	Birth Rate of Population (‰)	4.4	4.1
* 人口自然增长率 (‰)	Natural Growth Rate of Population (‰)	-1.5	-1.2
城镇单位从业人员（万人）	Persons Employed in Urban Units (10 000 persons)	2.36	2.14
# 在岗职工	On-post Staff and Workers	1.82	1.81
* 区县生产总值（亿元）	Gross Domestic Product (100 million yuan)	43.66	49.62
第二产业	Secondary Industry	10.86	12.08
# 工　业	Industry	9.97	10.75
第三产业	Tertiary Industry	32.80	37.54
区县生产总值增速 (%)	Increase Rate of Gross Domestic Product (%)		11.9
区县增加值（亿元）	Value Added of District (100 million yuan)	39.11	46.66
区县增加值增速 (%)	Increase Rate of Value Added of District (%)	20.2	17.9
一般预算区级财政收入（万元）	General Budgetary Government Revenue at District Level (10 000 yuan)	30382	37302
一般预算区级财政支出（万元）	General Budgetary Government Expenditure at District Level (10 000 yuan)	60566	76855
# 教育经费支出	Operating Expenses for Education	20879	26581
* 固定资产投资（万元）	Investment in Fixed Assets (10 000 yuan)	160039	110535
规模以上工业企业	Industrial Enterprises above Designated Size		
单位数（个）	Number of Units (unit)	42	39
从业人员（万人）	Employment (10 000 persons)	0.27	0.28
总产值（万元）	Gross Output Value (10 000 yuan)	65301	53243
主营业务收入（万元）	Principal Business Revenue (10 000 yuan)	63051	56659
利润总额（万元）	Total Profits (10 000 yuan)	628	756
资产总值（万元）	Total Assets (10 000 yuan)	48720	48930
负债总额（万元）	Liabilities (10 000 yuan)	27156	27474
社会消费品零售总额（万元）	Retail Sales of Consumer Goods (10 000 yuan)	508011	620656

23-6 续表 Continued

指　标	Item	2005	2006
*私营工商企业	Private Industrial and Commercial Enterprises		
户　数（户）	Number of Enterprises (unit)	1842	1884
从业人员（人）	Employees (person)	15472	16247
注册资本（万元）	Registered Capital (10 000 yuan)	153086	186840
总产值（万元）	Gross Output Value (10 000 yuan)	34033	40682
营业收入（万元）	Business Revenue (10 000 yuan)	70516	95063
*个体工商业	Individual Industrial and Commercial Enterprises		
户　数（户）	Number of Enterprises (unit)	9120	8553
从业人员（人）	Employment (person)	9215	8851
资　金（万元）	Fund (10 000 yuan)	22581	24231
营业额（万元）	Turnover (10 000 yuan)	127299	939728
实际直接利用外资（万美元）	Foreign Direct Capital Actually Used (USD 10 000)	1100	2500
吸引内资到位额（万元）	Actual Domestic Investment (10 000 yuan)	210340	300000
工业企业出口交货值（万元）	Delivery Value of Industrial Enterprises (10 000 yuan)	14745	17600
*小学校数（所）	Number of Primary Schools (unit)	30	30
*小学在校学生数（人）	Students Enrollment of Primary Schools (person)	16834	15656
*普通中学校数（所）	Number of Regular Secondary Schools (unit)	29	26
*普通中学在校学生数（人）	Students Enrollment of Regular Secondary Schools (person)	26393	24124
幼儿园数（所）	Number of Kindergartens (unit)	16	15
卫生机构数（个）	Health Care Institutions (unit)	89	78
#医院、卫生院	Hospital and Health Care Center	14	14
卫生机构床位数（张）	Beds (unit)	1044	1435
#医院、卫生院	Hospital and Health Care Center	1044	1114
新增再就业人员（人）	Newly Re-employment Person (person)	17592	24146
享受低保户数（户）	Number of Households Receiving Lowest Cost-of-Living (household)	10852	10800
发放低保金额（万元）	Cost of Lowest Cost-of-Living (10000 yuan)	2801	2844
*人均公共绿地面积（平方米）	Per Capita Public Green Areas (sq. m)	3.2	3.5

23-7 塘沽区基本情况
BASIC STATISTICS OF TANGGU DISTRICT

指　标	Item	2005	2006
*户籍户数(万户)	Registered Households (10 000 households)	17.62	17.97
#农业户	Agricultural Households	2.37	2.42
*户籍人口(万人)	Registered Population (10 000 persons)	48.85	50.13
1.农业人口	Agricultural Population	6.03	6.05
非农业人口	Non-agricultural Population	42.81	44.08
2.男	Male	25.18	25.83
女	Female	23.66	24.3
*人口出生率(‰)	Birth Rate of Population (‰)	7.5	5.2
*人口自然增长率(‰)	Natural Growth Rate of Population (‰)	3.0	0.7
城镇单位从业人员(万人)	Employment Personnel in Urban Units (100 persons)	3.56	3.78
#在岗职工	On-post Staff and Workers	3.27	3.5
*乡村从业人员(万人)	Rural Employment Personnel (10 000 persons)	2.68	
#农林牧渔业	Farming, Forestry, Animal Husbandry and Fishery	0.68	
*区县生产总值(亿元)	Gross Domestic Product (100 million yuan)	388.67	518.18
第一产业	Primary Industry	1.77	1.44
第二产业	Secondary Industry	237.77	373.84
#工　业	Industry	205.10	343.18
第三产业	Tertiary Industry	149.13	142.90
区县生产总值增速(%)	Increase Rate of Gross Domestic Product (%)		29.4
区县增加值(亿元)	Value Added of District (100 million yuan)	89.79	117.13
区县增加值增速(%)	Increase Rate of Value Added of District (%)	20.7	28.3
一般预算区级财政收入(万元)	General Budgetary Government Revenue at District Level (10 000 yuan)	108465	159900
一般预算区级财政支出(万元)	General Budgetary Government Expenditure at District Level (10 000 yuan)	147046	202654
#教育经费支出	Operating Expenses for Education	30934	44634
*固定资产投资(万元)	Investment in Fixed Assets (10 000 yuan)	3475198	4663476
年末实有耕地面积(万公顷)	Cultivated Land (year-end) (10 000 hectare)	0.48	
农林牧渔业总产值(万元)	Gross Output Value of Farming, Forestry, Animal Husbandry and Fishery (10 000 yuan)	48369	40144
农林牧渔业总产值增速(%)	Increase Rate of Gross Output Value of Farming, Forestry, Animal Husbandry and Fishery (%)	7.7	-17.0
粮食产量(万吨)	Total Yield of Grain (10 000 tons)	0.41	0.37
水产品产量(吨)	Total Yield of Aquatic Products (ton)	25970	21402
蔬菜总产量(万吨)	Total Yield of Vegetables (10 000 tons)	5.95	4.81
*农村居民人均年纯收入(元)	Per Capita Annual Net Income of Rural Households (yuan)	7932	8729
*农村居民人均生活消费支出(元)	Per Capita Annual Expenditure for Consumption of Rural Households (yuan)	4618	5077
#食品支出	Expenditure for Food	2034	2138

23-7 续表 Continued

指　标	Item	2005	2006
农村人均住房面积（平方米）	Per Capita Floor Space of Rural Households (sq. m)	24.5	24.7
规模以上工业企业	Industrial Enterprises above Designated Size		
单位数（个）	Number of Units (unit)	147	133
从业人员（万人）	Employment Personnel (10 000 persons)	1.36	1.40
总产值（万元）	Gross Output Value (10 000 yuan)	597553	761549
主营业务收入（万元）	Principal Business Revenue (10 000 yuan)	560805	730694
利润总额（万元）	Total Profits (10 000 yuan)	19913	20610
资产总值（万元）	Total Assets (10 000 yuan)	735694	864262
负债总额（万元）	Liability (10 000 yuan)	436661	539093
社会消费品零售总额（万元）	Total Retail Sales of Consumer Goods (10 000 yuan)	708694	810358
* 私营工商企业	Private Industrial and Commercial Enterprises		
户　数（户）	Number of Enterprises (unit)	4020	5068
从业人员（人）	Employees (person)	28871	36638
注册资本（万元）	Registered Capital (10 000 yuan)	650247	1006226
总产值（万元）	Gross Output Value (10 000 yuan)	137004	166621
营业收入（万元）	Business Revenue (10 000 yuan)	251465	307232
* 个体工商业	Individual Industrial and Commercial Enterprises		
户　数（户）	Number of Enterprises (unit)	15424	17079
从业人员（人）	Employment (person)	19681	22716
资　金（万元）	Fund (10 000 yuan)	73084	76782
营业额（万元）	Turnover (10 000 yuan)	285910	346070
实际直接利用外资（万美元）	Foreign Direct Investment (USD 10 000)	8707	11505
吸引内资到位额（万元）	Actual Domestic Investment (10 000 yuan)	290000	145557
工业企业出口交货值（万元）	Delivery Value of Industrial Enterprises (10 000 yuan)	258039	301613
* 小学校数（所）	Number of Primary Schools (unit)	57	52
* 小学在校学生数（人）	Students Enrollment of Primary Schools (person)	33033	33814
* 普通中学校数（所）	Number of Regular Secondary Schools (unit)	36	33
* 普通中学在校学生数（人）	Students Enrollment of Regular Secondary Schools (person)	25312	24280
幼儿园数（所）	Number of Kindergartens (unit)	88	87
卫生机构数（个）	Health Care Institutions (unit)	174	150
# 医院、卫生院	Hospital and Health Care Center	28	29
卫生机构床位数（张）	Beds (unit)	2219	2290
# 医院、卫生院	Hospital and Health Care Center	2017	2047
新型农村合作医疗覆盖率 (%)	New Rural Cooperative Medical Service Overlay Rate (%)	86	89
新增再就业人员（人）	Newly Re-employment Person (person)	13302	12777

23-8 汉沽区基本情况
BASIC STATISTICS OF HAN'GU DISTRICT

指　　标	Item	2005	2006
*户籍户数（万户）	Registered Households (10 000 households)	6.39	6.54
#农业户	Agricultural Households	1.56	1.64
*户籍人口（万人）	Registered Population (10 000 persons)	16.91	17.09
1.农业人口	Agricultural Population	4.55	4.61
非农业人口	Non-agricultural Population	12.36	12.48
2.男	Male	8.57	8.64
女	Female	8.34	8.45
*人口出生率(‰)	Birth Rate of Population (‰)	7.2	7.6
*人口自然增长率(‰)	Natural Growth Rate of Population (‰)	1.5	1.4
城镇单位从业人员（万人）	Employment Personnel in Urban Units (100 persons)	1.23	1.31
#在岗职工	On-post Staff and Workers	1.18	1.24
*乡村从业人员（万人）	Rural Employment Personnel (10 000 persons)	2.64	2.70
#农林牧渔业	Farming, Forestry, Animal Husbandry and Fishery	1.57	1.63
*区县生产总值（亿元）	Gross Domestic Product (100 million yuan)	35.84	43.26
第一产业	Primary Industry	3.31	3.52
第二产业	Secondary Industry	19.00	23.10
#工　业	Industry	15.59	17.95
第三产业	Tertiary Industry	13.52	16.64
区县生产总值增速(%)	Increase Rate of Gross Domestic Product (%)		16.8
区县增加值（亿元）	Value Added of District (100 million yuan)	24.08	29.62
区县增加值增速(%)	Increase Rate of Value Added of District (%)	19.2	20.1
一般预算区级财政收入（万元）	General Budgetary Government Revenue at District Level (10 000 yuan)	17930	22964
一般预算区级财政支出（万元）	General Budgetary Government Expenditure at District Level (10 000 yuan)	37350	46174
#教育经费支出	Operating Expenses for Education	10008	12161
*固定资产投资（万元）	Investment in Fixed Assets (10 000 yuan)	221041	266198
年末实有耕地面积（万公顷）	Cultivated Land (year-end) (10 000 hectare)	0.42	0.41
农林牧渔业总产值（万元）	Gross Output Value of Farming, Forestry, Animal Husbandry and Fishery (10 000 yuan)	80803	86304
农林牧渔业总产值增速(%)	Increase Rate of Gross Output Value of Farming, Forestry, Animal Husbandry and Fishery (%)	5.3	6.8
粮食产量（万吨）	Total Yield of Grain (10 000 tons)	0.41	0.32
水产品产量（吨）	Total Yield of Aquatic Products (ton)	26449	25863
蔬菜总产量（万吨）	Total Yield of Vegetables (10 000 tons)	3.33	3.34
*农村居民人均年纯收入（元）	Per Capita Annual Net Income of Rural Households (yuan)	7535	8298
*农村居民人均生活消费支出（元）	Per Capita Annual Expenditure for Consumption of Rural Households (yuan)	4424	5014
#食品支出	Expenditure for Food	1584	1830

23-8 续表 Continued

指　标	Item	2005	2006
农村人均住房面积（平方米）	Per Capita Floor Space of Rural Households (sq. m)	26.2	29.1
规模以上工业企业	Industrial Enterprises above Designated Size		
单位数（个）	Number of Units (unit)	93	93
从业人员（万人）	Employment Personnel (10 000 persons)	1.14	1.17
总产值（万元）	Gross Output Value (10 000 yuan)	252615	305471
主营业务收入（万元）	Principal Business Revenue (10 000 yuan)	250027	303850
利润总额（万元）	Total Profits (10 000 yuan)	5779	7397
资产总值（万元）	Total Assets (10 000 yuan)	205201	239275
负债总额（万元）	Liability (10 000 yuan)	136265	163075
社会消费品零售总额（万元）	Total Retail Sales of Consumer Goods (10 000 yuan)	137861	152243
* 私营工商企业	Private Industrial and Commercial Enterprises		
户　数（户）	Number of Enterprises (unit)	1104	977
从业人员（人）	Employees (person)	14908	10348
注册资本（万元）	Registered Capital (10 000 yuan)	99031	149680
总产值（万元）	Gross Output Value (10 000 yuan)	80415	90847
营业收入（万元）	Business Revenue (10 000 yuan)	79639	93683
* 个体工商业	Individual Industrial and Commercial Enterprises		
户　数（户）	Number of Enterprises (unit)	6260	5060
从业人员（人）	Employment (person)	5428	5060
资　金（万元）	Fund (10 000 yuan)	7046	5959
营业额（万元）	Turnover (10 000 yuan)	107090	123917
实际直接利用外资（万美元）	Foreign Direct Investment (USD 10 000)	3389	3900
吸引内资到位额（万元）	Actual Domestic Investment (10 000 yuan)	36800	96800
工业企业出口交货值（万元）	Delivery Value of Industrial Enterprises (10 000 yuan)	49358	73592
* 小学校数（所）	Number of Primary Schools (unit)	23	21
* 小学在校学生数（人）	Students Enrollment of Primary Schools (person)	10361	9488
* 普通中学校数（所）	Number of Regular Secondary Schools (unit)	15	15
* 普通中学在校学生数（人）	Students Enrollment of Regular Secondary Schools (person)	10647	10325
幼儿园数（所）	Number of Kindergartens (unit)	19	25
卫生机构数（个）	Health Care Institutions (unit)	15	15
# 医院、卫生院	Hospital and Health Care Center	8	7
卫生机构床位数（张）	Beds (unit)	992	930
# 医院、卫生院	Hospital and Health Care Center	972	930
新型农村合作医疗覆盖率 (%)	New Rural Cooperative Medical Service Overlay Rate (%)	80.2	70.7
新增再就业人员（人）	Newly Re-employment Person (person)	5000	6100

23-9 大港区基本情况
BASIC STATISTICS OF DAGANG DISTRICT

指　标	Item	2005	2006
*户籍户数（万户）	Registered Households (10 000 households)	13.20	13.44
#农业户	Agricultural Households	3.58	3.66
*户籍人口（万人）	Registered Population (10 000 persons)	35.46	36.97
1.农业人口	Agricultural Population	10.40	10.44
非农业人口	Non-agricultural Population	25.06	26.53
2.男	Male	18.49	19.24
女	Female	16.97	17.73
*人口出生率(‰)	Birth Rate of Population (‰)	11.8	10.2
*人口自然增长率(‰)	Natural Growth Rate of Population (‰)	8.2	6.5
城镇单位从业人员（万人）	Employment Personnel in Urban Units (100 persons)	2.01	2.33
#在岗职工	On-post Staff and Workers	1.98	2.14
*乡村从业人员（万人）	Rural Employment Personnel (10 000 persons)	4	
#农林牧渔业	Farming, Forestry, Animal Husbandry and Fishery	1.6	
*区县生产总值（亿元）	Gross Domestic Product (100 million yuan)	245.03	280.97
第一产业	Primary Industry	1.67	1.72
第二产业	Secondary Industry	196.41	231.19
#工　业	Industry	188.05	217.37
第三产业	Tertiary Industry	46.95	48.06
区县生产总值增速(%)	Increase Rate of Gross Domestic Product (%)		11.5
区县增加值（亿元）	Value Added of District (100 million yuan)	70.18	82.66
区县增加值增速(%)	Increase Rate of Value Added of District (%)	16.3	15.0
一般预算区级财政收入（万元）	General Budgetary Government Revenue at District Level (10 000 yuan)	50838	61386
一般预算区级财政支出（万元）	General Budgetary Government Expenditure at District Level (10 000 yuan)	96104	102620
#教育经费支出	Operating Expenses for Education	34422	40067
*固定资产投资（万元）	Investment in Fixed Assets (10 000 yuan)	564834	910631
年末实有耕地面积（万公顷）	Cultivated Land (year-end) (10 000 hectare)	1.34	
农林牧渔业总产值（万元）	Gross Output Value of Farming, Forestry, Animal Husbandry and Fishery (10 000 yuan)	40657	43399
农林牧渔业总产值增速(%)	Increase Rate of Gross Output Value of Farming, Forestry, Animal Husbandry and Fishery (%)	8.5	6.7
粮食产量（万吨）	Total Yield of Grain (10 000 tons)	4.31	4.55
水产品产量（吨）	Total Yield of Aquatic Products (ton)	7585	7652
蔬菜总产量（万吨）	Total Yield of Vegetables (10 000 tons)	3.21	3.02
*农村居民人均年纯收入（元）	Per Capita Annual Net Income of Rural Households (yuan)	7577	8349
*农村居民人均生活消费支出（元）	Per Capita Annual Expenditure for Consumption of Rural Households (yuan)	5242	4967
#食品支出	Expenditure for Food	1761	1839

23-9 续表 Continued

指　标	Item	2005	2006
农村人均住房面积（平方米）	Per Capita Floor Space of Rural Households (sq. m)	30.32	35.61
规模以上工业企业	Industrial Enterprises above Designated Size		
单位数（个）	Number of Units (unit)	200	209
从业人员（万人）	Employment Personnel (10 000 persons)	2.50	2.40
总产值（万元）	Gross Output Value (10 000 yuan)	1160650	1389895
主营业务收入（万元）	Principal Business Revenue (10 000 yuan)	1217614	1388105
利润总额（万元）	Total Profits (10 000 yuan)	33117	45012
资产总值（万元）	Total Assets (10 000 yuan)	967648	1023166
负债总额（万元）	Liability (10 000 yuan)	639925	653391
社会消费品零售总额（万元）	Total Retail Sales of Consumer Goods (10 000 yuan)	341300	383425
*私营工商企业	Private Industrial and Commercial Enterprises		
户　数（户）	Number of Enterprises (unit)	1948	2465
从业人员（人）	Employees (person)	16713	20728
注册资本（万元）	Registered Capital (10 000 yuan)	247244	443861
总产值（万元）	Gross Output Value (10 000 yuan)	93685	66045
营业收入（万元）	Business Revenue (10 000 yuan)	107409	107078
*个体工商业	Individual Industrial and Commercial Enterprises		
户　数（户）	Number of Enterprises (unit)	4952	5600
从业人员（人）	Employment (person)	10900	12781
资　金（万元）	Fund (10 000 yuan)	22106	24364
营业额（万元）	Turnover (10 000 yuan)	108440	112596
实际直接利用外资（万美元）	Foreign Direct Investment (USD 10 000)	5399	7020
吸引内资到位额（万元）	Actual Domestic Investment (10 000 yuan)	182850	330000
工业企业出口交货值（万元）	Delivery Value of Industrial Enterprises (10 000 yuan)	339046	369343
*小学校数（所）	Number of Primary Schools (unit)	32	40
*小学在校学生数（人）	Students Enrollment of Primary Schools (person)	24660	25573
*普通中学校数（所）	Number of Regular Secondary Schools (unit)	39	39
*普通中学在校学生数（人）	Students Enrollment of Regular Secondary Schools (person)	28633	29817
幼儿园数（所）	Number of Kindergartens (unit)	61	74
卫生机构数（个）	Health Care Institutions (unit)	14	14
#医院、卫生院	Hospital and Health Care Center	14	14
卫生机构床位数（张）	Beds (unit)	950	985
#医院、卫生院	Hospital and Health Care Center	950	985
新型农村合作医疗覆盖率(%)	New Rural Cooperative Medical Service Overlay Rate (%)	46.0	61.0
新增再就业人员（人）	Newly Re-employment Person (person)	12568	12005

23-10 东丽区基本情况
BASIC STATISTICS OF DONGLI DISTRICT

指 标	Item	2005	2006
* 户籍户数（万户）	Registered Households (10 000 households)	12.45	12.82
# 农业户	Agricultural Households	7.48	7.70
* 户籍人口（万人）	Registered Population (10 000 persons)	31.82	32.35
1. 农业人口	Agricultural Population	19.76	19.85
非农业人口	Non-agricultural Population	12.06	12.50
2. 男	Male	16.00	16.22
女	Female	15.82	16.13
* 人口出生率 (‰)	Birth Rate of Population (‰)	7.9	7.7
* 人口自然增长率 (‰)	Natural Growth Rate of Population (‰)	4.3	4.3
城镇单位从业人员（万人）	Employment Personnel in Urban Units (100 persons)	3.83	4.03
# 在岗职工	On-post Staff and Workers	3.57	3.97
* 乡村从业人员（万人）	Rural Employment Personnel (10 000 persons)	9.96	10.38
# 农林牧渔业	Farming, Forestry, Animal Husbandry and Fishery	1.8	1.89
* 区县生产总值（亿元）	Gross Domestic Product (100 million yuan)	172.75	203.02
第一产业	Primary Industry	3.82	4.09
第二产业	Secondary Industry	104.24	120.94
# 工 业	Industry	95.88	107.56
第三产业	Tertiary Industry	64.69	77.99
区县生产总值增速 (%)	Increase Rate of Gross Domestic Product (%)		14.4
区县增加值（亿元）	Value Added of District (100 million yuan)	102.21	115.60
区县增加值增速 (%)	Increase Rate of Value Added of District (%)	14.6	9.9
一般预算区级财政收入（万元）	General Budgetary Government Revenue at District Level (10 000 yuan)	97988	131002
一般预算区级财政支出（万元）	General Budgetary Government Expenditure at District Level (10 000 yuan)	104696	132466
# 教育经费支出	Operating Expenses for Education	19110	22356
* 固定资产投资（万元）	Investment in Fixed Assets (10 000 yuan)	1325078	1637341
年末实有耕地面积（万公顷）	Cultivated Land (year-end) (10 000 hectare)	1.3	1.13
农林牧渔业总产值（万元）	Gross Output Value of Farming, Forestry, Animal Husbandry and Fishery (10 000 yuan)	86202	92202
农林牧渔业总产值增速 (%)	Increase Rate of Gross Output Value of Farming, Forestry, Animal Husbandry and Fishery (%)	11.9	4.8
粮食产量（万吨）	Total Yield of Grain (10 000 tons)	1.20	0.97
水产品产量（吨）	Total Yield of Aquatic Products (ton)	21291	21017
蔬菜总产量（万吨）	Total Yield of Vegetables (10 000 tons)	21.83	21.66
* 农村居民人均年纯收入（元）	Per Capita Annual Net Income of Rural Households (yuan)	8634	9500
* 农村居民人均生活消费支出（元）	Per Capita Annual Expenditure for Consumption of Rural Households (yuan)	5433	5302
# 食品支出	Expenditure for Food	2042	2068

23-10 续表 Continued

指　标	Item	2005	2006
农村人均住房面积(平方米)	Per Capita Floor Space of Rural Households (sq. m)	31.83	32.18
规模以上工业企业	Industrial Enterprises above Designated Size		
单位数(个)	Number of Units (unit)	247	300
从业人员(万人)	Employment Personnel (10 000 persons)	4.55	4.68
总产值(万元)	Gross Output Value (10 000 yuan)	1904805	2468373
主营业务收入(万元)	Principal Business Revenue (10 000 yuan)	1886821	2389159
利润总额(万元)	Total Profits (10 000 yuan)	82534	135806
资产总值(万元)	Total Assets (10 000 yuan)	1497727	2063234
负债总额(万元)	Liability (10 000 yuan)	725330	1106073
社会消费品零售总额(万元)	Total Retail Sales of Consumer Goods (10 000 yuan)	404461	444211
*私营工商企业	Private Industrial and Commercial Enterprises		
户　数(户)	Number of Enterprises (unit)	4554	4688
从业人员(人)	Employees (person)	38155	40856
注册资本(万元)	Registered Capital (10 000 yuan)	627268	783612
总产值(万元)	Gross Output Value (10 000 yuan)	741081	815825
营业收入(万元)	Business Revenue (10 000 yuan)	622440	841059
*个体工商业	Individual Industrial and Commercial Enterprises		
户　数(户)	Number of Enterprises (unit)	7779	7551
从业人员(人)	Employment (person)	14407	14573
资　金(万元)	Fund (10 000 yuan)	28305	30184
营业额(万元)	Turnover (10 000 yuan)	174530	223410
实际直接利用外资(万美元)	Foreign Direct Investment (USD 10 000)	8348	10820
吸引内资到位额(万元)	Actual Domestic Investment (10 000 yuan)	183686	231269
工业企业出口交货值(万元)	Delivery Value of Industrial Enterprises (10 000 yuan)	651002	670707
*小学校数(所)	Number of Primary Schools (unit)	42	40
*小学在校学生数(人)	Students Enrollment of Primary Schools (person)	25397	25342
*普通中学校数(所)	Number of Regular Secondary Schools (unit)	27	23
*普通中学在校学生数(人)	Students Enrollment of Regular Secondary Schools (person)	16893	16163
幼儿园数(所)	Number of Kindergartens (unit)	61	66
卫生机构数(个)	Health Care Institutions (unit)	18	15
#医院、卫生院	Hospital and Health Care Center	12	12
卫生机构床位数(张)	Beds (unit)	722	722
#医院、卫生院	Hospital and Health Care Center	700	700
新型农村合作医疗覆盖率(%)	New Rural Cooperative Medical Service Overlay Rate (%)	95.0	100
新增再就业人员(人)	Newly Re-employment Person (person)	2230	6022

23-11 西青区基本情况
BASIC STATISTICS OF XIQING DISTRICT

指　标	Item	2005	2006
*户籍户数(万户)	Registered Households (10 000 households)	11.96	12.32
#农业户	Agricultural Households	8.46	8.72
*户籍人口(万人)	Registered Population (10 000 persons)	31.48	33.24
1.农业人口	Agricultural Population	23.14	23.31
非农业人口	Non-agricultural Population	8.34	9.93
2.男	Male	15.61	16.54
女	Female	15.87	16.70
*人口出生率(‰)	Birth Rate of Population (‰)	10.7	9.3
*人口自然增长率(‰)	Natural Growth Rate of Population (‰)	5.1	5.4
城镇单位从业人员(万人)	Employment Personnel in Urban Units (100 persons)	4.33	4.31
#在岗职工	On-post Staff and Workers	3.39	3.87
*乡村从业人员(万人)	Rural Employment Personnel (10 000 persons)	11.48	
#农林牧渔业	Farming, Forestry, Animal Husbandry and Fishery	3.74	
*区县生产总值(亿元)	Gross Domestic Product (100 million yuan)	229.65	269.77
第一产业	Primary Industry	6.43	6.57
第二产业	Secondary Industry	164.83	192.97
#工　业	Industry	161.61	188.24
第三产业	Tertiary Industry	58.39	70.23
区县生产总值增速(%)	Increase Rate of Gross Domestic Product (%)		13.7
区县增加值(亿元)	Value Added of District (100 million yuan)	123.68	149.55
区县增加值增速(%)	Increase Rate of Value Added of District (%)	18.8	17.3
一般预算区级财政收入(万元)	General Budgetary Government Revenue at District Level (10 000 yuan)	112110	148452
一般预算区级财政支出(万元)	General Budgetary Government Expenditure at District Level (10 000 yuan)	154484	171528
#教育经费支出	Operating Expenses for Education	16015	21073
*固定资产投资(万元)	Investment in Fixed Assets (10 000 yuan)	1088194	1886729
年末实有耕地面积(万公顷)	Cultivated Land (year-end) (10 000 hectare)	1.53	1.51
农林牧渔业总产值(万元)	Gross Output Value of Farming, Forestry, Animal Husbandry and Fishery (10 000 yuan)	133256	136063
农林牧渔业总产值增速(%)	Increase Rate of Gross Output Value of Farming, Forestry, Animal Husbandry and Fishery (%)	-1.5	2.1
粮食产量(万吨)	Total Yield of Grain (10 000 tons)	4.57	4.34
水产品产量(吨)	Total Yield of Aquatic Products (ton)	50645	50789
蔬菜总产量(万吨)	Total Yield of Vegetables (10 000 tons)	36.57	37.12
*农村居民人均年纯收入(元)	Per Capita Annual Net Income of Rural Households (yuan)	8810	9696
*农村居民人均生活消费支出(元)	Per Capita Annual Expenditure for Consumption of Rural Households (yuan)	4099	4475
#食品支出	Expenditure for Food	1524	1628

23-11 续表 Continued

指　标	Item	2005	2006
农村人均住房面积（平方米）	Per Capita Floor Space of Rural Households (sq. m)	27.19	28.52
规模以上工业企业	Industrial Enterprises above Designated Size		
单位数（个）	Number of Units (unit)	478	528
从业人员（万人）	Employment Personnel (10 000 persons)	10.82	9.44
总产值（万元）	Gross Output Value (10 000 yuan)	3376196	4000623
主营业务收入（万元）	Principal Business Revenue (10 000 yuan)	3001988	3844506
利润总额（万元）	Total Profits (10 000 yuan)	142979	177077
资产总值（万元）	Total Assets (10 000 yuan)	2942340	3212174
负债总额（万元）	Liability (10 000 yuan)	1728928	1882787
社会消费品零售总额（万元）	Total Retail Sales of Consumer Goods (10 000 yuan)	181532	510216
* 私营工商企业	Private Industrial and Commercial Enterprises		
户　数（户）	Number of Enterprises (unit)	3882	4334
从业人员（人）	Employees (person)	70420	76427
注册资本（万元）	Registered Capital (10 000 yuan)	584825	2030244
总产值（万元）	Gross Output Value (10 000 yuan)	463532	498209
营业收入（万元）	Business Revenue (10 000 yuan)	479106	515549
* 个体工商业	Individual Industrial and Commercial Enterprises		
户　数（户）	Number of Enterprises (unit)	5820	7152
从业人员（人）	Employment (person)	10298	11917
资　金（万元）	Fund (10 000 yuan)	28629	51941
营业额（万元）	Turnover (10 000 yuan)	277126	294919
实际直接利用外资（万美元）	Foreign Direct Investment (USD 10 000)	19010	23552
吸引内资到位额（万元）	Actual Domestic Investment (10 000 yuan)	154049	190200
工业企业出口交货值（万元）	Delivery Value of Industrial Enterprises (10 000 yuan)	729061	577600
* 小学校数（所）	Number of Primary Schools (unit)	38	38
* 小学在校学生数（人）	Students Enrollment of Primary Schools (person)	17402	16650
* 普通中学校数（所）	Number of Regular Secondary Schools (unit)	15	13
* 普通中学在校学生数（人）	Students Enrollment of Regular Secondary Schools (person)	16456	15899
幼儿园数（所）	Number of Kindergartens (unit)	64	65
卫生机构数（个）	Health Care Institutions (unit)	15	17
# 医院、卫生院	Hospital and Health Care Center	11	11
卫生机构床位数（张）	Beds (unit)	700	760
# 医院、卫生院	Hospital and Health Care Center	700	760
新型农村合作医疗覆盖率 (%)	New Rural Cooperative Medical Service Overlay Rate (%)	91.5	92.3
新增再就业人员（人）	Newly Re-employment Person (person)	4194	6920

23-12 津南区基本情况
BASIC STATISTICS OF JINNAN DISTRICT

指　标	Item	2005	2006
* 户籍户数 (万户)	Registered Households (10 000 households)	13.78	14.33
# 农业户	Agricultural Households	9.58	10.02
* 户籍人口 (万人)	Registered Population (10 000 persons)	38.07	39.06
1. 农业人口	Agricultural Population	27.69	27.98
非农业人口	Non-agricultural Population	10.38	11.08
2. 男	Male	19.05	19.55
女	Female	19.03	19.51
* 人口出生率 (‰)	Birth Rate of Population (‰)	8.5	7.7
* 人口自然增长率 (‰)	Natural Growth Rate of Population (‰)	5.5	4.1
城镇单位从业人员 (万人)	Employment Personnel in Urban Units (100 persons)	3.75	3.78
# 在岗职工	On-post Staff and Workers	3.62	3.67
* 乡村从业人员 (万人)	Rural Employment Personnel (10 000 persons)	13.4	
# 农林牧渔业	Farming, Forestry, Animal Husbandry and Fishery	3.37	
* 区县生产总值 (亿元)	Gross Domestic Product (100 million yuan)	103.13	117.27
第一产业	Primary Industry	2.83	2.99
第二产业	Secondary Industry	70.01	72.74
# 工　业	Industry	47.62	58.11
第三产业	Tertiary Industry	30.29	41.54
区县生产总值增速 (%)	Increase Rate of Gross Domestic Product (%)		10.9
区县增加值 (亿元)	Value Added of District (100 million yuan)	85.7	105.62
区县增加值增速 (%)	Increase Rate of Value Added of District (%)	15.3	20.2
一般预算区级财政收入 (万元)	General Budgetary Government Revenue at District Level (10 000 yuan)	63602	82566
一般预算区级财政支出 (万元)	General Budgetary Government Expenditure at District Level (10 000 yuan)	100953	121314
# 教育经费支出	Operating Expenses for Education	17564	19540
* 固定资产投资 (万元)	Investment in Fixed Assets (10 000 yuan)	336448	310534
年末实有耕地面积 (万公顷)	Cultivated Land (year-end) (10 000 hectare)	1.46	
农林牧渔业总产值 (万元)	Gross Output Value of Farming, Forestry, Animal Husbandry and Fishery (10 000 yuan)	58445	61887
农林牧渔业总产值增速 (%)	Increase Rate of Gross Output Value of Farming, Forestry, Animal Husbandry and Fishery (%)	3.3	4.3
粮食产量 (万吨)	Total Yield of Grain (10 000 tons)	2.34	1.97
水产品产量 (吨)	Total Yield of Aquatic Products (ton)	14348	20406
蔬菜总产量 (万吨)	Total Yield of Vegetables (10 000 tons)	12.63	12.27
* 农村居民人均年纯收入 (元)	Per Capita Annual Net Income of Rural Households (yuan)	7884	8688
* 农村居民人均生活消费支出 (元)	Per Capita Annual Expenditure for Consumption of Rural Households (yuan)	4709	5615
# 食品支出	Expenditure for Food	1708	2132

23-12 续表 Continued

指 标	Item	2005	2006
农村人均住房面积（平方米）	Per Capita Floor Space of Rural Households (sq. m)	25.35	26.67
规模以上工业企业	Industrial Enterprises above Designated Size		
单位数（个）	Number of Units (unit)	445	416
从业人员（万人）	Employment Personnel (10 000 persons)	7.43	6.7
总产值（万元）	Gross Output Value (10 000 yuan)	2203477	2986256
主营业务收入（万元）	Principal Business Revenue (10 000 yuan)	2133141	3105675
利润总额（万元）	Total Profits (10 000 yuan)	116814	191528
资产总值（万元）	Total Assets (10 000 yuan)	1732169	1956981
负债总额（万元）	Liability (10 000 yuan)	1038763	1108016
社会消费品零售总额（万元）	Total Retail Sales of Consumer Goods (10 000 yuan)	194473	546226
* 私营工商企业	Private Industrial and Commercial Enterprises		
户 数（户）	Number of Enterprises (unit)	3378	3977
从业人员（人）	Employees (person)	41688	44544
注册资本（万元）	Registered Capital (10 000 yuan)	488123	708586
总产值（万元）	Gross Output Value (10 000 yuan)	1355067	1850254
营业收入（万元）	Business Revenue (10 000 yuan)	1064709	1750200
* 个体工商业	Individual Industrial and Commercial Enterprises		
户 数（户）	Number of Enterprises (unit)	8254	8658
从业人员（人）	Employment (person)	16069	17260
资 金（万元）	Fund (10 000 yuan)	25545	28163
营业额（万元）	Turnover (10 000 yuan)	646517	738556
实际直接利用外资（万美元）	Foreign Direct Investment (USD 10 000)	12232	12937
吸引内资到位额（万元）	Actual Domestic Investment (10 000 yuan)	155822	185830
工业企业出口交货值（万元）	Delivery Value of Industrial Enterprises (10 000 yuan)	465026	504798
* 小学校数（所）	Number of Primary Schools (unit)	43	43
* 小学在校学生数（人）	Students Enrollment of Primary Schools (person)	25814	24232
* 普通中学校数（所）	Number of Regular Secondary Schools (unit)	20	18
* 普通中学在校学生数（人）	Students Enrollment of Regular Secondary Schools (person)	19281	18989
幼儿园数（所）	Number of Kindergartens (unit)	41	84
卫生机构数（个）	Health Care Institutions (unit)	16	15
# 医院、卫生院	Hospital and Health Care Center	12	11
卫生机构床位数（张）	Beds (unit)	553	553
# 医院、卫生院	Hospital and Health Care Center	529	529
新型农村合作医疗覆盖率 (%)	New Rural Cooperative Medical Service Overlay Rate (%)	80.0	81.9
新增再就业人员（人）	Newly Re-employment Person (person)	3107	1984

23-13 北辰区基本情况
BASIC STATISTICS OF BEICHEN DISTRICT

指　标	Item	2005	2006
*户籍户数(万户)	Registered Households (10 000 households)	12.51	12.88
#农业户	Agricultural Households	7.12	7.23
*户籍人口(万人)	Registered Population (10 000 persons)	33.02	34.22
1. 农业人口	Agricultural Population	19.81	19.64
非农业人口	Non-agricultural Population	13.21	14.58
2. 男	Male	16.53	17.12
女	Female	16.48	17.10
*人口出生率(‰)	Birth Rate of Population (‰)	8.9	8.8
*人口自然增长率(‰)	Natural Growth Rate of Population (‰)	4.4	4.1
城镇单位从业人员(万人)	Employment Personnel in Urban Units (100 persons)	3.57	3.64
#在岗职工	On-post Staff and Workers	3.31	3.37
*乡村从业人员(万人)	Rural Employment Personnel (10 000 persons)	11.49	11.56
#农林牧渔业	Farming, Forestry, Animal Husbandry and Fishery	2.94	2.76
*区县生产总值(亿元)	Gross Domestic Product (100 million yuan)	193.43	216.48
第一产业	Primary Industry	6.19	6.62
第二产业	Secondary Industry	138.34	145.28
#工　业	Industry	136.72	143.06
第三产业	Tertiary Industry	48.89	64.57
区县生产总值增速(%)	Increase Rate of Gross Domestic Product (%)		9.2
区县增加值(亿元)	Value Added of District (100 million yuan)	135.18	158.15
区县增加值增速(%)	Increase Rate of Value Added of District (%)	16.3	13.4
一般预算区级财政收入(万元)	General Budgetary Government Revenue at District Level (10 000 yuan)	92430	117394
一般预算区级财政支出(万元)	General Budgetary Government Expenditure at District Level (10 000 yuan)	113068	93683
#教育经费支出	Operating Expenses for Education	20578	24078
*固定资产投资(万元)	Investment in Fixed Assets (10 000 yuan)	428433	513698
年末实有耕地面积(万公顷)	Cultivated Land (year-end) (10 000 hectare)	1.85	1.85
农林牧渔业总产值(万元)	Gross Output Value of Farming, Forestry, Animal Husbandry and Fishery (10 000 yuan)	128135	137048
农林牧渔业总产值增速(%)	Increase Rate of Gross Output Value of Farming, Forestry, Animal Husbandry and Fishery (%)	4.6	5.8
粮食产量(万吨)	Total Yield of Grain (10 000 tons)	5.32	5.24
水产品产量(吨)	Total Yield of Aquatic Products (ton)	13512	13056
蔬菜总产量(万吨)	Total Yield of Vegetables (10 000 tons)	32.03	30.50
*农村居民人均年纯收入(元)	Per Capita Annual Net Income of Rural Households (yuan)	8776	9665
*农村居民人均生活消费支出(元)	Per Capita Annual Expenditure for Consumption of Rural Households (yuan)	4910	5096
#食品支出	Expenditure for Food	1888	1881

23-13 续表 Continued

指　标	Item	2005	2006
农村人均住房面积（平方米）	Per Capita Floor Space of Rural Households (sq. m)	35.18	33.04
规模以上工业企业	Industrial Enterprises above Designated Size		
单位数（个）	Number of Units (unit)	559	505
从业人员（万人）	Employment Personnel (10 000 persons)	8.95	7.82
总产值（万元）	Gross Output Value (10 000 yuan)	4630026	5581721
主营业务收入（万元）	Principal Business Revenue (10 000 yuan)	4624924	5708342
利润总额（万元）	Total Profits (10 000 yuan)	299059	253550
资产总值（万元）	Total Assets (10 000 yuan)	3920535	4234328
负债总额（万元）	Liability (10 000 yuan)	2330997	2536908
社会消费品零售总额（万元）	Total Retail Sales of Consumer Goods (10 000 yuan)	432805	491476
* 私营工商企业	Private Industrial and Commercial Enterprises		
户　数（户）	Number of Enterprises (unit)	4998	5785
从业人员（人）	Employees (person)	53553	62975
注册资本（万元）	Registered Capital (10 000 yuan)	749868	1098372
总产值（万元）	Gross Output Value (10 000 yuan)	241853	325681
营业收入（万元）	Business Revenue (10 000 yuan)	578394	883184
* 个体工商业	Individual Industrial and Commercial Enterprises		
户　数（户）	Number of Enterprises (unit)	6610	7676
从业人员（人）	Employment (person)	11827	13840
资　金（万元）	Fund (10 000 yuan)	26751	28465
营业额（万元）	Turnover (10 000 yuan)	471744	431642
实际直接利用外资（万美元）	Foreign Direct Investment (USD 10 000)	17766	21342
吸引内资到位额（万元）	Actual Domestic Investment (10 000 yuan)	104441	118772
工业企业出口交货值（万元）	Delivery Value of Industrial Enterprises (10 000 yuan)	1200000	1440000
* 小学校数（所）	Number of Primary Schools (unit)	44	42
* 小学在校学生数（人）	Students Enrollment of Primary Schools (person)	17467	17097
* 普通中学校数（所）	Number of Regular Secondary Schools (unit)	20	20
* 普通中学在校学生数（人）	Students Enrollment of Regular Secondary Schools (person)	15657	15894
幼儿园数（所）	Number of Kindergartens (unit)	109	116
卫生机构数（个）	Health Care Institutions (unit)	17	18
# 医院、卫生院	Hospital and Health Care Center	13	14
卫生机构床位数（张）	Beds (unit)	667	854
# 医院、卫生院	Hospital and Health Care Center	667	854
新型农村合作医疗覆盖率 (%)	New Rural Cooperative Medical Service Overlay Rate (%)	100	100
新增再就业人员（人）	Newly Re-employment Person (person)	4013	3181

23-14 武清区基本情况
BASIC STATISTICS OF WUQING DISTRICT

指 标	Item	2005	2006
*户籍户数（万户）	Registered Households (10 000 households)	25.60	26.16
#农业户	Agricultural Households	20.09	20.41
*户籍人口（万人）	Registered Population (10 000 persons)	81.72	82.49
1.农业人口	Agricultural Population	69.24	69.44
非农业人口	Non-agricultural Population	12.48	13.05
2.男	Male	40.96	41.31
女	Female	40.76	41.18
*人口出生率(‰)	Birth Rate of Population (‰)	9.7	9.1
*人口自然增长率(‰)	Natural Growth Rate of Population (‰)	3.3	4.0
城镇单位从业人员（万人）	Employment Personnel in Urban Units (100 persons)	6.36	6.75
#在岗职工	On-post Staff and Workers	6.35	6.71
*乡村从业人员（万人）	Rural Employment Personnel (10 000 persons)	37.29	37.56
#农林牧渔业	Farming, Forestry, Animal Husbandry and Fishery	19.85	19.28
*区县生产总值（亿元）	Gross Domestic Product (100 million yuan)	148.49	156.26
第一产业	Primary Industry	21.65	21.67
第二产业	Secondary Industry	65.29	73.10
#工 业	Industry	60.22	64.57
第三产业	Tertiary Industry	61.55	61.49
区县生产总值增速(%)	Increase Rate of Gross Domestic Product (%)		2.4
区县增加值（亿元）	Value Added of District (100 million yuan)	114.54	134.28
区县增加值增速(%)	Increase Rate of Value Added of District (%)	15.1	14.4
一般预算区级财政收入（万元）	General Budgetary Government Revenue at District Level (10 000 yuan)	77473	110021
一般预算区级财政支出（万元）	General Budgetary Government Expenditure at District Level (10 000 yuan)	145158	192608
#教育经费支出	Operating Expenses for Education	36236	43018
*固定资产投资（万元）	Investment in Fixed Assets (10 000 yuan)	507834	593698
年末实有耕地面积（万公顷）	Cultivated Land (year-end) (10 000 hectare)	8.99	8.96
农林牧渔业总产值（万元）	Gross Output Value of Farming, Forestry, Animal Husbandry and Fishery (10 000 yuan)	504587	502835
农林牧渔业总产值增速(%)	Increase Rate of Gross Output Value of Farming, Forestry, Animal Husbandry and Fishery (%)	6.2	-2.1
粮食产量（万吨）	Total Yield of Grain (10 000 tons)	59.57	60.99
水产品产量（吨）	Total Yield of Aquatic Products (ton)	54456	55522
蔬菜总产量（万吨）	Total Yield of Vegetables (10 000 tons)	142.37	142.37
*农村居民人均年纯收入（元）	Per Capita Annual Net Income of Rural Households (yuan)	7045	7780
*农村居民人均生活消费支出（元）	Per Capita Annual Expenditure for Consumption of Rural Households (yuan)	3031	3295
#食品支出	Expenditure for Food	1175	1210

23-14 续表 Continued

指　标	Item	2005	2006
农村人均住房面积（平方米）	Per Capita Floor Space of Rural Households (sq. m)	24.0	25.8
规模以上工业企业	Industrial Enterprises above Designated Size		
单位数（个）	Number of Units (unit)	439	446
从业人员（万人）	Employment Personnel (10 000 persons)	8.45	7.92
总产值（万元）	Gross Output Value (10 000 yuan)	1859243	1990654
主营业务收入（万元）	Principal Business Revenue (10 000 yuan)	1757513	1938372
利润总额（万元）	Total Profits (10 000 yuan)	151600	157873
资产总值（万元）	Total Assets (10 000 yuan)	1768530	2042234
负债总额（万元）	Liability (10 000 yuan)	964138	1087261
社会消费品零售总额（万元）	Total Retail Sales of Consumer Goods (10 000 yuan)	401545	490951
* 私营工商企业	Private Industrial and Commercial Enterprises		
户　数（户）	Number of Enterprises (unit)	2647	4216
从业人员（人）	Employees (person)	27500	31785
注册资本（万元）	Registered Capital (10 000 yuan)	622500	1096863
总产值（万元）	Gross Output Value (10 000 yuan)	270900	293500
营业收入（万元）	Business Revenue (10 000 yuan)	364500	394900
* 个体工商业	Individual Industrial and Commercial Enterprises		
户　数（户）	Number of Enterprises (unit)	19479	17316
从业人员（人）	Employment (person)	25400	24527
资　金（万元）	Fund (10 000 yuan)	55800	47947
营业额（万元）	Turnover (10 000 yuan)	154350	167200
实际直接利用外资（万美元）	Foreign Direct Investment (USD 10 000)	13529	16224
吸引内资到位额（万元）	Actual Domestic Investment (10 000 yuan)	276631	350000
工业企业出口交货值（万元）	Delivery Value of Industrial Enterprises (10 000 yuan)	725000	836000
* 小学校数（所）	Number of Primary Schools (unit)	182	174
* 小学在校学生数（人）	Students Enrollment of Primary Schools (person)	51856	56846
* 普通中学校数（所）	Number of Regular Secondary Schools (unit)	51	49
* 普通中学在校学生数（人）	Students Enrollment of Regular Secondary Schools (person)	47105	46453
幼儿园数（所）	Number of Kindergartens (unit)	239	264
卫生机构数（个）	Health Care Institutions (unit)	43	43
# 医院、卫生院	Hospital and Health Care Center	36	36
卫生机构床位数（张）	Beds (unit)	1340	1335
# 医院、卫生院	Hospital and Health Care Center	1221	1216
新型农村合作医疗覆盖率 (%)	New Rural Cooperative Medical Service Overlay Rate (%)		91.2
新增再就业人员（人）	Newly Re-employment Person (person)	16300	18690

23-15 宝坻区基本情况
BASIC STATISTICS OF BAODI DISTRICT

指　标	Item	2005	2006
* 户籍户数(万户)	Registered Households (10 000 households)	20.37	20.73
# 农业户	Agricultural Households	15.45	15.60
* 户籍人口(万人)	Registered Population (10 000 persons)	65.28	65.71
1. 农业人口	Agricultural Population	54.84	54.86
非农业人口	Non-agricultural Population	10.44	10.85
2. 男	Male	32.96	33.17
女	Female	32.33	32.54
* 人口出生率(‰)	Birth Rate of Population (‰)	9.8	9.6
* 人口自然增长率(‰)	Natural Growth Rate of Population (‰)	-1.1	4.7
城镇单位从业人员(万人)	Employment Personnel in Urban Units (100 persons)	2.99	2.56
# 在岗职工	On-post Staff and Workers	2.99	2.54
* 乡村从业人员(万人)	Rural Employment Personnel (10 000 persons)	25.67	26.82
# 农林牧渔业	Farming, Forestry, Animal Husbandry and Fishery	13.58	13.81
* 区县生产总值(亿元)	Gross Domestic Product (100 million yuan)	75.01	91.42
第一产业	Primary Industry	13.47	13.78
第二产业	Secondary Industry	28.74	37.33
# 工　业	Industry	25.29	34.53
第三产业	Tertiary Industry	32.80	40.31
区县生产总值增速(%)	Increase Rate of Gross Domestic Product (%)		18.5
区县增加值(亿元)	Value Added of District (100 million yuan)	74.26	81.97
区县增加值增速(%)	Increase Rate of Value Added of District (%)	16.7	8.0
一般预算区级财政收入(万元)	General Budgetary Government Revenue at District Level (10 000 yuan)	35326	49392
一般预算区级财政支出(万元)	General Budgetary Government Expenditure at District Level (10 000 yuan)	74173	99940
# 教育经费支出	Operating Expenses for Education	25540	30700
* 固定资产投资(万元)	Investment in Fixed Assets (10 000 yuan)	320166	385039
年末实有耕地面积(万公顷)	Cultivated Land (year-end) (10 000 hectare)	7.61	7.61
农林牧渔业总产值(万元)	Gross Output Value of Farming, Forestry, Animal Husbandry and Fishery (10 000 yuan)	318680	329224
农林牧渔业总产值增速(%)	Increase Rate of Gross Output Value of Farming, Forestry, Animal Husbandry and Fishery (%)	6.7	3.3
粮食产量(万吨)	Total Yield of Grain (10 000 tons)	40.52	43.49
水产品产量(吨)	Total Yield of Aquatic Products (ton)	35280	35788
蔬菜总产量(万吨)	Total Yield of Vegetables (10 000 tons)	60.85	56.63
* 农村居民人均年纯收入(元)	Per Capita Annual Net Income of Rural Households (yuan)	6692	7382
* 农村居民人均生活消费支出(元)	Per Capita Annual Expenditure for Consumption of Rural Households (yuan)	3191	3389
# 食品支出	Expenditure for Food	1028	1292

23-15 续表 Continued

指　标	Item	2005	2006
农村人均住房面积(平方米)	Per Capita Floor Space of Rural Households (sq. m)	22.0	23.4
规模以上工业企业	Industrial Enterprises above Designated Size		
单位数(个)	Number of Units (unit)	359	292
从业人员(万人)	Employment Personnel (10 000 persons)	7.13	5.78
总产值(万元)	Gross Output Value (10 000 yuan)	605162	770206
主营业务收入(万元)	Principal Business Revenue (10 000 yuan)	624572	774470
利润总额(万元)	Total Profits (10 000 yuan)	18993	23932
资产总值(万元)	Total Assets (10 000 yuan)	514255	632534
负债总额(万元)	Liability (10 000 yuan)	361842	379613
社会消费品零售总额(万元)	Total Retail Sales of Consumer Goods (10 000 yuan)	374358	429204
* 私营工商企业	Private Industrial and Commercial Enterprises		
户　数(户)	Number of Enterprises (unit)	1568	1782
从业人员(人)	Employees (person)	69200	69840
注册资本(万元)	Registered Capital (10 000 yuan)	259329	351495
总产值(万元)	Gross Output Value (10 000 yuan)	268392	177000
营业收入(万元)	Business Revenue (10 000 yuan)	52098	165000
* 个体工商业	Individual Industrial and Commercial Enterprises		
户　数(户)	Number of Enterprises (unit)	14396	13437
从业人员(人)	Employment (person)	31579	31542
资　金(万元)	Fund (10 000 yuan)	76502	98400
营业额(万元)	Turnover (10 000 yuan)	278744	283000
实际直接利用外资(万美元)	Foreign Direct Investment (USD 10 000)	3342	2029
吸引内资到位额(万元)	Actual Domestic Investment (10 000 yuan)	307651	360998
工业企业出口交货值(万元)	Delivery Value of Industrial Enterprises (10 000 yuan)	375214	379204
* 小学校数(所)	Number of Primary Schools (unit)	134	135
* 小学在校学生数(人)	Students Enrollment of Primary Schools (person)	50189	44602
* 普通中学校数(所)	Number of Regular Secondary Schools (unit)	49	48
* 普通中学在校学生数(人)	Students Enrollment of Regular Secondary Schools (person)	54269	49351
幼儿园数(所)	Number of Kindergartens (unit)	153	140
卫生机构数(个)	Health Care Institutions (unit)	46	46
# 医院、卫生院	Hospital and Health Care Center	41	41
卫生机构床位数(张)	Beds (unit)	1155	1155
# 医院、卫生院	Hospital and Health Care Center	1155	1155
新型农村合作医疗覆盖率 (%)	New Rural Cooperative Medical Service Overlay Rate (%)		81.7
新增再就业人员(人)	Newly Re-employment Person (person)	3000	5235

23-16 宁河县基本情况
BASIC STATISTICS OF NINGHE COUNTY

指　标	Item	2005	2006
*户籍户数（万户）	Registered Households (10 000 households)	11.28	11.43
#农业户	Agricultural Households	7.70	7.78
*户籍人口（万人）	Registered Population (10 000 persons)	36.74	36.89
1.农业人口	Agricultural Population	27.97	27.94
非农业人口	Non-agricultural Population	8.77	8.95
2.男	Male	18.65	18.73
女	Female	18.08	18.16
*人口出生率(‰)	Birth Rate of Population (‰)	9.5	9.9
*人口自然增长率(‰)	Natural Growth Rate of Population (‰)	4.1	4.7
城镇单位从业人员（万人）	Employment Personnel in Urban Units (100 persons)	1.77	1.77
#在岗职工	On-post Staff and Workers	1.76	1.76
*乡村从业人员（万人）	Rural Employment Personnel (10 000 persons)	11.39	
#农林牧渔业	Farming, Forestry, Animal Husbandry and Fishery	6.5	
*区县生产总值（亿元）	Gross Domestic Product (100 million yuan)	55.55	61.80
第一产业	Primary Industry	12.09	14.04
第二产业	Secondary Industry	24.55	27.35
#工　业	Industry	22.45	24.97
第三产业	Tertiary Industry	18.90	20.41
区县生产总值增速(%)	Increase Rate of Gross Domestic Product (%)		8.6
区县增加值（亿元）	Value Added of District (100 million yuan)	54.86	58.63
区县增加值增速(%)	Increase Rate of Value Added of District (%)	15.0	4.4
一般预算区级财政收入（万元）	General Budgetary Government Revenue at District Level (10 000 yuan)	32144	29958
一般预算区级财政支出（万元）	General Budgetary Government Expenditure at District Level (10 000 yuan)	55877	58405
#教育经费支出	Operating Expenses for Education	15065	16750
*固定资产投资（万元）	Investment in Fixed Assets (10 000 yuan)	150000	296319
年末实有耕地面积（万公顷）	Cultivated Land (year-end) (10 000 hectare)	3.87	
农林牧渔业总产值（万元）	Gross Output Value of Farming, Forestry, Animal Husbandry and Fishery (10 000 yuan)	260128	288320
农林牧渔业总产值增速(%)	Increase Rate of Gross Output Value of Farming, Forestry, Animal Husbandry and Fishery (%)	13.3	10.8
粮食产量（万吨）	Total Yield of Grain (10 000 tons)	8.83	8.89
水产品产量（吨）	Total Yield of Aquatic Products (ton)	16475	18382
蔬菜总产量（万吨）	Total Yield of Vegetables (10 000 tons)	40.28	37.74
*农村居民人均年纯收入（元）	Per Capita Annual Net Income of Rural Households (yuan)	6911	7650
*农村居民人均生活消费支出（元）	Per Capita Annual Expenditure for Consumption of Rural Households (yuan)	2860	3023
#食品支出	Expenditure for Food	1333	1447

23-16 续表 Continued

指 标	Item	2005	2006
农村人均住房面积（平方米）	Per Capita Floor Space of Rural Households (sq. m)	24.0	23.8
规模以上工业企业	Industrial Enterprises above Designated Size		
单位数（个）	Number of Units (unit)	196	139
从业人员（万人）	Employment Personnel (10 000 persons)	2.70	2.16
总产值（万元）	Gross Output Value (10 000 yuan)	808078	779800
主营业务收入（万元）	Principal Business Revenue (10 000 yuan)	759999	779690
利润总额（万元）	Total Profits (10 000 yuan)	58945	82000
资产总值（万元）	Total Assets (10 000 yuan)	493642	572861
负债总额（万元）	Liability (10 000 yuan)	302151	353461
社会消费品零售总额（万元）	Total Retail Sales of Consumer Goods (10 000 yuan)	216601	260003
* 私营工商企业	Private Industrial and Commercial Enterprises		
户 数（户）	Number of Enterprises (unit)	1565	1560
从业人员（人）	Employees (person)	14131	13536
注册资本（万元）	Registered Capital (10 000 yuan)	362228	384266
总产值（万元）	Gross Output Value (10 000 yuan)	109715	131652
营业收入（万元）	Business Revenue (10 000 yuan)	38789	46548
* 个体工商业	Individual Industrial and Commercial Enterprises		
户 数（户）	Number of Enterprises (unit)	7220	6989
从业人员（人）	Employment (person)	9601	9447
资 金（万元）	Fund (10 000 yuan)	17256	17974
营业额（万元）	Turnover (10 000 yuan)	186050	180605
实际直接利用外资（万美元）	Foreign Direct Investment (USD 10 000)	2552	3884
吸引内资到位额（万元）	Actual Domestic Investment (10 000 yuan)	62735	316355
工业企业出口交货值（万元）	Delivery Value of Industrial Enterprises (10 000 yuan)	350000	60924
* 小学校数（所）	Number of Primary Schools (unit)	63	61
* 小学在校学生数（人）	Students Enrollment of Primary Schools (person)	26921	25381
* 普通中学校数（所）	Number of Regular Secondary Schools (unit)	30	30
* 普通中学在校学生数（人）	Students Enrollment of Regular Secondary Schools (person)	31013	28383
幼儿园数（所）	Number of Kindergartens (unit)	140	140
卫生机构数（个）	Health Care Institutions (unit)	88	56
# 医院、卫生院	Hospital and Health Care Center	8	8
卫生机构床位数（张）	Beds (unit)	550	569
# 医院、卫生院	Hospital and Health Care Center	550	569
新型农村合作医疗覆盖率 (%)	New Rural Cooperative Medical Service Overlay Rate (%)		76.7
新增再就业人员（人）	Newly Re-employment Person (person)	4100	6100

23-17 静海县基本情况
BASIC STATISTICS OF JINGHAI COUNTY

指　标	Item	2005	2006
*户籍户数(万户)	Registered Households (10 000 households)	17.30	17.64
#农业户	Agricultural Households	13.23	13.41
*户籍人口(万人)	Registered Population (10 000 persons)	52.27	52.88
1.农业人口	Agricultural Population	43.07	43.35
非农业人口	Non-agricultural Population	9.20	9.53
2.男	Male	26.63	26.95
女	Female	25.64	25.93
*人口出生率(‰)	Birth Rate of Population (‰)	9.8	9.7
*人口自然增长率(‰)	Natural Growth Rate of Population (‰)	4.1	3.9
城镇单位从业人员(万人)	Employment Personnel in Urban Units (100 persons)	2.89	2.66
#在岗职工	On-post Staff and Workers	2.83	2.61
*乡村从业人员(万人)	Rural Employment Personnel (10 000 persons)	16.16	
#农林牧渔业	Farming, Forestry, Animal Husbandry and Fishery	7.50	
*区县生产总值(亿元)	Gross Domestic Product (100 million yuan)	129.52	148.17
第一产业	Primary Industry	12.79	12.72
第二产业	Secondary Industry	82.86	92.97
#工　业	Industry	79.75	89.48
第三产业	Tertiary Industry	33.88	42.48
区县生产总值增速(%)	Increase Rate of Gross Domestic Product (%)		11.4
区县增加值(亿元)	Value Added of District (100 million yuan)	85.18	99.90
区县增加值增速(%)	Increase Rate of Value Added of District (%)	14.5	14.1
一般预算区级财政收入(万元)	General Budgetary Government Revenue at District Level (10 000 yuan)	36167	43906
一般预算区级财政支出(万元)	General Budgetary Government Expenditure at District Level (10 000 yuan)	70653	83878
#教育经费支出	Operating Expenses for Education	22037	25231
*固定资产投资(万元)	Investment in Fixed Assets (10 000 yuan)	240556	228520
年末实有耕地面积(万公顷)	Cultivated Land (year-end) (10 000 hectare)	6.92	
农林牧渔业总产值(万元)	Gross Output Value of Farming, Forestry, Animal Husbandry and Fishery (10 000 yuan)	259824	264538
农林牧渔业总产值增速(%)	Increase Rate of Gross Output Value of Farming, Forestry, Animal Husbandry and Fishery (%)	10.2	1.1
粮食产量(万吨)	Total Yield of Grain (10 000 tons)	29.94	26.63
水产品产量(吨)	Total Yield of Aquatic Products (ton)	26293	27929
蔬菜总产量(万吨)	Total Yield of Vegetables (10 000 tons)	41.64	33.06
*农村居民人均年纯收入(元)	Per Capita Annual Net Income of Rural Households (yuan)	6692	7377
*农村居民人均生活消费支出(元)	Per Capita Annual Expenditure for Consumption of Rural Households (yuan)	3301	3629
#食品支出	Expenditure for Food	1186	1247

23-17 续表 Continued

指　标	Item	2005	2006
农村人均住房面积（平方米）	Per Capita Floor Space of Rural Households (sq. m)	26.5	26.7
规模以上工业企业	Industrial Enterprises above Designated Size		
单位数（个）	Number of Units (unit)	301	261
从业人员（万人）	Employment Personnel (10 000 persons)	5.38	4.53
总产值（万元）	Gross Output Value (10 000 yuan)	3117986	3120730
主营业务收入（万元）	Principal Business Revenue (10 000 yuan)	2429013	3360314
利润总额（万元）	Total Profits (10 000 yuan)	128072	151624
资产总值（万元）	Total Assets (10 000 yuan)	1779997	1735432
负债总额（万元）	Liability (10 000 yuan)	1302744	1078572
社会消费品零售总额（万元）	Total Retail Sales of Consumer Goods (10 000 yuan)	250848	286228
* 私营工商企业	Private Industrial and Commercial Enterprises		
户　数（户）	Number of Enterprises (unit)	3087	3194
从业人员（人）	Employees (person)	26487	27632
注册资本（万元）	Registered Capital (10 000 yuan)	705086	1000491
总产值（万元）	Gross Output Value (10 000 yuan)	494006	532906
营业收入（万元）	Business Revenue (10 000 yuan)	353330	366204
* 个体工商业	Individual Industrial and Commercial Enterprises		
户　数（户）	Number of Enterprises (unit)	10331	9997
从业人员（人）	Employment (person)	23698	22113
资　金（万元）	Fund (10 000 yuan)	60973	30193
营业额（万元）	Turnover (10 000 yuan)	168600	167390
实际直接利用外资（万美元）	Foreign Direct Investment (USD 10 000)	4488	4368
吸引内资到位额（万元）	Actual Domestic Investment (10 000 yuan)	94528	104700
工业企业出口交货值（万元）	Delivery Value of Industrial Enterprises (10 000 yuan)	196601	284839
* 小学校数（所）	Number of Primary Schools (unit)	97	96
* 小学在校学生数（人）	Students Enrollment of Primary Schools (person)	40445	40478
* 普通中学校数（所）	Number of Regular Secondary Schools (unit)	52	52
* 普通中学在校学生数（人）	Students Enrollment of Regular Secondary Schools (person)	41391	42597
幼儿园数（所）	Number of Kindergartens (unit)	257	252
卫生机构数（个）	Health Care Institutions (unit)	109	109
# 医院、卫生院	Hospital and Health Care Center	24	24
卫生机构床位数（张）	Beds (unit)	1267	1275
# 医院、卫生院	Hospital and Health Care Center	1218	1226
新型农村合作医疗覆盖率 (%)	New Rural Cooperative Medical Service Overlay Rate (%)	58.5	62.8
新增再就业人员（人）	Newly Re-employment Person (person)	3091	3039

23-18 蓟县基本情况
BASIC STATISTICS OF JIXIAN COUNTY

指　标	Item	2005	2006
* 户籍户数（万户）	Registered Households (10 000 households)	24.29	24.81
# 农业户	Agricultural Households	18.83	18.98
* 户籍人口（万人）	Registered Population (10 000 persons)	80.70	81.21
1. 农业人口	Agricultural Population	68.69	68.67
非农业人口	Non-agricultural Population	12.01	12.54
2. 男	Male	41.11	41.38
女	Female	39.59	39.83
* 人口出生率 (‰)	Birth Rate of Population (‰)	6.7	6.8
* 人口自然增长率 (‰)	Natural Growth Rate of Population (‰)	-0.5	1.6
城镇单位从业人员（万人）	Employment Personnel in Urban Units (100 persons)	4.59	4.56
# 在岗职工	On-post Staff and Workers	4.16	4.00
* 乡村从业人员（万人）	Rural Employment Personnel (10 000 persons)	32.32	
# 农林牧渔业	Farming, Forestry, Animal Husbandry and Fishery	16.31	
* 区县生产总值（亿元）	Gross Domestic Product (100 million yuan)	109.57	124.32
第一产业	Primary Industry	19.11	19.95
第二产业	Secondary Industry	55.09	59.19
# 工　业	Industry	51.60	52.60
第三产业	Tertiary Industry	35.37	45.18
区县生产总值增速 (%)	Increase Rate of Gross Domestic Product (%)		10.5
区县增加值（亿元）	Value Added of District (100 million yuan)	83.53	95.52
区县增加值增速 (%)	Increase Rate of Value Added of District (%)	14.2	11.7
一般预算区级财政收入（万元）	General Budgetary Government Revenue at District Level (10 000 yuan)	48009	55722
一般预算区级财政支出（万元）	General Budgetary Government Expenditure at District Level (10 000 yuan)	83004	99932
# 教育经费支出	Operating Expenses for Education	25961	30433
* 固定资产投资（万元）	Investment in Fixed Assets (10 000 yuan)	265033	318134
年末实有耕地面积（万公顷）	Cultivated Land (year-end) (10 000 hectare)	5.4	
农林牧渔业总产值（万元）	Gross Output Value of Farming, Forestry, Animal Husbandry and Fishery (10 000 yuan)	445053	463516
农林牧渔业总产值增速 (%)	Increase Rate of Gross Output Value of Farming, Forestry, Animal Husbandry and Fishery (%)	4.5	4.1
粮食产量（万吨）	Total Yield of Grain (10 000 tons)	41.22	45.58
水产品产量（吨）	Total Yield of Aquatic Products (ton)	27421	27876
蔬菜总产量（万吨）	Total Yield of Vegetables (10 000 tons)	101.30	88.87
* 农村居民人均年纯收入（元）	Per Capita Annual Net Income of Rural Households (yuan)	6693	7383
* 农村居民人均生活消费支出（元）	Per Capita Annual Expenditure for Consumption of Rural Households (yuan)	2757	2958
# 食品支出	Expenditure for Food	1025	1085

23-18 续表 Continued

指　　标	Item	2005	2006
农村人均住房面积(平方米)	Per Capita Floor Space of Rural Households (sq. m)	23.7	23.7
规模以上工业企业	Industrial Enterprises above Designated Size		
单位数(个)	Number of Units (unit)	136	151
从业人员(万人)	Employment Personnel (10 000 persons)	5.48	2.88
总产值(万元)	Gross Output Value (10 000 yuan)	672280	347406
主营业务收入(万元)	Principal Business Revenue (10 000 yuan)	626705	323524
利润总额(万元)	Total Profits (10 000 yuan)	26252	8053
资产总值(万元)	Total Assets (10 000 yuan)	264662	341698
负债总额(万元)	Liability (10 000 yuan)	236560	262484
社会消费品零售总额(万元)	Total Retail Sales of Consumer Goods (10 000 yuan)	236560	279172
* 私营工商企业	Private Industrial and Commercial Enterprises		
户　数(户)	Number of Enterprises (unit)	1091	1250
从业人员(人)	Employees (person)	17200	17653
注册资本(万元)	Registered Capital (10 000 yuan)	97000	128790
总产值(万元)	Gross Output Value (10 000 yuan)	83800	86006
营业收入(万元)	Business Revenue (10 000 yuan)	50400	63016
* 个体工商业	Individual Industrial and Commercial Enterprises		
户　数(户)	Number of Enterprises (unit)	14659	12075
从业人员(人)	Employment (person)	23000	21191
资　金(万元)	Fund (10 000 yuan)	30100	38302
营业额(万元)	Turnover (10 000 yuan)	116000	146601
实际直接利用外资(万美元)	Foreign Direct Investment (USD 10 000)	2737	3215
吸引内资到位额(万元)	Actual Domestic Investment (10 000 yuan)	110000	135000
工业企业出口交货值(万元)	Delivery Value of Industrial Enterprises (10 000 yuan)	500100	51377
* 小学校数(所)	Number of Primary Schools (unit)	130	127
* 小学在校学生数(人)	Students Enrollment of Primary Schools (person)	61833	57157
* 普通中学校数(所)	Number of Regular Secondary Schools (unit)	70	68
* 普通中学在校学生数(人)	Students Enrollment of Regular Secondary Schools (person)	65973	61682
幼儿园数(所)	Number of Kindergartens (unit)	205	200
卫生机构数(个)	Health Care Institutions (unit)	449	448
# 医院、卫生院	Hospital and Health Care Center	32	32
卫生机构床位数(张)	Beds (unit)	1368	1368
# 医院、卫生院	Hospital and Health Care Center	1368	1368
新型农村合作医疗覆盖率(%)	New Rural Cooperative Medical Service Overlay Rate (%)		85.6
新增再就业人员(人)	Newly Re-employment Person (person)	2070	3509

附：2006 年第二次全国残疾人抽样调查天津市主要数据公报

天津市第二次全国残疾人抽样调查领导小组
天津市统计局
2006 年 12 月 26 日

经国务院批准，我国进行了第二次全国残疾人抽样调查。在第二次全国残疾人抽样调查领导小组统一领导下，按照全国统一的调查方案，天津市第二次全国残疾人抽样调查领导小组组织实施了我市的调查。经过两年多的充分准备，我市于 2006 年 4 月 1 日开始全面调查，通过调查工作人员的艰苦努力，调查的各项任务已基本完成。现将初步汇总的主要数据公布如下：

一、调查的基本情况

本次调查采取分层、多阶段、整群概率比例抽样方法，在我市各区县抽取 88 个乡（镇、街道），176 个调查小区，平均每个调查小区 420 人左右。

本次调查标准时间为 2006 年 4 月 1 日零时，入户调查时间自 2006 年 4 月 1 日起至 5 月 31 日结束。在市政府和各区县政府直接领导下，组织了 18 个调查队、354 名调查员、144 名各科医生、21 名统计员以及 2112 名陪调员，逐户进行询问登记、筛查和残疾评定，现已全部完成入户调查、复查和调查质量的核查工作。

我市共调查了 24446 户、72351 人，调查的抽样比为 6.93‰。入户见面 62104 人，占调查总人数的 85.84%；按照《第二次全国残疾人抽样调查残疾筛查方法》，7 岁以上疑似残疾人筛出率为 11.39%，疑似残疾人检查率达到 99.69%。

二、残疾人数及其比例

根据调查初步汇总，被调查户中有残疾人的家庭共 3523 户，确定视力、听力、言语、肢体、智力、精神和多重残疾共 3958 人。其中，视力残疾 451 人，听力残疾 832 人，言语残疾 58 人，肢体残疾 1519 人，智力残疾 303 人，精神残疾 252 人，多重残疾 543 人。

本次调查结果显示，我市残疾人占总人口的比例为 5.47%，据此推算 2006 年 4 月 1 日零时我市各类残疾人的总数为 57.0 万人。各类残疾人的人数及各占残疾人总人数的比重分别是：视力残疾 6.5 万人，占 11.40%；听力残疾 12.0 万人，占 21.05%；言语残疾 0.8 万人，占 1.40%；肢体残疾 21.9 万人，占 38.43%；智力残疾 4.4 万人，占 7.72%；精神残疾 3.6 万人，占 6.32%；多重残疾 7.8 万人，占 13.68%。

与 1987 年第一次全国残疾人抽样调查比较，我市残疾人口总量增加，残疾人比例上升，残疾类别结构变动。影响这一变化的因素有，两次调查间人口增长与结构变动、社会与环境变化、残疾标准修订等，更深入的分析有待于在详细数据汇总和更全面的资料收集后进行。

三、调查质量评价

在入户调查、复查完毕后，我市按照《事后质量核查工作细则》进行核查，核查结果符合调查方案要求。经全国评估专家委员会对我市调查实施过程和数据质量进行综合评估，认定本次调查是一次成功的调查，数据真实可信。调查获得的丰富数据，将为我市经济社会和残疾人事业的发展提供可靠依据。

注：1. 本公报为初步汇总数。

2. 本次调查登记对象为具有中华人民共和国国籍并居住在中华人民共和国境内大陆的常住人口，残疾人按照《第二次全国残疾人抽样调查残疾标准》评定。

企业采风

Brief Introduction of Enterprises

中国统计出版社最新资料书简目

(仅供参考，以最后出书为准)

中国统计年鉴-2007
中国统计摘要-2007
国际统计年鉴-2007
2007中国发展报告
中国区域经济统计年鉴-2007
长江和珠江三角洲及港澳特别行政区统计年鉴-2007
中国社会统计年鉴-2007
中国第三产业统计年鉴-2007
中国城市统计年鉴-2006
中国劳动统计年鉴-2007
中国人口统计年鉴-2007
中国工业经济统计年鉴-2007
中国建筑业统计年鉴-2007
中国城市（镇）生活与价格年鉴-2007
中国商品交易市场统计年鉴-2007
中国连锁餐饮企业统计年鉴-2007
中国连锁零售业统计年鉴-2007
中国能源统计年鉴-2007
全国农产品成本收益资料汇编-2007
中国贸易外经统计年鉴-2007
中国基本单位统计年鉴-2006
中国民政统计年鉴-2007
中国农村统计年鉴-2007
中国农村住户调查年鉴-2007（中文）
中国农村住户调查年鉴-2007（英文）
中国县（市）社会经济调查年鉴-2007
中国农产品价格调查年鉴-2007
中国经济普查年鉴-2004
中国百强县（市）发展年鉴-2007
中国教育经费统计年鉴-2006
中国农村全面建设小康监测报告-2007
中国农村贫困监测报告-2007
中国国内生产总值核算历史资料（1952-2004）
中国高技术产业统计年鉴-2007
中国科学技术协会统计年鉴-2007
工业企业科技活动资料-2007
中国棉花年鉴-2006

2004年经济普查年鉴系列
2005年中国1%人口抽样调查系列资料

北京统计年鉴-2007
天津统计年鉴-2007
河北经济年鉴-2007
山西统计年鉴-2007
内蒙古统计年鉴-2007
辽宁统计年鉴-2007
吉林统计年鉴-2007
黑龙江统计年鉴-2007

上海统计年鉴-2007
江苏统计年鉴-2007
浙江统计年鉴-2007
安徽统计年鉴-2007
福建统计年鉴-2007
江西统计年鉴-2007
山东统计年鉴-2007
河南统计年鉴-2007
湖北统计年鉴-2007
湖南统计年鉴-2007
广东统计年鉴-2007
广西统计年鉴-2007
海南统计年鉴-2007
重庆统计年鉴-2007
四川统计年鉴-2007
贵州统计年鉴-2007
云南统计年鉴-2007
西藏统计年鉴-2007
陕西统计年鉴-2007
甘肃年鉴-2007
青海统计年鉴-2007
宁夏统计年鉴-2007
新疆统计年鉴-2007
新疆生产建设兵团统计年鉴-2007
石家庄统计年鉴-2007
唐山统计年鉴-2007
邯郸统计年鉴-2007
张家口经济年鉴-2007
呼和浩特经济统计年鉴-2007
包头统计年鉴-2007
沈阳年鉴-2007
大连统计年鉴-2007
长春统计年鉴-2007
吉林市社会经济统计年鉴-2007
四平统计年鉴-2007
延吉统计年鉴-2007
哈尔滨统计年鉴-2007
齐齐哈尔经济统计年鉴-2007
黑龙江垦区统计年鉴-2007
上海浦东新区统计年鉴-2007
南京统计年鉴-2007
苏州统计年鉴-2007
无锡统计年鉴-2007
常州统计年鉴-2007
徐州统计年鉴-2007
南通统计年鉴-2007
盐城统计年鉴-2007
镇江统计年鉴-2007
江阴统计年鉴-2007

杭州统计年鉴-2007
宁波统计年鉴-2007
绍兴统计年鉴-2007
台州统计年鉴-2007
舟山统计年鉴-2007
温州统计年鉴-2007
金华统计年鉴-2007
嘉兴统计年鉴-2007
湖州统计年鉴-2007
安庆统计年鉴-2007
福州统计年鉴-2007
厦门经济特区年鉴-2007
福州经济技术开发区年鉴-2007
南昌经济社会统计年鉴-2007
上饶经济社会统计年鉴-2007
九江经济统计年鉴-2007
济南统计年鉴-2007
青岛统计年鉴-2007
潍坊统计年鉴-2007
郑州统计年鉴-2007
洛阳统计年鉴-2007
三门峡统计年鉴-2007
南阳统计年鉴-2007
武汉统计年鉴-2007
宜昌统计年鉴-2007
十堰统计年鉴-2007
荆州统计年鉴-2007
长沙统计年鉴-2007
广州统计年鉴-2007
东莞统计年鉴-2007
惠州统计年鉴-2007
深圳统计年鉴-2007
南宁统计年鉴-2007
柳州经济统计年鉴-2007
来宾统计年鉴-2007
海口统计年鉴-2007
成都统计年鉴-2007
贵阳统计年鉴-2007
昆明统计年鉴-2007
西安统计年鉴-2007
兰州年鉴-2007
庆阳年鉴-2007
银川统计年鉴-2007
乌鲁木齐统计年鉴-2007
吐鲁番统计年鉴-2007

新疆调查年鉴-2007
内蒙古经济社会调查年鉴-2007

(京)新登字041号

图书在版编目(CIP)数据

天津统计年鉴. 2007/天津市统计局编.
-北京：中国统计出版社,2007.6
ISBN 978-7-5037-5127-1

Ⅰ.天…
Ⅱ.天…
Ⅲ.统计资料-天津市-2007-年鉴
Ⅳ.C832.21-54

中国版本图书馆CIP数据核字(2007)第049513号

天津统计年鉴—2007

作　　者/天津市统计局
责任编辑/郑淼淼
E-mail/yearbook@stats.gov.cn
责任校对/李立新　戴　华
封面设计/天津市河图广告传播有限公司
出版发行/中国统计出版社
通信地址/北京市西城区三里河月坛南街57号　中国统计出版社
邮　　编/100826
电　　话/(010)63376907
印　　刷/精一印刷（深圳）有限公司
经　　销/新华书店
开　　本/890×1240毫米　1/16
字　　数/110万字
印　　张/35印张
印　　数/1-5000册
版　　别/2007年8月第1版
版　　次/2007年8月第1次印刷
书　　号/ISBN 978-7-5037-5127-1/F·2427
定　　价/280.00元(含光盘)

本书附同版本CD-ROM一张，光盘内容以书面文字为准。

升级改造后的邮政11185客户服务中心

翻开中国邮政史，有一个地方格外引人注目，像一颗璀璨的明珠在邮政历史长河中熠熠生辉，它就是天津。天津是中国近代邮政的发祥地，是中国第一套邮票大龙邮票首发地。120多年来，天津邮政历尽坎坷，自强不息。今天，天津市邮政局已有从业员工 9000 余人，资产总额 12.46 亿元，邮电支局（所）457 处。尤其是从 2004 年以来，天津市邮政局结合天津实际和邮政行业的特点，认真贯彻落实科学发展观，提出了“超常规、大手笔、高水平、跨越式”的发展思路及“三年三大步，六年翻一番”的奋斗目标。全局干部职工解放思想，转变观念，深化改革，开拓创新，使企业得到了持续、快速、健康、协调发展。邮政业务总收入 2004 年完成 8.29 亿元，增长 9.7%，增幅居全国第四位；2005 年完成9.45 亿元，增长14.09%，增幅跃居全国第三位；今年1—10 月增长18%，增幅跃居全国第一位，预计到年底完成 11 亿元，可实现“三年三大步，六年翻一番”的第一阶段目标。

In the history of post, a city took one of the most places of China, which likes a beautiful pearl, shining in the past hundreds of years. This is Tianjin. Tianjin is the cradle land of China modern post history, which is also the cradle land of the first series of “dragon” stamps. In these 120 years, Tianjin Post Office has strove to become stronger constantly. Now, it has more than 9000 staff, 457 sub-post & telecommunication offices and the total assets value 1246 million yuan. Especially from 2004, according to the characters of Tianjin city and the post industry, in order to implement the scientific and evolutive notion, Tianjin Post Office brings forward a develop guideline of “exceeding routines, big scopes, high levels and rapid development” and a develop object of “three steps in three years, doubled in six years” . All the staff keep innovating and reforming, which help the enterprise develop continually, rapidly, healthy and harmoniously. In 2004, the total income is 829 million yuan, up 9.7%. The increase range is the 4th place in China. In 2005, the total income is 945 million yuan, up 14.09%. The increase range rises to the 3rd place. This year, from January to October, the total income increases 18% and the increase range is high to 1st place. It is predicted that the total income can reach 1100 million yuan and the first step of “three steps in three years, doubled in six years” can also be realized.

天津邮政在全国首开端午节“亲情粽”免费寄递活动

天津邮政代理电信业务专厅

北京2008年奥运会合作伙伴
OFFICIAL PARTNER OF THE BEIJING 2008 OLYMPIC GAMES

中国网通（集团）有限公司
天津市分公司

中 国 网　宽 天 下　Tianjin Communications Corporation

中国网通（集团）有限公司天津市分公司（以下简称“天津网通”）是中国网通旗下分公司，是北京2008年奥运会固定通信服务合作伙伴，是天津地区实力雄厚的基础电信运营商。

天津网通为客户提供固定电话、小灵通、宽带业务，近期还包装推出了“亲情1+”、ICT、“宽带商务”、“宽视界”、“2008宽带酒店”、IDC等产品和业务。目前天津网通拥有500万客户。

天津网通致力于向客户提供更为标准化、亲情化、差异化的服务，全利推进政府信息化、企业信息化、行业信息化、农村信息化、社区信息化、家庭信息化、个人信息化，为提高天津的信息化水平做贡献，引领全市人民早日进入数字新时代、畅享数字新生活。

Tianjin Communications Corporation is subordinated to China Network Communications Corporation. It is a predominant telecommunications operator in Tianjin and the fixed telecommunications service partner for the 2008 Olympic Games.

Our businesses include fixed telecommunications, PHS and wideband network services. Currently, CNC has developed services such as “family 1+”, ICT, wideband business, broad vision, 2008 wide-band rummery, and IDC. At present, the number of our telephone users hits the mark of 5 million.

Striving to contribute to the information level in Tianjin, CNC is dedicated to provide more and more standardized, considerate, diverse services for our clients and devoted to making our government, enterprise, industry, country, community, family and individuals obtain information more convenient so as to lead the whole municipalities into the great new era of digit.

地址：天津市和平区新兴路27号
Add: No. 27 Xinxing Road, Heping District,Tianjin

邮政编码 Postal Code: 300052
电话 Tel: +86 22 27830083,10060
传真 Fax: +86 22 27839927

http://www.tj.cnc.cn
http://www.online.tj.cn
http://www.cncmax.tj.cn

China unicom 中国联通
让一切自由连通
CDMA网
GSM网
Anycall
SAMSUNG
三星W579
一机双网，同时在线
全球网络，任你畅游！
世界体操冠军：李大双
世界体操冠军：李小双
世界风
时刻连通
中国联通以创新精神突破技术瓶颈，世界风双网双待横空出世，真正实现CDMA与GSM两种网络同时处于待机状态，无须切换，两网自由连接，在两种不同网络的技术优势支持下，让您与世界时刻自由连通！让您更能享受到CDMA网络“低辐射、高清晰、上网快、防窃听”的领先功能，让沟通成为享受！
三星W579
酷派728B
酷派288
大显C8000
UT斯达康T66
CECT C828
海信D806
中兴H500
* 网上直销：www.hicdma.com
* 总承销商：联通华盛通信技术有限公司
客户服务热线10010 话费查询热线10011
WWW.tj10010.com 中国联通天津分公司

坐落在天津市解放北路的中国银行天津市分行

2006年是中国银行股份有限公司天津市分行近百年历史上极不平凡的一年。随着中国银行在海内外资本市场整体的成功上市，天津中行进入了一个崭新的发展阶段。

这一年里，依托地区经济高速增长的发展机遇和奥运合作伙伴的契机，天津中行充分发挥中国银行国际业务领域的品牌优势，切实转变经营理念和增长方式，以“资本约束优先、质量控制优先、效益考核优先、战略重点有限”为原则，加快结构调整和战略转型，加强产品组合和业务创新，稳步推进信息科技、风险管理和内控体系建设，在国际结算、外汇资金等传统优势业务继续保持市场领先的同时，电子银行、个人理财业务取得长足的发展。依托遍布全市的近20家VIP客户理财中心和多元化、专业化的财富管理服务，“中银理财”的品牌已经逐步深入人心。

2007年，天津中行将牢牢把握滨海新区开发开放的历史发展机遇，继续推进以市场为导向、以客户为中心的经营战略，加快开发适应客户需求、附加值高、有比较竞争优势的产品，发挥多元化和国际化的业务优势，全方位创建民族金融业的优势品牌，提升服务质量，保持盈利增长，实现全面、协调、可持续的发展，为股东创造更大的价值回报，为客户提供高品质的金融服务，使“中国银行”的百年品牌不断焕发新的生机。

The year 2006 is an unusual year for Tianjin Branch of BOC (Bank of China) in its hundred-year history. With the success of IPO in national & international capital market, Tianjin Branch of BOC has taken a new step of development.

In this year, with the chance of growth of area economy and cooperation as an Olympic Games Partner, Tianjin Branch took advantages of brand credit in foreign settlement and changed management concepts and growth mode. According to the principle of “capital restriction priority, quality control priority, benefit assessment priority and tactic point limited”, Tianjin Branch expedited structure adjustment and strategy revolution, enhanced production combination and operation innovation, and improved the construction of information technology, venture management and inner-control systems. While keeping ahead in the traditional operation of international settlement and foreign exchange, etc., Tianjin Branch made a full development in online banking and personal finance. Depending on the nearly 20 VIP personal finance centers and multi-directional, professional wealth management service, the brand of “BOC Wealth Management” became more and more famous.

In 2007, Tianjin Branch will take the chance of the development of Binhai New Area, insist on the strategy of market-oriented and customer-centered and developed the products with high added value and competition advantages. Taking advantages of multi-direction and international settlement, Tianjin Branch will set up a national finance brand to improve the service quality, keep the increase of revenue, realize a complete, harmonious and continuable development, create more value for shareholders, provide high quality financial service for clients, and make sure the hundred-year BOC will be full of vigor and vitality.

中国银行滨海分行营业大楼

中国银行股份有限公司天津市分行理财中心

中国银行股份有限公司天津市分行营业大厅

企业名称：中国银行股份有限公司天津市分行
Name: Tianjin Branch of BOC
企业地址：(中国)天津市和平区解放北路80号
Add: No. 80 Jiefangbei Road, Heping District, Tianjin
邮政编码 Postal Code: 300040
客户服务电话 Tel-Service: 95566

Beijing 2008
PICC
中国人保财险
北京2008年奥运会合作伙伴
OFFICIAL PARTNER OF THE BEIJING 2008 OLYMPIC GAMES
PICC
中国人民财产保险股份有限公司
铸金牌服务 为梦想护航
PICC—58 年光辉历史，中国最大财产保险公司；
中国第一家海外上市金融国企；
中国保险业唯一 2008 年奥运合作伙伴；
营业网点最强大的保险品牌公司。
人保大厦
全天候 直销直惠 金牌保险服务
我公司从 2007年开始启动“全天候”(95518 电话直销+人保电子商务网www.e-picc.com.cn+PICC人保短信平台+全市各区县支公司营业网点）直销直惠金牌保险服务。为方便广大个人客户，提供最快捷、最优惠的柜台业务服务，在所属区县公司营业厅实行双休日正常营业。
一、营业时间：周一至周五，早 8:30 至下午 5:00
周六至周日，早 9:00 至下午 4:00
二、双休日营业对象：个人直接客户
三、双休日营业范围：
1. 承保机动车辆保险，投资保障型保险产品，家庭财产保险，各种个人意外、健康、责任保险，各种保险卡业务（以上业务可享受柜台直接优惠）。
2. 受理各种保险赔案，支付个人已结直接赔款（大额赔款请预约）。
3. 保险咨询，接受预约上门保险服务。
欢迎您明明白白买保险，清清楚楚领赔款

党委书记、董事长：孙宁豫　　十六大代表、总经理：刘云生

天津钢管集团有限公司是中国目前最大的石油套管生产基地，拥有世界先进的生产技术和装备。公司已通过了美国 API 石油学会认证、ISO9001 质量体系标准认证、ISO14001 环境管理体系认证、OHSAS18001职业安全健康管理体系认证，同时还先后通过了17个国家和壳牌、美孚等 48 家国际大石油公司的认证。目前，石油管材国内市场占有率达到 50%，产品出口到 70 多个国家和地区。

集团公司建有国家级技术中心和先进的钢管实验生产线，研制生产了抗腐蚀、热采井、高抗挤毁、特殊扣等一批高技术含量、高附加值新品，形成了具有自主知识产权的 TP 产品系列，其中 50 余项科研成果填补了国内空白。石油套管成为“中国名牌产品”，无缝钢管成为“中国名牌出口商品”。公司除生产无缝钢管以外，还生产石油钻杆、彩涂钢板、不锈钢薄板、铜线材、不锈钢管以及高压气瓶产品。公司还拥有华北地区最大的大型冶金机电设备制造企业，可以设计、制造各种大型工业炉、各类水电、风电、发电和港口机械等设备。

天津钢管集团有限公司先后获得了“国家质量管理卓越企业”、“第九届国家级企业管理现代化创新成果一等奖”、全国“五一”劳动奖状等荣誉，企业跻身中国企业 500 强，中国制造业 500 强和进出口企业 500 强。

地址: 天津市东丽区津塘公路396号
Add: No. 396 Jintang Highway, Dongli District, Tianjin
邮政编码 Postal Code: 300301
电话 Tel: +86 22 24802625
传真 Fax: +86 22 24360649
http://www.tpco.com.cn

石油套管

168厂生产线

套管生产线

天津钢管集团有限公司

Tianjin Pipe Group Corporation Ltd.

Tianjin Pipe Group Corporation Ltd. (TPCO) is the largest OCTG production base in China and possesses international advanced production technology and equipment. It has passed the certification of API Petroleum Institute, the certification of ISO9001, ISO14001 environmental management system and the certification of OHSAS18001 profession safety management system. It also has passed the certification of 17 countries and 48 international petroleum corporations. In present, petroleum pipe occupies 50 percent of domestic market, its products exports to more than 70 countries and regions.

TPCO has built technology center of national level and advanced production line of steel pipe. It can produce a series of hi-tech new products, and has formed the TP series products with autonomic intellectual property, of which, more than 50 scientific research results fill in the gaps of domestic related fields. Petroleum pipe become china famous product and seamless steel pipe become china famous export commodity. The corporation also produces steel plate, copper cash, high-pressure gas bottle and so on. It also has the largest metallurgical machinery & electric equipment enterprise in North China, which can produce large-sized equipment.

TPCO was awarded "national excellent enterprise on quality management" , first class national innovation award of 9th enterprise management modernization, and the national labor prize. It listed top 500 national enterprises, top 500 national manufacturers and top 500 imp. & exp. enterprises.

有限公司

Tianjin Iron & Steel Co., Ltd.

天钢是集烧结、炼铁、炼钢、连铸、轧钢生产工艺为一体的国有大型钢铁企业。2006年公司实现销售收入173.54亿元,同比增长46.10%;实现利税9.02亿元,利润6.16亿元,同比分别增长17.86%和18.14%。完成铁产量322.91万吨,钢产量301.09万吨,钢材产量270.27万吨。主要产品:连铸圆管坯、连铸方坯、连铸板坯、热轧中厚板、优质棒材、高速线材、中板、热轧带钢、炼钢和铸造用生铁等九大产品系列。

在市委、市政府的正确决策和领导下,天钢东移工程历经三年半的艰苦奋斗,于2006年5月2日3200m³高炉一次成功点火为标志,实现了全面成功投产,做到了当月投产当月盈利,当年投产当年盈利。一座年产炼铁、炼钢、轧材各400万吨生产能力的现代化钢铁联合企业屹立于滨海新区。东移工程全面投产形成了产品定位高档化、精品化;工艺技术装备大型化、连续化、自动化;资源能源利用节约化;环境保护清洁化;劳动生产率高效化;生产经营集约化等六大优势,成为我市工业经济一个新的增长点。

3座120t转炉

3500mm双机架中厚板轧机

地址:天津市东丽区津塘公路398号
Add: No. 398 Jintang Road, Dongli District, Tianjin
邮政编码 Postal Code: 300301
电话 Tel: +86 22 84366800
传真 Fax: +86 22 84366820

优质棒材生产线

Tianjin Iron & Steel Co., Ltd. is a large-sized state-owned enterprise in iron refining, steel refining, steel rolling and so on. In 2006, the company gained sales income 17.354 billion yuan, up 46.10% and paid tax 0.902 billion yuan, up 17.86% and made a profit of 0.616 billion yuan, up 18.14%. It produced iron, steel, rolled steel totally 3229.1 thousand tons, 3010.9 thousand tons, 2702.7 thousand tons, respectively. The nine main products include: continuous cast round, continuous casting billet, continuous casting slab, hot rolled plate, high quality bar, high speed wire, etc..

Under the lead of the municipal party committee and the municipal government, 3200m³ blast furnace fired successfully at the first time on May 2th 2006 indicated that the eastward moving of Tianjin Iron & Steel Co., Ltd. had finished after three years' endeavor and was able to make production across the board so as to make a profit as early as it was put into use. Now, a modern Iron & Steel united enterprise that is capable of producing steel, iron, rolled steel locates in the Binhai New Area. The eastward moving project makes products refined, equipments large-scaled and atomized, resource economized, environment clean, labor productivity efficient and production intensive. Consequently, the company is making contribution to the development of industry economics of Tianjin city.

高速线材生产线

双高炉外景

天津天铁炼焦化工有限公司

Tianjin Tiantie Coking & Chemical Co., Ltd.

董事长、总经理、党委书记：朱德升

天津天铁炼焦化工有限公司（原天津市第三煤气厂），为天铁冶金集团有限公司的子公司，具有独立法人地位，法人代表朱德升。公司座落于天津滨海工业区，距天津新港仅23公里，北临京山铁路、津塘公路、京津塘和唐津高速公路等主要交通干线，交通运输十分便利，地域优势十分突出，是中国北方重要的商品焦生产和出口基地，是天津滨海冶金工业区的煤气能源供应基地，是天津市最大的机焦生产企业。

天铁炼焦化工有限公司以天铁集团为依托，以京津唐地区为腹地，面向国内国际两个市场，大力实施品牌战略，产品畅销国内外，以优质的产品质量和良好的企业信誉，在国内和国际焦炭市场赢得很高的信誉度和美誉度，是中国焦化行业的知名企业，是中国焦化行业协会常务理事单位，已通过质量、环境和职业健康安全管理体系认证。是国家公告的第一批74家符合"焦化行业准入条件"的企业之一，是国家商务部对口直接发放焦炭出口许可证的48家单位之一。

天铁炼焦化工有限公司，于2000年10月建成投产，项目总投资16亿元，占地面积1460亩，拥有两座JN60-89型50孔6m焦炉，并配有相应的水、电、热力、备煤、回收等辅助设施，生产工艺及设备均采用国内外先进技术，生产管理采用计算机集中控制监测系统。现日产煤气120万m^3；年产焦炭突破100万吨；每年可回收焦油4.4万吨、粗苯1.2万吨、硫磺1880吨、外供煤气15000万m^3；年生产需耗洗精煤140万吨、动力煤10万吨。

2000年以来，天津天铁炼焦化工有限公司分别获得各级政府部门和相关组织授予的"纳税先进企业"、"重合同守信誉AAA企业"、"节能优秀企业"、"爱国卫生先进单位"等多项光荣称号。

天铁炼焦化工有限公司以"造福员工、奉献社会"为己任，坚持以人为本，把企业的"求真求实求发展、创业创新创一流"的愿景与员工的劳动愿望有机融合，真正使"企业的每一个细胞都活跃起来"，创造了一个"人品与精品同在，赢信和赢利共存"的和谐局面。"造一流人才、出一流产品、创一流业绩"、为天津实施"三步走"战略和天津冶金工业的发展贡献力量。天津天铁炼焦化工有限公司在搞好现有企业生产经营的同时，积极规划企业的中长期发展目标，竭诚希望与国内外企业共谋发展，共创辉煌。

Tianjin Tiantie Coking & Chemical Co., Ltd. is one of the subsidiaries of Tianjin Tiantie Metallurgical Group Co., Ltd.. It has an independent corporation status and the juridical person is Zhu Desheng. The company is located in the Binhai New Area in Tianjin, which is only 23 kilometers from new Tianjin port and quite close to Jingshan Railway, Jingtang Railway, Jingjintang high way and Tangjin highway. So, the transportation is rather convenient and the territorial advantages are extraordinarily remarkable. The company is an important base of coke production and exportation in the North of China, the base of gas supply to the Tianjin Binhai Metallurgical Industry Area and the biggest enterprise of organic coke production in Tianjin.

Tianjin Tiantie Coking & Chemical Co., Ltd. relies on the Tiantie Metallurgical Group, depends on Jingjintang Areas, faces to national and global market, and implements brand strategy, which wins good credit in many countries. The company is quite famous in the coking & chemical industry of China, and it is also the standing director of China Coking & Chemical Association. It has already passed the quality, environment and professional health standard certification, which is also one of the first 74 enterprises to meet the "coking & chemical industry entry standards".

The company was found in October 2000, with a total investment of 1600 million yuan. It occupies 1460 mu, has 2 JN60-89 coke furnaces of 6 m with corresponding equipment of water, electricity, power, stored coal and recycle. All the technology and instruments are of international advanced level and the information systems are used in controlling and management. Every day, it can produce gas 1200 thousand m^3. Every year, it can produce 1 million tons coke; recycle 44 thousand tons tar, 12 thousand tons benzene and 1880 tons sulfur; supply gas 150 million m^3; consume 1400 thousand tons refined coal and 100 thousand tons power coal.

Since 2000, Tianjin Tiantie Coking & Chemical Co., Ltd. has been granted "excellent taxpayer", "enterprise with good credit of AAA grade", "successful enterprise of economized energy", "advanced unit of sanitation" and many other titles.

The company insists on "benefit staff and contribute to society", combines the enterprise wishes of "factuality and development, innovation and advanced" and the working desire of staff to establish a harmonious environment of "good credit and good quality, more honors and more profits", and tries best to make contributions to Tianjin 3-step strategy and Tianjin metallurgical industry. While improving the operation and production quality, it also make the development of programming actively. The company welcome other enterprises to cooperate and develop together.

焦炉出焦场景

造福员工 奉献社会

地址：天津市东丽区无瑕街 Add: Wuxia Street, Dongli District, Tianjin

邮政编码 Postal Code: 300301

电话 Tel: +86 22 24367546 传真 Fax: +86 22 24367647

天津市天铁轧二制钢有限公司

Tianjin Tiantie Zhaer Steel Production Co., Ltd.

王福祥　天津市天铁冶金集团副总经理
天津市天铁轧二制钢有限公司党委书记、董事长

Tianjin Tiantie Zhaer steel production Co., Ltd. is a wholly-owned subsidiary company under Tiantie metallurgy group and a large national calss-2 enterprise that the main production is steel products for building and the special steels. The company has over 510 million RMB of Government assets and 23120 thousand square meters of plot area, with 4 sub-plants, a subsidiary business company and a joint-stock company of rolling cold coils, Becoming a National Large-scale integrated enterprise which annual capacity 180 thousand iron, 2 million tons steel billet, 2million tons steel product.

The company enjoys solid technical power, advanced equipment, reasonable process and first-class quality. It passed the certification of ISO9002 quality assurance system in 1995. In February 2002; the company passed the certification of ISO10012 measurement validation system. In November 2003, it passed the certification of ISO9001 quality assurance system version 2000. The double anchor brand hot-rolled ribbed steel bars for the reinforcement of concrete manufactured by our company was awarded the honor title of Tianjin high-quality product. In August 2004, such five products as hot-rolled deformed bars, screw thread steel bars for the concrete, round bar, flat bar and seamless tube blank were rated as the top level AAA for quality credit. And in 2004, these products won the national production quality inspection exemption certificate for year 2004 to 2007. In November 2004, it passed the certification of ISO9001 (GB/T 19001), ISO14001 (GB/T24001), OHSAS18001 (DB/T28001) quality, environment, working health safe "a system of the three standard" management system. At same time won the assurance certification.

Our company is a domestically well-known manufacturer specialized in steel bars, our "Double Anchor" brand products are excellent in appearance and stable in performance, and are widely used in some large capital construction projects involved in railway, bridge and key water conservancy in China, especially, these products have exported to Hong Kong, Southeast Asia, Australia, Africa, Canada and so on , win favorable comments from the all.

天津市天铁轧二制钢有限公司是天津天铁冶金集团下属的全资子公司，国有资产5.1亿元，占地面积23.12万平方米。公司现有4个生产分厂，一个商贸子公司和一个冷轧薄板股份公司。2006年公司参股迁安市荣信工贸有限责任公司形成战略合作伙伴，建立了稳固的原料基地，是一个年产18万吨铁、200万吨钢、200万吨材的大型联合企业。

公司技术力量雄厚，设备先进，工艺合理，品质一流，1995年11月通过ISO9002质量体系认证，2002年2月通过了ISO10012计量体系认证，2003年11月通过2000版ISO9001质量体系认证。公司生产的"双锚牌"热轧带肋钢筋获"天津市优质产品"的称号，2004年8月我公司生产的"双锚牌"五大系列产品荣获中国产品质量协会认定的最高产品质量信誉AAA证书。并再次获得04—07年度产品质量国家免检证书。2004年11月通过了ISO9001(GB/T19001)；ISO14001(GB/T24001)；OHSAS18001(DB/T28001)质量、环境、职业健康安全"三标一体"整合管理体系认证，并获得证书。

我公司是国内知名的钢材专业生产企业，公司生产的"双锚牌"系列产品，外形优良，性能稳定，在国内一些大的铁路、公路、桥梁、水利枢纽等项目建设中得到广泛应用，并且出口香港、东南亚、澳大利亚、非洲、北美等多个国家和地区，受到国内外用户的好评。

连轧生产线

厂区大门

天津市中北钢丝绳有限公司

Tianjin Zhongbei Steel Wire Rope Co., Ltd.

天津市中北钢丝绳有限公司（原天津市中北钢丝绳厂）始建于1971年，是钢丝、钢丝绳的专业制造厂。天津市冶金质量协会、中国标准化协会冶金标准化分会理事、中国钢结构协会线材分会理事单位。

本公司坐落在天津市西青区津杨公路，占地面积4万平方米，其中建筑面积2.1万平方米。现有生产设备65台套，检试验设备19台套，总资产6700万元。共有7个生产车间，8个职能部室，员工260人。

企业资信为AAA级。1997年通过中国（长城）质量保证中心的ISO9002质量体系认证；2000年通过ISO9002质量体系的复评审核；2003年通过2000版ISO9001质量管理体系的复评审核。镀锌钢丝绳通过中国船级社的工厂及产品认可；矿用钢丝绳通过国家煤炭安全产品标志认证。其中重要用途钢丝绳、电梯用钢丝绳获得冶金产品质量认证证书。Φ10mm、Φ12mm、Φ13mm电梯用钢丝绳通过天津OTIS电梯有限公司寿命试验合格，各项试验指标符合试验大纲要求。

本公司为新版《镀锌钢绞线》YB/T5004-2001标准的主要起草单位。并为新版《电梯用钢丝绳》GB8903和《电梯钢丝绳用钢丝》YB/T5198标准的主要起草单位之一。

本公司技术工艺先进、设备精良，具有完备的理化检测手段。主要产品有钢丝绳（光面、镀锌）、电梯用钢丝绳、镀锌钢绞线、架空绞线用镀锌钢线及稀土锌铝合金镀层钢丝、钢绞线等，年生产能力达20000吨。生产的“中北牌”系列产品质量稳定，寿命周期长。产品实物质量历年来在国家金属制品质量监督检验中心、国家电梯质量监督检验中心、国家电力部检测中心及天津市质量监督检验站15站连续检测中全部合格，并获得2001年“国家级权威检验合格国家监督抽查合格好产品”称号。产品行销国内24个省、市、自治区，广泛用于铁路、煤矿、石油、化工、机械、电梯、渔业、船舶、电力、邮电等行业，得到各有关客户的一致好评。

Tianjin Zhongbei Steel Wire Rope Co., Ltd., used to be Zhongbei Steel Rope Factory, built in 1971, is a special enterprise of steel wire and steel wire rope, which has listed as one standing committee member of Tianjin Metallurgy Quality Association, Metallurgy Standardization Association of China Standardization Association and Wire Stock Association of China Steel Construction Association.

The company is located in Jinyang highway, Xiqing district, Tianjin, with land area about 40,000 m^2, construction area about 21,000 m^2. At present, inside company, there are product equipment 65 sets and ispection instruments 19 sets, total assets 67,000 thousand yuan, with 7 workshops, 8 offices and 260 staff.

With enterprise qualification about AAA, in 1997, it passed ISO9002 quality certification system by China (Great Wall) Quality Center; in 2000, it passed retesting of ISO9002 quality system certification; in 2003, it passed retesting of ISO9001 (2000) quality system certification. Steel wire rope of galvanization was approved by China Shipping Union and awarded with product license; mineral steel wire rope was approved by safety by National Coal Inspection Bureau; elevator steel wire rope and important steel wire rope was approved by metallurgy production quality certification; 10 mm, 12 mm and 13 mm elevator steel wire rope passed life test of Tianjin OTIS Elevator Co., Ltd..

The company is the main drafter of *galvanization steel stranded cable* YB/T5004-2001 Standard and one of the main drafters of *elevator steel wire rope* GB8903 and *elevator steel wire* YB/T5198 Standard.

Zhongbei is of advanced technology, excellent equipment and perfect rational testing measurement. Its products consist of steel wire rope (of smooth or galvanization), elevator steel wire rope, galvanization steel stranded cable, steel-cored aluminum galvanization steel wire with annual output about 20,000 tons. Zhongbei series products have good qualities and long life, which passed the examination of National Quality Supervision & Examination of Wire Products, National Elevator Inspection and Testing Center and 15 Tianjin Supervision & Examination Centers, and acquired “Good Product of National Selective Examination”. Up to now, products have been sold to 24 domestic provinces, cities, or municipalities, which are widely used in the fields of coal, petro, chemistry, mechanism, railroad, ocean, elevator, electricity as well as telecommunication. They are highly praised by client.

电梯绳车间

检测中心

合股

地址：天津市西青区中北镇津杨公路
Add: Jinyang Highway, Zhongbei Town, Xiqing District, Tianjin
邮政编码 Postal Code: 300380
电话 Tel: +86 22 27913018, 6593
传真 Fax: +86 22 27392873 27945409
http://www.zhbgss.com
E-mail: zhbgs@zhbgss.com

中国石油大港油田公

PetroChina Dagang Oilfield

总经理：何树山

党委书记：赵玉建

大港油田公司是中国石油下属的，以油气勘探开发为主营业务的特大型油气田企业。公司总部位于国家“十一五”重点开发开放建设区——天津市滨海新区，距北京 190 公里，距天津国际机场 70 公里，距天津新港 40 公里，地理位置优越，海陆空交通发达，往来便捷，是环渤海经济圈的重要组成部分。

大港油田公司东临渤海，西接冀中平原，东南与山东毗邻，北至津唐交界处，地跨津、冀、鲁 25 个区、市、县。总勘探面积 18716 平方千米，年原油生产能力 530 万吨，年天然气生产能力 3 亿立方米。截至 2006 年底，累计生产原油 1.37 亿吨，累计生产天然气 167.8 亿立方米。

目前，大港油田公司拥有资产总额 164.2 亿元，有员工 12961 人，其中博士 35 人、硕士 206 人、本科 1840 人、大中专 4293 人，管理和专业技术人员 4408 人。

今后一个时期，大港油田公司将全面贯彻落实科学发展观，始终遵循“奉献能源、创造和谐”的企业宗旨，抓住发展机遇，立足大港探区，瞄准大场面，寻求大突破，实现大发展，努力把大港油田建设成大油气田。

PetroChina Dagang Oilfield Company is a large-sized enterprise subordinated to PetroChina Company and engaged in exploring crude oil and natural gas. The headquarters locates in Tianjin Binhai New Area which is one of the districts our nation puts great attention to developing and opening during the fifteen period, 190 kilometers away from Beijing city, 70 kilometers away from Tianjin International Airport and 40 kilometers away from Tianjin Port. The geography position is superior and the transportation linked with railway, airway, highway and the waterway is very convenient. All of this makes it one of the important components of the economical circle around Bohai Sea.

The company is situated in Dagang, with Bohai Sea on the east, Jizhong plain on the west, Shandong province on the southeast, and border of Tianjin and Tangshan on the north. Its extraction field covers 25 regions, cities and counties of Tianjin city, Hebei province and Shandong province with total areas of 18,716 square kilometers and produces crude oil, natural gas of 5300 thousand tons and 0.3 billion steers per year respectively. By the end of 2006, it has produced crude oil of 0.137 billion tons and natural gas 16.78 billion steers.

大港油田公司愿与国内外朋友友好往来，精诚合作，共谋发展

At present, the total asset of Dagang Oilfield Company has reached 16.42 billion yuan. There are 12,961 working staff, including 35 doctors, 206 masters, 1,840 undergraduates, 4,293 from junior college and technical secondary school, 4,408 managers and technical personnel.

From now on, the company will carry out the concept of scientific development throughout, follow the tenet of “Offering energy sources, Creating harmonious”, grasp the opportunity of development, depend on Dagang Oilfield, look for breakthroughs and dedicate to developing the Dagang Oilfield into Dagang gas field.

地址：天津市大港区三号院
Add: The Third Yard, Dagang District, Tianjin
邮政编码 Postal Code: 300280
电话 Tel: +86 22 25971708
传真 Fax: +86 22 25915115

海上作业平台

公司机关楼

中国石油大港石化公司

PetroChina Dagang Petrochemical Corporation

大港石化公司是中国石油天然气股份有限公司直属的地区分公司。目前公司有 2200 多名员工，固定资产原值 30.39 亿元，净值 18.04 亿元，原油一次加工能力 500 万吨/年，拥有燃料油、润滑油两条生产线，能够生产汽油、柴油、润滑油、液化气、丙烯、低硫石油焦、MTBE 等 11 大类 40 余种产品，年销售收入超过 120 亿元。

地处油田，毗临海港，身在高效市场的大港石化公司，紧紧抓住天津滨海新区开发开放的良好机遇，坚持"做精做细、做好做强"的发展理念，不断深化管理体制、运行机制改革，积极推进技术创新，大力提升盈利能力和竞争实力，努力实现企业的持续、有效、快速、协调发展，全力建设国内领先、国际一流的大型炼油基地。

PetroChina Dagang Petrochemical Corporation is directly under PetroChina Natural Gas Ltd.. Now, the company has 2,200 employees and its fixed asset amounts to 3.039 billion Yuan and net value is 1.804 billion Yuan. We have a capacity of processing 5000 thousand tons crude oil annually and have two product-lines of fuel oil and lubricant oil that are able to produce 40 products of 11 kinds, including gasoline, diesel oil, lubricant, LPG, propylene, MTBE, etc..

The company situated in an oil field and near the port, will grasp the opportunity of development and the open of Tianjin Binhai District, stick to the tenet of "More finer, More stronger ", strengthen reformation of the management system, push the technology creativity and enhance our ability of competition so as to develop the company consistently, quickly, effectively and harmoniously and construct the top-ranking large-scaled refinery of our country.

500 万吨完善配改一期工程投产典礼

地址：天津市大港区三号院花园东路口
Add: The East Joint of Huayuan Road, The Third Yard, Dagang District, Tianjin
邮政编码 Postal Code: 300280
电话 Tel: +86 22 25921144

做精做细、做好做强

中国石油大港油田集团有限公司
PetroChina Dagang Oilfield Group Co., Ltd.

党委书记：李文强

董事长、总经理：秦永和

中国石油大港油田集团有限公司以石油工程技术服务、加工制造、油气合作开发、工程建设、化工延伸、辅助生产为主营业务，具有油气勘探开发、工程技术服务、油气田钻采设计施工、石油装备和产品制造、管道路桥工程设计施工等较强能力和丰富经验。

截至 2005 年底，拥有资产总额 106 亿元；拥有主要生产装备 5000 余台（套）。拥有各类专业技术人才 12650 多人，其中：中国石油天然气集团公司级高级技术专家 3 人，享受政府特殊津贴专家 4 人，教授级专家 13 人。

中国石油大港油田集团有限公司坚持科技兴企，强化技术创新，加大科技投入，形成了大位移井、水平井综合配套技术，深井、超深井综合配套技术，发现和保护油气层综合配套技术、井下作业综合配套技术，浅海系列海工工程技术，储气库建设综合配套技术，石油钻采机械产品生产技术等独具大港特色的技术系列及众多专项技术。

凭借先进的技术和过硬的作风，中国石油大港油田集团有限公司市场领域不断拓宽，技术服务和施工作业队伍遍布国内各油田，并进入委内瑞拉、阿塞拜疆、俄罗斯、菲律宾、印尼、伊朗、格鲁吉亚、突尼斯、卡塔尔、苏丹、墨西哥、孟加拉、巴基斯坦等国际市场和泛华、赵东、菲利普斯等国内反承包市场。2005 年实现主营业务收入 64.17 亿元，位天津市百强企业前列，其中外部市场收入达到总收入的 51.73%。

PetroChina Dagang Oilfield Group Co., Ltd. is a large company of petroleum technology service, oil & gas exploitation, project construction and assistant production, which has strong ability and enough experiences in oil & gas survey, technology service, oil field design & construction, oil equipment production, pipeline project design and construction, etc..

By the end of 2005, the company has a total asset of 10.6 billion, more than 5000 main equipments

A. 机关办公大楼

B. 墨西哥浅钻井施工现场

C. 在突尼斯施工的 50D 钻机

D. 钻机配套中心全景

and 12650 technical personnel, among which, 3 senior technologists of China National Petroleum Corporation level, 4 experts gotten government special allowance, 13 experts of professor level.

The company insists on technology innovation, increasing technology input. Now it has mastered the integrated technology of Dagang character in the field of mega reach well, horizontal drain hole, deep well, super deep well, oil & gas discovery, borehole operation, natural gas storage, oil drilling and exploitation.

Resorted to advanced technology and well-knit style, the company has extended its market to all the national oil fields, and has entered the global market of Venezuela, Russia, Philippine, Indonesia, Iran, Tunis, Mexico, Bengal, Pakistan and so on, and the contract market of Fanhua, Zhaodong and Philips. In 2005, the revenue of main business has reached 6.417 billion yuan, of which, the revenue from foreign market takes 51.73%. The company has come into the first hundred enterprises of Tianjin.

地址：天津市大港区三号院
Add: The Third Yard, Dagang District, Tianjin
邮政编码 Postal Code: 300280
电话 Tel: +86 22 25922240
http://eip.dg.cnpc

中油华北销售大港分公司

PetroChina Northern Marketing Dagang Company

中油华北销售大港分公司组建于2000年10月，是中国石油天然气股份有限公司华北公司旗下的成品油资源型企业，公司位于天津市东南部的大港油田，濒临渤海，近距天津市区、北京、塘沽和大港油田炼油厂（大港石化公司），优越的地理位置和便捷的交通，使得大港分公司成为集地付、铁路发运、水路（管输）发运为一体的多功能型成品油资源型企业，辐射范围达天津、北京、河北大部、陕西、山东西北部、上海、江浙、广东、福建等地。

总经理：王多宏

公司领导班子

公司现有员工110人，机构精简，队伍精良，销售成品油的付油设施齐备、系统先进，方式主要有：

地付——公路外运油库库容达15000立方米，有14个付油鹤位，年付油能力达120万吨，汽车配送按150公里效益半径可辐射到天津、河北、山东等地区。

铁路发运——以中油大港石化分公司千米桥油库为依托，总库容10.2万立方米，设计年周转能力80万吨，具有库容大、品种齐全、辐射面宽、调运能力强等特点。

水路（管输）发运——以中油大港石化分公司塘沽南疆码头油库为依托，总库容 13.5 万立方米，具备下海、上岸、返输、与周边油库联网等多种功能，成品油年吞吐量60万吨。

公司成立以来，始终坚持以经济效益为中心、以实现双赢为目的、以深化内部管理为基础、以人为本图发展的工作方针，始终发扬团结、敬业、诚信、创新的企业精神，拥有团结务实、开拓创新的领导班子、积极向上的员工队伍、科学规范的规章制度。

随着大港分公司今后的不断成长，公司全体员工将始终如一地以满腔热情投入到环渤海经济区域的快速发展当中，为实现滨海新区的腾飞做出更大贡献！

PetroChina Northern Marketing Dagang Company established in October 2000, engaged in providing oil products, subordinates to Northern Company of PetroChina Compnay. The company locates in the Dagang oil field in the southeast Tianjin among which there are Bohai Sea, Tianjin, Beijing, Tanggu and Dagang oil field refinery factory (Dagang Petrochemical Company). With the advantageous geographical position and convenitent transportation, the company has developed into a multifunctional enterprise providing oil products by railway and sea. The business fields have extended to Tianjin, Beijing, most of Hebei province, Shanxi province, northwestward of Shandong province, Shanghai province, Guangdong province and Fujian province, etc..

There are 110 excellent employees and advanced equipments in the company. We provide oil products in three ways:

By road–we have a oil depot with a volume of 15000 steers and 14 intake depots so as to pay oil 1.2 million tons per year. The service reaches Shandong province, Hebei province and Tianjin city according to 150 kilometers benefit radius.

By railway–depending on the Qianmiqiao oil depot with a volume of 0.102 million steers and turn over capacity of 0.8 million tons per year, the service has a characteristic of large capacity and riot varieties.

By sea–relying on the oil depot with a volume of 0.135 million steers on the Tanggu Nanjiang Port of Petro China Dagang Petrochemical Company, the service has many functions and owns a oil products throughput of 0.60 million tons per year.

The company centers on getting benefits and aims to obtaining win–win. Basing on deep management, the regulations become more standardized and the leadership carries forward the spirit of solidarity, honesty and innovation as well as the employees do.

With the development of our company, all of the staff will devote to making more contributions to the development of Binhai New Area.

大港分公司公路外运油库

火车发运

海上发运

天津大学建筑设计规划研究总院

Tianjin University Academy of Architecture Devise and Layout Research

院长：洪再生 教授 日本工学博士

Dean: Professor Hong Zaisheng, Doctor of Engineering Awarded in Japan Established

- 总顾问：彭一刚 教授 中国科学院院士
  Consultant-in-Chief: Professor Peng Yigang, China, Academician
- 党总支书记：杨昌鸣 教授 博士
  Party Branch Secretary: Professor Yang Changming, Doctor
- 副院长：徐长安 于敬海
  Vice Dean: Xu Chang'an Yu Jinghai

本院创建于1958年，是国家甲级建筑设计、甲级城市规划设计、甲级工程咨询单位。本院依托于国家重点大学人才优势、学科优势和技术优势，凭借先进的技术装备和严谨的工作作风，近年来在全国范围完成各种类型、各种规模的建筑设计、城市规划设计屡获各类奖项，受到项目委托单位的好评。

本院现有一线设计人员180余人，其中45人为国家一级注册建筑师，35人为国家一级注册结构师，15人为国家注册城市规划师，拥有硕士学位的人员占全院总人数的40%以上。专业配套齐全，人员素质较高，使本院在教育和科研建筑、旅游和疗养建筑、办公和商贸建筑以及大型医院建筑、体育建筑设计和城市规划、古建筑保护规划等方面都有不同凡响的建树。其中,"威海甲午海战馆"、"深圳世界之窗"、"深圳欢乐谷"等项目在国内外均有影响，并且在天津海河开发重大项目的国际竞赛中，先后获得一、二等奖。此外在工业建筑设计、古建筑复原设计、设计监理、深基坑支护以及建设项目策划和可行性研究等方面也具有较强的实力，并取得了较好的业绩。

2005年是中国近代第一所大学——天津大学建校110周年，"实事求是"作为天津大学的校训，已经深深的融入本院的企业文化与服务理念之中。特色鲜明、风格独具的天津大学建筑设计规划研究总院，愿为中国的城市建设精心勾绘最具地方特色、最具竞争力、最具时代精神的发展蓝图。

Established in 1958, Tianjin University Academy of Architecture Devise and Layout Research is one of the national first-rank institutes of architecture devise, urban layout and project counseling. Supported by the advantage of talent, knowledge and technology from national key university TJU and by its advanced technique and rigorous style in work, the academy has won several awards in architecture devise and urban layout nationwide.

At present, there are 180 designers working in the Academy, among which 45 are national first-class registered construction designers, 35 are national registered civil planners; and 40% of them hold the Master's degree. Thanks to a complete range of specialties and a high-caliber team, the Academy specializes in a wide domain, including education and research architectures, gymnasium devise and urban layout, protection of archaic architecture, such as "Weihai Museum of Sino-Japanese War", "Shenzhen Window of The World", "Shenzhen Happy Valley". We are awarded the first-class and second-class prize in the Tianjin Haihe Development Project International Contest. Besides, we are also adept in devising of industrial architecture, renewal of archaic architecture, design supervision and feasibility research.

Tianjin University, the first educational institution of higher learning in China, has been there 110 years by 2005 whose motto, "Seek Truth from Facts", has also permeated into the academy's enterprise culture and service notion. Tianjin University Academy of Architecture Devise and Layout Research, with its brilliant and inimitable characteristic, would like to draw a blue print for domestic city construction with the utmost competitiveness and time spirit.

地址：天津市南开区卫津路92号　Add: No. 92 Weijin Road, Nankai District, Tianjin　邮政编码 Postal Code: 300072
电话 Tel: +86 22 27404753　传真 Fax: +86 22 27401845　E-mail: td_design@126.com

中国民航大学

Civil Aviation University of China

1951年9月25日，军委民航局第二民用航空学校在天津宣告成立。这所由毛泽东主席任命校长、周恩来总理选定校址的学校，奠定了中国民航大学的第一块基石。

建校55年来，中国民航大学已为民航、社会和国防现代化建设培养各类人才4万余人，孕育出的一代代莘莘学子占中国民航职工总人数的六分之一，工程技术和管理人才的三分之一。中国所有涉及民航业务的单位、国际民航组织等机构都有来自中国民航大学的学生，中国民航大学的校友们已经成为中国民航高级管理和技术领域的一支中坚力量。

今天的中国民航大学已发展成为中国唯一一所民航学科专业门类齐全、将航空科学技术与交通运输工程两大学科群交叉融合的高等学府。学校位于津门之畔，渤海之滨，占地110余万平方米，直属中国民航总局，以培养民航高级工程技术和管理人才为主，在校学生13000余人。学校致力于为中国民航持续快速发展提供强有力的人才、科技支持，被誉为中国民航人才的摇篮、科学技术研究的中心、国际文化交流的窗口。

当前的中国民航大学正在向国内知名、国际民航界有较大影响的教学研究型民航大学阔步前行!

On September 25th of 1951, The Second Aviation Academy, which was under the leadership of the Civil Aviation Administration of the Central Military Commission of the P. R. China, was proclaimed the founding in Tianjin. This Academy is the first footstone of Civil Aviation University of China, with its first principle appointed by Chairman Mao Zedong, and the location decided on by Premier Zhou Enlai.

During the past 55 years after it was founded, CAUC has supplied civil aviation industry, society and the national defense modernization with over 40,000 outstanding talents. The number of the trained students of the university has occupied 1/6 of the total number of the entire faculties of China's civil aviation industry, 1/3 of the personnel of engineering technology and management. There gathered the students of Civil Aviation University of China in every corner of China's civil aviation business, including ICAO and most of the branches of international aviation companies and organizations. The alumni of CAUC have become the backbone of the industry both in the field of management and technology.

The present CAUC has grown to be the only university of its kind with all the necessary disciplines in civil aviation and it well integrates the two disciplinary groups–Transportation and Aviation Science & Technology. The university locates at the seashore of Tianjin and gets near to the Bohai Bay, which occupies approximate 1.1 million square meters. The university is directly under the leadership of CAAC, which concentrates itself on training the senior talents of engineering and management. Now CAUC has a full-time student population of about 13,000. The university devotes itself to providing great support of personnel and science & technology for the rapid and sustainable progress of China's aviation industry. Therefore, the university is renowned as the cradle of talents for China's civil aviation, the scientific and technological research center of the industry, and the window of the civil aviation cooperation and exchange.

The current CAUC is marching forward to be a national famous university integrating teaching and researching together, which will have a great influence in the international aviation industry!

中外专家在校研讨空客A320飞机

B737 模拟机

许春生教授主持的“民航发动机使用可靠性研究”获国家科技进步二等奖

中国大冢制药有限公司

China Otsuica Pharmaceutical Co., Ltd.

由日本大冢制药株式会社和中国医药集团总公司所属中国医药工业公司和中国医药对外贸易公司共同投资，于1984年5月17日正式投产，为中国第一家中外合资制药企业。现有员工六百余人，产品行销国内二十七个省市自治区，已形成了遍及全国的销售网络。

作为第一家引进PP塑瓶输液的制药企业，经过二十年的发展，现已拥有聚丙烯、聚乙烯瓶装输液、PP共挤膜软袋输液、塑料安瓿注射液多品种多规格最新技术生产线，生产4大类46个品种输液产品及治疗青光眼及抗眼疲劳滴眼液产品和塑料安瓿水针剂。以“COP”为著名商标的输液产品以其严格的品质控制标准，使系列输液在临床安全使用二十年无一例热源反应，成为了安全输液的标志和典范。中国大冢以药品的高品质赢得了广大医务人员和患者的信赖。

公司输液产品于1986年荣获国家质量金质奖；1988年入选“全国十大最佳合资企业”第五名；先后荣获医药制造业“十佳品牌”、“最佳企业”和“全国外商投资双优企业”称号；连续5年被评为天津市外商投资知识密集技术密集型企业；2003年还荣获全国“五一”劳动奖状和天津市“十五”立功先进集体称号，高海春总经理并荣获天津市劳动模范称号。

在中日双方股东的全力支持下，公司业绩连年持续增长，中国大冢正以快速发展的步伐，将继续保持在中国基础输液领域的领先地位，同时为中国临床输液治疗作出新的贡献。

地址：天津市西青经济开发区南河工业园

Add: Nanhe Industry Park, Xiqing Economic Development Zone, Tianjin

邮政编码 Postal Code: 300382

电话 Tel: +86 22 23982883

http://www.chinaotsuka.com.cn

China Otsuica Pharmaceutical Co., Ltd. was invested by Japan Otsuica Pharmaceutical Co., Ltd., China Pharmaceutical Industry Company and China Pharmaceutical Foreign Trade Company and was put into operation on May 27, 1984. It is the first joint venture pharmaceutical enterprise in China. Now, there are more than 600 employees, the products have sold to 27 provinces over the whole country.

It is the first enterprise to import PP plastic transfusion bottle, after 20 years' development, it has put on many new production lines, such as polypropylene & polyethylene bottle transfusion, PP soft transfusion bag, plastic injection liquid and so on. I can produce 46 kinds of 4 types transfusion products, eye drops and plastic injection products. With the famous brand of "COP", the transfusion products resort to its strict standard, has made the series of the transfusion used safely for 20 years, and has become the mark and mirror of the safe transfusion. Its products have won the reliance of medical personnel and patients.

The transfusion products have been awarded the national golden prize in 1986. It came into "the top 10 joint venture of china" in 1988. The corporation has been awarded "the top 10 brand" "the best enterprise" and the "excellent enterprise of foreign investment" , has been awarded dense knowledge and technology enterprise of foreign investment in Tianjin for the successive 5 years. In 2003, it has been awarded the "National Labor Day Prize" and "The Advanced Unit of Tianjin in the Tenth Five-year Paln Period". The manager, Mr. Gao Haichun was awarded the working model of Tianjin.

With the support of the shareholders of China and Japan, the corporation grew year by year. It continues to develop and will sustain the leading level in transfusion field and contributes a lot for transfusion treatment in China.

天津太平洋医药科技集团是集医药制剂、化学制药、化工原料进出口贸易为一体的综合性集团公司。下属企业有天津太平洋制药有限公司、太平洋化学制药有限公司、外环化工有限公司、太平洋药店等。

集团公司主要生产、销售中西药制剂，自有商业设施租赁。原料药（非普拉宗、盐酸二甲双胍、依替膦酸二钠、包醛氧淀粉、藻酸双酯钠等）；货物及技术进出口业务。医药技术开发、技术转让、技术服务；建筑材料、机电产品、金属材料批发兼零售；集中供热服务；以自有资金对科技业、房地产业、商业进行投资；投资咨询；进出口业务等。

Tianjin Pacific Pharmaceutical Technology Group is a concentration of pharmaceutical preparations medical technology, pharmaceutical chemistry, chemical raw materials for import and export trade into an integrated group. Pacific Enterprises subsidiary Tianjin pacific Pharmaceutical Company Ltd., Pacific Ocean Chemical Pharmaceutical Co., Ltd., External Loop Chemical Industry Co., Ltd., Pacific Ocean Drugstore, etc..

The group company mainly produces, sells Chinese and Western medicine preparation, own commercial facilities are leased. Raw materials medicine (Feprazone, Metformin Hydrochloride, Etidronate disodium, Coated aldehyde oxystarch, Alginidetum Natricum, etc.); goods and technological import and export business. Technological development of medicine, technological transfer, technological service; Construction material, electronic product, metal material whole sale and retail; Central heating service; Make the investment to science and technology industry, real estate, commerce with the own fund; Investment consultation; Import and export business, etc..

文化园—科技集团

文化园—网球场

地址：天津市解放南路外环线 17 号桥
Add: Beside the 17th Bridge, Jiefang South Outer Ring Road, Tianjin
邮政编码 Postal Code: 300385
电话 Tel: +86 22 83983875

董事长：王周喜

总经理：马白玉

2006年是“十一五”计划的开局之年，城投集团坚持以科学发展观为指导，围绕“三步走”战略和“五大战略举措”，全力做好城市基础设施的资金组织，全年新签订融资合同额204.75亿元，融资到位额188.1亿元，完成固定资产投资212.8亿元，实现了“十一五”计划的开门红，较好地发挥了城建投融资平台的作用。

2006年，城投集团各重点建设项目推进顺利，一批基础设施竣工投入使用，大幅提升了天津市的整体城市载体功能：海河综合开发持续推进，大沽桥、保定桥、奉化桥建成通车，完成了光华桥、解放桥的改造，拓宽改造了一批临河道路，完成堤岸改造12.5公里，建成钟楼公园等6处临河绿地；京沪高速天津段全线通车，开工建设了京津高速二线、蓟平高速，新增高速公路通车里程91公里；快速路新增通车里程40公里，建成12座人行天桥和6座泵站，累计通车里程达到160公里；轨道交通项目全面提速，地铁一号线实现了通车试运营，地铁二、三号线试验段工程进展顺利，东站枢纽全面开工，京津城际轨道工程全速推进；环境整治项目持续展开，实现快速路等绿化134万平方米，河东桥园建筑主体工程完工，水处理业务从单一污水处理拓展到供水和再生水领域，成功进入贵州、湖北等外地水务市场，全年实际污水处理量达到4.4亿立方米，同比增长45%；城市路网建设成效显著，全年建成道路18条、通车总里程32.8公里，竣工公交场站15座，完成南运河整治6.1公里和8公里沿河道路，天津市的整体面貌改观巨大。

2007年，城投集团将继续围绕“用好城市资源、服务天津发展”这个主题，以刚刚完成的企业重组为契机，以“三创一建”为目标，以构建现代化综合交通体系、增强天津的对外辐射能力为重点，进一步加快高速公路、市区快速路、地铁、城际铁路、公交场站、大型风景区等项目建设。加大直接融资、资源整合和存量盘活的力度，增强集团创利能力，加快集团由单一融资平台向既是投资主体又是赢利企业的转变，实现城投集团在更高水平上又好又快地发展壮大。

2007年城投集团的主要工作目标是：完成固定资产投资146亿元，力争170亿元，实现融资到位额180亿元，其中直接融资突破50亿元。

1 | 2
3

1. 泰园公园全景
2. 津蓟高速公路
3. 杭州污水处理厂

意式风情区

"The 11th five-year plan" Period begins in 2006. Tianjin Infrastructure Investment Group sticked to following the guidance of the view of scientific development and encircling the "Three-step" strategy and the "Five strategies". The group had a good beginning of "The 11th five-year plan" and performed a good function as an investment platform of urban construction by doing the city infrastructure's capital organization well, making new financing contracts of 20.475 billion yuan, absorbing capital of 18.81 billion yuan and investing fixed assets 21.28 billion yuan.

In 2006, the group's important projects ran smoothly so that a set of infrastructures has been putting into use that enhanced the Tianjin city's function as a carrier. Comprehensive development of Haihe River has been pushing persistently; Dagu Bridge, Baoding Bridge and Fenghua Bridge have been putting into use. The reconstruction of Guanghua Bridge and Jiefang Bridge had been finished. Some roads near rivers were widened. A total of 12.5 km bank were rebuilt. 6 greenbelts including Belfry Park were built on rivers. The Tianjin section of the Beijing-Shanghai expressway could be used totally and the Beijing-Tianjin expressway line 2 and Jiping expressway began to be constructed which made the newly available expressway reach 91 km and the thruway 40 km, with 12 pedestrian bridges and 6 pumping stations built so that roads open to traffic reached 160 km totally. The railway traffic project was performed post so that the Subway Line1 had tested its operation and the test projects of Line 2 and Line 3 got along well as well as the Beijing-Tianjin railway project did while the eastern railway station was started to build. At the same time, environment renovation project was performed, including greening thruway 1.34 million m^2, finishing Hedongqiao Park main construction project, developing the water-treatment operation from single sewage-treatment operation to water regeneration and water supply field, entering Guizhou water market, treating sewage 0.44 billion m^3 which increased by 45 percent. The city's roads were constructed effectively. The group had constructed 18 roads and 15 bus stations while it renovated southern canal 6.1 km and roads along the river 8 km. Thus, 32.8 km had been opening to traffic and the city's traffic improved greatly.

In 2007, Tianjin Infrastructure Investment Group will encircle the subject

地铁高架路

海河 直沽桥

快速路卫津南路立交桥

海河 金汇桥

of "Using city source well, providing service for Tianjin's development", grasping the chance of recomposition finished yet, aiming at "Creation one, Construction one". The group will put emphases on constructing modern comprehensive traffic system and enhancing Tianjin radiant intensity by means of constructing expressways, thruways, subways, railways between cities, bus stations and large beauty spots, etc.. Besides, the group tends to grow fast by increasing the amount of direct financing, resource integration and stock-in-trade, strengthening the ability of gaining profit and transforming the company from single financing platform to both investment main body and profitable enterprise.

In 2007, the group aims at obtaining fixed asset 14.6 billion yuan and shooting at 17 billion yuan, gaining financing 18 billion yuan in which the direct financing exceeds 5 billion yuan.

建设中的东站交通枢纽

地址：天津市南开区卫津南路 76 号
Add: No. 76 Weijinnan Road, Nankai District, Tianjin
邮政编码 Postal Code: 300381

铁道第三勘察设计院

The 3rd Railway Survey & Design Institute

党委书记：王洪宇

院长：刘为群

铁道第三勘察设计院（简称铁三院）成立于1953年，是以铁路、公路、城市轨道交通等勘察设计为主的国家大型综合设计院，技术力量雄厚，专业齐全。铁三院综合实力在全国勘察设计百强中名列前茅，拥有对外经营权，通过了英国劳氏质量认证公司ISO9001质量管理体系、OHSAS18001健康安全管理体系和ISO14001环境管理体系认证，是全国勘察设计单位推行全面质量管理的第一个达标单位，多次被评为AAA级信用等级企业。

铁三院将秉承"诚信为本，追求卓越"的企业核心理念，坚持以人为本，不断开拓创新，竭诚为广大客户创造更多的价值，与客户一起共同实现新的发展。

Established in 1953, the 3rd Railway Survey & Design Institute is a large-sized national comprehensive institute in railway, road and subway surveying and designing. The company has advantages in both technology and specialty. Measured from comprehensive strength, the company can enter the first level of national 100th advanced enterprises. With foreign business license, the company passed ISO9001 Quality Standard System Certification, OHSAS18001 Health & Security Standard System Certification and ISO14001 Environmental Standard System Certification, which make the company to be the first enterprise implementing completely quality management in design industry. It also obtains "AAA" grade credit.

Holding the principle of "Honesty is our root, excellence is our object", the company will insist on human-oriented and innovated, continue making contributions to clients, and make new development together.

地址：天津市河北区中山路10号
Add: No. 10 Zhongshan Road, Hebei District, Tianjin
邮政编码 Postal Code: 300142
电话 Tel: +86 22 26273722
传真 Fax: +86 22 26355912
http://www.cr-tsdi.com.cn

天津泰达建设集团有限公司

TianJin TEDA Construction Group Co., Ltd.

天津泰达建设集团有限公司（Tianjin TEDA Construction Group Co., Ltd.）——“泰达建设”是以房地产开发为主业的大型企业集团，并具有物业管理、基础设施建设、装修装饰等综合能力，总资产逾100亿元，控股参股十多家企业，作为主发起人发起组建了津滨发展股份有限公司。泰达建设旗下的两家建设部一级资质房地产开发企业，已经累计投资数百亿元，竣工项目100余个，完成开发面积近500万平米的商品住宅、60万平米的商业项目以及40万平米的标准工业厂房，获得了相当高的市场知名度和美誉度。

天津泰达建设集团有限公司获得的部分荣誉：

- 天津市首批参与发起承诺销售“放心房”活动的企业之一；
- 多次获得“天津市优秀企业”、“开发区明星企业”等荣誉称号；
- 1994年起至今，连续12年获得天津市“守合同重信誉单位”称号；
- 2001年、2003年、2005年连续三次被评为“天津市房地产开发企业二十强”之首；
- 2006年进入全国房地产开发百强企业行列。

天津泰达建设集团滨海分公司成立于2001年12月11日，是天津泰达建设集团的直属分公司。

公司自成立以来，立足于滨海新区，以房地产开发为主业，不断提升产品品质与服务质量，以高尚品质打动人，以真诚服务感动人，务实求效，勇于创新，以诚心打造建筑经典，以空间承载品味个性。

经过多年努力，滨海分公司在滨海新区逐渐建立起了良好的市场口碑，相继成功开发了滨海·金融街、滨海·翠亨康庭、滨海·天江公寓、滨海·大学城、滨海·爱丽榭等一系列精品项目。公司所开发的“滨海”系列产品曾多次荣获“中国百佳经典楼盘奖”、“绿色节能示范建筑奖”、“投资天津经典楼盘奖”等多项荣誉，并且在滨海新区率先成立了业主俱乐部——滨海会。

公司多年以来一直坚持立足滨海新区、走可持续发展道路的经营模式，倡导“三大核心理念”，即：以创造客户价值为中心的产品理念，建立规范、高效的现代企业体制的制度理念，打造专业、专注精英团队的人才理念。目前公司已经汇聚了一大批高素质专业人才，并与国内外知名建筑设计、景观设计、营销策划、物业管理公司建立了广泛的合作关系。滨海分公司坚持以行动践行承诺，兢兢业业，孜孜以求，力求为客户提供卓越的品质和周到的服务，为滨海新区城市建设和地区居住品质的提升贡献力量。

Tianjin TEDA Construction Group Co., Ltd. is a big enterprise group whose main business is real estate and other comprehensive ability of estate management, infrastructure construction and decoration. With more than 10 billion yuan total assets and shares of more than 10 enterprises, the company established Jinbin Development Co., Ltd.. Two real estate development enterprise of the first level approved by China Construction Ministry under TEDA Group, have finished several ten billions investment, more than 100 constructed projects, commercial house with developed area of 5 million sq. m, 600 thousand commercial projects and 400 thousand standard industry buildings, which brought a lot of honors and credit to the company.

The honors include: One of the first enterprises participated in the launch of “assured houses” sales; Be awarded the name of “Excellent Enterprise in Tianjin” and “Star Enterprise in Development Area” for many times; Continually gained the name of “Good Credit Unit” for 12 years since 1994; Be appraised to be the first position of “20 Big Enterprises of Real Estate Industry in Tianjin” for continually 3 times in 2001,2003 and 2005; Be listed in the 100 big enterprises in the national real estate industry.

Binhai Subsidiary of the Group was established on December 11th, 2001, which is directly subordinate Tianjin TEDA Construction Group Co., Ltd..

Since established, Binhai Subsidiary has based on Binhai New Area, initiated from real estate industry as main business, continually developed the quality of products and service, used innovation and effective work to construct classical buildings, and used space to express personality and social taste.

After working hard for many years, Binhai Subsidiary earned good credit in Binhai New Area and developed a series of demonstration buildings, including Binhai Finance Street, Binhai Cuihengkang Courtyard, Binhai Tianjiang Mansion, Binhai Campus City, etc.. The Binhai series buildings were awarded “China 100 Classic Buildings”, “Green Energy Conservation Demonstration Buildings”, “Classic Buildings for Investment in Tianjin” for many times. The subsidiary also took the lead in establishing “Binhai Club” the owners' club.

For many years, the company consisted in the operation mode of sustainable development based on Binhai New Area, and sponsored 3 principles: the production principle of consumers' value-centered, the system principle of normative, efficient modern enterprise system, and the human principle of special, elite teamwork. Now, the company has already attracted a lot of high quality professions and cooperated with plenty of famous construction design companies, landscape design companies, marketing companies and estate management companies at home and abroad. Binhai Subsidiary insisted on keeping promise, providing excellent service and products to consumers and tried best to make contributions to the living condition and construction of Binhai New Area.

建筑经典，鉴赏生活；
建筑以人为本，空间承载个性；
一沙一石，用建筑传承历史；
一言一行，凭诚信筑就基业。

天佳市政公路工程有限公司

Tianjia Municipal Highway Engineering Co., Ltd.

董事长、党总支书记：宋金和

总经理：樊兆强

天津天佳市政公路工程有限公司是隶属于天津城建集团有限公司的国有施工企业。公司始建于1951年，具有经建设部核准的市政公用工程施工总承包、钢结构工程专业承包、桥梁工程专业承包一级资质。公司主要承建市政道路工程、桥梁工程、隧道工程、公共广场工程、污水处理工程、泵站工程，储气罐工程等市政公用工程，及钢结构桥梁、钢结构网架结构等钢结构工程。

五十多年来，公司通过在工程建设领域的实战锻炼，通过在建筑行业的点滴积累，以优质求信誉，以信誉促发展，在业内树立了品牌。公司先后承建了天津刘庄斜拉桥钢梁制安工程、金钢桥改建工程、温州新西山水厂工程、廊坊大容积储气罐工程、保定桥工程，参与了北安桥工程、友谊路立交工程、张贵庄立交工程、卫津南立交工程等诸多重点工程项目建设，并将经营范围拓展到城市道路、自来水、污水处理、高速公司等多个领域，同时也将市场经营领域拓展到温州、西安、呼和浩特等省市。

为适应社会主义市场经济的发展，于2000年喜迁新址，建成了占地53000多平米的现代化厂房及车间，并更名为天佳市政公路工程有限公司。

公司通过不懈地努力拼搏，用实力打响了品牌，参建的工程项目曾获得中国建筑工程鲁班奖七尊，中国土木工程协会詹天佑大奖二尊，中国市政工程金奖五枚和一系列社会荣誉，在天津市和全国施工企业中享有盛誉。

天佳公司承建的天津解放桥改造工程

Tianjia Municipal Highway Engineering Co., Ltd. established in 1951, is a state-owned construction enterprise that subjects to Tianjin Infrastructure Construction Group. The company that is authorized by the construction department has first-class qualification in undertaking general municipal public project, professional steel structure project, and bridge engineering project. Its main business include municipal public project and steel structure project, such as bridge project, tunnel project, public square project, sewage treatment project, pumping station project, gas tank project and steel structural bridge, steel structural netted structure.

In recent fifty years, the company has developed with the credit gained from high quality so as to set up our brand in the field. The company has constructed many projects, such as Tianjin Liu village cable-stayed Bridge, reconstruction of Jingang Bridge, Wenzhou Xinxishan water works, Langfang gas tank project, Baoding Bridge. It also joined the construction of many main projects, including Bei'an Bridge, Youyi road flyway, Zhanggui village flyway, and Weijin south flyway. Its business fields have extended to roads, tap water, and sewage treatment, high-speed company. At the same time, it has entered the market of Wenzhou, Xi'an, Huhehaote, etc..

To fit the development of socialistic market economy, the company moved and built modern workshops 53000 squares in 2000 and was renamed as Tianjia Municipal Highway Engineering Co., Ltd..

The company has high reputation because it has been awarded Luban prize seven times, Zhantianyou prize twice, Gold Cup prize of China municipal engineering five times, etc..

天佳公司承建的温州新西山水厂工程

天佳公司承建的天津海河保定桥桥梁工程

天佳公司承建的天津崂山道人行天桥工程

天津城建隧道股份有限公司

Tianjin Urban Construction Tunnel Co., Ltd.

董事长：张玉明

总经理：王顺来

天津城建隧道股份有限公司是专门从事隧道施工的企业，具有专业施工企业承包和生产经营能力，是集工程施工、技术研发、大型专业设备租赁、技术咨询为一体的专业化公司。公司注册资本7000万元人民币，总资产3.6亿元。

隧道公司的组建是天津城建集团面对竞争日益激烈地市场，为提高集团整体实力而实施的重大战略举措。目前公司拥有六台Φ6.34m土压平衡式盾构机，设备拥有量全国领先。同时公司还从挪威引进了MSS-65型造桥机，从意大利引进了十台旋挖钻机，能够施工最大孔径3m，深110m，同时具备地下连续墙0.6-1.2m宽，与同类设备相比具有国际先进水平。

隧道公司先后参与了天津市地铁一号线工程，天津市城市快速路海河大桥、北京地铁5号线东直门立交、广西桂林永福发电厂工程、宁波大唐乌江山发电厂工程等一大批重点工程建设，拥有雄厚的技术实力和具有世界先进水平的施工设备。

公司目前正在参加天津轻轨盾构段施工和天津站交通枢纽改造工程等一批重点工程建设，明年将投入沈阳地铁盾构施工，今后的各项合作和施工项目已经确立，公司全体员工将以团结、求实、创效、发展的工作标准，积极投入工程建设，为天津乃至国家“十一五”战略目标的全面完成做出隧道公司的贡献。

Tianjin Urban Construction Tunnel Co., Ltd. is a professional construction enterprise with strong ability of engineering and operation, whose fields have been expanded to project construction, R&D, equipment rent and technology consultation and so on. The register capital of the company is 70 million yuan and the total asset is 360 million yuan.

The foundation of company is an important strategic action for Tianjin Urban Group to improve the competition capability and adapt to the competitive market. Currently, the company has 6 shield machines with soil pressure equilibrium of Φ6.34 m, which makes the company get into first class in China. The company also fetch in a MSS-65 bridge fabrication machine from Norway, 10 hydraulic piling rigs from Italy that can make the max diameter to be 3 m, the max depth to be 110 m with the continuous underground wall of 0.6~1.2 m.

The company has constructed a lot of projects, such as Tianjin No. 1 Subway, Tianjin Haihe Bridge, Beijing Dongzhimen Cloverleaf Junction of No. 5 Subway, Guilin Yongfu Power Plant and Ningbo Wujiangshan Power Plant. Both the technology and the equipments have all reached the advanced level of the world.

Now, the company has taken the project of Tianjin light rail shield and rebuilding of Tianjin railway station. The next year, it will start the construction of Shenyang subway shield. According to the principle of "comity, factuality, effective and development", all the staff will work actively and make contribution to the eleventh five-year plan period.

2号盾构机

成型隧道

中法合营王朝葡萄酿酒有限公司

Sino-French Joint-Venture Dynasty Winery Ltd.

王朝公司地下酒窖

中法合营王朝葡萄酿酒有限公司始建于 1980 年，是我国第二家、天津市第一家中外合资企业，合资的外方为法国人头马亚太有限公司和香港国际贸易英得利有限公司。

公司从国外引进了具有国际先进水平的葡萄酒生产设备和技术，拥有国际酿酒名种葡萄原料种植基地近 3 万亩，建立了国家级技术开发中心，有强劲的科技开发能力。公司现生产三大系列 100 多个品种具有欧洲风格的葡萄酒，生产能力为 5 万吨 / 年，是亚洲地区规模最大的全汁高档葡萄酒生产企业。

公司始终重视产品质量，使王朝酒享誉海内外。王朝酒曾获十四枚国际金奖、八枚国家金奖，被布鲁塞尔国际评酒会授予国际最高质量奖。农业部将王朝酒确定为无污染、无公害、无病毒、营养丰富的绿色食品。自 1998 年以来，王朝酒连续九年在全国市场同类产品销量上遥遥领先。目前王朝酒在国内干酒市场的占有率近 50%，并被指定为国宴用酒，供应 231 个我国驻外使领馆；产品还远销美国、加拿大、英国、法国、日本、澳大利亚等二十多个国家和地区。随着王朝酒知名度的不断提高，企业的无形资产价值也在不断提升，2006 年经评估王朝酒的品牌价值已达 30.07 亿元人民币。

公司具有现代化的管理运营机制，1989 年被批准为国家二级企业；1996 年通过了 ISO9002 质量管理体系认证；2000 年取得了 ISO14001 环境管理体系认证；“王朝”被国家工商总局评定为中国“驰名商标”；2001 年《王朝高档干红葡萄酒酿造技术与原料设备保障体系的研制与开发》荣获国家科技进步二等奖，成为我国酿酒行业唯一获此殊荣的企业；《提高企业竞争力的优化管理》荣获国家企业管理现代化创新成果二等奖；2002 年王朝酒被国家质检总局认定为“免检产品”和“中国名牌”称号。2005 年 4 月荣获由中国食品工业协会认定的“中国葡萄酒 A 级产品标志”；公司还连续多年获得天津市优秀外商投资企业、天津市优秀企业、全国双优外商投资企业、中国食品行业质量效益型先进企业、全国质量效益型先进企业等荣誉称号。

王朝公司通过研发新技术，吸引优秀人才等措施，五年内将王朝打造成中国最大的葡萄酒产业基地之一，让天津王朝酒香飘世界。公司将建成现代化、国际化的一流大型企业集团。

地址：天津市北辰区津围公路 29 号
Add: No. 29 Jinwei Highway, Beichen District, Tianjin
邮政编码 Postal Code: 300402
电话 Tel: +86 22 26998888, 0838
传真 Fax: +86 22 26990996

酒的王朝

Sino-French Joint-Venture Dynasty Winery Ltd. established in 1980, is the second Chinese foreign joint venture ever set up and is also the first such joint ventures in Tianjin. The foreign investors are French Remy Martin Asia-Pacific Ltd. and Hong Kong International Trading Yingdeli Ltd..

The company has introduced equipments and technologies with international advanced level and has plantation of 30 thousand acres with international known breed of brewing grape. It has founded the technology development center and has a strong capability of developing new technology. At present, the company produces 100 kinds of European-style wine belonging to three series and is able to produce 50 thousand tons per year. It is the largest-size high-quality 100% wine production company in the Asian region.

The company always pays attention to the quality of products so that the dynasty wine is known to the world. The dynasty wine was awarded with fourteen international gold prizes, eight national gold prizes and the International Highest Quality Prize by CMB. The wine is also defined by the ministry of agriculture as pollution-free, virus-free and nutritious green food and has sold best in the national market in consecutive nine years since 1998. Now, the dynasty wine has obtained a percent of 50% to the national dry red wine market and is designated as the state banquet wine providing to 231 consulates in foreign countries, together with more than 20 countries and regions, such as America, Canada, Britain, France, Japan and Australia.

As the reputation of the dynasty wine is growing, the value of intangible estates is increasing. It is estimated that the brand value of the dynasty wine has reached 3.007 billion yuan in 2006.

The company has modernized management and operating system. In 1989, it was authorized as national secondary enterprise and obtained certificates of IS09002 quality controlling system in 1996, ISO14001 environmental management system in 2000. In 2001, *The Development and Exploiture of Dynasty High-quality Dry Red Wine Brewing Technology and Material Equipment Guarantee System* was awarded the second-class prize of national technology progress, the solitary enterprise in national brewing industry and the *Optimized Management to Improving Enterprise Competition* obtained the second-class national innovation award of enterprise management modernization. In 2002, the dynasty wine was authorized as "Check-free Product" and "China Name Brand". In April 2005, it is awarded with "China A rank Wine" by China Food Industry Association. The company was awarded with "Tianjin excellent foreign invested enterprise", "Tianjin excellent enterprise", "National double-excellence foreign invested enterprise", "China advanced enterprise of quality and profit in food industry " and "National advanced enterprise of quality and profit" etc..

The dynasty company tends to be one of the China largest wine production base in five years by means of developing new technology and recruiting excellent person with ability and a modernization, internationalized topping large-sized enterprise.

王朝至尊橡木桶干红葡萄酒

王朝至尊橡木桶干红葡萄酒是酿酒师严格按照国际葡萄与葡萄酒组织(O.I.V.)酿酒法则，采用国际先进的酿造工艺及酿酒设备，与天津燕山山脉南麓和宁夏贺兰山东麓产区得天独厚的土壤、气候条件孕育出的名贵酿酒葡萄赤霞珠与美乐的完美结晶。经除梗破碎、浸渍发酵、木桶陈酿、低温窖藏、有效地去除了不利酿造的物质，保留和提高了葡萄中的营养成分、香味物质及优美的色泽。

其特点：呈深宝石红色；具有优美和谐的果香、酒香及橡木香味；口感醇厚协调、圆润柔顺、余韵均衡持久、风格典型独特。此酒为佐餐酒，饮用时最佳温度16–18摄氏度；建议饮用前1小时开瓶透气；在食用烧烤煎炸肉类食品时配以此酒最为适宜。

环发之巅　财富风云

众星环极 商务之巅

财以类聚，人以群分。环渤海发展中心坐落于天津“国宾区”，是天津金融地脉所在，也是天津市涉外酒店最集中的区域和天津罕有的多功能综合区域。环发中心与五星级酒店喜来登、水晶宫、津利华、天津宾馆为邻；天津大礼堂、国展中心、友谊商厦、友谊风情街、银河广场等政经文娱场所分布左右。俯瞰经济风云际会，细察商业烟聚波属。环发中心让精英与精英为伍，让您和财富一起思考，与智者比邻而居。

厚积渤发 天时地利

环发中心区域干线纵横，大道迎宾。与机场、高速路、港口快速相连，使您体会出门即达目的地的畅快。不论是动脉大路还是微细循环，都具有随时的顺畅。我们在尽最大努力给您舒适的环境的同时，为您节省最宝贵的时间。环发中心让您占尽天时地利，坐拥政通人和。

海纳百川 若市门庭

环发中心区域出身显赫，财富聚集。友谊路区域业已成为国内顶级商圈之所在。高密度的商业资本，浓厚的商业氛围，成为众多商业巨贾置地逐鹿的首选。目前进驻该地区的有中资银行 13 家，保险公司 7 家，证券信托公司 3 家，形成天津经济的无形巨手，这里是天津最接近财富的地方。我们用最博大的胸怀，换来最繁荣的商机。

奋发蹈厉 大气磅礴

环发中心以恢弘的气度，树立五星级酒店式写字楼的典范。地下 2 层车库，1 ~ 3 层为商业裙楼，4 ~ 28 层为酒店公寓式写字楼，板式内廊结构，空间大气开合，间隔自由，规整和个性完美统一，单层平面建筑面积达 1563.17 平米，专为集团总部、金融企业、上市公司、行政机关等大中型商办机构设计。作为首屈一指的商务楼层，恰到好处。绝版典雅，不可复制。我们的目标是让环发中心成为财富精英的 ID CARD。

大展经纶 万千气象

环发中心主体建筑巍峨高耸，俯瞰周遭一线楼群，放眼迎宾馆万亩绿色，鸟瞰津河一带波涛。这里正是天津绿肺所在，我们将公园搬进您的办公室。让您感受不一般的办公品质。主体建筑与两栋 4 层联体附楼形成 U 型皇家龙椅之型，王气尽显，富贵若揭。环发中心外檐构饰拜占庭风格三段式腰线，线条流畅俊朗，色块浩然大气。大有泰山绝顶我为峰的气势。

大中至正 精益求精

环发中心内部按照五星级酒店标准规划建造。以人为本，阳光设计。三级分区总控系统中央空调，冷暖双制；全楼热水循环供应系统，一应俱全。任意多点智能化宽频网络，全铝断桥隔热双层镀膜玻璃窗；8 部全明高速电梯贯通上下，300 个停放车位方便出入，IC 卡自动门禁系统……让您感受真正的高科技生活，现代化办公。我们将最优质的服务送达每一个角落，让您在工作中释放激情，让心情和财富一起高涨。

指点江山 天津财富心地标

环发中心建成伊始，便吸引了国家开发银行、浦东发展银行、华夏银行等大区级金融机构的眼光，随后天房集团、天歌纺织、恒安人寿等大型公司管理总部也竞相入驻。环发中心已成为天津 CBD 投资价值的优秀典范，形成聚合金融、产业资本，联袂政商文化和智力经济的强大磁场。在第三次经济浪潮席卷天津之时，我们给您提供叱咤风云的崭新领地；我们相信独具慧眼并独树一帜的财经资本大师，一定是新大陆的发现者。指点主流经济，英雄呼之欲出。环发中心将见证您缔造财富的传奇。

时代的责任是给胜利者一个显赫的位置

……任是给成功者一个优质的环境……

天津市东达房地产开发有限公司

Tianjin Dongda Real Estate Development Co., Ltd.

总经理：牛世清

天津市东达房地产开发有限公司组建于1992年，主营房地产开发和商品房销售。公司成立之初，总经理牛世清以独到的眼光洞察了大直沽蕴藏的城市发展优势和潜在的开发价值，主动向政府请缨，承担了因人口稠密、基础设施落后而令许多开发商望而却步的大直沽地区的危改任务。从此，东达公司就确立了“六负责”的企业精神——对历史、对未来、对环境、对现实、对子孙、对政府负责。放眼今天，短短十来年的时间，大直沽地区已旧貌换新颜，成为名符其实的现代化城区了，这些变化可以说离不开牛总经理及东达全体员工的努力奋斗。

东达开发公司代表楼盘神州花园位于河东区中环线与六纬路交口处，地处市中心，比邻海河东岸，可谓海河岸边的璀璨明珠！总建筑面积318100平方米，总占地面积138700平方米，绿化率35%。为提高小区的生活环境质量体现以人为本的规划设计思想，在项目热卖的同时公司也在不断的完善各种配套设施，深化服务，建立了集游泳、餐饮、副食、乒乓球、台球、健身、休闲为一体的神州会馆，不仅充实了百姓的生活空间，还为20余名下岗职工安排了岗位。特别是“绿色蔬菜进小区”工程，为业主送来了方便与健康，受到了业主的广泛好评。神州花园以其独特的设计和建设，曾获得了众多的奖项，其中特别值得一提的是获得联合国环境规划署颁发的“中国国际花园社区”大奖，进一步证明了神州花园在天津房地产项目中的独特、领先地位。

Tianjin Dongda Real Estate Development Co., Ltd. was established in 1992. Its main business is real estate development and commercial houses. General manager, Mr. Niu Shiqing has an insight into the development advantages and potential value of Dazhigu area, and initiatively led the company to take charge of development of Dazhigu area. From then on, the company set up a enterprise spirit of "6-responsibilty" to history, to future, to environment, to realism, to offspring and to government. In ten years, with the hardwork of Mr. Niu and all staff, Dazhigu area has changed to a real modern city.

A representative real estate of Dongda, Shenzhou Garden, is located at the crossing of Middle Cycle Road and Liuwei Road of Hedong District. With the location of city center and Haihe River east bank, Shenzhou Garden could be called a beautiful pearl of Haihe River Bank. The construction area is 318.1 thousand sq. m, the total area is 138.7 thousand sq. m, and coverage rate of afforestation is 35%. In order to improve the quality of living environment, the company continuously increases the supporting infrastructure, enhances the service, and set up Shenzhou Guildhall with swimming, dining, table tennis,billiards, body shaping and many other refreshment. Not only service for people's living, but also provide jobs to 20 more off-laid staff. Especially the project of "Green vegetables come into block", brings convenience and health, which is welcomed by all the owners. Because of the unique design and construction, Shenzhou Garden has gained a lot of rewards, including "International Garden Block" reward issued by United Nations Environment Program, which proves the leading position of Shenzhou Garden in Tianjin real estate industry.

地址：天津市河东区大直沽八纬路直沽园
Add: Zhigu Garden, Bawei Road, Dazhigu, Hedong District, Tianjin
邮政编码 Postal Code: 300170

天津双街置业集团有限公

TIANJIN SHUANGJIE REAL ESTATE GROUP CO., LTD.

董事长：刘春海

张立昌书记视察

天津市北辰区双街镇双街村位于天津中北部，全村总人口为1644人。其中：农业人口1356人，非农业人口288人；拥有可耕土地800余亩。

改革开放以来，在村党支部书记刘春海同志的带领下，始终坚持“开拓创新、锐意进取”的理念，做实发展，不断壮大集体经济的实力，走出了一条以发展工业致富农民，以发展农业龙头项目带动农户，以建设“双街新家园”实现和谐发展的道路。

双街村发生了翻天覆地的变化，截止到2005年底，集体积累由原来的900万元增加到6亿多元，村民人均收入由2000多元，增加到18000多元。为全村年满18岁以上的村民全部上了养老保险；凡男满55周岁、女满50周岁的村民，每月发给500元的养老金，给种了一辈子地的农民解决了养老问题。实行了新型农村合作医疗，并随着村集体经济实力的不断增强，将农民医药费的报销比例由原来的33%提高了一倍。为满足村民不断增长的精神、文化需求，先后投资180万元建起老年活动中心、图书馆、村民健身活动基地；翻修了村民学校、文化活动室、村民服务中心。为了给村里的孩子们营造更好的学习和成长环境，投资500多万元，建成了5000平方米的花园式幼儿园；建成并投入使用占地面积65亩的市级模范小学，圆了农家孩子不出

和谐发展 实力推进社会主义新农村建设
——进取中的双街村

Develop Harmoniously to Improve the Conduction of New Socialist Countryside
——The Shuangjie Country in Progress

村就能上重点学校的梦想。一个经济发展、生活富裕、乡风文明、环境优美、管理民主的社会主义新农村已展现在人们面前。

The Shuangjie Country, which belongs to the Shuangjie County of Beichen District in Tianjin City, is located in the middle and north part of Tianjin. It has a total population of 1644, among which, agricultural population are 1356 and non-agricultural population are 288. And the area of cultivated land is 800 mu.

Since reforming and openning to the outside world, under the leadership of Secretary Liu Chunhai of country branch of CCP, Shuangjie Country insists on the idea of "Exploration and innovation, progressing bravely", develops the collective-owned economy, helps the rural people to get rich through the developing of industry and agriculture, establishes the "Shuangjie new home" and then realizes harmonious development.

Shuangjie Country has already made a huge change. By the end of 2005, the collective fund has increased from 9 million yuan to more than 600 million yuan, and the per capita average income has increased from about 2000 yuan to more than 18000 yuan. All the people aged 18 and over have gotten pension insurance. Men aged 55 and over and women aged 50 and over can get 500 yuan for pension every month. Through this way, Shuangjie Country solved the problem of old people dependency. The new rural cooperative medical care has also been put into practice. With the developing of the collective-owned economy, the reimbursement ratio of medical expenses has been doubled from 33%. In order to satisfy the increasing spiritual and cultural demand, Shuangjie Country has invested 1.8 million thousand yuan to build activity center for aged people, library and fitness center; rebuild school, cultural training room and service center. In order to conduct a better environment for children to study and grow, more than 5 million yuan was invested to build a kindergarten of 5000 square meters. A city-level exemplar primary school of 65 mu has also been built and used, which makes the rural children can get into the key school without leaving country. In a word, a new socialist countryside with developing economy, affluent living, rural custom civilization, graceful circumstance and democratic management has been established.

天津市北辰区双街村村委会　Shuangjie Village Committee, Beichen District, Tianjin

地址: 天津市北辰区京津公路西侧双街新城　Add: Shuangjie New Town, West of Beijing-Tianjin Highway, Beichen District, Tianjin

电话 Tel: +86 22 26973815

总经理：齐俊平

天津南开房地产开发公司成立于1984年，是天津市首批全民所有制的房地产开发企业，注册资金2000万元，为房地产开发二级企业，主要从事商品房开发及销售。我公司下辖建筑装饰工程公司和物业管理公司各一个，共有员工50人，专业技术人员占全部员工的70%。

公司成立以来，曾多次参加了天津市重点规划改造项目，如三级跳坑、危陋平房改造等，先后开发了义兴里、慎兴南里、西横堤、黄河道向阳路拥军里、连心里、天明西里1、2、3期、八里台禄达花园等五十多万平方米的商品房住宅及小区，销售率达到100%，创造了较好的经济效益和社会效益，在市区房改、危改中发挥了积极作用，95年被天津市政府评为房地产开发二十强企业。我公司现正积极的开拓市场，转换管理机制寻求更大的发展。公司坚持创新、发展、勤奋、务实的企业精神，恪守“质量第一、信誉第一”的企业宗旨，发扬国营企业“重合同，守信誉”的优良传统，以人为本，为广大客户营造一个温馨舒适的住宅，用我们的微笑、用优质的服务为更多的朋友提供一块属于自己的天地。

我公司的质量方针：

精心设计造舒适住宅，规范管理创一流品牌。

质量方针综合概括了我公司主营方向，致力于改善普通百姓居住条件的企业理念和市场经济条件下的“质量兴业”，是公司严格贯彻的准则，也是一定时期力争实现的目标。

▲精心设计造舒适住宅

在合理控制造价和执行国家建设标准的基础上，依靠科技进步，通过精心规划、精心设计、精心施工和科学管理，建设规划合理、设计新颖、功能齐全、设施配套、质量优良、环境优美，满足普通百姓住房改善需求，具有天津特色并适度超前的城市住宅小区，实现经济、社会、环境三个效益的统一。

▲规范管理创一流品牌

适应市场竞争需要，以质量为生命线，建精品、打品牌，树立“全市争领先”目标意识。坚持按施工规范和优良标准组织指导施工，生产产品。突出强调每道工序、每一环节都必须严格按规范和标准办事，有针对性消除质量通病，采取有效措施保证按规范标准贯彻始终。运用政治、经济、行政、法律多种手段确保创优达标。采用先进的管理手段，推陈出新，以优异的产品质量、服务质量，满足社会需求，使顾客满意。

公司历来建筑项目：

公司自1984年成立以来，曾多次参加了天津市重点规划改造项目，如三级跳坑，危陋平房改造等，先后开发了义兴里（43000平方米）、慎兴南里（2100平方米）、西横堤（116000平方米）、彩霞里（25000平方米）、耕耘里（5000平方米）、中医学院（3000平方米）、西南角（32000平方米）、北草坝（10000平方米）、黄河道向阳路拥军里、连心里（总共72000平方米）、天明西里1、2、3期（110000平方米）、仁善里、鸿远里（47076平方米）、八里台禄达花园（19958平方米）等五十多万平方米的商品房住宅及小区。

近几年来我公司开发了：

凯旋苑假日风情街

大港区是天津市滨海新区的重要组成部分，是一个以油田和石油化工为主体的产业的新型滨海城区。大港区区位优势明显，距北京165公里，距天津新港28公里，距天津滨海国际机场40公里，而且均有高速公路或高等级公路相连，交通极为便捷。

假日风情街踞守大港城区中心和繁华商业圈，东接上古林海鲜街，西连永明路已经成型的商业街，前方为润泽园别墅区，后方为高档住宅小区凯旋苑。项目配套完善，设施齐备。共46套沿街门面房，每套独立成店，而又聚店成市。本项目为纯粹的商业用房，二层建筑上部并没有住宅，层高达7.5米，可以满足各种业态使用。建筑面积14445平方米。

假日风情街是您商业经营、投资置业的上佳之选。

博雅轩（人才公寓）

我公司对原万华股份公司名下的印铁制罐厂进行开发，该项目坐落在红旗路中环线边，位置具佳，属市区中心地带，东临交通便利的中环线，南侧、西侧为住宅小区，北临雅安道已逐步形成的小商品、餐饮街，附近有车站、电子一条街、大型超市等。该项目总占地3.52公顷（约52.8亩），建筑面积93306平方米，及住宅、办公一体。

宝龙湾家园

该项目坐落在南开四马路与西关大街交口处，东至广开二马路，西至广开四马路，北至西关大街，南至清华祠大街。建筑面积约227216.45平方米。该项目地处市中心繁华地带，周边重点中小学、大型商场超市、医院齐全、交通便利。该项目规划为高低错落有致的板式高层，绿化率达到40%—50%。目前此项目在前期开发中。

董事长兼总经理：邢克实

福及子孙 功德无量

龙鑫公司不辱使命，誓把中山路建成天津特色文化商贸街

龙鑫公司创建于 2005 年 10 月份，是河北区委、区政府为振兴河北区经济而成立的正处级经济实体，公司将遵照区委、区政府的重大决策，有计划、有步骤地实施中山路的改造，准备利用 3 至 5 年的时间，通过开发改造将中山路建设成为集商务、商贸、文化、体育、娱乐、餐饮、旅游等为一体的特色文化商贸街。

中山路不仅曾是天津政治、经济、文化和商业的中心，而且在天津城市发展史上具有重要的地位。改造工作涉及五大工程：开发改造工程、历史文化估计修复改造工程、灯光夜景工程、环境工程和街景立面整修工程。总规划用地 29.6 万平方米、高级公寓 19.24 万平方米、中高档住宅 23.26 万平方米，涵盖商业购物、商务办公、餐饮娱乐、体育健身、文化旅游等多个领域。

吴振、张再旺、聂璧初、刘晋峰等十三位市级老领导应邀视察中山路开发改造工作，对改造中山路文化商贸街的决策给予充分肯定。

河北区区委书记张同庆多次听取中山路开发改造有关情况的汇报，并明确指出："整体规划，分步实施，抓住机遇，突破重点" 16 字方针，为中山路开发改造指明了方向。薛新立区长、马德香副主任、崔志勇副区长、李跃进副部长、杜翔主任等到龙鑫公司进行调研慰问，肯定了龙鑫公司成立以来取得的成绩。

"有朋自远方来，不亦乐乎。" 龙鑫公司董事长兼总经理邢克实表示："我们真诚欢迎海内外有识之士投资参与中山路的开发建设，我们将提供优惠的政策和优质服务。同时，也殷切地希望河北区各单位和父老乡亲，关心中山路改造，支持中山路改造，共同为重塑中山路的辉煌、发展河北区经济作出贡献。"

Tianjin Longxin Real Estate Development Co., Ltd. was founded in October, 2005. It is a economic unit which is set by Hebei District Committee and Hebei District Government in order to improve development of Hebei District. According to the decision of the district committee and government, the company implements the rebuilding program of Zhongshan Road step by step. It is going to cost 3–5 years to change Zhongshan Road into a street with unique characters of culture and commerce, which combines business, commerce, culture, entertainment, catering and tourism together.

Zhongshan Road not only is the political, economic, cultural and business center, but also has important status in the development of Tianjin City. The rebuilding program contains five big projects: exploitation and rebuilding, restoring of scenic spots and historical sites, illumination and night–sight, environment project and refit of street scene. The program will occupy 296 thousand square meters totally, which includes 372.3 thousand square meters business establishments, 410 thousand square meters plaza and restaurants, 192.4 thousand square meters luxury mansions and 232.6 thousand square meters dwelling houses of middle and top grade. It will involve shopping, business, catering, entertainment, body fit, tourism and many other areas.

Wu Zhen, Zhang Zaiwang, Nie Bichu, Liu Jinfeng and other 9 former municipal leaders were invited to inspect the rebuilding progress of Zhongshan Road, and they all praised the decision of Culture & Commerce Street.

The secretary of Hebei District Zhang Tongqing debriefed the rebuilding progress for many times. He brings forward a guideline of 16 characters and makes a direction for the future development. When president Xue Xinli, vice–director Ma Dexiang, vice–president Cui Zhiyong, vice–minister Li Yuejin and director Du Xiang of Hebei District visited Longxin Realty Corporation, they all commended the achievements since it established.

The chairman of board and general manager Xing Keshi said: "Welcome to invest to the construction of Zhongshan Road. We will provide favorable policy and services of high quality. Meanwhile, we hope all the units and people of Hebei District will help the rebuilding of Zhongshan Road and make contributions to the economic development."

2003 年 4 月 2 日，戴相龙市长在南开区委书记刘长顺的陪同下考察鑫茂集团

Originally established in 1993, it was registered Tianjin Xinmao Scien–Tech. Investment Group Co., Ltd. on Dec 26, 2000 with its registered capital of 223 million yuan. It is mainly engaged in Scien–tech. Park establishment, Hi–tech. industry investment as well as small & medium–sized industry incubation operation. It locates on 16 Rongyuan Road, Tianjin Hi–tech. Park.

The group holds a listed company–Xinmao Science & Technology Co., Ltd. which has already been listed by Shenzhen Stock Exchange At moment , the group has 2,400 staff and 42 subordinates with its total assets reaching 24 hundred million yuan. Until now, the group has already formed its “Tri–Pillar Industry” mode which takes Scien–tech. Park exploitation & construction as its “Domain Industry”. The “Tri–Pillar Industry” includes Scien–tech. Park Exploitation & Construction, Scien–tech Industry Operation concentrating on Business incubation, investment & development relying on Scien–tech. Park’s capability; Hi–Tech. Industry Operation like IT software, digital tech., space tech. etc.; Related Service Industry like estate management , business–trade and cultural service.

2006 年 10 月 10 日，天津鑫茂鑫风能源科技有限公司股东签约仪式

鑫茂科技园·军民两用技术产业基地鸟瞰图

天津市热力公司

Tianjin Heat Power Company

天津市热力公司是我市集中供热的骨干企业，中国城镇供热协会常务理事单位。公司成立于 1985 年，是天津市成立较早的供热企业，当年在体院北小区建设 3 万平方米的供热示范工程，拉开了我市集中供热的序幕。如今公司下设 6 个供热管理所，20 个供热站，承担 5 万多户居民的供热任务，供热规模约 700 万平米。按照一业为主，多角化经营的原则，公司相继成立了供热设计室、保温管厂、宾水酒楼、康健园洗浴等多经单位。二十多年来，公司始终坚持“服务人民、奉献社会”的服务理念，牢固树立“辛苦我一人、温暖千万家”的企业精神，按照“安全运行、均衡供热、诚信服务、用户满意”的质量方针，突出主题抓发展，严格规范抓管理，以人为本抓育才，立足用户抓创建，为天津市的供热事业做出了应有的贡献。

近几年来，公司领导班子以“三个代表”重要思想为指导，牢固树立科学发展观的思想，按照构建和谐社会、和谐企业的要求，带领广大干部职工奋力拼搏、锐意创新，开始了热力公司“二次创业”的历程，进入了一个新的上升期，形成了金谷园、华苑产业园区、水上国际村等区域 40 平方公里、2000 万平方米以上的控规。07 年热力公司将以更加崭新的精神风貌，确定发展工作目标，全力抓好科学发展，除继续完善 3 个热源基地的基本建设及设备安装配套外，还要再完成供热管网的铺设、换热站的建设，重视热力企业文化建设，提炼、形成具有热力特色的精神文化体系，提高职工综合素质，增强企业凝聚力，叫响“天津热力”品牌，树立良好的企业形象；大力推进热力科技创新，狠抓节能减排工作，提高全员职工节能减排意识，制定节能减排工作目标，实现公司节约发展、清洁发展、安全发展和可持续发展，为实现天津市“十一五”节能减排目标做贡献；瞄准全国一流管理水平，打造企业优势，夯实各项基础管理工作，提高企业的市场竞争能力和控制能力，在供热运行、服务、经营、能耗等方面跨入全国先进行列，为热力公司又好又快持续健康发展奠定坚实基础。

Tianjin Heat Power Company is a key enterprise of Tianjin central heating. It is also a standing flat of China District Heating Association. The company founded in 1985 is one of the earliest heating enterprises in Tianjin, which started the history of Tianjin central heating with the heating demonstration construction of 30 thousand m². Now, the company has 6 heating offices and 20 heating stations. It afford the heating load of 50 thousand households with the heating space of 7 million m². According to the principle of profession and multi-operation, the company set up heating design department, heat preservation pipe factory, Binshui restaurant and Kangjianyuan bathroom orderly. For 20 years, the company insist on the idea of "service for the people, contribute to the society", builds up the enterprise spirit of "tire myself, warm others", establishes quality guideline of "secure operation, balanced heating, creditable service, satisfying customers", takes development, management, training, innovation as the most important things, and makes a lot of contributions to the development of Tianjin heating projects.

In the recent years, the leading group takes "Three Represents" as the director principles, implements the scientific and evolutive notion, and leads all the staff to work hard. The company has started the second entrepreneur, come into a new ascending period and founded a controlling space of 40 sq. km., 20 million m² including Jingu Village, Huanyuan Industry District and International Country, etc.. In 2007, the company will make a new developing target, continue consummating the construction of three heating bases and instruments installations, finish the laying of heating network and heating exchanging stations. Making a point of enterprise culture construction, the company will establish a culture system with heating characters, increase the comprehensive quality of staff, and enhance the coherence of enterprise. It will improve the heating technology innovation, try its best to save energy and reduce the discharge, and make sure the company can realize economice development, clean development and secure development, which supports Tianjin "11th-five years" energy-saving & discharge-reducing target. Also, the company will advance the management level, build up enterprise superiority, increase the market competition and controlling ability, try to enter the national advanced rank of heating operation, service, circulation and energy use, and settle a stable base for good, quick, sustaining and robust development.

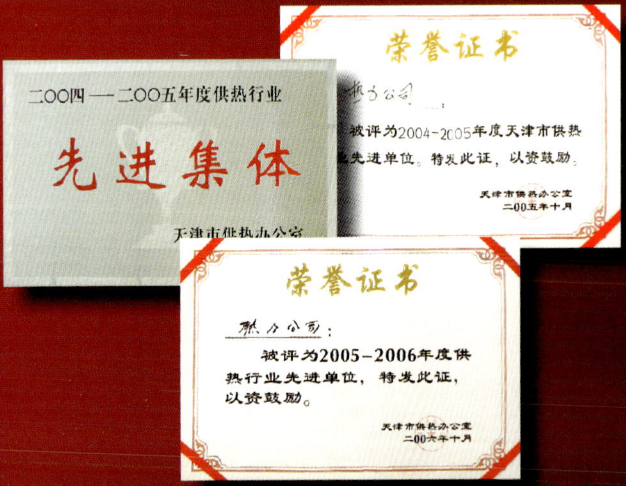

地址：天津市河西区宾水道 49 号
Add: No. 49 Binshui Road, Hexi District, Tianjin
邮政编码 Postal Code: 300060
电话 Tel: +86 22 23010532
传真 Fax: +86 22 23010532

天津送变电工程公司

Tianjin Electric Power Transmission & Transformation Engineering Corporation

总经理：张嘉利

党委书记：周顺起

天津送变电工程公司成立于1953年，是具有国家一级资质的电力工程公司总承包施工企业。50多年来，他们无私奉献，努力拼搏，优质高效地完成了数十项国家和天津市重点工程，为华北电网建设和改善天津市城乡人民生活水平做出了巨大的贡献。连续16年被天津市政府授予“守合同、重信誉”企业，其企业资信和建筑信誉等级均为“AAA”企业。2005年被评为全国“质量安全先进企业”，“中国企业诚信经营示范单位”和“全国企业文化建设先进单位”等光荣称号。

现在，天津市电网建设“十一五”规划的高潮期正在向我们走来，天津送变电工程公司全体干部、职工紧紧围绕“一强三优”、“三抓一创”的工作思路，牢固树立强烈的事业心和使命感，以超前的意识、一流的技术和先进的管理，积极投入到天津电网建设实践中来。

他们决心以诚信为基石，不断提升服务意识，提高竞争能力，打造精品工程，树立一流的品牌和良好的社会形象，让政府放心，让用户满意，为天津市经济发展和滨海新区的腾飞做出更大的贡献。

Tianjin Electric Power Transmission & Transformation Engineering Corporation, which was founded in 1953, is a power engineering construction enterprise of national first grade. Since its establishment, the company finished a lot of key projects of the nation and Tianjin City, and made great contributions to the construction of power net in North of China and the improvement of People's living conditions. The company was granted the “honor construction and abide by its words” unit for 16 years continuously. Both the enterprise credit and the construction quality were honored “AAA” grade. In 2005, the company obtained the title of “Advanced Enterprise in Quality and Security”, “Model of Enterprises with Good Credit in China”, “Enterprise with Good Culture in China” and so on.

Now, the upsurge of the “Eleventh-five” construction of Tianjin power net is coming. According to “One Predominance and Three Advantages” and “Three Improvement and One Innovation”, all the staff of Tianjin Power Transmission Corporation will do best to the construction of Tianjin power net with enhanced responsibility, advanced technology and good management.

The company has decided to keep good credit, increase service routines, strengthen the ability of competition and build top-ranking projects. They will set a topping brand and make a good image, which can satisfy the government and the consumers, and then do more contributions to the development of Tianjin City and Binhai New Area.

地址：天津市河东区卫国道122号
Add: No. 122 Weiguo Road, Hedong District, Tianjin
邮政编码 Postal Code: 300161
电话 Tel: +86 22 24565026
传真 Fax: +86 22 24565026

天津市重点工程静海迎丰220kV变电站

河北清苑500kV变电站电器安装

刘房子经济发展总公司

Liufangzi Economy Development General Company

总经理：田东平

刘房子为我市西北部一颗璀璨的明珠，被市政府评为市级明星小康村。地理位置优越，与津霸公路、中环线、外环线、子牙河形成环围。远期规划前景宏大，在9平方公里的辖区内，780余户近2700人正以饱满的热情迎接二十一世纪的挑战。

改革开放十几年的发展，村经济已初具规模。现有村办集体企业十几家，三资企业数家；农业生产逐步走上科学、规模、效益型，现已形成的津霸公路刘房子村商业一条街，为第三产业的发展起到了促进作用。工业产值在村经济的比重日渐上升，已初步形成农、工、商合理发展，相互促进，比翼齐飞良性循环之势。

几年来教育事业得到长足发展。同时加大了社会福利、社会保障的投入。村容、村貌焕然一新，治安良好，民风纯朴，已实现精神文明与物质文明的共同发展。

刘房子领导正用战略眼光审视自己，以高度责任感率领全体人民共同努力、继往开来。

地址: 天津市北辰区津

…Highway, Beichen District, Tianjin

邮政编码 Postal Code: 300400

电话 Tel: +86 22 26654384

建设竣工后的高级别墅一角

Liufangzi, as a shining star in Northwest Tianjin, is a municipal level well-off star town with good geographic location, connected with Jinba Highway, Middle-Ring Road, Extra-Ring Road and Ziya River, having a good developing potential. In its 9 square kilometers area, there are more than 780 families, nearly 2,700 people, who are heartedly welcoming the challenge of the 21st century.

After more than 10 years, development since the reform and opening to outside, the town's economy becomes scaled. There are over 10 township collective enterprises and several joint ventures in the town. Its agricultural production is becoming scientific efficient and on scale, a commercial street is set up in the town near Jinba Expressway, which plays an important role in the development of its tertiary industry. Its development of agriculture, industry and service industry become coordinated with each other.

与天津商学院联建的教学楼

Its education has also gotten improved rapidly. Its input in social welfare and social protection system is also enlarged. The town's environment and outlook are changed freshly which is socially securitied and civilized. The town is also realized co-development of spiritual and material civilization.

The leaders of the town are inspecting themselves strategically, and leading its people to work hard together and success the past and looking forward the future. We are heartedly looking forward to actively cooperating with friends in different walks to achieve an excellent future.

天津海洋开关厂车间一角

党委书记：王志杰

天津市公路养路费征稽处（简称征稽处），负责全市几十万辆机动车的养路费征收和稽查管理工作。2006年全市养路费收入达到18亿余元，为加快天津市市政公路事业发展和城市基础设施建设做出了较大贡献。征稽处坚持以人为本的科学发展观，走可持续发展之路，通过确立费收工作中心，实施科技兴费战略，全市征稽所（站）已实现计算机联网征费，用生产力的飞跃带动征费管理的规范。征稽处坚持一手抓费收源头，一手抓队伍建设人头的工作方针，既向科技要效益、向管理要效益、向依法行政要效益，又向文明优质服务要效益。通过倡导"服务人民，奉献社会"征稽精神，和"倾心相助，诚心解难，暖心服务，温馨待人"的服务准则，不断拓展征稽文化的内涵，加快队伍整体素质的提高，努力塑造新时期交通征稽人的良好社会形象，打造一支让政府放心，让群众满意的行政执法队伍。2000年，征稽处被市委、市政府授予天津市模范集体荣誉称号；2002年，被共青团中央授予"全国青年文明号"称号，2004年被交通部评为"先进集体"，并连续被天津市评为"九五"、"十五"立功先进集体。

Tianjin Road Toll Collection & Audit Office (Collection & Audit Office for short) is in charge of road toll collection, checking and management of hundreds of thousand vehicles in Tianjin. In 2006, total revenue from road toll has reached 1.8 billion yuan, which made a lot of contribution to Tianjin municipal road development and infrastructure facilities construction. Collection & Audit Office insists on scientific development approach of "people oriented" and takes the way of sustainable development. With the establishment of working center and the implement of "invigorating toll through science and education" strategy, all the collection & audit stations has realized collection and audit through network, which improved the standardization of collection management in virtue of productivity development. Persisting in the same important status of toll payer and working staff, Collection & Audit Office make benefits from technology, management, legal administration and better services. Adhering to the spirit of "service the People and make contribution to the society" and guideline of "help others full-heartedly, solve difficulties sincerely, provide services warmly and welcome customers friendly", the office keeps on expanding the collection & audit culture, improving the whole makings of working staff and shaping a good society figure of transportation toll collector & auditor in new period, and then sets up a administrative law executing procession which can satisfy the government and people. The office was awarded "Tianjin Exemplary Collectivity" by Municipal Committee and Municipal Government in 2000; in 2002, was awarded "National Civilized Youth" by Communist Youth League Committee; in 2004, was listed in "Advanced Collectivity" by Ministry of Communications; and was awarded advanced collectivity by Tianjin City in "the 9th five-year period" and "the 10th five-year period" continually.

征稽处党委召开庆"七一"总结表彰大会

征稽处开展知识竞赛活动

征稽处职工进行军事化培训

COATS

天津津英纺纱有限公司系天津纺织品集团进出口股份有限公司和天津棉纺七厂与英国高士集团合资经营企业，于1988年成立，而后进一步扩展规模，相继成立天津李七庄纺纱有限公司和天津津高捻线有限公司，并于2004年将津英、李七、津高三公司吸收合并为津英纺纱有限公司；合资期限为50年，投资总额已达4,300余万美元，中外方各占50%；拥有50,000多纱锭、13,000多倍捻锭和4,500多长丝捻线锭；年出口创汇3,000万美元；是具有一定规模、较强竞争能力和世界一流技术装备的合资经营企业。

本公司原料以进口为主，产品以出口为主，自1990年6月14日相继开业以来，累计出口创汇近3.3亿美元，实现利润4,600余万美元。十五年来，公司一直在盈利中运营，在国际市场激烈竞争中不断发展。一个两头在外，大进大出，且初具规模并在国际市场上具有较强竞争力的中英合资企业，在阔步前进。

李鹏总理、有关国家首脑要员以及我市主要领导和国家有关部门领导人，均先后莅临公司参观视察。公司开业运营以来，连年荣获国家及市政府授予的“双优”、“最佳”外商投资企业、“天津市工业百强企业”、“天津市人均出口创汇前十名企业”、“天津市优秀企业”等荣誉称号，并于1991年跨入“中国规模最大的500家外商投资工业企业”行列。2000年6月，天津市政府又单独对在1990—1999年度连续十年荣获各类先进称号的津英纺纱等八家公司，颁发奖牌，予以表彰。

Tianjin Jinying Spinning Co., Ltd. established in 1988, is a joint-venture enterprise invested by Tianjin Textile Group Imports and Exports Ltd., Tianjin No. 7 Cotton Textile Factory and U.K. Coats plc Group. The company was founded as the combination of Tianjin Liqizhuang Spinning Ltd. and Tianjin Jingao Twist Thread Ltd. in 2004. The time limit of joint venture is 50 years and total investment capital is of 43 million yuan at equal share of 50% each. It has more than 50,000 spindles, 13,000 times twist spindles and 4,500 twisted filament yarns and earns foreign exchange of 30 million dollars through export annually. Now, the company has great ability of competition with top-ranking equipments.

The company pays most attention to importing raw material and exporting products. It has earned foreign exchange of 330 million dollars though export and has made profits of 46 million dollars from June 14, 1990 until present. During the 15 years, the joint-venture enterprise has been developing and making profits consistently.

We received a lot of visitors from central and municipal government, including Premier Li Peng and many senior officials. The company has received a lot of awards every year, such as “Double Excellent”, “Double Good” enterprise with foreign investment, “100 leading Industrial Enterprises in Tianjin”, “The Top 10 Enterprises of Earning Foreign Exchange Though Export Per Capita” and “Excellent Enterprise of Tianjin”. In 1991, the company also listed in the “Largest 500 Industry Enterprises in Tianjin”. In June 2000, Tianjin government prized Jinying Spinning Co., Ltd. and other seven companies who received special award of achievement for consecutive 10 years.

地址：天津市西青区李七庄津涞公路南
Add: South Jinlai Road, Liqizhuang, Xiqing District, Tianjin
邮政编码 Postal Code: 300381
电话 Tel: +86 22 83912847, 2940
传真 Fax: +86 22 83913935
E-mail: tjjysc@public1.tpt.tj.cn

天津市侯台商贸集团有限公司

Tianjin Houtai Trade Group

侯台科技园座落于天津市西青区中北镇，是天津市西青经济开发区的组成部分，占地 4 平方公里，位于天津市区西侧，紧邻天津市外环线 500 米绿化带。

- 园区位置优越，距首都北京120 公里、天津机场30公里、天津新港40公里，交通便利。
- 园区各种基础配套设施完备，陕气入津减压调度总站位于园区北侧，天津市第四污水处理厂位于园区南侧。
- 园区以标准厂房出租方式招商。以电子信息、生物医药、精密机械、新型材料等高新技术产业项目为主。
- 园区引入现代工业物业管理模式，为企业生产经营活动提供高效、便捷、全程、优质的服务。

With an area of 4 square kilometers, Houtai Technological Park is located in Zhongbei Township, Xiqing District, Tianjin Municipality, which is a part of Xiqing Economic Development Area. It stands at the west of Tianjin Municipality, near to Tianjin section of Beijing-Shanghai expressway and 500-meter greenbelt of Tianjin outer ring road.

The park has superior regional location. It is 120 kilometers away from Beijing (the capital of China), 30 kilometers from Tianjin Airport and 40 kilometers from Tianjin New Harbor. It has convenient transportation.

The main control office of natural gas drawed from Shanxi Province in Tianjin situated in the north of the Park and The Fourth Sewage Treatment Plant of Tianjin lies in the west of the Park. The Park has basic conditions to set up all kinds of facilities.

The Park will attract investors by the way of renting standard workshop. Many high and new technology industrial projects are encouraged, such as electronic information, biological medicine, precise machinery, etc..

The Park adopts modern industrial manage style to provide efficient, convenient, whole-course and high-quality services for enterprises.

地址: 天津市复康西路碧欣路
Add: Bixin Road, Fukangxi Road, Tianjin
邮政编码 Postal Code: 300384
电话 Tel: +86 22 23079566
传真 Fax: +86 22 23079566
http://www.tjhtjt.com